SURVEY AND OPINION RESEARCH:

PROCEDURES FOR PROCESSING AND ANALYSIS

JOHN A. SONQUIST

University of California
Santa Barbara, California

WILLIAM C. DUNKELBERG

Purdue University
West Lafayette, Indiana

PRENTICE-HALL, INC., Englewood Cliffs, New Jersey 07632

Library of Congress Cataloging in Publication Data

SONQUIST, JOHN A
Survey and opinion research.

Bibliography.
Includes index.
1. Social science research. 2. Social surveys—Data processing. 3. Public opinion polls—Data processing. 4. Social surveys—Statistical methods. 5. Public opinion polls—Statistical methods. 1. Dunkelberg, William C., joint author. II. Title.
H62.S724735 001.4′3 76-47022
ISBN 0-13-878264-4

To
Hanne, Barbara,
Eric, Cathy, Kristi, Eric, and Kevin

10 9 8 7 6 5 4 3 2 1

Printed in the United States of America

PRENTICE-HALL INTERNATIONAL, INC., *London*
PRENTICE-HALL OF AUSTRALIA PTY. LIMITED, *Sydney*
PRENTICE-HALL OF CANADA, LTD., *Toronto*
PRENTICE-HALL OF INDIA PRIVATE LIMITED, *New Delhi*
PRENTICE-HALL OF JAPAN, INC., *Tokyo*
PRENTICE-HALL OF SOUTHEAST ASIA PTE LTD., *Singapore*

CONTENTS

PREFACE

Interviews and questionnaires as data collection tools have become major approaches to the collection of information for basic research, for policy development, and in support of business decision making. Regardless of the final objectives of a study, the disciplinary orientation of the analyst, or the eventual use of survey data, there are data management and statistical computation tasks that are common to every use. Computers can be employed to advantage throughout the process of converting newly-received data into meaningful statistical summarizations. The effective sequencing of combined manual and computer-based processing operations is the subject of this book.

The discussion begins at the point where completed data collection schedules are in the hands of the analyst, and takes the reader through each of the steps required to prepare the statistical analyses. The topics treated here include:

- organizing the data processing
- determining the data storage structures
- preparing data for encoding into machine-readable form (editing)
- designing and using codes for transcribing data (coding)
- controlling the consistency and quality of data
- constructing scales and indices
- shepherding the data through commonly used statistical computations
- managing the project

Of particular interest to readers new to the use of computer-based statistical analysis techniques are the sections dealing with data structures (Chapter 2), code construction (Chapter 4), negotiating with the computer center (Chapter 9), and the basic ideas underlying the use of statistical programs (Chapter 8). Both new and experienced practitioners will find the sections on the computation of indices and of Guttman, Thurstone, and Likert scales useful (Chapter 7). Those whose knowledge of set theory is minimal will find helpful the discussion of this topic and how it applies both to quality control (Chapter 6) and to index and scale construction (Chapter 7).

A major audience for this book are the many computer science professionals whose systems are used by social scientists. Depicted here are the tasks that almost every social science computer user has ahead when he or she walks into the user-services department of the computer center. Not every such person knows exactly what is required to transform raw data into usable statistical summarizations. This book can help the computer scientists understand what it is that most social science computer users seek to accomplish.

We have chosen to organize these materials more as a handbook than as an expository introductory text. And we have tried to avoid burdening the beginners where possible by placing more complex material toward the end of each of the chapters. Probably the best use, in an educational context, is as a handbook for students carrying out actual research projects. Early draft sections of the transcript have been used to train both graduate and undergraduate students at a university level. Rather than place introductory concepts such as set theory in a separate appendix, we have placed this type of material in the chapters dealing with the tasks for which these concepts are most relevant. After all, most of us learn abstract ideas best when we must use them immediately.

This handbook organization will, we hope, make this text quite useful to novice and master practitioners alike. Both the checklists of topics to remember when setting up runs on a computer program (Chapter 8), and the suggestions for topics to be covered by computer center user-service personnel in orientation sessions for survey staff members represent procedural refinements that many of us learn at considerable time and cost and then forget when we turn our attention to other matters. Masters need checklists; but novices need explanations. Experienced analysts should find that they can give this book to an intelligent, but inexperienced assistant, ask that person to read it, and anticipate a significant upgrading of that person's contribution to the success of the project. It should be possible to give a section like the one on quality control to a programmer with a good computer science background but little experience with this particular type of data management, with the full expectation that he or she will be able to handle the logical problems correctly.

Although the emphasis may appear to be on larger-scale survey projects, prospective users of survey data collection techiques will find that the basic steps outlined here are essential ingredients for successful management of even the smallest project. Each section alerts the reader to steps that might be combined or otherwise simplified for smaller projects.

This book seeks to codify and make available the more than ten years of combined experience in handling research data accumulated by the authors while at the Survey Research Center, Institute for Social Research, University of Michigan. These roles included study director, computer programmer, developer of statistical software, computing facility administrator, and research assistant. The research technology presented here has been tested and debugged by many —and it works. We have sought to present it from a practical day-to-day point of view, digressing to introduce technical questions when it is important for them to be known in order to deal with the problem at hand.

We have made no attempt to treat specifically the data generated by experiments. These may produce information collected by computer-controlled instruments on a real-time basis, a vastly different data management task. Yet, these data are generally supplemented by questionnaires and interviews and are analyzed using statistical techniques similar to those treated here. To that extent the problems are similar.

Many generous people have helped us to select and assemble these materials. Most, such as the students in our research methods classes over the years, must go unnamed, but we can acknowledge our most recent benefactors. Rensis Likert, Angus Campbell, George Katona, James Morgan, John Lansing, Charles Cannell, and Joan Scheffler all contributed immeasurably to the development of the technology reported here. Gregory Marks, Duane Thomas, Stewart Robinowitz, Judith Rattenbury, Neal van Eck, Nancy Baerwaldt, Frank Stafford, and Jay Schmiedeskamp also played major roles. We are grateful to those who read various drafts of the manuscript, or parts of it, and whose suggestions were most helpful: Edmund Meyers, Robert B. Smith, James A. Davis, Bradford Smith, Anthony Shih, Robert Poolman, Laura Klem, and Sandy Hendricks. Karl Karlstrom and Margaret McAbee of Prentice-Hall provided fine editorial guidance.

The price a family pays for an author's manuscript is a high one. All put up with unpredictable ups and downs and a sometimes random-appearing obsession with completing the manuscript. We express our gratitude and indebtedness to our wives and children by dedicating this book to them.

JOHN A. SONQUIST
Santa Barbara, California

WILLIAM C. DUNKELBERG
West Lafayette, Indiana

SURVEY RESEARCH AND THE COMPUTER

Surveys are undertaken for a wide variety of reasons. In some cases, the purposes of the survey may be simply to describe the characteristics of a population. Alternatively, the analyst may be interested in collecting information relevant to the evaluation of the effects of a program of action, for instance, to determine the impact of a new program of teaching in a school system or the effect of an advertising campaign. Other studies may search out relationships between variables and have as an objective the generation of explanatory models. Still others are aimed at the testing of hypotheses which are very explicit and are precisely specified by theory.

In most cases, survey objectives are multiple. If a population is to be described, there may be both long- and short-run objectives. For example, one may wish to maximize the usefulness of the data to other researchers after a specific research objective has been met.[1] Census surveys trace the changes in the characteristics of important subgroups in the American population over time as well as provide short-run information on the numbers of various types of persons in area subdivisions. Surveys are also used to study various aspects of human behavior with a view to obtaining explanations of why the behavior occurs. They are often aimed at assessing the reasons why some people act differently than others. Several sets of behavior patterns may be investigated simultaneously in a survey, possibly by different investigators.

The central objectives of a survey can usually be identified as being focused on one or two of four main goals: testing hypotheses, evaluating programs, describing populations, or building models of human behavior. Other objectives

[1] For example, see Katona et al. (1971).

may include conceptual clarification, development of highly reliable scales, and other methodological improvements.[2]

Most surveys usually have as a central objective a search for relationships between variables. They seek evidence in support of alternative explanations for differences between people's behavior. Some of these explanations may take the form of hypotheses which are very precise and explicit, and which guide the research inquiry. Others are derived from a mixture of sometimes vague theory and experience, and generally contain statements of what are essentially cause-and-effect relationships (although they may be phrased in other terminology). When cause-and-effect relationships are studied, statistical controls are used to establish contrast groups. Alternatively, matching procedures may be used to approximate experimental designs. When designs like this are used, the survey logic is generally deductive in nature. The data processing reflects the hypothesis and model-testing objectives of the project.

In other cases, the study objectives may be concerned merely with the determination of the existence of patterns of relationships between variables, with no reference to causation. This is often an objective in the purely descriptive work undertaken in the early stages of research in a particular subject area. Here, the analyst may seek to discover if there are configurations of traits or "ideal" types among the respondents.

Survey methods are often combined with more informal procedures to evaluate the impact of a particular program. In this case, the objectives often include determination of the multiplicity of the effects of the program, institutional procedure, or policy. Studies of this type are very similar to hypothesis-testing studies, but often the hypotheses are stated only implicitly and are derived from the practical objectives to the program being evaluated, rather than from theory. A variety of procedures may supplement survey methods to enable untangling the effects of the program itself from the confounding effects of participant self-selection and other factors. Such a study generally seeks answers to the questions: "To what extent did the program achieve its objectives?"; "Was this because of what they did or because of some confounding factors?"; and "What, if anything, else happened?"

Other studies employing survey methods have as their primary function the seeking of accurate descriptions of selected populations, organizations, or other social groups. At times, special sampling procedures may be used to insure adequate representation of special groups in the population, which are specifically related to the study objectives.

Descriptive studies may be concerned with such complex phenomena as needs, attitudes, and opinions. They often employ the same statistical methodologies as do explanatory studies, which seek to discover quantitative relationships among specified variables, except that their objective is not to use these

[2] For a further and much more complete discussion of survey objectives, see Fellin et al. (1969).

correlations as the basis for the formulation of ex post facto explanatory models. Rather, population description studies are concerned primarily with questions of fact and often attempt to determine the extent of the differences between important population subgroups with reference to a set of characteristics. It is of some importance for the statistical processing of these studies that the question of *why* such differences may occur is an objective for one study and not for another.

Other studies are explicitly concerned with the discovery of interrelationships among variables with a view to answering the question "Why are people different?" This is, perhaps, the most frequent use of survey methods. The correlations discovered form the basis of ex post facto explanatory models of human behavior, which are then used to generate ideas for future investigation, resulting in further refinement of the complex models. Since the objective of such studies is to explain why differences in behavior occur, causality or some equivalent is an important concept. Relevant variables are suggested by theory and experience. However, in many cases only the very general nature of their probable association is suggested, and the formulation of hypotheses is not very precise. Often a large number of potentially relevant variables are included in the study. In many cases where this happens, an objective is the isolation of variables that have predictive value. This contrasts with the descriptive objective of constructing a taxonomy which looks only to the recurrence of different configurations of values of specific variables. Often these two objectives are combined in the same study, together with one or two more specific hypotheses to be tested. These factors all affect the statistical processing (and thus the computing) required for the study.

Survey methods are also used in conjunction with experimental studies. Thus, interviewing techniques or other systematic data-collection procedures may be used to obtain and record the values of variables relevant to the experimental situation. In particular, the experimenter may use pre- and post-experiment survey instruments to obtain and measure the values of the variables important to the experiment. Generally, these variables do not include the independent variable, which is recorded simply by noting which of the control or experimental groups each subject is in. However, experimenters often must also try to control for the effects of other potentially relevant variables, and may use survey data collection methods extensively to obtain systematic, quantitative data from subjects before and after the experiment. The use of survey methods in connection with experiments also influences the nature of the statistical analysis. Control over the number of subjects in each group makes possible the use of analysis-of-variance models that would not be feasible using ordinary random-sampling methods.

Survey methods may also be used in research designs that are primarily exploratory. Even though the particular study may not be primarily concerned with providing precise quantitative descriptions of the distributions of variables in a particular population, the researcher may still use this type of description for exploratory purposes. In seeking to develop hypotheses or increase his familiarity with a phenomenon, laying the basis for more precise future research, or while clarifying or modifying concepts, a researcher may use empirical quantitative measures as well as more informal and qualitative exploratory methods. Sometimes exploratory studies use a form of experimental manipulation in approximating an experimental strategy. These studies sometimes have as their objective the locating of variables that are potentially related to an important independent variable. In studies in which the objective is exploratory, survey methods are sometimes combined with experimental manipulation in order to sift through the many variables that may be related to the crucial dependent variable.

Surveys of all these types often employ multistage probability sampling methods to obtain representativeness with efficient data collection, and they generally obtain a large number of measures. In some cases, the surveys may be repeated from time to time to obtain information on trends. Sometimes the same individuals are interviewed at several points in time (a "panel" study).

Once the desired correspondence between measured indices (and their encoded representations) and the concepts of the analyst has been achieved, the task of computing statistics begins in earnest. It is in statistical computing, for reasons to be discussed below, that computing equipment found its earliest and most frequent usage in survey research. A large number of computer programs have been written whose function is to recode and transform variables, scales, and indices, and to compute and report the statistics necessary for interpretive analysis. These range from simple frequency-distribution programs to complex multivariate-analysis-program packages. The analyst is faced with an embarrassment of riches and often must choose among many procedures.

On the other hand, all programs have important restrictions on the way in which data presented to them may be encoded. It is not at all uncommon for the researcher to find that there are a number of existing statistical programs which will do almost what is wanted (but not quite), or to find that there exists a program that will do exactly what is wanted, but that the data do not have the proper configuration and hence are not compatible with the program.

Perhaps the most important effect that electronic computing equipment has had on the processing of survey data has been to make the use of complex multivariate statistical techniques possible, even easy. If a thorough knowledge of what programs are available (including their data input requirements and output options) is possessed by the researcher when he or she is designing the study, plans can be made to make use of these powerful techniques and data can be collected with this in mind.

There is much to be said (but not here) about the statistical techniques that have been programmed and are available as general-purpose "canned" routines on most large computers. These include, among others, programs for computing frequency, distributions, medians, percentage distributions, means, standard deviations, various nonparametric measures, multivariate analysis of variance, multiple regression, factor analysis, canonical correlations, discriminant-function analysis, and exact sampling errors for means and proportions based on multistage probability samples.[3] In addition, complex "hill-climbing," clustering, threshold, and other search algorithms have been programmed which employ heuristics for isolating patterns of relationships between variables or similarities between units. Newly developed techniques for analyzing structures of units representable by digraphs have also been programmed. Programs for the analysis of data collected over time and conceptualized as discrete-time Markov processes have been developed.

But the survey researcher's problems in doing statistical analysis are simple in comparison with the tasks faced in getting the data ready for entry into an available program. First, the programs that will perform the computations required for the particular configuration of statistical survey processing must be located—or one must face the arduous task of writing the necessary programs. This latter alternative is not suggested for the researcher whose primary objective is completion of a research project rather than program development.

Given the large number of programs available, the researcher's best strategy in gaining access to the needed statistical programs involves becoming connected at an early stage of the research process to the informal communication channels existing around each computing installation. The technology of computing and the uses already made of computers in the social sciences have long since outstripped the ability of existing formal communication channels to transfer timely information about what programs are available to the scientist with a problem.

Despite the fact that computer manufacturers and some scientific and professional organizations have attempted to catalogue and index the programs that have been written, most information about what is available locally is still transmitted by word-of-mouth. Therefore, it is necessary to find out who the local statistically-oriented computer users are and who would be likely to have developed solutions to data-processing problems soon to be encountered by the project. This means crossing the disciplines of sociology, political science, psychology, statistics, economics, engineering, anthropology, and education (among others) to locate computer users with similar statistical interests and useful programs in private libraries. These can supplement the general-purpose programs now commonly maintained at local computer centers. A last alternative on the horizon is the possibility of remote access through computer networks[4] to powerful software designed specifically for processing survey data.

This does not mean that formal channels of communication about statistical programs should be written off as useless. The lists of available programs

[3] For an extended discussion of available social-science software, see Anderson (1974).

[4] For example, see Meyers (1972, p. 176).

usually maintained by a computing installation and by its larger users is the best starting place and will generally produce information about programs in most general use locally, as well as leads to other sources of programs. Research organizations that use computing facilities also maintain files of available statistical programs, which may or may not be listed in the computing center's library file. Lists of programs available from computer manufacturer's "user organizations" are generally maintained by the computing installation itself and are often good sources of statistical programs that can be used with survey data.

When one is in the middle of a research project it is advisable to use programs developed for a local computer rather than to obtain and try to adapt programs written elsewhere. This is especially true if the programs proposed for alteration were written for a computer of a different size or for one made by a different manufacturer. Problem-oriented compiler languages differ sufficiently between computers that a considerable rewriting of programs is usually necessary, often at a large expense of time and money. This rule applies, but with considerably less force, to programs written elsewhere for an identical computer.

PROCESSING THE DATA—AN OVERVIEW

The best place to start exploring the logic of a research effort is at the end. What the researcher hopes to accomplish or discover is the prime determinant of the structure of the tasks, even when this work is simple and purely descriptive. This is especially true when the researcher must determine exactly which data to collect rather than searching through and selecting from data that already exist. Probably the biggest part of the survey cost is the data collection, particularly when the samples are representative of large geographic areas. Errors made in the data-collection process are generally irreparable; it is too expensive to go back to all respondents in a sample to ask new questions or to ask a question differently. Consequently, it is essential that the design of the study be evaluated carefully, that the hypotheses to be tested be carefully prespecified, and that the behavioral models and assumptions be well identified. All of these considerations determine the form of questions and instruments to be used; and the latter must be carefully designed and effectively pretested if possible, since they determine the structure of the data that are to be processed. It is in this sense that the research process must literally begin at the end, with the objectives of the study and the data and computational power required to meet these objectives.

There may be yet other factors that affect the design of the research. For example, some information (such as education) might be collected to evaluate the quality of the representativeness of the sample, even though it is not a variable posited to be important for the behavior to be studied. The inclusion of certain basic variables also vastly increases the usefulness of data to other researchers, frequently at negligible cost to the designer of the survey. Some types of information also increase the compatibility of the data collected with other information sources (for example, identifying census tracts). Even peripheral objectives affect the data-processing requirements.

The technology to be used to transfer the data from the instrument to the storage media also influences the form of the questions and the questionnaire and thus the data processing; machine-readable interview schedules are an example. The design of the data collection usually involves more than the technical arrangement of the survey instrument, the most important differences being the decision to use closed- rather than open-ended questions (generally viewed as a loss of information). The result of these decisions is an instrument which, when applied to a respondent sample, generates the data about which this book is concerned.

Clearly, the data processing is closely interrelated with other phases of the research process. The steps that make up the conduct of a survey are summarized in Figure 1-1. They are not of equal importance or detail but will serve to indicate our focus.

Conceptualization and Study Design. Clearly, an error at the design stage—for example, the omission of a question to tap an important variable (if uncorrected before the final version of the questionnaire goes out into the field)—would be very costly and very likely uncorrectable. It is especially important in this type of research that, early in the process, a great deal of time be devoted to detailed planning. Hypotheses to be tested must be specified in as much detail as possible, since all the data required must be identified prior to the actual construction of the questionnaire. Very specific decisions about the form of the data must also be made at this point (e.g., whether to collect income data in categories or to ask for the dollar amount). Other things being equal, it is desirable to collect data in the form that maximizes the investigator's flexibility at later stages in the research process. This is limited by financial and interview-length considerations, of course. The basic data structure, as well as specific details of its form, are determined here.

Pretesting and Data Collection. Some type of pilot study or pretest is generally advisable prior to the actual conduct of a survey. A small-scale survey gives the researcher an advance opportunity to see failures in question design; to see if questions appear to measure what one wishes to measure; to see if the codes designed as rules for categorizing the data and transferring them from the questionnaire to machine-readable storage medium are properly designed; to find out whether the questionnaire is too long, or too short; to ascertain whether or not questions have an optimal ordering; and to locate technical mistakes made in layout or inadequate directions in the instrument. Many serious errors can be avoided by taking the time to make an adequate pretest. When pretesting is

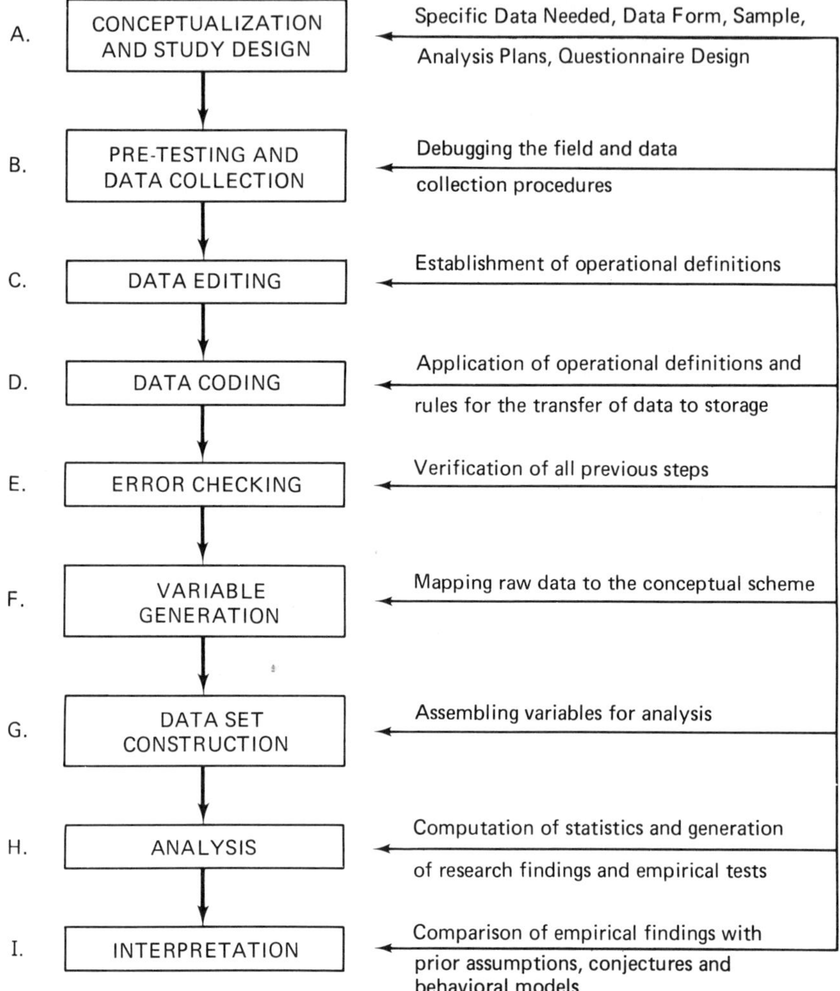

Figure 1-1 Overview of the Stages in Survey Research

complete, the data-collection phase starts in earnest. Computer-based procedures must fit together with manual procedures and can be tried out here.

Data Editing. Prior to actually transferring information from the instrument to the data-storage media, it is generally advantageous to *edit* the completed questionnaire, especially if the instrument is long or complicated. At this point, interviewer errors (failure to complete the questionnaire or to follow directions) can be caught, and consistency checking and variable generation can be accomplished. For example, one might check reported monthly payments times the number of remaining payments against reported remaining installment debt in a question sequence on automobile purchases, or check to see that rugs purchased by the respondent were recorded in the questionnaire section on "additions and repairs to the home" rather than in the "durable goods expenditures" section of a buying survey. Obviously this distinction depends on operational rules and definitions based on concepts from the study design stage of the process. Chapter 3 treats this process in detail.

Data Coding. Data coding is the process of transferring the data from the instrument to the data-storage media, usually punched cards.[5] Some variable construction can be combined with this process; for example, coding the actual value of family income as well as number denoting an income category. However, for studies of any size it is generally advisable to separate the two functions. The rules for categorizing, recording, and transferring the data are called *codes.* The code indicates which computer-readable characters will represent the data in the storage media. Figure 1-2 illustrates a typical section of a code. In this example the first field (located in the first three columns of the punched card) contains a three-digit identification of the study (in this case, 753). Such identification is essential where more than one study is being processed at the same time. It facilitates quick identification of the data deck. A *deck number* appears in columns 4 and 5 of every card and is essential when there is more than one card of data per unit of observation. Columns 6 through 9 uniquely identify the respondent. Columns 7 through 12 contain the actual amount of family income as reported in the questionnaire. Column 13 is an example of the type of variable generation that can occur in the coding process. The coder ascertains which category actual income falls in and records ("codes") the corresponding number indicated by the code.

Column 14 records the response to a question about debt. The amount of debt owed is coded in columns 15 through 19. If no debt is owed (the code for column 14 is 5 or 9), the coder is instructed to code a 0 in columns 15 through 19. If it is not ascertained whether or not any debt is owed, there is assumed to be none. This is typical of the kinds of decisions that must be made prior to the coding of the data.[6] If income is a crucial variable, all questionnaires where income was not ascertained might be deleted from the sample. Or, more likely, income might be "assigned," in which case a value is simply provided based on other data, such as age, education, and occupation—again an illustration of the operational decisions that must be made and that are dependent on earlier stages of the process.

Column 20 illustrates another useful method of identifying the data

[5] Often the coding process would first involve transfer of the data in their coded form to 80-column code sheets, which are then used for keypunching.

[6] There was no "not ascertained" (N.A.) code specified for family income in columns 7 through 12.

Column	
1 – 3	Study Number (753)
4 – 5	Deck Number (01)
6 – 9	Interview Number
7 – 12	Q1: Family Income XXXXXX (code amount in dollars)
13	Bracket; Total Family Income (Field in 7–12) 1. Under $5,000 2. $5,000 – $9,999 3. $10,000 – $14,999 4. $15,000 or more
14	Q2: Whether has Debt 1. Has Debt 5. Owes no debt 9. Not ascertained
codes 0 in col. 15-19 (for codes 5 and 9)	
15 – 19	Q3: Amount of Debt Owed XXXXX (code amount in dollars) 99998 Don't know amount 99999 Owes debt, amount not ascertained
20	Q4: Do You Plan to Buy a New Car in the Next Twelve Months? 1. Definitely will buy 2. Probably will buy 3. Maybe, uncertain 5. Will not buy 9. Not ascertained
code 0 in col. 21 (for codes 5 and 9)	
21	Q5: What Kind of Car Will It Be? 1. Sedan or hardtop 2. Stationwagon 3. Jeep 7. Other 8. Don't know (D.K.) 9. Not ascertained (N.A.) 0. Inappropriate (coded 0 in col. 20)
22	Q6: Family Size 1. One 2. Two 3. Three 4. Four 5. Five 6. Six 7. Seven or more 8. D.K. 9. N.A.

Figure 1-2 A Study "Code"

represented in a field; the actual question asked is used as the identifying heading. Column 21 illustrates the use of a residual category, a 7, to handle infrequent or unimportant answers. Again, it is the study design and the objectives that determine which data are to be specifically identified and which are to be lumped into residual categories. Coding is discussed in Chapter 4.

Error Control. Checking the data for completeness and consistency when they are finally in machine-readable form is essential if variable generation and analysis are to be free of unnecessary trouble and confusion. For example, consider the code 4 appearing in column 14 of a data record described by Figure 1-2. What does it mean? It means somebody "goofed" and one will have lost some information if it is not corrected. What is the meaning of a five in column 14 and 01000 in columns 15 through 19? Clearly, one or the other must be incorrect. Was column 14 miscoded, or was there a stray pencil mark in column 16 of the code sheet which was used to punch the data from? These are examples of more obvious errors and inconsistencies. Less obvious are the following:

1. 9 coded in column 22. Was the answer really not ascertained, or did the coder mean 9 family members?
2. 090000 in columns 7 through 12. Is it really a very high income family, or is it a transcription error for a family with a $9000 income?

These kinds of problems are more difficult to spot but are no less troublesome. Chapter 6 deals with these problems and outlines detailed procedures for coping with them.

Variable Generation. Just which variables must be constructed from the basic data depend on the analyses to be performed. These, in turn, were determined by the study design and its hierarchy of objectives. The variable-generation process can be very complex, involving the construction of indices based on multivariate analyses; or it may be very simple, such as the "bracketing" of a field variable. Column 13 is an example of the latter, a *bracket code* for the field in columns 7 through 12. In either case, the importance of having the data "clean" (i.e., having eliminated inconsistent or erroneous codes and other errors) is obvious. One cannot, for all units of analysis, construct a variable "definitely intends to buy a new station wagon in the next 12 months" (coded 1 in column 20 and 2 in column 21) with confidence, if there are some observations coded 4 in column 21 (type of car)! It is difficult enough to deal with the legal codes available. For example, just how should one handle those coded 8 in column 21? Or, if "definitely" is dropped from the description of the variable to be constructed, how is "intends" to be defined? Shall we include only those coded 1, or shall we include those coded 1, 2, and 3? These are issues that arise from an attempt to operationalize a concept and to implement that conceptualization in a code that maps numbers onto the categories that one wishes to use. What is done at this stage, then, depends on early work done during the study design as well as technical work done to ensure the quality of the data and the accuracy of the codes. The accuracy of the codes as a descriptor of the data contained in the storage media is a prerequisite for everything that follows. Chapter 7 discusses this phase of the study.

Data-Set Construction. When the survey is large and/or there are large numbers of variables per unit of observation, file management becomes an important problem. Consider, for example, a survey containing 2000 respondents with 15 cards of basic data per unit. Reading all these data into the computer for each analysis can be quite expensive. Furthermore, if new variables must be generated (and this is generally the case), adding these to the main file only exacerbates the problem, especially if the variables added are of little use in other analyses.[7] In such cases, it is frequently more efficient to work with subsets of the units or variables being studied. The disadvantage is that if a required variable has not been included in the subset you are using, it must be reconstructed. Chapter 7 treats the uses of subfiles.

Analysis. The next step in the process, analysis, is the heart of the entire project. It is at this stage that hypotheses are tested and discoveries are made about the behavior of the units of analysis. The initial study design has guided the entire process—what data were to be collected, in what form, and how they were to be transformed. Now the design dictates how the large number of variables will be analyzed (i.e., how these variables are to be related to each other and, operationally, what models and techniques will be used to test for and to validate the expected results). Chapter 8 explores the relationships among the data structure, the study objectives, and the statistical analysis.

Interpretation. Now the process has gone almost full circle. The researcher is again examining initial hypotheses, conceptual models, and conjectures, this time with the research findings to shed light on the processes described in the conceptualization and the study design. In this book, we shall touch only briefly on issues related to interpretation.

Subsequent chapters deal with the data-processing aspects of all of these issues in more detail, identifying the problems that the researcher is likely to encounter and presenting tested methods of coping with them. They develop an overall procedure for the handling of survey data which, hopefully, will minimize wasted time and will ensure that the data are as clean as possible when the analysis and interpretive stages are reached.

7 Despite the fact that analysis programs frequently have options enabling the analyst to construct variables at the time a statistical analysis is being run, it is generally useful to devote a block of time early in the study to variable generation.

SCHEDULING THE PROCESSING STEPS

One additional topic remains in this overview of the survey analysis process—scheduling. To avoid costly delays in processing the data, a fairly detailed schedule of activities should be established. An example is shown in Figure 1-3. The schedule presented begins with the completed questionnaire, the interviewers' instruction book, and an inventory of specific data-collection

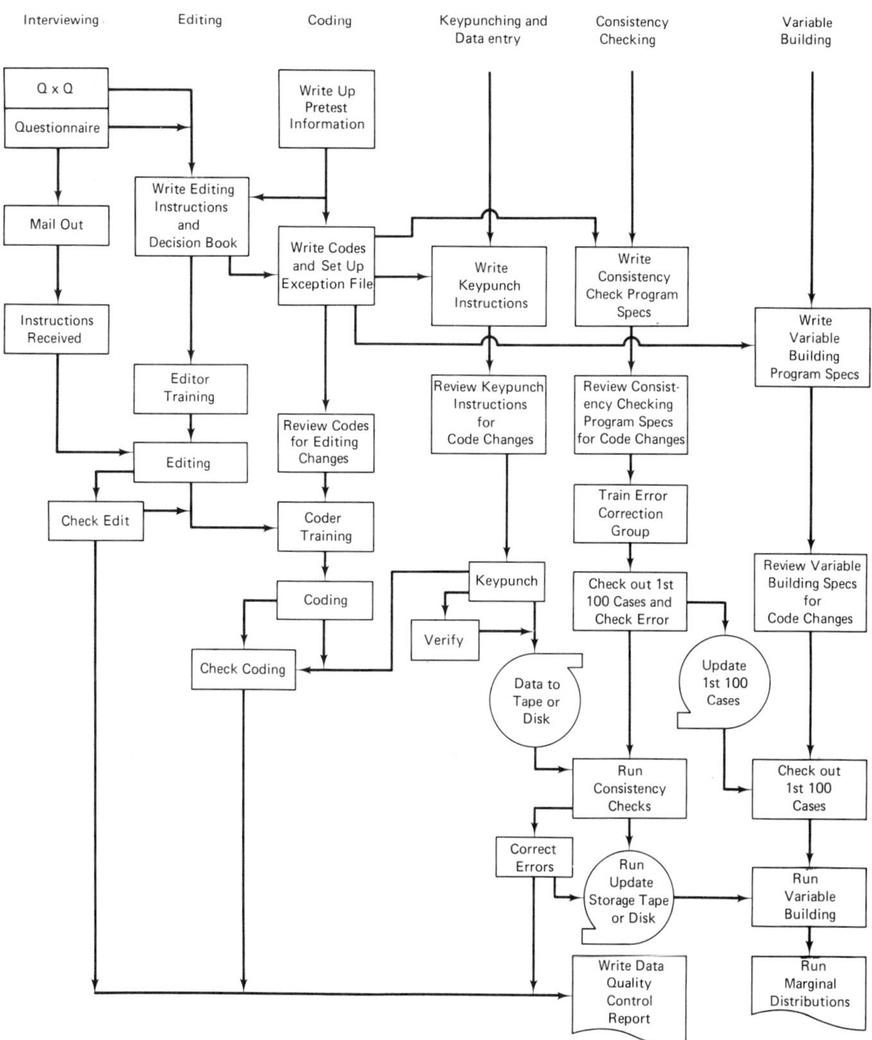

Figure 1-3 An Overview of File Conversion

objectives defined for each individual question. The pretest will have been done prior to finalization of the questionnaire. Materials are mailed out and the interviewing begins. Interviews will begin to come back to the researcher not long after interviewing starts (almost immediately if a local survey or a telephone interview is being conducted). Once enough actual interviews are available, the editors for the study should begin training, if the process is complex enough to warrant the division of labor. Then regular editing of the interviews should start promptly. This requires that the editors' instruction book be completed by this date. The length of time needed to prepare the book will dictate how much earlier its preparation should have begun. The research staff should check-edit in the earlier stages of the editing to make sure that the editors and the interviewing procedures are working properly, to discover any errors being systematically made, and to discover incompetent editors.

Once some of the interviews have been edited, coder training and coding can commence. Again, this requires completed code books, and their preparation should have started early enough to ensure their availability. Clearly, any delay in these activities is transmitted to all subsequent work schedules. Information from the pretest may provide valuable guidelines for code construction and for writing editors' instructions. As in the editing process, coding output should be checked by the research staff in the early stages of the process to ensure that no major problems persist.

As soon as a reasonable number of interviews have been coded, keypunching or other transcribing to machine-readable form may start. Consistency checking programs and variable-generation programs should have been set up with appropriate lead time so that when the first hundred or so interviews have been punched, they may be duplicated and used to check out the consistency-check and variable-generation programs.[8]

Once all the interviews have been coded and the data have been keypunched, it is recommended that a copy be made of the entire data set. A convenient method is to write the data on tape (or make a duplicate deck) to be used as input to consistency checking and variable-generation programs. Although consistency checking and variable generation may be parts of a simultaneous process, they are shown here with variable generation *logically* following the consistency check, since it is much more difficult to generate variables properly when inconsistencies and illegitimate codes are present in the data.

Having completed the checking and correction of the data and the generation of new variables, the entire study should again be duplicated to provide protection against inadvertent loss or damage to the data-storage media. Again,

[8] Data should be duplicated and originals kept in their proper place in storage. Test data are often discarded when procedures are proved, and the risk of losing original data is too great.

the simplest way is to copy the data onto one or more computer tapes, particularly if tapes rather than cards are to be used as input to data-analysis programs. For smaller studies, duplicate card decks are sufficient. As will be noted later, it is desirable at this point to obtain frequency distributions on all the variables in the study (or at least the major variables). These will be invaluable in analyzing the data later and can serve as check references for the detection of errors.

DATA STRUCTURES

It is the purpose of this chapter to outline a conceptual framework to be applied to cross-sectional or survey data as an informational structure. One reason for undertaking this task at this point is to make clear the need for a systematic review of the types of data structures that the proposed project will generate *before* trying to fit them into survey data-processing programs that may never have been designed to accept them. In addition, the reader will gain some insight into the types of problems that arise in the handling of complex data structures. Most importantly, a vocabulary for discussing data and data *structure* is a prerequisite to grasping the fundamental ideas of data *processing*. Finally, setting forth systematically the matrix and list concepts that have evolved for dealing with simple data structures will provide (at least by contrast) a framework for making the problems of dealing with more complex structures explicit.[1] These concepts have evolved in dealing with practical problems that required writing programs having not only the mathematical sophistication of "scientific" computation, but also the input volume and logical complexity of commercial applications.

In the sections that follow, a set of concepts for thinking and talking about survey data structures is presented, with a review of some of the important departures from the more simple rectangular data structure most commonly generated by survey procedures, and a set of criteria for adequate solutions to the data-handling problems in survey-processing systems which must deal with complex data structures. Readers whose data can be adequately described in matrix and vector terms may wish to skip the section on list structures.

No attempt is made to deal with the broader questions of data structures

[1] For example, see Meyers (1973, Chap. 14).

generated by experimental or other means. Several excellent and comprehensive frames of reference have already been set forth for this purpose.[2] However, some of the concepts developed by these writers will be used in considering the type of data that is our primary focus: nonexperimental survey data ordinarily generated when public-opinion "poll" methods are used. The first step is an outline of a conceptual scheme for characterizing survey data.

MATRIX CONCEPTS

Before discussing basic conceptual informational structures, it will be useful to review some concepts generally used to organize survey data. The most useful concept employed by many developers of statistical and data-management programs is that of the *array*. The terms are mathematical, but the usage is colloquial, so we shall try to explain the usage and commonly understood meanings as they apply to survey data (see Figure 2-1).

A *scalar* is a single value, usually a number. In survey research, it is often the coded answer to a single question. The interviewer asks, "Do you usually think of yourself as a Republican, a Democrat, or what?" The response, "I'm an Independent," might well be recorded as a "3" for "Independent." Not all coded answers are necessarily recorded as numbers, however. The answer to a question identifying one attribute of a respondent, the state of residence, might be recorded as "CALIF." Thus, the value taken on by a scalar need not be a member of the set of real numbers. Its value may be drawn from the set of integers, the set of real numbers, or it may be a configuration of alphanumeric characters.

A *vector* is an ordered array of scalars. In a survey, data are usually collected as a vector. Questions are asked of the respondent in a fixed order, and there are good reasons for maintaining this order in the coding process. One knows which scalar corresponds to which variable (question) because of its location in the ordered list. The first scalar in the vector is typically a respondent identification number, the scalar values of the study variables following in a predetermined order. Sometimes for methodological reasons the order in which questions are asked is varied, depending on the respondent's answers; however, during the coding process a fixed order is generally established. Meyers (1971) terms this a "bucket" format. Every interview is coded as a vector. Each coded attribute of the respondent is recorded in a fixed position in the vector. One vector is coded for each respondent. Of course, there are variations to this pattern, and we shall consider them later. The point here is that every vector has the same ordering of information as every other one—we do not code "age" as the first element in the vector for the first respondent and as the ninth element in the vector for the second respondent.

2 For example, see Coombs (1964) and Torgerson (1958).

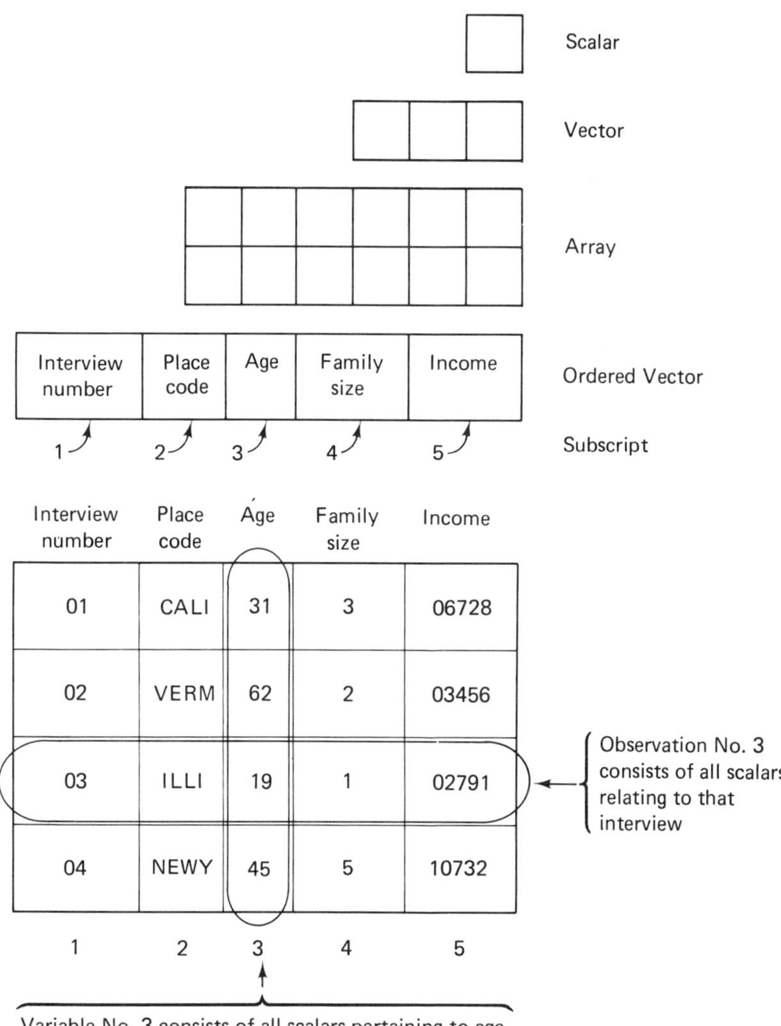

Figure 2-1 Scalars, Vectors, and Matrices

Thus, one can always identify a *variable* by its *subscript*. The latter is simply a number attached to each scalar that represents its location in the vector: first, second, third, and so on. A vector has a *length*, the number of scalars in the vector. A scalar is sometimes called an *element* when it is a member of a vector.

Vectors are sometimes termed *row* or *column* vectors, depending on whether they are logically recorded from left to right or from top to bottom. In most (but not all) representations of survey data, we shall refer to *units of analysis* (observations) as row vectors and to *variables* (attributes measured by the study) as column vectors.

A vector is an array with one *dimension*. An array with more than one dimension is called a *matrix*. An alternative way of viewing a matrix is as a group of vectors all of the same length. If they are row vectors, one has a conceptual scheme that is convenient for representing a survey in which each row is a respondent and each column contains answers to a particular question. This is a two-dimensional rectangular array. The length of the horizontal dimension (the number of columns) is related to the number of respondent attributes for which measures were obtained. The length of the vertical dimension (number of rows) is the number of respondents interviewed. A rectangular array is the most commonly used framework for organizing survey data.

Arrays with three or more dimensions can be envisioned. The most common third dimension is time. Data are collected from the same individuals at two or more points in time. Array terminology generally assumes that all the vectors comprising the array have the same length and that there are not any "holes" in the middle.[3]

DATA ORGANIZATION

Three important aspects of survey methodology are particularly affected by the theoretical structure of the data: (1) the sample design, (2) the data-collection strategy, and (3) the structure and form of actual data records. The first two problems are not systematically treated in this book. The third point, however, encompasses much of the material in the remaining chapters. If the reader has not completed (1) and (2) for a project under way, this discussion should be of additional benefit. The logical structure of the data is crucial to the determination of the units to be interviewed, how they are selected, whether there are single or multiple units of analysis per interview unit (e.g., the interview unit may be a dwelling unit which contains several units of analysis: family units, spending units, adult units), and other parameters of the sampling process. The data-collection strategy includes such decisions as who is interviewed, how many times each unit is interviewed, what kinds of data are to be collected (e.g., the data required to decompose each interview unit into units of analysis), the way answers are recorded, and related decisions.

It would probably be easiest, in most cases, if the operational form of the data structure were identical to the logical data structure. However, there are other important considerations which preclude this, including the requirements of data-analysis programs and the need to make the coding process as efficient

[3]It should be noted that we refer here to the structure inherent in the relationships between the data elements themselves and not to the way in which they must be organized for entry into survey data-processing programs that accept only rectangular data.

as possible. Thus, the researcher must often find creative ways to represent complex data structures in the context of much simpler storage patterns, most commonly the rectangular array. This chapter will describe several alternative conceptual data structures commonly found in research methodologies and discuss the process of rectangularizing the conceptual data structure for ease of coding and analysis.

Rectangular Data Structures

The simplest structure generated by a conventional cross-section survey is one response for each respondent to each of a set of questions. Every question results in exactly one answer, and every respondent is asked every question (refusals to answer a question have their own code as a response). The answers are represented by single values of a set of variables purporting to measure relevant attributes of that respondent at that point in time.

This structure can be conveniently represented as a data matrix A, illustrated in Figure 2-2. It constitutes the simplest form a set of survey data usually takes. The row subscript, i, varies over the observations $1, 2, 3, \ldots, N$, and the column subscript, j, varies over the variables $1, 2, 3, \ldots, V$. Each element, a_{ij}, is the value of the jth variable for the ith observation. This matrix is sometimes termed an *object-attribute* matrix.

It is important to note that what constitutes an observation (object) is a decision made consciously or unconsciously by the researcher at the beginning of the study. It may not necessarily coincide with either the sampling unit or the data-collection unit. For instance, one might decide to study automobile accidents using the accident as the unit but collect data by interviewing individual drivers. The decision to design the study so that the data-collection unit is not the same as the analysis unit may lead to considerable processing problems if the computer programs to be used were not designed to cope with this type of data organization. Similarly, variables need not correspond exactly to questions asked; several questions may be used to code a single variable, or several variables may be coded from the same answer.[4]

These considerations lead us to define an *atomic data element* as the value of an *attribute* defined for an *object* at one point in *time* by means of a specific *set of stimuli*, using a particular research *instrument* administered by a particular *interviewer*. We have seen that attributes and objects are the usual two dimensions of a rectangular data matrix. Generating a data matrix at several points in time, using alternative instruments, or recording data from several interviewers in different rows of the matrix generally complicates the data structure and the processing and analyses. Ordinarily, other matrix dimensions, such as time or alternative instruments, are collapsed during coding or other-

[4] For a further discussion, see Chapter 4.

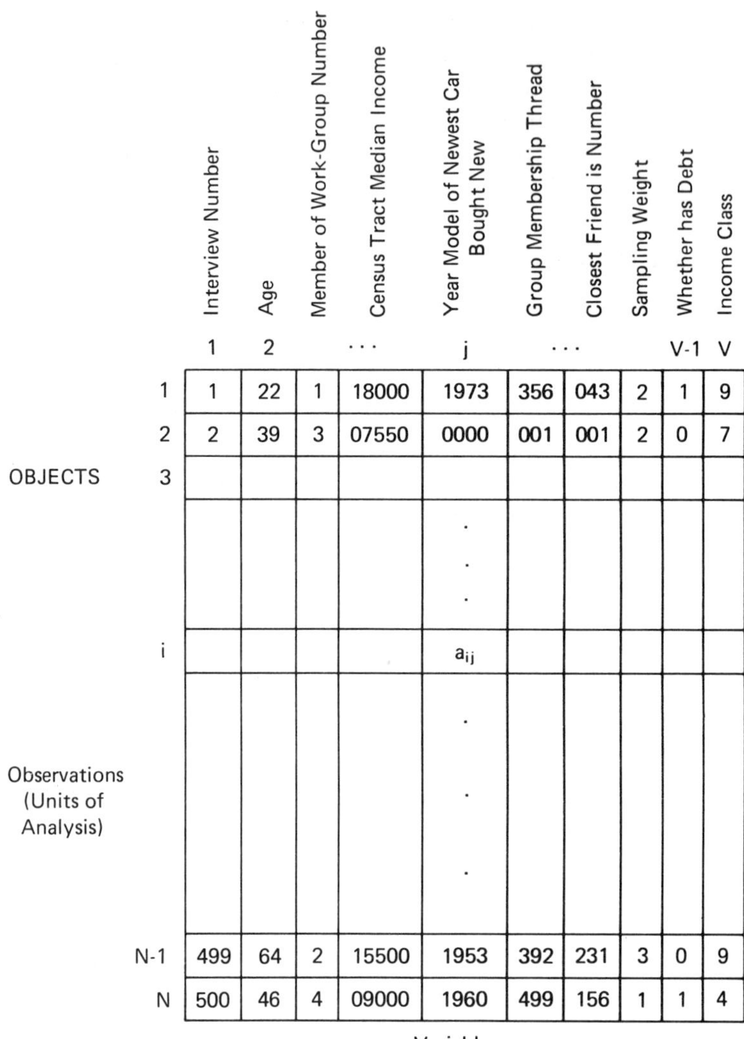

	Interview Number	Age	Member of Work-Group Number	Census Tract Median Income	Year Model of Newest Car Bought New	Group Membership Thread	Closest Friend is Number	Sampling Weight	Whether has Debt	Income Class
	1	2		. . .	j		. . .		V-1	V
1	1	22	1	18000	1973	356	043	2	1	9
2	2	39	3	07550	0000	001	001	2	0	7
3										
					. . .					
i					a_{ij}					
					. . .					
N-1	499	64	2	15500	1953	392	231	3	0	9
N	500	46	4	09000	1960	499	156	1	1	4

Figure 2-2 A Two-Dimensional Cross Section Data Matrix "A"

wise simplified to create a rectangular structure. It is this type of rectangular structure, a data matrix with N rows and V columns, that most statistical-survey-analysis programs will accept (Figure 2-2).[5]

These rectangular data matrices are usually stored row-wise; that is, the

[5] This type of data corresponds to that referred to by Coombs (1964 p. 28) as Q-II single-stimulus data.

physical representation of the data in their associated storage medium involves storing all the values for the variables for one unit, or row, in one *storage record* (e.g., one card in a deck of punched cards). The second record contains all the variables for the next unit. The matrix is usually stored from left to right, and if the rows are too long to fit into one physical record, several records are used (e.g., several cards per interview). This is the way data are usually collected when survey methods are used, and it is a natural way (although not necessarily the most efficient one) of organizing the data matrix for computer storage and processing.[6]

Variables in these arrays are of two basic types—*raw* or *derived*—according to whether they are simply coded answers to questions or the result of some mathematical and/or logical transformation of the original data. Creation of a derived variable on a permanent basis results in the addition of a new column to the matrix. Sometimes respondents must also be added to the data base, resulting in the addition of new rows. Research designs sometimes call for the investigation of several types of objects in a single study. Hence, many data matrices may be generated by one study. These may need to be concatenated together or otherwise combined for some purposes, and it is from this need that what have come to be called "data-management problems" arise.

A study by Katona et al. (1966) provides an illustration of a complex data base with many types of objects. The study generated eight data matrices used for analyses with various purposes. The units of analysis included family heads, cars owned by family heads, spending-unit heads, cars owned by spending-unit heads, household durable goods items bought during the calendar year by families, cars scrapped during the year by families, characteristics of the counties in which the interviews with family heads were taken, and characteristics of the census tracts in which these interviews were taken. One additional matrix, a "noninterview" array, contained one row for each address in the sample at which no interview was obtained. Observations made by the interviewer as to the house type, geographical location, type of neighborhood, and so on, were incorporated into this last file. Since these same observations were obtained for both interview and noninterview addresses, evidence of bias in the sample with respect to these known characteristics could be assessed. This required extraction of the relevant information about primary family units for each address and concatenation of this with the noninterview matrix. The result was a matrix with one row for every address in the original sample. Construction of this array permitted comparison of the characteristics of addresses from which interviews were obtained with those from which no interviews were obtained.

If the study design calls for returning to all or to selected respondents one or more times (a reinterview), the dimensionality of the data matrix is increased by one (see Figure 2-3). Succeeding waves are recorded "in back" of the two-dimensional matrix of data from the first wave. The subscript t of the

6 For a discussion of column-wise ("vat") storage, see Meyers (1973).

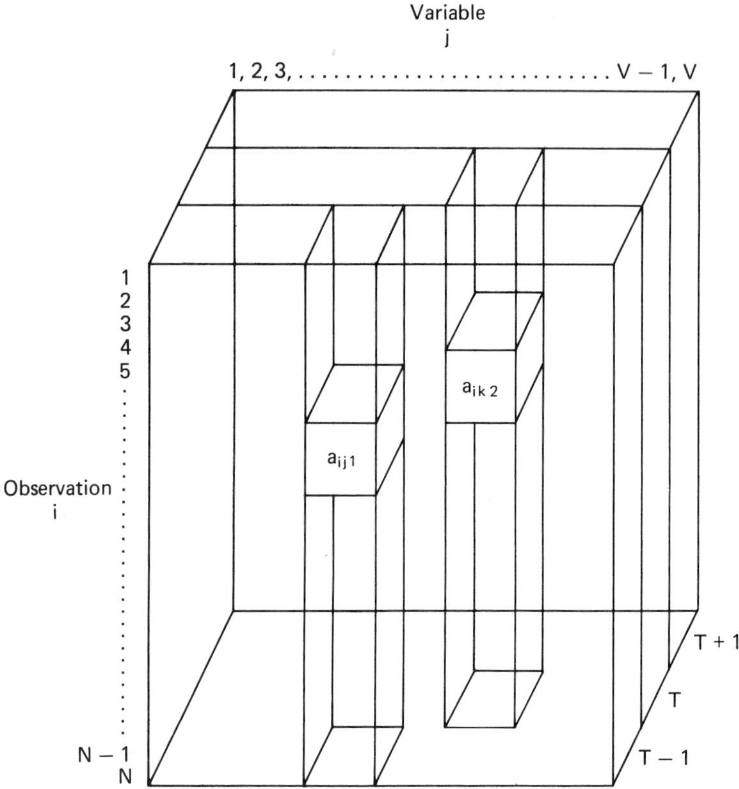

Figure 2-3 A Three-Dimensional Data Matrix "A"

third dimension ranges over the number of times the questionnaire was administered.[7]

Types of Variables

Variables are used for various purposes in the analyses, so the contents of each column in the data matrix differ in the way in which they are used. Variables may be identifiers, weights, attributes, or relational indicators. A unit *identifier* (e.g., interview number) is always required, since the physical storage of the data in computer-readable form always requires *at least* two copies of

[7] This object–attribute–time matrix actually has three more dimensions, which are ordinarily collapsed (as they are here). These extra dimensions are *instruments*, *observers*, and *repeated administrations* of the interview stimulus materials within one time period (perhaps by the use of alternative forms of several questionnaires used in varying sequences). Data-collection procedures in which these other dimensions are not collapsed will almost necessitate the use of special-purpose data-management programs to alter data to fit existing statistical programs.

the data matrix (counting the interview schedule itself). If more than one study is being processed in the same computer installation, other columns would generally be devoted to the study identification. Several additional identifiers might also be required if the study design calls for multiple data matrices. They would permit mapping the rows of one matrix into those of another; for example, a matrix containing one row for each automobile owned by the families in the study would normally contain both an automobile identification number and a reference to the number of the family, or row in the family matrix, which owned the car.

If the sample design obtains information at different sampling rates from several strata (or if some observations are deemed more reliable than others), *weight* variables may be established in the data matrix. The later use of the weight is to permit statistical analysis of the data in which each row is treated as multiple copies of itself with the number of copies being determined by the weight. Weights are not always integral, since they are sometimes normalized to sum to the sample size.

Attributes are of several types. The most common are the coded *answers* to questions posed in the survey (e.g., the respondent's age). Similar in form are those variables which are logical or mathematical *functions* of other variables. Sometimes the study design calls for *summary* variables reflecting the respondents' position in the distribution of the attribute (e.g., percentile score on an achievement test). A measure may be recoded from summarizing the attributes of a number of rows in another matrix, which are then all associated with the row in question (e.g., the year model of the newest car owned by a particular family requires a search of the automobile object-attribute matrix). A *contextual* variable records a characteristic of the environment in which the observation exists (e.g., median income of the census tract in which the family resides).

Sometimes the value of a variable will identify the respondent as a member of a particular interacting or socially interrelated group of people (e.g., as a member of a particular work group, union local, or high school clique). In this case the variable is said to be *relational.* It shows where that observation is positioned in the system of relationships among the set of objects being studied. The information is recorded by coding the identification number(s) of the object(s) to which the unit in question is related (e.g., the interview number of that person named as "best friend").

Further mention will be made of this type of relational data later, since its use is becoming more widespread in survey studies of organizations and other face-to-face groups.[8] It is important to note here that relational data, whether specifying the existence of a relationship to another object in the same data matrix, or to an object in another data matrix, *cannot be handled* by ordinary survey data-processing techniques as generally implemented in most available

[8] This type of interacting group is contrasted with a group that is really only statistical in its nature, like a sample of consumers who have no real contact with each other.

programs, and thus require special programming and management procedures.

All the above-mentioned types of variable have exactly one value per observation. However, theory may require the collection of data that are to be kept in other forms. Perhaps, at some point in the future, the verbatim recording of respondents' answers to questions will be put in machine-readable form as the usual mode of storing data. However, only one general type of multiple-valued variable appears to be relatively common at the time of writing. This takes the form of an ordered *list* of values and corresponds to Coombs' (1964) type Q-1 data. For example, respondents may be asked to rank a series of alternative policies from most to least preferred, or be asked which magazines they read. The result is a variable whose value is an ordered or unordered list of scalars, and which may be of varying lengths for different respondents (see Figure 2-4). This type of response cannot be recorded as a single value in a cell of the data matrix of the type discussed above. Instead, such a variable is generally coded as a set of *dummy variables* (each having the value 1 or 0) or as a fixed-length vector or list in which each answer (up to some predetermined

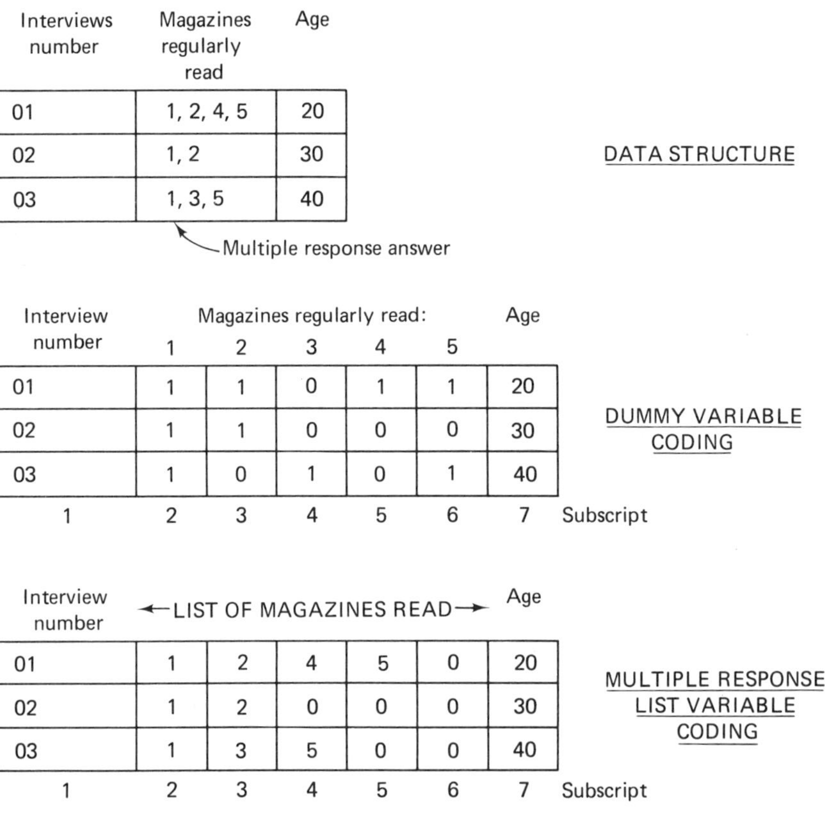

DATA STRUCTURE

Interviews number	Magazines regularly read	Age
01	1, 2, 4, 5	20
02	1, 2	30
03	1, 3, 5	40

Multiple response answer

DUMMY VARIABLE CODING

Interview number	Magazines regularly read: 1	2	3	4	5	Age
01	1	1	0	1	1	20
02	1	1	0	0	0	30
03	1	0	1	0	1	40
1	2	3	4	5	6	7 Subscript

MULTIPLE RESPONSE LIST VARIABLE CODING

Interview number	←LIST OF MAGAZINES READ→					Age
01	1	2	4	5	0	20
02	1	2	0	0	0	30
03	1	3	5	0	0	40
1	2	3	4	5	6	7 Subscript

Figure 2-4 Multiple Response Variable

number of answers) is represented as a single value in a series of variables. Short lists are then padded. The *series* must then be identified as a *multiple-response group*, or *list variable*. The length of the vector is generally set equal to a predetermined maximum number of anticipated responses. Additional responses from loquacious respondents simply are not coded, although priority coding schemes may be used to ensure that responses of certain types are not overlooked simply because they occurred late in the respondent's string of answers.[9] This is not always a particularly desirable coding arrangement, but it is resorted to in order to force data that are more properly represented by a list structure into the rectangular matrix format demanded by most statistical programs.[10]

More complex data matrices occur with a frequency that makes a careful examination of the capabilities of a system of statistical programs contemplated for use mandatory. Some analysts may wish to obtain paired comparisons of all stimuli in a set (in our example, they are simply ranked along one dimension). This would require a data matrix in which the elements were themselves triangular matrices, or possibly square and not symmetrical! An analyst with this type of data would almost certainly need the regular services of a competent programmer whose function would be to convert this type of data into a rectangular form suitable for input to available programs, or to write analysis programs for which it would be acceptable.

Our reason for dwelling on concepts for describing the data that can be generated by a survey is to provide a vocabulary for assessing one's own proposed data structure in order to anticipate possible problems that might be encountered in converting it into a form suitable for entry into available analysis programs. To make this minimum vocabulary basically complete, the concept "list" must be added to the terms already treated. The concept has been alluded to in our previous discussions, but now must be formally treated. Readers whose data are completely described by matrix and vector concepts may wish to postpone reading this discussion of list structures.

List Data Structures

When applied to a set of atomic data elements, a *list structure* provides a clear and precise way of representing *relationships* among these elements. This contrasts with the array, which has its primary use in representing the *attributes* of objects.[11] We shall illustrate the typical ways in which these kinds of data structures arise in the course of a survey and note what has to be done to convert data in which the logical structure is more easily conceptualized in terms of

[9] See Chapter 4 for a discussion of priority coding and Chapter 5 for an example.

[10] A better concept for use in designing statistical programs to process survey data might be that of a data matrix in which the elements were represented as unordered (or ordered) lists of scalars, not simply the single scalar values.

[11] Clark (1969) suggests four kinds of list structures: simple lists, two-way threaded lists, branching lists, and re-entrant lists. The reader is referred here for an extended discussion.

lists into rectangular *array* form for processing. The need for these concepts increases as more research is done which involves the analysis of group structures as well as the study of correlations between individual attributes.

One typical structure that arises in survey data is composed of units possessed by or which comprise members of a larger structural unit. This may simply occur because data are collected from one respondent about an entire house or family; but the family has several subunits, which may constitute units of analysis relevant for the study. For instance, in a study focusing on employment, persons over age 16 who are not in school and are either working or looking for work may be the relevant units of analysis. Or, each family may own one or more automobiles and the study objectives may call for summarizing data over automobiles. In both these cases, the unit of data collection comprises several subunits, which are the focus of the analysis. The larger unit can be represented by a list structure.

In other cases, we shall need the concept of a tree-like structure because the response to a single stimulus simply generates more than one piece of information. In this case, the list depicts a series of relationships between the respondent and the set of all possible types of codable answers.[12] In still other situations, the list structure depicts the relationships between objects, or people, or sets of people constituting the analysis units.

Figure 2-5 represents responses to a single question as a list. There are really three elements in the list, not four, since the fourth response is a "sign-off" by the respondent that no more information is forthcoming.

Figure 2-6 represents the use of a list structure to depict the relationships among the sampling, interviewing, and data-analysis units. Such a structure might well arise in a study of labor-force participation. The type of list structure used to characterize the data in Figure 2-7 is becoming more prevalent as survey methods are being used to study natural groupings of interacting people. For instance, it may be of importance to note where people sit relative to one another around a conference table if it affects their relationships with one another and the nature of their interactions. The two-way list representation of the data allows a complete reconstruction of who sits next to, or across from, another participant, as well as their spatial relationships to the leader. What is not depicted is the entire matrix of relationships. By making assumptions about the seating arrangements relative to the leader, all the spatial information can be recovered.[13]

Figure 2-8 is a more complex downward-branching list, a tree structure of the type that is required when a subunit "belongs to" (or, in this case, "is used by") more than one of the larger units. An analysis of the automobile

[12] Since the responses are ordered, the data could be analyzed as the type identified by Coombs (1964) as Q-I preference data.

[13] This list can also be seen to be hierarchical, even though note is kept of who sits to the left of each person as well as to the right.

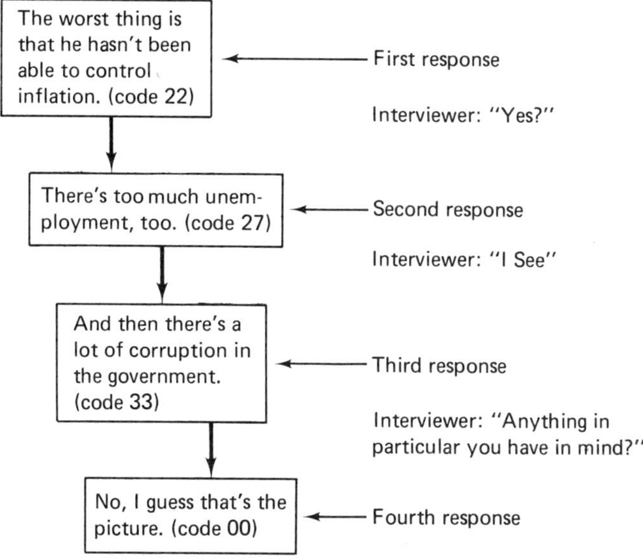
Interviewer: "Why is it that you feel the President has done a really lousy job?"[1]
The worst thing is that he hasn't been able to control inflation. (code 22)
First response
Interviewer: "Yes?"
There's too much unemployment, too. (code 27)
Second response
Interviewer: "I See"
And then there's a lot of corruption in the government. (code 33)
Third response
Interviewer: "Anything in particular you have in mind?"
No, I guess that's the picture. (code 00)
Fourth response
[1] Note: It is assumed that respondent is the head of the family.

Figure 2-5 A Simple List: Reasons for Disapproval of the President's Handling of his Job

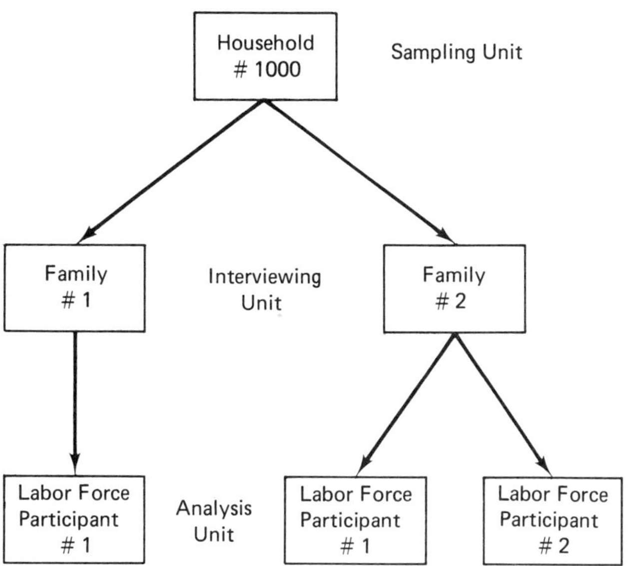
Household # 1000
Sampling Unit
Family # 1
Interviewing Unit
Family # 2
Labor Force Participant # 1
Analysis Unit
Labor Force Participant # 1
Labor Force Participant # 2

Figure 2-6 A Branching List—Tree

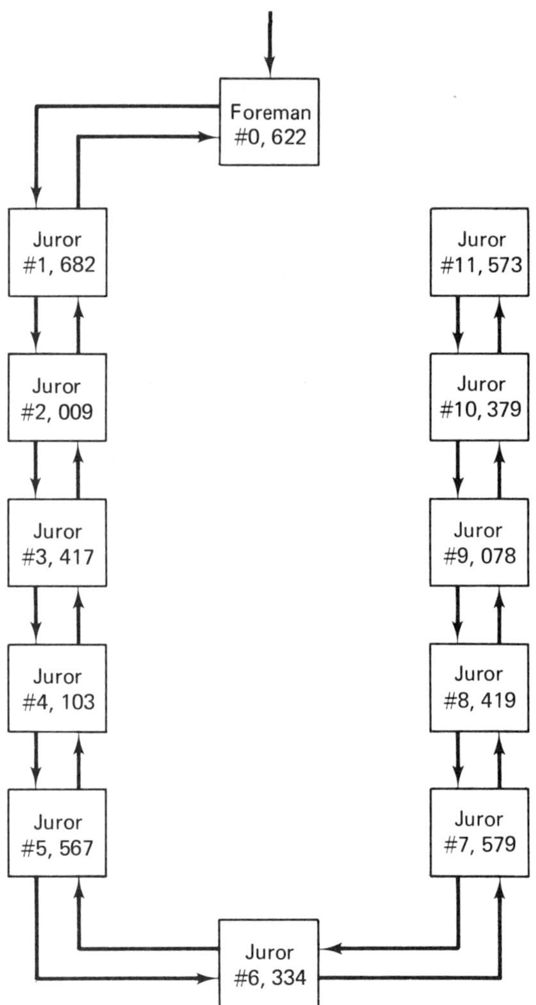

Figure 2-7 A Two-Way List Showing the Positions of Jurors around a Table

data for Spending Unit No. 1 in Family No. 3 would require information on Car No. 2 as well as on Car No. 6.

The most complex type of tree structure likely to occur in surveys is that required to depict the sociometric structure of a group of persons in a school classroom or an industrial work group. The structure is not necessarily hierarchical in nature, although some analysis algorithms will treat it as such.[14] Figure 2-9 illustrates the basic data drawn in a sociogram.

[14] For a review of relational-analysis algorithms, see Gleason (1969).

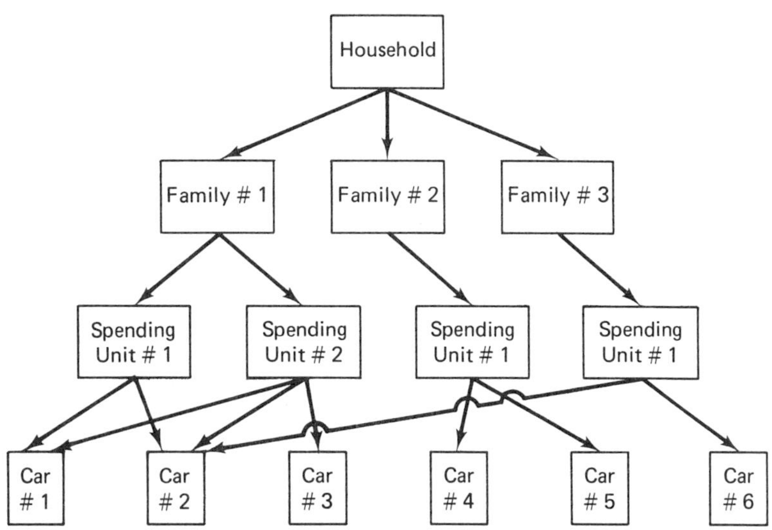

Figure 2-8 Downward Multi-Branching Tree Structure (re-entrant)

Tree Structures

A few simple rules will permit the analyst to represent (code) information in a way that will facilitate the handling of that portion of it for which a tree structure is a more appropriate conceptualization than an object-attribute matrix:

1. Give every individual data-analysis unit an identifying number sufficient to identify it uniquely.
2. Record these identifying numbers as list variables in the records of the units linked to it.
3. Where linkage is indeterminate (since several units stand in the same relationship to the subunit in question), record the unique identifier in *each* of the units to which it is linked.

These ideas can best be explicated by giving a few examples. Figure 2-10 illustrates the types of identifiers that are typically required. For each list variable (multiple-response), a maximum number of responses are provided for, and the empty portions of the list are filled up with "inapplicable" codes.[15] Example a. illustrates a typical list variable in which a single question generates multiple answers. A series of coded answers are listed in a set of fields that provide for up to five possible answers. The coded responses are given in the order

[15] We shall go over the details of the use of inapplicable codes in Chapter 4.

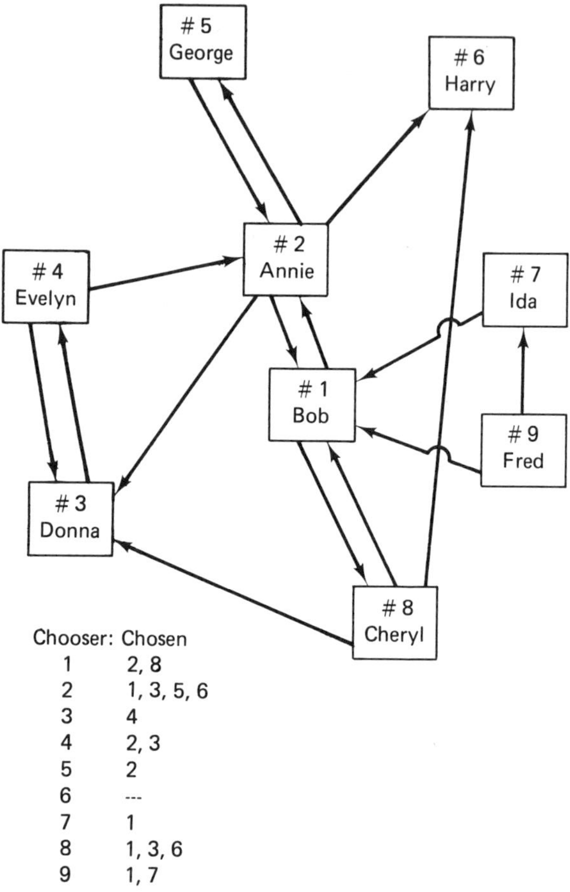

Figure 2-9 Digraph Structure Depicting a Clique (the numbers are simply person identifiers)

in which the respondent gave them during the interview, and the remaining spaces are filled with zeros, that code having been reserved for that purpose. The information is stored in a record for the family. The respondent may have been the "family head" or other family member. In any case, the response is used to characterize the family's attitude toward the president.

Example b. illustrates the type of identification that would be required in a file containing records for each labor-force participant for which the data were gathered by means of one interview per family in each sampled household. Each family would have a variable whose value was the number of labor-force participants (example c.).

If a number of decision-making groups such as juries were studied, the configuration of participants around the discussion table could be recorded

	Variable:	Code Sequence:	Code Located In Record for:
a.	Why president has done a poor job. (up to 5 responses coded)	1000, 22, 27, 33, 00, 00	Family # 1000
b.	Identification for first labor force participant in family number 2 in household number 1000	1000, 2, 1	Labor force participant
c.	Number of labor force participants in family # 2	1000, 2, 2	Record for family # 2 with identification
d.	Jury configuration: (foreman listed first)	622, 682, 009, 417, 103, 567, 334, 579, 419, 078, 379, 573	Record for a given jury
e.	Jurors sitting on left and right sides on jury with foreman # 622	417, 622, 009, 103	Record for juror # 417
f.	Automobiles used (identified by number) by family # 3 in household # 1000 (assume maximum 5)	1000, 3, 2, 6, 0, 0, 0	Family # 3 in household # 1000
g.	Persons chosen by Bob (person # 1) (assume maximum number is 5)	1, 2, 8, 0, 0, 0	Record for person # 1, Bob
h.	Sex of persons choosing Donna[1] (assume maximum number of 5)	3, F, F, F, 0, 0	Record for person # 3, Donna

[1] This would ordinarily be coded with digits instead of alphabetic characters (e.g., 1, female; 2, male, etc.)

Figure 2-10 Examples of Coded Values for List Variables

as in example d. If the foreman is always listed first and the participants are listed counterclockwise, the whole seating arrangement can be reconstructed. It is assumed that one record per jury is desired.

Example e. illustrates another method for recording positional information if the analysis is to proceed first by summarizing over the behavior of a single juror. The attributes of the persons on either side can also be recorded as part of the immediate environment (i.e., as contextual attributes).

The data structure represented in Figure 2-7 represents a somewhat more difficult problem, since, although each family "belongs" to exactly one household and each spending unit "belongs" to exactly one family, the same "belonging-to-one" pattern is not the case for the use of the automobiles owned by the three families who live together.[16] For this reason, the identifiers assigned to automobiles cannot simply consist of serial identifiers starting with the number 1 *within each family*. Rather, they must be identifiers that will connect the car with the smallest unit within which it can be uniquely assigned serially (i.e., the household). Example f. provides an illustration.

Relational Data

Figure 2-9 depicts the type of data that is most difficult to handle with most computer programs ostensibly designed to cope with survey data. It arises when the purposes of the study include the analysis of *relations* between objects or entities. Thus, research designs aimed at discovering the paths through which rumors travel, and those designed to isolate informal cliques and subgroups in work situations, suffer from the same problem; one can obtain such data using survey methods and record them (examples g. and h.), but the usual programs cannot analyze them.

These structures can be recorded using the same type of question which elicits a simple list variable. In this case, one asks for the reasons "why you don't like the way the president is doing his job" or "which magazines do you read?". In the other, the questions are aimed directly at eliciting information about the respondents' relationships with other persons in an identifiable interacting group of persons.[17] "Who are your closest friends in the class?" or the question "To whom do you go for advice about how to solve technical problems on your job?" are typical examples. In Figure 2-10, examples g. and h. illustrate the types of information that may be generated as relational list variables. The identifiers of the names, persons, or other units are placed in a list which may or may not be ordered and which provides for up to some prespecified number of choices.

PROCESSING COMPLEX STRUCTURES

From the preceding discussion, the reader can see that a number of problems may be encountered when coding list variables generated using survey procedures. When coding decisions are made, an arbitrary plan to ignore some of the responses must be made in order to fit the data into a fixed-length format. Usually the last-mentioned ones are disregarded. However, a priority code may be set up to ensure that if certain persons (responses) are, in fact, mentioned,

[16] This example is not actually so unrealistic as might be supposed at first glance, if we refer to use, not ownership of the automobiles.

[17] Coombs (1964) designates this type of relational data as Q-III.

their names (response categories) are recorded. If measures of popularity or characteristics of best friends are to be recorded, it may be advantageous to code these variables directly from the assembled sets of several questionnaires rather than resorting to extremely complex computer procedures that almost certainly will have to be written as special-purpose programs. The size of the data base, as usual, should influence the method chosen. The larger the data base, the more to be gained by using the computer.

We shall not attempt to deal with the statistical analysis of list-structure variables in this section. Rather, we shall simply note that two operations are generally necessary for rectangularizing a file with the desired units of analysis and the desired variables when the file contains list-structured data. Since many list structures are hierarchical, a means of aggregating data from smaller units into attributes of the larger units is generally needed. Conversely, the capability for imputing downward to each smaller unit the characteristics of the larger unit of which it is a part is also needed. The operations are complementary. For example, one may need to characterize a family by the most prestigious job held by any one of its labor-force participants. Conversely, if the unit of analysis to be studied is the individual, it may also be desirable to characterize each labor-force participant according to certain attributes of the larger family unit of which he is a member (e.g., the most prestigious job held by any one of its labor-force participants).[18]

The conversion of sociometric choice data into a rectangular file that can be used for conventional statistical analysis is a complex process and will depend almost completely on the specific analysis objectives of the study. Only a few general points will be made here. First, the desired output must generally be a rectangular file with one record per desired analysis unit. Second, the respondent will generally be characterized by measures of position in the network of relationships or by summary measures of the attributes of the people in the subgroups of which he or she is a member. For example, one may classify a worker according to the proportion of his clique members who are union members. The crucial point for the data processing is that this cannot be done until analysis of the matrix of relationships has *already* taken place to determine the respondent's position in the network, to isolate the subgroups comprising his particular social-environmental niche, to compute the summary measures for the relevant subgroups of members, and to add this information to the data vector. This means that the raw data in list-variable form must be transformed into an *adjacency matrix* for analysis (see Figure 2-11).[19] Then the results of that analysis must be returned to rectangular form as contextual variables. Some examples of these types of measures include characterizing a respondent according to

[18] The criteria for the *choice* of a data-analysis strategy that involves the aggregation of subunit or subsystem attributes and analysis at a higher level rather than calculating higher-level system attributes and imputing them downward for analysis is beyond the scope of this discussion.

[19] See Gleason (1969).

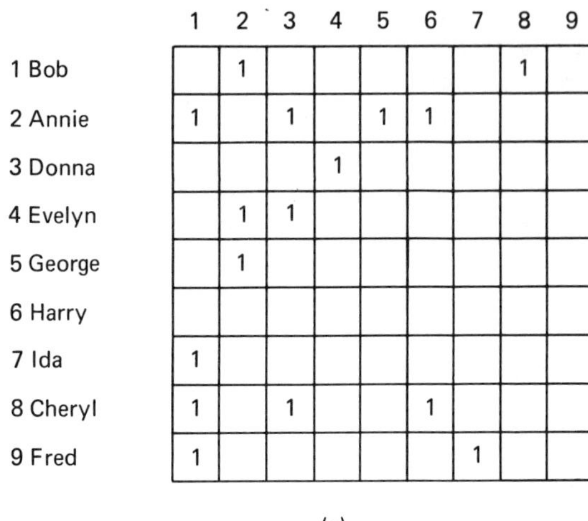

	1	2	3	4	5	6	7	8	9
1 Bob		1						1	
2 Annie	1		1		1	1			
3 Donna				1					
4 Evelyn		1	1						
5 George		1							
6 Harry									
7 Ida	1								
8 Cheryl	1		1			1			
9 Fred	1						1		

(a)

Chooser:	Chosen:
1	2, 8, 0, 0
2	1, 3, 5, 6
3	4, 0, 0, 0
4	2, 3, 0, 0
5	2, 0, 0, 0
6	0, 0, 0, 0
7	1, 0, 0, 0
8	1, 3, 6, 0
9	1, 7, 0, 0

(b)

Figure 2-11 List and Adjacency Matrix Representation of a Relational Structure

how many steps removed he or she is from the person most frequently designated by other members as the group leader, or the proportion of high-status persons among those who chose him.

Problems in Rectangularizing Data

Rectangularizing a data matrix often wastes space in the machine-readable files. When the data are rearranged into array form, portions of rows and columns will be missing. Figure 2-12 illustrates an irregular three-dimensional array that must be filled out and rearranged in order to complete the rectangularization process. Several operations must be accomplished. First, data were collected at two points in time, so the "back row" time T_2 data will have to be brought "forward" and placed "next to" the data from time T_1. Second, one

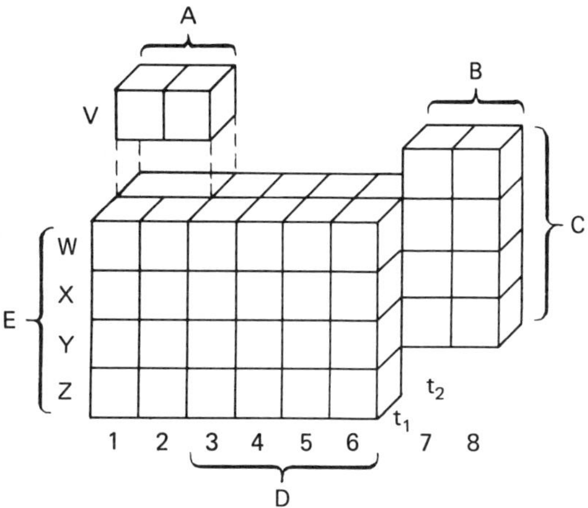

A. Variables 1 and 2 which had to be collected at time t_2 for Unit V, because Unit V wasn't interviewed at time t_1.
B. Variable 7 and 8 collected for V, W, X, Y at time t_2.
C. Wave two data units V, W, X, Y collected at time t_2.
D. Variables 3, 4, 5, 6, for which data was collected at both time t_1 and time t_2 but note t_2 values not collected for Z.
E. Units W, X, Y, Z interviewed at time t_1;

Figure 2-12 Irregular Three-Dimensional Data Array

respondent, *Z*, could not be reinterviewed, and all the data for time T_2 are missing for that respondent. It must be "dummied in" as missing data. Third, a new respondent was interviewed at time T_2 and certain "face sheet" or "demographic" variables (which, for everyone else, had been collected at time T_1) had to be collected from this respondent at time T_2. Finally, certain other questions were added at time T_2 which had not been asked at time T_1, requiring more dummying of missing values.[20]

In Figure 2-12, *A* illustrates the variables originally collected at time T_1 that had to be collected for the new person *V* added to the sample at time T_2; *B* represents the new questions 7 and 8 asked at time T_2; *C* represents the set of interviews collected at time T_2, persons *V*, *W*, *X*, and *Y*; and *D* represents the variables collected at both time periods. It is important to note that these variables, 3, 4, 5, 6, were collected at time T_1 for person *Z* but were not collected at time T_2, since *Z* was not interviewed at that time. *E* represents the set of interviews *W*, *X*, *Y*, and *Z* interviewed at time T_1.

Figure 2-13 depicts the same irregular three-dimensioned data array in

[20] We have not shown other problems which could also occur in situations like this, including changes in the wording of the questionnaire, or in the forms of the questions used to generate the information that is supposed to be common between the two time periods.

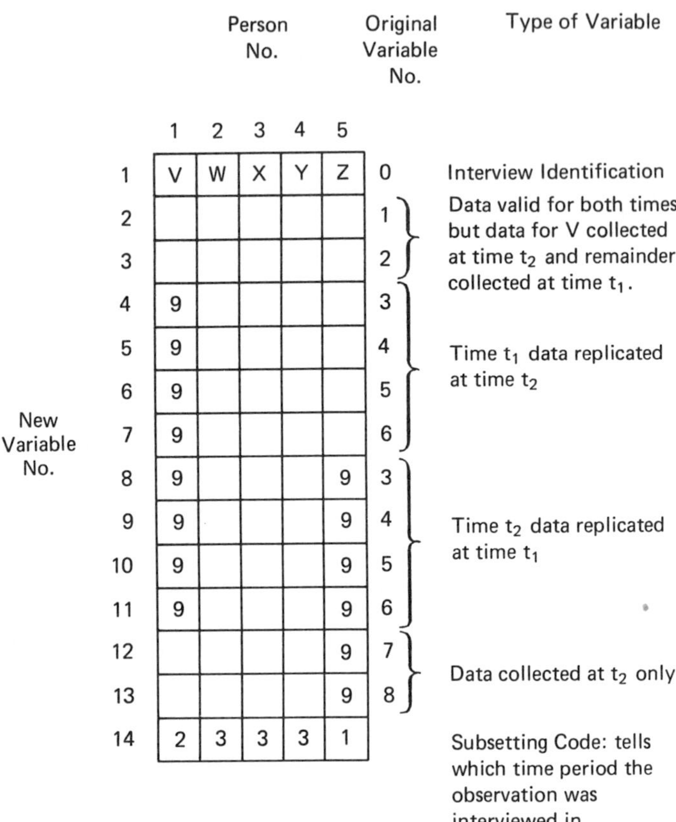

Figure 2-13 Rectangularization of an Irregular Three-Dimensioned Array

rectangularized form.[21] The missing sections of the array have been dummied in with missing data codes. The data valid for both times, but collected for observation V at time T_2, have been placed in the data matrix as though they had come from time T_1 (under the assumption that information about region and urbanization of area lived in, for example, can be validly collected at any time). A code has been added to every observation which has the value 1 if the data were collected only at time T_1, the value 2 if the data were collected only at time T_2, and the value 3 if the data were collected at both times.

Placed in this form and stored one logical record per observation, the following subfiles can be obtained:

[21] Note that the matrix has been turned sideways so that people appear in columns and variables appear in rows for ease in placing the diagram on the page. Some computer programs also use this transposed form of the data matrix in storage. See Meyers (1973) for an example.

1. Panel data matrix:
   (a) Observations: all those coded 3 in variable fourteen
   (b) Variables: one through eleven and fourteen
2. First-wave (time T_1) data matrix:
   (a) Observations: all those coded 1 or 3 in variable fourteen
   (b) Variables: one through three, four through seven, fourteen
3. Second-wave (time T_2) data matrix:
   (a) Observations: all those coded 2 or 3 in variable fourteen
   (b) Variables: one through three, and eight through fourteen

At this point, the analyst is in the position, to be able to assess the existence and importance of discrepancies between each individual respondent's answers at time T_1 and at time T_2 and can also analyze each wave separately. Unfortunately, manipulating the individual files from time T_1 and T_2 to produce the rectangularized file may, in many cases, require special-purpose computer programs.

We have indicated the types of research designs and data collection procedures that may require considerable advance planning to get the data into the form required by the analysis programs to be used, and suggest that analysts with such problems plan to budget their staff funds to include a competent computer programmer. Even if the necessary capabilities are available in the statistical "package," a careful examination of the program's data-manipulation capabilities, together with a review of the utility programs available at any computer center, will be required very early in the life of the project if unnecessary and probably costly delays are to be avoided.

Strategies in Solving Rectangularization Problems

Rectangularizing a data set has one major advantage—it works; that is, it permits the analyst to use available statistical packages. However, it wastes space in files and input–output time which may be very costly. Compatibility with most analysis programs is purchased at the cost of records which may be heavily padded with "inapplicable" or "no answer" values. The records may be very long and unwieldy, further increasing costs because of the excessively large amount of computer storage that must be devoted to input and output. Furthermore, clerical costs associated with making and keeping up-to-date codes for several files are heavy, since several sets of codes have to be made and updated when new variables are added to the files.

The worst of the problems appears to be the high costs associated with computer input and output. When records are stored row-wise, every time any variable is used in a run, all the data for the whole study must be read into the computer. Since computer billing procedures often include charges for input and output, serious consideration needs to be given to methods reducing the volume of data passed through when two or more time periods are used in a rectangularized file. These problems can be partially offset by using variable-length records and omitting the padding, but this will generally restrict the number of data-analysis programs available to the analyst. In addition, the preliminary processing required to rectangularize the file is often costly in and of itself, and, if not carefully controlled for errors, can be a source of problems that are laced through the subsequent analyses.

Codebook management is particularly complicated because of the large number of variables and the duplicate files that are required. Confusion inevitably arises unless names for time T_1 and T_2 variables are carefully identified.

On the other hand, the advantages of rectangularization include easy access to flexible variable-generation routines and a wide variety of statistical programs. Once rectangularization has taken place, the survey staff is in familiar territory in setting up computer runs, an additional advantage that is not to be taken lightly.

The alternatives include writing special-purpose programs to handle almost all the data processing for the study; writing special-purpose programs to rectangularize subsets of the data from the main data base, which is kept as close to its original form as possible; or a complete rewrite of the currently available statistical systems for processing survey data. Eventually each large-scale statistical system should include provision for handling multiple units of analysis, aggregation and imputation procedures, storage of data by variable instead of by observation, adequate treatment of list variables, and inclusion of provisions for handling relational data. This will doubtless have to await the next generation of survey data-processing software.[22]

[22] For examples of aggregation and imputation capabilities, see Shanks (1973) and Rattenbury et al. (1973). Meyers (1973) illustrates the use of storage by variable instead of by observation. Rattenbury (1973) illustrates the embryonic relational capabilities currently available in one statistical system, OSIRIS III.

EDITING

The primary purpose of the editing process is to ensure that the information in the questionnaire is ready to be transferred to data storage. It is the first step in processing after the completion of the interview. The editing strategy should be designed to ensure completeness, consistency (logical, conceptual, and administrative), and clarity and readability. Where errors cannot be corrected, they are at least recorded. Editing procedures should establish the completeness of the sample and interview. Every eligible respondent should be interviewed—and no others. Assignments must be made for missing information, where appropriate.

Although the consistency of the data can be checked systematically later by use of a computer, errors detected immediately after the interview process can be corrected more easily. Correction may require contact with the interviewer (and reliance on the interviewer's memory) or it may require recontacting the respondent. Interviewers may be able to clarify many problems from memory if they are contacted soon enough after completing the interview. Logical consistency requires that figures balance and that the respondent's answers to one set of questions agree with the answers to another set (e.g., that a female respondent is not asked her "wife's age"). Conceptual consistency simply means that a concept such as "installment debt" has the same components for each respondent (e.g., that debt on cars has not inadvertently been omitted for some respondents). In addition, editing procedures can be aimed at ensuring administrative consistency. If there are problems in administering the questionnaire (e.g., confusing directions to the interviewer), these can be detected early by the editing process and corrected before many interviews are incorrectly done.

A further objective is to ensure clarity and "readability" of the interviews.

Answers may not have been recorded completely enough for unambiguous classification by a coder, or some of the interviewers' handwriting may be illegible. Again, quick contact with the interviewer may clarify the problem and recover information that would otherwise have been lost.

Finally, editors may generate summary statistics about the quality of information in the questionnaire. They function to feed back information about interviewing errors to the field staff and to provide the research staff with information about the quality of the data being collected.

Mail interviews lend themselves least to this type of editing process. Once they are in the hands of the respondent (indeed, once they are mailed), it is practically impossible to make any structural, procedural, or administrative changes. For this reason, extensive pretesting is especially important for this kind of survey.

On the other hand, telephone interviews, particularly if run under the supervision of the researcher, can be subjected to almost simultaneous editing. Questions, interviewing techniques, probes, and so on, can be changed quickly and easily. There is also better control over the interviewers (e.g., their style, the probes used), since they frequently are all located in one place (or concentrated in several places). Field supervision is made much easier.

Personal interviews fall somewhere in between. There can be no "simultaneous" editing of the interview as in telephone interviews. In addition, personal interviews are often more complicated than either mail or telephone interviews. Thus, the editing process may be more complex.

Editing personal interviews generally requires several steps (some or all of which are also appropriate for mail or telephone interviews). The first stage is editing by the interviewers. After each interview or at the end of each day the interviewer should check through completed questionnaires, looking for errors and omissions. Frequently, any errors found can be corrected from memory (although here, and more so at later times, there is danger of biasing the data when relying on the memory of the interviewer). If necessary, this is probably the best time to recontact the respondent.

Sometimes field supervisors are used in the interviewing edit. In addition to being responsible for all interviewing in a specified geographic area and for collecting completed interviews to return to the central office, they would conduct the second edit, checking the interviews before sending them on to the central office and noting any problems or potential problems which could not be corrected at that point.

The final edit comes when the interviews are received by the researcher. It may actually occur in two parts. First, a technical edit (similar to those already conducted) may be performed by the field personnel receiving interviews from the field supervisors. The main objective is to review the adequacy of the field procedures used by the interviewer. Second, a project-directed edit is conducted, which is more concerned with the quality of the data, with its general internal consistency, and with missing data (generally refusals to answer certain questions). This process is usually more complicated and time consuming. It is usually not possible to correct errors found here by going back to the respondent (except for data checked early in the process), because the field work is likely to have been completed. However, early feedback can help to prevent the recurrence of errors.

There are some problems that arise during interviewing which can either be dealt with by an adequate editing procedure or which can at least be identified so that the researcher can take account of them later. These include:

1. Improper field procedures
   (a) Wrong questionnaire form used.
   (b) Interview inadvertently not taken.
2. Incomplete interviews
   (a) Questions not asked.
   (b) Directions not followed (proper segments of the questionnaire were not administered).
3. Improperly conducted interviews
   (a) The wrong respondent interviewed (e.g., son instead of father).
   (b) Questions misinterpreted by interviewer or respondent.
   (c) Evidence of bias or influencing of answers.
   (d) Failure to probe for adequate answers or the use of poor probes.
   (e) Interviewer apparently does not understand what type of responses constitute an answer to the actual question asked; or does not understand what the objective of the question is, and thus accepts an improper frame of reference for the respondent's answer.
   (f) Interviewer's illegible writing and/or style.
   (g) Interviewer recorded information which identified a respondent whose anonymity should have been protected.
   (h) Other evidence of need for training or instructions to be given to interviewer (e.g., failure to write down probes, wrong abbreviations, failure to follow directions).
4. Technical problems with the questionnaire or interview
   (a) Space was not provided for needed information.
   (b) The presence of unanticipated or unusually frequent extreme responses to questions, indicating a possible need for rewording of certain questions.
   (c) Inappropriate or unworkable interviewer instructions not detected in the pretest.
   (d) The order in which questions were asked introduces confusion, resentment, or bias into the respondent's answers.
5. Respondent rapport problems
   (a) Frequent refusal to answer certain questions.

   (b) Reports of abnormal termination of the interview (or presence of hostility) due to sensitive questions.
   (c) Evidence that respondent and interviewer are playing the "game" of "What answer do you want me to give?"
   (d) Evidence that the presence of other people in the interview situation is causing problems.

6. Consistency problems that can be isolated and reconciled
   (a) Contradictory answers (e.g., reports no savings in one section of the interview but reports interest from bank accounts in another section).
   (b) Misclassification (e.g., mortgage debt improperly reported as installment debt).
   (c) Impossible answers (e.g., reports paying $600 for a new Edsel in 1970—the car should have been recorded as a "used" car; or weekly income reported on the income-per-month line).
   (d) Unreasonable (and probably erroneous) responses (e.g., reports borrowing $2000 for two years to buy a car but reported monthly payments multiplied by 24 months are less than $2000; or house value is reported as being $90,000 while income is $2000 per year and the respondent claims less than a high school education).
7. Information that can be generated for use in later randomizing or assignment of missing information

The technical edit is best conducted by those who supervised the interviewing. It seeks to establish completeness, legibility, and general administrative consistency. The second edit, dealing with more complex questions of consistency, missing data, and the like, is best left to the direction of the substantive research staff, since these problems are more closely related to the design of the study and are best reviewed under close control and with a specially trained staff. A well-planned and organized editing operation can save both money and data in a sample survey, ensuring better reliability and increased ease in working with the data at later stages.

Even a small study must deal with the problems defined by the editor. The difference between the small study and a large one is that the researcher performs the task instead of organizing and supervising a production staff employing a division of labor.

ORGANIZING THE EDIT

Effective editing requires a systematic procedure for assessing interview quality. Unless the editing required is trivial, a book or manual of editors' instructions will have to be produced for use in production editing. The organization of this manual should follow the structure of the questionnaire (by section or topic). Each section in the instruction book should be preceded by a checklist, which alerts the editor to the important questions to be checked, outlines calculations and assignments to be made, and gives book references and any source tables to be used.

Whenever possible, each section should deal with questions in the order in which they appear in the questionnaire. Definitions, rules, concepts, tests of reasonableness, and examples should be included. Here are some examples of specific editing requirements included in the instruction book of a typical survey:

1. The total price reported as being paid for a car must equal the sum of reported amounts for cash paid, amount borrowed, and the trade-in allowance within 10 per cent, or $100, whichever is smaller. Figures must be adjusted if this condition does not hold.

The calculation of reasonableness could easily be done by computer once the data were transferred to a machine-readable storage medium. However, correction of errors frequently requires judgment and/or other information in the questionnaire (not all of which will be coded) not available to the computer and would which require pulling out the interview at a later date and correcting the data. This kind of trade-off must be considered when designing the editors' instructions.

2. Capital-gains income is not included in the concept of regular income used in the study. It should be edited out if included and reported in a section on miscellaneous income receipts (exact question references should be given).
3. Wall-to-wall carpeting and built-in appliances are to be excluded as purchases of durables and moved to the section on additions and repairs (specific question references here) since they are permanent and will likely remain in the home when sold (and are reflected in the reported value of the house).

Examples 2 and 3 illustrate types of editing that require alterations of the data to make them consistent with the concepts used in the study. Thus, although a built-in appliance is a durable good, it is important to the study that this be included as part of the house (perhaps to avoid double counting of assets if the built-ins are included in the reported value of the house). In Example 2 it appears that the study is interested in "usual" income as a separate concept or perhaps wishes to test the hypothesis that two types of income are treated differently by consumers.

4. Cars jointly owned or cars used by family members away from home must be excluded from the interview if there is a nonzero probability that the other owner or user is an eligible respondent in the study.

Here, editors must be concerned with the sample design and the quality of the sample and the data by eliminating a car that might have been counted twice in the sample.

Many of these problems are resolved by using information provided by the interviewer in addition to the normal response to the question. This information takes the form of marginal notes or attached explanations and is rarely recorded in machine-readable form. When this kind of information must be used, computerized editing techniques will not be satisfactory. The importance of well-trained interviewers is evidenced by the fact that the reporting of relevant facts is crucial to the reconciliation of these kinds of problems. The interviewer should only report the facts, leaving the interpretation to the editing and research staffs.

The success of the editing process depends heavily on a clear formulation of the concepts and objectives in the study design in the editing instructions. Including in the instruction book the reasoning behind the rules the editor is to apply improves his or her ability to edit the study meaningfully.

For very large studies, editing may be a long and very complicated procedure. At some point, it is even advantageous to divide the editing into two or more parts, because the success of editing depends heavily on the familiarity of the editor with the instruction book and the procedures. The division can be made on several criteria. Easiest is a simple division based on sections of the instrument. (Some editors do the first half, others do the second half.) It may also be advantageous to divide the work to be done on a conceptual basis (all the editing of financial data might be done by one group of editors, the rest of the questionnaire by a second group).

The Editors' Instruction Book

Assembled as a loose-leaf notebook, this editor's instruction book should contain check-lists of things to do, explanations of study objectives, information about definitions to be applied to the data, and such tables as may be needed for assigning missing data. Where possible, such aids as indexing tabs, marginal notes, boxes drawn around items, and reminders should be used.

Figure 3-1 provides a suggested outline for an editors' instruction book. Its four main sections—an overview of the study, an overview of the premachine processing of the interview data, a general introduction to editing, and specific instructions for the task to be accomplished—make possible its use both as a training and reference document. It assumes that editors are likely to be short-term temporary employees who must be trained and who will not necessarily be familiar either with research techniques or the substantive area of the study.

The purpose of including sections on study objectives and on the administrative handling of interviews before and after the editors see them is to facilitate the enlistment of the editing staff as active participants in an enterprise whose objectives they will take over as their own. The general introduction to editing should be included both for training purposes and to make possible its use as a manual to which procedural questions can be referred as production editing progresses.

I. Introduction: What the Study is about; an overview
   A. Overall objectives
   B. Sample design, units of analysis
   C. Kinds of variables and specific concepts used in the study
II. Overview of the sequence of operation on an interview
   A. Interviewing steps
   B. Receipt of the completed interviews
   C. Editing procedures
   D. Coding operations
   E. Conversion to machine readable form
III. A general introduction to editing
   A. Specific editing objectives, an explanation
      1. Assessment of extent to which concepts have been applied correctly and consistently
         a. Sampling
         b. Interviewing
      2. Locating and reporting the extent and sources of systematic sources of errors or discrepancies in the interviews.
         a. Sources: interviewer, respondent, instrument, other
         b. Potential corrective actions by: editor, interviewer, interviewing supervisor, study staff
         c. Use of editing decision book
         d. Guidelines for solving problems by referral to interviewer, editor action, or involvement of supervisory staff
      3. Making the interview clear, consistent and simple for coders
   B. Specific editors' tasks
      1. Assessing correct and consistent application of concepts
         a. Application of rules
         b. Balancing quantitative data
         c. Checking for consistency of data
         d. Review of improbable answers
      2. Corrective actions
         a. Performed by editor
            (1) Deleting improper material
            (2) Moving information to proper section, splitting items
            (3) Assigning factual data
            (4) Handling of "no answer" or "inapplicable" categories
         b. Types of problems to be referred to interviewers for information or another call to the respondent
         c. Circumstances requiring designation of an interview as "refusal" or other non-interview; removal of an interview from sample

Figure 3-1 Outline for an Editors' Instruction Book

3. Clerical tasks aimed at making the interview clear, consistent and simple to code
   a. Checking arithmetic; balancing
   b. Rounding numbers
   c. Handling of over-the-field amounts
   d. Stamped boxes
   e. Changing qualified answers
   f. Conversion of time data

C. Rules for editing
   1. Writing in green pencil
   2. Never erase interviewers entries
   3. Explanatory notes to coders
   4. Recording assumptions and decisions
   5. Conventions for coding: zeroes, numbers, NA's, inapplicable, negative, over-the-field values
   6. Abbreviations

IV. Detailed instructions for editing, by interview section. Overview of editing tasks in the current study. Organization of the interview by topic, overview of research objectives of each section and overview of editing tasks in each section as they relate to these objectives.
   A. Editing instructions for first interview section
      1. Checklist of tasks and index to section
      2. List possible assignments
      3. Introduction to the interview section
         a. Specific study of objectives
         b. Concepts used in the section
      4. Detailed explanation of each checklist item
         a. Definition
         b. Notation
         c. Rules for applying concepts
         d. Corrective actions to be performed
         e. Other clerical tasks to be performed
         f. Error reporting actions to be undertaken
         g. Coding to be performed
            (What to do and how to do it)
      5. Assignment tables to be used with this section
   B. Instructions for other interview sections B., C., etc.

V. Dated copies of editing instruction updates

Figure 3-1 (cont'd.) Outline for an Editor's Instruction Book

Editor Training

To accomplish their tasks effectively, editors must be carefully trained prior to the beginning of production editing. Using interview pretest results, the research staff should prepare several practice interviews for editor training. Each of these dummy interviews should contain answer patterns that reflect conceptual and procedural problems similar to those the editor will face in actual production. After a discussion of the objectives of the study and the concepts underlying the measures in the instrument, all editors should begin actually carrying out the editing instructions using the first practice interview. When completed, the research staff and the editors jointly go over the practice interview, reinforcing the process of applying the concepts of the study in the editing, explaining what should have been edited (or left alone), and going over the reasons why. This procedure is repeated for as many practice interviews as the research staff has prepared. (This should depend on the complexity of the data-collection procedures and the experience of the editing staff.) Editor training is an important part of the processing of survey data. The more familiar the editors are with the study, the more uniform the measures of the concepts of the study will be. It is also important for editors to know when not to edit, since imposition of their own perceptions, beliefs, and attitudes on the respondent's protocol is hardly what is desired. Hence, more caution is required in editing responses to questions ascertaining attitudes and beliefs than when handling those reporting behavior.

Production Editing: An Overview

Once editors are trained and have become familiar with the editors' instruction book, the production editing process can begin. First, a procedure for keeping track of the status and location of all interviews should be established. When possible, all interviews should be kept securely in a central location and signed out by the editors working on them. Storage in packs of 10 interviews, each pack in a large envelope, is a convenient method. The first and last interview numbers in the pack and the study identification are written on the outside of the envelope. The interview numbers identifying the pack are written in one corner of the envelope for easy visibility when the envelope is filed.

Figure 3-2 shows an example of a sign-out sheet for use with a divided editing process. The sign-out sheet indicates the editing status of each pack of interviews and also the editor responsible for that pack. Its use minimizes delays and helps keep the editing process an orderly one. It also records information that can easily be used later to assess and control editing cost, and it facilitates the check-editing process. Each editor should write his or her initials on every interview edited. A colored pencil should be used on the interview so that the editing notes can be distinguished from those of the interviewer.

As a rule, interviews should never be taken away from their pack except to be sent back to the interviewer for completion or to answer a question. If one has to be removed, a sheet of paper should be inserted into the pack to mark temporarily the position of that interview. The date, reason for removal, the remover's name, and an explanation of the whereabouts of the interview is recorded on the paper, which should be removed when the interview is returned.

When a problem arises that is not covered adequately by the instruction book, the editor should check the Editors' Decision book (discussed in the next

Study: # 752 Political Attitudes Editing Sign-Out Sheet

	Edit I		Check Edit I		Edit II		Check Edit II	
Interview number	Editor's Initials	Date Completed	Editor's Initials	Date Completed	Editor's Initials	Date Completed	Editor's Initials	Date Completed
0001-0009	WCD	5/1	JS	5/2	PJ	5/7		
0010-0019	DE	5/2	AT	5/3				
0020-0029								
0030-0039								
0040-0049					JS			
0050-0059					RB	5/3	WCD	5/6

Figure 3-2 Editing Sign-Out Sheet

section) to see if an identical or similar problem has already been encountered and a procedure decided upon for coping with it. If it has, the appropriate steps to take will be spelled out in the decision book. If not, a research project staff member should be consulted and these steps worked out and recorded in the decision book the first time they are used.

Research staff members should work closely with the editors, especially in the early stages of the editing process, for it is then that the meaningfulness of the data is evaluated in terms of the concepts of the study. Any changes made in the procedures should serve to improve a variable as a measure of a concept in the study design. The researcher should be continuously concerned with assessing the adequacy of the editing instruction and the effectiveness of the editors' training. The objective is an understanding of the quality of the data collected and the measurement problems that were encountered.

Each member of the research staff should edit 10 or 20 interviews and should check-edit extensively, especially early in the editing process. Checking should continue through the end of the editing. Check-editing is simply a re-edit of interviews already completed by the production editing group. Generally, this should be done by members of the research staff familiar with the study design and concepts. Any mistakes should be pointed out to the editor who has made them. If all editors seem to be missing some fundamental points, it may be useful to have an editors' meeting to go back over certain parts of the editing. This is a good idea once every few days, anyway. Feedback is essential if the editors' performance is in any way deficient.

Editors and check editors should always write down all their work on the interview itself so that any changes they make can be understood easily. If they use the editors' decision book in editing a particular interview, references to it (or to any other source or basis for the decisions) should be noted. All writing on the interview should be done with a colored pencil to distinguish it from the interviewer's writing.

Editors' Decision Book

As is typical when dealing with individual cases, there will always be problems which are not covered adequately by the editors' instruction book. These problems generally require a decision by the researcher. Figure 3-3 illustrates the type of decision that might be made and recorded. Since the same or very similar problems are likely to arise all through the editing process, it is useful to maintain a detailed log of the disposition of all problem cases. This is the role of the Editors' Decision Book.

Interview number	Problem:
799	Husband taken out as head of household, staying with daughter in another dwelling unit for the winter. (Initials: A.T.)
346	Husband is on freighter bound for Saigon as non-military ship's cook. Decision: take him as head of family unit. He is not non-sample nor can he be double-counted. (Initials: J. S.)
0082	Housing value given as $10,000, but is grocery store with living quarters in rear; with no other information given one half of this value was assumed for value of living quarters. (Initials: W. D.)
0092	I split a $20,000 value the same way as the interview 0082 above, and for the same reasons. (Initials: R. R.)

Figure 3-3 Examples of Editing Decisions

Although such a book could take many forms, a simple and effective procedure is to cut up a blank questionnaire and paste each question or block of questions (precoded or yes/no questions rarely require individual attention) on a blank sheet of paper, leaving plenty of space for notes after each question. The sheets should be organized in order of appearance of the questions in the instrument. A loose-leaf book should be used to permit the insertion of additional blank pages or a page with a question originally excluded because it was not expected to generate problems. Index tabs facilitate locating each section.

When confronted with a special problem, the editor can check the appropriate page of the decision book to see if an identical or similar problem has already been solved. If it has, the editor has a guide to solving it. If not, the editor consults with the research staff to develop a procedure for solving it. When the problem is resolved, the following information should be entered on the page that contains the appropriate question or question sequence:

1. The interview number of the problem respondent.
2. The question (or series of questions) that was the source of the problem.
3. The data given by the respondent (figures or the response given).
4. The decision that was made. Include all calculations and assumptions and the reasons (evidence from other questions) for making them.
5. The decision maker's name.

The book should be reviewed by the research staff at regular intervals and at the end of the editing process. Provision should be made for a final review of the decision book, and a final report on the editing should be written by the study staff members responsible for the editing. This report should summarize the decisions made, point out troublesome facets of the questionnaire, and provide a quantitative error and cost summary.

The advantages of such a system are clear. Once an editing decision is made and recorded, it provides a guide to other editors for the solution of identical or similar problems. This minimizes unnecessary interruptions of the research staff and ensures that problems are handled consistently among editors. The decision book also provides the research staff with information about the quality of data and ways in which each question might be improved if and when that question is used again. It is a valuable asset in the later interpretation of statistics with unexpected values.

Editing on the Computer

Editing operations which are straightforward and require only data that are normally coded from the interview can sometimes be accomplished convientiently on the computer. This requires correcting the data after they have been punched onto cards, rather than before, but computer-based survey-data-manipulation systems sometimes provide suitable capabilities.

The advantages of computer-based editing procedures may outweigh the difficulties in some circumstances:

1. A computer edit can be very fast (if the necessary programs have been prepared in advance).
2. The procedure is not subject to the kinds of errors that an editing staff would make.
3. It may be possible to correct the errors as they are detected if the rules for correction can be operationalized in advance.

4. Only those interviews with errors would have to be handled manually, saving a great deal of time (but yielding less "feel" for the data).
5. The error-assessment algorithm would be consistently applied for all respondents.

Sometimes such a process can be combined with the variable-building operation on the computer. The larger the data base, the more helpful such procedures may be.

Yet, there are disadvantages:

1. Except for assignment of missing data, editing after the coding process may severely complicate code design and coding procedures, since one of the major purposes of editing is to ensure that the responses to questions are within the bounds of the codes. Thus, if editing on the computer is planned, its impact on the coding process must be carefully considered.
2. Opportunities to do editing on the computer may be restricted, since editing procedures rarely lend themselves to the precise logic required for programming; frequently much of the information needed (e.g., interviewer comments and the additional comments of the respondent) will not even be coded. (On the other hand, after inconsistencies have been cleaned up and the data are in machine-readable form, assignment of missing information using a computer program is often very satisfactory.)

Coding and Variable Building During Editing

Many of the variables that will have to be generated from the basic data are best coded at the editing stage, for one or more of the following reasons:

1. The process of conceptually editing the data accomplishes a large part of the work required to build the variable.
2. Building the variable requires the pulling together of data from noncontiguous locations in the questionnaire and/or the use of outside information.
3. Individual elements of the variable must be edited and made consistent with the final variable constructed, and a fair amount of judgment is involved.
4. The sample is very small and/or the number of variables to be built are relatively few in number.

5. The computer technology available cannot easily handle the construction.

These problems are considered further in Chapter 4.

Editing Missing Information

Missing data present one of the major problems in the processing of much survey data. They are first encountered by the research staff in the editing stage. The most common source of missing data is the refusal of the respondent to answer particular questions in the interview. Questions in a survey are sometimes quite personal, and people may be sensitive about answering them (financial questions, for example). Or a respondent simply may lack the necessary information to answer a question. For some questions, of course, this itself is information to the researcher. But in many cases, a "don't know" is lost information (the amount of money in savings accounts, the price paid for a car, the length of time unemployed, and so on). As will be pointed out in Chapter 4, it is often useful to distinguish in coding between the don't know (D.K.) responses and the refusals or otherwise not ascertained (N.A.) data.

Another major source of missing data (N.A. type) is the failure of the interviewer to ask questions, follow directions, or write legibly. Failure to probe enough to get a response that is, in fact, an answer to the question as asked is also a source of N.A.'s. When detected, this needs to be called immediately to the attention of the interviewing staff. Many of these problems will have been eliminated by field edit, but some problems will invariably get through undetected.

If missing data occur frequently in an interview or there is an unacceptable amount on the very important variables in the study, a decision must be made as to whether the interview is worth keeping. So little information may be presented as to warrant its rejection and classification as a nonresponse. This problem is disturbingly frequent in surveys that deal with issues that are sensitive to respondents.

The most frequent method of dealing with missing data is to allow it to stand as is. Special code values are simply set aside for missing data in the code used to classify the data. In this case, the function of the editor may be simply to assess whether information is missing and to mark ambiguous responses clearly for the coders. This is the easiest way to deal with the missing data but presents problems for analysis at later stages. For example, if all respondents who were N.A. on any one of 10 predictors being used in an analysis were excluded from that analysis, half of the sample might be eliminated. With rare exceptions, respondents with missing data on a dependent variable in an explanatory analysis are always excluded.

Another method of dealing with missing data at the editing stage is to eliminate it by "assigning" a reasonable value to the variable. As an example, consider a respondent who has answered 199 of 200 questions in the interview but has refused to reveal his income. But income is one of the crucial variables in the study. Should the interview be thrown out? Part of the answer depends on the importance of the variable in the study, but completely discarding the interview generally is not a very good alternative. Too much other good information, gathered at considerable expense, would be lost. To avoid the technical problems of handling missing data later, a value might be assigned by the editor for income for each such respondent. Two things would be needed to make a reasonable assignment. First, there would have to be other data in the questionnaire that are correlated with income. Age, sex, occupation, education, and house value are good examples. Second, an exact relationship between these variables and income must be specified. Such data might be available from recently conducted surveys, or government statistics, or if necessary could be determined from known data in this survey (much more difficult since it requires early processing of data).

One procedure sometimes used is quite simple, requiring only an "actuarial" table for assigning a value. Figure 3-4 is an illustration of how income might be assigned using information about age and education. The cells of this table are merely sample means from a previous survey containing age, education, and income. A simple table look-up yields the mean value of income for a particular age–education group. A more sophisticated procedure might use the results of a multiple regression of income on age, education, occupation, and other variables. As the number of predictors rises, however, so does the probability that one of them will also be among the missing data in the interview.

	Education					
Age	0-6	7-8	9-11	12	College	N.A.
Under 24	3000	5000	6000	8000	12000	5000
25-34	4000	6000	7000	9000	14000	9000
35-44	5000	7000	8000	10000	16000	10000
45-54	7000	9000	10000	12000	19000	12000
55-64	5000	7000	8000	11000	17000	11000
65 and over	3000	5000	6000	9000	14000	9000
N.A.	5000	7000	8000	10000	15000	10000

Figure 3-4 Mean Income by Age and Education

For evaluative purposes, it is a good idea to keep track of the total number of assignments made in each individual interview. An allowance for this should be made in designing the code. Editors are instructed to enter the "number of assignments made" in a coding box stamped at the end of the interview. For individual variables of crucial importance, it may also be a good idea to note the fact that its value has been assigned. A code can be established for that, and the fact that it is assigned should be marked so that it is obvious to the coder from the editor's notes (e.g., assigned values could be noted with a large "A" written next to the value in the editor's green pencil).

A large number of assignments for a particular variable can have undesirable effects on its characteristics. As an extreme example, consider the effect of assigning all the values of income in a survey because all respondents refused to reveal the information. Then there would only be 42 values of income in the entire study, those shown in the income assignment table. The variable would have a drastically reduced variance and have no variance within age and education groups. This is hardly a desirable property. Thus, for use in the analysis stage in interpreting results, the number of assigned observations may be an important piece of information. It is generally desirable to code whether or not each of the crucially important independent variables has been assigned for that interview.

One solution is to use random-number tables combined with tables of means in a procedure that adds randomly chosen constants to the table values so as to maintain known levels of variation in those cells. Alternatively, if use of assignment tables based on other variables would lead to circularity in the logical reasoning behind explanatory analyses being conducted in the study, assignment by means of randomly chosen constants alone might be preferable. Thus, population values can be estimated from previous sample statistics based solely on that variable. The choice would depend on study objectives. Such procedures are better adapted to implementation in a computer program but are mentioned here because with only one or two variables for which assignments are to be made, manual procedures would be simpler. It is important to note that if computer analysis programs cannot deal selectively with missing values in the fashion desired by the researcher, some assignment procedure is needed. This means that computer program capabilities need to be investigated *before* editing takes place, not afterward.

In a large study, it is unlikely that it will be practical to assign all missing data, unless a straightforward randomizing procedure is available. For many of the variables, the effort would not be worthwhile. If a variable is to be used as a major dependent variable in the study, it is generally best not to assign many of its values.

Where assignments are to be made, the necessary information must be provided in advance and assignment tables constructed and included in the appropriate places in the editors' instruction book. Frequently, assignments must be made in two stages. First, an assignment must be made as to whether or not the respondent has a particular characteristic (such as debt). This requires a probabilistic statement about the incidence of the characteristic. For instance, a random number in the range 00–99 could be used as follows:

Has Debt	No Debt
00–48	49–99

The division is based on known data showing that previous studies of the incidence of debt estimate that 49 per cent of all U.S. families have debt. If a usable response to a yes/no question about debt (such as "Do you owe any money. . . ?") is not obtained, the editor can check off the next number from a random-number table, assign "yes" if the number is between 00 and 48, or assign "no" if the number is 49 to 99. The assignment is noted by checking the "yes" or "no" box in the interview with the editor's green pencil (and marking an A beside it to note an assigned value).

If "yes" is assigned (or was already checked but the amount was not supplied), the amount of debt owed must then be assigned. This can be accomplished using a procedure similar to that shown for the assignment of income. If "no" was assigned, the "amount" question is simply marked "assigned inappropriate" [INAP (A)].

EDITING OBJECTIVES

An editor has three specific objectives:

1. To assess the extent to which the concepts of the study have been applied correctly and consistently.
2. To locate and report the extent to which the application of concepts and required procedures deviates from that prescribed, and take action to correct them where appropriate.
3. To perform the clerical tasks needed to make the interview clear, consistent, and simple for the coders.

Proper Application of Concepts

An important aspect of the application of the conceptual scheme employed in any study lies in the definitions used in the sampling and interview procedures. A typical editor's task is to review the interviewer's implementation of these concepts from the information found in the interview. Was the dwelling unit from which the interview was obtained part of the population of such units as defined by the study (e.g., a permanent residence rather than a summer home or a hotel)? Were all the listed occupants residents of that dwelling unit according to the study's definitions of resident? Is there any evidence that someone was overlooked? Who is the "head" of each family? Were all the interviews that should have been taken actually obtained from this dwelling unit? Were the right respondents chosen? Did the interviewer follow prescribed procedures for listing all the family members in the proper sequence for each interview? Information from the "listing boxes" on the front or "face" sheet of each interview is combined with data from a "thumbnail" sketch of the interview situation and answers to factual and substantive questions, to provide an answer to the question "Was the sampling done properly?"

The concepts of the study must also be applied correctly by the interviewer to the interviewing process itself. Was the correct sequence of questions followed? Sometimes certain questions are to be asked only of retired persons, persons "in the labor force," or female respondents. Sections improperly asked will generally be marked "inapplicable" and those omitted may be marked "no answer," or the questionnaire might be returned to the interviewer for completion if several crucial sections are missing. In each case, information bearing on whether or not the procedures were followed correctly must be provided for in the interview schedule. Clear definitions of such things as "What is a dwelling unit?", "What is required if this dwelling unit is to be considered the 'residence' of a given person?", and "What configurations of people living together are to be considered a family?" must be provided by the research project staff in the instruction book.[1]

In assessing the adequacy of the interviewer's applications of the substantive concepts of the study in factual questions, the editor must assemble information from various portions of the interview that appear to bear on the topic and determine what information is actually to be used, omitting the remainder from consideration. For instance, the 1966 Survey of Consumer Finances attempted to measure the amount of debt incurred on additions and repairs to housing during the calendar year.[2] Included were: interior remodeling and improvements, rugs or drapes costing $300 or more, plumbing and gas installations, electrical wiring and fixtures, built-in electrical appliances, heating and cooling systems, attachments such as awnings, improvements to the house exterior, and landscaping and grounds improvements. Excluded were: debts incurred before or after the specific time period, improvements on rental or other business property, and debts already counted as mortgage debt. Editors were required to scan several sections of the questionnaire to locate debts reported in several different places, determine whether the debts were incurred

[1] For instance, in the 1966 Survey of Consumer Finances (Katona et al., 1967) the study population consisted of the primary and secondary families living in dwelling units within the 48 states of the continental United States and the District of Columbia, exclusive of dwellings on military reservations. The sample was selected from the 74 PSU's of the SRC national sample. Eligible respondents were heads of families; however, interviews were taken with a spouse if one was present, rather than treating respondent absence as a noninterview situation. Dwelling units were defined as two or more rooms with a separate entrance from the outside or from a common hallway, one or more rooms in an established hotel or apartment building, or one or more rooms with cooking facilities more permanent and substantial than a hot plate. Old people's homes, sanitariums, convents, or other institutions containing 10 or more unrelated families, or transient hotels and motels, were not included in the sample. However, trailers, houses, apartments, living quarters over garages, and rooming houses were included. Persons defined as residents included live-in servants, students home between terms, and servicemen home on leave; excluded were people in the hospital, persons away on business, and people in prison. A family was defined as a group of persons living together in the dwelling unit and related by blood, marriage, or adoption. The head of the family was designated as the husband if the adults in the family consisted of husband and wife only, and was usually the husband, otherwise. However, it was required that the designated head be the person best acquainted with the family finances, usually the main wage earner.

[2] For the question asked, see Katona et al. (1967, p. 279).

during the time period in question, delete those that referred to property rented out or used for business purposes or which were for furnishings instead of additions and repairs (e.g., rugs or drapes under $300 in price), delete debts from back taxes, unpaid utility bills, and so on, and add up the total debt incurred given the study definitions. We shall have more to say about applying study concepts and definitions later.

Reporting and Correcting Errors

The second major task of the editor is to locate and report the extent and sources of systematic errors and discrepancies in the interview. These errors may be due to the interviewer, the respondent, the interview schedule itself, the instructions to the interviewer, or other sources. Where the task simply requires applying procedures already worked out and listed in the editors' instruction book, no special reporting is generally needed unless there appear to be more errors than expected, or errors appear to be concentrated among particular interviewers or types of respondents. When interviews frequently need to be sent back to the interviewers for completion, or where frequent entries in the decision book indicate a major source of trouble, changes in interviewing procedures are probably warranted if they can still be implemented. Then, increased attention must be given to editing this part of the interview.

In many cases, corrective action can simply be taken by the editor by deleting improper material, moving information to the proper section of the questionnaire, or assigning missing data. In other cases he or she will have to decide whether to refer the problem to the study director or to the field staff for handling by the interviewer; in some cases, the interview may have to be designated a "refusal" by the study director if a large amount of information is clearly insufficient or obviously falsified.

Many of the editor's reporting functions can be handled by means of the editors' decision book. Others (e.g., those relating to interviewer malfunctioning) can be handled by instructing editors to make up a file of 3- by 5-inch cards, one for each error. The card contains the number of the interview on which the error was found, the question in error, the type of error made, the editor's initials, and the date. Types of errors reported in this fashion might include: (1) bad sampling or wrong respondent, (2) incomplete interview, (3) wrong section of questions asked, (4) inadequate probes used, (5) repeated acceptance of responses that did not provide an answer to the question, and (6) illegible handwriting. If interactive computer terminals are available, such a file can be kept on-line. Periodic review permits locating troublesome interviewers or interview sections. The types of errors reported in this fashion would undoubtedly vary with the subject matter of the interview and the experience of the interviewing staff. Of course, such feedback can be used to modify interviewer behavior if the field schedule permits. Otherwise, it merely would be used to pinpoint problems that had to be left as no-answer responses.

Making Clerical Adjustments

The third important set of tasks routinely performed by the editor is all those clerical operations needed to make the interview clear and simple to code. This includes checking any arithmetic that may have been performed by the interviewer; balancing such quantities as monthly payments, interest paid, down payment, and total price of purchases; rounding amounts to the nearest $100 or whatever; assigning codes to values too large to fit into the field established for them; changing qualified answers to specific terminology (e.g., "a few" = "4"); and converting time data to the proper period (e.g., weekly to monthly income figures).

This overview of the specific objectives of editing has pointed out the kinds of things that editors do when assessing the quality of an interview. Concepts need to be applied correctly and consistently, the extent and sources of error must be located and reported, and various clerical tasks must be performed to get the interview ready for coding. A more detailed description of some of these tasks follows.

Examples of Editing Operations

This section illustrates the kinds of things that editors actually do, and presents some examples of techniques that have been used successfully. Some of the editing operations from the 1968 Survey of Consumer Finances will be used to illustrate typical tasks that require the application of concepts, provide examples of various corrective actions, and suggest the specific kinds of clerical tasks that can be performed routinely.

There are four types of specific editing operations related to assessing the consistency of application of the concepts of the survey. These include assessing the interviewer's actual implementation of the survey procedures, seeing that quantitative data "balance" in cases where this is required, checking for consistency between qualitative answers, and reviewing the possible explanations for improbable answers.

There is no interviewing area in which the proper application of concepts is as important as in the definition of the sampling frame and the selection of respondents to be interviewed. If the conceptual scheme defining the sampling frame and the units of interviewing are improperly or inconsistently applied, none of the data collected may be of much use, even if the respondents answered questions accurately and willingly. Hence, a typical first task for the editing operation is to make sure that from the evidence in the interviews the sampling and listing were done properly. Its primary purpose is to make sure that, using the study definitions, all members (and only members) of the dwelling unit or other sampling unit being interviewed are entered in the listing boxes. In addition, the family-unit composition of the dwelling unit would ordinarily be determined and pre-coded, the interviewer's decisions reviewed as to the designation of the "head" of each family, and a check carried out to make sure that the proper person was interviewed. The details of this procedure are illustrated in the example in Chapter 5.

As an editor goes about his or her duties, it may be discovered that the interview being worked on should not have been taken. For instance, if the study sampled people aged 18 and over, and a 17-year-old was interviewed, the interview should be discarded. If the sample is one of dwelling units and a man whose house is not in the sample is interviewed in his place of business, those data should be discarded. In these cases, the reason for the discard is that the data were not from the desired population. However, in other cases, either the interviewer or the respondent created a situation in which the data generated by the interview are of such poor quality as to be useless. There are two requirements for handling this type of situation: (1) an explicit rule should be written that is applied uniformly, and (2) the rule should involve only the bad information on those variables deemed to be of critical importance to the study. These rules should be applied consistently so as not to bias the sampling procedures. The study director sets the rules.

Another example of editing to ensure proper application of concepts is the set of procedures associated with the editing of information on consumer discretionary debt in the 1967 Survey of Consumer Finances.[3] The survey sought to measure the amount of certain kinds of consumer expenditures during 1967 on a family basis, the amount of debt incurred during 1967, and the total amount of debt owed by each family. It is important to note that the concern was only with certain kinds of expenditures and debt, which required classifying and measuring these separately. Hence, the editors were required to make two major decisions for each item of expenditures and debt contained in the interview (including the thumbnail sketch). These decisions were: (1) whether the item was the type of expenditure that was to be measured, and, if so, (2) whether the information was to be left in the section of the interview in which it was elicited, or moved and recorded in another section for coders to use there. Because the patterns of consumer expenditures and debts are so varied and because neither the respondent nor the interviewer should attempt to classify the debt information according to detailed study concepts during the interview, the editing job was a complex one.

To facilitate the interviewing process, debt questions were spread among five sections of the questionnaire. But for study purposes debts were classified according to a set of very specific categories, purposes for which the debts were incurred. Types of debt included: (1) mortgages (housing), (2) passenger cars, (3) housing additions and repairs, (4) major household durable goods, and (5) other discretionary personal consumer debt. All nonmortgage debts were further classified into installment and noninstallment debt, and all were subdivided according to whether they were acquired during the preceding calendar year.

[3] See Katona et al. (1968).

However, because of the study objectives, not all kinds of debts were to be measured. Excluded was debt incurred in situations in which the consumer had little or no choice. For example, editors deleted debts for medical or dental expenditures, and for taxes and back taxes. In addition, since the study focused on the financial transactions of people in their roles as consumers rather than producers, the debts measured were those incurred in acquiring and using things in their private lives, not those incurred primarily to make a living. Thus, debts associated with investments, or for farm machinery, or with renovating rooms to rent were excluded. Figure 3-5 shows the breakdown of debt used.

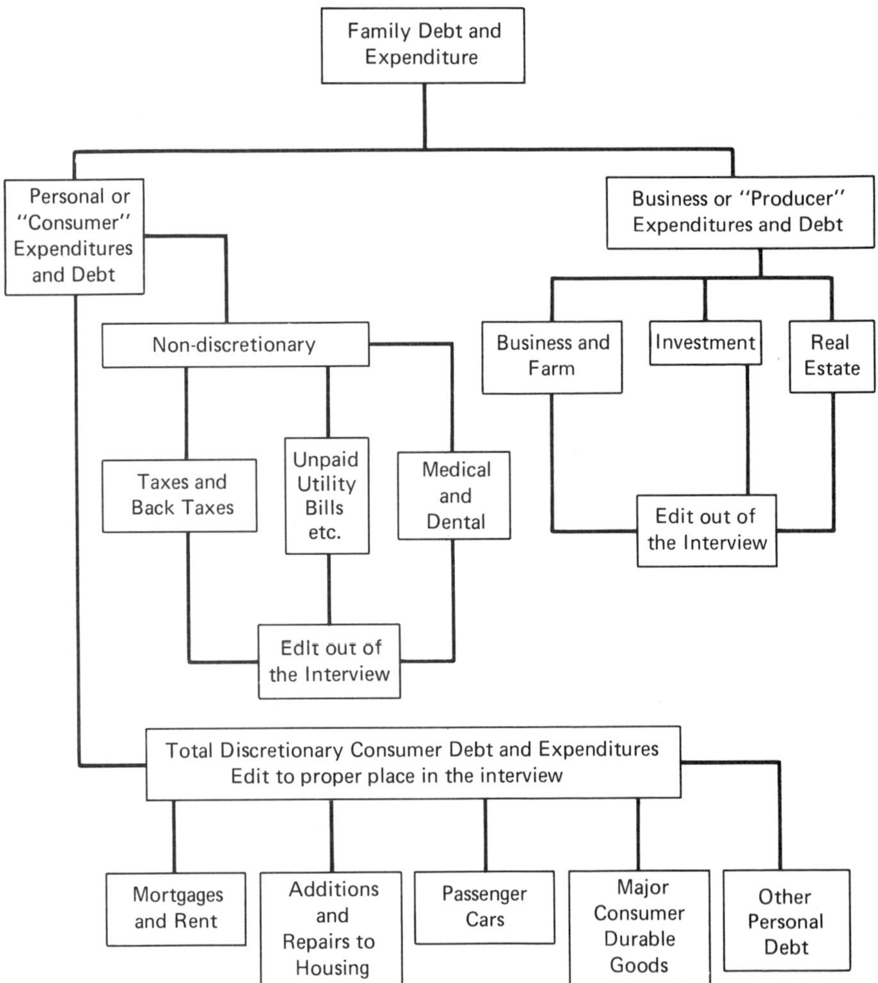

Figure 3-5 Classifying Types of Debt

The study further subdivided private discretionary consumer debt into such categories as mortgages on living quarters and grounds, installment debt and revolving accounts, and informal debts to friends or relatives. Mortgages (any loans using real estate as collateral) were included unless they were incurred for business, farming, or investment purposes. Installment debt was defined as all private discretionary nonmortgage debt of the family owed to financial or commercial institutions and subject to two or more regular payments. Debts owed to individuals or nonfinancial/noncommercial institutions were included with noninstallment debts. Revolving accounts were classified as installment debt. Noninstallment debt included private discretionary nonmortgage debts owed to financial or commercial institutions which were not subject to more than one regular payment. It also included all debt owed to individuals or other types of organizations. Thirty-day charge accounts were not considered debt unless they were in arrears; 30-day notes to a bank or loan company were considered noninstallment debt. Debts to friends or relatives were considered noninstallment debt if the respondent indicated that he felt an obligation to repay the debt. Debts between members of the same family unit were excluded from the interview.

How the debt was classified depended on the nature of the purchase with which it was associated. For instance, additions to housing were defined as items more or less permanently attached to the house or property which added to its value. Repairs included normal upkeep and maintenance of the house or property and of additions to it. Rules were established for dealing with questionable items; for instance, gas stoves and refrigerators were not considered additions unless they were built-ins.

Clearly, the types of decisions required of the editing staff are complex when concepts to be used in the analysis are as complex as the "amount of installment debt outstanding."[4] If trends over time are to be studied, concepts must be kept constant, and any changes in them documented. Thus, the more complex surveys become, the more important are these efforts directed toward conceptual clarity and consistency.

When respondents are asked for financial information, balancing the responses can lead to more accurate data. For instance, in obtaining information about items on which debt was incurred, respondents will generally know what their down payment was and what their monthly payment schedule is. But they may not know exactly what the price was that they actually paid for the article in question if there was a trade-in. This is particularly true of automobiles. By reviewing the consistency of this kind of factual information, the editor can contribute significantly to its accuracy.

The task of balancing quantitative information is illustrated by the automobile-debt editing procedures used in the 1968 Survey of Consumer Finances.

[4] For example, see Table 2-3 in Katona et al. (1968, p. 28).

For cars purchased prior to 1967, it was desired to record the amount of money still owed on the car, if any. For cars purchased during the calendar year or in early 1968, a complete picture of the financial transaction was an important objective. Respondents were asked a lengthy series of questions about their current transactions, including the price of the car, the down payment, the amount borrowed, the payment schedule, and the amount received in trade from old cars.[5] For cars purchased earlier, only the payment schedule and remaining debt were ascertained. For these older cars, one editing task was to determine whether the amount of the monthly payment times the number of remaining payments equaled the amount stated by the respondent that he had left to pay, at least within the range of plus or minus one payment. If the resulting figure exceeded the reported remaining debt by more than one payment, the latter was adjusted upward on the assumption that the information about the size of the payments and the number remaining was more accurate. If the product understated the reported amount by less than two payments, the discrepancy was assumed to be due to a "balloon" note (a large final payment due in a lump sum) and the last payment treated as two payments (i.e., the reported number of payments was increased by one and all debt reported was treated as installment debt). If the discrepancy equaled two or more payments, the difference was treated as noninstallment debt. This procedure facilitated consistency and accuracy in reporting levels of aggregate remaining installment debt. The example in Chapter 5 details the editing procedures dealing with automobile debt.

Other editing tasks associated with Survey of Consumer Finances car debt illustrate the next major editing task to be treated in our discussion of the consistent application of concepts. This is the task of checking answers to questions to isolate and reconcile answers that are inconsistent with one another. Several kinds of inconsistencies may occur:

1. The interviewer fails to ask a section of questions that should have been asked. The answers must be marked "no answer" so that coders do not inadvertently code "does not apply," or assignments must be made. *Example:* The family reports owning two cars, but the interviewer forgot to ask the sequence of questions pertaining to debt on the second car.
2. The interviewer asked a sequence of questions that should not have been asked. The answers should be changed to "inapplicable" so that coders do not inadvertently code substantive answers. *Example:* The editor discovers that an absent family member is incorrectly listed as being a member of the dwelling unit. Questions eliciting information about his contributions to family income as a member of that dwelling unit should be marked "inapplicable."

[5] For the exact details of the questions asked, see Katona et al. (1968, p. 255).

3. Obviously inconsistent answers are recorded. One is clearly erroneous, and a judgment must be made as to which is the most likely candidate to be changed. *Example:* Respondent reports purchasing a "new" Edsel automobile in 1970. This cannot be, since Ford stopped making these many years earlier.

In each case, the editor alters (rewrites) one of the answers on the interview in colored pencil. Coders will use the altered version.

This final example also illustrates the fourth type of editing activity concerned with the application of concepts—reviewing the interview for improbable answers. These may be due to the interviewer inadvertently writing down an incorrect answer, to misinterpretation of the question, or to other miscommunication between interviewer and respondent. The problem is to find out which. The following examples illustrate some of the types of problems that may be encountered:

> A farm laborer who was unemployed for half of the year reports income from wages and salaries of $9100; the interviewer transposed the digits ($1900) when he wrote the figures down.
>
> A building contractor reports purchasing a new Oldsmobile for $1000; the interviewer has also noted that he traded in a year-old car; she had recorded the cash payment in the blank reserved for the total price of the new purchase.
>
> There is a discrepancy between the total price reported for a car purchase and the amount borrowed by a well-to-do doctor; a note in the thumbnail sketch calls attention to the fact that the respondent traded in a 30-foot sailboat when she bought her new Buick.

Corrective Procedures and Documentation

This review of the editor's conceptual assessment tasks suggests that a number of corrective actions can be taken at this stage. In some cases these are simply carried out. In others, they are recorded in the editors' decision book. If the problems are really serious, the interview may have to be sent back to the interviewer or called to the attention of senior study personnel. Tasks that can often be performed by the editor include deleting improper material, moving information to the proper section, splitting items, assigning or assuming factual data, and noting down how coders are to treat "no answer" or "inapplicable" categories to specific questions. What is to be recorded or to be the subject of review by the study director should depend on the experience that the staff has with surveys and on their familiarity with the subject matter under study.

Deleted items are never erased. When necessary, they are marked for deletion by circling them. Interviewer's entries must always be left readable, even when deleted. A note must always be placed next to the deleted item explaining why it has been deleted. Responses are deleted usually because they do not constitute a valid answer to the question asked.

Sometimes it is necessary to delete an item from one part of the questionnaire and re-record it elsewhere. When this is done, the original entry is circled and marked to be moved. Then it is written (in colored pencil) in the new place. It is very important that an explanatory note be written next to the deleted response, telling where it was moved to and why, and another note written next to it in its new place, telling where it came from.

Explanatory notes are used whenever a decision is made, the reasons for which might not be readily apparent to the coder. They should explain the decision briefly, but fully. Conscientious coders should bring mysterious or incomprehensible problems back to the editor for explanations and aid in handling.

When factual items are being edited, it may be necessary to "split" the response. The presence of much "splitting" may indicate the need for more precise instructions to interviewers for getting enough detail as a result of their probes to obviate the need to divide answers. For example, an editor reports:

> Respondent's house value was reported at $19,500, but this included two separate buildings, one of which is used for his furniture business. . . . Since there is no other information about the relative sizes of the buildings, I split the total reported value in half to use as the value of the residential section.

Another editor reports:

> The respondent said that he spent $3000 to redecorate the inside of his house and remodel his kitchen. . . . I assumed $500 as redecorating (repairs) and $2500 as remodeling.

Any action would have been arbitrary in these cases and the goal was (1) to approximate the real state of affairs as closely as possible, (2) to apply similar rules in similar situations, and (3) to find out how much of this kind of trouble there was. Such editing operations are based on the available information.

Sometimes estimates can be made which at least put bounds on the splitting rules. In the 1967 Survey of Consumer Finances, prices paid for a number of consumer-durable-goods items were required to be split if reported as an aggregate total. The relative prices of the items listed were estimated using mail-order catalogs and then the total price mentioned by the respondent was divided up accordingly, categorizing each item in terms of the conceptual scheme chosen. As noted earlier, where explanation or hypothesis testing is the purpose rather than description, the criteria for deciding whether or not to use procedures such as splitting of responses depends on the objectives of the study.

When a respondent does not know the information asked for, or refuses to give it, or when the interviewer has forgotten to ask the question, a codable response to the question is not present. This may also occur when the interviewer simply fails to probe enough to obtain a meaningful response. In most cases the editor identifies it as not ascertained by writing N.A. in colored pencil where the response should have been (the exceptions that concern assignments will be explained below). All questions that are contingent upon the question N.A.'d are then "INAP'ed" (marked "inappropriate") by the editor by drawing a large × or diagonal line through the area in which the contingent responses should have been and writing INAP across the area. Figure 3-6 illustrates this.

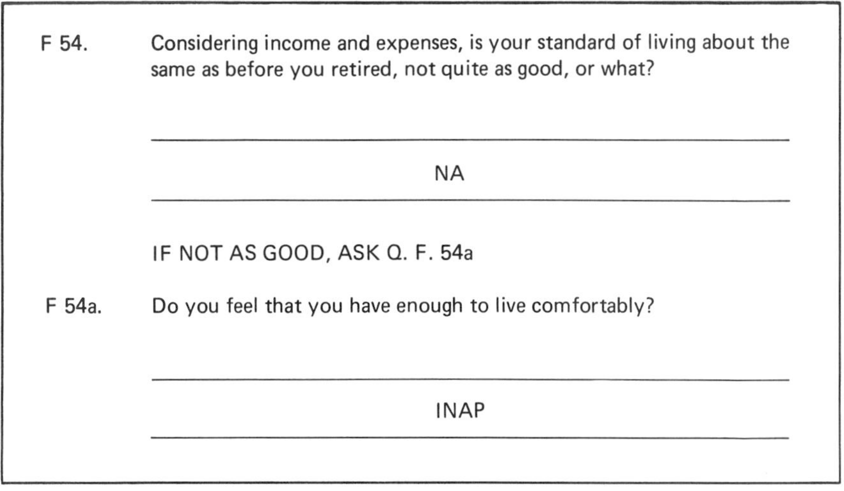

F 54. Considering income and expenses, is your standard of living about the same as before you retired, not quite as good, or what?

NA

IF NOT AS GOOD, ASK Q. F. 54a

F 54a. Do you feel that you have enough to live comfortably?

INAP

Figure 3-6 Editing Missing Information and Inapplicable Sections (Used by permission of the Survey Research Center of the Institute for Social Research, The University of Michigan.)

In other cases, some questions might be left blank because the interviewer instructions require that these questions not be asked in certain circumstances (see IF NOT AS GOOD in Figure 3-6). In these cases, the question(s) should be INAP'ed in the manner described.

For some important variables, it may be desirable to *assign* missing values rather than to establish a special code for them. This is required if the computer programs to be used cannot accept missing data codes. Assigning missing values will often be advantageous if the purpose of the study is largely descriptive, and it has some advantages even if hypothesis testing and explanation are purposes of the study. Of course, in the latter case care must be taken not to permit correlations to become spuriously inflated by the assignment procedure.

Assignments are made *only* where the editor is instructed to make them and are always made from the procedures established for that purpose. Any other attempt to supply missing information is not an assignment but an *assumption*. Whenever an assignment is made, an indication (e.g., a large printed A placed slightly above and to the right of the value) that the value is assigned should be made.

There are two types of assignments: *control-question* assignments and *value* assignments. Control-question (e.g., "Do you owe any money?") assignments are often based on percentages of respondents who answered one way or another to that question in previous studies. They usually involve the use of random-number tables. Missing-value assignments associated with these control-question assignments are usually based on proportions for different subclasses of respondents computed from previous data.

Value assignments (e.g., "How much money do you owe?") can be made using other information in the questionnaire in assignment tables of the type presented earlier. When an editor knows with some degree of certainty from other information in the interview that the regular assignment is way out of line, a conference with the editing supervisor can be held and an *adjusted assignment* made and recorded in the Editors' Decision Book. These are not recorded as assignments, since they are based on particular criteria rather than on a general rule. They should be considered as assumptions and so marked in the decision book. In all cases, the important thing about the treatment of the assigned item is that it be consistent with the study aims and purposes.

Editing Conventions

One editing task is to make life easy for coders. This section explains the details of what the editor actually does in carrying out this task. Editors, not coders, should check and balance interviewer arithmetic, round numbers, deal with over-the-field amounts, adjust qualified answers, and make time period adjustments. To do these tasks consistently requires adjusting rules for treating data, and communication rules as well.

Here is a list of typical instructions that would ordinarily be included in an editors' manual or instruction book:

1. Write only in green pencil (coders use blue, study staff uses red or some other distinctive color). Do not use ink.
2. Never erase an interviewer's entries. When necessary, delete them by circling. Interviewer's entries must be readable even when deleted.

Notes must be placed by deleted items explaining why they have been deleted.

3. Explanatory notes are also used whenever a decision is made that might not be apparent to the coder. The note should briefly, but fully, explain the decision. Editing should not appear mysterious, or the careful coder will bring the problem back to the editor for aid and explanation.
4. In most cases, the editor establishes the "N.A." (not ascertained) status of a question by writing "N.A." where the response should have been. (The exceptions to this concern assignments.)
5. Questions that are contingent upon an N.A.'d question should be "INAP'ed" (marked "inappropriate" for this respondent) by the editor by drawing a large × or diagonal line through the area in which the contingent response should have been recorded and writing INAP across the area. In other cases, a question (or questions) will have been left blank because the interviewer is not supposed to ask those questions of this respondent. In this case, the question(s) should be INAP'ed as above. Even though the interviewer has already N.A.'d and INAP'ed the questions, it is generally desirable for the editor to redo them, since green pencil is more noticeable to the coders.

Figure 3-7 lists some commonly used editing abbreviations.

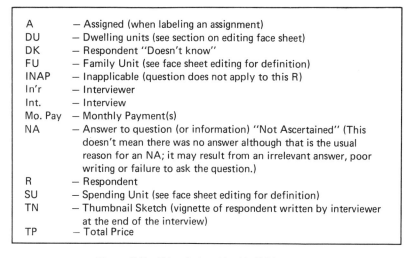

A	– Assigned (when labeling an assignment)
DU	– Dwelling units (see section on editing face sheet)
DK	– Respondent "Doesn't know"
FU	– Family Unit (see face sheet editing for definition)
INAP	– Inapplicable (question does not apply to this R)
In'r	– Interviewer
Int.	– Interview
Mo. Pay	– Monthly Payment(s)
NA	– Answer to question (or information) "Not Ascertained" (This doesn't mean there was no answer although that is the usual reason for an NA; it may result from an irrelevant answer, poor writing or failure to ask the question.)
R	– Respondent
SU	– Spending Unit (see face sheet editing for definition)
TN	– Thumbnail Sketch (vignette of respondent written by interviewer at the end of the interview)
TP	– Total Price

Figure 3-7 Abbreviations Used in Editing

An example from Katona et al., (1969) will illustrate the checking and balancing of interviewers' arithmetic. In an automobile purchase transaction:

1. (Net outlay) = (total price paid) − (cash from trade-in or sale)
2. (Remaining installment debt) +/− (one payment) = ($ monthly payment) × (number of payments left to be made)
   If monthly payment times the number of payments is greater than remaining installment debt (RID) by more than one payment, edit the RID to be equal to the monthly payment times the number of payments. If monthly payment times the number of payments is not greater than the RID by more than one payment, or is less than RID, leave all numbers the way they are. Round to the nearest $10.

Frequently, amounts given in dollars need to be rounded. A typical rounding rule is to round to the nearest unit (e.g., dollar) as follows:

$.01–.49	round down to the smaller whole dollar
$.50	round to the nearest *odd* whole dollar
$.51–.99	round up to the larger whole dollar

The usual procedure in setting up codes for a study is to allocate a field of sufficient width (in characters) to accommodate the largest (absolute) values that are expected to appear. For instance, an income field of five characters (XXXXX) might be allocated for "total yearly family income." Ordinarily, this will suffice, but sampling procedures do sometimes yield extreme cases (e.g., someone turns up with $190,000 in yearly income). These are termed *over-the-field* amounts. A reasonable editing procedure might be (1) to see if there were anything in the interview to indicate that an interviewer had intended to write $19,000 or if the larger figure seemed correct; (2) if correct, to record (99998) as the value of the field (99999 having been reserved as a missing-data code); and (3) to record this fact in the editors' decision book. The datum is designated as an over-the-field amount.

Sometimes codes are set up to take exact figures, but interviewers and respondents do not always provide exactly what is needed. Systematic treatment of *qualified answers* is no substitute for adequate questionnaire design and interviewer instructions, but it permits use of what information has been collected with a minimum introduction of unsystematic and ad hoc biases. It is the editor's job to produce exact figures where needed. Here are some useful rules:

1. About, I guess, maybe, possibly, around $50, etc.—leave as is ($50).
2. Between $50 and $100, etc.—use the midpoint ($75).
3. At least, a little over (under), slightly over (under), just over (under) $50, $50+, $50−increase (decrease) by 10 per cent ($45, $55).

4. More (less) than \$50—increase (decrease) by 20 per cent (\$40, \$60).
5. Well over (under), quite a bit over (under), much more (less) than \$50—increase (decrease) by 20 per cent (\$40, \$60).
6. "A few" or "several"—four (4), unless you can make a better estimate from the available information. This applies to "a few hundred" or "several thousand" also.
7. "A couple"—two (2), unless you can make a better estimate. This is also better than an assignment. It also applies to "a couple of hundred."

If many such responses are found to come from a particular interviewer, more training may be necessary.

Sometimes respondents give an amount stated in a different time period than that asked for. For instance, the interview may ask "How much rent do you pay each month?" and the respondent, who pays his rent weekly, says "\$40 per week." It makes no sense whatsoever for the interviewer to ask the respondent to convert his answer. It is far better to wait and convert the response to the desired unit during the editing. Where possible, use of precalculated tables will speed up the editing process. If this is not feasible, desk calculators can be used. One month equals $4\frac{1}{3}$ weeks.

WHERE IT ALL FITS TOGETHER

Once the interviews have been edited, the next major step in the process is the coding, a systematic, question-by-question content analysis, and the transferral of the data to the storage media in their now more complete and consistent form. Coding techniques are explored in Chapter 4.

It is probably safe to assert that all surveys require some sort of editing procedure, even the simplest mail or telephone survey. When a minimum amount is needed, the editing may be done at the same time the coding is accomplished, possibly by the same people. But then decisions will still have to be made, information condensed, multiple answers reduced to a single datum, and vague answers made more specific through arbitrary assumptions. A division of both time and labor is probably a better choice in most cases.

This chapter pointed to the importance of editing as data quality control by pointing out the relationship between formal, explicit editing procedures and the design and objectives of the study. The importance of good editing for the prevention of serious problems later in the analysis cannot be stressed too strongly.

An overview of the whole editing process is shown in Figure 3-8. Many of the steps can be taken well in advance of the actual receipt of the interviews

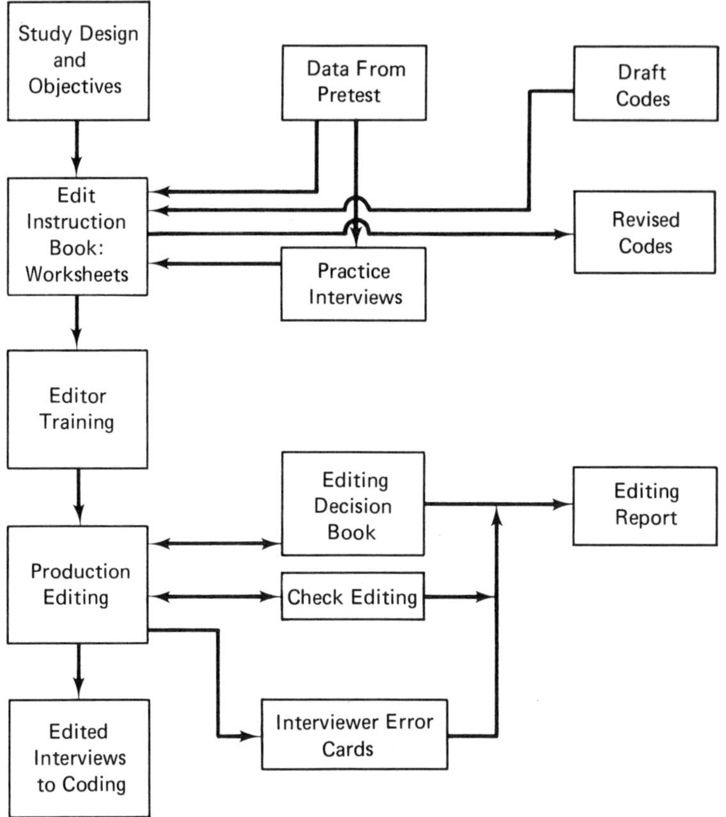

Figure 3-8 Steps in Editing: Overview

from the field, expediting the processing of the information. In smaller studies they can be combined into a single editing–coding step, and some steps possibly will not even be needed. Yet, experience, some of it "bitter," indicates that later steps in the processing and analysis of survey data will be either more or less time consuming, difficult, and costly, depending on how well the procedures and principles discussed here were implemented.

CODING AND CODE CONSTRUCTION

"Coding" is a term generally used to describe the process of interpreting, classifying, and transferring information from the survey instrument to the data-storage medium. Often the encoded information is transferred to a *code sheet*, a large paper ruled with 80 columns corresponding to the 80 columns of a data card with a capacity of about 20 cards of data (20 rows). From this sheet, the data cards are punched. The coding process is frequently carried out simultaneously with editing, but the two processes are considered separately here.

The code is a systematic framework for classifying responses to questions and assigning them to mutually exclusive categories that represent each variable included in the study. It is the set of rules used for transferring information from the instrument to the storage medium. Thus, the code represents one part of the operational form of the concepts to be used in the analysis stages of a study. The questionnaire and the interviewing and editing instructions form the remainder. After the information has been converted into a machine-readable form, the code defines the meanings of the numerical representations contained in the storage medium. Both the research staff and any others desiring to use the study will rely on the code to explain the meaning of the numerical data representations (e.g., a code may define the meaning of a 1 punched in column 27 as meaning that the respondent is married). It is crucial, then, that the construction of the code be carried out with an eye to the objectives and concepts of the study as well as to the restrictions imposed by the technology to be used for analysis. A poorly constructed code not only slows up the coding process (raising costs) but, more importantly, compromises the quality of information in and the usefulness of the study.

This chapter does not deal with the principles of content analysis and classification. The reader will find extended treatments of these in Simon (1969),

Roth (1966), Lansing and Morgan (1971), Galtung (1967), and in other writings. We shall focus here on the technical details of how coding actually gets done.

CODE DESIGN CONSIDERATIONS

The code used to govern the transfer of data to the storage media should be designed with each of the specific research objectives of the study in mind. The researcher should not be in the position of being unable to construct a particular variable or compute a particular statistic only because of carelessness in transferring the data from the instrument to the storage medium. Since the code is also the primary source document for the information in storage, successful data retrieval and use depend on the completeness of the documentation in the code.

The form taken by the code is influenced by the data-storage medium used. The most common form of data storage is still the 80-column punched card. Each of the 80 columns may be punched in the "0" to "9," "+," and "—" rows. Combinations of these punches represent the alphameric characters that are legitimate on standard computers. As will be seen more clearly later, there are advantages to representing a variable on cards using the set of integers in the range 0–9 (e.g., many tabulating programs produce 10 × 10 tables).

The basic point to be made is that the code design is influenced to a significant degree by the nature of the physical storage medium to be used and the types of analysis programs available, together with their input requirements. When only a counter–sorter was available, for example, the one-column representation ("+" and "—," as well as the 0–9 codes) of a variable proved to be particularly convenient. Today, however, most processing is done with computers, and the one-column restriction on code values is of less importance; and the use of the "+" and "—" characters should definitely be avoided.

Identification Fields and Code Structure

If more than one punch card is required to hold all the data for a single respondent, it is necessary to identify each card completely and systematically. The cards to be coded and the variables on them should be organized to match the sequence of items in the questionnaire. Figure 4-1 illustrates one set of identification fields that has been found to work well.

Columns 1 to 3 on every card in this study carry the same identification number or letters.[1] This will hopefully distinguish the cards from all others with

[1] Even if there is only one card per respondent, some identification of the study is highly desirable to distinguish one's own cards from those belonging to others at the computer center.

Column Number	Description
1-3	Study number or identification (xxx) (STUDY)
4-5	Card number (xx) (DECK)
6-9	Interview or respondent number (INT)
10	Wave number (use only if a reinterview) (WAVE)
11-80	Data codes

Figure 4-1 Code Structure for a Data Card

which they might conceivably be mixed. The identification is shown on the code form as a constant. If two cards were required to code each respondent, the latter would have a card 01 and a card 02. This is shown in columns 4 and 5. The respondent's identification or interview number (usually assigned in the sequence in which the interview was received) is in columns 6 to 9, generally numbered serially from 0001. Special series interviews may be numbered in the 7000 and 8000 ranges, and 9000 series numbers are often used for incompleted interviews as a convenient method for accounting for all of the addresses in the sample frame. Column 10 can be used to record precisely when the data were obtained during the conduct of a multiwave reinterview study.

Coding Unequal-Length Data Records

Occasionally, sets of information are required that do not apply to some respondents but involve several cards of data for others. Information about car ownership is a case in point; some respondents do not own a car while others may own as many as six. If one full card is needed to hold the data for one car, some respondents will need one "car card" and others will need as many as six.

Getting such data coded is not a particularly difficult task; all that is required is repeated application of the code to the data until all the multiple observations are coded. It is advantageous for at least one car card to be coded for every family, even though some may own no car. Multicar families have one card for each car. The code might be structured as in Figure 4-2. Each car owned by the respondent has been labeled by an editor according to a specific car-sequencing rule. This identification appears in colored pencil at the top of the column of data for this car.

There are two kinds of data in the code: (1) variables that describe the respondent (such as car ownership and interview number), and (2) variables that describe the car (such as car I.D. and year model). The respondent-descriptive variables will be the same on all car cards for a given family, while the car descriptive data will vary. A small part of the data set might look like that in Figure 4-3.

Variable Number	Column Number	Description
1	1-3	Study number (772)
2	4-5	Deck Number (05)
3	6-9	Interview number (FAMILYNO)
4	10	Car I.D. (CARNO)
		(Coder: use green numbers at the top)
		1. owns no car; first car
		2. second car
		3. third car etc.
5	11	Car ownership (CO)
		(Q.C2) How many cars do you and your family living here own?
Code 0 in col. 12-13		0. none
		1. one
		etc.
		7. seven or more
		8. D.K.
		9. N.A.
6	12-13	Year model of car owned (MODEL)
		(Q.C12) What year model is it?
		00. Inap.; owns no car
		45. 1945 model or earlier
		xx. code model year
		98. D.K.
		99. N.A.

Figure 4-2 Code for Car Ownership Data

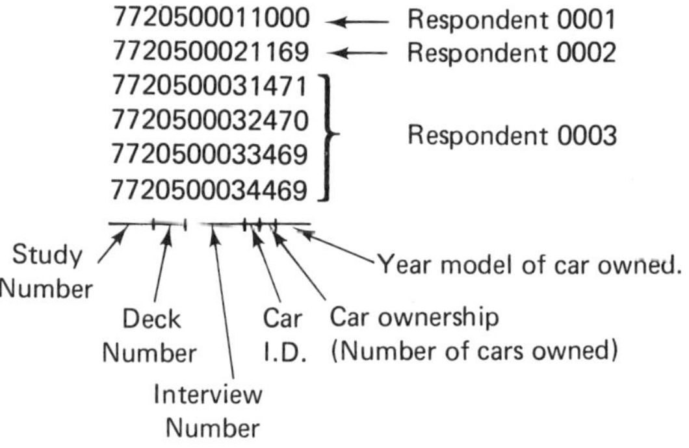

Figure 4-3 The Car Ownership Data File

Each row represents a partially filled card. There is at least one card for every respondent, even if no car is owned. The first three columns contain "772"; this will appear on all cards in the study. Columns 4 and 5 contain the card number "05"; this will be the same on cards coded with this code format (i.e., on all car cards). Columns 6–9 contain the interview number; this will be different for each respondent but the same for each car owned by the respondent. Column 11 describes the number of cars owned by the respondent; this, too, will be the same for all cars owned by the respondent (e.g., column 11 is always "4" for all cards coded for respondent number 0003).

Column 10, however, will be different for each car owned (a decision made by the editor), as will columns 12 and 13 since they describe the car, not the respondent. In essence, using the car number code is equivalent to adding a fifth number to the four-digit interview number in columns 6–9 that converts the unit of analysis from families to cars. Thus, car number one is 00031 in columns 6–10, car number two is 00032, and so on. This number will uniquely identify each car in terms of the respondent who owns it.

Principles of Code Construction

The following guidelines for the code construction process will apply to most studies.

1. The order of the data in the code should correspond as closely as possible to the order of questions in the questionnaire.

This minimizes the amount of skipping around that the coder must do, speeding up the coding process and reducing the potential for coding errors. The sequence of variables can be arranged for analysis purposes more easily after the data have been transcribed to the storage medium.

2. When answers to a question are precoded in the instrument, make sure that the code established for the question is equivalently and consistently numbered to avoid coding errors.

Figure 4-4 illustrates a question and its associated code.

3. Each coded variable (usually in one-to-one correspondence with a question in the instrument) should contain:
   (a) a description of the variable and the unique name to be used as a mnemonic reference in statistical computer programs,
   (b) the question number of the source of the data in the questionnaire, and, where appropriate, the page number on which it appears,
   (c) the exact wording of the question and all interviewer instructions that pertain to it,
   (d) a precise definition of the code values to be used in transferring information to machine-readable storage,
   (e) the column number(s) in which it is to be recorded,
   (f) space for entering additional variable-number information for identifying the variable when used in analysis.

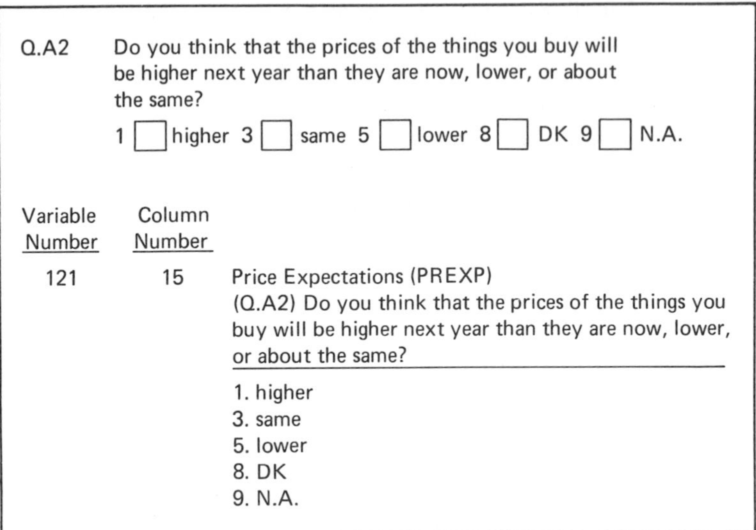

Q.A2 Do you think that the prices of the things you buy will be higher next year than they are now, lower, or about the same?

1 ☐ higher 3 ☐ same 5 ☐ lower 8 ☐ DK 9 ☐ N.A.

Variable Number	Column Number	
121	15	Price Expectations (PREXP) (Q.A2) Do you think that the prices of the things you buy will be higher next year than they are now, lower, or about the same? 1. higher 3. same 5. lower 8. DK 9. N.A.

Figure 4-4 A Typical Attitude Question and Its Associated Code

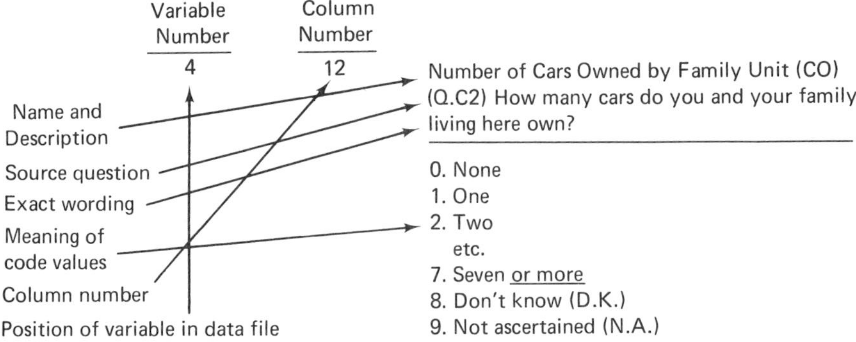

Figure 4-5 Contents of the Code for a Variable

Figure 4-5 provides an example of these five types of information.

4. Codes should be well spaced to avoid confusion; be sure to leave room for explanatory notes to be added later by hand.

A code should never be typed so that it is broken in the middle and then continued on a subsequent page. This invites coding errors and gains nothing but a page or two of paper.

5. Always preserve as much of the original detail in the data as feasible.

Physical storage is usually relatively inexpensive, so preserving the original data ensures maximum flexibility in analysis. This also enhances the usefulness of the study to other researchers who may be interested in other forms of the variables. It also helps maintain compatibility with other studies. For example, consider a study in which only the distinction between being over and under age 65 was meaningful but in which that question was not asked directly. Age is often simply recorded in actual years. The use of one of two alternative codes might be considered. Figure 4-6 illustrates the choices. One alternative records the actual age in years as reported by the respondent. The other provides the age information exactly in the form needed by the study but precludes use of age in any other form, either by the study designers or by others. If, at some time subsequent to the coding, the researchers decided that it would be desirable to compare the over-65 group with those near retirement, say, aged 55 to 64, they would find it necessary to recode the original interviews, an expensive and time-consuming process.

Minimizing the amount of variable building done by the coders (e.g, age in years being transformed into a dichotomous variable) also increases the speed at which the coding process takes place and eliminates one major source of coding error.[2] Unless variable building in the coding process is essential, it should be avoided. This is discussed further in a later section.

Variable Number	Column Number	
42	30	Age of Family Head (AGEH) (Q.A15) How old are you now?
		1. Under 65 5. 65 or older 8. D.K. 9. N.A.

(a)

Variable Number	Column Number	
42	30-31	Age of Family Head (AGEH) (Q.A15) How old are you now?
		xx. code age in years 97. 96 or older 98. D. K. 99. N.A.

(b)

Figure 4-6 Alternative Age Codes

2 An unpublished study of the coding procedure for one survey indicated that most coding errors were made when coders had to transform a field variable (such as age or income) into a set of class intervals.

6. Make sure that the values used to define codes are standard computer characters, acceptable as input to all of the computing equipment and programs that you plan to use.

The choice of code values begins with a consideration of the legal character set on the computer to be used for processing and analysis; it also requires knowing the input requirements of the data-management and statistical-analysis programs that are to be used. Many analysis programs will only accept numbers as input. This programming practice usually restricts the code values to the integers 0–9. *Do not use multiple punches and punching patterns outside the character set acceptable by the programs you expect to use.* When in doubt, use positive integers and zero for nominal and ordinal scales and identifiers, and code positive and negative real numbers for variables measured at the interval and ratio levels.

One of two basic character sets are in use in most computer facilities. They are shown in Appendix I.

7. Establish codes both for missing data and for over-the-field values where needed. Do not leave missing information blank.

As pointed out in Chapter 3, there is a difference between a refusal to answer and failure to answer due to lack of information. The fact that a respondent did not know the answer to a question, or had no opinion, is frequently a valuable piece of information to the study, and it is desirable to differentiate between these two responses in the code if this is the case. Figure 4-7 presents conventions used successfully by many studies. The code values actually used, of course, should depend on the requirements of the computer programs available locally.

Consider a data field of one column. The code value 8 is reserved for "don't know" (D.K.) types of responses. The code value 9 is used to code refused information, questions not asked by the interviewer, those left blank, and all otherwise not ascertained (N.A.) information. If the data field exceeds one column, the rightmost digit is an 8 or a 9 and the remainder of the field to the left is filled in with 9s. For example, if a field is six digits long, the don't-know responses are coded 999998, and the not-ascertained group are all coded 999999.

Field widths should be planned to eliminate the over-the-field problem if possible, since truncation results in a loss of potentially valuable information. An allowance for the unexpected should be included in the code, however, since the problem cannot always be avoided. In a one-column code, a 7 is often reserved to represent values of the variable too large to be recorded in the field. In this case, it means "seven or more." In the case of a six-digit field, 999997 would mean that amount or more.

Code Value	Abbreviation	Explanation
9	NA	The question was not asked but should have been; the question was misunderstood by the respondent; the answer made no sense; the answer was so general that it fitted into many categories (unless the code provides a general category for such responses)
8	DK	Respondent does not have an answer or an opinion (and says so); respondent is equivocal or uncertain, giving no clear response (unless "uncertain" is assigned another code value)
7		Other (a residual response category); over the field amount (7 or more for example) in a one column code
0	INAP	The question was not appropriate and was therefore not asked; none, a value of zero as the proper response to the question

When fields are more than one column in length, a proper number of 9s or 0s should be used in front of the proper code. For example, in a 4 column field, the NA code would be 9999, the DK code 9998, the over the field code 9997 and the INAP code would be 0000. 0009 could not exclusively represent the missing data code as it is also a legitimate value for the field. Other missing data codes can be used if these are not compatible with the analytical programs to be used.

Figure 4-7 Suggested Coding Conventions

8. Maintain consistency between everyday meanings of words and the way numbers are used in the code.

This speeds up the coding process and helps minimize coding errors. Figure 4-8 illustrates common conventions for yes/no answers and the use of zero code values; Figure 4-9 illustrates the use of spacing, directionality of scaling, and a rule for numerical codes. Coders will still tend inadvertently to use 8 and 9 to correspond to the values 8 and 9 even when they are reserved for D.K. and N.A. categories. If the variable in question is an important one, all 8 and 9 code values should be verified in the consistency checking of the data. See Chapter 6 for further discussion.

9. Keep field codes consistent with single-column codes.

Fields (variables with values exceeding one character in width, such as income and age) can often conveniently be coded as illustrated in Figure 4-10. Note that the examples have much in common. Each provides a zero code (with the appropriate number of characters) for answers of zero, and for coded values to be recorded when the question is inapplicable to the respondent. Each provides for D.K.s, refusals, or other answers that fail to provide information in response to the question (N.A.s). This convention is consistent across all vari-

a. Yes/no questions might always be coded to separate INAP's, yes, no, don't know, and no-unsure responses, e.g.

Have you stopped beating your wife?

0. INAP.; Not married
1. Yes, have stopped
5. No, have not stopped
8. Don't know whether have stopped or not
9. Not ascertained; no answer

b. 0 should *always* mean zero, none, or inappropriate question for this respondent.

c. Scales should always run in the same direction:

1. Better	More	Higher	Faster
3. Same	Same	Same	Same
5. Worse	Less	Lower	Slower
8. D.K.	D.K.	D.K.	D.K.
9. N.A.	N.A.	N.A.	N.A.

Figure 4-8 Code Conventions for Yes/No, Zeroes, and Directionality

a. Use spacing to mark important distinctions:
   1. Very favorable
   2. Favorable

   3. Neutral response

   4. Unfavorable
   5. Very unfavorable
   8. D.K.
   9. N.A.

b. Numerical codes (like the number of children) should always correspond to code values as much as is possible:
   0. None
   1. One
   2. Two
   3. Three
   etc.
   7. Seven <u>or more</u>
   8. D.K.
   9. N.A.

Figure 4-9 Code Conventions for Spacing and Numeric Codes

ables to provide a systematic framework for dealing with missing data. Codes for responses too large to fit in the allotted space are provided (e.g., the code of 999997 for income). Finally, codes that will receive little use (such as car year models prior to 1945) are combined into one value.

Sometimes variables will contain a decimal point—for example, questions about interest rates paid on mortgages. Usually, decimal fractions are ignored or rounded when measuring data with large magnitudes (e.g., house value or debts owed). To record them, even if given by some respondents, would lend

Variable Number	Column Number	
207	65-70	Family Income (INCOMEF) (Q.G17) How much was your total family income in 1972? 000000. No income in 1972 xxxxxx. Code amount in dollars 999997. $999997 or more 999998. D.K. 999999. N.A.
208	20-21	Year model of newest car owned (YRNWC) (Q.C12) What year model is it? [Coder: code year model of car labeled #1 in green at left margin.] 00. INAP.; owns no car 45. 1945 model or earlier. xx. code model year. 98. D.K. 99. N.A.

Figure 4-10 Two Examples of Field Codes

a spurious indication of precision to most error-ridden survey data. Yet, for some variables, such as responses to a question about interest rates, the fractional part of the answer is crucial and must be retained. The general coding procedure is to drop the decimal point for coding purposes. It takes up unnecessary space, makes for unnecessary writing, and can easily be restored when the data are read into the computer. An example is shown in Figure 4-11. The data can be reconverted later if the actual decimal figure is required. Handwritten decimal points are easily confused with a blank by keypunch operators.

10. Make sure that the categories used to make up the code for a particular question are, in fact, mutually exclusive and completely exhaustive (i.e., there must be one and only one code value for each respondent for every variable in the study).

Column Number	
56	Interest paid on mortgage (INTRST) (Q.B5) What rate of interest do you pay on your mortgage? 00. INAP.; does not own xx. code interest rate multiplied by 10 Example: if respondent reports 3.7% code 37. 97. 9.7% or more 98. D.K. 99. N.A.

Figure 4-11 Coding Decimal Points

11. When the codes 0–9 are inadequate for representing the range of responses to a question measured at the nominal level, organize code values into meaningful major classifications, each with more detailed subclassifications. This can easily be represented as a two-digit code.

Figure 4-12 provides an example. A question from a political survey, its responses can be classified into several major categories: economic, political, and social reasons. Within each of these broad classifications, one can isolate more specific subgroups. These can be conveniently organized for coding and analysis as illustrated in Figure 4-13. Notice that in column 30, a code of 1 implies an economic reason, a 2 implies a political reason, and a 3 implies a social reason. Column 31 provides detail about the type of reason.

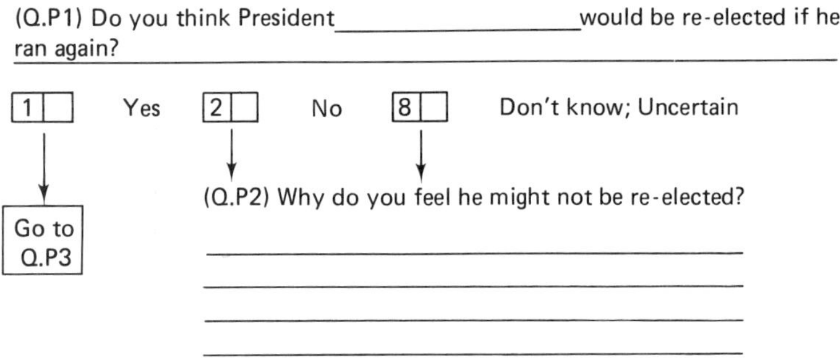

Figure 4-12 A Question from a Political Survey

Respondents may well give more than one answer in response to this type of question. The code allows for the recording of up to two mentions, the first in columns 30 and 31 and the second in columns 32 and 33. More could be included by repeating the same code for columns 34 and 35, and so on. A common practice is to accept as the "first mention" the first response recorded by the interviewer unless a "priority" is placed on a later-mentioned response. First mentions are generally assumed to reflect the most important reason or issue to the respondent. Reasons beyond two in this example would simply be ignored by the coder.

The priority response can be illustrated by recourse to one class of responses. Suppose, in the study, it is important to identify respondents citing war as an issue. To remind the coder to flag such a response, regardless of whether the respondent had mentioned it first or not, it is identified as a priority response. The coder is instructed to search all responses given and to record this one first, if it appears at all. Uninteresting responses might also be flagged as "low priority" to discourage them from appearing when other alternatives are available.

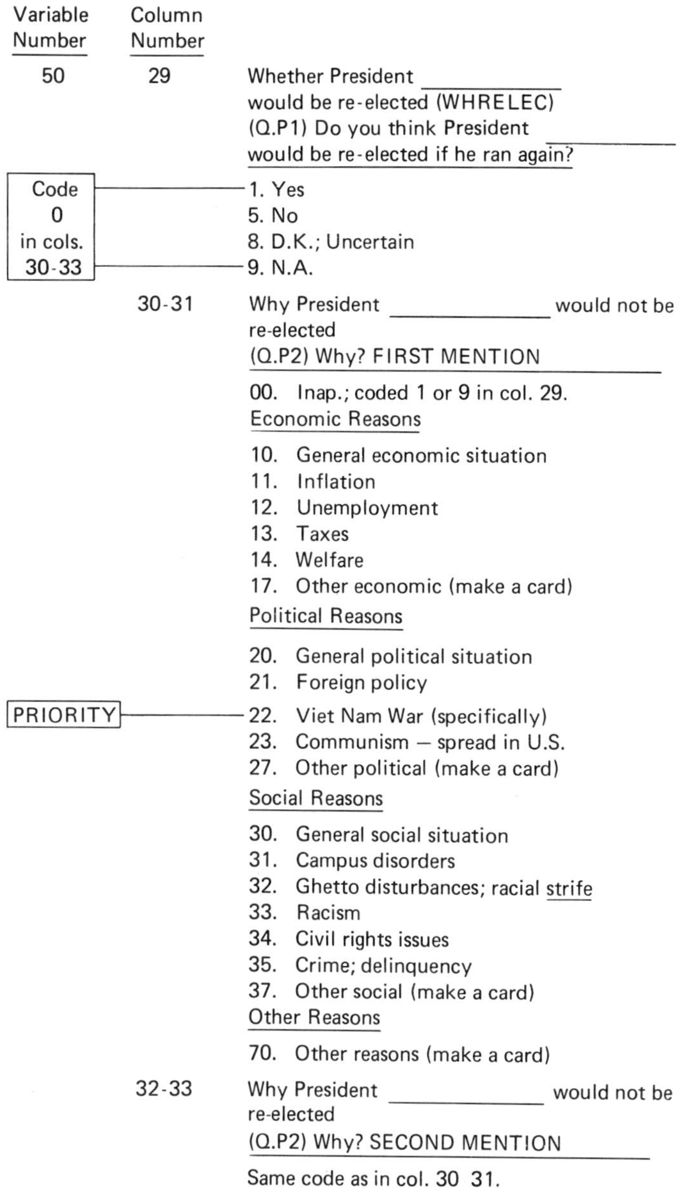
Variable Number	Column Number	
50	29	Whether President ______ would be re-elected (WHRELEC) (Q.P1) Do you think President ______ would be re-elected if he ran again?
Code 0 in cols. 30-33		1. Yes 5. No 8. D.K.; Uncertain 9. N.A.
	30-31	Why President ______ would not be re-elected (Q.P2) Why? FIRST MENTION
		00. Inap.; coded 1 or 9 in col. 29.
		Economic Reasons
		10. General economic situation 11. Inflation 12. Unemployment 13. Taxes 14. Welfare 17. Other economic (make a card)
		Political Reasons
		20. General political situation 21. Foreign policy
PRIORITY		22. Viet Nam War (specifically)
		23. Communism — spread in U.S. 27. Other political (make a card)
		Social Reasons
		30. General social situation 31. Campus disorders 32. Ghetto disturbances; racial strife 33. Racism 34. Civil rights issues 35. Crime; delinquency 37. Other social (make a card)
		Other Reasons
		70. Other reasons (make a card)
	32-33	Why President ______ would not be re-elected (Q.P2) Why? SECOND MENTION
		Same code as in col. 30 31.

Figure 4-13 An Example of a Reasons Code

12. Use contingency boxes.

The code example illustrated in Figures 4-12 and 4-13 uses a contingency box to aid the coder and speed the coding process. The screening question, Q. P1, is designed to shunt away respondents who expect reelection. No more information is desired of them and Q. P2 is not to be asked of them (i.e., it is inappropriate and should be coded as such). The contingency box directs the coder to code 0s in all columns relating to reasons the current president is not expected to be reelected. Thus, the coder need not even read through this part of the code for respondents coded 1 or 9 in column 29. This procedure can save a great deal of time if a detailed section with many questions follows.

13. In designing code structure, keep in mind the kinds of statistical analyses to be done.

Use of least-squares procedures (e.g., multiple regression) may require continuous variables, not class intervals. Ranking or ordering may be required rather than variables coded at the nominal level. Again, it must be emphasized that codes should be designed with the analysis in mind, not vice versa.

Codes for Open- and Closed-Ended Questions

Any type of survey instrument will generally be made up of two basic types of questions: open- and closed-ended. Figure 4-14 gives two examples. *Open-ended questions* are characterized by the lack of any preformed response structure associated with them. Basically, the interviewer simply writes down

(Q.A4) What is your opinion about the effects of inflation on business conditions?

____

____

(Q.G14) How much was your total family income last year? $__________

(Q.A4) What is your opinion about the impact of inflation on business conditions?

Improve business conditions	☐ 1
Makes conditions worse	☐ 3
No impact	☐ 5
Other	☐ 7
No opinion; don't know	☐ 8
No answer	☐ 9

(Q.G15) How much was your total family income last year?

Under $5000	☐ 1
$5000 – 9999	☐ 2
$10,000 – 14,999	☐ 3
$15,000 or more	☐ 4
Don't know	☐ 8
No answer	☐ 9

Figure 4-14 Alternative Question Formats Dealing with Inflation and Income

the respondent's exact comments. Such questions involve extensive preparation in code construction prior to the coding process, as well as well-trained interviewers.

At the other extreme is the precoded, or *closed-form, question.* Here, the answers are predetermined in form. The interviewer must force the respondent's answer into one of the categories, either by on-the-spot interpretation or by probing if the first answer cannot be pigeonholed satisfactorily. (The "other" category is often omitted from such questions to help force a substantive answer.) This structure is often less desirable than the open-ended alternative, especially if the question has never been used before on a large scale. The problem is that the interviewer must not only conduct the interview, but also code answers simultaneously, not an easy task. Moreover, interviewers must also develop ad hoc rules for dealing with ambiguous responses, a task better left to the study staff if the same rules are to be applied to responses from all persons interviewed.

On the other hand, if a question has been used frequently, its response pattern and useful code categories have become well known, and the question has been shown to elicit relevant answers, then such a structure often results in good information at minimal cost. Certain forms of questions, of course, lend themselves to this type of structure—yes/no questions, for example.

The rigidity of such forced-choice structures can be reduced considerably by including an "other" code category as a possible response for which the interviewer records an answer verbatim when it does not fit into the predetermined choices easily. This adds an open-ended part to the question. At a minimum, the researcher can see what kind of information the precoded structure is missing and has the option of adding new codes to isolate frequent responses that appear in the "other" category. The code-construction task is a simple one for forced-choice questions. The answer categories are simply tagged with numbers.

When open-ended questions are used and there has been little or no prior experience with the question, constructing a reasonable code may be particularly difficult. The first piece of information available is the intent of the question. It was presumably included in the instrument to measure something, and the researcher ought to have at least some expectations of the kinds of responses desired. Typically, however, some respondents will interpret a question differently than intended or perceive it as referring to a different topic. This is one of the biggest sources of error in both question and code design and is a likely occurrence since the education levels and social background of researcher and respondent are often quite different. Thus, questions almost always elicit some unanticipated answers.

The second source of information for code construction, the pretest, will generally provide hints as to how to deal with these unanticipated answers. The researcher reviews responses to the question that are given by a small group of respondents like those intended for study, writes them on cards, and then sorts them into piles using a rule based on characteristics the responses have in common. Reasonable answers not anticipated earlier can now be incorporated into the code. Rules for handling and classifying certain important or unexpected types of responses should also be developed at this time.

The third source of information about the adequacy of the code design comes from the early stages of the actual coding process and entails feedback to the researcher regarding responses that are seen to fit poorly into the code. Periodic reviews may indicate the need for code revisions and recoding earlier interviews.

THE CODING PROCESS

After the codes have been designed, the production coding can start. This section discusses coder training, the production coding process, quality control, complex coding tasks, and the difficulties that can be expected.

Coder Training

If a special coding staff is to be used in processing the study, it is beneficial to spend some time training them before they begin work on actual edited interviews. For this purpose, the research staff should prepare one or two practice interviews—questionnaires made up by the research staff in duplicate so that all coders working on the study will be practice-coding the same interview. The few hours of time invested in training pay off highly in the reduction of coding errors. The objectives of coder training are to demonstrate the consistent and proper application of codes and to encourage the proper use of administrative procedures.

Prior to actually working on the practice interviews, the research staff should spend some time with the coders, discussing the study itself, its objectives, the sample, how the questions will be used in analysis, what kinds of answers are expected, and likely sources of problems in coding (the editing process will provide some hints). Coders should also be told of any departures from normal coding procedures or normal card or question structure that the study requires.

The practice interview should contain difficult problems for the coders to deal with, as well as a straightforward production coding assignment. If data with a complex structure are to be coded, problem cases reflecting the range of structures expected should intentionally be built into the practice interview by the research staff. Each practice interview should be worked on by all coders. Then, in a group, the coders and the research staff should go over each one, discussing procedures for dealing with different data structures and the concepts underlying the procedures and decision rules. The result is to enlist coders' intelligent cooperation in handling the problems that inevitably arise during production coding and to establish pathways of communication between coders and the research staff (Roth, 1970).

Production Coding

Once a sufficient number of interviews have been edited and the coding staff has been trained, production coding can begin. Coding should still be monitored closely early in the process to ensure quick correction of any procedural or conceptual difficulties. A reasonable system must be designed for keeping track of interviews if several coders are working on the project. A simple extension of the sign-out system discussed in Chapter 3 works well, showing at a glance the status of each bundle of interviews (additional columns could be used to check keypunch and verification status). An example is shown in Figure 4-15. All interviews can be kept in a central location, and coders can easily tell which interview packs are available for coding.

Interview Number	Editor	Date Completed Editing	Check	Editing	Coder	Date Completed Coding	Check	Coding
0001-0009	JS	6/1	AT	6/1	RJ	6/1	AT	6/1
0010-0019	WCD	6/2	GH	6/2	RJ	6/2	AT	6/2
0020-0029	JN	6/1			DN	6/2		
0030-0039	WCD	6/3						
0040-0049	JS	6/4	GH	6/4				
0050-0059								
0060-0069								

Figure 4-15 A Control Log for Editing and Coding

Coding Quality Control

The researcher must establish systematic ways to get feedback about the coding process. In particular, one needs information about how well the codes designed by the researcher are classifying the data. In addition, feedback on coder performance is crucial.

If a code does not correspond well to the pattern of answers being received, alterations may have to be made. Moreover, the whole project will benefit from hearing coders' observations about the coding process. For previously used questions, there is not liklely to be much trouble. Most of the problems with the code will have been worked out in earlier surveys. However, new questions and questions whose responses can change over time will require closer attention. Questions about politics or economic conditions often have codes that rapidly become obsolete.

A useful method for getting data about the coding process, which does not entail continuous interruptions of the research staff by the coders, is to use memo cards. Coders are instructed to fill out a 3- by 5-inch file card each time a response does not fit the code well, or difficulty is encountered in deciding the category in which to place the respondent. An instruction to "make a card" each time the "other" code category is selected can be used to generate information about potential obsolescence of codes.

The content of the card should include the interview number, the question number, the date the card was made, the response given by the respondent, the disposition made by the coder (i.e., the code value assigned), and the coder's name. These cards should have a fixed format to facilitate hand sorting. Coders should be encouraged to make such a card any time there is uncertainty about the disposition of the case. The cards should be collected in a central location and read by the research staff at least twice a day. The procedure provides immediate feedback to coders and timely information to the research staff about code adequacy. If a suitable message-switching program is available on interactive computer terminals, this can profitably be used instead of 3- by 5-inch cards.

If a code is failing to match the response patterns accurately, there are several courses of action available to the researcher as the messages are reviewed. First, a new code value can be added if possible. The research staff should issue a written, dated, code-change sheet to all coders. This ensures that everyone receives information about the change. Then, using the information from the coder messages, the affected interviews can be corrected on their code sheets. If an entire new code must be designed, similar procedures are followed. Another alternative is to wait until the end of the study, examine all the messages, and make decisions about code changes at that point. With recorded information about the interview number, the response, and the existing code value, corrections to the machine-encoded data can be made. All code changes should be recorded and publicized promptly. One copy of the code, labeled "master copy," should be maintained by whoever is in charge of coding.

Extensive *check coding* should be performed early in the coding process, especially if coders have had little or no prior coding experience. It is performed on a sample taken from each pack of interviews. Check coding is simply a second coding of an interview, performed by a member of the research staff or by an experienced coder. The data record of the check coder is compared to the original coded data. Then all differences are noted, discussed, and reconciled between the coder and the check coder. This discussion provides the former with immediate feedback on performance and provides the latter with information about difficulties with the code or the concepts used in the study. If possible, all of the early interviews should be check-coded. Once coders become experienced and comfortable with the procedures, fewer errors will be made, and the sampling rate can be reduced gradually to about 10 per cent. Check coders should compile statistics showing the extent and nature of the unreliabilities.

The purpose of check coding is to catch errors early, gain information about where corrective coder training should take place, help the coders to apply codes consistently and correctly, and to maintain consistency with data and concepts from other studies. The process generates information for the study director about the frequency and type of errors in the study's variables. It serves administratively to indicate who is performing poorly and needs help.

As noted several times in this chapter, it is advisable to keep the coding process as simple as possible. This helps minimize the number of coder errors. If there is very little (and only simple) variable building to be done, or some data are needed very quickly, or if the variables are of a type that is not easily subjected to the clean and simple logic of the computer, some variable building may be combined with the coding process. It is even better, sometimes, to perform some coding operations during the editing phase.

Other than the mapping of verbal responses into code categories, the most common type of variable building done by coders is the conversion of data in fields (such as family income or age) to a set of class intervals. The coder transcribes the actual value into a field, looks up the bracketed value, and codes it in a subsequent column on the code sheet. This activity, a major source of coder errors, is actually best left to the computer. It is far better to devote the coding to tasks ill-suited to computer processing. For instance, coders can better be asked to generate indices or summary codes that require a subjective reading of several responses in detail. Information about the conduct of the interview may even be required, such as the probes used (these should have been carefully recorded by the interviewer), or the total number of refusals to answer questions occurring in the entire interview.

Whenever possible, it is best to let coders interpret verbal responses, to depend on editors for accuracy checks, and to depend on computing equipment for tasks that require the repeated application of well-defined rules to unambiguous data. When careful judgment is needed or procedures are used that require dealing with many exceptions, it is advisable to establish a division of labor that assigns one or two coders to work only on those tasks. In many cases, scheduling considerations will dictate that these activities be carried out together with the editing operations (i.e., ahead of the main bulk of the coding). Such tasks include occupation coding and worksheet procedures of the kind needed to study such detailed concepts as income and debt.

Complex Coding and Variable Building

When coding tasks require enough specialized skill to warrant special treatment, the time-tested principle of the division of labor is appropriate. In addition, some tasks may require such a level of understanding of the basic study concepts and sampling and field procedures as to warrant attaching them to the editing rather than to the coding phases. On a large project, this may mean that they are performed by different individuals; on a small one, this distinction would not be made. But even here, setting aside a specific block of time to accomplish these tasks rather than working them in with the rest of the coding or editing will often pay off in time saved and in errors not committed. The tasks most suited to being segregated are those that require either the application of very complex codes, those that are associated closely with the sampling procedures, or those in which information must be compiled from various parts of the interview.

Establishing a code value for the respondent's occupation and the industry in which he or she works are typical examples of tasks that have been found to have low reliability. The coder must spend the time necessary to develop familiarity with the complex codes frequently used and to develop the skills required to cope with unusual cases that are difficult to classify. One coder doing all the occupation coding will generally do a better job than many coders, each coding only a few interviews.

In studies that use complex family structure concepts like the "spending unit", it may be desirable for the editing staff to do the coding.[3] This is especially true if the editors must examine the interview to determine that exactly the right number of interviews have been obtained. Editing decisions about these questions may require discarding the interview or sending the interviewer back for an additional one. At the decision point, the editor has at his or her fingertips all the information about who lives at the dwelling unit and is in a propitious position to code that information. Moreover, it is often best to hold problem cases like this from further coding until the sampling questions have been resolved. Thus, family-structure concepts and dwelling-unit occupancy concepts are natural candidates for coding by the editing staff. The codes are simply written in coding boxes on the questionnaire for later transcription by a coder, along with the rest of the information.

Where worksheets or other complex information-collating aids are used, the principle of the division of labor can again be invoked to the benefit of the error count and the man-hour tally for the study. In most cases, editors can be trained to perform the worksheet computations at the end of the checks for errors. The editor picks up information from various points for transfer to a worksheet upon completion of a scan of the interview for inconsistencies and for data that need to be edited out or moved. The question of occupation coding illustrates the uses of coding boxes and worksheets. It is an extremely complex task requiring sorting through a considerable amount of verbiage to seek three types of information:

1. the type of work the person does (i.e., occupation or job),
2. the nature of the industry or business in which the person is employed,
3. whether or not he or she is self-employed.

[3] For instance, one possible definition of a "spending unit" is: "Members of a family forming a subgroup who pool their incomes for most spending and budgeting purposes." A married woman and her husband who live with her parents might, in some cases, meet this definition. For an example, see Katona et al. (1965).

Lacking any of these essential elements, a typical coder brings to bear subjective biases, and the resulting classifications are often incorrect and unreliable.

Classifying and coding occupational information requires familiarity with the codes to be used, plus knowing something about set theory and its applications. It requires the ability to apply rules, a skill at grasping similarities and differences, and a considerable amount of persistence. The coder must learn to postpone judgments until assembly and interpretation of all the available evidence have been completed, and all alternative code categories have tentatively been explored. Only then can high levels of accuracy and reliability be achieved.

Occupation coding starts by scanning the verbal descriptions of the kind of work performed to determine whether both an "occupation" and an "industry" have been reported. For example, "clerk in a supermarket," "bank teller," and "telephone company lineman" all contain both kinds of information. "Truck driver," "salesman," and "sociologist" only define the respondent's occupation. "Steelworker," "works in a grocery store," and "automobile plant" inform the coder only about industry. In some cases, a company name may be given, which is a clear indication of an industry; but in these days of conglomerates, this level may not be an accurate industry indicator. The matter should be taken up with the editing supervisor, and the decisions recorded in the editors' decision book. Generally, if two jobs are reported, the first-mentioned one would be coded unless there were clear indications that it is not the respondent's primary job.

Alternatively, an occupation title may be consistent only with a particular industry, or with some type of manufacturing industry, and so on. In such cases, the coder can apply the most detailed code available (e.g., "manufacturing, unspecified"), even though specific industry information was not actually present in the interview. When only occupation is specified, it will generally be necessary to leave industry information as "missing data." If only industry is indicated, occupation would generally receive editorial attention and a recorded decision.

If the verbal description contains no clear-cut occupational title, it is necessary to check occupational titles for codes that are thought to be appropriate, or synonymous. In this case, consistency between the description of the occupation given in the codes and that in the interview schedule is sufficient. If a quick search yields no obvious solution, then an editorial decision must be made and recorded. Where scanning indicates both an occupation and an industry, both pieces of information enter the coding process.

Certain occupations are particularly troublesome to code. Two of the most frequently appearing offenders are "engineer" and "foreman." Many occupational titles include the word "engineer" but do not imply a professional with college training in engineering. A foreman in a craft occupation is generally given only the code for his craft.

A useful compilation of information on the coding of occupational status measures appears in Robinson, Athanasiou, and Head (1969). Figure 4-16 gives

Occupation Categories

Code 3-digit codes from the U.S. Department of Commerce Census of occupations, 1960 Edition.

Professional and Technical (000-195)

01. Accountants and Auditors (000)
02. Clergymen (023)
03. Teachers – secondary and primary (182-184)
04. Teachers – college, librarians, principals (030-060, 111)
05. Dentists (071)
06. Physicians and Surgeons (162)
07. Engineers (080-093)
08. Lawyers and Judges (105)
09. Social and Welfare Workers (165, 171)
10. Other Medical and Paramedical – Chiropractors, Optometrists, Osteopaths, Pharmacists, Veterinarians, Nurses, Therapists, and Healers (022, 152, 153, 160, 194, 150, 151, 193)
11. Scientists, Physical and Social – e.g., Chemists, Physical and Biological Scientists, Statisticians, etc. (021, 130-145, 171-175)
12. Technicians – Airplane Pilots and Navigators, Designers, Dieticians and Nutritionists, Draftsmen, Foresters and Conservationists, Funeral Directors, Embalmers, Photographers, Radio Operators, Surveyor, Technicians (medical, dental, testing, n.e.c.) (012, 072, 073, 074, 103, 104, 161, 164, 181, 185, 190-192)
13. Public Advisors – Editors and Reporters, Farm and Home Management Advisors – Editors and Reporters, Farm and Home Management Advisors, Personnel and Labor Relations Workers, Recreation and Group Workers, Religious Workers (075, 102, 153, 165, 175)
17. Other Semi-Professional or Professional (with college degree) –e.g., Architects
18. Other Semi-Professional (no college degree)
19. Professional, NA what type

Self-employed Businessmen. Managers and Officials (R. 250-289)

21. Self-employed Business man, Owner or Part-owner, "Large" Business (earned more than $10,000 in 1963)
22. Self-employed Businessman, Owner or Part-owner, "Small" Business (earned less than $10,000 in 1963)
23. Self-employed Business, NA what size
28. Other Managers, Officials, and Proprietors
29. Manager, Official or Proprietor, NA what type

Clerical and Sales (Y, Z, 301-360, S, 380-395)

30. Bookkeeper (310)
31. Stenographers, Typists, and Secretaries (345, 360, Z)
32. Other Clerical (Y, 301-360)
33. Sales, Higher-status traveling or "outside" goods (381, 382)
34. Sales, Higher-status traveling or "outside" services (380, 385, 393, 395)
35. Sales. "Inside" Sales. Salesman, Clerk (S)
36. Sales. Lower-status "outside" sales. Hucksters, Peddlers, Newsboys (383, 390)
37. Other Sales
38. Clerical, NA what type (Y, Z, 301-360)
39. Sales, NA what type (S, 380-395)

Figure 4-16

Skilled Workers (Q, 401-554)

41. Self-employed Artisans and Craftsmen
42. Foremen (430)
48. Other Craftsmen and Kindred Workers
49. Skilled Workers, NA what type

Semi-skilled. Operatives and Kindred Workers (T, W, 601-721)

51. Operatives and Kindred Workers

Service Workers (555, 801-890, P)

61. Protective Service Workers – Firemen, Marshalls and Constables, Policemen and Bailiffs (850-854)
62. Other Protective Service (860)
63. Members of Armed Service – Enlisted men, NA whether enlisted or officer (555)
64. Members of Armed Service – Officers (555)
65. Private Household Workers (P, 801-803)
68. Other Service Workers (810-842, 874-890)
69. Service Worker, NA what type

Unskilled Laborers (U, V, X, 901, 905, 960-973)

71. Farm Laborers (U, V, 901, 905)
78. Other Laborers (X, 960-973)
79. Unskilled, NA what type

Farm Operators (N, 222)

81. Farm Managers (222)
82. Farm Owners and Tenants (N)
89. Farmers, NA what type

Unemployed and Students

91. Unemployed with private income (Rentier)
92. Student (IF R is a part-time day student, classify here rather than by occupation. If R is studying nights, classify by occupation)
93. On Strike (code occupation and unemployment times as for general unemployed)
94. Other general unemployed

Retired

95. Retired

Housewife

96. Housewife (If R works part-time outside home, R should be classified according to part-time occupation)
99. NA

NOTE: Coding of part-time farmers. Depends on classification of head. (1) If land is farmed part-time but only non-farm job is mentioned, non-farm job is coded. (2) Apparent farm workers who work on small farms while maintaining non-farm jobs are coded non-farm. (3) Farm heads who appear to be picking up non-farm work on side are coded "farm". In general, depends on coder estimate of primacy. Where all else is equal (or unknown) code by first mention.

Figure 4-16 (cont'd.)

a useful detailed occupation code, based on one developed by the Inter-University Consortium for Political Research, and derived from the three-digit codes set forth in the Department of Commerce Census of Occupations, 1960 edition.

If information must be assembled from various parts of the interview, coders may need to employ *coding boxes* as aids. These are useful devices for identifying the results of complex procedures that generate only a few final coded values. For instance, in the 1966 Survey of Consumer Finances (Katona et al., 1967), it was desired to code the total dollars spent in 1965 on additions and repairs to housing. A number of questions elicited information about each expenditure. Calculators were used to compute the total expenditures falling under the concept, and editors recorded the results in a five-character box stamped with a rubber stamp or preprinted in a certain place on the interview form. Figure 4-17 illustrates the use of a stamped box to record total additions and repairs to housing.

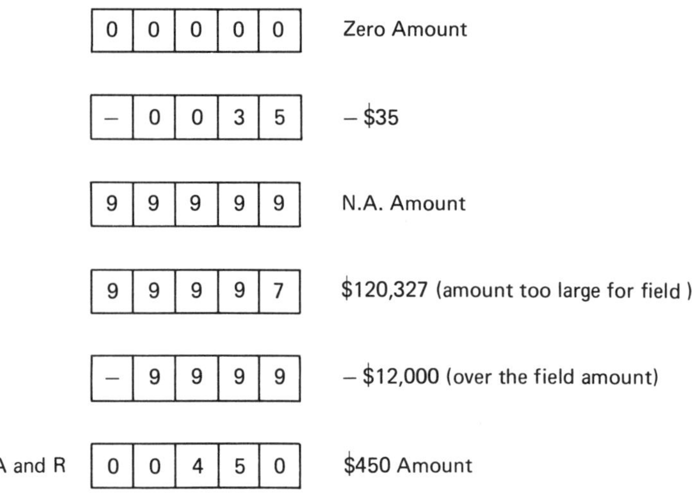

Figure 4-17 A Stamped Box: Additions and Repair to House

A coding box always has the required number of characters set forth in the editing instructions and represents the field exactly as the coder will code it. It is labeled by writing a mnemonic identifier beside it (e.g., "A & R" for "additions and repairs") and the computed amount is entered into it. The box is always stamped in a specific place in the interview, not randomly. Any such boxes are always coded. They would be filled with 0s where inappropriate. The exact handling of N.A. and over-the-field amounts must conform to local computer-program requirements. These must be determined before procedures for using coding boxes can be developed.

Sometimes a very large amount of information scattered all through the interview must be collected, manipulated, and coded to produce variables more closely conforming to the study's analytic concepts. Information is often scattered, simply because questions should be asked in a sequence that makes sense to the respondents. For example, it makes sense to ask about debt on additions and repairs to housing in a section of an interview that deals with housing. Another section dealing with automobile purchases and ownership would contain information on debt for this type of item. Still another section may deal specifically with debt in the context of a discussion of purchases of other consumer durable goods, such as furniture or sports equipment. If these individual debt items are to be grouped together to obtain measures corresponding to specific economic concepts, such as "remaining installment debt incurred during the previous year," the information must be brought together in one place and then added up. It would seem reasonable to do this after the basic data have been coded in machine-readable form; a computer could be used. But the process requires complex judgments at the time the coding is done, so worksheet procedures that are supported by a calculator prove more satisfactory.

The 1966 Survey of Consumer Finances Debt Worksheet illustrates one type used in collating information (see Figure 4-18). (The questionnaire that generated these data is reproduced in Katona et al., 1967.) The coder performs the following steps:

1. he or she enters interview identification information at the top of the worksheet and initials it;
2. debt associated with business operations is edited out (i.e., is not transferred to the worksheet);
3. the remaining installment debt incurred in 1965 and that incurred in other years is entered in the lightly shaded areas above the four-digit boxes; (Assignments are made if necessary. Information is obtained from various parts of the questionnaire.)
4. remaining noninstallment debt is likewise entered;
5. all amounts in the lightly shaded rectangles are summed and entered in the subtotal boxes (additions and repairs, cars, durable goods, and other);
6. the subtotals are summed horizontally, and the results are entered in the remaining total debt column;
7. the remaining total debt column is coded using the indicated codes;
8. the subtotals are summed vertically to obtain 1965 and non-1965 installment debt, remaining total debt, and total remaining installment debt;

9. checks are made for assignments, and the existence of these is coded;
10. all additions are rechecked.

Upon completion of the worksheet, it is placed between the pages of the inter-

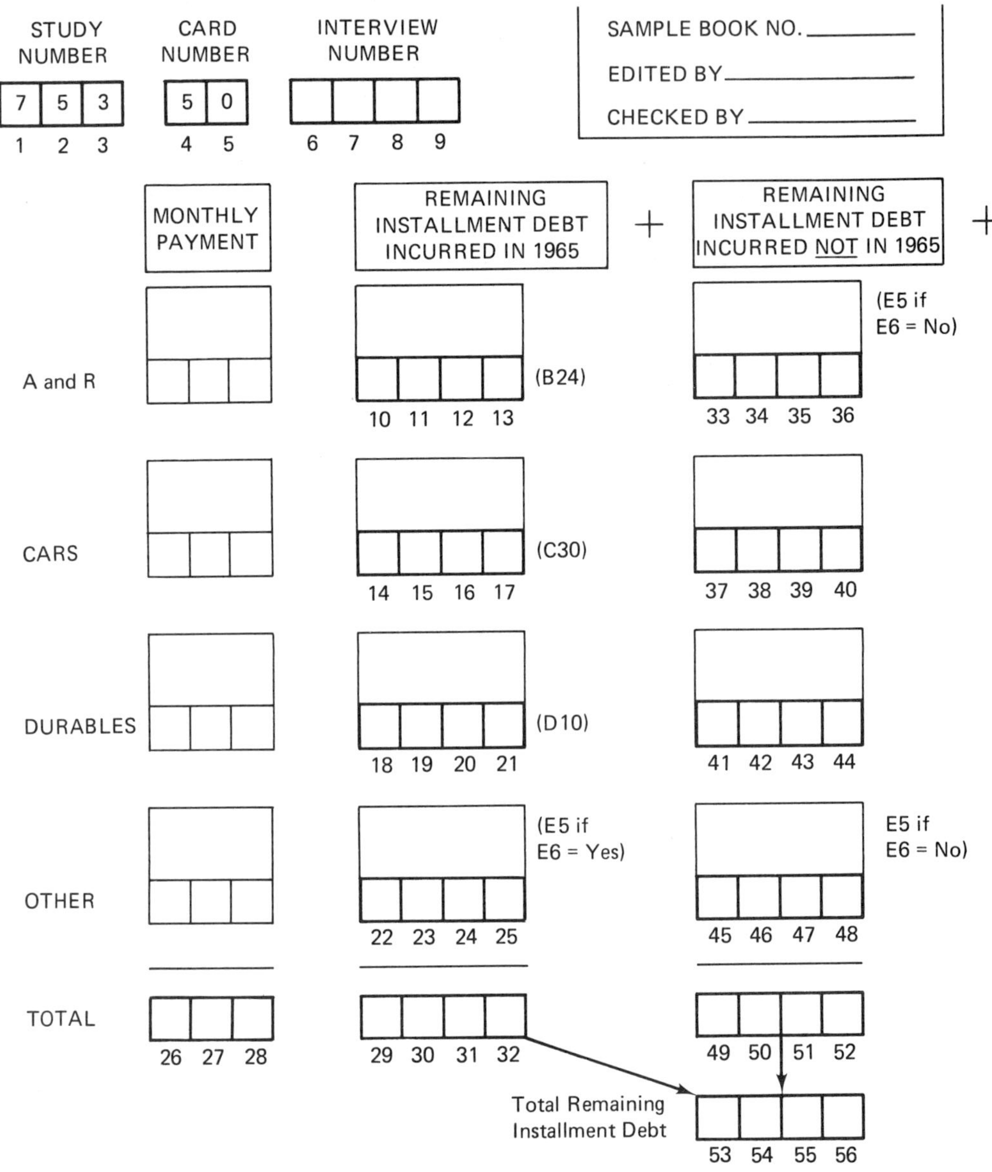
STUDY NUMBER 7 5 3 (1 2 3)
CARD NUMBER 5 0 (4 5)
INTERVIEW NUMBER (6 7 8 9)

SAMPLE BOOK NO. ______
EDITED BY ______
CHECKED BY ______

	MONTHLY PAYMENT	REMAINING INSTALLMENT DEBT INCURRED IN 1965	+	REMAINING INSTALLMENT DEBT INCURRED NOT IN 1965	+
A and R		10 11 12 13 (B24)		33 34 35 36 (E5 if E6 = No)	
CARS		14 15 16 17 (C30)		37 38 39 40	
DURABLES		18 19 20 21 (D10)		41 42 43 44	
OTHER		22 23 24 25 (E5 if E6 = Yes)		45 46 47 48 E5 if E6 = No)	
TOTAL	26 27 28	29 30 31 32		49 50 51 52	

Total Remaining Installment Debt 53 54 55 56

Figure 4-18

(Used by permission of the Survey Research Center of the Institute for Social Research, The University of Michigan.)

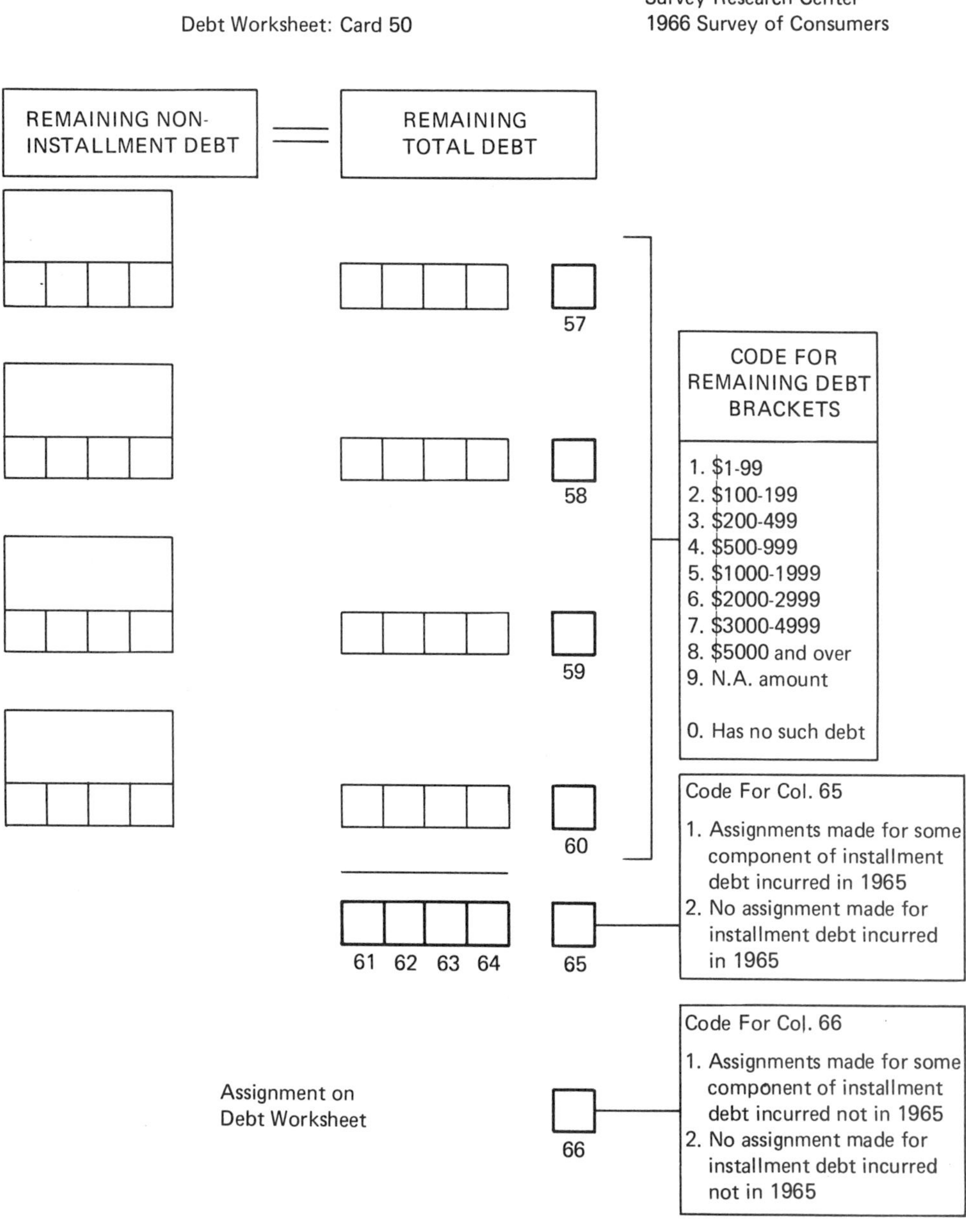

Figure 4-18 (cont'd.)

view, and both are returned to the pack of interviews for checking. The debt information is now in a concise form readily transcribed into machine-readable form with a minimum of errors. It seems likely that this type of manual procedure will persist for some time despite recent improvements in automated source data-acquisition procedures.

Difficulties Faced by the Coder

Although this book does not really attempt to deal with the issue of questionnaire construction, it does have something to say on that subject as it relates to the successful processing and transferral of the data to machine-readable form. Some examples of problems that coders face will be illustrated here.

A common coding problem related to question order is illustrated by the first series of questions and hypothetical answers presented in Figure 4-19. The hypothetical intent of the first question is to find out why people think that we will have an economic recovery in the near future. Those who do not expect a recovery are not asked questions 2 and 3 (although, in principle, they could be). The problem here is that the question structure does not make it clear whether or not Q.3 relates back to Q.1 or to Q.2. Thus, answer B is a meaningful answer to Q.3 and could easily be coded (assuming a well-defined code) as an answer to it. Answer A, however, relates to the timing of the upswing and is not really a good answer to the question. This presents the coder with difficulties that take extra time to resolve and could have been avoided simply with better question construction. Placing Q.3 ahead of Q.2 would avoid this problem, making the coding easier and obtaining better data. Answers such as

Q.1 Do you think we will have good times in the economy soon?

[1 YES | X] [5 NO |] GO TO Q.4. [8 DK: Uncertain |]

Q.2. About when will that happen? IN THE NEXT FEW MONTHS

Q.3. Why is that? (A) BECAUSE WE ARE ALREADY IN AN UPSWING
BECAUSE THE GOVERNMENT IS SPENDING A LOT OF MONEY

Q.4. Do you think that over the next few months the rate of inflation will be reduced or that the level of unemployment will rise?

NO

Q.5. Have you heard any favorable news about the stock market lately?

NO

Q.6. Do you think we might have a recession next year? YES

Figure 4-19 Coding Problems

"I heard it on TV" would still result, but the probability of a meaningful answer would be raised. Good question structuring leads to clearer and more easily codable responses, fewer coding errors, and minimizes coder judgment.

Another coding nightmare is posed by Q.4 of Fig. 4-19. How is the coder to view this? NO, the rate of inflation will not be reduced? NO, the level of unemployment will not rise? NO, neither will happen? NO, both will happen?

Q.5 is an example of what happens when the likely response pattern of the respondent is not considered. There are many interesting possibilities: NO, heard nothing about the stock market lately; NO, heard nothing favorable about the stock market lately; NO, don't pay any attention to news about the stock market. Whatever the results, they surely must be interpreted in light of the troubles with the question used to generate them. The problems could be discovered through the coder-message technique or by pre-testing the questionnaire.

The way in which people use verb tenses can create problems for the coder also. For example, consider the meaning of the answer to Q.6: YES, we might, but it is very unlikely; YES, it is sure to happen; and everything in between. A NO answer would have similar interpretational problems: NO, we'll never have one; NO, not next year, but perhaps the year after that; NO, not next year, but we'll definitely have one soon.

Other questionnaire design practices present problems for coders. Precoding responses with numbers that do not correspond to other conventions used in coding leads to errors (e.g., establishing the code 1 to mean "none"). So does placing questions in a part of the questionnaire where they are improperly asked of respondents (e.g., asking "Is it useful for you to own two or more cars" of all respondents). If this is not supposed to be asked of non-car-owning respondents, the coder must continually check car ownership before deciding whether to code an INAP. or N.A. for a missing response. Mistakes such as these greatly increase the time and costs required for coding and increase the probability of errors and the unnecessary infusion of coder judgments into the study.

ON TO THE NEXT STEP

This completes our discussion of the coding process, although later chapters will refer to the issues raised here. The document that we have termed the "code" will provide the basis for the design of all the analyses and the interpretation of all output produced by the statistical analysis programs. Every survey, regardless of its size, needs some sort of code that at least describes the structure of the data in the storage medium. The procedures and principles described in this chapter are well tested and will help to ensure the quality of the data and the researcher's ability to use them easily at later stages in the research process.

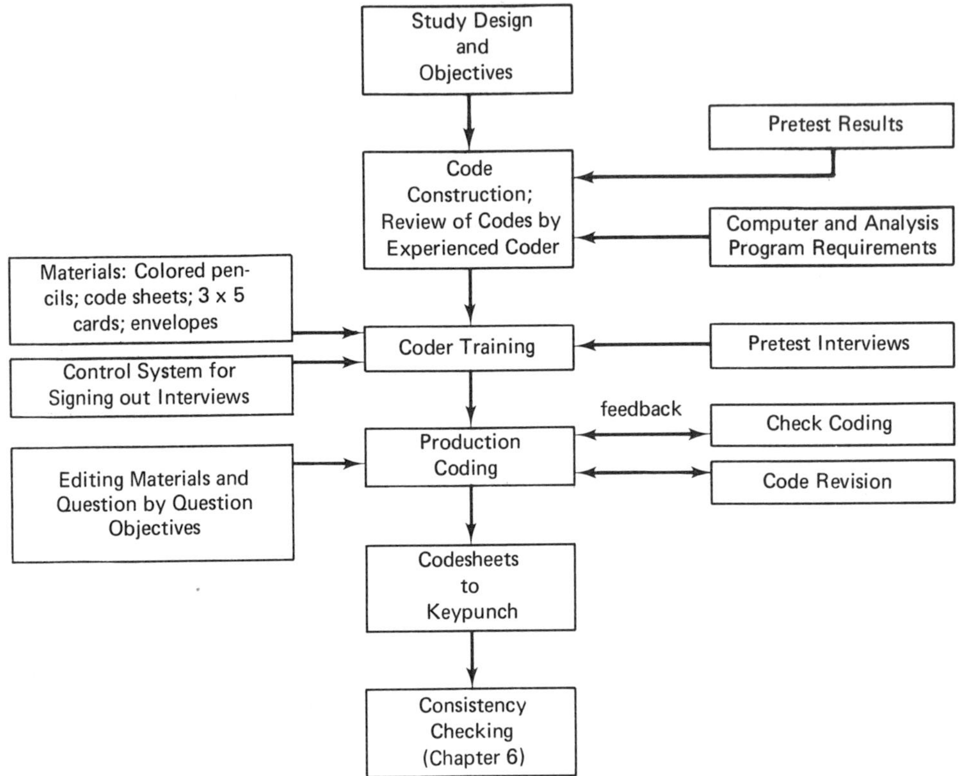

Figure 4-20 An Overview of the Coding Process

Not all the steps described here and summarized in Figure 4-20 will need to be fully implemented for all surveys. Size and complexity determine what must be done. But, for the most part, all the tasks discussed here must be performed to some degree, even if only by a single person. Good documentation, systematic procedures, and quality code construction are always prerequisites to successful analysis of the data.

At this point in the process, the data have been transferred to the storage medium, transformed from the interview through the use of the code. For some small studies, analysis will be the next step. For most, however, more work remains. The data, now on cards or some storage equivalent, will contain transcription errors and logical inconsistencies. Analysis of such "dirty" data as these is usually unnecessarily expensive and time consuming (some computer runs fail, and successful ones cannot be interpreted). In most cases, a simple cleaning of the data will prevent many problems and will be cost-effective. In others, a larger consistency-checking effort will be required. These processes are the subject of Chapter 6.

AN EXAMPLE

To give the reader a feel for the application of the principles discussed so far, an example follows. The displays include:

1. a questionnaire
2. an 80-column single-card description of each card in the study
3. a code for the data in the questionnaire
4. editors' instruction book
5. editors' decision book
6. a listing of the coded data.

The questionnaire is a condensed version of the 1968 Survey of Consumer Finances conducted by the Economic Behavior Program of the Survey Research Center, The University of Michigan. A report of the findings of the study and a full reproduction of the questionnaire are given in Katona et al. (1969). All the supporting documentation presented in this chapter is adapted from that actually used in the processing of the study and is reproduced by permission of The Survey Research Center of the Institute for Social Research, The University of Michigan.

The Questionnaire

Although questionnaire design is not the subject of this book, the questions included in the example do illustrate a wide variety of question types and nesting styles, tested organization of interview directions (e.g., skip instructions, probes), and layout (e.g., use of boldface type, wide margins), all of which have considerable relevance for the data processing.

The first page of the questionnaire describes the unit being interviewed and provides the basic information needed to identify the proper respondents. Other identifying information is on the face sheet, including the sample book number (a unique number identifying this address in the sample), a geographic identifier, and information about when and for how long the interview was taken.

The questions begin with Section A, General Attitudes. A few examples are shown, illustrating pre-coded and open-ended types of questions. Special instructions to the interviewer are included for Q.A5 to ensure that a proper answer is given by the respondent. Coding problems posed by this type of open-ended question were discussed in Chapter 4.

Section B deals with housing. Of particular interest here are the guides to the interviewer included in the questions (e.g., Q.B2) and in the margin of the page (e.g., to the left of Q.B2 and Q.B5). Note that sub-questions are indented and that arrows and skip instructions guide the interviewer through the section (Q.B8, Q.B9, and Q.B3 are examples).

At the end of the sequence on housing are several boxes, labeled HS, HV, and R. They will hold the data on housing status, house value, and rent. Editors determine the proper numbers to be written in the boxes. The code contains instructions to the coder to pick up information about these variables here rather than in questions B3, B5, and B7. The organization of questions B10 and B15 is quite similar.

Section C gathers extensive information about car ownership, with special emphasis on recent purchases of cars. An interviewer must be reasonably well trained to properly handle a more complex sequence such as this, even though the instructions are quite explicit. Again, several boxes are provided for use by editors and coders. Where detailed answers are needed or a particular context is required, special instructions are given (e.g., Q.C6 and Q.C9).

Section D deals with family income. In terms of the detail collected, it is quite complex. The interviewer is again guided through the section with boldface skip instructions and directional arrows. Income from all major sources received by each family member is ascertained. The interviewer performs some arithmetic during the interview and checks with the respondent regarding the accuracy of the results. Most of the data collected in this section are building blocks for such concepts as total family income, earned income, transfer payment income, and capital income. Questions are asked in detail to preserve flexibility for later analysis, and to make sure that the respondent does not inadvertently overlook a major income source.

Sections E and F call for other demographic information about the family unit not recorded on the face sheet. Section F is strictly observational and includes the interviewer's evaluation of the reliability of the information in the questionnaire. Some data will be available and can be used for evaluative purposes (e.g., the response-rate analysis) even if the interview is not completed.

The last page of the instrument, the thumbnail sketch, provides the interviewer with the opportunity to record observations on the respondent and the interview. It is frequently used to explain complex problems and situations and to provide additional data that might be useful in interpreting answers to particular questions. This section is often invaluable to the editors and frequently provides some interesting insights into the data.

Editors' Instruction Book

The beginning of the editors' instruction book should contain a general statement about the study, its objectives, and the respondents. This need not be especially detailed, since this same material should be well covered in editor training, but it may serve as a useful reminder to the editor. The introduction should also describe the structure of the manual and general editing procedures (e.g., the concept of missing data, assignments, and random-number tables). No example of the introduction is included here, since these topics are covered in Chapter 3. The example begins with Section I, FACE SHEET and LISTING BOX.

The first page of each section is the CHECKLIST. It provides a brief outline of the major concerns of the section for the editor, lists specific checks and calculations to be performed, and sets forth procedures to be followed in evaluating the data in the instrument. When missing data must be assigned, possible assignments are listed with references to the appropriate statistical tables for use in making them. Once an editor becomes familiar with the procedures, he may rarely have to look at anything but the checklist, if it is well structured.

The pages following the CHECKLIST detail the editors' job in each task. Within each major checklist heading, important concepts, calculations, and steps are noted at the left margin opposite the detailed explanation of the procedure. This makes it simple to locate sections dealing with a particular problem.

Important concepts are carefully spelled out in the instructions. For example, the definitions of a family unit (FU), a dwelling unit (DU), and a primary family unit are set forth in Section I. In Section III, additions and repairs to the home are carefully distinguished from durable goods. These operational definitions are reinforced by editor training, which deals with the more general objectives and measures in the study.

Typical problems and special cases are noted and illustrated in each section, along with an outline of the procedures for dealing with them. Principles and concepts to be applied are set forth. In Section I, the treatment of family members not at home is carefully spelled out. In Section II, the treatment of trailer owners and other special problems, such as the housing status of sharecroppers, is discussed. The treatment of interval responses (such as "between $8000 and $10,000" as a response to the house-value question) and how to deal with split ownership are covered. Section IV explains how to deal with the joint ownership of a car as well as with cars used principally by family members not living at home.

Editors must frequently perform variable building in the editing process, since complex judgments may be required for some variables, or the calculations necessary to generate them must be performed as a matter of course in their task of assessing the consistency and reliability of the data. Items J7 through J11 provide a good example of such a procedure. Qualitative, judgmental evaluations of the reliability of the data are required. Imputations are made where necessary. Valuable information may be gleaned from interviewer notes in the margins or in the thumbnail sketch.

Another editing example is the income worksheet. Here, editors are not only involved in variable building but also code several variables. Cards 06 and 07 for this example study would be punched directly from these worksheets. The editors' instructions specify where in the questionnaire the data are to be found and where on the worksheet they are to be entered. Calculations for subtotals and totals are outlined, and where to put the results is set forth. Results to be eventually transcribed onto punched cards are entered in boxes tagged with column numbers. This technique provides an organized and efficient framework for structuring a computer check on the arithmetic performed after all the editing decisions have been made and all numbers entered on the form.

Card Layout Form

Each data deck contains a large number of specific pieces of information, potentially as high as 80. It is difficult to locate specific information by thumbing through pages of codes to find the desired data. Facilitating this is the major use of the 80-column card layout form. Each of the six codes in the example study is preceded by such a form. It functions as an index to the data.

The general nature of the information contained on a card of data is at the top of the page (e.g., DEMOGRAPHICS, ATTITUDES, HOUSING). Once the subject area is located, the STUDY and DECK identification numbers are easily located. The body of the form then shows the contents of the card column by column. This makes locating data relatively simple.

In early phases of the study, draft codes are organized according to the anticipated sequence of questions in the study, and the card layout form is used with them in setting up a first view of what the study data file structure will be. The filled-out form also finds uses in consistency checking, variable building, and analysis phases of the study. Several 80-column layouts can be combined to represent a tape or disk record.

The first two columns provide a space to indicate the original source of the data on the card. This is particularly useful during the building of variables and indices or when work decks are to be constructed that contain data from several sources.

A third column provides for assigning a sequence number to the variables on the deck. On card 01, for example, there are 35 variables in 56 columns. A variable number, ranging from 1 to 35, is assigned to each and is useful in mapping the data into the format requirements of computer programs. In practice, sequencing of variables will take one of several forms, depending on the mode of data storage selected by the researcher. In the example here, the variables are numbered sequentially from 1 to 120, a form consistent with the large number of variables for each record usually found in tape or disk files. If card formatting were to be maintained (wasting much space on each card), the variable sequencing for each card would begin with 1.

Even more useful for assembling format information for input to the computer is the field-size column. This indicates the actual number of characters taken up by each field. Thus, using FORTRAN INTEGER mode, the first seven variables could quickly be formatted as (I3,I2,I4,3I1,I2). If it is later desired to pick up the last variable, number 35, for input, the proper format could easily be stated, since the layout form tells exactly where to skip to pick up, NEIGHBORHOOD as (I3,I2,I4,3I1,I2,T55,I2). If other information were desired, the form could easily be altered to include it.

Card Codes

Data codes are shown in detail for the example questionnaire and illustrate many of the principles discussed in Chapter 4. Beginning with card 01, the identification is spelled out first, starting with the study number, the deck number, and the interview number. Then the coder is instructed to pick up the six-digit number in the upper right-hand corner of the face sheet, a four-digit number immediately beneath it, and the interviewer's identification number from the label. The first two numbers are put on the instrument by the field staff when the questionnaire is received in the office. The data are taken from a cover sheet accompanying the interview, which indicates the actual address from which it was taken. This cover sheet is immediately separated from the interview when it is received to prevent inadvertent identification of the respondent. The information contained in the six-digit sample book number and the four-digit place code number is interpretable using the codes for columns 10–19. After entering the interviewer's identification number, the coder is instructed to turn to page 4 of the code to begin the substantive information starting in column 29.

The code for card 01, column 45, indicates how simple coding rules can be used to assist the coders. The 3 $\times$ 3 box will significantly reduce the number of coding errors. Card 02, columns 11-12 and 13-14, illustrate the use of the two-column response code. Here, a first digit of 1 or 2 indicates a reason for the respondent's belief that the family unit will be better off; those beginning with 5 or 6 denote reasons for being worse off. Up to two mentions are to be recorded (as noted in the margin of the code), so the code for columns 11 and 12 is repeated in columns 13 and 14.

The use of the contingency box is illustrated throughout the code example. Column 12 of card 05 makes use of several of the instructions contained in boxes in the left-hand margin. Such instructions speed up the coding process considerably and cut errors by eliminating unnecessary reading by the coder and by removing a decision about the applicability of a series of questions. These instruction boxes are also useful in setting up consistency checks, for they indicate clearly which codes in a particular column are consistent with zero codes elsewhere.

When information is not coded directly from the sequence of questions, these deviations are carefully pointed out to the coder. Thus, after coding card 01, column 45, the coder is told to turn to Section E, where he begins coding question E1 according to the code for column 46. The information in card 02, columns 14–16, comes from the "R" box at the bottom of the page. Similarly, columns 18–23 come from the "HV" box. Both were filled in by the editor. The car identification coded in card 04, column 10, is the be found ". . . ABOVE COLUMNS FOR Q.C5."

Editors' Decision Book

Only one example page from the Editors' Decision Book is shown in Figure 5-1. All problem resolutions are recorded on these pages to provide

Editor	Interview Number	Car Number	
WCD	0062	1	TP = 3000 AB + TI + CASH = 5000 Payment x Months = 1200, AB = 1000, looks OK CASH = TI = 2000 Decision: CASH = 0, probably sold car and used cash proceeds
JS	0263	1	TP = 2000, CASH = 1000, AB = 0, TI = 1000, T'NAIL indicates that R borrowed 1000 from credit union to buy the car. Decision: CASH = 0, AB = 1000
AT	1076	1	TP = 3500, AB + TI + CASH = 3900 AB = 2400, TI = 0, CASH = 1500 Decision: AB = 2000 since payment x months = 2400, AB reported includes finance charges

Figure 5-1 Editing Decisions

information to the editors and to document the way in which the question was interpreted.

Data Listing

To illustrate the end product, data card sets for several interviews are shown in Figure 5-2. The study number (772), the deck numbers, and the interview number are easily identified in the first nine columns. The remaining information, transferred to cards from the questionnaire via the coding instructions, represents the basic data of the study. Still to come are the variable-building procedures that will transform it into more complex descriptions of the unit of analysis used here, the family.

```
                        CARD COLUMNS
00000000011111111112222222222333333333344444444445555555555
12345678901234567890123456789012345678901234567890123456789
___________________________________________________________
                      FIRST INTERVIEW

77901000100302011103633019763033142411120185012288123203
77902000111019150000
779030001771000000920001134407300004500
77904000112106811251268375041150012505000000000000000
7790500012125008750212500875000000000000000000000
7790600013000000000000000000003000088000000000206
___________________________________________________________
                      SECOND INTERVIEW

77901000210103211124463931102028131301120212010977246708
77902000231255111356
779030002545018050000003196200000000000
779040002120000000000000000000000000000000000000000000
77905000212000070000000000000000000000000000000000
7790600020000000000000000000003000088000000000206
___________________________________________________________
                      THIRD INTERVIEW

77901000301101211121731481060030235001210363040040012607
7790200035525355253500000
779030003996012010000003454400000000000
779040003111062621312650000000000000000000000000000000
77905000307500000000000000000000000000002500000000
77906000307500000000000000250001000080000000000107
___________________________________________________________
```

Figure 5-2 Three Interviews on Cards

QUESTIONNAIRE

1968 SURVEY OF CONSUMERS

1. Interviewer's label

2. PSU ______________

3. Your Interview No. ______________

4. Date ______________

5. Length of Interview ______________ (Minutes)

INTERVIEWER: LIST ALL PERSONS, INCLUDING CHILDREN LIVING IN THE DWELLING UNIT, BY THEIR RELATION TO THE HEAD.

6. All persons, by relation or connection to head	7. Sex	8. Age	9. Family Unit No.	10. Indicate Response By Check ✓
1. HEAD OF DWELLING UNIT			1	
2.				
3.				
4.				
5.				
6.				
7.				
8.				
9.				
10.				
11.				
12.				

A: GENERAL ATTITUDES

A1. (Once again) We are interested in how people are getting along financially these days. Would you say that you and your family are better off or worse off financially than you were a year ago?

1. BETTER NOW ↓ | 3. SAME ↓ | 5. WORSE NOW ↓ | 8. UNCERTAIN ↓

A2 Why do you say so?____________________________________

____

A3. Are you people making as much money now as you were a year ago, or more, or less?

1. MORE NOW | 3. ABOUT THE SAME | 5. LESS NOW

A4. During the last few months, have you heard of any favorable or unfavorable changes in business conditions?____________________________________

(IF YES) A5. What did you hear?______________________________

____

IF NOT CLEAR WHETHER SOME CHANGE R MENTIONS IS FAVORABLE OR UNFAVORABLE, PROBE: "Would (MENTION CHANGE) be favorable or unfavorable?" AND NOTE "favorable" OR "unfavorable".

B: HOUSING

B1 Now I'd like to talk with you about things here at home. I am particularly interested in any changes which may have occurred in your housing since last year at this time. When did you move into this (house/apartment)?

_____________ (YEAR)

B2 How long have you lived here in (COUNTY NAME, e.g., BRONX) county?

_____________ (YEARS)

B3. Do you (FAMILY UNIT) own this (home/apartment), pay rent, or what?

☐ OWNS OR IS BUYING THIS (HOME/APARTMENT) – (GO TO Q. B7)

☐ PAYS RENT ON THIS (HOME/APARTMENT) – (GO TO Q. B5)

☐ NEITHER OWNS NOR RENTS THIS (HOME/APARTMENT)

Continued

(IF NEITHER OWNS NOR RENTS)

B4. How is that? ______________________

____

(TURN TO Q. B8)

(IF RENTS)

B5. About how much rent do you pay a month? $________

B6. Do you rent it furnished or unfurnished?

[1.] FURNISHED   [5.] UNFURNISHED

(TURN TO Q. B8)

(IF OWNS OR IS BUYING)

B7. Could you tell me what the present value of this house (farm) is? I mean, about what would it bring if you sold it today?

$______________

(ASK EVERYONE)

B8. Generally speaking, do you think now is a good time or a bad time to buy a house?

[1.] GOOD   [3.] PRO-CON   [5.] BAD   [8.] DON'T KNOW

B9 Why do you say so? ______________________

____

HS ☐   HV ☐☐☐☐☐☐ (DOLLARS)   R ☐☐☐ (DOLLARS)

ADDITIONS AND REPAIRS

(ASK EVERYONE)

B10. Did you have any expenses for work done on this (house and lot/apartment) in 1968 – things like upkeep, additions, improvements, or painting and decorating? (FARMERS – EXCLUDE FARM BUILDINGS; LANDLORDS – EXCLUDE INCOME PROPERTY)

☐ YES   ☐ NO – (TURN TO Q. C1)

Continued

B.11 What was done? — — anything else? (ENTER WORK DONE) ——→			
B12. When did you buy it? B13. How much did it cost? B14. Did you borrow or finance any of it?	______(MONTH) $______ 1. YES ↓ 5. NO → GO TO BOX A	______(MONTH) $______ 1. YES ↓ 5. NO → GO TO BOX A	______(MONTH) $______ 1. YES ↓ 5. NO → GO TO BOX A
(IF YES TO B 14) B15. How much did you borrow or finance?	$______	$______	$______

BOX A	(INTERVIEWER: REPEAT Q'S B11 - B15 FOR EACH ADDITION OR REPAIR MENTIONED' USE MARGINS FOR EXTRA A/R

ADD + REP

COST ☐☐☐☐

(DOLLARS)

BOR A and R

☐☐☐☐

(DOLLARS)

C. CARS

C.1. This next set of questions is about cars. Altogether, how many people are there in your family living here who can drive? ______DRIVERS

C.2. Do you or anyone else here in your family own a car?

☐ YES ☐ NO (TURN TO SECTION D).

C.3. Altogether, how many cars do you and your family living here own?______(CARS)

(IF 2 OR MORE) C.4 How long have you had more than one car in the family?__(YEARS)

Continued

(INTERVIEWER: ASK REST OF PAGE FOR EACH CAR OWNED BY FU)

Now I'd like to ask a few questions about the car (s) you have now.	CAR #	CAR #	CAR #
C5. What year model is it?	19 ____	19 ____	19 ____
C6. What make of car is it? (2 WORD ANSWER)			
C7. Is it a 2-door sedan, a 4-door sedan, a station wagon, convertible, or what?			
C8. Is it a compact, regular size, something in-between, or what?			
C9. Who usually drives this car? (RELATION TO HEAD)			
C10. Did you buy this car new or used?	1. NEW 2. USED	1. NEW 2. USED	1. NEW 2. USED
C11. In what year did you buy it?	19 ____	19 ____	19 ____

LIST CARS BOUGHT IN 1967 OR 1968 (FROM Q. C11), AND ASK C12-C22 FOR EACH CAR.

Now about the cars you bought in 1967 or already this year ––

SHOW BLUE CARD 2 TO RESPONDENT LIST MODEL YEAR AND MAKE →	CAR #	CAR #	CAR #
C12. What was the total price of this car?	$ ____	$ ____	$ ____
C13. When did you buy it	____ (MON)	____ (MON)	____ (MON)
TP	□□□□	□□□□	□□□□
C14. When you bought this car did you trade-in or sell a car?	1. YES / 5. NO	1. YES / 5. NO	1. YES / 5. NO
C15. (If TI or SALE) How much did you get for it?	$ ____	$ ____	$ ____
TI	□□□□	□□□□	□□□□
C16. How much did you pay down in cash?	$ ____	$ ____	$ ____

Continued

C17. Did you borrow or finance part of the total price?	5. NO 1. YES ↓	5. NO 1. YES ↓	5. NO 1. YES ↓
(IF BORROWED) C18. How much did you borrow, not including financing charges?	$______	$______	$______
AB	☐☐☐☐	☐☐☐☐	☐☐☐☐
C19. How much are your payments and how often are they made?	$______ per ______	$______ per ______	$______ per ______
C20. How many payments did you agree to make altogether?	______	______	______
C21. How many payments have you made?	______	______	______
C22. How many payments do you have left to make? RID ☐☐☐☐	______	______	______

D. INCOME

D1 In this survey of families all over the country, we are trying to get an accurate picture of people's financial situation.

☐ FARMER (AS MAIN JOB) ☐ NOT FARMER (GO TO Q. D5)

D2.	What were your total receipts from farming in 1967, including soil bank payments and commodity credit loans?	$______(A)
D3.	What were your total operating expenses, not counting living expenses?	$______(B)
D4.	That left you a net income from farming of (A – B) . . . is that right?	$______

Continued

(ASK EVERYONE)

D5. Did you or anyone else in the family living here own a business at any time in 1967, or have a financial interest in any business enterprise?

☐ YES ☐ NO – (GO TO Q. D9)

D6. What kind of business is it? ____________________

____

D7. Is it a corporation or an unincorporated business or do you have an interest in both kinds?

1. CORPORATION – (GO TO Q. D9)

2. UNINCORPORATED 3. BOTH 8. DON'T KNOW

D8. How much was your (family's share of the total income from the business in 1967 . . . that is, the amount you took out plus any profit left in? $ ________

D9. How much did you (HEAD) receive from wages and salaries in 1967, that is, before anything was deducted for taxes or other things? $ ________

D10. In addition to this, did you (HEAD) have any income from overtime, bonuses, or commissions?

☐ YES ☐ NO – (GO TO Q. D12)

D.11 How much was that? $ ________

D12. Did you (HEAD) receive any other income in 1967 from:

(IF YES TO ANY ITEM, ASK, "How much was it?" AND ENTER AMOUNT AT RIGHT)

(IF NO, ENTER "0")

NOTE: SHOW CALCULATIONS, IF ANY

a. professional practice or trade . . . . $ ________
b. farming or market gardening, roomers or boarders . . . . $ ________
c. dividends . . . . $ ________
d. interest, trust funds, or royalties, rent . . . . $ ________
e. social security . . . . $ ________
f. other retirement pay, pensions, or annuities . . . . $ ________
g. any other sources, like family allotments, unemployment compensation, welfare, or help from relatives . . . . $ ________
h. anything else ________________ . . . . $ ________
(SPECIFY)

Continued

D13. (INTERVIEWER: CHECK BOX)

☐ MALE FU HEAD HAS WIFE ☐ MALE FU HEAD HAS NO WIFE (TURN TO Q. D17) ☐ FEMALE FU HEAD (TURN TO Q. D17)

D14. Did your wife have any income during 1967?

☐ YES ☐ NO (TURN TO Q. D17)

D15. Was it income from wages, a business, or what? Any other income?

(SOURCE) (SOURCE)

D16. How much was it before deductions? $ ________ + $ ________ = $ ________

D17. (INTERVIEWER: SEE FACE SHEET FOR ANYONE (OTHER THAN HEAD AND WIFE) AGED 14 OR OLDER AND CHECK BOX)

☐ NO ONE 14 OR OLDER (EXCEPT HEAD AND WIFE) – (GO TO SECTION E)

☐ OTHER FAMILY MEMBERS 14 AND OLDER

LIST OTHER FU MEMBERS 14 AND OLDER BY RELATION TO HEAD AND AGE →						
D18. Did (MENTION MEMBER) have any income during 1967?	☐ NO ☐ YES		☐ NO ☐ YES		☐ NO ☐ YES	
(IF YES TO Q. D18) D19. Was it from wages, pension, interest, a business, or what? (ASK SOURCES a . . . h)	SOURCE	SOURCE	SOURCE	SOURCE	SOURCE	SOURCE
D20. How much was it?	$ ______	$ ______	$ ______	$ ______	$ ______	$ ______

Continued

D21. Are you (HEAD) working now, unemployed or laid off or what?

1. RETIRED

2. PERMANENTLY DISABLED

3. HOUSEWIFE

4. HANDLES OWN INVESTMENTS ONLY

5. STUDENT

6. WORKING NOW

7. UNEMPLOYED; SICK; LAID OFF

8. RETIRED AND WORKING; RETIRED AND UNEMPLOYED

OTHER (EXPLAIN)____

____

____

____

E. INFORMATION ABOUT FAMILY

(ASK EVERYONE)

E1. Now I have just a few more questions. Are you (HEAD) married, single, widowed, divorced, or separated?

1. MARRIED	2. SINGLE	3. WIDOWED	4. DIVORCED	5. SEPARATED

(2–5: GO TO Q. E3)

(1. MARRIED:) E.2 How long have you been married? ______ YEARS

(ASK FOLLOWING QUESTIONS FOR BOTH HEAD AND WIFE)

		(HEAD)	(WIFE)
E3. How many grades of school did you (HEAD) finish?		______ (GRADES)	______ (GRADES)
(IF MORE THAN 8)	E4. Have you had any other schooling?	☐ NO (GO TO SEC. F) ☐ YES ↓	☐ NO (GO TO SEC. F) ☐ YES ↓
(IF YES TO Q.E4)	E5. What other schooling did you have?	______ (COLLEGE, SECRETARIAL BUSINESS, TRADE SCHOOL, NURSING, ETC.)	______ (COLLEGE, SECRETARIAL BUSINESS, TRADE SCHOOL, NURSING, ETC.)
	(IF ANY COLLEGE) E6. Do you have a college degree?	☐ NO (GO TO SEC. F) ☐ YES ↓	☐ NO (GO TO SEC. F) ☐ YES ↓
	(IF YES TO Q.E6) E7. What degree(s) do you have?	______	______

(INTERVIEWER: CHECK TO MAKE SURE Q's 2, 3, 4, 5 ON PAGE 1 ARE COMPLETE. REMEMBER TO FINISH OBSERVATION SHEET AND THUMBNAIL SKETCH.)

END

Thank Respondent

F. OBSERVATION DATA

(INTERVIEWER: BY OBSERVATION ONLY)

F1. Sex of Head of Family Unit: ☐ MALE ☐ FEMALE

F2. Sex of Respondent: ☐ MALE ☐ FEMALE

F3. Race: ☐ WHITE ☐ NEGRO ☐ OTHER (specify)__________

F4. Number of calls:__________

F5. Who was present during interview:____________________

F6. TYPE OF STRUCTURE IN WHICH FAMILY LIVES:

☐ TRAILER
DETACHED SINGLE FAMILY HOUSE
☐ 2-FAMILY HOUSE, 2 UNITS SIDE BY SIDE
☐ 2-FAMILY HOUSE, 2 UNITS ONE ABOVE THE OTHER
☐ DETACHED 3-4 FAMILY HOUSE
☐ ROW HOUSE (3 OR MORE UNITS IN AN ATTACHED ROW)
☐ APARTMENT HOUSE (5 OR MORE UNITS, 3 STORIES OR LESS)
☐ APARTMENT HOUSE (5 OR MORE UNITS, 4 STORIES OR MORE)
☐ APARTMENT IN A PARTLY COMMERCIAL STRUCTURE
☐ OTHER (Specify)__________

F7. NEIGHBORHOOD: Look at 3 structures on each side of DU but not more than 100 yards or so in both directions and check as many boxes as apply, below.

☐ VACANT LAND ONLY
☐ TRAILER
☐ DETACHED SINGLE FAMILY
☐ 2-FAMILY HOUSE, 2 UNITS SIDE BY SIDE
☐ 2-FAMILY HOUSE, 2 UNITS ONE ABOVE THE OTHER
☐ DETACHED 3-4 FAMILY HOUSE
☐ ROW HOUSE, (3 OR MORE UNITS IN AN ATTACHED ROW)
☐ APARTMENT HOUSE (5 OR MORE UNITS, 3 STORIES OR LESS)
☐ APARTMENT HOUSE (5 OR MORE UNITS, 4 STORIES OR MORE)
☐ APARTMENT IN A PARTLY COMMERCIAL STRUCTURE
☐ WHOLLY COMMERCIAL OR INDUSTRIAL STRUCTURE
☐ OTHER (Specify)__________

F8. If Respondent's answers to factual questions (house value, income, etc.) seem badly out of line with your observations, please note below.

____

____

____

(USE NEXT PAGE FOR THUMBNAIL SKETCH)

THUMBNAIL SKETCH

EDITING INSTRUCTION BOOK

SECTION I: FACE SHEET AND LISTING BOX (Items 1 - 10)

CHECK LIST

A. INITIAL INTERVIEW
B. READ THUMBNAIL
C. CHECK LISTING BOX AND EDIT OUT NON-DU MEMBERS
D. CHECK TO SEE IF "HEAD" IS CORRECTLY DESIGNATED

E. CHECK AGE AND SEX OF HEAD IF NA
F. CHECK TO SEE WHETHER INTERVIEW SHOULD HAVE BEEN TAKEN OR CONSTITUTES A REFUSAL

POSSIBLE ASSIGNMENTS

	Q. Ref.	Assign. Table #
Age	Face sheet Q.7	Take to editing supervisor

EXPLANATION OF CHECKLIST

Initials A. WRITE YOUR INITIALS ON THE INTERVIEW AT THE TOP LEFT OF FACE SHEET

Thumbnail B. READ THE THUMBAIL ON LAST SHEET FOR ADDITIONAL INFORMATION OR LOCATION TROUBLE SPOTS IN THE INTERVIEW. UNDERLINE USEFUL INFORMATION IN GREEN.

C. CHECK LISTING BOX AND EDIT OUT NON-DU MEMBERS

1. The listing box should contain all persons living in the Dwelling Unit, at the same time the Interviewer first had contact with the household. (If necessary, date of first contact may be obtained from the cover sheet.)

2. It should not include visitors or persons (like students away at school) who are not living in the DU currently. If there is a doubt about whether to include someone see DU TABLE

3. Edit out non-DU members by circling in green and writing an explanatory note.

DU TABLE (TO DETERMINE DU MEMBERS)

PERSONS "STAYING" IN SAMPLE UNIT AT TIME OF FIRST CONTACT

Place of residence here	Place of residence elsewhere?	Member of the DU?	Examples
Yes	No	Yes	(a) Just "lives here" (b) Lodger (c) Servant; living in
Yes	Yes	Yes*	(a) Has country home or town house. (b) Has summer home or winter home. (c) Student living here while at school, or soldier while in service. (d) Home on military leave or school recess.
No	No	Yes	(a) Waiting completion of new home. (b) Takes turns staying with children, or parents.

PERSONS ABSENT FROM SAMPLE UNIT AT TIME OF FIRST CONTACT

Place of residence here	Place of residence elsewhere?	Member of the DU?	Examples
Yes	No	Yes	(a) Traveling Salesman on the road. (b) Railroad man on a run. (c) In general hospital. (d) On vacation or visiting. (e) Absent on business.
Yes	Yes	No*	(a) Has country home or town house. (b) Has summer home or winter home. (c) Away at school or in service. (d) In prison or nursing home or special hospital.

*IF "DON'T KNOW" ON ANY OF THESE CRITERIA, INCLUDE IN THE DWELLING UNIT.

BASIS OF THE DU TABLE: FINAL TEST OF DU MEMBERSHIP AND INTERVIEWABILITY.

In cases where the situation is too complex to be determined by the DU Table, the final test, and basis of the DU Table is whether or not the person could have, theoretically speaking, been interviewed somewhere else at the time that the Interviewer WENT TO THE DU FOR THE FIRST TIME.

In order to ascertain the date of the Interviewer's first call it is necessary to obtain this information from the cover sheet in the Field Office. See a Check Editor or Supervisor for this – do not do it yourself.

DEFINITIONS FOR USE WITH ITEM D AND E

DU	1. Dwelling Unit (DU): A sampling unit which is: a. A one family house or half of a two family house or b. An apartment or flat in an apartment house or other building or c. A trailer (as long as it has cooking facilities) or d. Living quarters in back of stores, over garages, etc. or e. A rooming house. We do not sample institutions such as old people's homes, sanitariums, convents, military bases, dormitories, etc., which contain ten or more unrelated families.
FU	2. Family Unit (FU): A Family Unit is a group of persons living in the same dwelling unit who are related to each other by blood, marriage or adoption. Each FU should be interviewed: if a DU contains a man and his wife and a roomer there are 2 FU's and we should have 2 interviews for the DU.
FU Head	3. Head of FU. Each FU has a person designated as head by the following: 1. If there is one adult in the family, he (she) is the head. 2. If the family contains exactly two adults, who comprise a married couple, then the husband is always the head. 3. In all other cases, apply to the adults in the FU the following rules in the order in which they are listed. 4. a. Whoever provides the income which constitutes the major share of the financial support for the family. If several adults share equally in the financial support, then of those . . . b. Whoever earns the most money (is the major earner). If no one adult earns more than the others, then . . . c. Whoever is working (or looking for work). d. If absolutely none of the above steps selects one person, then the "head" is the person whose age is closest to 45.
Primary FU	4. Primary FU: If there is more than one FU in a Dwelling designate as Primary FU the one which: a. contains the DU owner or b. (if FU rents home) contains the member who pays the rent or c. (if jointly owned or rented or "neither owns nor rents" see B3) has the member with the highest income or d. has the older head IN THE ABOVE ORDER OR PRIORITY
Secondary FU	5. Secondary FU: after designating the Primary FU (above) each other FU is considered a secondary FU.

D. CHECK TO SEE THAT "HEAD" IS CORRECTLY DESIGNATED

Our Interviewers are instructed to interview the Head of each FU unless permission to substitute someone else is given. If you find an interview in which the Interviewer has considered and/or designated the wrong person as head of an FU (see definition) take the interview to the Editing Supervisor. If the Editing Supervisor agrees that the wrong head was designated, the entire interview will have to be edited to correct for this; the information for the correct head being edited into those places where information for the head is called for, etc.

DU COMPOSITION EXAMPLE

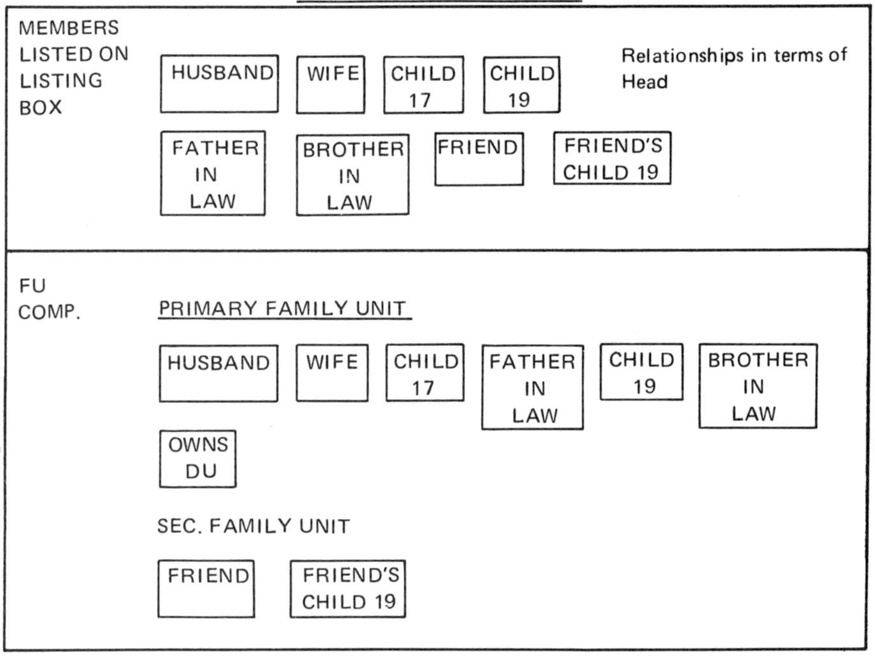

MEMBERS LISTED ON LISTING BOX	HUSBAND / WIFE / CHILD 17 / CHILD 19 FATHER IN LAW / BROTHER IN LAW / FRIEND / FRIEND'S CHILD 19	Relationships in terms of Head
FU COMP.	PRIMARY FAMILY UNIT HUSBAND / WIFE / CHILD 17 / FATHER IN LAW / CHILD 19 / BROTHER IN LAW OWNS DU SEC. FAMILY UNIT FRIEND / FRIEND'S CHILD 19	

Head's Age and Sex

E. CHECK AGE AND SEX OF HEAD IF NA

We are most anxious to have the age and sex of each FU Head. If it does not appear in Qs. 7 - 8 of the listing box on the face sheet, see if you can determine it from the Thumbnail or other information in the interview and enter it in the listing box. If you still cannot determine age or sex of Head, bring the interview to the Editing Supervisor.

Continued

F. SPECIAL NOTE CONCERNING WHETHER INTERVIEW SHOULD HAVE BEEN TAKEN:

1. If you find an interview taken:
   1) at a place which does not fit out definition of a Dwelling unit
   2) where someone was interviewed who was not a member of the Family Unit being interviewed.
   3) where the respondent was not living in the Dwelling Unit at the time the Interviewer first went to the DU.
   4) where the family for which the interview is being taken did not live in the Dwelling Unit at the time the Interviewer first went to the DU.

Take these interviews to the Editing Supervisor. The decision whether to accept them or not will have to be made at a higher level.

2. If you find an interview for a DU which contains more FU's than the interviewer was aware of, take the interview to the Editing Supervisor who should check with Field Office on it.

SPECIAL NOTE CONCERNING INTERVIEWS WHICH ARE REFUSALS:

In certain cases an Interviewer will take an interview which, because essential information (i.e. Income, Mortgage, Assets) has been refused, we may consider a total refusal. If in doubt about a refusal, the Study Director makes the decision. Take all refusals to the Editing Supervisor.

NOTE: WE DO NOT EDIT SECTION A

SECTION II: HOUSING (B1-B9)

Check List

EDITING CHECK LIST

A. CHECK YEAR MOVED IN AND ASSIGN IF NA

B. CHECK HOUSING STATUS, ASSIGN IF NA

C. PRECODE HOUSING STATUS

D. CONVERT RENT TO MONTHLY FIGURE (IF NECESSARY) AND ASSIGN IF NA

E. DETERMINE HOUSE VALUE, ASSIGN IF NA

F. FILL IN HV BOX

G. FILL IN R BOX

Assignments

	Question	Assignment Table
A. YEAR MOVED IN	B1	B1
B. Housing Status	B3	B2
C. Rent	B5	B3
D. House Value	B7	B4

Continued

EXPLANATION OF CHECK LIST

B1:
Year Moved
In

A. CHECK YEAR MOVED IN AND ASSIGN IF NA

1. We want here the year the house was moved into which may be different from the year it was bought. Assume year given is correct unless Interviewer notes a discrepancy.
2. If NA assign from table B1.

B3:
Housing Status

B. CHECK HOUSING STATUS. ASSIGN IF NA
We want here the Housing Status for the FU being interviewed – you may code "owns" even if the Head is not the owner as long as the owner lives in the DU.

Check to see that housing status is consistent with the following rules:

Secondary FU's cannot be the sole owners

1. Secondary FU's cannot be the sole owners of the houses that they live in. If they do lay claims to home ownership the FU Composition Code may have to be changed. Find the primary FU interview corresponding to the secondary. If the primary FU lays no claim to ownership and the secondary does, then the primary FU should be the secondary and the secondary should be the primary FU. Check with the Editing Supervisor to make sure you are correct.

Joint Owners

2. Joint owners are primary and secondary FU's who legitimately share ownership of a house or primary FU's who share ownership with someone outside the DU. Include owners of co-op apartments.

Trailer Owners

3. Check Q. F6 to see whether DU is a house trailer, if not specified by interviewer in Section B.
   a. Trailers are treated as houses except that they cannot have mortgages or house equity (debt should be edited out).
   b. Eliminate any ground (or lot) rental.
   c. If trailer value is N.A., assign a value of $2850.

Share Rent

4. Secondary FU's who share rent should be labelled "shares rent with primary."

Share Croppers and Tenant Farmers

5. Share-croppers and tenant farmers are given an ownership status code separately from that which applies to non-farmers. If someone claims to be a share-cropper or tenant, check his occupation code, precoded in green in Sec. D, or see the occupation precoder.
   a. If the code is 05911, check the "Pays Rent" box at B3, write "tenant farmer" next to it and N.A. the Rent Amount at B5. Do not assign Rent Amount.
   b. If this code is not 05911, he is not a tenant farmer or share cropper; edit as ordinary rent.

Continued

Neither Owns Nor Rents

6. Neither owns nor rents are those who:
   a. Receive rent as part of their pay.
   b. Someone who has sold the house in which they live, have not moved out as yet, but pays no rent.
   c. Someone who receives housing as a gift from someone outside the DU or from the Primary FU.

Both Boxes Checked

7. "Both owns and rents" is a situation:
   a. Where a man rents the dwelling he lives in now but owns a home somewhere else. Here again, it is the residence he currently occupies that counts, and he is a renter. The home he owns is real estate (which may be providing rental income – check the income schedule).
   b. R now rents his home but has built or bought (or is building) a home into which he is about ready to move, only the "rent" box should be checked. Wherever R is currently living is coded.

Precode Housing Status

C. PRECODE THE HOUSING STATUS

in green to the left of the boxes for Q.B3, according to the following code:

HOUSING STATUS CODE:

(Q.B3. B4.F6) Do you (FU) own this home or pay rent or what?

Owns:

1. Own home (containing one or two DU's); owns farm alone.
2. Owns apartment building (three or more DU's) or building with both commercial and living quarters in which R lives. (If apartment building has 10 or more DU's be sure R is also coded as owning an unincorporated business – see D5 - D8).
3. Joint owner; owner of cooperative apartment; joint farm owner or cooperative farmer.
4. Owns trailer.

Rents:

5. Pays rent, excluding FARMERS (see Code 7) (unless they rent a house in town where they live).
6. Shares Rent of DU (code for both primaries and secondaries).
7. Tenant farmer; sharecropper; farmer who rents farm for cash and/or crops (if farmer owns home in town and rents farm, code "1". If farmer rents home in town and owns farm code "5").
8. Neither owns nor rents (includes secondaries who pay no cash but who supply food and/or pay utility bills).
0. Other – see Editing Supervisor and note problem in Editing Decision Book.

Continued

B5:
Rent

D. CONVERT RENT TO MONTHLY FIGURE AND ASSIGN IF NA.

1. We want the most recent rent paid, not the year's average rent.
2. Convert rental payments to a monthly basis, if necessary.
3. If rent is NA, assign a rental value from Table B3, unless R is a tenant farmer.

Special Cases

1. Share croppers and tenant farmers: Edit Rent to NA – Do not assign.
2. Unrelated secondary roomers and boarders: If R says he pays a lump sum for both room and board, edit half of what he pays as rent. (If amt. is NA do not halve the assignment.)
3. Joint renters: If two or more FU's share the rent of a DU, the share paid by the secondary FU's should be deleted, labelled "shares rent with primary" and Marked "0". The total paid for the DU should appear in primary's interview.
4. Utilities payments: If R pays for utilities separately and itemizes them, we want to exclude them; otherwise accept rental figure as given.
5. Trailer: Lot rental and utility connection rental are not included in this section. We do want to include people who actually rent a trailer.

B7, B9
House value

E. DETERMINE HOUSE VALUE. ASSIGN IF NA

1. House value includes that of the house and lot; for farmers, the house, farm buildings and land.
2. If R buys a house furnished, do not attempt to separate out the value of the furnishings.

House Value Assignment

3. If House Value is NA, assign from table B4 unless house owned is a trailer then assign $2850.

Problem Cases

1. If Range is given code the midpoint; if R says he's been offered $8000 but wouldn't take less than $10,000, code the midpoint.
2. If R mentions only the value assessed at for tax purposes, take it in New York City and Boston, double it elsewhere.
3. If the value reported is for property jointly used for business and owner-occupancy, split the value (and mortgage debt) on the basis of available information for the case at hand and record problem in editing decision book.
4. If value reported is the total value for a multiple family dwelling split according to best available information and record situation in Editing Decision Book.
5. If a primary and secondary FU share the ownership of a house, total house value should be entered on the primary FU's questionnaire and deleted on the secondary's Interview. with an explanatory note.

ASSIGNMENT OF MISCELLANEOUS HOUSING ITEMS

Q. B1 What year did you move into this house (apartment)? Use random number table.

Table B1

1942 or earlier	00-06
1943-52	07-19
1953-57	20-30
1958-62	31-52
1963	53-59
1964	60-65
1965	66-76
1966	77-96
1967-1968	97-99

Q. B3 Do you own this home, pay rent, or what? (Primary Family) Use random number table.

Table B2

Family Income	Owns	Rents	Neither
Under $1000	00-51	52-83	84-99
$1000-1999	00-45	46-83	84-99
$2000-2999	00-49	50-85	86-99
$3000-3999	00-49	50-89	90-99
$4000-4999	00-48	49-89	90-99
$5000-5999	00-55	56-91	92-99
$6000-7499	00-61	62-94	95-99
$7500-9999	00-72	73-97	98-99
$10,000-14, 999	00-80	81-98	99-99
$15,000 or more	00-83	84-98	99-99

Q. B5 Assignment of Monthly Rent

Table B3

Income	Rent Payments
Under $3000	$ 50
$3000-4999	70
$5000-5999	75
$6000-7499	80
$7500-9900	90
$10,000 or more	120

TABLE B4

ASSIGNMENT FOR HOUSE VALUE*

Family Income	(Belt Code 1) Central Cities of 12 largest SMSAs	(Belt Code 2) Central Cities of other SMSAs	(Belt Code 3) Suburban Areas of 12 largest SMSAs	(Belt Code 4) Suburban Areas of other SMSAs	(Belt Code 5) Adjacent Areas	(Belt Code 6) Outlying Areas
Under $3000	$16,700	$ 9,900	$12,800	$12,000	$ 9,300	$ 9,200
$3000-4999	$13,900	$11,700	$15,400	$15,900	$11,000	$13,600
$5000-7499	$16,200	$12,800	$15,800	$14,500	$13,300	$15,400
$7500-9999	$18,400	$15,200	$18,700	$15,100	$14,500	$15,800
$10,000 or over	$22,800	$21,500	$24,800	$25,500	$22,300	$32,100

*If FU owns a trailer with value NA, assign $3300 in all cases.

Note: Belt code is the third digit from the left of the 4-digits written on the "Place Codes" line in the box on the first page of the questionnaire.

F. FILL IN "HV" BOX

1. Enter amount from B7 in HV Box.
2. Renters and "neither owns nor rents" will be coded 0 in HV Box.

G. FILL IN "R" BOX

1. Enter amount from B5 in R Box.
2. Home owners and "neither owns nor rents" will be coded 0 in R Box.

SECTION III: ADDITIONS AND REPAIRS Q. B10-B15

Check List

EDITING CHECK LIST

NOTE: INITIAL FACE SHEET IN UPPER RIGHT TO THE LEFT OF "JAN-FEB 1968"

A. EDIT OUT NON-1967 ITEMS
B. EDIT OUT FARM AND BUSINESS ITEMS

C. EDIT OUT NON-A and R ITEMS (DURABLES, FURNISHINGS)
D. MAKE NECESSARY ASSIGNMENTS
E. ENTER AMOUNTS IN BOXES

Assignments

POSSIBLE ASSIGNMENTS

	Q. Ref.	Table #
WHETHER A and R	B.10	B5a
WHETHER DEBT	B.14	B5b
RID (TOTAL A and R RID)	B15	B6

Introduction

In this section we are interested in totalling what the FU spent on additions and repairs during 1967 on the home R lives in, or on the lot. We include summer or winter homes, and any house R lived in personally during the yea

Definition of Addition or Repair

An A and R item is something which is added to the living quarters or lot and becomes a permanent part of them, thus adding to their value. An A and R item is not normally taken with the FU if the FU should move to another place (as are durables or furnishings) but is left behind in the old living quarters as a permanent installation.

An A and R expenditure is an expenditure to purchase, install, build, replace, repair, or maintain an A and R item.

ADDITIONS AND REPAIRS

EXAMPLES OF A and R ITEMS

1. INTERIOR REMODELING AND IMPROVEMENTS:

   Ceilings
   Closets
   Entrances
   Plaster Walls
   Rooms
   Stairs
   Partitions
   Finishing basements, rooms, additions
   Floors
   Painting
   Cabinets (built-in)
   Inlaid linoleum
   Tiling
   Shelves (built-in)
   Wall paneling or papering
   "Remodeling" or "renovating"
   Exterminating
   Wall-to-wall carpeting (see below)

2. RUGS, CARPETS, OR DRAPES COSTING $300 OR MORE:

   If cost is less than $300 these are assumed to be furnishings and should be edited out.

   Rugs and carpets costing $300 or more are assumed to be wall-to-wall carpeting and are additions for (home) owners.

Continued

3. PLUMBING AND GAS INSTALLATIONS: (This includes all plumbing and gas lines and all fixtures and built-in appliances permanently attached to them — if largely electrical).

   Bathroom fixtures
   Garbage disposal units
   Humidifier — for owners
   (Durable for renters)
   Hot water heaters (and systems)
   Incinerators (built-in)
   Sinks
   Water Softeners
   Wells and pumps

   > Gas cooking stoves and refrigerators are not permantly attached and are not additions unless built-in

4. ELECTRICAL WIRING AND FIXTURES:

5. BUILT-IN ELECTRICAL APPLIANCES:

   Built-in:

   Ovens
   Ranges
   Refrigerators
   Dishwashers

   > If not known whether built-in, assume not — then they are durables

6. HEATING, COOLING AND VENTILATING SYSTEMS:

   Air ducts
   Central air conditioning, built-in (room-type installed in windows) are durables
   Exhaust and vent fans, built-in
   Furnaces
   Heating systems
   Humidifiers — for owners, only — (Durables, for renters)
   Radiators and other major parts of a heating system
   Space heaters — for owners only — (Durables for renters)

7. ATTACHMENTS:

   Awnings
   Doors
   Screens
   Shutters
   Storm windows and doors
   TV antennas (also FM antennas)
   Venetian blinds
   Windows

Continued

8. IMPROVEMENTS TO HOUSE EXTERIOR:
   Chimneys
   Garages
   Gutters
   Insulation
   Porches
   Roofs
   Siding
   Weather stripping

9. LANDSCAPING AND GROUNDS IMPROVEMENTS:
   Driveways
   Fences
   Fireplaces
   Landscaping
   Lawns
   Patios
   Shrubbery
   Sidewalks
   Tennis Courts
   Trees (Planted)
   Swimming Pools

> Sewers, installation of City Water, Street Paving and Curbing are not A and R and should be edited out: including debt.

10. ADDITION OF LAND AND BUILDINGS:

    Addition of Land – If it is adjacent to the property of FU dwelling and not used for farm or business purposes

    Barns
    Cabins
    Garages
    Sheds
    Etc.

    } On legitimate A and R property and not used for business purposes.

    Special Cases: The following items are additions for home owners and belong in the A and R section, but should be edited out for non-owners

    Drapes $300 and over
    Furnaces
    Garbage disposals
    Unlaid linoleum
    Rugs or carpets $300 and over
    Storm windows
    Venetian blinds
    Waterheaters and softeners

EXPLANATION OF CHECKLIST

NON-1967	A. EDIT OUT NON-1967 ITEMS In section B we want only A and R items purchased in 1967 for homes lived in during 1967. Therefore delete from Section B: 1. A and R in 1968 2. A and R in 1966 or earlier 3. A and R on homes for personal use not lived in during 1967. } IF DEBT: EDIT OUT
	B. EDIT OUT FARM AND BUSINESS EXPENDITURES AND DEBTS: We want here only expenditures and debts on FU's personal living quarters. 1. Edit out completely any expenditures and debt:
Farm A and R	a. made on farm buildings (except for the house which FU lives in and its immediate grounds). 2. Edit out of B money borrowed for expenditures:
Rental Property	a. made to create or maintain homes, apartments or rooms for which the FU receives or intends to receive rental income.
Property Used By Another FU Rent Free	b. made to create or maintain homes, apartments, or rooms for which the FU receives no rental income but which is (or would be) a separate DU in terms of our sampling (i.e. is used rent free by aged parents).
Business Property.	c. made on business property even if such property is attached to the DU, such as a beauty shop, an office, a store, etc.
Non-A and R Items	C. EDIT OUT NON-A and R ITEMS: using the previous definition and the EXAMPLES OF ADDITIONS AND REPAIRS TABLES.
Assignments	D. MAKE NECESSARY ASSIGNMENTS for missing information, using appropriate assignment tables B5a-b and B6 at the end of this section. NOTE: if you use B6 that is an assignment for total Rid for all A and R in this section.
A and R Boxes	E. ENTER AMOUNTS IN BOXES: Cost of all Additions and/or Repairs is entered in the "ADD + REP" Box. Total debt owed (B15 for all items bought) is entered in the "RID A and R" Box.

Continued

TABLES B5a, b
ASSIGNMENTS FOR A AND R

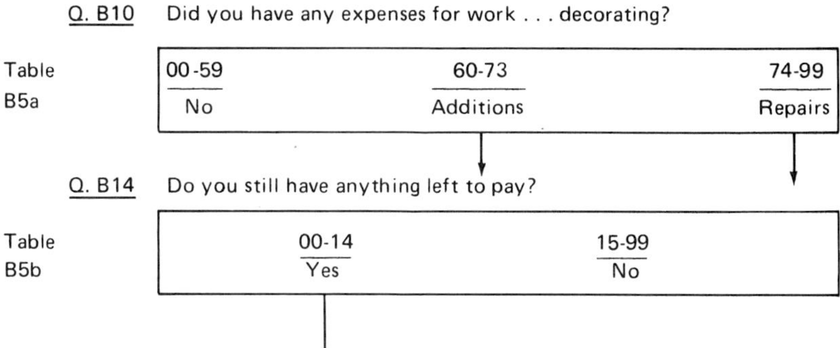

TABLE B6
ASSIGNMENTS FOR A AND R RID

Family Income	Amount All Ages
Under $3000	$260
$3000-4999	350
$5000-7499	620
$7500-9999	650
$10,000 and over	870

SECTION IV: CARS QC1. - C22:

EDITING CHECK LIST

A. CHECK WHETHER OWNS (C2) AND NUMBER OF CARS (C3)
B. EDIT OUT OR MOVE VEHICLES AS NECESSARY

FU OWNS AT LEAST ONE CAR

D. NUMBER ALL CARS; USE "FIRST CAR" RULES IF FU OWNS MORE THAN ONE CAR.
E. CHECK PLACEMENT OF CAR INFORMATION ON PAGES 8-11 BY YEAR OF PURCHASE.
F. CHECK CAR NUMBERING AND CAR IDENTIFICATION ON PAGES 8-11.
G. EDIT YEAR MODEL, MAKE, BODY STYLE, SIZE – FOR ADEQUACY OF RESPONSE (C5-8); MAKE ASSIGNMENTS WHERE NECESSARY.
H. IDENTIFY PRINCIPAL DRIVER (C9).
I. ASSIGN C10 (NEW/USED) AND C11 (YEAR BOUGHT) IF NECESSARY.

CARS BOUGHT IN 1967 OR 1968

Check for gifts, disconnected transactions, cars not delivered. Check for debt on TI, payment in kind, wreck, cash from another sale.

J. 1. EDIT TOTAL PRICE: DETERMINE FROM NADA BOOK IF N.A.
2. ENTER PRICE IN TP BOX.
3. ASSIGN WHETHER TRADE-IN (C14) FROM TABLE C4; ASSIGN TI VALUE IF NECESSARY: ENTER AMOUNT IN TI BOX.
4. EDIT CASH (C15); ASSIGN WHETHER CASH FROM TABLE C5.
5. EDIT WHETHER BORROWED (C17); ASSIGN FROM TABLE C6.
6. BALANCE FINANCING INFORMATION: CASH + TI + AB = TP.
7. CONVERT PAYMENTS TO MONTHLY BASIS
8. CHECK AMOUNT BORROWED (C18) $<$ PAYMENT (C19) x MONTHS (C20)
9. EDIT AB BOX
10. CHECK PAYMENT MONTHS: C20 = C21 + C22
11. ENTER REMAINING INSTALLMENT DEBT IN RID BOX

ASSIGNMENTS

K. CODE "CA" (CAR ASSIGNMENT) AT TOP OF CAR SECTION IF ASSIGNMENTS MADE

POSSIBLE ASSIGNMENTS	Q. Ref.	Table No.
WHETHER OWNS	C2	C1
NUMBER OF CARS OWNED	C3	C1
INCOMPLETE MAKE IDENTIFICATION	C6	CC, CI
BOUGHT NEW/USED	C10,	C2
WHEN PURCHASED	C11	C3
1967-1968 PURCHASES		
TOTAL PRICE	C12	See Editing Supervisor
WHETHER TRADE-IN/SALE	C14	C4
TRADE-IN/SALE AMOUNT	C15	See Editing Supervisor
WHETHER CASH (bought 1967-1968)	C16	C5
WHETHER BORROWED OR FINANCED	C17	C6
REMAINING INSTALLMENT DEBT	—	C7

INTRODUCTION

This section is concerned only with privately owned passenger cars. Make sure that the relevant information for each car is in the proper space in the interview. Please take careful note of any comments written on the margins or in the Thumbnail Sketch. These are often useful in resolving problems that arise in this section.

A. CHECK WHETHER OWNS (C2) AND NUMBER OF CARS (C3)

Number of Cars Owned

The correct number of cars should be checked in Q.C3. Missing information about "whether owns" and "number of cars owned" should be assigned, using Table C1.

* If FU owns no cars, zero out the TP, TI, AB boxes and skip to Section D

B. EDIT OUT OR MOVE VEHICLES AS NECESSARY.

Section C (1-22) is concerned only with privately owned passenger cars and station wagons.

INCLUDE

1. Include in C1-C22:
   a. jeepsters, jeep station wagons;
   b. cars owned by unincorporated business owners;
   c. privately owned cars used partly for business;
   d. all other privately owned passenger cars.

EXCLUDE

2. Edit out any debt on:
   a. trucks, pick-ups, pick-up campers;
   b. Jeeps, Scouts, Broncos.

Continued

EXCLUDE

3. Edit out of interview:
   a. cars provided to FU by incorporated businesses;
   b. cars not in running order;
   c. cars not licensed or planned for license in 1968;
   d. cars or trucks not owned by this FU.

   Edit out any debt associated with these exclusions.

Doubtful Cases

If there is any doubt as to whether a car is a station wagon or a truck (e.g., Ford Econoline, Chevy Greenbrier, V.W. Microbus, International Carryall or Travelall), see the editing supervisor. If it has windows for rear seat passengers it's a station wagon. If not, it's a truck and edited out.

FU OWNS AT LEAST ONE CAR

D. NUMBER ALL CARS IN SECTION C. USE "FIRST CAR" RULES IF FU OWNS MORE THAN ONE CAR.

"First Car"

1. FU owns only 1 car. Number it one.
2. FU owns 2 or more cars. Determine "First Car" by the following:
   a. The one purchased in 1967; if any. If two or more cars bought in 1967 choose the most expensive one.
   b. If no car bought in 1967, the latest model year (regardless of purchase year) is the first car. (1968 purchases have no special priority.)
   c. If the year models are the same, take the most expensive.
3. Using the same rules, again, determine the second, third and fourth cars, etc. Cross off the interviewer's numbers as necessary. Number all cars in Section C.

E. CHECK PLACEMENT OF CAR INFORMATION BY YEAR OF PURCHASE.

Where Cars Are Listed

Make sure that only cars bought in 1967 or 1968 are listed in C12-C22. Edit information to proper places as necessary.

F. CHECK NUMBERING AND CAR IDENTIFICATION

Numbering and Identification

1. Check to make sure that cars are adequately identified ('62 Corvair, '58 Ford, etc.) at the tops of the pages. Use information from C5 and C6.

   If the FU has two cars of the same make and year, additional identification information must be used (value is a good criterion — check the NADA books). See Supervisor if necessary.
2. Check that Interviewer has not moved cars to different columns. If so, make sure they are properly identified and numbered.

FU OWNS AT LEAST ONE CAR

G. EDIT YEAR MODEL, MAKE, BODY STYLE, SIZE — FOR ADEQUACY OF RESPONSE (C5-8); MAKE ASSIGNMENTS WHERE NECESSARY.

Year (C5)

1. Year model:
   a. If C5 is NA and car brought used: leave it as it is.
   b. If C5 is NA and car was purchased new, edit C5 to equal C11.

Continued

Make (C6) 2. If R gives a two-word answer to C6, accept it — it need not be consistent with his answer to C8 (size). However, if a one-word answer is given to C6, then use the answer to C8 to complete the description of the make of car, according to the following rules:

If C8 is "Compact and C6 is:	Edit C6 to:
Buick	Buick Special
Mercury	Comet
Chevrolet	(see Table CC)
Oldsmobile	F-85
Ford	Falcon
Plymouth	Valiant
Studebaker	Lark
Dodge	(see Table CC)
Pontiac	Tempest
Rambler	(see Table CC)
If C8 is "something in; between" and C6 is:	**Edit C6 to:**
Buick	Buick Special
Mercury	Comet
Chevrolet	(see Table CI)
Oldsmobile	F-85
Ford	Fairlane
Plymouth	Valiant
Studebaker	Lark
Dodge	Dart
Pontiac	Tempest
Rambler	(see Table CI)

Do not alter cases other than those listed above — if there appears to be a problem, see the Editing Supervisor.

Body (C7) 3. If a Corvette is described as a "Coupe," edit it to "Sports Car." In the case of any other problems, see the Editing Supervisor, but normally this question will not need editing.

Size (C8) 4. DO NOT EDIT C8 UNDER ANY CIRCUMSTANCES. We accept R's response to this question. Do not make it consistent with the make of the car.

FU OWNS AT LEAST ONE CAR

H. IDENTIFY PRINCIPAL DRIVER (C9).

Principal Driver (C9) 1. We want C9 to refer to a specific relationship to the head. Such answers as HEAD, WIFE, and SON 21 are acceptable. Answers such as "R" should be edited to an acceptable form. Give age of son, daughter, if necessary for complete identification.

Continued

2. If the main driver is outside the FU, see Editing Supervisor and refer to P. 763 edit decision book. If the car could have been picked up in another interview as owned we don't want it, unless it would be picked up there as a calendar year gift.

I. ASSIGN C10 (NEW/USED) AND C11 (YEAR BOUGHT) IF NECESSARY.

New/Used (C10)

1. To assign C10 (if NA) when C11 is NA use Table C2.
2. To assign C10 if C11 (year of purchase) is known (not assigned):
   a. If the year bought (C11) is one year before model year (C5) or same as model year, assume car was bought new.
   b. If year bought (C11) is one or more years after model year (C5), (ex.: 1964 model bought in 1965); assume car was bought used.
3. To assign (C11) (year bought) use Table C3. Be sure that the contingency instructions followed in C11-C22 correspond to the assigned year.

CARS BOUGHT IN 1967 OR 1968

Planned Purchase

If R only intends to buy the car mentioned in C12-C22, but has not yet finalized the transaction, edit the information out.

Price (C19)

J1 EDIT TOTAL PRICE: DETERMINE FROM NADA BOOK IF NA.

Total price (C12) can be assigned form NADA books if it is NA. Use the NADA books as follows:

a. Check state of interview on face sheet and find the regional book which includes that state (use either April or October ed.) Use "Jan. 1968" NADA books for 1968 models bought new.
b. Look up the make, model, and year in the book and use Amount:
   New Car = A.D.P. column
   Used Car = Avg. Ret. column
   Assume second lowest "price line."
c. Add for optional equipment (on new only):
   $400 (original equipment price) in South and Southwest
   $200 (original equipment price) elsewhere.

"Pack" Price

If price is reported by R including extra fees, service charges, documentary fees, etc., this is called "Pack." Do not attempt to separate these items out but use the "pack" price.

Gift

If the car was a gift to this FU, mark it gift and use 0000 as the price.

J2 ENTER PRICE IN TP BOX.

Consistency of price information

Check consistency of price information as follows:

a. If no borrowing:

TI + CASH = TP

b. If there was borrowing:

TI + CASH + BORROWING = TP

If sum is within $50 or less of the TP leave all figures as they appear.
If sum is over $50 (more or less) off see editing supervisor (or put in problem box)

CARS BOUGHT IN 1967 OR 1968

J3. ASSIGN WHETHER TRADE-IN (C14) FROM TABLE C5. ASSIGN TI VALUE IF NECESSARY; ENTER AMOUNT IN TI BOX.

Trade-In — a. Check the validity of the information at C14.
The following rules apply:

Connected Transaction — 1. Trade-ins or sales directly involved with a purchase are included here. The proceeds from an independent (noted as such by Interviewer) sale or scrapping of a car should be edited out and C16 adjusted if necessary.
If R trades in 2 cars on one purchase, C14 should equal sum for both cars.

Wrecks — 2. A wrecked car paid for by insurance should be considered a trade-in or sale unless it was scrapped. Adjust C16 if necessary.

Payment in Kind — 3. Trucks, boats, etc., traded in on a car are "payment in kind". Label them as such, "zero" the trade-in amount and add the amount to Cash (C16).

Debt Owed on Trade-In — 4. Debt still owed on a trade-in must be subtracted from trade-in value.

Sale Receipts Reported as TI and Cash — Some respondents who sell (not trade) their old cars report the proceeds twice — once as proceeds from the sale, and once as Cash paid for the new car. This may explain some discrepancies in price. See Editing Supervisor if it looks like this is the case.

Whether Trade-In NA — b. Assign C14 (whether trade-in) from Table C4 if it is NA.

TI Amount NA — c. Assign C15 from NADA books if NA. Use NADA books as described above (J1) for cars traded in except use the wholesale column for obtaining trade-in value.

Edit TI Box — d. Enter amount of trade-in or sale in the TI Box.

J4. EDIT CASH (C15); ASSIGN WHETHER CASH FROM TABLE C5

Cash NA — Assign whether cash from Table C5 if NA. We do not assign amount of cash; see Supervisor to determine if it can be deduced.

Cash — Check to make sure the cash outlay does not include money received from an associated sale of a car. It could include insurance money from a car which was scrapped.
Insurance money from a wrecked car which was traded in (but not scrapped), however, is included under trade-in.

Double Counting — Sometimes R borrowed money from the bank for the down payment on the car and then went down to the dealer and paid "cash" for his car. This is all borrowed money. Be on the lookout for it; otherwise cash and borrowing will be double-counted.

CARS BOUGHT IN 1967 OR 1968

J5. EDIT WHETHER BORROWED (C17); ASSIGN FROM TABLE C6.

If C17 (whether borrowed) is NA assign from Table C6. We do not assign amount borrowed; see Supervisor to determine if amount can be deduced.

Inclusion of Financing Charges — Question C18 asks for amount borrowed not including financing charges, fees, interest, etc. If these charges are reported we want to exclude them — see Supervisor.

Continued

J6. BALANCE FINANCING INFORMATION.

Balancing the Financing Information

If financing charges are properly excluded from the report of amount borrowed (C18), then:

TI + CASH + BORROWED = TOTAL PRICE

If does not balance (+ or – $50) put in problem box. NOTE: if it exceeds total price there may have been debt on an old car which was re-financed and included in the amount borrowed in the payment schedule. Reduce the TI so it balances if there is evidence of this.

J7. CONVERT PAYMENTS TO MONTH BASIS (C19-C22) AND CHECK PAYMENT SCHEDULE.

Conversion to Monthly Pmts.

a. Convert all payments to a monthly basis. Make adjustments in C19-C22.

Checking the Pmt. Schedule

b. Check that the number of payments made (C21) plus the number yet to make (C22) equals the number originally contracted for (C20).

C21 + C22 = C20

J8. CHECK AMOUNT BORROWED (C18). (PAYMENTS x MONTHS) > AB

Checking Inclusion of Interest

Financing charges may run quite high on cars. Since we asked for the amount borrowed exclusive of these charges, the following relation should hold:

Monthly payment times TOTAL months to pay should be larger than amount borrowed.

This should exceed the AB by an amount equal to 5-25% of the amount borrowed (depending on the length of debt).
If it equals amount borrowed (C18), then financing charges have probably been included in the answer to C18. See Editing Supervisor. If it is less than amount borrowed there is either an error in reporting or there may be two loans, only one of which has been mentioned. See Editing Supervisor.

CARS BOUGHT IN 1967 OR 1968

AB Box

J9. EDIT AB Box

If there was any borrowing, determine the amount borrowed (not including financing charges) for 1967 and 1968 car buyers and enter in "AB" box below C18.

AB | | | | |

J10. CHECK PAYMENT MONTHS

Payments made (C21) and payments left to make (C22) should equal total payments (C20). Adjust C21 and C22 to equal C20 unless the answer to C20 was unreasonable in J8. Then see Editing Supervisor.

Continued

J11. CALCULATE REMAINING INSTALLMENT DEBT

1. Multiply monthly payment (C19) by months left to pay (C22) to get Remaining Installment Debt (RID). Add for each car owned and enter sum in RID Box

   RID = C19 x C22

2. If C19 or C22 are NA, assign RID Box from Table C7. Put and "A" beside the RID Box.

ASSIGNMENTS

K. CODE "CA" (CAR ASSIGNMENTS)

Precode a 1 digit code for car assignments at the beginning of the CAR section as follows:

1. At least one assignment for cars now owned by this FU (denoted by "A")
5. No car assignments on cars now owned by this FU (no "A"s in Sec. C).

Label this code "CA = ".

TABLE C
ASSIGNMENTS FOR CARS

Table No

Q. C3. How many cars do you and your family living here own?

Table C1

Income	None	One	Two	Three
Under $3000	00-50	51-93	94-98	99-99
$3000-4999	00-23	24-79	80-98	99-99
$5000-7499	00-10	11-66	67-96	97-99
$7500-9999	00-04	05-52	53-95	96-99
$10,000-14,999	00-02	03-21	22-81	82-99
$15,000 and over	00-00	01-11	12-62	63-99

Q. C10 Did you buy your car new or used?

Table C2

	First Car		Additional Car	
Income	New	Used	New	Used
Under $3000	00-29	30-99	00-20	21-99
$3000-4999	00-34	35-99	00-20	21-99
$5000-7499	00-42	43-99	00-25	26-99
$7500-9999	00-50	51-99	00-35	36-99
$10,000-14,999	00-64	65-99	00-40	41-99
$15,000 and over	00-80	81-99	00-60	61-99

Q. C11 What year did you buy it?

Table C3

First Car		Additional Cars	
1967-68	1966 or Earlier	1967-68	1966 or Earlier
00-43	44-99	00-16	17-99

Continued

TABLE CC
MAKE OF CAR FOR "COMPACTS"*

C6. What make of car is it?

	Year Model				
	1966-68	1965	1964	1963	1962-1960
Chevrolet					
Corvair	00-64	00-52	00-48	00-45	00-65
Chevy II	65-99	53-99	49-99	46-99	66-99
Rambler					
Classic	00-38	00-28	00-53	00-67	–
American	39-99	29-99	54-99	68-99	–
Dodge					
Dart	00-99	00-99	00-99	00-99	—
Lancer	–	–	–	–	00-99

TABLE CI
MAKE OF CAR FOR "INTERMEDIATES"*

C6. What make of car is it?

	Year Model				
	1966-68	1965	1964	1963	1962-1960
Chevrolet					
Chevy II	00-25	00-33	00-28	00-60	00-99
Chevelle	26-99	34-99	29-99	61-99	–
Rambler					
Classic	00-38	00-55	00-53	00-75	–
American	39-99	56-99	54-99	76-99	–
Dodge					
Coronet	00-99	00-99	–	–	–
Dart	–	–	00-99	00-99	–
Lancer	–	–	–	–	00-99

*Answer to C8 – "Is it a compact, or regular-size or something in between or what?

Ref: 1965 *Automotive News Almanac* (Detroit), page 40.

CARS BOUGHT IN 1967 OR 1968

Q. C12 What was the total price of this car?

See Editing Supervisor if NA to Q. C12. (NADA)

Continued

Q. C13 . . . did you trade in or sell a car? (Car bought in 1967-1968)

Table C4

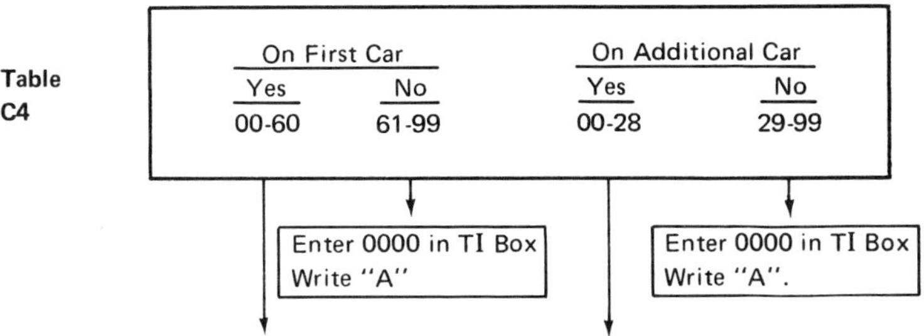

Q. C14 What did you get for the trade in or sale?

See Editing Supervisor if NA to Q. C15 (NADA)

Q. C15 How much did you pay down in cash? (Car bought in 1967-1968)

(Whether paid any cash)

Table C5

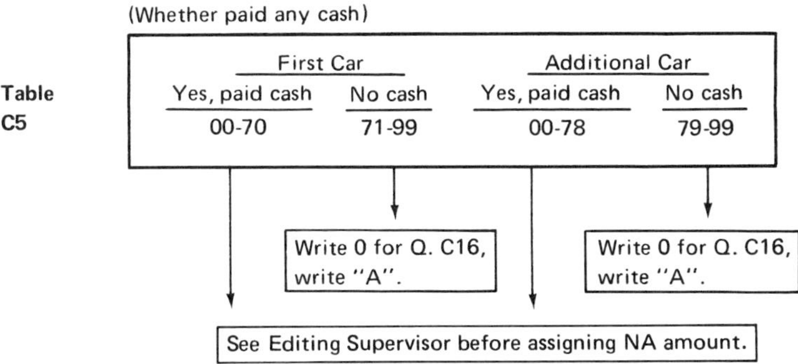

CARS BOUGHT IN 1967 OR 1968

Q. C17 Did you borrow or finance part of the total price? (Car bought in 1967 or 1968)

(Whether borrowed)

Table C6

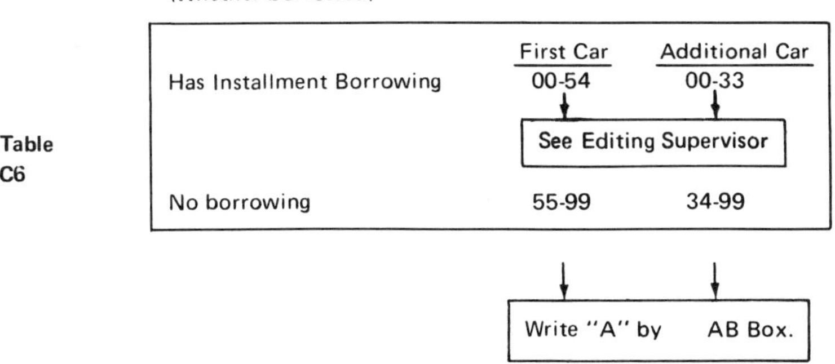

First Car
Additional Car
Has Installment Borrowing
00-54
00-33
See Editing Supervisor
No borrowing
55-99
34-99
Write "A" by AB Box.

TABLE C7

REMAINING INSTALLMENT DEBT
CONTINGENT ON "YES" TO Q.C17

	Age of Head			
Family Income	18-34	35-54	55-64	65 and over
Under $3000	$ 660	$ 640	$ 670	$ 550
$3000-4999	870	820	730	810
$5000-7499	1070	1090	990	870
$7500-9999	1090	1100	1440	1630
$10,000 and over	1390	1520	1440	1680

NOTE: ASSIGNMENT REPRESENTS ALL CAR DEBT FOR FU AND IS ENTERED ONLY ON THE DEBT WORKSHEET.

NOTE: If this assignment appears to be much higher or lower than the possible debt it represents, see the Editing Supervisor

SECTION V: INCOME WORKSHEET

Editor's Checklist

CHECKLIST

CARD 05

A. ENTER INTERVIEW NUMBER AND YOUR INITIALS
B. TRANSFER INCOME OF HEAD, WIFE, AND OTHERS FROM SECTION D TO WORKSHEET AND LABEL "OTHERS."
C. TOTAL INCOME ACROSS AND ENTER IN "ENTIRE FU" BOXES
D. TOTAL INCOME DOWN AND ENTER IN LINES 3, 7, 10 AND 15 FOR EACH PERSON AND THE ENTIRE FU
E. TOTAL BOXES A, B, C AND E. ENTER TOTAL IN BOX F AND CHECK WITH TFI IN INTERVIEW IN SECTION D.

CARD 06

F. ENTER INTERVIEW NUMBER
G. ENTER DOLLAR BRACKET CODES IN BOXES 10-19

H. CODE NUMBER OF MINOR AND MAJOR EARNERS IN BOXES 46-47
I. CODE WHETHER FU OWNS A BUSINESS IN BOX 48
J. CODE INCOME ASSIGNMENTS IN BOX 49

POSSIBLE ASSIGNMENTS

Assignments

NOTE: ALL ASSIGNMENTS ARE MADE WHEN EDITING SECTION D. THESE ASSIGNMENTS ARE THEN TRANSFERRED TO THE WORKSHEET AND LABELLED WITH A BLOCK "A".

Continued

NOTE: On Income Worksheets, all heavy-lined boxes must be filled in!

EXPLANATION OF CHECKLIST

Interview Number Initial Interview

A. ENTER INTERVIEW NUMBER IN BOXES 6-9 AND ENTER YOUR INITIALS IN SPACE PROVIDED

Transfer Income

B. TRANSFER THE INCOME FROM SECTION D TO THE INCOME WORKSHEET AND LABEL "OTHERS".

1. The income from D4, D8, D9, D11, and D12a-h should be transferred to the column labelled "Head" (unless another FU member has unincorporated business income).
2. D9 and D11 are combined on line 1 when transferring to worksheet.
3. Income from other self-employment (D12a) should appear on line 2.

Wife

4. Transfer the wife's income components in D16 to the column labelled "wife".

Others

5. When there are "others" with income in the FU, identify each in the box at the top of each column according to his age and relationship with the Head (e.g., "son, 18", "father, 69").
6. Include here income earned in 1967 by FU members now deceased. Write above those columns "deceased husband" or whatever.

No Wife, or Others

7. If there is no Wife or Others in the FU, or they are present but had no income, a single vertical line may be drawn through those boxes except the heavy lined boxes which are to be filled in with zeroes.

Total Entire FU Income

C. TOTAL INCOME ACROSS AND ENTER IN "ENTIRE FU" BOXES. TOTAL EACH LINE ACROSS FOR HEAD, WIFE AND OTHERS AND ENTER TOTALS IN "ENTIRE FU" BOXES.

Total Income Each Person

D. TOTAL INCOME DOWN AND ENTER IN LINES 3, 7, 10, 14. DO THIS FOR EACH PERSON AND FOR ENTIRE FU. REMEMBER THESE BOXES MUST ALWAYS BE FILLED IN.

Total Family Income

E. ADD BOXES A, B, C, and D TOGETHER AND ENTER TOTAL IN BOX E.

Int. Number

F. ENTER THE 4-DIGIT INTERVIEW NUMBER IN BOXES 6-9

Code Dollar Brackets

G. ENTER DOLLAR BRACKET CODES IN BOXES 10-19.

Using the Dollar Bracket Code on the worksheet, enter the proper code number in boxes 10-19. In all cases, the dollar amount in the Entire FU column is the one to be coded.

H. CODE NUMBER OF MINOR AND MAJOR EARNERS IN BOXES 46-47

Code Minor Earners

1. Enter the number of FU members (including Head and Wife) whose income was $1-599 in Subtotals A and B (i.e., when lines 3 and 7 are added) in Box 46. This is not the same as the number of tax returns.

Continued

Code Major Earners

2. Enter the number of FU members (including Head and Wife) whose income was $600 or more in Subtotals A and B (i.e., when lines 3 and 7 are added) in Box 47.

Code Whether Owns Business

I. CODE WHETHER FU OWNS A BUSINESS IN BOX 48
Using code given on worksheet, enter proper code to indicate Business Ownership for FU. (See D5 and D7).

Code Income Assignments

J. CODE INCOME ASSIGNMENTS IN BOX 49
Using the code on the worksheet enter the proper code which indicates any income assignments, and for whom, in Box 49.

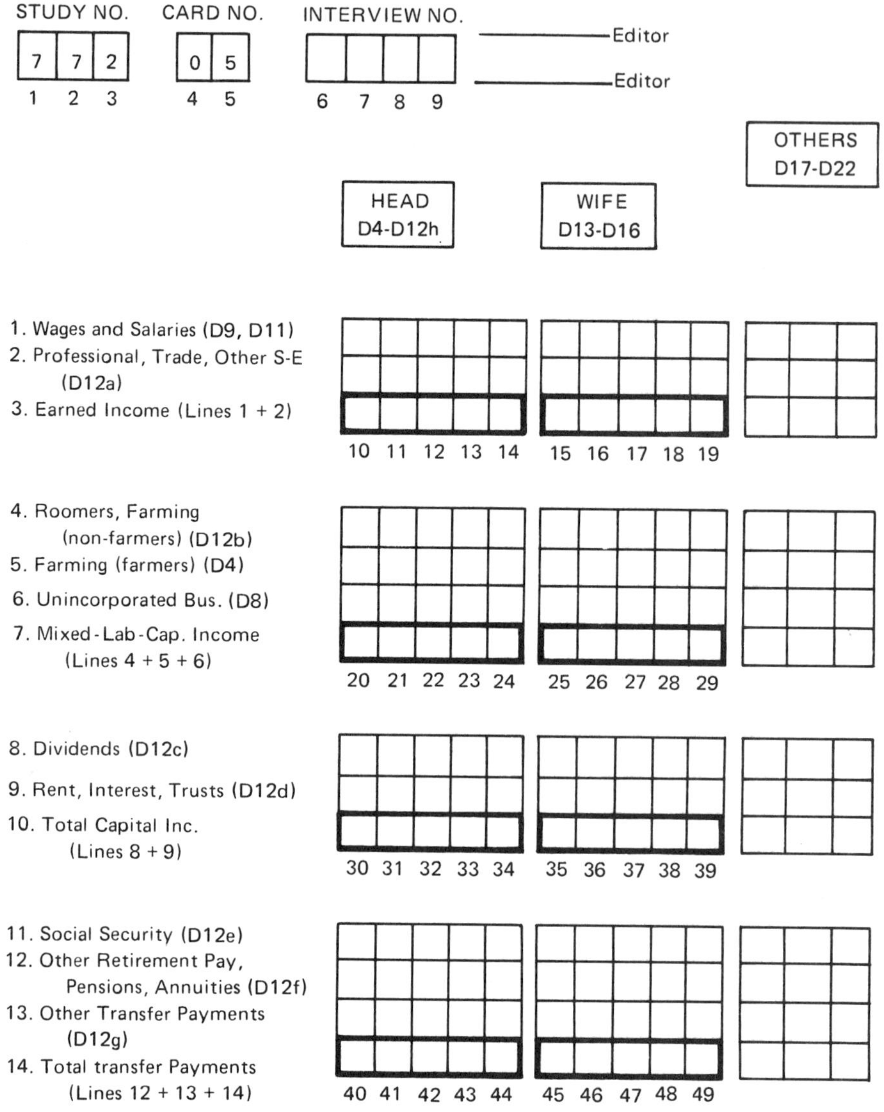

1968 Survey of Consumers
Project 45772
INCOME WORKSHEET – I

STUDY NO.	CARD NO.	INTERVIEW NO.
7 7 2	0 5	
1 2 3	4 5	6 7 8 9

____________Editor

____________Editor

	HEAD D4-D12h	WIFE D13-D16	OTHERS D17-D22
1. Wages and Salaries (D9, D11)			
2. Professional, Trade, Other S-E (D12a)			
3. Earned Income (Lines 1 + 2)			
	10 11 12 13 14	15 16 17 18 19	
4. Roomers, Farming (non-farmers) (D12b)			
5. Farming (farmers) (D4)			
6. Unincorporated Bus. (D8)			
7. Mixed-Lab-Cap. Income (Lines 4 + 5 + 6)			
	20 21 22 23 24	25 26 27 28 29	
8. Dividends (D12c)			
9. Rent, Interest, Trusts (D12d)			
10. Total Capital Inc. (Lines 8 + 9)			
	30 31 32 33 34	35 36 37 38 39	
11. Social Security (D12e)			
12. Other Retirement Pay, Pensions, Annuities (D12f)			
13. Other Transfer Payments (D12g)			
14. Total transfer Payments (Lines 12 + 13 + 14)			
	40 41 42 43 44	45 46 47 48 49	

1968 Survey of Consumers
Project 45772
INCOME WORKSHEET – II

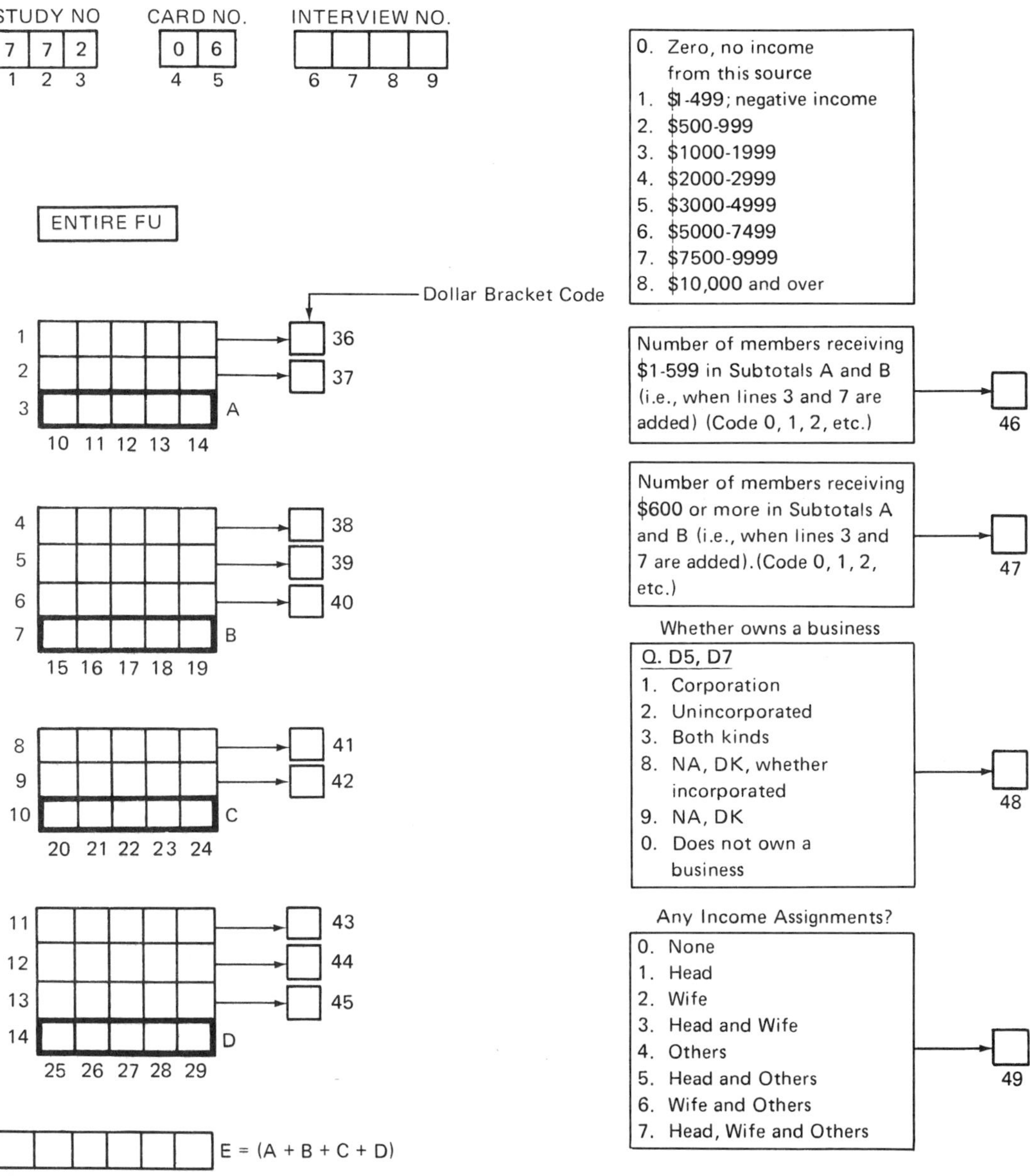

STUDY NO 7 7 2 (1 2 3)

CARD NO. 0 6 (4 5)

INTERVIEW NO. (6 7 8 9)

ENTIRE FU

Dollar Bracket Code

1 → 36
2 → 37
3 A
10 11 12 13 14

4 → 38
5 → 39
6 → 40
7 B
15 16 17 18 19

8 → 41
9 → 42
10 C
20 21 22 23 24

11 → 43
12 → 44
13 → 45
14 D
25 26 27 28 29

E = (A + B + C + D)
30 31 32 33 34 35

0. Zero, no income from this source
1. $1-499; negative income
2. $500-999
3. $1000-1999
4. $2000-2999
5. $3000-4999
6. $5000-7499
7. $7500-9999
8. $10,000 and over

Number of members receiving $1-599 in Subtotals A and B (i.e., when lines 3 and 7 are added) (Code 0, 1, 2, etc.) → 46

Number of members receiving $600 or more in Subtotals A and B (i.e., when lines 3 and 7 are added). (Code 0, 1, 2, etc.) → 47

Whether owns a business

Q. D5, D7
1. Corporation
2. Unincorporated
3. Both kinds
8. NA, DK, whether incorporated
9. NA, DK
0. Does not own a business

→ 48

Any Income Assignments?

0. None
1. Head
2. Wife
3. Head and Wife
4. Others
5. Head and Others
6. Wife and Others
7. Head, Wife and Others

→ 49

SECTION VI: E: INFORMATION ABOUT THE FAMILY

Editor's Checklist

EDITING CHECK LIST
A. CHECK MARITAL STATUS
B. CHECK YEARS MARRIED
C.

E1: Marital Status

A. CHECK MARITAL STATUS

1. Check to see that marital status agrees with the face sheet. If not, look through the interview to determine which is correct.
2. If Head of FU is currently married, but spouse is not living in this DU, circle out "married" and precode a "6" in the left margin.

E2: Years Married

B. CHECK YEARS MARRIED

1. If length of time married is given in months, convert to nearest number of years. If R has been married less than one year, convert to one year.

SECTION VII: F: OBSERVATION SHEET

EDITOR'S CHECK LIST

Editor's Checklist

A. CHECK SEX OF HEAD OF FU
B. CHECK SEX OF RESPONDENT
C. CHECK RACE OF RESPONDENT
D. CHECK WHO WAS PRESENT
E. CHECK TYPE OF STRUCTURE
F. CHECK TYPE OF NEIGHBORHOOD

F1: A. CHECK SEX OF HEAD OF FU

Check to see that the sex of the FU Head in Q. F1 agrees with the face sheet.

F2: B. CHECK SEX OF R

Check to see that the sex of the Respondent agrees with the face sheet.

F3: C. Check Race of Respondent (if NA see Supervisor)

F5: D. CHECK WHO WAS PRESENT

Check to see that F5 includes the respondent, does not include the Interviewer and that all persons are listed by Relationship to Head.

F6: E. CHECK TYPE OF STRUCTURE

There should be just one box checked in Q. F6. If more than one is checked, edit out all but one. You can probably determine which one is right by checking Qs B3-B7.

F7: F. CHECK TYPE OF NEIGHBORHOOD

Any number of boxes may be checked except edit out "Vacant land ONLY" if other boxes are checked.

DATA CODES AND 80-COLUMN CARD FORMS

SINGLE CARD FORM

Project Number: 772	Project Name: Survey of Consumers	
Project Director: Phone:	Card Layout By: Phone: Date:	
Deck Number: 01	Source Document:	Trf. from Cards:

Remarks: Example of card layout for Deck 01: Demographics

Columns 1-40

FROM Card	FROM Col		POSSIBLE CODES V	Name	Field Size
		1 2 3	1	Study Number (772)	3
		4 5	2	Deck Number (01)	2
		6 7 8 9	3	Interview Number	4
		10	4	Geographic I. D.	1
		11	5	Primary Sampling Unit	1
		12	6	Urbanization Code	1
		13 14	7	Dwelling Unit P.S.U. Identific	2
		15	8	County Code	1
		16	9	Secondary Selection	1
		17	10	Belt Code	1
		18	11	Size of City	1
		19	12	Distance from City	1
		20 21 22 23 24 25 26 27 28	13	Interviewer Social Security Number	9
		29	14	Interview Date	1
		30 31 32	15	Length of Interview	3
		33	16	Sex of F.U. head	1
		34 35	17	Age of F.U. head	2
		36 37	18	Age of wife	2
		38	19	Is respondent head?	1
		39	20	Sex of respondent	1
		40	21	Number of Adults	1

Columns 41-80

FROM Card	FROM Col		POSSIBLE CODES V	Name	Field Size
		41	22	Adults over 65	1
		42	23	Children under 16	1
		43	24	Age, youngest child	1
		44	25	Age, oldest child	1
		45	26	Age/sex, head	1
		46	27	Marital status, head	1
		47 48	28	Years married	2
		49	29	Education, head	1
		50	30	Education, wife	1
		51	31	Race	1
		52	32	Number of calls	1
		53	33	Who present	1
		54	34	Type of structure	1
		55 56	35	Neighborhood	2
		57			
		58			
		59			
		60			
		61			
		62			
		63			
		64			
		65			
		66			
		67			
		68			
		69			
		70			
		71			
		72			
		73			
		74			
		75			
		76			
		77			
		78			
		79			
		80			

Survey Research Center
Economic Behavior Program

Study 772
January 1968

1968 Survey of Consumer Finances
Card 01
N = 2677

FACE SHEET: DEMOGRAPHIC PAGE

Variable Number	Column Number	
1	1-3	Study Number (45772)
2	4-5	Card Number (01)
3	6-9	Interview Number (4 digits: in upper left hand corner of face sheet)
	10-15	Sample Book Number (6 digits) in upper right hand corner of face sheet in green.

Columns 10-12 indicate PSU: column 13-14 assigned serially to DU's from a particular PSU; column 15 indicates PSU county code.

	16-19	Place Codes (4 digits) in upper right hand corner of face sheet under Sample Book Number
	20-28	Q.1. Interviewer's Social Security Number (9 digits: on address label in upper left of face sheet)

CODERS: TURN TO COLUMN 29

10-15

STANDARD PSU CODE (Arranged in Numerical Order. See below for details of this code)

001-002	Los Angeles City	301-302	Baltimore City
003-004	Los Angeles suburbs	303-304	Baltimore suburbs
011-012	San Francisco and Oakland Cities	311-312	Washington City
013-014	San Francisco suburbs	313-314	Washington suburbs
101-102	Chicago City, north	365-366	Harris, Tex.
103-104	Chicago suburbs	375-376	Atlanta, Ga.
111-112	Chicago City, south	385-386	Jefferson, Ky.

[Fourteen examples are shown; other detail omitted]

Variable Number	Column Number	
		Details of Standard PSU Codes (Columns 10-12) (See Sampling Memo # 3, November, 1966)
4	10	Identification of Geographic Region

Self-Representing PSU's

0. West for 12 largest PSU's
1. North Central for 12 largest PSU's
2. Northeast for 12 largest PSU's
3. South for All PSU's

Non-Self-Representing PSU's

4. South for Other PSU's
5. South for Other PSU's
6. North Central for Other PSU's
7. North Central for Other PSU's
8. West for Other PSU's
9. Northeast for Other PSU's

Variable Number	Column Number	
5	11	This digit in combination with the region identification code (col. 10) uniquely identifies a PSU in all cases except Chicago and New York. Codes for the Chicago PSU are: 10, 11. Those for New York are: 20, 21, 22, 23 San Diego and San Bernardino though selected as one PSU, have separate interviewing staffs. They are coded 805 and 806.
6	12	Urbanization Code

Self-Representing PSU's (12 largest SMSA's or consolidated areas)

1-2. Central Cities
3-4 Suburbs

Non-Self-Representing PSU's

5-6. Standard Metropolitan Statistical Areas (Including a city or twin cities totally — SMSA's), 50,000 or more population by 1960 Census
7-8 NON-SMSA PSU's

Variable Number	Column Number	
7	13-14	Identification Number arbitrarily assigned serially to D.U.'s from a particular PSU (not by date of interview).

Variable Number	Column Number	
8	15	County Code This code can be used to identify the county in the PSU where the interview was taken. It is used in combination with cols. 10-11.

STATE	COUNTY	PSU	PSU CODE	COUNTY CODE
Alabama	Montgomery	Montgomery	44_	1
Arizona	Maricopa	Maricopa	83_	1
Ark.	Clark	Clark	53_	1
	Mississippi	Mississippi	51_	1
	Pulaski	Pulaski	42_	1
Calif.	Alameda	San Francisco	01_	2
	Contra Costa	San Francisco	01_	4
	[Remaining detail omitted]			

Variable Number	Column Number	
	(16-19)	Place Codes (line 2 of box at top of face sheet)
9	16	"Secondary Selection". This is an identification code and can be used only in conjunction with the PSU code in Cols. 10-12 0.Panel Members who moved outside their P.763 or P.772 segment
10	17	"Belt" (1960 Census classifications) 1. Central cities of 12 largest SMSA'S 2. Central cities of other SMSA's 3. Suburban areas of 12 largest SMSA's 4. Suburban areas of other SMSA's 5. Adjacent areas 6. Outlying areas 9. Panel members who moved outside their P.763 or P.772 segment
11	18	Size of place (1960 Census classifications) Panel members who moved outside their P.763 or P.772 segment, it was assumed that they lived in their post office address. The Size of Place was looked up from the 1960 Census. 1. Central Cities of the 12 largest SMSA's 2. Cities 50,000 and over, exclusive of the central cities of the 12 largest SMSA's 3. Urban places 10,000-49,999 4. Urban places 2,500-9,999; urbanized areas not included in above codes 5. Rural, in an SMSA PSU 6. Rural, not in an SMSA PSU 9. N.A.

Variable Number	Column Number	
12	19	Distance from the Center of the Central City
13	20-28	Q1. Interviewer's Social Security Number (9 digits) (address label in upper left of face sheet)
14	29	Q4. Date of Interview
15	30-32	Q.5. Length of Interview
16	33	Q7. Sex of Head of Family Unit (from listing box)
17	34-35	Q8. Age of Head of Family Unit (from listing box)

12 — 19 — Distance from the Center of the Central City

1. 0.0-0.9 (Note: this should properly be read 0.0 through 0.9999 . . .)
2. 1.0-1.9
3. 2.0-3.9
4. 4.0-5.9
5. 6.0-7.9
6. 8.0-9.9
7. 10.0-14.9
8. 15.0-24.9
9. 25 miles or more
0. All addresses in non-SMSA PSU's and all addresses in Central Cities of the 12 largest SMSA's. Panel members who moved outside their P.763 or P.772 segment.

13 — 20-28 — Q1. Interviewer's Social Security Number (9 digits)
(address label in upper left of face sheet)

14 — 29 — Q4. Date of Interview

0. January 10 or before
1. January 11-17
2. January 18-24
3. January 25-31
4. February 1-7
5. February 8-14
6. February 15-21
7. February 22-28
8. March 1-7
9. March 8 or later

IF NA, CODE DATE ON COVER SHEET IN F.O. IF NOT THERE, CODE DATE STAMPED BY F.O.

15 — 30-32 — Q.5. Length of Interview

Code actual number of minutes (e.g., "1 hour and 10 mins. = 70 mins.
999. NA

16 — 33 — Q7. Sex of Head of Family Unit (from listing box)

1. Male
2. Female
9. NA

Check against Q.F1, page 34

17 — 34-35 — Q8. Age of Head of Family Unit (from listing box)

Actual age in years (0-96)
97. 97 years and older
99. NA

If NA see Supervisor for assignment

Variable Number	Column Number	
18	36-37	Q8. Age of Wife of Head (from listing box)

Actual age in years (0-96)
97. 97 years or older
99. NA
00. INAP., Head of FU is not married.

19	38	Q9-10. Is R the Head of his Family Unit? (from listing box)

1. Yes, R is the Head of Family Unit.
2. No, R is the wife of the Head.
3. Both Head and Wife present and acting as respondents.
4. R is someone else in the Family Unit.
8. Other
9. NA

20	39	Q7-10. Sex of Respondent (from listing box)

1. Male
2. Female — Check against Q.F2,
3. Both – (two or more respondents)
9. NA

21	40	Number of Adults in this Family Unit (from listing box)

Adults are persons 18 years and older or who are married.

1. One
2. Two
3. Three
4. Four
5. Five
6. Six
7. Seven
8. Eight or more
9. NA

22	41	Number of adults aged 65 or older in this FU (from listing box)

0. No adults in this FU aged 65 or older.
1. One
2. Two
3. Three
4. Four or more
9. NA

Variable Number	Column Number	
23	42	Number of children (under 18) in THIS FU (from listing box)

1. One
2. Two
3. Three
4. Four
5. Five
6. Six
7. Seven
8. Eight or more
9. Number of children NA
0. No children under 18 NA whether any children

NOTE: Include all in FU regardless of whether Head is parent or not. This question refers only to children under 18 years.

Code 0 in cols. 43-45

Variable Number	Column Number	
24	43	How old are they? (from listing box)

AGE OF YOUNGEST CHILD UNDER 18

1. Less than two years
2. 2 years up to 2.99 years
3. 3 years up to 3.99 years
4. 4 years up to 4.99 years
5. 5 years up to 5.99 years
6. 6 years up to 8.99 years
7. 9 years up to 13.99 years
8. 14 years up to 18 years
9. NA
0. INAP., coded 0 in Col. 42

If there is just one child, code it both as the youngest in col. 43 and the oldest in col. 44.

Variable Number	Column Number	
25	44	How old are they? (from listing box)

AGE OF OLDEST CHILD UNDER 18

1. 0 up to 5.99 years
2. 6 up to 9.99 years
3. 10 up to 12.99 years
4. 13
5. 14
6. 15
7. 16
8. 17
9. NA
0. INAP: coded 0 in col. 42

Variable Number	Column Number	
26	45	Sex, Age of Children in the FU 15, 16 or 17 years old

(from listing box) (BROTHERS AND SISTERS OF HEAD ARE CODED HERE)

0. Has no boys or girls 15, 16, or 17 years old; INAP., coded 0 in col. 42
1. Has no boys and 1 girl 15, 16 or 17 years old.
2. Has no boys and 2 or more girls 15, 16 or 17 years old.
3. Has 1 boy and no girls 15, 16 or 17 years old.
4. Has 1 boy and 1 girl 15, 16 or 17 years old.
5. Has 1 boy and 2 or more girls 15, 16 or 17 years old.
6. Has 2 or more boys and no girls 15, 16 or 17 years old.
7. Has 2 or more boys and one girl 15, 16 or 17 years old.
8. Has 2 or more boys and 2 or more girls 15, 16 or 17 years old.
9. NA how many boys and girls 15, 16 or 17 years old.

GIRLS 15-17	BOYS 15-17: 0	1	2+
0	0	3	6
1	1	4	7
2+	2	5	8

CODER: PLEASE TURN TO SEC. E OF INTERVIEW

27 46 Q. E1. Marital Status of Head

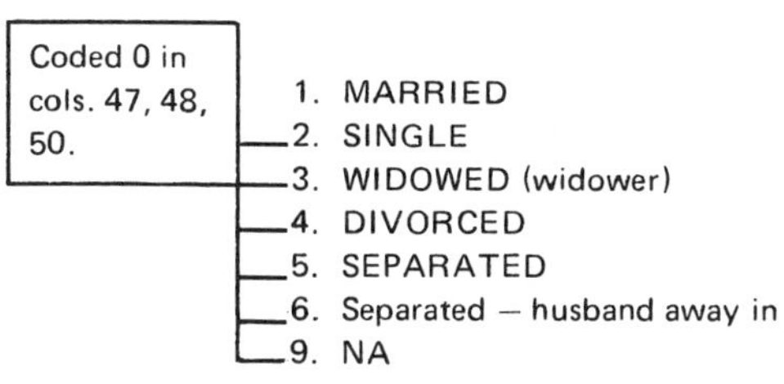

Coded 0 in cols. 47, 48, 50.

1. MARRIED
2. SINGLE
3. WIDOWED (widower)
4. DIVORCED
5. SEPARATED
6. Separated – husband away in service
9. NA

28 47-48 Q. E2. How long have you been married?

Code actual number of years.

00. Not married; coded 2-6, 9 in col. 46
01. One year or less
99. NA; DK

Variable Number	Column Number	
29	49	Q. E3-7. Education of Head of Family Unit

If head has 8 grades or less of education and also some non-college training, code the number of academic grades.

1. 0-5 grades
2. 6-8 grades
3. 9-11 grades; some high school plus non-college schooling
4. 12 grades; completed high school (12 years)
5. Completed high school plus other non-college training
6. College, no degree (include junior colleges)
7. College, Bachelor's degree
8. College, advanced or professional degree
9. NA; DK

30	50	Q. E3-7. Education of Wife of Family Unit

If wife has 8 grades or less of education and also some non-college training, code the number of academic grades.

1. 0-5 grades
2. 6-8 grades
3. 9-11 grades; some high school plus non-college schooling
4. 12 grades; completed high school (12 years)
5. Completed high school plus other non-college training
6. College, no degree (include junior colleges)
7. College, Bachelor's degree
8. College, advanced or professional degree
9. NA; DK
0. INAP., coded 2-6, 9 in col. 46; no wife. Husband in service, wife temporary head.

CODER: PLEASE TURN TO SEC. F

31	51	Q. F3. Race

1. WHITE
2. NEGRO
3. OTHER

32	52	Q. F4. Number of Calls

1. One
2. Two
3. Three
4. Four
5. Five
6. Six
7. Seven
8. Eight or more
9. NA

Variable Number	Column Number	
33	53	Q. F5. Who was present during the interview? (Do not include interviewer)

1. Head only
2. Wife only
3. Head and wife only
4. Head and somebody else (not wife)
5. Wife and somebody else (not husband)
6. Head and wife and somebody else
7. Somebody else; R is someone other than wife or head
9. NA

34	54	Q. F6. Type of structure in which family lives

1. TRAILER
2. DETACHED SINGLE FAMILY HOUSE
3. 2-FAMILY HOUSE, 2 UNITS SIDE BY SIDE.
4. 2-FAMILY HOUSE, 2 UNITS ONE ABOVE THE OTHER.
5. DETACHED 3-4 FAMILY HOUSE
6. ROW HOUSE (3 OR MORE UNITS IN AN ATTACHED ROW)
7. APARTMENT HOUSE (5 OR MORE UNITS, 3 STORIES OR LESS)
8. APARTMENT HOUSE (5 OR MORE UNITS, 4 STORIES OR MORE)
9. APARTMENT IN A PARTLY COMMERCIAL STRUCTURE
0. OTHER (Make a card)

35	55-56	Q. F7 Neighborhood. Look at 3 structures on each side of DU but not more than 100 yards or so in both directions and check as many boxes as apply, below.

> CODER: Code the highest density type of residential housing mentioned – i.e. code the box checked that corresponds to the largest numerical code.

01. VACANT LAND ONLY.
02. TRAILER
03. DETACHED SINGLE FAMILY HOUSE
04. 2-FAMILY HOUSE, 2 UNITS SIDE BY SIDE
05. 2-FAMILY HOUSE, 2 UNITS ONE ABOVE THE OTHER.
06. DETACHED 3-4 FAMILY HOUSE.
07. ROW HOUSE (3 OR MORE UNITS IN AN ATTACHED ROW)
08. APARTMENT HOUSE (5 OR MORE UNITS, 3 STORIES OR LESS)
09. APARTMENT HOUSE (5 OR MORE UNITS, 4 STORIES OR MORE)
10. APARTMENT IN A PARTLY COMMERCIAL STRUCTURE
11. WHOLLY COMMERCIAL OR INDUSTRIAL STRUCTURE
12. OTHER (Make a card)
99. NA

SINGLE CARD FORM

Project Number: 772

Project Name: Survey of Consumers

Project Director:
Phone:

Card Layout By:
Date:

Deck Number: 02

Source Document:

Trf. from Cards:

Remarks: Example of card layout for Deck 02: Attitudes

Columns 1-40						Columns 41-80					
FROM			POSSIBLE CODES			FROM			POSSIBLE CODES		
Card	Col		V	Name	Field Size	Card	Col		V	Name	Field Size
		1	36	Study Number (772)	3			41			
		2						42			
		3						43			
		4	37	Deck Number (02)	2			44			
		5						45			
		6	38	Interview Number	4			46			
		7						47			
		8						48			
		9						49			
		10	39	Financial Condition	1			50			
		11	40	Reason Why — First	2			51			
		12						52			
		13	41	Reason Why — Second	2			53			
		14						54			
		15	42	Making More Now	1			55			
		16	43	News — Business Cond.	1			56			
		17	44	What News — First	2			57			
		18						58			
		19	45	What News — Second	2			59			
		20						60			
		21						61			
		22						62			
		23						63			
		24						64			
		25						65			
		26						66			
		27						67			
		28						68			
		29						69			
		30						70			
		31						71			
		32						72			
		33						73			
		34						74			
		35						75			
		36						76			
		37						77			
		38						78			
		39						79			
		40						80			

1968 Survey of Consumer Finances

CARD 02
N = 2677
ATTITUDES, EXPECTATIONS

Variable Number	Column Number	
36	1-3	STUDY NUMBER (772)
37	4-5	CARD NUMBER (02)
38	6-9	INTERVIEW NUMBER (4 digits: upper right of face sheet)
39	10	Q. A1. We are interested in how people are getting along financially these days. Would you say that you and your family are better off or worse off financially than you were a year ago?

1. BETTER NOW
3. SAME
5. WORSE NOW
8. UNCERTAIN, D.K.
9. N.A.

40	11-12	Q. A2. Why do you say so?
41	13-14	REASONS FOR MAKING FU BETTER OFF

CODE UP TO TWO MENTIONS

10. Better pay: raise in wages or salary on present job, promotions, higher commissions, change to higher paying job (include Armed Forces induction or discharge).
11. Higher income from self-employment or property: higher business profits or farm income, higher dividends, royalties or rents, more income from professional practice or trade.
12. More work, hence more income: Head (or wife) started working (again), more members of family working, higher income, N.A. why.
13. Increased contributions from outside FU: (from private individuals government pension, relief or welfare, gifts).
14. Lower Prices: decrease in cost of living.
15. Lower taxes.
16. Decreased expenses: fewer people to be supported by FU; spending less, N.A. whether 14 or 16.
18. High interest rates; tight credit.
19. Better asset position: more savings, business or farm worth more, has more business, farm, or personal assets, stock went up,
20. Debt, interest or debt payments low or lower; have paid, is paying bills.
21. Change in family composition means higher income or better off (except 16 or inheritance); got married, etc.

LOW PRIORITY — 27. Other reasons for making FU better off: greater security (job more permanent, psychological security), greater opportunities, higher standard of living, have more things, future outlook improved, got insurance.

Variable Number	Column Number	
	11-12, 13-14 (cont.)	(Q.A2) Why do you say so?

REASONS FOR MAKING FU WORSE OFF

50. Lower pay: decrease in wages or salary on present job, change to lower paying job (include Armed Forces, induction or discharge).
51. Lower income from self-employment or property: lower business profits or farm income, lower dividends, royalties or rents, less income from professional practice or trade.
52. Less work, hence less income: head unemployed, laid off, sick, retired, on strike, unsteady work, less overtime, fewer members of FU working, lower income N.A. why.
53. Decreased contributions from outside FU.
54. Higher prices: increase in cost of living: prices rise faster than income.
55. High, higher taxes.
56. High interest rates; tight credit.
58. Increased expenses: more people to be supported by FU; spending, more N.A. whether 54, 55, 56 or 58.
59. Worse asset position: savings used up wholly or partly, less business, farm or personal assets.
60. Debt: interest, debt, or debt payments high or higher.
61. Change in family composition means lower income or worse off (except 58); divorced, death, etc.
62. Stock market: stocks declined in value.
67. [LOW PRIORITY] Other reasons for making FU worse off: less security (job less permanent, psychological insecurity), fewer opportunities (dark future outlook), lower standard of living.
99. N.A. (use only in Cols. 11-12)
00. No change, no pro-con reason given, no second mention.

42 15 (Q. A3) Are you people making as much money now as you were a year ago, or more, or less?

1. MORE NOW
3. ABOUT THE SAME
5. LESS NOW
9. D.K., N.A.

43 16 Q. A4 During the last few months, have you heard of any favorable or unfavorable changes in business conditions?

1. Yes
5. No — Code 0 in col. 17-18 19-20
9. N.A. — Code 0 in col. 17-18 19-20

Variable Number	Column Number	
44 45	17-18, 19-20	Q. 5. During the last few months, have you heard of any favorable or unfavorable changes in business conditions? (IF YES) What did you hear?

CODE UP TO TWO MENTIONS

FAVORABLE CHANGES

Government, defense (any reference to war, code 11 or 12)

LOW PRIORITY

10. Elections, new president, politics.
11. More or continuing defense production, military spending (international situation getting worse).
12. Less defense production, military spending; relaxation of international tensions; peace negotiations; bombing halt.
13. Poverty program, aid to Appalachia, Great Society programs will continue to increase.
14. Other government programs continuing or increasing.
15. Government spending (other than defense) reduced; cut in space program, foreign aid, government programs.
16. Tax changes.
18. Government spending (general); budget, deficits; fiscal responsibility.
19. Government steps to improve business conditions; balance of payments; government economists, monetary authorities, etc.
17. (Other) references to government, not codable above.

Employment and purchasing power

21. Consumer demand is (will be) high (except autos – code 26); people want to buy, are buying.
22. Purchasing power is (will be) high; people have money to spend; wages are high; any kind of income high or higher.
23. Employment has risen, is rising; more overtime; plenty of jobs or work around; unemployment declining.
24. Population increase.
25. Low (lower) debts; high (higher) assets.
26. Automobile demand is (will be) high, higher.
27. (Other) references to employment and purchasing power, not codable above.

Prices

30. Interest rates higher. Credit harder to get.
31. Lower prices; prices aren't rising; stable prices.
32. Higher prices; inflation; prices rising.
33. Easier money; credit is easy to get; interest rates declined.
34. Price changes have been balanced by wage changes.
35. Profits high, higher.
36. Profits low, lower.
38. Stock market.
39. Devaluation of pound (makes imports cost less, etc.).
37. (Other) references to prices, not codable above.

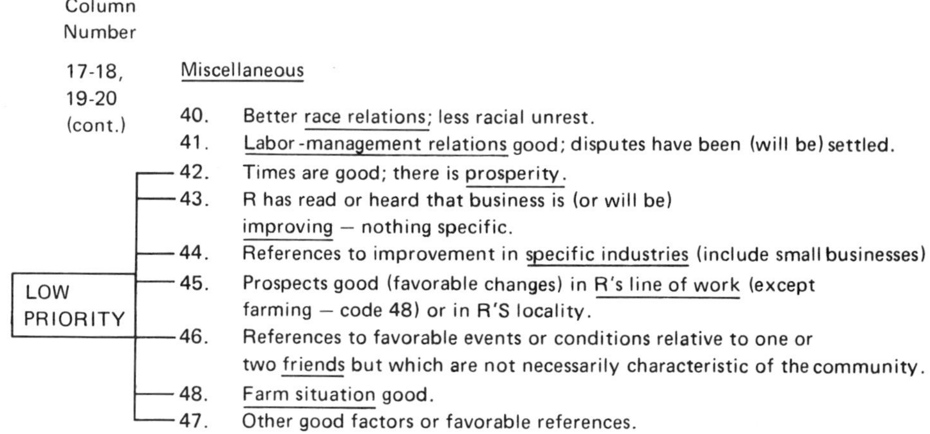

Column Number

17-18, 19-20 (cont.)

Miscellaneous

40. Better race relations; less racial unrest.
41. Labor-management relations good; disputes have been (will be) settled.

LOW PRIORITY:

42. Times are good; there is prosperity.
43. R has read or heard that business is (or will be) improving — nothing specific.
44. References to improvement in specific industries (include small businesses)
45. Prospects good (favorable changes) in R's line of work (except farming — code 48) or in R'S locality.
46. References to favorable events or conditions relative to one or two friends but which are not necessarily characteristic of the community.
48. Farm situation good.
47. Other good factors or favorable references.

UNFAVORABLE CHANGES

Government, defense (any reference to war, code 51 or 52)

LOW PRIORITY:

50. Elections, new president, politics.

51. More or continuing defense production, military spending, (international situation, Vietnam getting worse).
52. Less defense production, military spending; relaxation of international tensions; peace negotiations; bombing halt.
53. Cut in poverty program; other Great Society programs decreasing.
54. Other government programs, space program, foreign aid, continuing or increasing.
55. Other government programs, space program, foreign aid will be cut; government spending reduced.
56. Tax increases.
58. Government spending (general); budget, deficits; fiscal irresponsibility.
59. (Other) references to government, not codable above.

Employment and purchasing power

61. Consumer demand is (will be) low; people don't want to buy, aren't buying; people are saving their money.
62. Lack of purchasing power; people don't have money to spend; low incomes.
63. Drop in employment; high or higher unemployment; layoffs less overtime; people are working short hours.
64. Population increase.
65. High (higher) debts.
66. Automation.
68. Shutdown of plants and factories.
69. Demand is saturated; people have what they need, don't have to buy; stores are overstocked, inventories are high.
67. (Other) references to employment and purchasing power, not codable above

Column
Number

17-18, 19-20 (cont.)

Prices

71. Prices are falling, will fall, are too low; deflation.
72. Prices are high, too high, won't fall; inflation.
73. Tight money; credit hard to get; interest rates rising, are too high.
74. Wages lag behind prices.
75. Profits high; too high.
76. Profits low, falling; businesses losing money.
78. Stock market; decline in stock prices.
79. Problems with the dollar or gold; world monetary troubles.
77. Other price references, not codable above.

Miscellaneous

80. Bad race relations; racial unrest; riots; civil disorders.
81. Strikes, union demands, labor unrest.
82. Recession is coming; has set in; business activity has turned down.
83. Good times can't last; decline is inevitable – nothing specific.

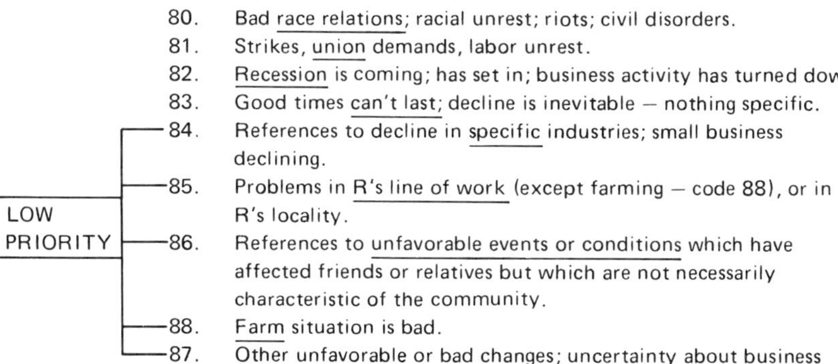

84. References to decline in specific industries; small business declining.
85. Problems in R's line of work (except farming – code 88), or in R's locality.
86. References to unfavorable events or conditions which have affected friends or relatives but which are not necessarily characteristic of the community.
88. Farm situation is bad.
87. Other unfavorable or bad changes; uncertainty about business conditions.
97. Elections, N.A. whether favorable or unfavorable.
98. Change, N.A. whether favorable or unfavorable.
99. N.A. what heard; N.A. whether heard (use only in Cols. 30-31).
00. Has heard of no changes; no second mention.

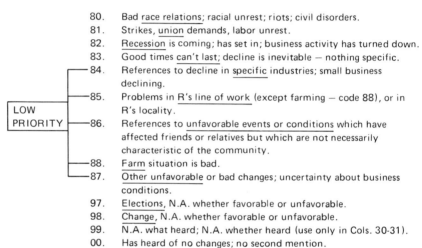

SINGLE CARD FORM

Project Number: 772	Project Name: Survey of Consumers	
Project Director: Phone:	Card Layout By: Phone:	Date:
Deck Number: 03	Source Document:	Trf. from Cards:

Remarks: Example of card layout for Deck 03: Housing

Columns 1-40

FROM			POSSIBLE CODES		
Card	Col		V	Name	Field Size
		1 2 3	46	Study Number (772)	3
		4 5	47	Deck Number (03)	2
		6 7 8 9	48	Interview Number	4
		10	49	Year Moved in	1
		11	50	Years in County	1
		12	51	Housing Status	1
		13	52	Neither Own/Rent	1
		14 15 16	53	Monthly Rent	3
		17	54	Furnished-Unfurnished	1
		18 19 20 21 22 23	55	House Value	6
		24	56	Good Time to Buy House	1
		25 26	57	Reason Good/Bad — First	2
		27 28	58	Reason Good/Bad — Second	2
		29 30	59	Month of Largest A and R	2
		31	60		1
		32 33 34 35	61	Total Amount Borrowed on A and R	4
		36 37 38 39	62	Expenditures on Additions and Repairs	4
		40			

Columns 41-80

FROM			POSSIBLE CODES		
Card	Col		V	Name	Field Size
		41			
		42			
		43			
		44			
		45			
		46			
		47			
		48			
		49			
		50			
		51			
		52			
		53			
		54			
		55			
		56			
		57			
		58			
		59			
		60			
		61			
		62			
		63			
		64			
		65			
		66			
		67			
		68			
		69			
		70			
		71			
		72			
		73			
		74			
		75			
		76			
		77			
		78			
		79			
		80			

Survey Research Center
Economic Behavior Program

Study 772
January, 1968

1968 SURVEY OF CONSUMERS
CARD 03
N = 2677

HOUSING: ADDITIONS AND REPAIRS

Variable Number	Column Number	
46	1-3	Study Number (772)
47	4-5	Card Number (04)
48	6-9	Interview Number (4 digits)
49	10	(Q. B1) When did you move into this (house/apartment)?

1. 1944 or earlier
2. 1945-1954
3. 1955-1959
4. 1960-1964
5. 1965
6. 1966
7. 1967
8. 1968
9. 1969

50 11 (Q. B2) How long have you lived in ________________ (County name)?

1. 25 years and over; 1944 or earlier
2. 15-24 years; 1945-1954
3. 10-14 years; 1955-1959
4. 5-9 years; 1960-1964
5. 4 years; 1965
6. 3 years; 1966
7. 2 years; 1967
8. 1 year; 1968 (4 months-1 year)
9. 0-3 months; 1969

If R says "All my life" code from age on face sheet.

(NA or DK, code same as B1)

HOUSING STATUS

51 12 (HS BOX) Do you (FU) own this home or pay rent or what? (Q. B3, B4, F6)

Owns:

Code 0 in cols. 13-17 (codes 1-4):

1. Owns home (containing one or two DU's) own farm alone.
2. Owns apartment building (three or more DU's or building with both commercial and living quarters in which R lives.
(If apartment building has 10 or more DU's be sure that R is coded as owning an unincorporated business.)
3. Joint owner; owner of cooperative apartment; joint farm owner or cooperative farmer*
4. Owns trailer

Rents:

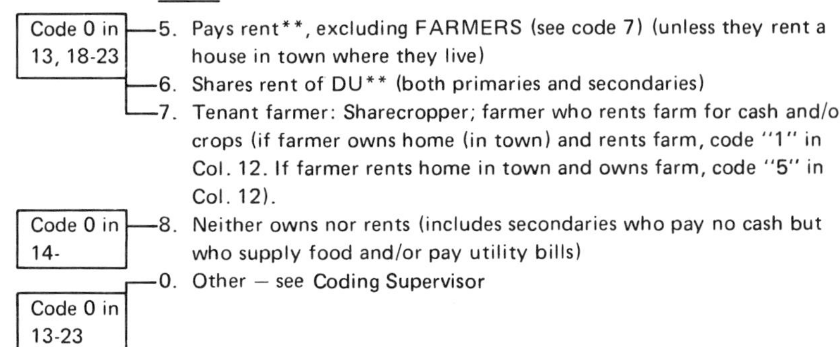

Code 0 in 13, 18-23

5. Pays rent**, excluding FARMERS (see code 7) (unless they rent a house in town where they live)
6. Shares rent of DU** (both primaries and secondaries)
7. Tenant farmer: Sharecropper; farmer who rents farm for cash and/or crops (if farmer owns home (in town) and rents farm, code "1" in Col. 12. If farmer rents home in town and owns farm, code "5" in Col. 12).

Code 0 in 14-

8. Neither owns nor rents (includes secondaries who pay no cash but who supply food and/or pay utility bills)

Code 0 in 13-23

0. Other – see Coding Supervisor

HOUSING STATUS N.A. – SEE CODING SUPERVISOR

* If primary FU shares ownership of 1 DU with another FU, code total house value to primary FU, and zero out house value on secondary's card. If 2 FU's co-own 2 or more DU's (coded 3 in Col. 12) see the Editing Supervisor for instructions if there is any question concerning Col. 12 code.

** Secondaries:

a. If a roomer, boarder, or otherwise sublets part of DU code "5" in Col. 12 and code amount of rent paid in Cols. 14-16.
b. If shares rent with a primary FU, code "6" in Col. 12 and zero out Cols. 14-16 (code total rent to primary).
c. If pays a single sum for room and board, code half of the total as rent in Cols. 14-16.

Variable Number	Column Number	
52	13	(Q. B4) (IF NEITHER) How is that?

Coded 8 in Col. 12

1. Servant; housekeeper
2. Farm laborer
3. Other person for whom housing is part of compensation (janitors, gardeners, nurses, etc.)
4. Persons for whom housing is a gift, paid for by someone outside of FU, owned by relative, pays no rent or only taxes
5. Sold own home, but still living there
6. Living in house which will inherit; estate in process
7. Living in temporary quarters (garage, shed, etc.) while home is under construction.
8. Other
0. Inap. Coded 1-7, or 0 in Col. 12

Variable Number	Column Number	
53	14-16	(R BOX) (IF RENTS) About how much rent do you pay a month? (Q. B5) Coded 5 or 7 in Col. 12; Coded 6 in Col. 12 if R is a Primary FU XXX. Code amounts in DOLLARS 999. Rent N.A. (for tenant farmers and sharecroppers only) 000. Inap., Coded 1-4, 6 (if secondary), 8 or 0 in Col. 12 [Box:] If R pays room and board code $\frac{1}{2}$ for rent. If secondary FU shares rent, attribute all rent to primary. If R is a tenant farmer or sharecropper and pays rent in both cash and crops, or crops only, code N.A.
54	17	(Q. B6) (IF RENTS) Furnished or Unfurnished? Coded 5-7 in Col. 12 1. Furnished (including semi-furnished) 5. Unfurnished 9. NA, DK 0. Inap., Coded 1-4, 8 or 0 in Col. 12
55	18-23	(HV BOX) Present Value or Cost of House (Q. B7) XXXXXX. Code amount in DOLLARS 000000. Inap., coded 5-8 or 0 in Col. 12
56	24	Q. B8. Generally speaking, do you think now is a good time or a bad time to buy a house? 1. GOOD 3. PRO-CON 5. BAD 8. DON'T KNOW 9. N.A. — [Code 0 in cols. 25-28]
57	25-26 27-28	Q. B9. Why do you say so? Reasons why now is a GOOD time to buy a house Prices; Credit [CODE UP TO TWO MENTIONS] 11. Prices are low, lower; prices are reasonable, stable, not too high. 12. Good buys available; buyer's market (oversupply of houses); difficult for sellers to find buyers; hard for other buyers to get credit. 13. Prices are going up; buy before prices are higher. 14. Prices won't get any lower (not codable 13) 15. Lower down payment. 16. Credit easy to get; easy money, N.A. if 15, 16, 17 or 18 17. Interest rates are low (now). 18. Credit will be tighter later; interest rates will go up. 19. Lower taxes, taxes will be higher later

Employment; Times

21. People can afford to buy now, purchasing power available, high employment; prosperity; people have money to spend; times are good.
22. Buying makes for good times, prosperity, high employment.

Column Number

25-26 27-28 (cont.)

Supply and Quality

31. Supply adequate; no shortages now; there may be shortages later; many houses on market, (no reference to influence on prices, deals)
32. Quality is good; better; may get worse.
33. New models have improvements, new features; are attractive.
34. Good selection; variety.

Other Good

LOW PRIORITY (41–47):

41. Seasonal references only.
42. R only says that if you need it and have the money, this is as good a time as any; if people need things, will buy them regardless of the times.
43. Population increase.
44. Renting is unfavorable (because of high rents apartment shortage, etc.)
45. Owning is always a good idea (because of investment or sentimental reasons)
46. Capital appreciation; buying a home is a good investment these days (because the value of houses will increase) reference to special or temporary circumstances which make houses a good investment. (Code under 44 reasons which imply that house ownership is always a good investment).
47. Other reasons (miscellaneous)

Reasons why now is a BAD time to buy a house

Prices; Credit

51. Prices are (too) high; higher; houses cost more than they are worth.
52. Seller's market.
53. Prices will fall later; will come down; are falling; will not rise; future uncertainty about prices
54. Higher down payment required.
55. Credit hard to get; financing is difficult.
56. Interest rate too high.
57. Tight money (answers not codable 54, 55, or 56)
58. Taxes are too high.

Variable Number	Column Number	

Employment; Times

61. People can't afford to buy now (low levels of employment; times are bad; don't have money to spend; people are too far in debt).
62. People should save money to hedge against uncertainty of times bad times ahead; employment too uncertain.

25-26, 27-28 (cont.)

Supply and Quality

71. Supply inadequate; poor selection.
72. Quality is poor; quality may be better later.
73. Poor designs; unattractive styling; new features or improvements will come later.

Other Bad

80. International situation; threat of war; cold war.

LOW PRIORITY (81–87):

81. R mentions only seasonal factors
82. Renting is favorable; rents are low.
83. Renting is always better than owning.
84. Capital depreciation: buying a house now is a bad investment (because the value of houses will decrease) references to temporary or special circumstances which make houses a bad investment. (Code under 83 responses that imply that home ownership is always a bad investment).
85. Difficult to get rid of present house; market poor.
87. Other reasons why now is a bad time to buy.

88. Better return on alternative investments.
99. N.A., D.K. reasons (use only in Cols. 25-26)
00. Inap., coded 9 in Col. 24; coded 8 in Col. 24 and no reasons given; no second mention.

ADDITIONS AND REPAIRS

59 29-30 (Q. B12) Month of largest single A and R expenditure in 1967

01. January
02. February
03. March
04. April
05. May
06. June
07. July
08. August
09. September
10. October
11. November.
12. December

99. Month NA, but some expenditure
00. Inap., no expenditure on additions and repairs — Code 0 in cols. 31-39

Variable Number	Column Number	
60	31	(Q. B.12) Quarter of 1967 with largest total A and R expenditures

1. First quarter (January-March)
2. Second quarter (April-June)
3. Third quarter (July-September)
4. Fourth quarter (October-December)
9. N.A. which quarter, but some expenditure
0. Inap., no expenditures on additions and repairs; coded 0 in cols. 29-30).

61	32-35	Total Amount borrowed on 1967 additions and repairs

(CODER: Code editor's figure in BOR box)

XXXX. Code amount in DOLLARS
9997. $9997 or more
9999. Amount NA, but some borrowing
0000. Inap., no borrowing in 1967

62	36-39	(ADD AND REP Box) Expenditure on Additions and Repairs in 1967

XXXX. Code amount in DOLLARS
9997. $9997 or more
9999. Amount NA, but some expenditure on additions
0000. Inap., no expenditure on additions or repairs; coded 0 in cols. 29-30.

SINGLE CARD FORM

Project Number: 772	Project Name: Survey of Consumers

Project Director: Phone:	Card Layout By: Phone: Date:

Deck Number: 04	Source Document:	Trf. from Cards:

Remarks: Example of card layout for Deck 04: Automobiles

FROM			POSSIBLE CODES		
Card	Col		X	Name	Field Size
		1 2 3	63	Study Number (772)	3
		4 5	64	Deck Number (04)	2
		6 7 8 9	65	Interview Number	4
		10	66	Car I.D.	1
		11	67	Number of Drivers	1
		12	68	Number of Cars Owned	1
		13	69	Years Multiple Owner	1
		14 15	70	Year Model	2
		16 17	71	Make of Car	2
		18	72	Style	1
		19	73	Size	1
		20	74	Usual Driver	1
		21	75	Bought New/Used	1
		22 23	76	Year Purchased	2
		24 25 26 27	77	Total Price Paid	4
		28	78	Quarter Bought Car	1
		29	79	Whether Trade In	1
		30 31 32 33′	80	Value of Car Traded In	4
		34 35 36 37	81	Amount Paid in Cash	4
		38	82	Whether Borrowed	1
		39 40	83	Amount Borrowed	2

FROM			POSSIBLE CODES		
Card	Col		X	Name	Field Size
		41 42			
		43 44 45	84	Monthly Payment	3
		46 47	85	Original Length of Debt	2
		48 49	86	Remaining Number of Payments	2
		50 51 52 53	87	Total Remaining Instalment Debt on Cars	4
		54 55 56 57 58 59 60 61 62 63 64 65 66 67 68 69 70 71 72 73 74 75 76 77 78 79 80			

1968 SURVEY OF CONSUMERS
CARD 04
N = 2677

F.U. AUTO OWNERSHIP; PURCHASES; AUTO DEBT AND "ADDITIONAL CAR" DETAIL

CODE CARD 04 EVEN IF NO CAR OWNED BY F.U. IF F.U. OWNS MORE THAN ONE CAR, CODE ONE CARD 04 FOR EACH ADDITIONAL CAR IN F.U.

Variable Number	Column Number	
63	1-3	Study Number (772)
64	4-5	Card Number (04)
65	6-9	Interview Number
66	10	Car Identification Number (NUMBER ABOVE COLUMNS FOR Q. C5)

Code 0 in Col. 13 — 1. Car NO. 1 (FIRST CAR): NO CAR IN FU

2. Car NO. 2
3. Car NO. 3

. . . etc.

Note: If R owns $\frac{1}{2}$ car with someone outside FU, code this FU as owning car

Variable Number	Column Number	
67	11	Number of Drivers in FU

(Q. C1) . . . Altogether, how many people are there in your family living here who can drive?

CODE NUMBER OF DRIVERS IN FU

0. No one in the FU can drive
1. One driver in FU
2. Two drivers in FU
3. Three drivers in FU

. . . etc.

NOTE: Include here all people who know how to drive.

9. N.A., D.K. number of drivers

Variable Number	Column Number	
68	12	NUMBER OF CARS OWNED BY FU

(Q. C2, C3) Do you, or anyone else in the family here own a car? Altogether, how many cars do you and your family living here own?

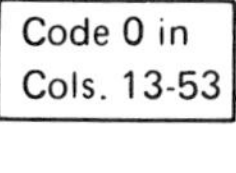
Code 0 in Cols. 13-53

CODE NUMBER OF CARS OWNED BY FU

0. No one in FU owns a car
1. FU owns one car
2. FU owns two cars
3. FU owns three cars
. . . etc.

Code 0 in Col. 13

NOTE: If R owns $\frac{1}{2}$ of car with someone outside FU, code this FU as owning car.

69	13	HOW LONG A MULTIPLE OWNER

(Q. C4) How long have you had more than one car in the family?

CODE NUMBER OF YEARS FU HAS OWNED TWO OR MORE CARS

0. Inap.; AND less than 1 year
1. 1 year (1.0-1.9)
2. 2 years (2.0-2.9)
3. 3 years (3.0-3.9)
4. 4 years (4.0-4.9)
5. 5 years (5.0-5.9)
6. 6 years (6.0-6 9)
7. 7-10 years (7.0-10.9)
8. Eleven or more years

9. D.K., N.A.

70	14-15	(Q. C5) What year model is it?

39. 1939 or earlier
40. 1940
41. 1941
42. 1942 (includes 1945)

NOTE: If adjacent year is given, e.g., either 1962 or 1963, code the earlier year.

xx. 1946-1968 (Code last two digits of year model)
99. D.K., N.A.
00. Inap., no cars owned by FU, coded 0 in column 12

Variable Number	Column Number	
71	16-17	(Q. C6) What make of car is it?
		MAKE OF CAR OWNED

58.	(Buick)	Electra, Riviera only
28.	(Buick)	Special (1961-1969 models)
36.	Buick	All other (or NA which of above)
51.	Cadillac	
56.	(Chevrolet)	Camaro
62.	(Chevrolet)	Chevelle
61.	(Chevrolet)	Chevy II
18.	(Chevrolet)	Corvair
11.	Chevrolet	All other or NA which of above (except Corvette – code 50; and Greenbriar – code 10)
53.	Chrysler	(except Imperial – code 54)

[Remaining detail omitted]

10. Other low priced domestic cars – Henry J., Hudson Jet, Willys, Crosley, Allstate, Econoline, Greenbriar, Travelall

20. Other low priced foreign made cars – English Ford, Saab, Austin, Fiat, Volvo, Hillman, Opel, Simca, Vauxhall, Taunus, DKW, Isetta, BMW, Morris, Nash Metropolitan, Toyopet, Peugeot, Skoda, Anglia, Prinz, Datsun, Toyota.

30. Other medium priced domestic cars (Kaiser, Checker)

59. Foreign made medium or high priced or sports cars (Porsche, Riley, Mercedes, Jaguar, M.G., Austin-Healy, Bentley, Alfa, Sunbeam, Triumph, Borgward, Citroen, Rover, Rolls

50. Other domestic high priced or sports cars (Corvette)

99. D.K., N.A. make

00. No one in FU owns a car, Coded 0 in Col. 12

Variable Number	Column Number	
72	18	(Q. C7) Is it a sedan (2-door or 4-door), a station wagon, a convertible, or what?

1. Sedan (2-door or 4-door), coupe, hardtop
2. Station Wagon
3. Sports Car, Convertible
7. Other
9. D.K., N.A.
0. No one in FU owns a car, Coded 0 in Col. 12

Variable Number	Column Number	
73	19	(Q. C8) Is it a compact, regular-size, something in-between, or what?

> Accept R's response to this question. Do not make it consistent with make of car.

1. Compact
3. "Middle-sized," "in-between"
5. Regular-size
9. D.K., N.A.
0. Inap., coded 0 in Col. 12

74	20	(Q. C9) Who usually drives this car? (RELATION TO HEAD)

1. Head, no one drives the car
2. Wife
3. Head and wife equally
4. Son or daughter
5. Other person(s) (for example: son-in-law)
8. Combination of the above
9. N.A.
0. Inap., coded 0 in Col. 12

75	21	(Q. C10) Did you buy this car new or used?

(N.A.'s are assigned by editors)

1. New
2. Used
0. Inap., no one in FU owns car, Coded 0 in Col. 12

76	22-23	(Q. C11) In what year did you buy it?

> NOTE: If adjacent year is given, e.g., either 1962 or 1963, code the earlier year.

(N.A.'s are assigned by editors)

> Code 0 in Cols. 24-53 — GO ON TO SEC. E (applies to codes 39 and xx)

39. 1939 or earlier

xx. 1940-1966
Code last two digits of year

68. 1967
69. 1968

> CODER: Go to Q. C12 and begin coding Cols. 24-58 (applies to codes 68 and 69)

00. No one in FU owns car, Coded 0 in Col. 12

77	24-27	TOTAL PRICE (TP BOX)

(Q. C12) What was the Total Price, of the car you bought in 1967 or 1968? (N.A. assigned) TP BOX EDITED IN GREEN

Coded 67 or 68 in Cols. 22-23

XXXX. Code amount in DOLLARS
9997. $9997 or more

0000. [Car was a gift] Inap., coded other than 67 or 68 in Cols. 22-23; Coded 0 in Col. 12.

Variable Number	Column Number	
78	28	Quarter of Year Bought Car (From Q. C13)
79	29	(Q. C14) (IF BOUGHT IN 1967-68 ONLY). Did you trade-in or sell a car car when you bought that one?
80	30-33	TRADE-IN OR SALE (TI BOX)
81	34-37	PAID IN CASH

78 28 Quarter of Year Bought Car (From Q. C13)

0. Inap., did not buy a car in 1967 or 1968

1. Jan., Feb., March, 1967
2. April, May, June 1967
3. July, Aug., Sept., 1967
4. Oct., Nov., Dec., 1967
5. Jan., Feb., March, 1968

9. N.A., D.K.

79 29 (Q. C14) (IF BOUGHT IN 1967-68 ONLY). Did you trade-in or sell a car car when you bought that one?

(NA's are assigned by editors)

1. YES, TRADED IN OR SOLD A CAR
5. NO — Code 0 in Cols. 30-33
0. Inap., this transaction not made in 1967 or 1968; coded 0 in Col. 12

80 30-33 TRADE-IN OR SALE (TI BOX)

(Q. C15) What did you get from Trade-in or Sale? TI BOX EDITED IN GREEN

Coded 67 or 68 in Cols. 22-23 (transaction made in 1967 or 1968)

XXXX. Code amount in DOLLARS
9997. $9997 or more
0000. No trade-in or sale. Inap., coded other than 67 or 68 in Cols. 22-23; coded 0 in Col. 12

81 34-37 PAID IN CASH

(Q. C16) How much did you pay down in cash
Coded 67 or 68 in Cols. 22-23. Code Gifts 0000

XXXX. Code amount in DOLLARS
9997. $9997 or more
–XXX. Negative amount
9999. Cash N.A.
0000. Cash paid; car was gift; Inap., coded other than 67 or 68 in Cols. 22-23; coded 0 in Col. 12

CODER: BEGIN CODING COL. 66-73 WITH Q. C34

COLS. 66-74 REFER TO CAR TRADED IN OR SOLD (CODED 1 IN COL. 29)

Variable Number	Column Number	
82	38	BORROWED OR FINANCED

(Q. 17) Did you borrow or finance part of the total price?

1. Installment or other borrowing on car purchased in 1967 or 1968
5. No installment or other borrowing on 1967-1968 purchase.
0. Inap., no one in FU owns car; Coded 0 in Col. 12

[Code 0 in Cols. 39-53 — applies to codes 5 and 0]

Variable Number	Column Number	
83	39-42	AMOUNT BORROWED (AB BOX)

(Q. C18) How much did you borrow, not including financing charges?
CODE FROM AB BOX, EDITED IN GREEN

XXXX. CODE AMOUNT IN DOLLARS

9997. $9997 or greater
9999. N.A., D.K.
0000. INAP., NO BORROWING

Variable Number	Column Number	
84	43-45	MONTHLY PAYMENT

(Q. C19) How much were your payments and how often were they made?

XXX. Code amount in DOLLARS per month
997. $997 or more
999. Payment amount not ascertained

000. Non-installment debt only; debt repaid by time of interview; Inap., coded 5 or 0 in Col. 38, coded 0 in Col. 12

Variable Number	Column Number	
85	46-47	ORIGINAL LENGTH OF DEBT

(Q. C21) How many payments did you agree to make all together?
XX. Code length in MONTHS (from incurrence until termination)

97. No repayment schedule; all non-installment debt
98. Revolving fund
99. Length of debt D.K., N.A.

00. Inap., car not purchased in 1967 or 1968 (coded other than 67 or 68 in Cols. 22-23); car not financed when bought in 1967 or 1968 (coded 5 in Col. 38); coded 0 in Col. 12 (no car in FU).

Variable Number	Column Number	
86	48-49	REMAINING LENGTH OF DEBT

(Q. C22) How many payments do you have left to make?

XX. Code length in MONTHS (Until loan will be repaid)
97. No repayment schedule; all non-installment debt
98. Revolving fund
99. Length of debt D.K., N.A.

00. Loan repaid by time of interview; no auto loan, coded 5 or 0 in Col. 38; coded 0 in Col. 12

87	50-53	REMAINING INSTALLMENT DEBT (RID BOX)

XXXX. Code amount of INSTALLMENT DEBT LEFT TO PAY IN DOLLARS
9997. $9997 or more
0000. Inap.; Loan repaid by time of interview; no auto loan; coded 5 or 0 in col. 38; coded 0 in col. 12.

NOTE: THERE CAN BE NO N.A. AMOUNTS FOR RID ON CARS.

SINGLE CARD FORM

Project Number: 772	Project Name: Survey of Consumers	
Project Director: Phone:	Card Layout By: Phone: Date:	
Deck Number: 05	Source Document:	Trf. from cards:

Remarks: Example of card layout for Deck 05: Income I

Columns 1-40

FROM			POSSIBLE CODES		
Card	Col		X	Name	Field Size
		1 2 3	88	Study Number (772)	3
		4 5	89	Deck Number (05)	2
		6 7 8 9	90	Interview Number	4
		10 11 12 13 14	91	Head's Earned Income	5
		15 16 17 18 19	92	Wife's Earned Income	5
		20 21 22 23 24	93	Head: Mixed Labor/Capital Income	5
		25 26 27 28	94	Wife: Mixed Labor/Capital Income	4
		29			
		30 31 32 33 34	95	Head: Total Capital Income	5
		35 36 37 38 39	96	Wife Total Capital Income	5
		40			

Columns 41-80

FROM			POSSIBLE CODES		
Card	Col		X	Name	Field Size
		41 42 43 44	97	Head: Total Transfer Payments	5
		45 46 47 48 49	98	Wife: Total Transfer Payments	5
		50 51 52 53 54			
		55 56 57 58 59 60 61 62 63 64 65 66 67 68 69 70 71 72 73 74 75 76 77 78 79 80			

1968 Survey of Consumer Finances
Card 05
N = 2677

FU INCOME WORKSHEET

> This card is coded on the Income Worksheet by the editors. Major components of income are assigned.

Variable Number	Column Number	
88	1-3	Study Number (772)
89	4-5	Card Number (05)
90	6-9	Interview Number (4 digits)
91	10-14	Q. D9, D11. D12a. Earned Income: HEAD Wage, salary, professional, trade and "other self-employment income. (Lines 1 + 2) XXXXX. Code amount in DOLLARS 99997. $99,997 or more 00000. Zero such income; no income from this source
92	15-19	D. D15, D16. Earned Income: WIFE Wage, salary, professional, trade and "other self-employment" income. (Lines 1 + 2) XXXXX. Code amount in DOLLARS 99997. $99,997 or more 00000. Zero such income; no income from this source
93	20-24	Mixed-Labor – Capital Income: HEAD XXXXX. Code amount in DOLLARS 99997. $99,997 or more 00000. Zero such income: no income from this source –XXXX. Negative amount to $-9999

Variable Number	Column Number	
94	25-29	Mixed-Labor-Capital Income: WIFE

XXXXX. Code amount in DOLLARS
99997. $99,997 or more
00000. Zero such income no income from this source
–XXXX. Negative amount to $-9999

95	30-34	Total Capital Income: HEAD

XXXXX. Code amount in DOLLARS
99997. $99997 or more
00000. Zero such income: no income from this source
–XXXX. Negative amount ot $-9999

96	35-39	Total Capital Income: WIFE

XXXXX. Code amount in DOLLARS
99997. $99997 or more
00000. Zero such income: no income from this source
–XXXX. Negative amount up to $-9999

97	40-44	Total Transfer Payments: HEAD

XXXXX. Code amount in DOLLARS
99997. $99997 or more
00000. Zero disposable income
–XXXX. Negative amount up to $-9999

98	45-49	Total Transfer Payments: WIFE

XXXXX. Code amount in DOLLARS
99997. $99997 or more
00000. Zero such income: no income from this source
–XXXX. Negative amount to $-9999

SINGLE CARD FORM

Project Number: 772	Project Name: Survey of Consumers	
Project Director: Phone:		Card Layout By: Phone: Date:
Deck Number: 06	Source Document:	Trf. from Cards:

Remarks: Example of card layout for Deck 06: Income II

Columns 1-40						Columns 41-80					
FROM			POSSIBLE CODES			FROM			POSSIBLE CODES		
Card	Col		X	Name	Field Size	Card	Col		X	Name	Field Size
		1	99	Study Number (772)	3			41	112	FU: dividends BKT	1
		2						42	113	FU: rent interest BKT	1
		3						43	114	FU: soc. sec. BKT	1
		4	100	Deck Number (06)	2			44	115	FU: other retir. BKT	1
		5						45	116	FU: other trans. BKT	1
		6	101	Interview Number	4			46	117	Minor earners	1
		7						47	118	Major earners	1
		8						48	119	Owns business	1
		9						49	120	Employment status	1
		10	102	FU: Earned Income	5			50			
		11						51			
		12						52			
		13						53			
		14						54			
		15	103	FU: Mixed Labor/ Capital Income	5			55			
		16						56			
		17						57			
		18						58			
		19						59			
		20	104	FU: Total Capital Income	5			60			
		21						61			
		22						62			
		23						63			
		24						64			
		25	105	FU: Total Transfer Income	5			65			
		26						66			
		27						67			
		28						68			
		29						69			
		30	106	FU: Total Income	6			70			
		31						71			
		32						72			
		33						73			
		34						74			
		35						75			
		36	107	FU: total wages BKT	1			76			
		37	108	FU: professional BKT	1			77			
		38	109	FU: roomer inc. BKT	1			78			
		39	110	FU: farm inc. BKT	1			79			
		40	111	FU: business inc. BKT	1			80			

Survey Research Center
Economic Behavior Program

Study 772
January 1968

1968 Survey of Consumers
Card 06
N = 2677
FU INCOME WORKSHEET (Brackets)

This Card is coded on the Income Worksheet by the Editors. Major components of income are assigned.

Variable Number	Column Number	
99	1-3	Study Number (772)
100	4-5	Card Number (06)
101	6-9	Interview Number (4 digits)
102	10-14	Earned Income: FU

Wage, salary, professional trade and "other self-employment" income (subtotal A)

XXXXX. Code amount in DOLLARS
99997. $99,997 or more
00000. Zero such income; no income from this source

103	15-19	Mixed-Labor-Capital Income: FU (Subtotal B)

XXXXX. Code amount in DOLLARS
99997. $99,997 or more
00000. Zero such income; no income from this source
–XXXX. Negative amount to $-9999

104	20-24	Total Capital Income: FU (Subtotal C)

XXXXX. Code amount in DOLLARS
99997. $99,997 or more
00000. Zero income
–XXXX. Negative amount up to $-9999

105	25-29	Total Transfer Payments: FU (Subtotal D)

XXXXX. Code amount in DOLLARS
99997. $99,997 or more

106	30-35	Total Income: FU (F = Subtotal A + B + C + D)

XXXXXX. Code amount in DOLLARS
999997. $999,997 or more
000000. Zero income
–XXXXX. Negative amount up to $-99,999

Variable Number	Column Number	
107	36	Total Wages: FU
		0. Zero, no income from this source 1. $1-499; negative income 2. $500-999 3. $1000-1999 4. $2000-2999 5. $3000-4999 6. $5000-7499 7. $7500-9999 8. $10,000 and over
108	37	Total Professional, Trade, Other Self-Employed: FU
		0. Zero, no income from this source 1. $1-4999; negative income 2. $500-999 3. $1000-1999 4. $2000-2999 5. $3000-4999 6. $5000-7499 7. $7500-9999 8. $10,000 and over
109	38	Total Roomers, Non-farmers Income: FU
		0. Zero, no income from this source 1. $1-499; negative income 2. $500-999 3. $1000-1999 4. $2000-2999 5. $3000-4999 6. $5000-7499 7. $7500-9999 8. $10,000 and over
110	39	Total Farm Income: FU
		(Code same as in col. 38)
111	40	Total Unincorporated Business Income: FU
		(Code same as in col. 38)
112	41	Total Dividends: FU
		(Code same as in col. 38)
113	42	Total Rent, Interest, Trusts: FU
		(Code same as in col. 38)

Variable Number	Column Number	
114	43	Total Social Security: FU
		(Code same as in col. 38)
115	44	Total "Other" Retirement Pay: FU
		(Code same as in col. 38)
116	45	Total "Other" Transfer Payments: FU
		(Code same as in col. 38)
117	46	Number of Minor Earners
		($1-599 when lines 3 and 7 are added)
		0. None 1. One . . . etc. 9. Nine or more
118	47	Number of Major Earners
		($600 or more when lines 3 and 7 are added)
		0. None 1. One . . . etc. 9. Nine or more
119	48	Whether own a business (Q. D5, D7)
		1. Corporation 2. Unincorporated 3. Both kinds 8. NA, DK whether incorporated 9. NA, DK 0. Does not own a business
120	49	Q. D21. Are you (HEAD) working now, unemployed, or laid off or what?
		1. Retired 2. Permanently disabled 3. Housewife 4. Handles own Investments Only 5. Student 6. Working now 7. Unemployed, sick, or laid off 8. Retired and working now; retired and unemployed, 9. N.A., D.K., See Supervisor before using this code.

CHECKING THE COMPLETENESS AND CONSISTENCY OF THE DATA

At this point in the process, the data have been transferred to the storage media, most likely 80-column punch cards. However, performing any analyses with great confidence in the completeness or technical quality of the data would overlook the likelihood that a large number of problems still exist in the data. Here is a list of major deficiencies that can be found in most survey data at this point, most with near certainty:

1. Failure to have contacted every address in the sample originally drawn. Some sort of interview should have been received from every address in the sample.
2. Wide variations in the response rate to the survey that are correlated with various population characteristics. This leads to bias in population estimates.
3. The existence of code values (punches in the cards) which are *invalid* (not members of the computer's character set) or *illegal* (not acceptable to the analysis programs to be used).
4. The existence of code values which are valid and legal, but which are not in the code for the variable in question. For example, a 7 recorded for a variable containing data that should be coded 1 (yes) or 2 (no) would be termed *wild*.
5. Missing or duplicate records. This is especially likely when several cards of data per observation are coded.
6. Inconsistencies in the data. For example, the response to a yes/no question about owing debt is coded "no," yet a nonzero value is recorded in the field containing the amount of debt owed.

The existence of these kinds of errors must be detected and must be corrected before analysis, or even variable building, can proceed.

There are many alternatives available to the researcher for dealing with these problems. This chapter makes two assumptions: (1) that all data were put on 80-column punched cards after coding and stored as card images, and (2) that a computer will be used to process the data. The discussion is geared to the most widely used technology and data-storage media but employs a conceptual structure which is easily applied when any kind of equipment is used. The principles set forth here apply regardless of how many interviews are gathered. Smaller projects simply require less formal and extensive recordkeeping and no division of labor. With only a few hundred interviews, using a computer for these tasks is a decided advantage over manual procedures. The gains are truly impressive if the study is larger.

If a study is very complex, it may be impractical to check for all possible inconsistencies. The researcher must decide which checks are essential and which are less important or can be best dealt with during the analysis phase of the study as problems arise. When checking is done on the computer, it is usually accomplished quickly; but, even here, large amounts of time can be consumed in the process of looking up and correcting inconsistencies when possible. Thus, there is always a need for a judicious selection of the checks to be made. The researcher should:

1. Decide what checks are to be made. Remember, the fewer the checks, the simpler the checking programs and the correcting process.
2. Write and check out the computer programs. Use data known to contain specific inconsistencies (contrived data are generally preferable).
3. Organize and flowchart the correcting process, including a specific procedure for making corrections in the data and recording what was done.

Figure 6-1 provides a rough overview of the consistency check process. Dating such a form would provide scheduling guidelines for the completion of many of the tasks required for this part of the processing operation. For example, all consistency-check programs should be written and checked out with test data prior to the time the actual data are available to be checked. If the checking is to be done in two parts, an estimate must be made as to when about half of the data will be out of the coding operation and be keypunched. This type of scheduling eliminates many lost days. Each step shown may be more than one operation. For example, if there are two decks of cards in the study, two wild-code checks will have to be run. It is sometimes desirable to set up a time table for the processing of each of the decks in the study.

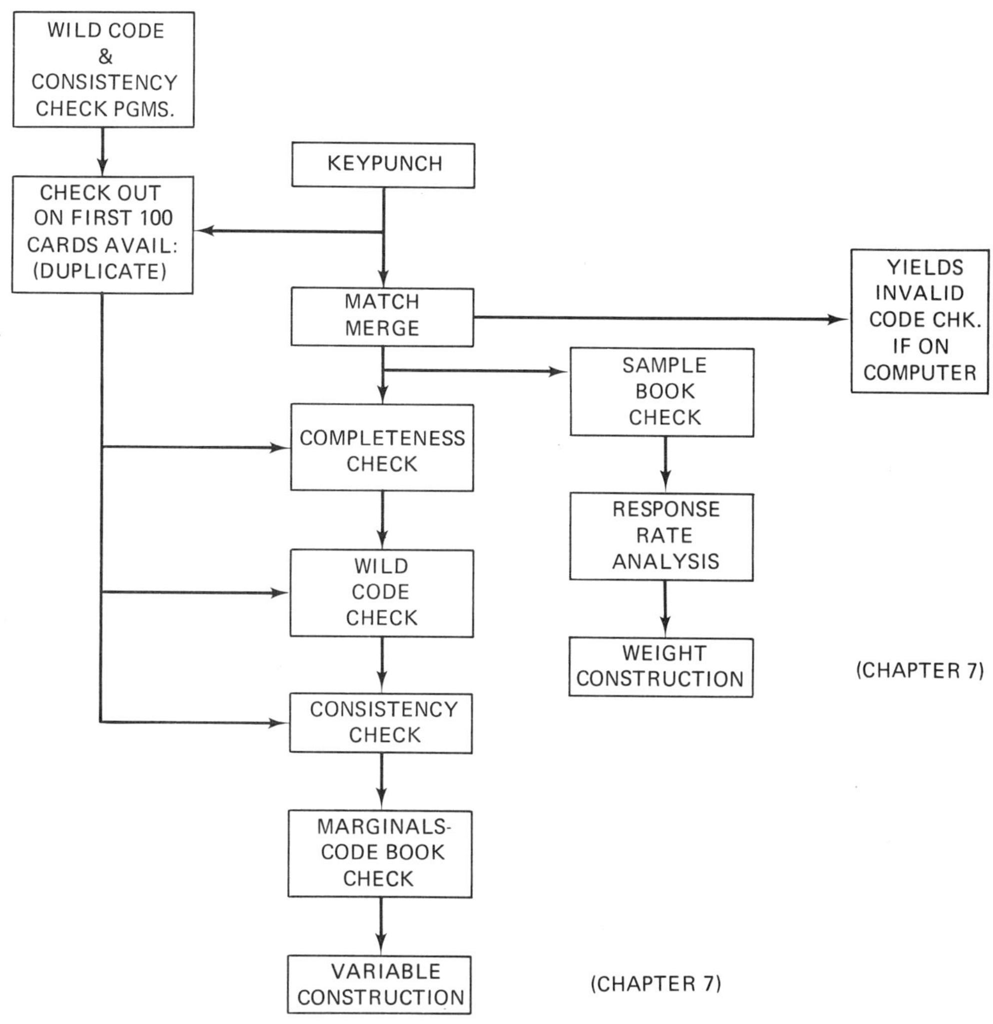

Figure 6-1 Consistency Checking Process

COMPLETENESS OF THE FILE

There are two major aspects of file completeness to be dealt with: (1) the number of cards contained in a deck must be correct; and (2) when there is more than one deck (i.e., more than one card of data per observation), there must be a one-to-one correspondence between the cards in each deck. (How the "correct" number of cards is determined, is discussed in the next section, "Sample Book Check".) At this point every member of the sample must be accounted for, either as a response with a complete set of data for that sample point, or as a nonresponse of one type or another. The number of cards in the master deck for the study should equal the number of sample responses.

If there is more than one data card per unit of analysis, the first step is to check that there are exactly the right number of cards for each respondent. Frequently, cards are punched twice or not at all. This may result from the keypunching or because coders miscopy interview numbers. Any such error results in parallel data files in which cards in one file have no matching counterpart in the others. For example, in a case with two cards per respondent, there should be a card 01 and a card 02 for each respondent, as illustrated in Figure 6-2. This file is perfectly *match-merged* on interview number. Card 01 for interview 0001 is followed by card 02 for that interview, cards 01 and 02 for interview 0002 follow, and so on. There are no missing or duplicate cards.

Data File
772010001XXXXX
772020001XXX
772010002XXXXX
772020002XXX
772010003XXXXX
772020003XXX

CARD 1

Column Number	Description
1-3	STUDY (772)
4-5	DECK NUMBER (1)
6-9	INTERVIEW NUMBER
10-14	DATA

CARD 2

Column Number	Description
1-3	STUDY (772)
4-5	DECK NUMBER (2)
6-9	INTERVIEW NUMBER
10-12	DATA

Figure 6-2 Match Merged File and Data Codes

Frequently, however, the data may look as in Figure 6-3 after they have been match-merged. This file illustrates some of the errors typically found in a match-merge check. Card 01 is missing for interview 0002, and there is a duplicate of card 01 for 0003 that was punched incorrectly but not removed after keypunching. Or, possibly, the missing card 01 for interview 0002 was mispunched as 0003. Card 02 for 0004 is missing, and there are duplicates of card 01 for interview 0005. Perhaps card 01 for 0005 was punched twice, or coders coded card 01 twice. All such errors and inconsistencies must be eliminated before the data can be processed further, especially if cross-card consistency checks are to be made.

Sample Book Check

For numerous reasons not discussed here, not all respondents in a sample will yield a usable interview. Consequently, there will not be a complete set of data for every analysis unit in the sample. (In Figure 6-2, a complete set of data is exactly one card 01 and exactly one card 02.) Thus, the data records must be

Data File	
772010001XXXXX	
772020001XXX	
	Card 01 for 0002 is missing.
772020002XXX	
772010003XXXXX	
	There are duplicates of Card 01 for 0003
772010003XXXXX	
772020003XXX	
772010004XXXXX	
	Card 02 is missing for 0004
772010005XXXXX	
772010005XXX	
	There are duplicates of Card 01 for 005 and Card 02 is missing or the deck number is incorrect.
772010006XXXXX	
772020006XXX	

Figure 6-3 Match Merged File with Errors

checked against the original sampling of respondents to ensure that every address and every respondent was contacted.

To facilitate such as check, units for which no interview is taken (a nonresponse) should be accounted for. A convenient method is a data card in a nonresponse file which indicates the sample identification number of the nonresponse and any other available information on the address of the sampled unit. This sample identification number should also be included on one of the regular data cards of each successfully completed interview (on card 01 or card 02 in our example). Once the missing and duplicate cards from the interview files have been resolved, the master data file can be match-merged with the nonresponse file on sample identification number. This should exactly match and completely exhaust the sample book list of addresses and respondents.

Response Rates and the Computation of Weights

There are several reasons for undertaking an analysis of the response rates. If data from the study are to be generalized, it is necessary to generate evidence of the extent to which those respondents reached differed from those not reached. Clearly, the differences must be measured with respect to those characteristics that the interviewer can verify without actually interviewing the potential respondent (such as housing status, region of residence, city size, race, and similar relatively observable data). The response-rate analysis produces control information that describes the extent to which the field procedures effectively generated the sample they were intended to produce. These data are a prerequisite to any decision about weighting actual responses for analysis, and they are essential to interpreting the findings of the study. Results may be subject to wide margins of error if the response rate is low, or if there are large differences in the response rate that are correlated with variables of particular interest to the study. Response rates often vary between rural and urban settings.[1]

The data needed for response-rate calculations consist of a file containing one record for each data-collection unit (usually one interview) that was generated during the field work. In a typical national sample of families, dwelling units might be sampled and then listings made of all families in the dwelling unit. Where several families live in a dwelling unit, one interview is obtained from a designated respondent in each family. The file needed for a response-rate analysis would consist of a record for each family, whether interviewed or not. Where the interviewer is unable to obtain an interview, a "cover" sheet is turned in for the family with any information about the lost interview that can be gained by observation or by questioning neighbors.

These records each contain the unique sample book number that defines that dwelling unit (i.e., segment, and primary sampling unit information), as well as data about the location of the unit and other relevant characteristics. These might include such factors as whether it is in a central city; how far it is from the city center; the interviewer's interview sequence number; the date it was obtained; the total number of calls made before the interview was obtained; length of the interview in minutes; county, state, and city codes; family-composition information; reasons an interview could not be obtained (e.g., house vacant, not a dwelling, not at home, respondent absent, refusal, noneligible respondent, etc.); type of structure; type of neighborhood; estimated monthly rent of dwelling unit; estimated family income of the missing family; estimated number of adults in the family; whether or not there is a married couple in the family; race of the head of the family; and age and sex of the head of the family. This is often coupled with the interviewer's rating of how good the information is upon which the estimates of these attributes are based.

When all these records are listed in ascending sequence according to their sample book numbers, it is then possible to make a one-to-one match with the sampling frame. This verifies that all the addresses have been visited, that there are no inconsistencies in the number of families reported at each address, and that there is exactly one interview or non-interview record for every family whose presence was detected in the interviewing process. This same file is used to determine to what extent there appear to be differences in the observed attributes of not-at-homes, refusals, and families from whom an interview was obtained.

If there are extensive and systematic differences in the response rates for various sample strata, it may be desirable to use weights to compensate for these

[1] For a further discussion, see Lansing and Morgan (1971, Chap. 3). Sometimes outside information can provide clues to the nature of nonresponse problems. In a study of credit-card users, credit application data provided information about those not responding to a mail questionnaire (Dunkelberg, 1973).

varying rates. If estimation of population parameters is a primary purpose of the study, then to the extent that respondents and nonrespondents differ on the characteristics to be estimated, weighting will provide some correction. On the other hand, if explanation and the study of correlations between variables is the purpose of the study, then weighting would only be required if there were reason to suspect that the absent non-responders may seriously influence the relationship between the variables to be studied. Lansing and Morgan (1971, pp. 233–236) argue that the more multivariate the analysis, the less likely it is to be affected by response-rate problems.

Figure 6-4 illustrates response-rate calculations. The array of sampled families is shown divided into primaries and secondaries. From these are subtracted the non-sample addresses and non-eligible respondents. The response rate, then, is simply one minus the proportion of non-interviews. Figure 6-5 illustrates this computation for a study in which interviews are obtained in urban and rural areas. The rate varies from 73 per cent in the central cities of the 12 largest Standard Metropolitan Statistical Areas (SMSA's) to 90 per cent in rural areas. The calculation procedure removes the nonsample records (i.e., unoccupied, not habitable, not occupied because of new construction, not a dwelling unit, no eligible respondent) from the file first. Then, using the interviews and the sample-but-no-interview records, the analysis is performed. The dependent variable is "disposition of the cover sheet." The proportion of interviews in each class of the independent variable shows the response rate directly (i.e., it shows the proportion of cover sheets that ended up as interviews rather than as refusals, not-at-homes, etc.).

A response-rate report should include definitions of the terms used in the computations, computational formulas, and comparisons of the sample statistics with other surveys over the same population, if possible. When possible, it should include an analysis of response rates classified by relevant variables. A non-response is generally defined as any failure to obtain a usable interview from an analysis unit that properly falls into the sample.

Sampled Families		5219
Addresses	5163	
Secondary Families	56	
Non-sample addresses		703
Non-eligible Respondent		659
Interviews		3165
Non-interviews (refusal, etc.)		692

$$\text{Response Rate } R = 1 - \frac{692}{5219 - 703 - 659} = \quad 82.1\%$$

Figure 6-4 Response Rate Computations
(Used with permission of The Survey Research Center of the Institute for Social Research, The University of Michigan.)

RESPONSE RATE

Size of Place (1960 Census Classification)	Interview + Non-interview	Interviews	Rate %
Central Cities of 12 largest SMSA's	557	405	72.7
Cities 50,000 and over (except central cities of 12 largest SMSA's)	863	665	77.1
Urban Places 10,000 – 49,999	665	550	82.7
Urban Places 2500 – 9999; urbanized areas not included above.	818	688	84.1
Rural, in an SMSA PSU	183	160	87.4
Rural, not in an SMSA PSU	771	697	90.4
TOTAL	3,857	3,165	82.1

Note: Response rate = Int's/Ints + Non-Ints.
Project 763 MTRS 107, 18

Figure 6-5 Response Rate by Size of Place
(Used with permission of The Survey Research Center of the Institute for Social Research of The University of Michigan.)

If, for a personal interview survey, the response rate is below 80 per cent and wide differences in rates exist between strata which could have an effect on study findings, then weighting often should be undertaken. If the computer programs to be used will not accept weights, then an "exploded" file (one in which interview records are physically reproduced the number of times indicated by the associated weight) should be developed after the wild-code and consistency-checking operations have been successfully completed. A random sample of interviews from each stratum is selected and reproduced to obtain the required number of observations in that stratum.

An example illustrates the need for weights and how they might be used. Suppose that a study is designed which is not primarily concerned with the behavior of people over 60 years of age. Yet, to put the findings in perspective, it might be deemed desirable to obtain data on the behavior of elderly respondents. To save money, only half of all respondents over 60 might be interviewed, yielding enough data to provide background statistics with adequate statistical accuracy. Thus, the first question asked of each potential respondent is his or her age. The interviewer is supplied with a random method for deciding whether or not to take the interview. When all interviews have been taken, there will be only about half as many respondents over 60 as there would have been if interviews had been taken with the entire sample.

Clearly, no correct estimate of the age distribution of the population can be made from the data as sampled. The proportion of elderly will be understated, and all other proportions correspondingly overstated. Moreover, population estimates of central tendency and dispersion of other variables cannot be made, since these are often correlated in unknown ways with age. Weighting provides a reasonable solution to this problem. Since the elderly included in the sample were selected randomly, we can assume that they were like the ones we did not interview. If we physically reproduce the data records of the over-60 respondents and add the duplicates to the sample, there would be an appropriate number of respondents in the over-60 category and our age distribution would then be a far better estimate of the population that we sampled originally. Basically, the procedure has assigned a weight of 2 to all respondents over 60, and a weight of 1 to all others. It is assumed that we have corrected the bias in the distributions of all other characteristics affected by our undersampling of the elderly, since those included in our sample are like those we did not interview. Other methods of dealing with weights will be discussed later in this chapter and in Chapters 7 and 8.

There are a few more sophisticated problems that have been introduced by this procedure, however. Suppose that the sample originally drawn was a simple random sample. Associated with this sample are means, proportions, variances, and so on, that can be used to estimate population values, provided that we actually adhere to simple random-sampling assumptions. For example, we might say that the mean age of the population was estimated to be 31 and attach an estimate of the sampling error of this statistic. Ordinarily, estimates of sampling error reflect the size of the sample for which the computed mean was computed. However, we have deviated from a truly random-sampling procedure by including only half of the respondents over age 60 and attaching a weight of 2 to them by duplicating their information. The effect of this has been to reduce, by unknown and possibly varying amounts, the variation of all the characteristics that we have measured. This causes us to overstate the reliability of our findings if we base our estimates of sampling errors on the downwardly biased standard deviations calculated from our data. An example illustrates the problem. Suppose that two elderly people both fell into our sample and lived next door to one another. At least some of their characteristics would be identical (e.g., city of residence), but others would not be. Our procedure would be likely to take one and omit the other. Then we would reproduce the one obtained, using it as an estimate of the one we omitted. The true differences between the two people are certainly not zero for most characteristics (e.g., their ages, income, family size, education). But our estimates would show no difference. This pattern would be reproduced over our entire group of over-60 respondents. Thus, we would have reduced the variance of each of these characteristics in our sample, and perhaps removed some of their explanatory power in a correlational analysis.

From this viewpoint, we can now see the nature of the problem that differential response rates present, an important difference being that one has much less control over the process that generates reduced variation. First, there is not one single characteristic, such as a procedure which selects half of the elderly, that we can use to explain the differences in response rates. For example, suppose that we have only half of the number of elderly people that we should, but it is because no elderly people living in big cities will open their doors for an interview, not because we have decided to interview every other one on a random basis. To simply double the number of over-60 respondents in this case is clearly a mistake. The over-60 respondents that live in central cities are better representative of those not interviewed than are the larger group of all respondents over age 60. So, it is better to weight the former. The difference between population estimates using these two alternatives to establish weights can be illustrated by considering what would happen if other variables were correlated with the non-response factors. For example, what if all respondents over 60 in the big cities had incomes twice as large as their rural counterparts? Clearly, there is a need for a careful response-rate analysis prior to analyzing the data. However, weighting is not a totally satisfactory way to deal with the problem of non-response. A variety of unmeasured characteristics may, in fact, be the factors determining response-rate differentials. Yet, a careful analysis and the use of weights is often adequate, and is superior to taking no corrective action.

A common procedure is to calculate weights as follows and to attach a weight variable to every valid interview in the file. Then all computations are carried out, using weighted formulas with appropriate corrections for degrees of freedom associated with significance tests and confidence intervals (Kish, 1965; Frankel, 1971).

1. Divide the population into k mutually exclusive strata according to the desired combinations of variables. Each stratum i has N_i observations.
2. Estimate the proportion p_i of the total population that should be represented by the ith stratum, $0 < p_i < 1$ for $i = 1$ to k.
3. Assign the weight w_i to all observations in the ith stratum such that $w_i = (p_i/N_i)N$.

This normalizes the sum of weights to the sample size. If the computer programs to be used require integer weights, however, this procedure must be supplemented by a further normalizing process which sets the smallest weight equal to 1 and rounds all other weights to the nearest integer. Weights should not be used which employ more than two digits because of the rounding error associated with the use of floating-decimal arithmetic in computing equipment. Keep the sum of weights as small as is consistent with adequate compensation for missing interviews. The mechanics of weight construction are discussed in Chapter 7.

Character Set Check

Invalid characters are all those punch combinations that are not acceptable to the devices to be used in processing and analysis. *Illegal* characters are those not acceptable to at least one of the computer programs to be used. *Wild* codes are those characters which are valid and possibly legal but which are not meaningful in the context of the code written to describe the data. For example, a 7 punched in a particular column may be valid and legal, but it has no meaning if the data in the column were to have been represented by a 1, 5, or 9 (perhaps a "yes," "no," or "not ascertained" code). An A would be valid (able to be read by the computer) but would probably be illegal to most statistical-analysis programs.

If the data are to be put on the computer for manipulation, then all invalid codes will be discovered by the computer as it is reading the data in for the first time. Most computer devices refuse to accept input that contains invalid codes. If they are frequent, this can be an expensive way to locate such codes (in terms of delays and expensive computer time used), but there is little alternative. The likelihood of the occurrence of such codes is low, as keypunch equipment produces only valid characters unless there is mechanical failure or the keypunch operator inadvertently double-punches a single column. The criteria used for judging whether a code is valid is the character set accepted by the processing equipment. (See Appendix I for generally accepted valid characters.)

Code *legality* depends on the input requirements of the computer programs to be used. Punches are legal if accepted as valid character input by all the programs to be used. An example of a valid character that is illegal is the character A punched in a numerical field being read with a numerical format (either integer or floating decimal). Computer programs designed to accept numerical data will reject such "illegal" characters, a good thing from the standpoint of error control. But having the program stop when such input is encountered can be expensive if such errors are numerous, and it is desirable to remove such characters before attempting to read the fields or columns that contain them. The alternative is to read them as alphanumeric characters first, and check them for legality.

The code book itself is the criterion for determining whether or not a legal character (or set of characters) in a field is wild. Wild codes are those that have no meaning in the context of the data code that has been established. This clearly includes all illegal as well as some legal characters.

The logic of the wild-code check is simple. The researcher specifies the set of acceptable (or unacceptable) legal characters for each column of the data card(s). This is compared against the observed contents of each column on the cards to determine the acceptability of each character. There are often library computer programs available for such checks. They typically print the identification fields of each data card that contains errors (e.g., interview and card number) and list the offending columns and the invalid codes.

Correcting the data is most often a largely manual task, first requiring that each interview be looked at to determine what the actual code value should be. Then the data cards must be corrected. Corrections can be made manually on the keypunch or by a program designed to look up the card in error and replace the offending character with one supplied by the researcher.

If the correction strategy has been laid out in advance, considerable time is saved. Input decks to be checked should be placed in ascending sequence on interview number, since the instruments are generally stored in the same order, and this makes for a straightforward job of looking up the errors.

Written corrections can often be made on the output of the wild-code check program for later punching as input to the file correction programs, or they can be set up on a worksheet to facilitate manual corrections using a keypunch. It may also be convenient to use a form that has space for column numbers and the new codes to be put in them, with spaces for noting the proper identification numbers of the interview and card deck to be altered.

The exact procedure for a wild-code check will depend on the options available locally for correcting the data file. If the data set is small, the process may often be quickly and conveniently carried out on a counter–sorter, using the code book to indicate the proper code values for each column. If a computer program is used, the changes will generally have to be collected, usually on a summary form, for keypunching or key entry through a computer terminal. Examples of two possible summary forms are shown in Figure 6-6. These provide good records of the actual changes made to the data, and should be kept and added to the processing memo files. The correction form, of course, assumes a particular kind of correction program. The form in the upper half of Figure 6-6 is useful as input to a correction program that requires the location of the interview and card number. It assumes that these data are correct and uses them to identify cards in the file to be corrected. Any problems with the interview and deck numbers should already have been eliminated in the merge checking. The program scans the correction card to see if new values are specified to be put into the specified data record. It then either writes a new record on tape or disk, or punches out a corrected card to physically replace the one in error. Numerous corrections can be made at one time, including the insertion of an entirely new record.

The lower half of Figure 6-6 illustrates the input to a correction program that makes only one correction at a time. More than one column can be corrected, however, as long as they are contiguous. Several lines (several input cards for the correction program) may be required to correct an individual record. These example forms are designed to facilitate preparation of punched-card input to a computer correction program. If the corrections are to be done

Interview number in 0 6 to 0 9 Deck number in 0 4 to 0 5

Column Number

```
0         1         2         3         4         5         6         7         8
12345678901234567890123456789012345678901234567890123456789012345678901234567890

030071                      7
170107                                 07500
050321          00000            99                       4     17500
011089                  27
071089                                     4           9999      9999
111089          2799           5      8        1               0000      0
```

INT				DECK		COL				NEW CODE				
0	0	7	1	0	3	2	9			7				
0	1	0	7	1	7	4	0	4	4	0	7	5	0	0
0	3	2	1	0	5	1	8	2	3	0	0	0	0	0
0	3	2	1	0	5	4	4	4	5	9	9			
0	3	2	1	0	5	5	8			4				
0	3	2	1	0	5	6	4	6	8	1	7	5	0	0
1	0	8	9	0	1	2	6	2	7	2	7			
1	0	8	9	0	7	4	4			4				
1	0	8	9	0	7	5	6	5	9	9	9	9	9	
1	0	8	9	0	7	6	6	6	9	9	9	9	9	

Figure 6-6 Two Examples of Wild Code Correction Forms

manually, other summarizing forms may be more useful. If a professional keypunching staff is to be employed, they should be consulted about the format of the correction inventory forms. Sometimes corrections can be made interactively, using a computer terminal and a "text editor" utility program. When this is available, it may well be the best choice.

It may be worthwhile to undertake part of the task of consistency checking the data while doing the wild-code check. Such variables as house value, income, and debt owed are subject to a particular kind of coding error, the misplaced digit. This can arise from failure to right-adjust a number in a wide field, or by transposing digits. For example, an income of \$7500 may be coded 750000 instead of 007500 in a field of six columns set aside for the purpose. Or an income of \$15000 might be coded 51000. In general, it pays to locate and verify extreme values that may appear in the study, as they will have a large impact on the computation of the statistics. One way to sort out the extreme cases is to specify certain characters as wild, when, indeed, they are technically acceptable. In the example just cited, any code other than 0, 1, or 2 might be specified as wild in the first column of the field. This would flag any respondent that had an income of \$300,000 or more for verification in the error-correction process.

Such a procedure is not all extra work, since there is a significant likelihood that the interview will have to be pulled to check other errors, especially if the study is fairly complex.

The final check on the quality of characters depends on the determination of their consistency as variables. Our emphasis here is on card columns only to the extent that they correspond to variables in the study. It is characteristics, not characters, that are the issue in this evaluation of the data. Any two or more variables in the study may have acceptable codes and yet be inconsistent with one another, owing to coding errors, editing errors, or errors made by the interviewer or respondent. For example, if the respondent reports that he owns no car, it is expected that all the data relating to the characteristics of the car owned will be zero, consistent with the fact that he owns no car. Yet, if he leased a car, the data on that make and model might incorrectly have been recorded by the interviewer. This error may then have been missed by the editor and coded by the coder. The wild-code check procedures would not uncover the problem, since 0 is an acceptable code for car ownership and nonzero codes are acceptable in the fields making up the variables MAKE and MODEL. This is the kind of error that the consistency check must uncover.

Before discussing consistency checking in detail, it is useful to summarize the discussion to this point regarding the codes that appear on the data cards or other storage media and the criteria used to evaluate the quality of the data. Note that the entire checking process might conceivably be attempted on one pass over the data, since a consistency-check procedure could be designed both to deal with wild and with illegal codes, as well as with inconsistencies. Often, however, the task would be too complex and even impossible if existing library programs must be used to do the checking. Anyway, there are advantages to breaking a large problem into smaller, manageable parts, especially if this facilitates dividing the work among several people. Figure 6-7 summarizes each step of the checking process and identifies the criteria used to evaluate the data.

CODE TYPE	CRITERIA
Valid or Invalid	The valid character set for the equipment to be used in processing the data.
Legal or Illegal	The set of characters that are acceptable to the computer programs that are to be used.
Wild or Acceptable	The set of characters used to identify information in the data code for the variable.
Consistent or Inconsistent	The logic of the data as organized in the data code for each variable in the study.

Figure 6-7 Criteria for Evaluating Character Quality

Wild-Code Check

Invalid and illegal code values will generally be detected in the process of loading the data onto a computer and attempting to execute some type of program using the data (such as a match–merge program). If this check has not been accomplished prior to this point, the possible existence of these types of errors must be kept in mind when constructing the wild-code check. Clearly, all illegal and invalid codes are included in the class of wild codes (those code values that are not included in the master data code as meaningful representations of information in the study).

In concept, the wild-code check is very simple. For each column containing data in the form of punches, the acceptable values can be identified in the code book. All columns containing wild codes should be flagged, the data checked in the original interview, and the errors corrected. The use of a counter-sorter best describes the process. The column indicator on the card sorter is set to the column to be checked. The cards are placed in the hopper and sorted. All cards are sorted into pockets of the sorter according to the code in the column to be checked. The code should agree with the distribution of cards in the sorter pockets. If there are cards in any pockets other than those corresponding to the code values, they are wild. Each erroneous card must be checked against the data in the original interview to ascertain the correct code value, and then it must be repunched.

A computer program designed to accomplish the same check is structured in essentially the same way. The program is supplied with lists of legal codes, one for each of the card columns to be checked. It reads a record, compares the contents of each such column against the corresponding list of legal codes, and flags all the errors detected. An image of each record having at least one error is printed, together with a set of indicators pointing out the columns in error. The printout of the error messages can then be employed in looking up the data in the original interviews and in recording the corrections made. The latter might also be transferred to a keypunch form with information showing the columns to be changed and the correct values to be used in fixing the offending card. The corrections are then punched onto cards. A keypunch may be used to duplicate the correct parts of the original deck and simultaneously to make the corrections needed, or the computer may be used to make the corrections. In either case, the corrected file is then run through the check a second time to ensure that the correction process worked satisfactorily.

The logic of the wild-code check is shown in Figure 6-8. An equivalent computer program can be equally simple, or very complex, depending primarily on the sophistication of the error diagnostics desired. A simple FORTRAN version is shown in Figure 6-9. It is designed to check card 2 in the example in Chapter 5. Only columns 10–20 are checked (columns 1–9 contain only identification numbers that will have been checked during the sample book listing).

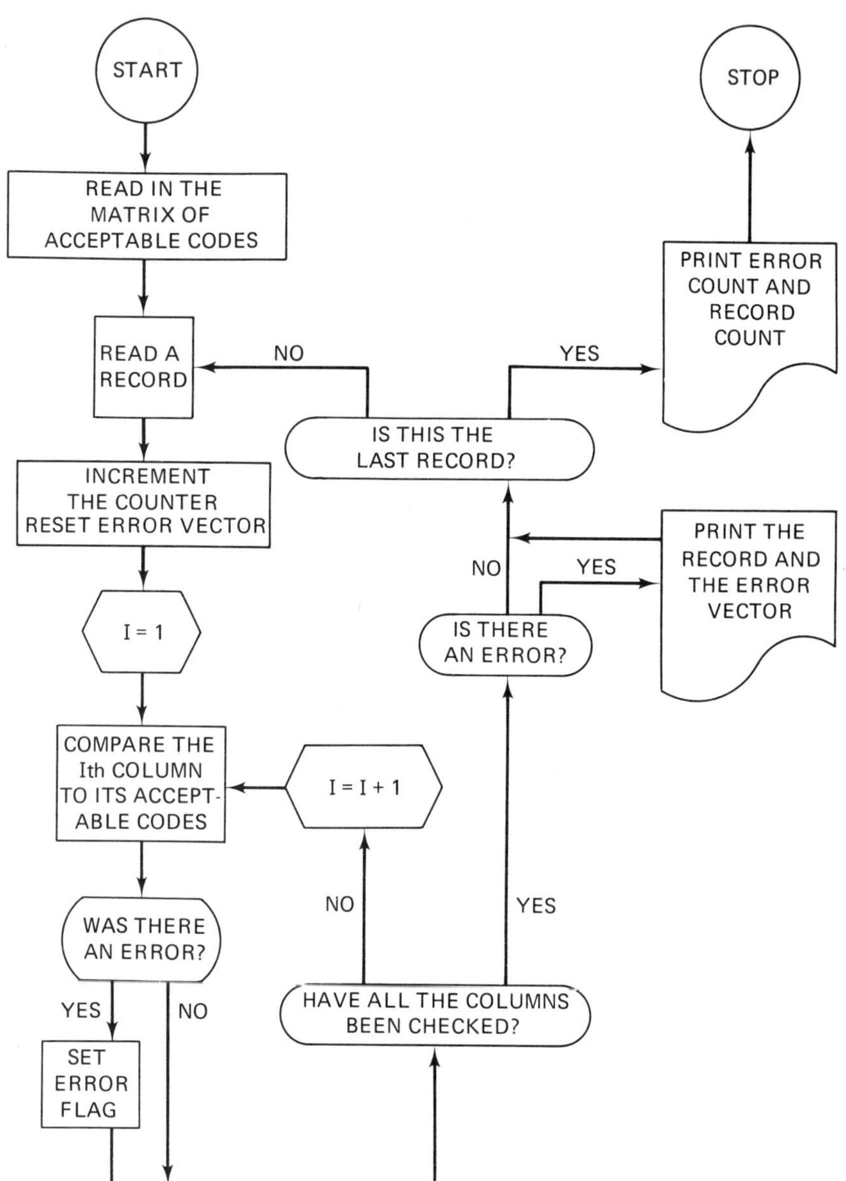

Figure 6-8 Wild Code Check Algorithm

The program was written to handle any number of records. Other columns could be checked by altering some of the limiting parameters in the program (e.g., array dimensions, loop limits). It would be very simple to check columns 10–80, for example, by changing the number 20 in every statement to the number 80,

```
C         PROGRAM TO WILD CODE CHECK CARD 2
          IMPLICIT INTEGER (A-Z)
C         DIMENSION THE ARRAYS AND ZERO OUT THE COUNTERS
          DIMENSION A(20, 11), C(20), E(20)
          CC=0
          ERCT=0
C         CC IS A COUNT OF THE RECORDS READ BY THE PROGRAM
C         ERCT IS A COUNT OF THE NUMBER OF RECORDS THAT ARE IN ERROR
C         READ IN THE LEGAL CODE VALUES FOR EACH COLUMN TO BE CHECKED
C         INSERT BLANK CARDS FOR COLUMNS NOT TO BE CHECKED
C         COLUMNS 1-2 OF EACH CARD MUST INDICATE THE NUMBER OF ACCEPTABLE
            CODE VALUES
C         COLUMNS 3-12 MUST CONTAIN THE ACCEPTABLE CODE VALUES, IN ANY
            ORDER, BUT WITH NO BLANK COLUMNS BETWEEN VALID CODES
C         THE PROGRAM ONLY CHECKS FOR THE INTEGER VALUES 0, 1, 2, 3, 4, 5, 6, 7, 8, 9
          CARDS MUST BE IN ASCENDING ORDER, CORRESPONDING TO THE COLUMNS TO
            BE CHECKED, FOLLOWED BY DATA DECK TO BE CHECKED
          DO 10, 1=1, 10
   10     READ (1, 11) (A(I,J), J=1, 11)
   11     FORMAT (I2), 10I1)
C         READ IN EACH RECORD ONE COLUMN AT A TIME (THE C ARRAY)
    1     READ (1, 15, END=999) (C(I), I=1, 20)
   15     FORMAT (20I1)
          CC=CC+1
C         STORE BLANKS IN THE ERROR INDICATOR ARRAY, E
          DO 5 I=1, 20
    5     E(I) = ' '
C         CHECK COLUMNS =0 TO 20. SET THE FLAG FOR A BAD RECORD TO 0
          BAD=0
          DO 50 I=10, 20
C         SET THE SCOPE OF THE ERROR CHECK LOOP EQUAL TO THE NUMBER OF
            ACCEPTABLE CODES FOR THE 1 TH COLUMN
          K=A(I, 1)
C         CHECK TO SEE IF THE COLUMN IS TO BE CHECKED
          IF(K.EQ.0) GO TO 50
C         SET THE FLAG FOR A BAD COLUMN IN A RECORD
          ERR=1
          DO 40 J=2, K
          IF(C(I). EQ.A(I,J)) ERR=0
   40     CONTINUE
          IF(ERR.EQ.1)E(I)='1'
C         IF ERR IS STILL 1, THE VALUE IN THE COLUMN FAILED TO MATCH ANY
C           OF THE ACCEPTABLE CODES SO A 1 IS PLACED IN THE APPROPRIATE
C           COLUMN OF THE E VECTOR TO BE PRINTED BELOW AN IMAGE OF THE
C           CARD. THIS FLAGS THE COLUMN IN ERROR. THE RECORD ALSO HAS
C           AN ERROR, SO BAD IS SET TO 1.
          IF(ERR.EQ.1)BAD=1
   50     CONTINUE
C         CHECK TO SEE IF THERE WERE ANY ERRORS. IF YES, PRINT THE RECORD
          IF(BAD.EQ.0)GO TO 1
          ERCT=ERCT+1
          WRITE(6,60)(C(I), I=1,20)
   60     FORMAT(1H0, 'WILD', 5X,20I1)
          WRITE(6, 70) (E(I), I=1, 20)
   70     FORMAT (1H , 'ERR IN', 3X, 20A1)
          GO TO 1
  999     WRITE (6, 1000) CC, ERCT
 1000     FORMAT (1H0, 'END', 5X, 'RECORDS=', I6, 5X 'NUMBER OF ERRORS=', I6)
          STOP
```

Figure 6-9 Wild Code Check Program and Legal Value Cards

```
Legal Code Value Cards For The Wild Code Check

     0513589

     06125690

     101234567890

     06125690

     101234567890

     041359

     03159

     101234567890

     101234567890

     101234567890

     101234567890
     ↑
     COLUMN 1
```

Figure 6-9 (cont'd.)

and by changing the loop statement to "DO 10 I = 1,70" so that 70 vectors of acceptable codes would be read instead of only 10. Additional lists of legal codes would have to be supplied at the end of the program, of course. Comment cards are used extensively in the program to explain the purpose of each instruction. This is useful to other staff members, and even helps the writer remember what the purpose of each line was.

Note that the lists of acceptable codes have a particular format that must be followed. The program expects that there will never be more than 10 acceptable code values. In this example, this might be the integers 0–9. (This could be changed by altering the dimension of the array A, the READ statement labeled 10, and the FORMAT statement labeled 11). The first element on the input card denotes the number of valid code values for the column in question. Two columns (1 and 2) are needed for this and the number is placed in them right-justified. Thus, for column 10, there are five valid codes (denoted 05 in columns 1 and 2). The codes are 1, 3, 5, 8, and 9. Any other value will be reported as wild.

The number of acceptable codes is used by the program to limit its comparisons to the number of acceptable values read in. This may vary with each column to be checked. The 10 cards together describe the acceptable values for columns 10–20 on card 2. The first two columns on each card always denote the number of acceptable values in the list, which then follow (in any order). There can be no blanks between the elements in the acceptable value list. Each card is read using format (I2, 10I1). There must be exactly one of these cards for each column being checked. The data to be checked follow the legal code cards.

An example of the output is shown below. The card image is printed out, preceded by the word "WILD." Each wild code is flagged with the number 1 printed underneath. When all cards have been processed, the program prints the number of records read and the total number of errors detected.

```
WILD       77202000211199812641
ERR IN                    1
WILD       77202000523260586874
ERR IN               11    1
END        RECORDS=   10     NUMBER OF ERRORS=  2
```

In the example, a wild code of 8 has been found in column 15 of interview 0002, card 02. In interview 0005, there were wild codes of 2, 3, and 8 in columns 10, 11, and 16, respectively. Any legal character could be used to denote the errors, an *, for example, by using it in place of the 1 enclosed in prime marks in the FORTRAN instruction immediately after the one labeled 40. If the printed output is properly spaced, the corrected values can be written directly on the computer ouput for use in making the actual corrections to the file. The printing of the card image might well be broken up to isolate the interview number and facilitate the reading of the error indicators. The program could be used to consistency-check also, since extreme values can be found by declaring large integers in the first column of a field as wild. For example, if the first column of the total price field has 7–9 declared wild, any reported price that exceeds $7000 will be flagged and can easily be checked for coding errors.

Once the wild-code check is complete, all errors detected in the data should be corrected before proceeding with any other checking. It is extremely difficult, usually, to write logic statements for consistency-checking purposes if one cannot be sure that the only code values present are acceptable. The importance of this will become more obvious as the strategy for consistency checking is set forth below. Since the data code is the source document for writing the consistency-check program, it must accurately describe the characters used to encode the data that are to be checked.

CONSISTENCY CHECKING THE DATA

The researcher should ask and answer several questions before beginning a consistency check of the data:

1. Which of the interrelated variables should be checked for inconsistencies? Some may be too vague to check, some not important enough,

others may have too small a probability of error, and still others will be essentially independent of the other variables in the study.

2. Have the results of the editing and coding processes been examined to identify problem areas that merit special attention in the consistency-check process? If there were frequent editing problems or coding questions regarding one or more variables, these are likely candidates for consistency problems. The Editors' Decision Book and the "make-a-card" procedure in coding provide this information.
3. Have all the corrections from the preceding steps been made? This makes the logic of the checks simpler.
4. Are there any tests of "reasonability" that should be made to help identify extreme cases that might be the result of miscoded information?
5. What is the logic of each check? In general terms, what are the directions of the implications contained in the consistency statements? If A implies B, does B also imply A?
6. Are there any checks that must be made across physical data-storage units (between card decks, for example)? If so, the data must be merged prior to the check.

Many of the variables in the study are not related to any other variable in a strictly logical way, as a rule. For example, family size may be related to car ownership in a correlational sense, but there is no strict rule relating the two and so a consistency check is not required. Yet, there are circumstances when this might be the case, however. In deciding which checks are necessary, one of the major sources of information will be the data code constructed for the study. In particular, each "contingency box" should be considered a candidate for checking. Usually, these boxes contain instructions to code zeros in fields that are not applicable if the respondent has answered a control question in a particular way. For example, the majority of variables on card 4 in our extended example are zeroed out if the respondent indicated that he did not own a car (0 code in column 12). If ownership of one car is reported, another contingency box instructs the coder to code 0 in column 23, the variable relating to multiple ownership. Similar examples can be found throughout the code. Such contingency boxes usually indicate checks that are worth making.

The information collected from the editing and coding process will also provide useful clues about possible relationships that should be consistency-checked. Reports of a large number of problems with a particular sequence in the questionnaire (e.g., the set of questions that measure total price, trade-in value, cash payments, and the amount borrowed in our autombile transaction) may indicate the need for a consistency check. A quick look through the editors' decision book will generally indicate which questions frequently presented problems. Similarly, if the coders had frequent problems classifying responses to particular questions, and these are logically related to other variables in the study, careful consistency checking may be in order. Information pertinent to deciding what to do can be found by examining the problem messages recorded by the coders during this phase of the study. These data will also provide insights into the precise nature of the consistency problem.

Logical Concepts in Consistency Checking

In Chapter 7, sets, propositions, and functions are discussed, with a view to developing a vocabulary for expressing the specifications for generating variables. The same vocabulary applies also to the selection of cases for inclusion in subfiles. In addition, it applies to consistency checks. Dealing with propositions about the values of variables, sets of observations for which these propositions are true, and actions to be taken upon recognition of true-or-false conditions, allows one to express clearly and concisely the logical relationships between variables that comprise the core of the consistency problem. This section presents summaries of two additional logical concepts of special importance for this phase of the data processing, and illustrates the ways in which they are used.

The expression $p \longrightarrow q$ means "p implies q." Another way of saying this is to assert that "if statement p is true, then statement q is also true." Statements of this form pertain to the coded values of the variables for a single interview. Any individual record can be inspected to see if, in fact, they are true for that record. If they are, the record is termed logically consistent. If at least one such statement is false for that record, it is termed inconsistent.

Some examples are "X coded 0 implies Y coded 0" and "AGE >= 21 IMPLIES VOTE68 NOT = 0." These statements reflect the way the data should have been gathered, coded, and keypunched. When an observation is examined, one can tell if the assertion is true or false when applied to it. If it is false, an error has been made somewhere along the line and some identifying information should be printed to indicate which observation is in error, and which requirements were not met. Then with the interview and the data record, the exact nature of the consistency problem can be ascertained and the data reconciled. An example will make the logical concepts clear. Assume that cash payments and borrowing money are the only methods of paying for a color-television set.

> Let p stand for "Respondent still owes money on it."
>
> Let q stand for "Purchased it by borrowing at least some of the price."

The logical connection between these two statements is that whenever p is true, then q must also be true. The truth table that defines this implication is shown

p	q	p → q
T	T	T
T	F	F
F	T	T
F	F	T

Figure 6-10 "Implication" Truth Table

in Figure 6-10. An observation in which the respondent is recorded as owing money ($p =$ true) and is also recorded as having borrowed ($q =$ true), passes the test (i.e., it is consistent). Passing the test is indicated by the T in the first row of the $p \longrightarrow q$ column of Figure 6-10. For this observation, p is true and q is true, so the assertion $p \longrightarrow q$ is also true and the observation meets the requirement.

When the respondent owes money ($p =$ true) but is recorded as never having borrowed ($q =$ false), there was an error in either interviewing, editing, coding, or keypunching. To reduce the symbolism to a more compact form, if $p =$ true and $q =$ false, then the assertion $p \longrightarrow q$ is false for this observation. It is inconsistent since it does not meet the requirement and must be corrected.

The configuration of the data in the fourth row of the truth table is as straightforward; the respondent owes no money now and did not borrow any. In the data, $p =$ false and $q =$ false, so for this condition the assertion $p \longrightarrow q$ is not contradicted by the data, and the observation passes the test.

The third row is less obvious. The respondent owes no money ($p =$ false), but there was some borrowed ($q =$ true). Should this be interpreted as an error? No. Logically, the debt could have been paid off by the time the interview was taken. The recorded answer pattern is consistent with the requirement that q implies p. When p is true, then q must be true, or else $p \longrightarrow q$ is false. However, when p is false, then q can be anything and still $p \longrightarrow q$ is always true.

The propositions p and q can be compound. For instance, p might well be of a form as complex as (r AND s AND (t OR u)). The reader may well ask "What about the reverse?" If $p \longrightarrow q$, is it also the case that $q \longrightarrow p$? There are other questions, too: does not-p imply not-q; does not-q imply not-p? An examination of the Venn diagram in Figure 6-11 provides the answers.

S is the set of interviews in the file. R is the set of people who paid some cash for a television set. Q is the set of people who incurred debt. P is a proper subset of Q (the set of those in Q who have paid off their debt).[2] Clearly, $p \longrightarrow q$, since in order to pay off a debt, it must have been incurred. However, $q \longrightarrow p$ is false, since there may be some who incurred debt who have not yet paid it off. The assertion not-p implies that not-q is also false, because the set of people

[2] The union of sets Q and R is all purchasers of television sets—those who paid cash, used credit, or made use of both. Their intersection includes only those who paid some cash and also incurred some debt.

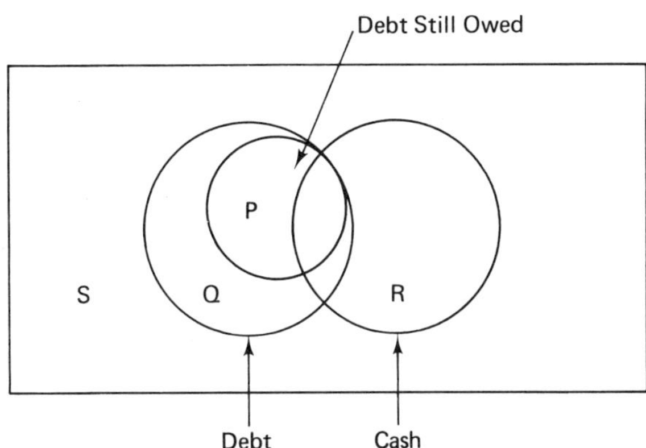

Figure 6-11 Venn Diagram of Debt and Cash Payment

who are outside *P* include some who are in *Q* (having incurred debt, but not having repaid it). The set of those outside *P* also includes some of those who are outside *Q* (either having paid only cash, or not having even bought a television set). However, the assertion not-q implies that not-p is true, since money never borrowed cannot be owed.

Since there are actually two consistency relations that can apply to these data ($p \longrightarrow q$ and not-$q \longrightarrow$ not-p), does it make sense to use both as tests? No, because one is the inverse of the other and therefore has exactly the same meaning (i.e., it is logically equivalent). The appropriate assertion, stated in the language of variables and values, would be something like

```
(TV_DEBT >0) IMPLIES (TV_PURCHASE_PATTERN  >= 2 )
```

where TV_PURCHASE_PATTERN is 0 if no TV set was bought, 1 if cash only, 2 if cash and borrowing, and 3 if borrowing only. The assertion would be true for each observation that met the logical requirement and false for each one that failed the test.

An examination of the truth table for all four of the implications we have considered (Figure 6-12) completes the discussion of the implication operator as a consistency-check concept. As noted above, $p \longrightarrow q$ is the same as not-$p \longrightarrow$ not-q, since their truth-table columns are identical. This means that either can be used interchangeably with the other, whichever seems to fit the problem better. One could have chosen to assert:

```
(TV_PURCHASE_PATTERN<2) IMPLIES (TV_DEBT = 0)
```

with the assumption that some inadvertent slip of the keypunch did not provide an occasional negative value for TV_DEBT.

p	q	p→q	q→p	$\bar{p}$	$\bar{q}$	$\bar{p}$→$\bar{q}$	$\bar{q}$→$\bar{p}$
T	T	T	T	F	F	T	T
T	F	F	T	F	T	T	F
F	T	T	F	T	F	F	T
F	F	T	T	T	T	T	T
Direct		Converse		Inverse		Contrapositive	

Figure 6-12 Truth Tables: Direct, Converse, Inverse, and Contrapositive

The four ways of stating an implication go in pairs: direct and contrapositive, converse and inverse. The inverse negates both p and q, the converse merely reverses the directionality of the relations, and the contrapositive does both. If the direct assertion is true, its contrapositive is true, but both its converse and inverse may be false. And if one of them is false, so is the other, because they are equivalent.

The reason for being so explicit about the differences between these four logical patterns is people's unfortunate tendency to think the inverse is the pattern equivalent to the direct assertion, rather than the contrapositive. The result is to write consistency-check assertions that detect large numbers of "errors" which are, in fact, consistent observations. A careful look at the Venn diagram shows that "(TV_DEBT = 0) IMPLIES (TV_PURCHASE_PATTERN > 2)" will not separate the erroneous cases from the good ones.

There is a second logical pattern that is of importance in developing a vocabulary of consistency checking. This is the operator "if-and-only-if," often abbreviated "iff," and also sometimes termed an "equivalence." It has the form

$$(p \longrightarrow q \text{ AND } q \longrightarrow p)$$

and is written $p \longleftrightarrow q$. Its truth table is shown in Figure 6-13.

If asserions p and q are both true, or if p and q are both false, the assertion $p \longleftrightarrow q$ is true, and p and q are said to be equivalent. In consistency-checking

p	q	p⟷q
T	T	T
T	F	F
F	T	F
F	F	T

Figure 6-13 "If and Only If" Truth Table

data, they are consistent if $p \leftrightarrow q$ is true (i.e., if the truth values of p and q match). If they do not match (i.e., if one is true and the other false), the consistency assertion is false. The iff consistency assertion requires that q be true if p is true, and false if p is false. If we find an observation such that q ever occurs without p or p ever occurs without q, then it is inconsistent and in error. All cases that have p must have q, and vice versa.

One may also say that the set of all observations for which p is true must be equivalent (identical) to the set for which q is true. In other words, the complement of P must be equivalent to the complement of Q. An example of an equivalence requirement is:

```
Q.6 Do you (HEAD) work for someone else, yourself, or what?

(   ) SOMEONE ELSE        (   ) BOTH SOMEONE ELSE AND SELF

(   ) SELF ONLY (Skip to Q.8).

Q.7 Do you belong to a labor union?    (   ) YES    (   ) NO
```

The consistency relation is: "Everyone who works at least part of the time for someone else should have been asked about labor-union membership, and everyone asked about union membership should have been recorded as working for someone else at least part of the time."

Assume that the codes for WORK_PATTERN are: (1) works for someone else, (2) works both for someone else and for self, (3) works for self only, (9) no information about work pattern, (0) inapplicable. Assume also that the codes for UNION_MEMBERSHIP are (0) inapplicable, (1) yes, (5) no, (9) don't know whether belongs to a union. The consistency assertion would read

```
UNION_MEMBERHIP = (1,5,9) IFF WORK_PATTERN = (1,2).
```

Union membership should be coded 1, 5, or 9 if and only if work pattern is coded 1 or 2. The reader may well ask at this point: "What about those people who don't work?" Clearly, neither of these questions should have been asked if that were the case, and both should have been coded zero. All the present requirement says is that those coded 1, 5, or 9 on union membership must be coded 1 or 2 on work pattern. If they are not coded 1, or 5, or 9, to be consistent they must be coded something other than 1 or 2 on work pattern. The reader should examine this case carefully to see how the no-answer categories for WORK_PATTERN are treated.

The implication and equivalence operators are the foundation of all the wild-code check and consistency-check phases of the study. A wild-code check is simply a less complicated proposition about the value of each variable taken one at a time. The consistency check assesses the truth of more complex propositions involving more than one variable. In each case, the assertion is applied to each observation and the values of the variables are checked. If the result is true, the observation passes that test. If, after all the tests have been performed, the observation has passed all of them, it is passed on down the processing stream. If at least one test has failed, the appropriate information is printed out and the interview can be pulled from storage to see what caused the inconsistencies. We now turn to a more detailed review of the use of this type of logical structure in practice.

Consistency Check Logic in Use

Consistency checks center on the relationships between variables in the study rather than on the contents of a particular column. An exception is the case where a variable occupies exactly one column. Whereas a simple wild-code check merely examines its value, the consistency check examines its contents in relation to values of another variable. More generally, each field is examined for inconsistent values. Those to which it is related need not be on the same punch card (or even in the same file), although this will usually be the case, since related questions are generally asked together and coded together.

For example, let A and B represent two variables in the study. If they have no logical relationship for the purposes of the study, no check is required. Alternatively, they may be logically related, but there exist no precise rules prescribing their relationship. Often, however, such rules can be stated. If a respondent says he owes no debt (variable A), the field describing the amount of debt owed (variable B) must be zero.

If a value of A requires a particular value of B ($A1 \longrightarrow B1$), a check can be made: If $A = A1$, then $B = B1$ is required. More precisely, if A has a value in the set of values comprising $A1$, then B must have a value in the set comprising $B1$ for a given observation to be consistent. If the variable "Whether has debt (yes/no)" has the value 5 (representing no), the variable "Amount of debt owed" must have the value zero. In a more concise notation, $(A = 5) \longrightarrow (B = 0)$.

In this example it also true that $B1$ implies $A1$; that is, if the amount of debt reported is zero, the questions relating to whether or not any debt was owed would have to have had "no" answers. Checking the observation to see that the requirement $(A = 5) \longrightarrow (B = 0)$ is met does not ensure that the requirement $(B = 0) \longrightarrow (A = 5)$ has also been met! Figure 6-14 will help to make this point clearer. The code values in Figure 6-14 are consistent with the code conventions established in our discussion of that phase. To check for all the possibilities, more than one error statement is required. Condition A1, NO DEBT, is represented by a code 5; condition A2 (YES, HAS DEBT), is a code 1; B1 (OWES NOTHING) is represented by 0000; and B2 (OWES XXXX) is represented by a positive nonzero number. The logical statements and the equivalent FORTRAN are as follows:

```
A1 -→B1    IF (A.EQ.5.AND.B.GT.0)
A2 -→B2    IF (A.EQ.1.AND.B.EQ.0)
```

		AMOUNT OF DEBT OWED	
		(B1) ZERO	(B2) NON-ZERO
WHETHER HAS DEBT	NO (A1)	CONSISTENT A = 5, B = 0	INCONSISTENT A = 5, B = XXXX
	YES (A2)	INCONSISTENT A = 1, B = 0	CONSISTENT A = 1, B = XXXX

Figure 6-14 Consistency Check Table for Existence and Amount of Debt

The first statement overlooks the possibility of $A = 1$ and $B = 0$. The second fails to cover the possibility of $A = 5$ and $B =$ XXXX, where XXXX is any positive nonzero number. However, if both checks are made, all types of inconsistencies will be handled properly. Either used alone would leave certain types of errors undetected.

In this example, the reverse implications also hold (i.e., $B1 \longrightarrow A1$ and $B2 \longrightarrow A2$), but this is not always the case. Consider a consistency check of the reported value of the wife's income and the employment status of the wife. It is true that if the wife is not working, her income as coded should be zero ($A1 \longrightarrow B1$). The reverse, that a code of zero in the income field means that the wife is not working, is simply not true. The respondent may be unmarried and "Wife's income" would be coded zero (inapplicable). Clearly, $B1$ does not imply $A1$. In this example, the consistency relationship is evidently more complicated. If the code also distinguishes between employed and unemployed women, the consistency check must allow for this. If there is a third code value which is used when the respondent is unmarried or is herself a woman, other types of statements would be required. This can be seen in Figure 6-15. The valid combinations are: ($A1$, $B1$), ($A2$, $B2$), and ($A3$, $B2$). If the code for the value of the wife's income included a nonzero category for "inappropriate," then the last consistency combination would be ($A3$, $B3$), where $B3$ is the code value for inappropriate respondents. Usually, however, such a nonzero code is not used, and a zero would simply be coded for these cases. The need to correct all the wild codes in the data file prior to the consistency check should be evident from all these considerations. If one cannot be sure what values might appear, it is surely more difficult to write the logic statements for the consistency check!

The exact form taken by the logic statements depends on how the data codes have been set up. It will generally be a good idea to construct such "contingency" tables when designing the consistency check, at least until thinking in set-theoretic terms has become second nature. Usually, logic statements couched in set-theoretic terms are straightforward to translate into a high-level

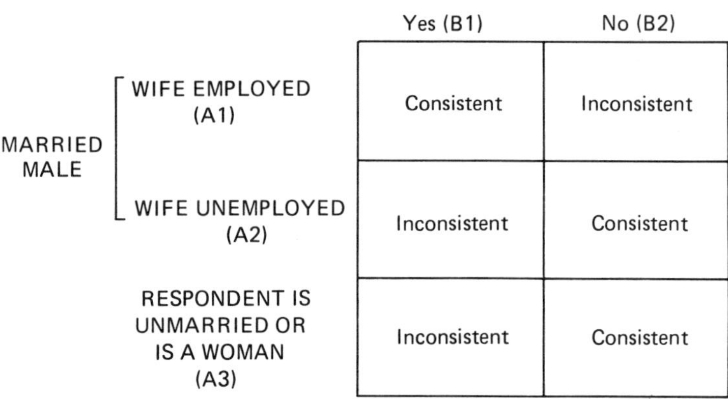

Figure 6-15 Consistency Check Table for Marital Status and Wife's Income

computer programming language. Some languages will even have the facility to perform an equivalence test with the use of one statement. A trap for the unwary is to use the two-way implication when it is inappropriate.

Cross-file and Reasonableness Checks

A more complex, type of check relates to the completeness of the file. It occurs when a variable number of records must be coded for each respondent. For example, in a consumer survey, one card might be coded for each major consumer durable good purchased by the household. For some households, this would be none; for others, maybe five or six. Respondents may have from zero to five or six such "trailer" cards, each describing a purchase, as well as the main decks of information for the household. The number of such cards required would depend on the total number of purchases, ordinarily coded on the master or "lead" card, which is always coded for everyone. Thus, the number of trailer cards must be consistent with the count of durable goods purchased which is reported on the lead card. A similar consistency-check problem would be posed for a study that coded a card for each car owned, or a card for each child in the family. In each case, the number of trailers varies from zero upward. Checks of this type generally require a special-purpose computer program written to read each master record together with its associated trailers. Although it appears relatively simple, the logic of this type of check is far more complex than that required for within-record checks.

A final category of checks can be characterized as those seeking to assess reasonableness. One example was presented in the discussion of wild-code checking checking for extremely large numbers in fields such as those recording income, house value, and so on. We saw that extremely large values can result from simple errors such as failing to use leading zeros when coding, or transposing digits (e.g., $1600 being recorded as $6100). Other tests of reasonableness can also be imposed. For example, one might flag as potential errors all cases in which the reported value of the respondent's home exceeded five times the reported annual income of the family. Such tests are ordinarily based on known relationships between variables and are simply designed to flag observations with a relatively high degree of probability of error so that they can be scanned manually.

Programs and Procedures

Ordinarily, the steps needed to check the data are simple, as were those for the wild-code check. The complexity comes from seeking sophistication in

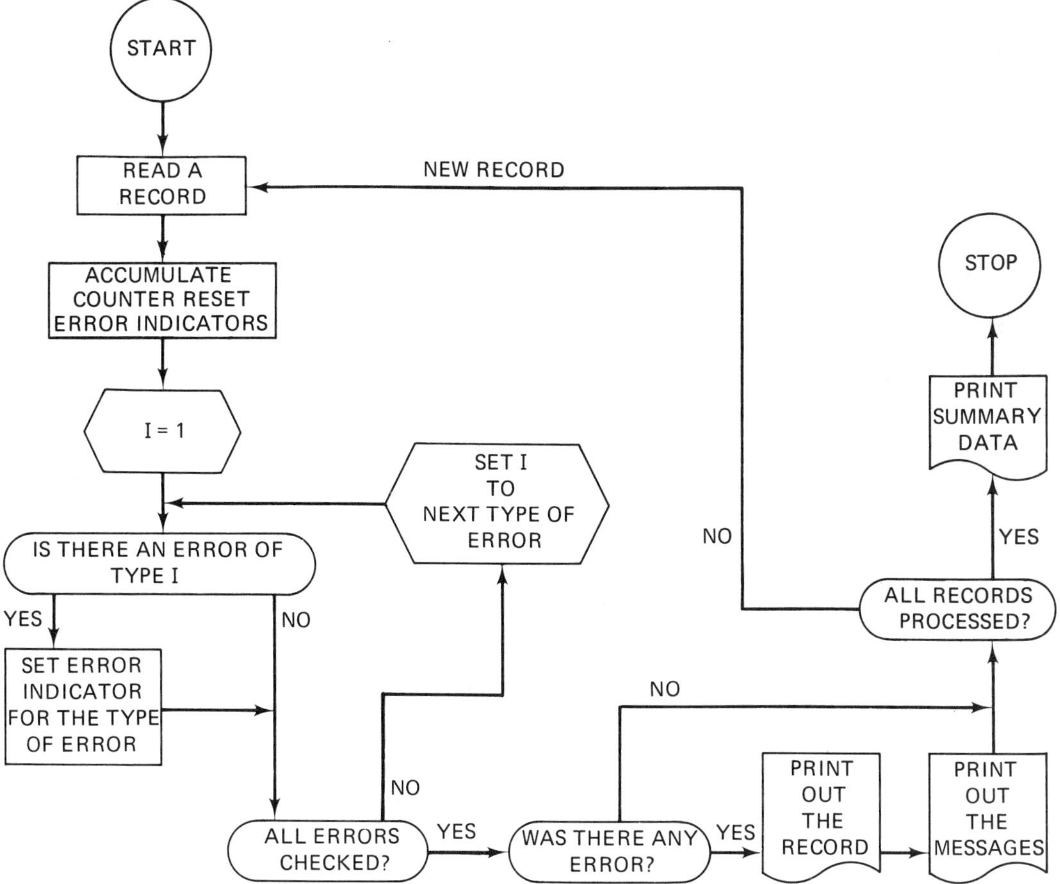

Figure 6-16 Consistency Check Algorithm

the output of the computer program to be used for the checking, and from performing many checks in the same program. A straightforward flowchart for a consistency-checking program is shown in Figure 6-16. The processing is record by record, with all error diagnostics for a given record printed out right after that record is processed.

A consistency-check program for card 04 from the example in Chapter 5 is shown in Figure 6-17. There are 10 basic errors that the program is designed

```
COLUMN
1             7
C             CONSISTENCY CHECK PROGRAM FOR CARD 04: AUTOMOBILES
C             ASSUMES THE LEAD/TRAILER CHECK HAS BEEN MADE
C             THE E VECTOR INDICATES THE TYPE OF ERROR, EC, THE COLUMN
C             IN ERROR. COL IS AN IMAGE OF THE RECORD.
              IMPLICIT INTEGER (A-2)
C             ESTABLISH PROPER DIMENSIONS, ZERO OUT COUNTERS
              DIMENSION E(10), EC(53), COL(53)
              CC = 0
              LEADCT=0
              ERCT = 0
C     1       READ IN A RECORD AS A SET OF VARIABLES
C             VARIABLE DEFINITIONS AND LOCATIONS
C             STUDY = STUDY NUMBER, READ FROM CARD 01, COLUMNS 1-3 (04:01-03)
C             DK = DECK NUMBER (04:04-05)
C             INT = INTERVIEW NUMBER (04:06-09)
C             ID = CAR I.D. (04:10)
C             CΘ = NUMBER OF CARS OWNED (04:12)
C             MΘ = YEARS MULTIPLE OWNER (04:13)
C             YRBT = YEAR BOUGHT CAR (04:22-23)
C             TP = TOTAL PRICE (04:24-27)
C             TIS = WHETHER TRADE-IN OR SALE (04:29)
C             TIS = AMOUNT OF TIS (04:30-33)
C             CASH = AMOUNT OF PAID IN CASH (04:34-37)
1         6   7
C             BOR = WHETHER BORROWED OR FINANCED (04:38)
C             AMTBOR = AMOUNT BORROWED (04:39-42)
C             MP = AMOUNT OF MONTHLY PAYMENT (04:43-45)
C             OLD = ORIGINAL LENGTH OF DEBT (04:46-47)
```

Figure 6-17 Consistency Check Program

```
COLUMN

C            RLD = REMAINING LENGTH OF DEBT (04:48-49)
C            RID = REMAINING INSTALLMENT DEBT
C            COL(I) = COLUMNS 13-53: MIGHT BE ZERO IF OWNS NO CAR OR BOUGHT
                     BEFORE 1967
             READ (5, 10, END = 999) STUDY, DK, INT, ID, CO, MO, YRBT, TP, TIS
        1    TI, CASH, BOR, AMTBOR, MP, OLD, RLD, RID, (COL(I), I=1, 53)
    10       FORMAT (I3, I2, I4, I1, 1X,2I1, I2, I4, IX,
        1    I1, 2I4, I1, I4, I3, 2I2, I4, T1, 53I1)
             CC = CC+1
C            COUNT NUMBER OF LEAD CARDS
             IF (ID.EQ.1) LEADCT = LEADCT + 1
             DO 5 I=1, 53
     5       EC(I) = 0
             DO 6 I=1, 10
     6       E(I) = 0
C            CHECK FOR NONOWNERS: COL 13-53 SHOULD BE ZERO. ERROR TYPE 1
             IF(CO.GT.0) GO TO 16
             DO 15 I = 13,53
             IF (COL(I).NE.0) EC(I) = 1
             IF (COL(I).NE.0) E(1)=0
    15       CONTINUE
             GO TO 110
1            7
C            ONLY CAR OWNERS GO THROUGH THIS SECTION
C            CHECK CONTINGENCY BOX FOR COL. 13. ERROR TYPE 2
    16       IF(CO.EQ.1.AND.MO.NE.0) E(2) = 1
             IF(CO.GE.2.AND.MO.EQ.0) E(2) = 1
             DO 20 I = 14, 23
             IF (COL(I).EQ.0) EC(I) = 1
             IF (COL(I).EQ.0) E(3) = 0
    20       CONTINUE
C            ABOVE, THE REVERSE IMPLICATION IS CHECKED
C            ERROR COLUMNS ARE FLAGGED (EC(I)=1) AND THE
C            TYPE OF ERROR IS NOTED (E(3)=1)
             IF (YRBT.GT.66) GO TO 25
C            IF CAR NOT BOUGHT 1967 OR 1968, COLUMNS 24-53 SHOULD BE ZERO.
             ERROR TYPE 4
             DO 21  I=24,53
             IF (COL(I).NE.0) EC(I) = 1
             IF (COL(I).NE.0) E(4)=1
    21       CONTINUE
             GO TO 110
```

```
COLUMN
C              IR CAR BOUGHT 1967 or 1968, TP AND TLS CANNOT BE ZERO. ERROR TYPE S
      25       IF (TP.EQ.0) E(5) = 1
               IF (TIS.EQ.0) E(5) = 1
C              TRADE IN CODES MUST BE CONSISTENT. ERROR TYPE 6
               IF (TIS.EQ.1.AND.TI.EQ.0) E(6) = 1
               IF (TIS.EQ.5.AND.TI.NE.0) E(6) = 1
1              7
C              IF BORROWING OCCURRED, GO TO PROPER CHECK SEQUENCE
               IF (BOR.EQ.1) GO TO 35
C              IF NO BORROWING, COLUMNS 39-53 SHOULD BE ZERO. ERROR TYPE 7
               DO 31 I=39, 53
               IF (COL(I).NE.0) EC(I) = 1
               IF (COL(I).NE.0) E(7) = 1
      31       CONTINUE
               GO TO 110
C              IF BORROWING OCCURRED, AB, MP, OLD, RLD SHOULD NOT BE ZERO. ERROR TYPE 8
      35       IF (AB.EQ.0) E(8) = 1
               IF(MP.EQ.0) E(8) = 1
               IF(OLD.EQ.0) E(8) = 1
               IF(RLD.EQ.0) E(8) = 1
               IF(RLD.EQ.0) E(8) = 1
C              PERFORM SOME QUALITATIVE CHECKS
               X = .1 * TP
               TP1 = TP+X
               TP2 = TP-X
               SUM = CASH + TI + AMTBOR
               IF (SUM.LT.TP2.OR. SUM.GT.TP1) E(9) = 1
C              THIS CHECKS TO SEE THAT CASH + TL + AMTBOR ADD TO TP WITH A 10%
               MARGIN. ERROR TYPE 9
               DEBT = RLD * MP
               DI = RID + MP
               D2 = RID - MP
               IF (DEBT.LT.D2.OR.DEBT.GT.D1) E(10) = 1
C              THIS CHECKS TO SEE THAT REMAINING INSTALLMENT DEBT
C              IS EQUAL TO THE PRODUCT OF MONTHLY PAYMENT
C              TIMES MONTHS LEFT TO PAY, WITHIN ONE PAYMENT
C              ERROR TYPE 10
C              CHECK TO SEE IF THERE WERE ANY ERRORS
```

Figure 6-17 (cont'd.)

```
      DO 100 I=1, 10
      IF(E(I).NE.0) GO TO 110
100   CONTINUE
      GO TO 1
C     NO ERROR, READ NEXT RECORD
C     ***
C     ERROR SEGMENT
C     PRINT OUT CARD IMAGE
110   WRITE (6,115) INT. ID, (COL(1), I = 1, 53)
115   FORMAT (IHO, 'ERROR, INT =', I4, √X, 'ID=', I2, 5X,  3I1)
      ERCT = ERCT + 1
C     IF ERROR INDICATOR NEEDED, PRINT IT OUT
      IF (E(1).EQ.1.OR.E(3).EQ.1.OR.E(4).EQ.1.OR.E(7).EQ.1) GO TO 116
      GO TO 120
116   WRITE (6,117), EC(I), I = 13, 53)
117   FORMAT (IHO, 41X, 41I1)
120   IF(E(1).EQ.1) WRITE (6, 501)
      IF(E(2).EQ.1) WRITE (6, 502)
      IF(E(3).EQ.1) WRITE (6, 503)
      IF (E(4).EQ.1) WRITE (6, 501)
      IF(E(5).EQ.1) WRITE (6, 505)
      IF(E(6).EQ.1) WRITE (6, 506)
      IF(E(7).EQ.1) WRITE (6, 501)
      IF(E(8).EQ.1) WRITE (6, 508)
      IF(E(9).EQ.1) WRITE (6, 509)
      IF(E(10).EQ.1) WRITE (6, 510)
501   FORMAT (1HO, 'THE INDICATED COLUMNS ARE NOT ZERO AND SHOULD BE')
502   FORMAT (1HO, 'CO AND MO ARE INCONSISTENT')
503   FORMAT (1HO, 'THE INDICATED COLUMNS ARE ZERO BUT SHOULD NOT BE')
505   FORMAT (1HO, 'TP OR TLS ARE ZERO AND SHOULD NOT BE')
506   FORMAT (1HO, 'TIS AND TL ARE INCONSISTENT')
508   FORMAT (1HO, 'AB, MP, OLD, RLD, RID: ONE OR MORE ARE 0 AND SHOULD NOT BE')
509   FORMAT (1HO, 'CASH + TI + AMTBOR NOT EQUAL TP + — 10%')
510   FORMAT (1HO, 'MP*RLD NOT EQUAL RID + — MP')
C     GO READ A NEW RECORD
      GO TO 1
C     ***END OF PROCESSING - ALL RECORDS READ
999   WRITE (6, 1000) CC, LEADCT, ERCT
      FORMAT (IH1, 'END, CC = ', I6, 5X, 'LEADS=', I6, 5X, 'ERRORS =', I6)
      STOP
      END
```

to look for. Whether or not each error occurred is indicated by the value of the corresponding elements in the vector *E*, which will be all zeros unless an error occurs. When an error is detected, the appropriate cell of the 10-cell *E* vector is set to 1. A 53-cell vector indicates columns that are in error. The latter is similar in function to the construction used in the wild-code check routine. It is named the EC vector, and is also filled with zeros before each record is processed. COL is the image of the record read in integer form. It also contains 53 cells, the number of columns of data on card 04.

Other features of the program are typical of those found useful in handling consistency-checking problems. All the variables receive definitions in comment statements and are identified as to location. Mnemonics are used for variable names. The latter facilitate writing the logic statements, since the variables involved are easily identifiable. As in the wild-code check, the input formatting procedure reads the data twice, once to pick up the variables and once to pick up a complete image of the card as a string of characters. Two-way checks are made for all variables where this logic applies. For example, if no car is owned, columns 13–53 are checked to make sure that they are zero. If a car is owned, they are checked to make sure that they do not contain zeros. Column 13 may be zero if one car is owned and is not checked by this set of statements. It receives checks in two other places. Each error type has a specific message to be printed, clearly identifying the problem. The implementation of instructions from the contingency boxes in the code is specifically checked by the program.

Correcting Errors

Once the consistency-check program has been run on the data file, the correction process is much the same as for the wild-code check. Each record in error will be printed out with a set of diagnostic comments pinpointing the errors found in the data. The interview schedules must then be reexamined to reconcile the inconsistencies. The corrections, if any, can then be noted right on the computer output, and this can be used either as a guide to a keypunch operator correcting the original data cards or as a source document for punching error-correction cards to a data-updating program.

It is advisable to complete the error-correction process before starting to generate constructed variables. When the latter involve several input variables, wild or inconsistent data can lead to numerous misclassifications or to cases that do not fit the specified logic of the variable-generation specifications and which are thereby dumped into the "miscellaneous" or "other" categories of the resulting variables. In any case, a serious loss of information and delayed schedules are likely if a decision is made to leapfrog this phase of the study.

The computer programming required to perform consistency checks illustrates the more general point that a significant portion of the data processing for a study often does not lend itself easily to generalization. Library programs are not always available to perform the data-management tasks with which this book is largely concerned. Some of the large-scale survey data-processing programs are exceptions, and researchers using them may find all the resources they need, but many analysts will need access to applications programming resources adequate to the task of accomplishing many of the jobs discussed here. In general, these programs are "one-shot" jobs; that is, they should be designed to do one special job and not as experiments in software design. A major design criterion is simplicity; another is to minimize the amount of programming time required. Since these programs will not be used over and over again, it does not matter if they make efficient use of the computer hardware. Elegant output is also unnecessary. Tricky coding is certainly to be avoided, as it is a source of debugging problems. On the other hand, it is highly desirable that the code reflect the logical structure of the processing problem. High-level languages, such as PL/1, ALGOL, or FORTRAN, are clearly indicated, as is the adoption of a program structure that is highly modular.

Since these programs become a part of the documentation of what was done to the data, readability and good documentation are of paramount importance. Although it is sometimes easier to use array notation in consistency-check (and in variable-building) programs, it is probably better to use mnemonics that describe individual variables. A survey staff member is better able to review the logic of a consistency-check program if the notation DEBT = 0 is used rather than the more obscure V(6) = 0. In fact, if the study staff puts these into the original code book, then codes, logic statements, and computer programs all use the same notation. Anything that will make for good documentation, reduce errors, and facilitate the checking of one person's work by another is desirable during these phases of the study.

MARGINAL DISTRIBUTIONS AS VERIFICATION

After the corrections have been made, it is useful to compute frequency distributions for all variables in the study and enter them next to the appropriate codes in the master code book. A simple way to obtain them is to run cross-tabulations on successive pairs of variables. With a little rearranging of this rule, many of the tables can be produced that will be needed later. These marginals provide the first direct information about the sample. The distributions of "face sheet" variables can easily be obtained. These distributions also provide information about the feasibility of studying in detail selected subgroups of the sample, since the actual number of cases should be recorded in the code book as well as the sample percentages.

Perhaps the most important use of marginals relates to the information they provide for verification of the results of later variable-building and analysis steps. In these later steps, the analyst should always verify that the correct number of cases, the proper population subgroup, was selected for the computation of statistics. With the marginals, this can frequently be accomplished simply by referring back to them. Marginals also provide information relevant to a final overall check on the wild-code and consistency-checking process. Any uncorrected wild codes will be discovered, as will be errors resulting from incorrect alterations during the consistency checks that result in substantial impacts on the distributions of variables that have been studied previously.

With this step complete, the data are now "clean." The contents of all columns of the data cards should be totally consistent with the values specified by the code book. All inconsistencies between variables have been reconciled, at least where these inconsistencies are important to the analysis. If all the data were now in the form desired for analysis, the researcher could proceed with that work. In most cases, however, some variables must still be constructed. If a maximum of detail has been preserved, the generation of alternative forms of class intervals and the like, and other summarizations of the detail, will be straightforward. The attention of the analyst will turn toward making the variables correspond as closely as possible to the study concepts. This variable-generation and scaling process is the subject of Chapter 7.

VARIABLE GENERATION

There are four main reasons why the construction of new variables and the establishment of subfiles frequently occupy a large part of the attention that the survey analyst gives to his data. First, the questions one can ask in a survey generally do not have a one-to-one correspondence with the concepts that one wishes to study. Thus, new variables must be constructed. Second, there are good reasons for coding and storing data in a detailed form, preserving as much of the original information as possible. Third, reformatting and alterations of the basic data are typically required in order to use the statistical techniques and computer programs available. Fourth, new variables sometimes have to be added to the data file based on information not collected during the interviewing process.

This chapter will review the factors that generate a need for the construction of new variables, explain the logical and mathematical manipulations fundamental to variable generation and work-file manipulation in survey processing, and review the measurement theory that underlies this process. It will illustrate the basic procedures that are used and discuss complexities in the study design that can seriously complicate the process. Finally, it will summarize some of the administrative strategies that can be used to help avoid making serious mistakes which can lead to invalid results and to countless wasted hours of labor.

MEASUREMENT CONCEPTS

The measurement paradigm that underlies the type of procedures discussed here includes the concepts of objects, attributes, magnitudes, quantities, measurement, and numbers. The paradigm is employed either explicitly or implicitly in almost all survey research.

An *object* is a measurable unit, such as a person, group, family, or other social system that has properties capable of gradations.[1] These properties, such as cohesiveness, age, location of residence, or race, are sometimes referred to as attributes. Attributes can be thought of as abstractions imposed by the investigator on the flux constituting the behavior being studied. An *attribute*, then, is an observable property capable of gradation.[2] *Magnitude* is the amount of an attribute present at the time of measurement. It refers to the possibility that two objects can be compared and that one object is said to have more of the attribute than the other. Presence or absence is the minimal distinction that can be made with respect to it. The *class* of all magnitudes of a particular kind defines that particular attribute, and a magnitude is simply one point in the ordered set of points constituting the attribute. Attributes have names, definitions, and rules for assigning numbers to points in the set. A *quantity* is a combination of an attribute and a magnitude. For example, "age" is an attribute, but 34 is a magnitude, applying to inches, apples, or years. Thirty-four years of age is a quantity. Relations between quantities occur when two objects are compared. Individual A is 34 years of age; individual B is younger, at 24 years of age; individual C is the same age, at 34 years.

Measurement pertains to an attribute (not all attributes are measurable). It is the assignment of numbers to represent the magnitude of one of the attributes of the objects. The properties of numbers that apply to the measurement process are: the name (set membership), order (ranking), distance, and origin (zero point).

For some attributes one can give empirical meaning to one or more of these properties of numbers. Then one can establish a one-to-one mapping between the number system and a series of objects that possesses the properties. In the measurement process, one uses information generated by the data-collection instrument to assign numbers to the objects so that the relationships between the assigned numbers reflect the relations between the objects with respect to the attribute in question. Torgerson (1958, p. 42) distinguishes four types of measurements according to whether or not the concepts of distance between points and an origin or zero point are invoked. They are: ratio measurement (distance and origin), interval measurement (distance but no origin), ordinal measurement (no distance and no origin), and a less frequently used type of operation in which an ordinal measure is anchored to a zero point (origin but no distance). Of course, the set-naming concept is always invoked. For example, everyone who lives in the Northwest is a member of the set of people assigned a magnitude of 1 for an attribute called "region of residence."

Davis (1971), in a useful discussion of variables, provides a clear rationale

[1] For a much more complete discussion, see Torgerson (1958, Chap. 1), Nunnally (1967), Blalock and Blalock (1968, Part 1), and Davis (1971).

[2] The extent to which these properties are stable and subject to agreement over time and between observers is an elusive question not dealt with here. For a provocative discussion, see Wilson (1971).

for tying together raw survey information from several questions into a measure of a concept. According to Davis, a variable has four facets: a name, a verbal definition, a set of categories, and a procedure for sorting observations into the categories. The categories are given identifiers, usually numbers. The verbal definition relates the name to the underlying attribute. The procedure for sorting observations into categories involves (1) a rule for generating raw questionnaire (or other) information using a set of stimuli common to all respondents (i.e., the instrument and interviewers' manual), and (2) mapping the information collected onto the set of numbers that is embodied in the code during the editing and coding stages of the research. When the mapping rules are sufficiently precise to be programmed, it makes sense to use computing equipment to implement them. This latter mapping process is commonly known as *variable generation*.

There are many examples of variables that do not correspond to the raw answer to a single question on a survey. In studying income inequality one may wish to examine the proportion of the total dollars of personal income in the sample held by a family. This is a ratio or share. For comparison purposes, measures must sometimes be converted to percentiles or expressed in standard-deviation units away from the mean. Others must be measured by multi-item scales in order to improve reliability, validity, and discriminatory power. In each case, coded data must be manipulated, usually by computer, to produce the variables needed for the analysis.

A particularly important reason for combining raw measures is that error is always present in the measurement process. Any given variable may not correlate very highly with the underlying attribute that it is presumed to measure. It may also be correlated with other attributes. Increasing the number of variables (each of which may be based on a separate question in the instrument) used to provide information for placing respondents on an underlying dimension and combining them into a scale may help to solve these problems. Under the assumptions used by this kind of measurement paradigm, the scaling increases the correlation of the resulting scale variable with the presumed underlying attribute, permitting finer discriminations among respondents and yielding increased reliability.[3]

In some cases a variable that is appropriate for representing an attribute logically involves combining a number of component-measured attributes in various ways (e.g., family life cycle). The attribute may be more easily measured by combining its components. Sums (e.g., "disposable income"—total family income from all sources net of approximate taxes) and ratios (e.g., ratio of family installment debt to disposable income) are typical of these types of variables. The analysis may require working with residuals from an additive multivariate technique to obtain a measure that is independent of background or other factors. The procedure for constructing this type of variable is quite complex.

[3] Nunnally, (1967, p. 56).

Contextual analysis methods that require classifying an observation according to the characteristics of its "environment" (e.g., membership in a high-producing work group), or studying the change in a variable over time, also require an extensive amount of processing of raw data to obtain the specific measures desired. All of these involve variable-generation procedures aimed at mapping raw data onto an attribute.

The multiplicity of objectives embodied in a survey also results in differing requirements for changing and modifying variables, since the same survey information may be used for a variety of purposes. One objective may be to develop and validate a scale; another may be to study the statistical behavior of several forms of the scale. Thus, the same variable may be used as an explanatory factor in one phase of the analysis and as a dependent variable in another, each use requiring slightly different forms of the variable.

Multiple study objectives require accurate, well-documented variable-generation procedures. The basic purposes of the study may include a variety of explorative, descriptive, model-building, and hypothesis-testing or model-verification objectives. In each case, the data generated in raw form by the survey instrument have to be mapped onto a set of categories that represents the concept to be studied. Careful documentation of the generation procedures used is required to minimize problems in the construction of new data codes and confusion in the use and interpretation of the constructed variables.

An additional reason why variable-generation procedures are used is that not all study objectives can (or should) be incorporated into the design at the beginning. New objectives invariably unfold during the analysis process. Thus, there are good reasons for gathering and recording raw data in the maximum amount of detail consistent with the budget, the current state of the recording and data-processing technology, and the study's main objectives. It makes good sense to try to tailor the variables to each individual analysis requirement rather than to lock the data at the beginning of the study into a particular form of each variable. If, instead, a maximum amount of detail is coded, one can generate multiple versions of the information as needed. This issue was discussed in detail in Chapter 4.

Another major class of reasons why variables have to be manipulated by computer prior to using them in an analysis arises from the inherent "dirtiness" of data and the requirements of computer programs to be used in analysis. Missing information sometimes has to be assigned or randomized. Formats have to be changed, character sets altered, and codes changed to meet the input requirements of statistical programs. Skewness or non-normality problems or non-linearity problems may have to be taken care of. Categories that contain only a few observations may have to be collapsed. The statistical procedures may require a one–zero dummy-variable or *z*-score representation of the variables. In each case, the appropriate sections of the data file have to be examined and acceptable versions of the information created.

Finally, variable generation and file manipulation are necessary because some required variables may be derived from a source other than the original interview or questionnaire. In some projects, the file must be matched record by record with another data base and certain variables obtained from the external file. For instance, in a panel study of university faculty members, salary information from central university payroll files could be added to the survey file. In a national sample survey, contextual information from census-tract tapes might be added to the survey file to permit classifying respondents by the median income of the neighborhood in which they resided.

All these factors make the variable-generation procedures used by the study staff of critical importance. It is important to note that mistakes made here will result in files that need to be re-created, statistics that must be redone, and reports that need to be rewritten (hopefully, before they reach publication). Errors are "laced" through the rest of the analysis if mistakes take place at this stage; hence, extreme care and good records are necessary.

We turn now to a more detailed consideration of the concepts and procedures that are an integral part of the variable-generation process.

Set Theory, Logic, and Functional Notation

Thinking about variable-generation problems in a survey requires a vocabulary. The purpose of this section is to help the reader learn to visualize variable-generation problems in terms of sets of observations and their unions and intersections. Using Venn diagrams can help clarify the nature of the logical manipulations to be performed and can facilitate the development of codes which have the properties of being mutually exclusive and completely exhaustive. An understanding of the basic principles of related logical propositions about the values of variables provides the basis for using the variable-generation commands provided by most data-management and survey-processing statistical packages. Functional concepts provide the basis for a convenient notation and a basis for understanding the differences between a computational rule and the procedure for accomplishing it.

The idea of a set of objects, a class of things, is one familiar to almost everyone. A herd of horses, a flotilla of ships, and a deck of cards are examples. Here the concern is with the set of observations in a file. Sets are given *names* —the H-BAR-H Herd, the Normandy Invasion Fleet, the Student Life Style Survey File Number One. Sometimes sets are defined by enumerating the list of objects comprising them: for example, $A =$ (ALEX, BOB CARL). More commonly, they are defined by a *rule* that everyone (hopefully) can agree on, such as "the set of all boys who live at 1077 Vernier." The rule includes them in the set because they all appear to have some property in common that defines them to the observer and his readers as objects which, for the observer's current purposes, should be classified together. In set A above there were three elements: ALEX, BOB, and CARL. If N is the set of boys in set A whose names begin with A or B, N is a subset of A, since every member of N is in A. Since there is at least one element in A which is not in N (CARL), we call N a *proper* subset of A.

Let G be defined as "all the girls who are in set A." But there are no girls in A. $G = \varnothing = (\quad) =$ the *null set* or the *empty set*. This empty set, $\varnothing$, is always a subset of every set. It is important to note that $\varnothing$ is not the same as zero (0) which is an element in the set of numbers. The *universe* of objects of the type we are talking about is referred to as S. For our purpose, this will generally be all the observations in the survey file.

Several new terms can now be defined terms:

$S =$ the file of survey interviews,
$R =$ set of all interviews in S obtained from rural areas,
$M =$ set of all interviews in S obtained from male respondents,
$M' =$ complement of M; those in S who are not male,
$R' =$ complement of R; those in our file S who are not rural,
$S' =$ the complement of everything in our file; $S' = \varnothing$, the empty set,
$\varnothing' = S$; our file, the complement of the empty set.

The symbol $\cap$ defines the *intersection* of two sets. In the file, all the interviews come either from the city or from a rural area. No interview can come from both areas. So we have *disjoint* subsets,

$$R \cap R' = \varnothing.$$

The symbol $\cup$ defines the *union* of two sets. Since the classification scheme is mutually exclusive and exhaustive, in our file we have

$$R \cup R' = S.$$

Figure 7-1 shows Venn diagrams which illustrate the two partially overlapping subsets of our file S. Figure 7-1(a) shows the set of rural interviews as the shaded area. The partial overlap with the set of interviews from male respondents can be seen in the diagram. In Figure 7-1(b) the complement, R', is shown. There are some interviews that are male and not in rural areas which are part of R'. Other males are in R. Figure 7-1(c) displays the union of the two subsets. There are some who have both characteristics and some who have only one. Figure 7-1(d) shows the intersection. This figure shows each region of the diagram expressed as the intersection of a subset or its complement with the corresponding subset or complement.

It is important to note that Rural and Male are not disjoint (mutually exclusive). Rather, they are partially overlapping; that is, $R \cap M \neq \varnothing$, the set of rural male people, is not empty. If two sets are disjoint, their intersection is the null set.

The union and intersection operators are *commutative* (i.e., the union of R and M is the same as the union of M and R). Likewise, the intersection of R

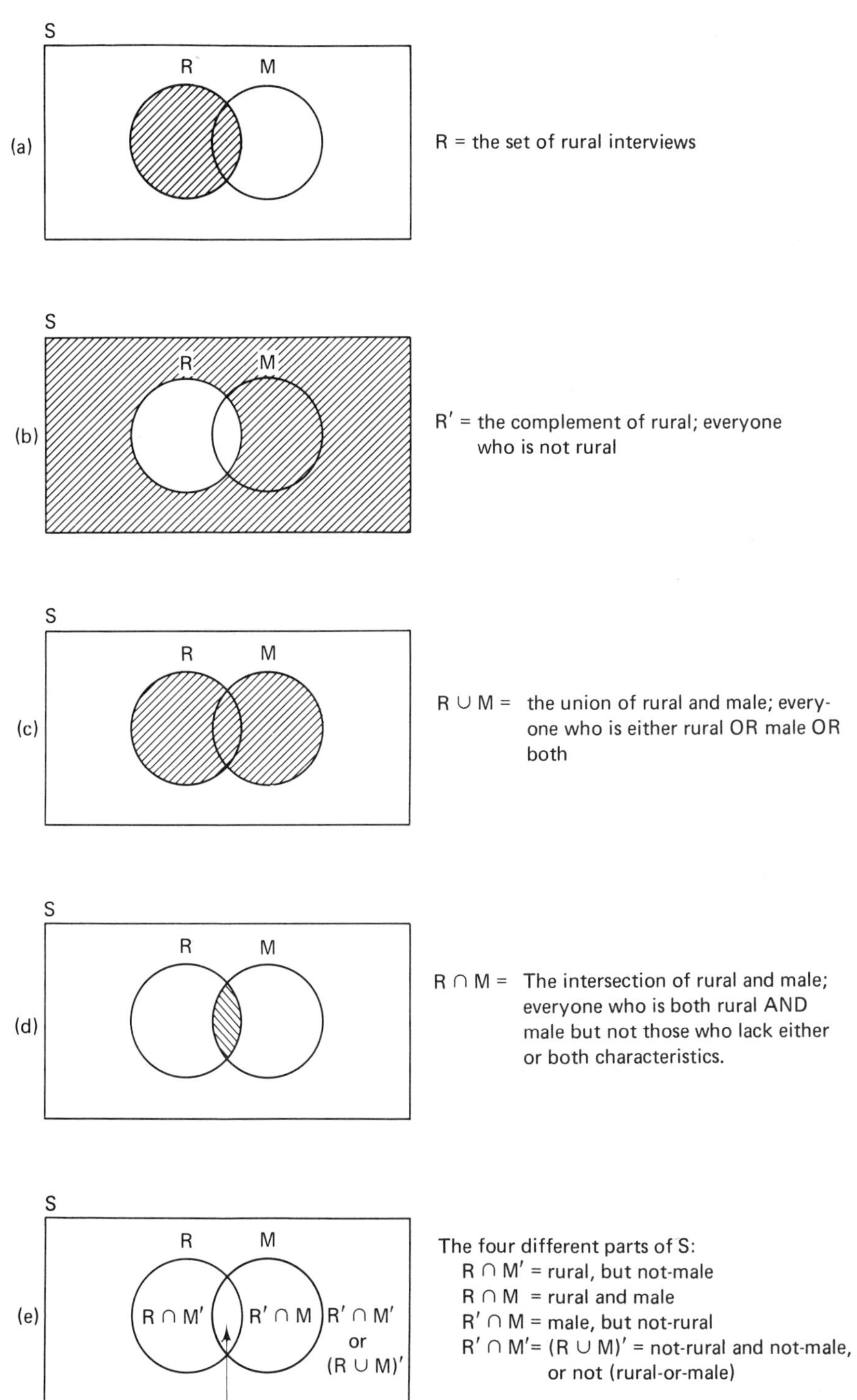
S
R
M
(a)
R = the set of rural interviews
S
R
M
(b)
R′ = the complement of rural; everyone who is not rural
S
R
M
(c)
R ∪ M = the union of rural and male; everyone who is either rural OR male OR both
S
R
M
(d)
R ∩ M = The intersection of rural and male; everyone who is both rural AND male but not those who lack either or both characteristics.
S
R
M
(e)
R ∩ M′
R′ ∩ M
R′ ∩ M′
or
(R ∪ M)′
R ∩ M
The four different parts of S:
R ∩ M′ = rural, but not-male
R ∩ M = rural and male
R′ ∩ M = male, but not-rural
R′ ∩ M′= (R ∪ M)′ = not-rural and not-male, or not (rural-or-male)

Figure 7-1 Sets, Intersections, and Unions

and M is the same as the intersection of M and R. Symbolically,

$$R \cup M = M \cup R$$

and

$$R \cap M = M \cap R.$$

With three sets, these relations still hold. Let T be the set of people in S over age 21. The result is shown diagramatically, in Figure 7-2, where

$$(R \cup M) \cup T = R \cup (M \cup T)$$

and

$$(R \cap M) \cap T = R \cap (M \cap T).$$

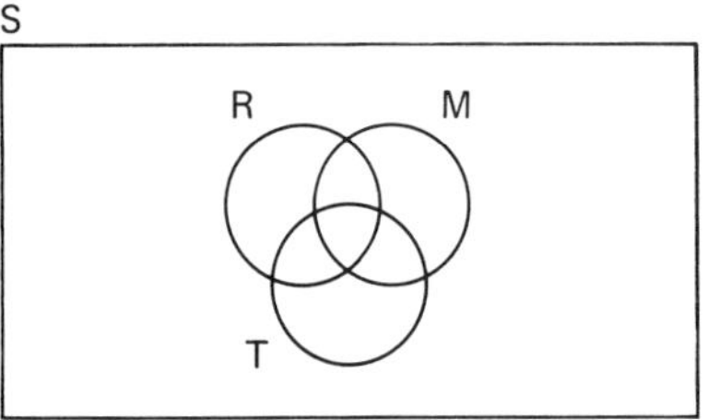

Figure 7-2 Three sets

One can see that the union operator $\cup$ behaves something like the logical operator OR and something like addition, since the areas comprising the two subsets are added together. The intersection operator $\cap$ is something like AND and, although it is less obvious, has a lot in common with multiplication. The union and intersection operators are commutative and *associative*. But, unlike multiplication and addition with numbers, the set operators have two *distributive laws*, not one. Thus,

$$R \cap (M \cup T) = (R \cap M) \cup (R \cap T)$$

and

$$R \cup (M \cap T) = (R \cup M) \cap (R \cup T).$$

In English, the first of these asserts that the set of rural people who are either male or over 21 is the same as combining the set of rural males with the set of rural people over 21. In the second case, when the set of rural people is combined with the set of males over 21, you get the same subset as taking the people who are either rural or male and who are also either rural or over 21. The reader is urged to find these subsets in the diagram. The usefulness of the diagrams and the symbols should be clear to anyone who has tried diligently to follow the imprecise English formulation of this example.

The empty set $\varnothing$ acts like a zero and the universal set S (which in this example is the entire survey file) acts like the number 1, but the analogy is not perfect:

$R \cup \varnothing = R$ (rural people + nobody = rural people),
$R \cap S = R$ (rural people who are in the S file = themselves),
$R \cap \varnothing = \varnothing$ (rural people who are members of some other set that is empty form an empty set),
$R \cup S = S$ (rural people plus the whole file = the whole file).

In the file everyone is either rural or not rural, so rural + nonrural = everybody:

$$R \cup R' = S.$$

There is no one who is both rural and not rural:

$$R \cap R' = \varnothing.$$

The usefulness of set theory in conceptualizing recoding problems has been illustrated by the examples. A set of observations is defined by a *rule*, a proposition or assertion about the values of the variables characterizing the observations as they appear in a file. The set is comprised of those observations in the file for whom the proposition is true. For example: Let T be the name of the set of observations in the file S such that the value of the variable "AGE" is greater than or equal to 21.

Note that we could have named the set 1. By naming it with a 1 and by naming its complement with a zero, 0, we would establish a recoding rule for a dummy variable.[4] A reasonable name for the variable would be "Whether aged 21 or older." T and T' together exhaust the file ($T \cup T' = S$), and there is no one who is in both T and T' ($T \cap T' = \varnothing$).

This logic is simply extended to trichotomies and to variables with more than three categories. A rule is written for each desired subset, such that the set of rules defines subsets that are mutually exclusive. For the last "none of the above" category, a rule is defined specifying the complement of the union of all the previously defined subsets. This is a foolproof scheme, needed because some of the "dirty" observations may not meet any of the list requirements (particularly if no consistency checking is done). For instance, with three classes, one defines subsets T_1 and T_2 and the residual class $T_3 = (T_1 \cup T_2)'$.

Propositions About the Values of Variables

Propositions about the values of variables are simply assertions that for any given observation, the proposition is true. The propositions assert that the relations and arithmetic expressions specified in the proposition hold. For any given observation, either they do or do not hold, and the proposition is either true

[4] For a discussion of the use of dummy variables in multiple regression, see Lansing and Morgan (1971) and Dunkelberg (1974).

(T) or false (F). The relationships are

$=$ equality,
$<$ less than,
$>$ greater than,
$\leq$ less than or equal to,
$\geq$ greater than or equal to,
$\subset$ a member of the set consisting of.

The arithmetic operators are

$+$ addition,
$-$ subtraction,
$\times$ multiplication,
$/$ division,
a^x exponentiation.

Some examples are

REGION $= 2$,
EDUCATION < 9,
AGE >17,
HUSBANDS_EDUCATION $\leq$ WIVES_EDUCATION $- 1$,
INCOME_SHARE $\geq .05 \times$ YEARLY_INCOME,
VOTE68 $\subset$ (1,2,4-6,9).

Rules for defining more complex sets of observations are established by linking two or more propositions about the values of variables together with a logical operator. For example, a proposition about age and one about residence can be combined as follows:

(1) AGE ≥ 21 AND RURAL $= 2$.
(2) AGE ≥ 21 OR RURAL $= 2$.

In the first case, a set F of all observations is defined such that, for all of its elements, the value of the variable whose name is AGE is greater than or equal to 21 and the value of the variable whose name is RURAL is exactly equal to 2. All observations for whom this compound proposition is true are members of this set. In the terms we have been using, it is the intersection of two larger subsets. Let M be the name of the set of observations such that AGE ≥ 21, and let R be the set such that RURAL $= 2$. Then F is the intersection of these two sets: $F = M \cap R$.

The rule defining F is the conjunction of the rules defining M and R. It is the first of the combined rules given above. The key word in the verbal description for the rule is "and." The logical operator in the formal description is AND. This operator is defined more carefully below.

The disjunction of the two rules gives $G = M \cup R$, which is the union of the associated sets. The key word here is "or" and we have the second of the two compound rules given above. The logical operator is OR.

Propositions about the values of variables, conjunctions, and disjunctions are analogous to the concepts of sets, intersections, and unions. The only difference is that the propositions have to do with the rules defining the sets of observations in the file rather than with the sets themselves. It is important to note the precise definitions of "and" and "or" in this context, since common English usage is not consistent.

The complement of the set F is F' and the proposition defining it, which as we noted above was (AGE $\geq$ 21 AND RURAL = 2), has an analogous property, negation. F' = NOT(AGE $\geq$ 21 AND RURAL = 2). F' is the set for which the original proposition is false; but put slightly differently, it is the set for which the negation of the original proposition is true.

Ordinary mathematical notation uses slightly different symbols for propositions than for sets. We summarize this. Let p be a proposition (such as AGE $\geq$ 21) and let q be a second proposition (such as RURAL = 2). Then

$p \wedge q$ means p AND q (conjunction),
$p \vee q$ means p OR q (disjunction),
$\bar{p}$ means NOT p (negation).

It is useful to list the truth tables for $\wedge$ and $\vee$. Each has a row for every combination of truth and falsity for the propositions p and q. It can be seen that the compound proposition $p \wedge q$ is true only when p is true and q is true (from examining the first row). Observations in the set F which is defined by the complex rule $p \wedge q$ will consist of those in the intersection of the set M (defined as those observations for which rule p is true), and the set R (defined as those observations for which rule q is true. If F were defined by the rule $p \vee q$, it would comprise the observations in the union of M and R (see Figure 7-3).

Two other aspects of the relationships between sets and the logic of propositions about variables are important, because they allow us to simplify the

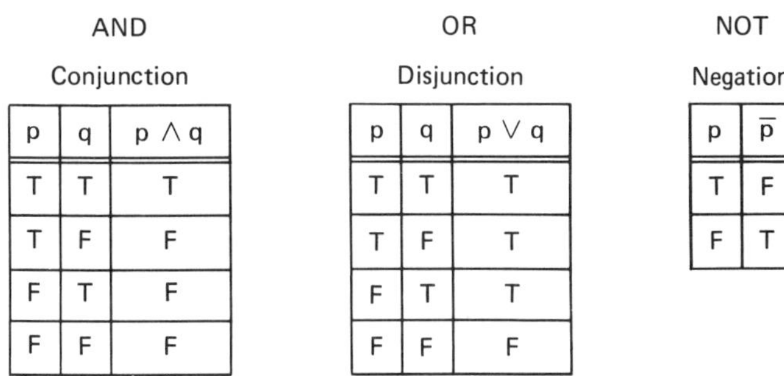

AND

Conjunction

p	q	p ∧ q
T	T	T
T	F	F
F	T	F
F	F	F

OR

Disjunction

p	q	p ∨ q
T	T	T
T	F	T
F	T	T
F	F	F

NOT

Negation

p	$\bar{p}$
T	F
F	T

Figure 7-3 Truth Tables for AND, OR, and NOT

way in which a complex expression is stated. We have:

Relations between sets:		Relations between propositions:
$(M \cap R)' = M' \cup R'$	and	$\overline{(p \wedge q)} = \bar{p} \vee \bar{q}$
$(M \cup R)' = M' \cap R'$	and	$\overline{(p \vee q)} = \bar{p} \wedge \bar{q}$.

These relationships, called *DeMorgan's laws*, simply state that when you negate an "and" proposition, you get an "or" proposition, and vice versa. Put in terms of sets, the complement of the intersection of two sets is the union of the complements taken separately; the complement of the union of two sets is the intersection of their separate complements. In the example, if you take out those over 21 (M) who are rural (R) and examine those whom you have left, it is the same group you would get by combining the nonmales with the nonrural people and examining the two together. The second relationship formalizes the process of removing people who are either male or rural and examining the remainder. The first selects for examination the nonmales together with the nonrural people.

This discussion has been couched in terms of the extraction of subsets from a file for examination or use in a subfile. It should now be clear to the reader that the logical procedures of extracting cases to create a work file are exactly analagous to those defining subsets in the variable-generation process. In the first case, those observations for which the proposition is true are selected. In the latter case, the appropriate subset identifier is stored as the value of a new variable, appended to each observation as the rule is applied to it, and the record is returned to the main file. Usually, the positive integers and zero are used as subset identifiers.

The pair of distributive laws that apply to sets also apply to the propositions defining them. If p, q, and r are propositions, then

$$p \vee (q \wedge r) = (p \vee q) \wedge (p \vee r)$$
$$p \wedge (q \vee r) = (p \wedge q) \vee (p \wedge r).$$

Figure 7-4 summarizes all the relationships about propositions. One illustration is as follows: If we define a subset of observations F which has a rule of the form $p \vee (q \wedge r)$, as given in column 5, then observations for which p is false, q is true, and r is false (row F) are *not* to be given the identifier 1, corresponding to membership in K, since the corresponding table entry in column 5 is false. They will be assigned 0. Nor are observations to be given the identifier 1 if the configuration of truth values is given by rows G and H. On the other hand, those observations for which the configuration of true and false patterns corresponds to that in rows (A) through (E) would be assigned a 1. An example of such a rule that might occur in a survey and which has the $p \vee (q \wedge r)$ form specified by column 5 is: Code as 1 all interviews from people who are either female or who are black and live in the South. Code the remainder as 0.

We have p = female respondent, q = black respondent, r = respondent living in the South. A female, white, living in the South would be coded 1 (row C), and a male, white, living in the South (row G) would not be given the desig-

	1	2	3	4	5	6	7	8	9	10	11
	p	q	r	q ∧ r	p ∨ (q ∧ r)	p ∨ q	p ∨ r	q ∨ r	p ∧ (q ∨ r)	p ∧ q	p ∧ r
(A)	T	T	T	T	T	T	T	T	T	T	T
(B)	T	T	F	F	T	T	T	T	T	T	F
(C)	T	F	T	F	T	T	T	T	T	F	T
(D)	T	F	F	F	T	T	T	F	F	F	F
(E)	F	T	T	T	T	T	T	T	F	F	F
(F)	F	T	F	F	F	T	F	T	F	F	F
(G)	F	F	T	F	F	F	T	T	F	F	F
(H)	F	F	F	F	F	F	F	F	F	F	F

Figure 7-4 Truth Table for *p*, *q*, and *r*

nation 1 and would fall into the complement of the set specified by the first rule, receiving a 0.

The allied concepts of implication, if and only if, converse, and contrapositive were discussed in Chapter 6. The discussion here illustrates the employment of set-theory concepts in conceptualizing the rules required for mapping answers to survey questions onto the set of numbers. Sets are defined by propositions about the values of variables. Another useful set of concepts comes from the mathematical idea of a function. This is the subject of the next section.

Functions and Variable Generation

This section introduces a number of additional concepts useful in conceptualizing variable-generation and recoding problems in survey analysis. Functional notation provides a clear and concise way of specifying mathematical transformations on raw data, and the concepts of domain and range provide a vocabulary for discussing the way in which logical information and mathematical transformation specifications have to be supplied to a computer during the variable-generation phase of the data processing.

One straightforward definition of a function is a rule that prescribes a unique value of y for each given value of x on a Cartesian plane. A function can also be thought of as a rule that maps elements from one set (x) onto those of another (y) so that no two elements in y come from the same element of the first. The first set (x) is referred to as the domain and the second set (y) is the range.

Figure 7-5 illustrates the notions of domain and range. For the survey analyst faced with a variable-generation task, the domain ordinarily corresponds to the values of the variables to be transformed. This will include missing data and "inapplicable" codes (as well as any "wild" codes that may yet be in the data)! The range defines the set of possible recoded values given the domain.

In Figure 7-5(a) the mapping is enumerated rather than being specified in functional notation. The use of functional notation is illustrated in Figure 7-5(b).

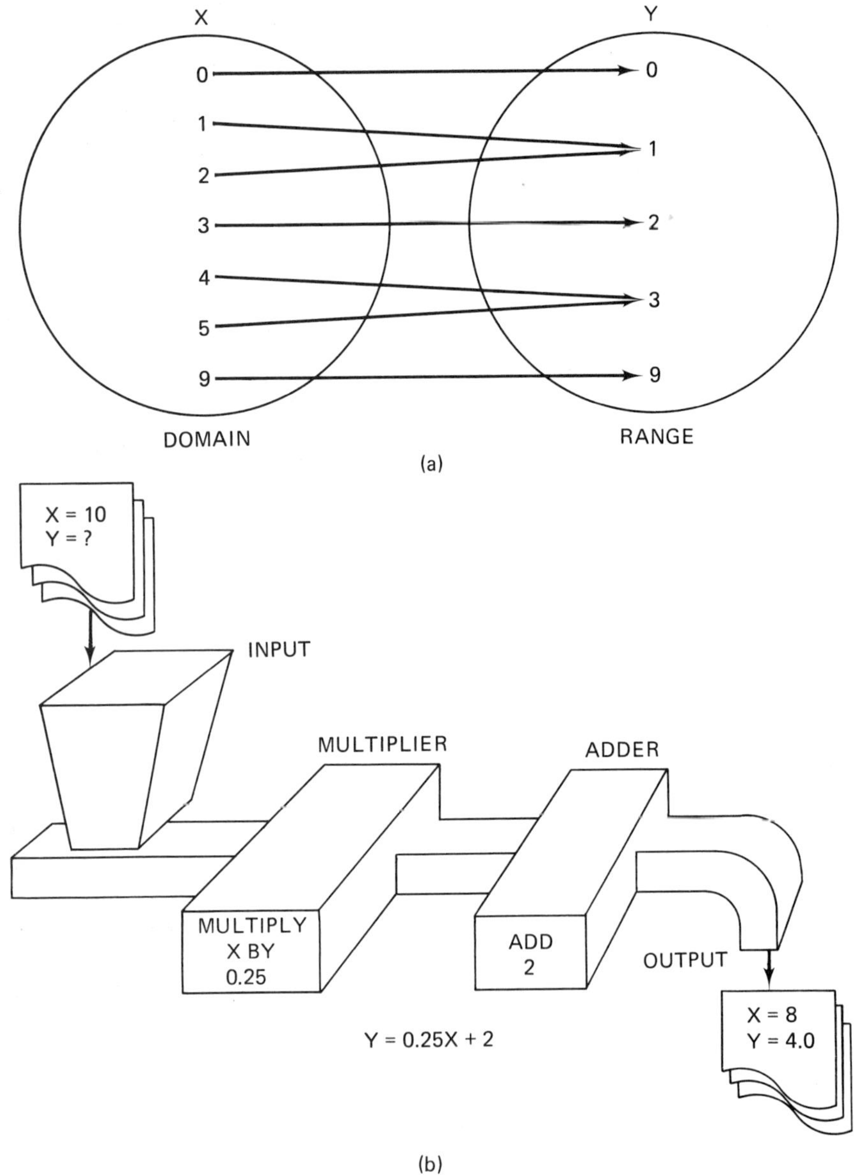

Figure 7-5 Functional Notation: Enumeration and Formula

Records are processed one at a time. The "machine" reads the value for x, applies the rule it has been programmed to use, and produces a value of y. In this illustration the machine accepts values of x and produces values of $y = .25x + 2$. An appropriate set of conditional statements would produce the mapping shown in Figure 7-5(a).

A function is completely specified by indicating its domain and its range, and either enumerating all the mapping arrows or writing an expression indicating all the mathematical relationships between input and output. Where data are nominal or ordinal, enumeration as a function definition is generally the appropriate method of notation. Where data are treated as interval or ratio scales, functional notation generally would be more satisfactory.

Figure 7-6 illustrates two of the types of functions commonly used in processing survey data. In Figure 7-6(a) the relationship is discontinuous at each end. This is the type of configuration that would occur if 0 were used to mean "This variable does not apply to this person," and 9 were used to mean "We don't know what the value of the variable is." The straight lines in between represent the treatment of applicable, known cases.

In Figure 7-6(b) a code consisting of five classes, an inapplicable code, and a missing-data code is "collapsed." The inapplicable and missing-data codes are retained, but the substantive categories are changed. This is the type of operation that would be used to put "strongly agree" and "agree" together on one side, group "strongly disagree" and "disagree" together on the other side, and leave the "undecided" group in the middle.

Generally, either enumeration or a combination of enumeration and formula notation will be used in working out the specifications for a recoding operation. Even when a formula can be used, the discontinuities in the function caused by the presence of inapplicable and missing data codes require some enumeration.

Functional notation can be extended to the case in which y is a function of several x's. For example,

$$Y = \sqrt{x_1^2 - x_2^2} \tag{7-1}$$

for the cases in which x_1 and x_2 are both valid data, with appropriate missing data codes for the cases in which one or both are "missing data" or "inapplicable." It is left to the reader to decide whether the domain of this function includes the cases for which the proposition $(x_1^2 - x_1^2) < 0$ is true.

When several nominal or ordinal variables are used to construct a function, enumerating the elements requires care, since all permutations and combinations of the codes that can appear in each of the x-variables have to be assigned y-values. For two or three x-variables, a cross-tabular format can be used which is similar to the row stubs on the truth table given in Figure 7-4. A single column is used, giving the y-values that are to be assigned for each combination of x-values.

The discussion has proceeded on the assumption that the values entering

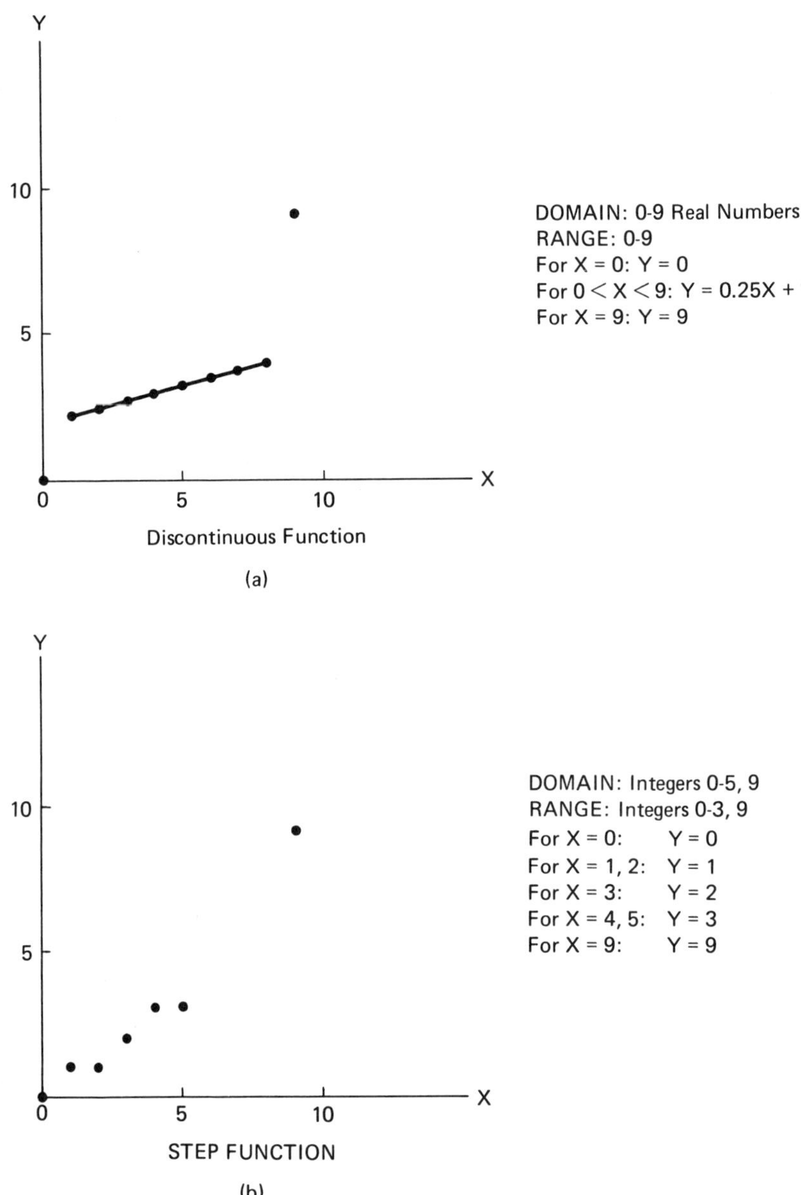

Figure 7-6 Functional Forms Typical of Those Found in Much Survey Data

into the computation of the function are constants, such as 1, 5, or 3, or are x-values available from the interview record. In this case the *algorithm*, or procedure for computing the function, starts with all the information present when the observation in question is processed. When all necessary information is not present, the procedure for computing the function may require two steps. In the example illustrated in Figure 7-6(a), a slope and an intercept were actually specified, on the assumption that these constants were available from past statistical analysis of the data or from theory or other a priori considerations.

However, many functions that we might want to use either require examination of each observation's position relative to others (e.g., percentile score) or computation of summary statistics from the file of observations to plug into the right places in the function. A z-score formula requires first knowing what the mean and standard deviation of the distribution is. This requires examining each observation and doing some computation. Then there is more computation after all the summations have taken place.

Writing down a function such as $z = (x - \bar{x})/s$ merely specifies a mapping rule—not a procedure for actually accomplishing the mapping; that requires prior computation of $\bar{x}$ and s. Whenever summations or examination of relative position are required, several steps, some involving the whole file of observations, are generally needed. These cautions apply to contextual variables, sometimes they apply to variables aggregated from subunits of the data, and generally they apply to variables representing changes over time. The important point here is to note that a mapping rule is not the same as a procedure for accomplishing the mapping.

We have been concerned with developing a vocabulary for talking about recoding and variable-generation problems. We used set theory and the ideas of union, intersection, and complement, the logic of propositions about the values of variables using relational and logical operators, and the concept of a function as a mapping rule with a domain and range. Remember that a mapping rule and the procedure for accomplishing it are not the same; each variable to be generated must have both defined.

TYPES OF GENERATED VARIABLES

It should be clear at this point that variable generation in survey analysis is not restricted to the mere collapsing of categories to facilitate the interpretation of a cross-tabulation. There are many types of function "machines" which can convert data as initially coded into a wide variety of forms. Which ones should be used in any given study will depend on the level of measurement achieved, whether data are collected on more than one unit of analysis, and whether or not the information is collected at two or more points in time. Obviously, this will also depend on the purposes of the analysis, the sophistication of the analyst, and the availability of suitable computer programs.

Figure 7-7 sets forth an outline of various types of generated variables. The rationale for the classification is the level of measurement that specifies the mathematical operations that typically would be employed in making transformations on the data and the type of summarization of the data required before

Summarization Required Over[1]	Type of Measurement Employed		
	Nominal	Ordinal	Interval or Ratio
None	Collapsed	Collapsed Adjacent Codes	Mathematical Transformation or Class Intervals
Variables	Typologies	Guttman Scale	Likert Scale Thurston Scale Ratios, sums
People	Contextual Configuration or Typology	Contextual Relation; Percentile	Contextual Variable; z-score, factor score, regression residual, share
Sub-units	Sub-unit configuration or typology	Sub-unit relational pattern, maximum, minimum, etc.	Sub-unit variable, sum, mean, variance, etc.
Time[2]	Turnover pattern	Change in rank, change in direction only	Numeric change score

[1] For simplicity summarization patterns over multiple-valued items, or trials has been omitted. These are further complicating factors, if present.

[2] In some cases summarization over two, or even three of these dimensions may be required before actual computation can occur.

Figure 7-7 An Overview of Types of Generated Variables

computation can take place. The need for summarization determines the number and type of steps that must first be performed on the data to compute the new variables.

The simplest case is the one in which no summarization is necessary and all the information needed is contained in a single variable. For nominal information, the only operations that are meaningful are those which accomplish the combining of sets. For instance, state codes might be combined into regions, or magazines grouped by type. Any subset can be combined with any other subset. Any mathematical transformation may be used and the scale's nominal properties remain invariant.

When the information is ordinal, only adjacent subsets can be combined (since the operators $<$ and $>$ now have meaning). Some examples include collapsing codes from percentile ranks and from single Guttman scale codes. Ordinal variables are invariant under any monotonic transformation.

When interval data are being transformed, any linear transformation will preserve the scale properties, and all four mathematical operators can be employed. The set combination operators, union and intersection, as restricted by ordinality to adjacent sets, can still be used.

When the variable in question is a ratio scale, only transformations where the scale is multiplied by a constant will preserve the ratio properties. All the logical relational and mathematical operators can be employed, as with interval data. It is useful to note that many transformations are undertaken specifically to change the ratio properties of such scales. One may prefer to analyze the square root of a positively skewed distribution or to work with logarithms of a variable instead of its original value. The objective might be to seek a form of the variable that is related linearly to another. Alternatively, one may apply only set and relational operators and establish an ordered set of class intervals for use in frequency distributions. A large fraction of the recoding done by survey analysts is of this code-collapsing or transformational type.

Computing new variables as functions of several others is somewhat more complex. At the nominal level this requires set-intersection (equality) operators applied to several variables. Examples include such typologies as family life cycle and type of mental illness. At the ordinal level, the less-than or greater-than operators are invoked among several variables. Guttman scaling procedures are illustrative of the type of variable-generation procedures for dealing with this type of data. At the interval or ratio level are found IQ score computations, Thurstone and Likert scaling procedures, and computations of ratios and sums.

In these examples, all the information is typically available in one place. Since most survey-data management systems store information with all the values for one unit at one period of time in one record, the computation can simply be done by reading the record, examining the variables in question, applying the rules, and writing out the results. When summarization has to take place first over people, times, or subunits, this is no longer the case. The variable-generation phase requires three steps: summarization over the requisite unit(s), computation of summary measures, and application to each observation of the information that is now available.

Summarization over people at the nominal level can be illustrated by a contextual variable characterizing each individual according to the modal class of observations in the group in which he interacts; for example, a variable indicating the predominant political-party affiliation in the county in which the respondent lives, or whether he is in a work group with a supervisor who is laissez-faire, autocratic, or democratic in his attitude toward workers. The data may come from other sources, or it may be generated by analyzing the study data. Summarization over people at the ordinal level is illustrated by the respondent's percentile position or rank on a variable among others in the study or in an important interacting subgroup. Contextual variables may also be computed at the interval or ratio-scale level. The most common types of variable generation requiring summarization over the whole group are those illustrated by the computation of *z*-scores, factor scores, or regression residuals.

Aggregation of data from subunits often present problems for survey analysts, because few survey data-management systems deal relatively easily with multiple units of analysis.[5] Examples of aggregation at the nominal level would include such variables as "whether any adult in the family has a blue-collar job" and "family owns at least one automobile bought new." At the ordinal level an example is "education level of most educated adult in the family." At the ratio-scale level, an example might be "age of the newest car that was purchased new by the family." The latter affords an excellent example of a variable that requires several rules applied to different subsets of the data. Its codes might include: (1) do not have a car, (2) have at least one car but it was not purchased new, (3) age in years of such a car, and (4) some type of required information was missing for at least one family member, so the new variable is "missing data."

Aggregation or summarization over time presents many of the same computational problems as that over contextual variables and subunits. Some examples of such variables include "vote pattern now and in last election" (nominal), "whether income went up or down during last 12 months" (ordinal), and "IQ change since kindergarten" (interval).

Of course, summarizations can take place over several dimensions. Summarization over variables and people (units) would be required to create a contextual Likert scale (e.g., adding up items to obtain the level of alienation in the respondent's work group). Summarization over variables and time would be required to create an IQ change pattern. Summarization over all three would be required to create a variable reflecting changes in factor-score patterns over time.

The most common strategy in dealing with complex summarizations that must be performed to compute indices reflecting contextual properties, changes over time, or properties of aggregated subunits is to restructure the file so that the requisite variables are present in a single logical record (i.e., so the file looks to the computer like a rectangular file for a single time period).[6] Then the generally available index construction and variable-generation routines available for those indices which require summarization only over variables can be employed. Keeping these larger issues in mind, we now turn to questions of more specific detail in the data processing that are related to the variable-generation process.

[5] There are exceptions: DATANAL, PICKLE, OSIRIS, and those based on COBOL code-generation techniques.

[6] Even this case ignores the possibility that multivalued variables may have to be dealt with (e.g., "Which magazines do you read?"). These introduce further complications which are handled only poorly by any currently existing survey data-management system when index construction problems are being considered.

OVERVIEW OF SCALING AND SCALE COMPUTATION

The nature of the computing process as it relates to survey analysis is ultimately determined by the nature of the measurement techniques that were employed in the data-collection process and by the specific analysis objectives at hand. This section presents a short discussion of measurement and relates it to several kinds of scaling operations that often precede use of the data in descriptive or explanatory survey analyses. Here the concern is primarily with the operations necessary to convert item responses into a scale, not with the analysis of the patterns of responses necessary to assess their dimensionality.[7]

The purpose of measurement is to quantify the attributes of objects, systems, persons, or other units of analysis. It requires applying a set of procedures according to a set of rules to obtain values of variables. These rules are standardized, in the sense that other investigators using the same ones should agree in the "amount" of the attribute present, given the same object. This permits replication, facilitates communication, and, like most cultural traditions, makes for economy of effort.

Not all concepts are matched by measurable variables, so obtaining a measure for the concept may require combining several variables. Of course, some concepts may not even be matched by any combination of measurable variables (e.g., "extrasensory perception"). On the other hand, a variable may pertain to more than one concept (e.g., "race" or "social class"), and thus it may present a problem of separation of effects for the analyst.

In the measurement process, numbers are assigned to objects to represent the quantity of each specific attribute thought to be present. Numbers are used as measures in at least three different ways, and the computing required will depend on the intended use of the numbers when they are assigned. Numbers are used:

1. As labels for individual objects. Here a real number, usually an integer, is simply assigned as a name and serves the purpose of distinguishing one individual object from another. Each object has its own identifying number (e.g., interview number 527).

2. As labels for classes of objects.[8] The number is a name representing a class of objects and, thus, is subject to the arithmetic and logical operations that can be performed with names. The objects in a single class are viewed as alike with respect to some attribute and, unlike

[7] The latter will be considered in Chapter 8.

[8] There is an important exception to this use of numbers for labels. For a useful discussion of "dummy-variable coding," see Cohen (1968) and Bottenberg and Ward (1963).

the above-mentioned use of numbers for names, many objects will be assigned the same number. Objects that do not possess this level of similarity on the attributes in question are given another number. Thus, this usage corresponds to what is commonly referred to as a "nominal" scale (e.g., males are coded 1, females as 2).

3. As labels for ordered classes of objects. The set of classes of objects is ordered from most to least with respect to an attribute. It is not known how much in an absolute sense any of the objects possesses the attribute, and there is no indication how far "apart" the objects are. The ordinal properties of the integers merely indicate the relative positions of the classes. This use is generally referred to as an ordinal measure (e.g., Guttman scale of alienation). In the extreme case there are no ties, and each class has exactly one element in it.
4. To measure distances between objects on the continuum represented by the attribute. The rank ordering of the objects is known, how far "apart" they are is known, but the absolute magnitude of the extent to which the attribute is present in each is not known (e.g., IQ, time, Likert scale or Thurstone scale not anchored at a zero point).
5. To indicate magnitudes relative to zero. The zero point is known for at least one of the objects. Rank ordering is known, as are distances between objects (e.g., height, weight, Likert or Thurstone scale with zero anchoring point). This is generally called a ratio scale.

It is important to note that for computational purposes, not all scale types are open to manipulation by means of any mathematical operator. With the appropriate operators come the associated mathematical techniques. Although it makes sense mathematically to add, say, five and three and then divide by two to get an average of four, it may not make sense logically in terms of the attribute measured by the numbers. This point is sometimes obvious and sometimes not; for instance, it is clearly ridiculous to compute $(5 + 3)/2 = 4$ if the attribute in question is "type of fruit"; five is the label for the class of apples and three is the label for the class of oranges. The level of correspondence between the mathematics and the notion of distance between points on an underlying attribute is not so obvious if the attribute is attraction toward "work group"; five on one item means "frequently eats lunch with other members," and three on another item means "sometimes eats lunch with supervisor."

In considering data transformations, it is important to know under what types of mathematical operations a scale will remain invariant. Invariance means that all the ratio, interval, or ordinal properties of the scale remain the same after the transformation has been performed. It remains the "same" scale, and the forms of its correlations with other scales and variables are not changed. Ordinal scales are invariant under any monotonic transformation. Interval scales are invariant under all linear transformations; ratio scales are invariant only under

Scale Type	Relational and Arithmetic Operators Assumed Applicable to the Scale	Scale Invarient Under:
Nominal	=	Any transformation
Ordinal	< = >	Any monotonic transformation
Interval[1]	< = > x / + −	Any linear transformation
Ratio	< = > x / + −	All transformation where scale is multiplied by a constant

[1]Strictly speaking the operators "x" and "/" can be applied to the intervals themselves if not to the values themselves; hence (c-d)/(a-b) would be legitimate even if c/a would not be.

Figure 7-8 Characteristics of Scales

multiplication or division by a constant.[9] Figure 7-8 summarizes the characteristics of these types of scales.

The logic of applying the mathematical and relational operators listed in Figure 7-8 is beyond the scope of our considerations. If the data fit the axioms of the measurement model used (and if the assumptions of the model seem reasonable), the measure has the properties of the scale generated by the application of the model, and the mathematical operators appropriate to that level of measurement can be used. The fit is a statistical problem; the reasonableness of the axioms often cannot be assessed until use of the scale reveals whether it turns out to be useful in research.[10]

There is some disagreement about the propriety of relaxing the extreme strictness of scaling assumptions and using mathematical transformation operators that are supposed to be reserved for "higher" levels of measurement, but it appears that the consequences are not always serious. Although it seems unwise to treat an ordinal scale (with no defined zero point) as though it were a ratio scale in order to produce aggregate estimates in a descriptive survey, correlations between variables and differences between group means appear to be little affected by monotone transformations. Thus, one would not care to estimate the total amount of discontent in a population using a Guttman scale ranging from very discontented (coded 5) to very pleased (coded 1), but using a Pearson product-moment correlation coefficient to relate discontent to dollar income probably would not result in a statistic whose value would mislead the analyst in an assessment of the relation between the two underlying attributes.

[9] For an informative discussion of invariance, see Nunnally (1967, Chap. 1).

[10] See Nunnally (1967).

Thus, if one is willing to assume that the scale used is at least monotonically related to the trait, product-moment and rank-correlation statistics will yield very similar results.[11] This is definitely not the case when slopes or other statistics heavily influenced by estimates of the shape of the functions are of interest.

As noted above, there are at least two sides to the question of whether mathematical manipulation of ordinal scales using addition, subtraction, multiplication, and division has desirable consequences. Can one legitimately average ratings, when the respondent was only asked to make ordinal judgments, in order to come up with an index combining the judgments from several items? The position to be taken here is that the answer should depend upon one's assessment of the long-run consequences for research of the mathematical manipulation of "questionable" scale items. According to Nunnally (1967), the gains outweigh the dangers. Keeping in mind that controversy over the question of ordinal versus interval measures is far from settled, we present a summary of the concepts that underlie the measurement model implied, by choosing to use the type of summated scales with which this chapter is primarily concerned.

The *trace line* of an item is a useful concept in explicating almost all measurement models that have to do with surveys in which one takes on the task of scaling respondents (as opposed to scaling items), as illustrated in Figure 7-9. The trace line of an item can be thought of simply as the plot of the expected values of the item scores that would be observed for respondents at various positions on the attribute. Figure 7-9(a) is a sharply rising monotonic response curve for a dichotomous item (the expected value is simply the proportion answering "yes" to the item). Two other trace lines are also illustrated, a nonmonotonic line approximating a normal distribution, Figure 7-9(b), the other almost linear. Figure 7-9(c) illustrates the trace for a five-category Likert-type item. The expected values are the mean of the responses for people at that point on the attribute. Of course, other shapes could be envisioned, including monotonically decreasing lines for negatively worded items.

Guttman Model

Figure 7-10 illustrates trace configurations that reflect the sets of assumptions forming the bases for Guttman, Thurstone, and Likert scaling models, respectively. In the Guttman model, persons responding positively to item 1 (the most extreme item) would also be expected to respond positively to items 2 and 3. Any respondent who responded negatively to item 1, but positively to item 2, would be expected to respond positively to item 3. He ranks "below" the former on the scale. The assumption made when using a Guttman scaling model is that a person at a given point on the attribute axis will tend to respond nega-

[11] See Nunnally (1967). However, Wilson (1971) takes an opposing view, arguing that in practice differing conclusions would be reached too frequently to justify "promoting" ordinal items (personal communication) and that hypotheses testing logic cannot rise above circularity unless independent justification for trace-line assumptions can be adduced.

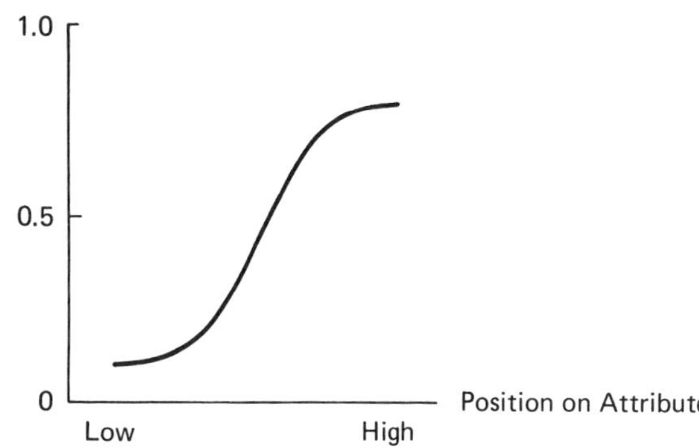

(a): Monotonic Trace Line with Steep Slope

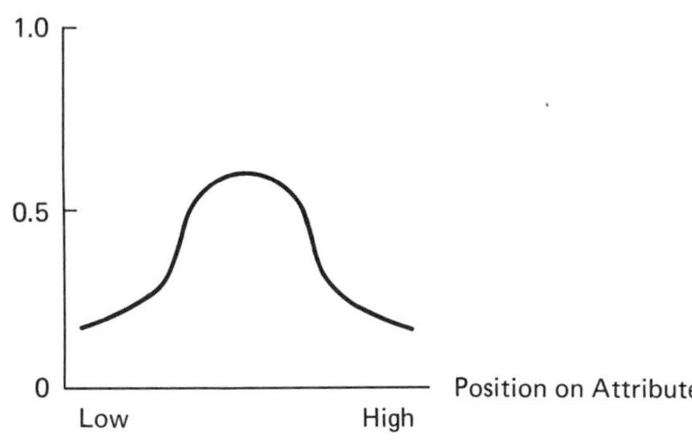

(b): Non-monotonic Trace Line

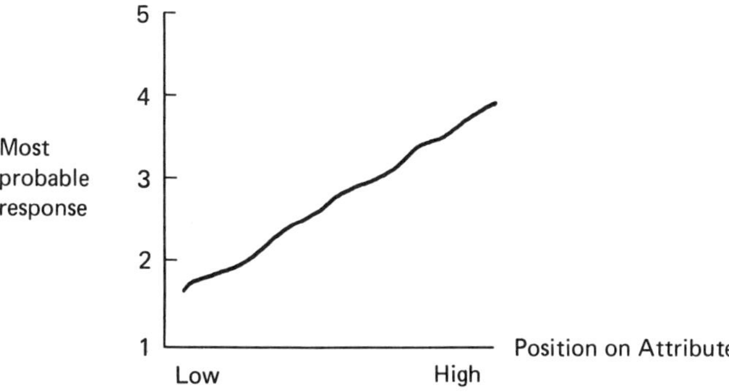

(c): Monotonic Trace Line with Gentle Slope and Approximately Linear

Figure 7-9 Three Types of Trace Lines

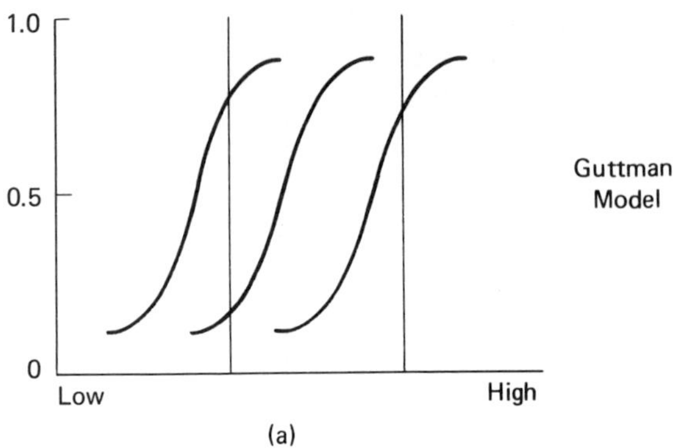

(a)

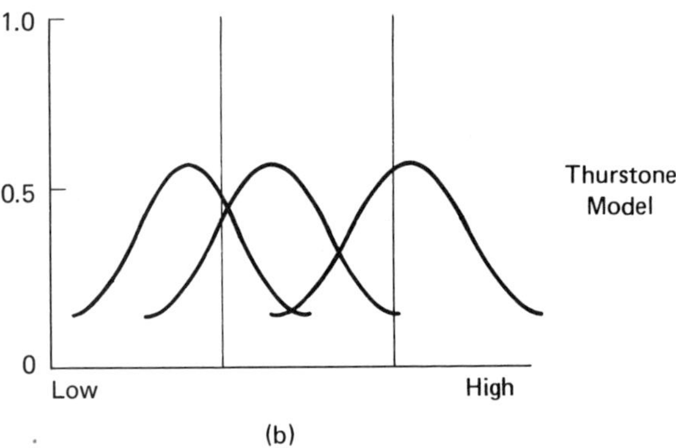

(b)

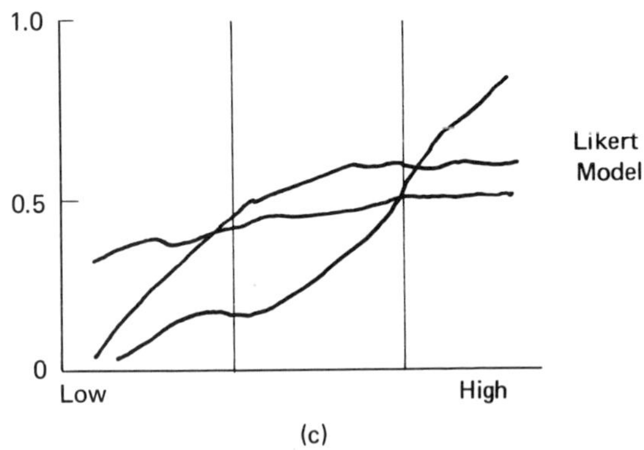

(c)

Figure 7-10 Assumed Trace Line Configurations for Guttman, Thurstone, and Likert Models

tively to all items whose trace lines rise at a point to the right of him and positively to those items whose lines rise at a point to the left of him. A further rather important assumption is that the items are "valid" (i.e., they all measure the attribute in question and not a variety of attributes). In addition, the items have to be worded so as to have the type of trace line shown. If the trace-line assumptions and the validity assumption can be presumed to apply to a set of items, they should form a triangular pattern of responses, such as that illustrated by Figure 7-11.

Person	Response Number 1	2	3	4	Scale Type
2	1	0	0	0	1
3	1	0	0	0	1
1	1	1	0	0	2
5	1	1	1	0	3
4	1	1	1	0	3
6	1	1	1	1	4
7	1	1	0	1	"Error"

Triangular pattern of positive and negative responses that fits the monotone scaling requirements for a Guttman scale.

Figure 7-11 Pattern of Agreement for Items

The actual logic used in practice is a little different. If the data fit closely the type of pattern shown in Figure 7-11, and if the validity assumption appears reasonable, then it is said that a Guttman scale for the underlying attribute has been developed. Some maverick respondents always mar perfection, however. In the illustration, person number seven displays a nonscale pattern that could be equally well assigned, without serious loss of information or misrepresentation, to scale types three or four.

The development of such a scale would have previously involved administering a collection of items that are presumed to have trace lines of the kind indicated to a group of people. Then by trial and error, cutting points would have been chosen (if the items are not dichotomous), and the data would have been arranged so as to produce a pattern as close as possible in shape to the required triangular pattern. Since there are several people generally at each scale point, the data matrix takes on the shape of a staircase. Items that tend to be associated frequently with nonscale configurations of responses are discarded, and the procedure is repeated until the best ordering of items and people is found.[12]

12 The trace-line assumptions for Guttman scaling have been severely criticized by Nunnally (1967). A review of the arguments is beyond the scope of the present treatment, and the reader is referred to this source.

In assigning Guttman scale positions to respondents, a frequently used method is simply counting the number of positive responses. This is often used when items are dichotomous. A more precise procedure is to determine the respondent's scale type and then assign the associated scale value. This is accomplished essentially by a computer-based table look-up procedure that

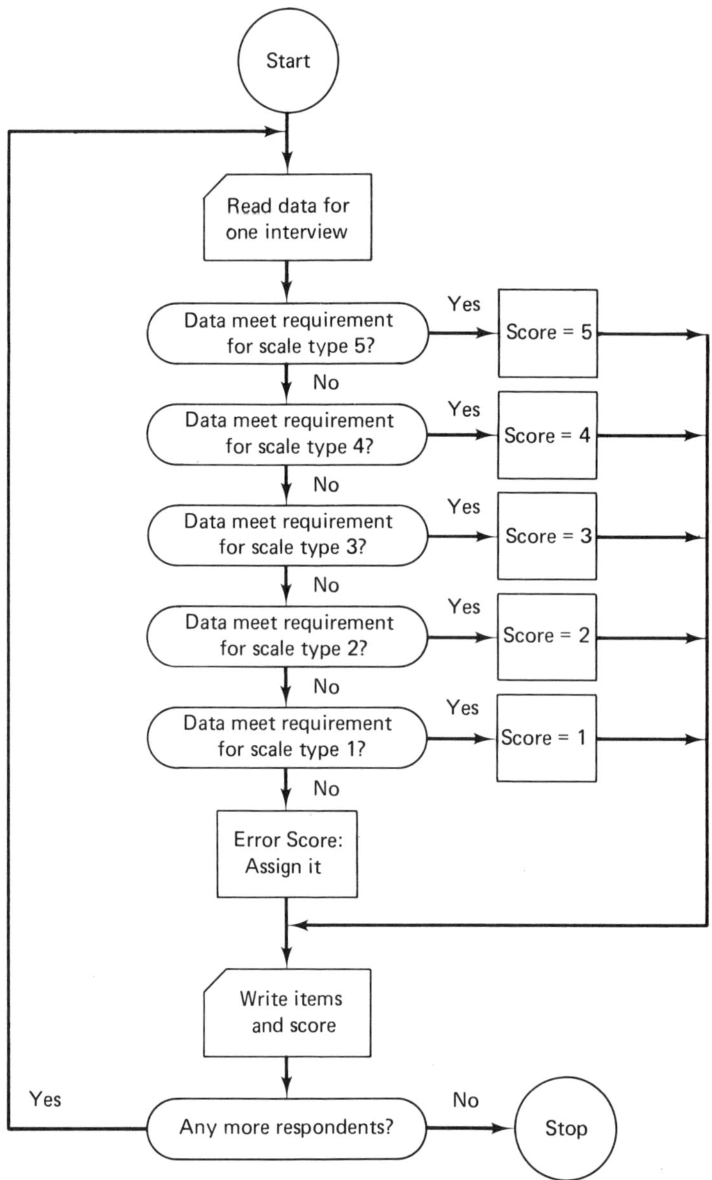

Figure 7-12 Computation of Guttman Scale

requires recognizing what pattern of responses is associated with a particular case and obtaining the matching scale value (see Figure 7-12). The problem again is those respondents who do not have perfect scale patterns. These may even constitute a fair proportion of the sample, possibly a majority. Even with high "reproductibility coefficients," these "mavericks" are troublesome.

One procedure for "rounding them up" satisfactorily is to assign the offender the score that corresponds to the perfect scale pattern most similar to his own.[13] This minimizes his error. However, this does not always yield an unambiguous solution. To resolve ambiguities, Borgatta and Hayes (1952) suggest assigning the average of the score of the alternative scale-pattern candidates. Henry (1952) favors assigning the maverick to the most frequent of the alternative perfect scale types. Riley et al. (1954) put forth the following rule: If the number of alternative types available for assignment is odd, assign the response to the middle type; if it is even, assign it to the type closest to the middle of the scale; or if the two are equidistant from the middle, assign it to the most negative of the two.

It is generally a good idea to inspect a small number of "maverick" interviews to gain some intuitive feel for the data. Figure 7-13 provides a guideline for information that must be assembled when constructing Guttman scale scores.

Thurstone Model

In contrast to the Guttman model, the Thurstone scaling model presupposes items that are written so that they have nonmonotonic trace lines; that is, it is assumed that at some point the trace line for each item changes its slope from positive to negative. Indeed, the Thurstone model assumes that the item traces approximate normality. Thus, any individual's probability of responding in the positive direction on the scale is assumed to be highest for those items whose trace line is high at the point on the attribute axis where that individual lies. Items that are either less positive or more positive than the individual's position will tend to be rejected. Items are chosen from a large number of attitude statements that have each been rated by a group of judges on, say, an 11-point scale as to how favorable or unfavorable they are on the attitude dimension. The mean of the judges' ratings is termed the item's scale "value." Items are then chosen upon which judges agree and which, taken together, span the entire range from positive to negative on the attitude dimension. A respondent's scale score is the average of the scale values of the items that he has responded to positively. Given the assumption that the judges make interval discrimination, the respondent's score appears as interval; hence, the term "equal-appearing intervals" is often applied to the resulting scale. Complete details are given by Edwards (1957), and Nunnally (1967) provides a critical evaluation. The details

[13] Similarity is measured by the number of item responses made by the maverick that would have to be changed in order for him to agree perfectly with the perfect scale pattern.

Checklist for Information to be Supplied when Constructing a Guttman Scale

A. Input Cases – subset definition
   1. File name and date: data to be used
   2. Definition of units of analysis for which scale is "defined"
   3. Subset of units of analysis to be used for which the measure is "defined" (rule for extracting subset)

B. Input Items – list
   1. Item identification (question, variable names, question number, etc.)
   2. Treatment of inapplicable and missing data codes
   3. Locations of fields in input records

C. Table-look-up information – mapping rules
   1. List of configurations and scale values to be assigned
   2. Cutting points for positive and negative treatment
   3. Rule for assigning "inapplicable" cases
   4. Rule for assigning cases with some missing information
   5. Rule for assigning non-scale types

D. Output – new variable
   1. File name
   2. Location of field in file, field width
   3. Code for the field and variable name

E. Examples
   1. Lowest scale value configuration
   2. Intermediate scale value configuration
   3. Highest scale value configuration
   4. Example of assignment of "inapplicable" case, missing information case and assignment of several non-scale-type cases.

Figure 7-13 Guttman Checklist

of the rather straightforward computer processing are given in Figures 7-14 and 7-15. All items are read for a given respondent. The scale values of those he agrees with are looked up in an internally stored table, and the results are averaged. Then the resulting index is added to the respondent's file together with the items.

Likert Model

Most scales currently in use in survey research appear to be based on the summation model originally set forth by Likert (1932). Like the other two models, this model assumes valid items (i.e., that almost all of the variation in each item score is due to the respondent's position on the same underlying attribute). Unlike other models, trace lines are assumed only to be monotonically related to the attribute. But the assumption is made that the lines are such that a summation of item scores is assumed to be approximately linearly related to it. The logic applies to items with multiple positions (i.e., five-point

Checklist of Information Required for Computing Scale Values of Respondents Using Thurstone Techniques

A. Input Cases
   1. File name and date: data to be used
   2. Definition of units of analysis for which scale is defined
   3. Subset of units of analysis to be used for which the measure is defined (rule for extracting subset)

B. Input Items
   1. Item identification (question number, variable names, question wording, etc.)
   2. Inapplicable and missing data codes
   3. Locations of fields in input records

C. Computation Information
   1. Scale value associated with each item
   2. Minimum number of items with no missing data that will permit computation of a scale score; rule for deciding how much missing data can be tolerated before scale score is assigned as missing data
   3. Formula for averaging item scale values
   4. Handling of decimal points and, where appropriate, zeroes and negatives

D. Output
   1. File name
   2. Location of field in file, field width
   3. Code, range, handling of decimal points, minus signs, N.A. and inappropriate codes

E. Examples
   1. Lowest possible scale value configuration
   2. Highest scale value configuration
   3. Maximum amount of missing data that still permits computation
   4. Amount of missing data that requires assignment of missing data
   5. Values supplied for an inapplicable case and a missing data case

Figure 7-14 Thurstone Checklist

scales) as well as to dichotomous items. Unlike the Guttman assumptions, each item is not assumed to have the same type of monotonic curve; on the contrary, it is expected that each monotonic trace line will have its own pattern of departures from linearity, but that when combined these will cancel each other out and the resulting combination will be approximately linear, especially if enough items are used. Thus, the assumptions of the model lead to a linear combination of items (e.g., their sum or average) and so to an interval scale, rather than one with merely ordinal properties. Adding an additional assumption, the existence of a zero point, leads to a ratio scale.

In addition to the reasonableness of its trace-line assumptions, other

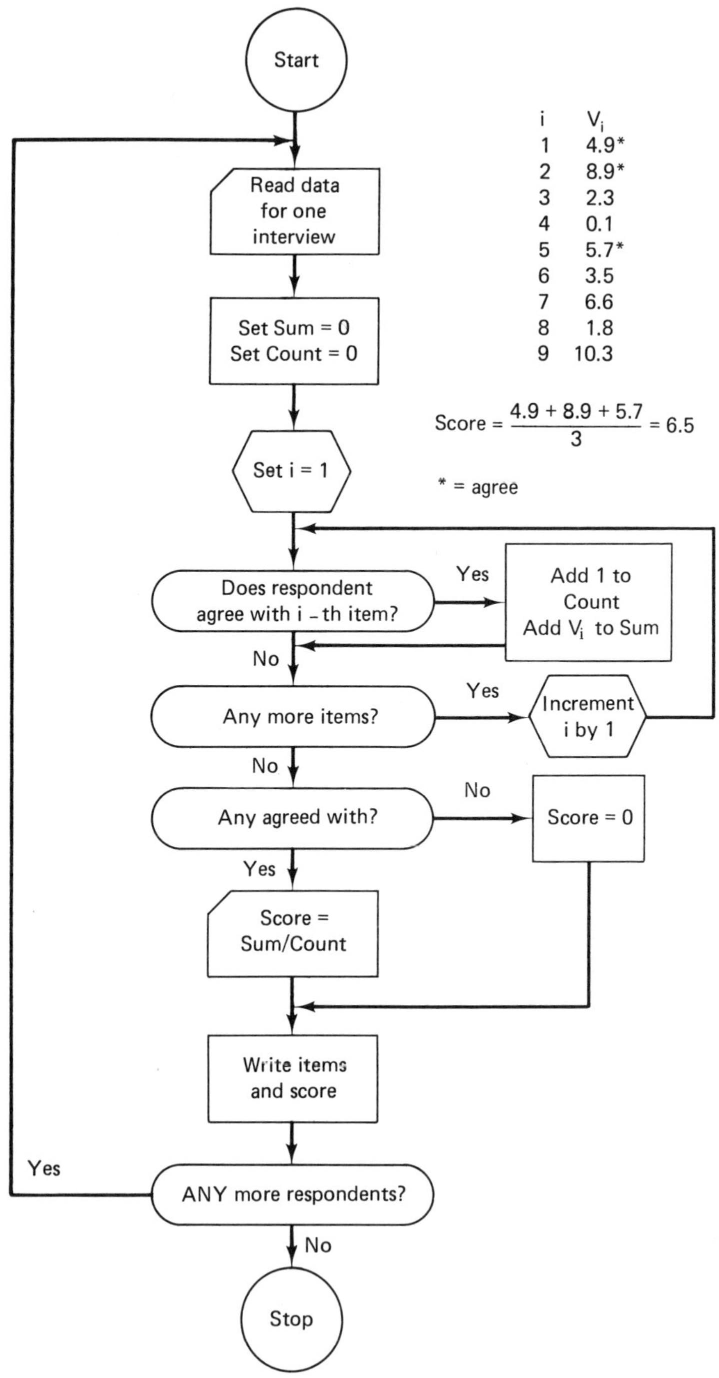

Figure 7-15 Computation of Thurstone Scale Scores

advantages of the model include the recognition that individual items tend to have considerable specificity and may possibly have considerable measurement error. The model allows for this in that individual items are not given undue weight. With enough items, Likert scales can apparently be made highly reliable, they are relatively easy to construct, and they can easily be adapted to many different kinds of measurement situations. The model appears intuitively reasonable.

Ordinarily, in computing scale scores, differential weighting of items is not used (Nunnally, 1967, p. 534); the exception is when a factor analysis has provided exact definitions of the relationships between items and an underlying factor structure to be used. The need to avoid error due to positive response sets in the data-collection phase of research often requires phrasing some items negatively, and thus reversing some item scores is generally necessary in the computation of the scale score. Missing data on some of the items are simply handled by omitting the item from computation of the scale score or by assigning the average of the items. Of course, if too many items are missing, the respondent must be declared N.A. for the scale. The analyst must decide which items or how many items missing shall be sufficient for the scale to be declared N.A. for that respondent.

Although Likert-scale construction is vastly simplified if all the items are designed to have the same number of response categories, in some cases it may be desirable to use items with differing numbers of response categories in a single Likert scale. There are two alternatives. One is to adopt cutting points on the basis of the most reasonable assumptions available and to collapse all items into dichotomies. This loses information. A better procedure is for the response categories to be normalized before an average score over the items is computed. Obviously, item ranges must be made equal before this can be done. One way to do this is to convert item scores into z-scores. A simpler procedure is to normalize all items to a range of 10. The following formula can be used:

$$S_{ij} = \frac{10(R_{ij} - .5)}{M_i}, \tag{7-2}$$

where S_{ij} is the normalized score for ith item for the jth respondent, R_i is the raw score made by the jth respondent on the ith item, and M_i is the largest score obtainable on the ith item.[14] The formula assumes that integers have been assigned to the M_i response categories as follows: $1, 2, \ldots, M_{i-1}, M_i$. The formula will result in nonintegral values, but this will not disrupt things, since the scores are to be averaged. An example will make the process clearer.

Two items are to be used in a scale of perceived job advancement opportunities. They are scored as follows:

[14] Note that actual range of the normalized scores is from .5 to 9.5; either 0 or 9.9 could be used as a missing-data code.

1. Is the company you work for a good one for a person who is trying to get ahead in life?
   (1) ____ Very good (2) ____ good (3) ____ All right
   (4) ____ Bad (5) ____ Very bad
2. In your company do employees have to fight for whatever they get?
   (1) ____ Always (2) ____ A lot of the time (3) ____ Some of the time (4) ____ Hardly ever

One of the items, say the first, will have to be reversed by subracting it from 1

Check List of Information Required for Computing Scale Values of Respondents Using Likert Techniques

A. Input Cases
   1. File name and date of data to be used as input
   2. Definition of units of analysis for which scale is defined
   3. Subset of units of analysis to be used for which measure is defined (include rule for extracting subset)

B. Input Items
   1. Item identification (question number, variable name, question wording, etc.)
   2. Inapplicable and missing data codes
   3. Locations of fields in input records

C. Computation Information
   1. Exact codes for each items to be used in the scale
   2. List of items that are to be reversed in direction and reversal instruction
   3. Cutting points if dichotomization is to be used
   4. Instructions for normalizing where needed
   5. Weighting procedures to be used, (specify unit weights if no weighting)
   6. Minimum number or pattern of items to be used in constructing scale (anything with less information is assigned missing data code)
   7. Formulas and rounding instructions
   8. Instructions for handling case in which all items are missing data or zero denominator occurs formulas
   9. Assignment procedures for missing items, where appropriate

D. Output Information
   1. File name
   2. Location of field file, field width
   3. Code: range, handling of decimal points, minus signs, missing data and inapplicable codes

E. Examples
   1. Reversal of scale
   2. Normalization example
   3. Maximum value and minimum value of scale using weighting procedures if any
   4. Example of patterns that would result in inapplicable, missing data and assignment
   5. Maximum amount of missing data that still permits computation

Figure 7-16 Likert Checklist

greater than its maximum. Both are to be adjusted to a 10-point scale. Assuming that a respondent answered the first item by checking "2" and the second by checking a "3," we would have

$$S_1 = \frac{10[(6 - 2) - .5]}{5} = 7 \tag{7-3}$$

$$S_2 = \frac{10(3 - .5)}{4} = 6.25. \tag{7-4}$$

The scale score is $(7 + 6.25)/2 = 6.6$ when rounded to one decimal. Figure 7-16 illustrates the computation. Figure 7-17 contains a checklist of information to be supplied when constructing a Likert scale.

We turn now to a consideration of computing procedures in variable generation.

PROCEDURES FOR GENERATING VARIABLES

Working out a procedure for generating new variables requires a close attention to detail and an awareness of the way in which the variables are to be used in the analysis, as well as technical computing knowledge. This section we shall outline the kinds of information that must be specified when the procedures for generating new variables are being worked out. Perhaps more mistakes are made at this point in survey research than at any other (except for the actual interviewing process). Hence, there is a real payoff for conscientious checking of drafted specifications. Here are the steps that must be performed and written down clearly and completely in preparing the logic statements and the code addition:

1. *Specify the population over which the new variable is to be defined.*
   (a) Specify the *units* (persons, families) to be used as (1) input and (2) output.
   (b) Specify the *group* of these units for which the resulting measure is *defined.* (For example: The variable "proportion of acute conditions attended by a physician" is defined only for people having at least one acute condition during the time period asked about in the interview.)
   (c) In writing the code for the new variable, allow one value (often zero is a good choice) to represent uniquely those cases where the concept (and thus the variable) does not apply. Write the rest of the rules for generating the new variable so that this code can never be generated by any other applicable condition.
2. *Define the fields to be used as inputs.* This information should include the file identification, the *location* (columns or character position), and

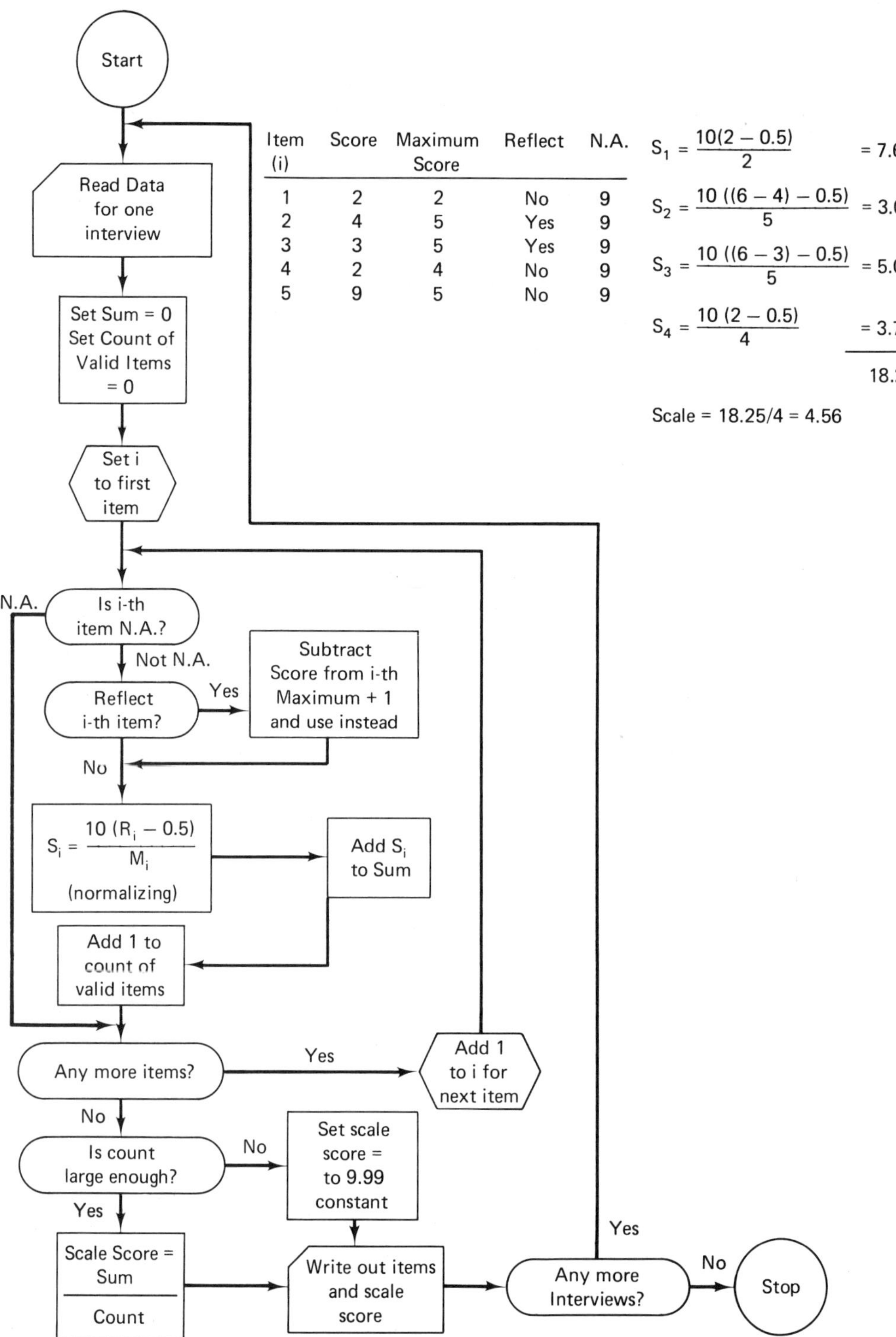

Figure 7-17 Likert Scale Score Computations

the character set used for the variable. The presence of *minus signs* and *inapplicable codes* in the input variables should be indicated. *Missing information* codes and *maximum and minimum values* of applicable codes should also be listed. These should comprise the entire range of codes logically *possible—not* merely those *expected. Decimal places* should be specified where applicable for input variables. A *complete code* for the variable should be supplied. Assign *names* to variables which are unique and not confusing.

3. *Define the fields to be used as outputs.* This should include *location*, number of *characters* (i.e., field width), *decimal-point location*, *possibility of negative (minus) values*, *inapplicable values*, and *missing information codes*. *Maximum* and *minimum* legal values should be specified and a *complete code* supplied. If *negative values* do not occur, specify this rather than not saying anything about minus signs.
4. Define the *units*, *subunits*, *times*, and so on, over which summarization must take place before computation can proceed. If summarization requires that the file be in a *sequence*, specify the fields to be used as *keys* for the ordering.
5. *Specify computation.* Use *formulas*, *constants*, *tables*, and *group definitions* to indicate what the computation is. In some cases this will require assigning values to certain classes of observation *in order*, so as to establish priorities. Generally, the specification is best if independent of the order. Each case in the sample should receive an *unambiguous value*. This is easily given by writing a series of pairs, each pair consisting of a group definition and a rule assigning a value to the new variable based on the inputs. Take care of all "expected" or "legal" values of the inputs first. Then specify what is to be done with unanticipated configurations of conditions in the data. Missing data codes and inapplicable codes should be treated as "anticipated." Specify what to do if the denominator of a fraction is zero (usually set the fraction = 0). Codes selected for all substantive answers, for "no answer," or for "inapplicable" must be chosen so that statistical programs to be used later will accept them.
6. *Generate test data.* Supply *test observations* and *precalculated answers*, run the program, and then check the results against the known answers. Include cases that will generate *missing-data codes*, *inapplicable codes*, some at the *bottom* of all legitimate ranges, and some at the *very top*. Various permutations of these conditions are desirable in a test setup. Time and money determine how much testing and verification of results can be done. A mistake made in generating variables will often require redoing or abandoning all statistics and tables based on those variables; hence, care is needed. Run marginal distributions, means, and so on, immediately for further checks.

7. *Provide adequate records.* Each step of the variable-generation process levels some sort of record of what was done. The best example would be the actual documentation produced by library programs or compilations of computer programs. If tabulating equipment is used, a set of instructions should be produced. These documents should be carefully organized and additional comments added when appropriate and kept as a permanent record of the data-transformation process. Each "job" (e.g., the construction of one or more variables with a library program) should receive a unique identifying number. All documents for the job should be *dated* and sequentially *numbered* (in the order in which steps are performed where relevant) and kept in a permanent file. For each new variable generated and added to the master file, a *dated* "code addition" should be made and added to the master code. The addition should refer to the job number and step that generated each variable.

Missing Data in Scale Computations

To create Likert scales, item responses are counted or summed. If some items are not present (respondent may say "*don't know*" to a given item), the scale must be set to "don't know" or the scoring formula must accommodate N.A.'s, usually by estimating the missing answer. One method is to replace the *missing* items with the average of those present. For example, if

$$S = \sum_{i=1}^{5} x_i \tag{7-5}$$

(i.e., the score is the sum of x_1, x_2, x_3, x_4, x_5) and x_4 is missing, we might replace x_4 with

$$\frac{x_1 + x_2 + x_3 + x_5}{4}. \tag{7-6}$$

This can be done if the *range of each item is the same.*[15] Alternatively, we may count items coded in the scale direction:

$$S = \prod_{i+1}^{5} (x_i = 1) \tag{7-7}$$

and the scale scores is the *count* of the number of items 1–5 in which the value of the item equals 1. (The number of "yes" responses might be an example.) A missing item can be replaced with a 1 or other value according to a *probability* determined from the known items. Suppose that x_4 is unknown and $x_1 = x_2 = x_5 = 1$. Then the probability that x_4 is 1 is equal to

$$\frac{1 + 1 + 1}{1 + 1 + 1 + 1} = \frac{3}{4} = .75,$$

[15] See the dicussion of normalizing ranges presented earlier in this chapter.

since 3 out of 4 known values are 1. Then x_4 is generated using a *random-number generator*. Then the total scale score is computed.

Missing information in Thurstone items constitutes no technical problem provided that one is willing to make an assumption similar to those required above—that the mean of the items on which there is no answer is no different from that of the items answered by the respondent, and that this is true for all respondents. The scale score is simply the mean of the scores for the items responded to. The extent to which this assumption may be justified will depend on the circumstances and the past history of nonresponse associated with the items. Missing information in Guttman items can be dealt with using one of the three procedures outlined earlier for dealing with nonscale types.

Probably the most satisfactory procedure for dealing with missing information in the components of a configuration measure such as family life cycle is to assign values to the components first. This has the advantage of preventing unreasonable ad hoc assumptions from entering the analysis in a form that has generally been forgotton by the time the final report for the study is being written. On the other hand, if reasonable assumptions can be made and if the amount of missing information is not large, the simplest procedure is to deal with the missing-data categories as a part of the computer program that generates the configuration.

An alternative method of deciding what to assign for any missing scale item is to choose a random number from a distribution with the same "shape" as the distribution of known cases for the *item*, to assign this number as the replacement for the missing value for the item, and then to compute the scale score as usual. For interval or ratio items this can be approximated by selection from a normal distribution with the same range, mean, and standard deviation as that of the known cases. If more accuracy is desired, skewness and other deviations from normality can be taken into account.

Selection of a subset of the known cases as a base for determining the shape of the random distribution from which the assignment is to be made further increases the accuracy, provided the criteria for selecting the distribution are known to be correlated with the item in question. However, as noted elsewhere, the objectives of the study must be taken into account in selecting these criteria, since selection of the distribution may bias findings if the study objectives involve model building, hypothesis testing, or any other explanatory objective.

When the purpose of the scale is descriptive and the variable is an important one, a good general rule is to use the most accurate estimating procedure consistent with time and budget. Otherwise, selection of a random number from a normal distribution with the same mean, standard deviation, and range as the known item scores is a reasonable and easy-to-implement choice.

Similar considerations apply to ordinal and nominal items. The hand-editing procedures described earlier, which involved assignment from probability tables, correspond to a more complex procedure that can easily be programmed for a computer, in which the item is assigned to one class if a generated random number is within one range, and to another class if it is larger or smaller. In this case random numbers from a flat distribution bounded by zero and 1 are used. The ranges taken together run from zero to 1 with widths corresponding to the proportion of known item scores that lie in the various class intervals.

The advantage of randomized procedures based only on the distribution of the offending item are that they enable conceptualizing N.A. cases as "white noise"—pure random information. In an explanatory study, this appropriately biases correlation coefficients downward. It may not be best for a descriptive study, however. In any case, none of these procedures is a good substitute for adequate interviewing and carefully thought out and pretested scales.

Variable Building: Examples

This section details the major steps usually followed in the process of variable construction. They may be summarized as follows:

1. Define the form of the variables desired, based on the research objectives and the concepts of the study. Operationally, this will yield a CODE ADDITION.
2. Elaborate the functional logic of the mapping rules for the variables desired, identifying all the input variables required and the relationships between them that will determine the values of the variables to be built. This is called the LOGIC STATEMENT. Check it thoroughly.
3. Translate the logic statement into the PROCEDURAL LANGUAGE of the variable-building technology (e.g., FORTRAN if you are writing your own program, or the logical statements of any library routine to be used). Have someone else check it thoroughly.
4. Check the routine on test data.
5. Execute the operation and add the new variables to the data file. Then recheck the results.
6. Update all records and codes, and file the variable-generation program in the permanent processing record for the project.

The following example illustrates the computation of a ratio:

Input Fields

1. Number of chronic conditions in 1964 per person (NO. CHR. 64). Card P columns 31 and 32, range 00–99. No missing data; no inapplicable cases (all persons used), no decimals. Defines "C"

2. Number of chronic conditions attended by a physician in 1964 per person (ATT.CHR.64); card P columns 33–44, range 00–99. No missing data; 00 in columns 31 and 32 indicates inapplicable case, no decimals. Defines "A"

Output Fields

3. Attendance ratio—index of attendance (CHR.ATT.R.64). Card P columns 68 and 69. Form XX, read as X.X, range 0.0 to 1.0. Decimal point not punched. Inapplicable indicated by 99. No missing data. Defines "CAR64"

4. Calculation of the ratio (CHR.ATT.R.64).
   (a) For all persons where $C > 0$ (there was at least one chronic condition) and where $P \leq C$:

$$\text{CAR64} = \frac{P}{C} \times 10,$$

   where P is the number of attended chronic illnesses in 1964 and C is the number of chronic illnesses. Compute to two decimal places, round to one place, and multiply to write out as X.X.
   (b) For all other cases, CAR64 = 99.
   (c) Whenever $P > C$, print "Family Number" in addition to CHR.ATT.R.64, P, and C.

5. Documentation:

Study 777   Card P   Code Addition   July 23, 1974

Variable Number	*Column Number*	*Description*
38	68–69	Ratio of chronic illnesses in 1964 attended by a physician (CHR.ATT.R.64) (Spec. Sheet 11, Step 4, July 23, 1974). Decimal X.X—range 0.0–1.0. Form XX, read as X.X. No missing data.
		00 Had conditions, no attendance
		XX Ratio of chronic illness attended to total chronic illness
		10 All conditions treated
		99 No conditions; inapplicable

A second example illustrates the collapse of the code "age in years" into a set of class intervals. The input file is that referred to above:

Age in Years (P: 35–36)	*AGELEV* (P: 70)
00–18	1
19–24	2
25–34	3
35–44	4
45–54	5
55–64	6
65–98	7
99 (missing information)	9

This procedure uses a set of *conditions* in the left-hand column and a set of corresponding *constants* describing the values of the new variables in the right-hand column. Thus, it illustrates the use of a step function.

A third example illustrates the use of several group definitions to compute an index:

For all persons—child care capability (CCC) is defined as follows:

1. Family has no children under age 14:
   CCC = 0 (inapplicable).
2. Family has children and there is at least one adult female (age over 18) in the house whose main activity is keeping house:
   CCC = 4.
3. Family has children and there is no adult female keeping house (*no* person who is female, over age 18, and keeps house), but there is at least one adult female working on a farm:
   CCC = 3.
4. Same as (3) except that all adult females present work other than on a farm or keeping house:
   CCC = 2.
5. Family has children but includes no adult females:
   CCC = 1.
6. Otherwise, CCC = 9 and print family number and input data.

In the next example, the variables that the researcher desires to add to his data file are (1) a set of class intervals for the age of the family head, (2) a life-cycle variable, and (3) a broad summary of region of residence for each respondent. The form of those variables is shown in Figure 7-18, which is an example of what the code addition might look like.

The next step is to spell out just how these new variables will be mapped and then constructed from the data presently contained in the study. This

Variable Number	Column Number		
36	57	Age of Family Head – Bracket (AGEB)	PGM01
		1. 18-24	
		2. 25-34	
		3. 35-44	
		4. 45-54	
		5. 55-64	
		6. 65 and over	
37	58	Family Life Cycle Categories (LC)	PGM01
		Under Age 45	
		1. Unmarried, no children	
		2. Married, 2 or more adults, no children	
		3. Married, 2 or more adults, youngest child under 6	
		4. Married, 2 or more adults, youngest child 6 or over	
		Age 45 or over	
		5. Married, 2 or more adults, has children	
		6. Married, 2 or more adults, no children, head in labor force*	
		7. Married, 2 or more adults, no children, head retired*	
		8. Unmarried, no children, head in labor force*	
		9. Unmarried, no children, head retired*	
		Any Age	
		0. Unmarried, has children	
38	59	Region of Residence (REGION)	PGM01
		1. Northeast	
		2. North Central	
		3. South	
		4. West	

* Unemployed people and housewives 55 years or over are considered retired; unemployed people and housewives under 55 are considered to be in the labor force.

Figure 7-18 Code Addition

requires the detailing of the logic and mathematics of the functions involved, keeping in mind the two fundamental requirements that the categories of the variables built must be mutually exclusive and exhaustive in all possibilities. For the variables used in this example, the mapping logic is shown in Figure 7-19. The first thing that should be noted is the information content of the logic statement:

1. All variables are assigned a meaningful name for easy reference (e.g., AGE, MSTAT, LC, AGEB, REGION).

2. The actual meaning of each name is included along with the mnemonic reference (e.g., "head's age," "marital status").
3. The location of each variable on the original data deck is identified (e.g., AGE, the age of the family head in years, is located in columns 34 and 35 of the data deck designated card 1; this is denoted 1: 34–35). The exact form of this identification will vary, depending on the storage medium used for the data (e.g., tape, disk, cards).
4. The sequence number of each variable is identified (e.g., AGE is V17, the seventeenth variable in the string of variables that make up the original data base). Again, the exact nature of this identification will depend on the medium of data storage that is selected and on the computer programs used.

The inclusion of such information helps the researcher ensure that he or she is using the correct variables in the study and greatly facilitates the checking

Family Life Cycle (LC)

Mapping Rule Application Sequence	AGE B V36 (1:57) (Age of Head)	MSTAT V27; (1:45) (Marital Status)	ADULTS V21 (1:40) (# Adults)	AGEYNG V24 (1:43) (Age Youngest)	EMSTAT V120 (6:49) (Employment Status)	LC (Life Cycle)	Category Label Under 45
↓	1, 2, 3	2-5	anything	0	anything	1	Single
	1, 2, 3	1	2-8	0	anything	2	Married, No Children
	1, 2, 3	1	2-8	1-5	anything	3	Married, Preschool
	1, 2, 3	1	2-8	6, 7, 8	anything	4	Married, No Preschool
							Over 45
	4, 5, 6	1	2-8	1-9	anything	5	Married, Children
	4, 5, 6	1	2-8	0	6-7	6	Married, No Children, Head Working
	4, 5, 6	1	2-8	0	1-5, 8, 9	7	Married, No Children, Head Retired
	4, 5, 6	2-5	anything	0	6-7	8	Single, Head Working
	4, 5, 6	2-5	anything	0	1-5, 8, 9	9	Single, Head Retired
	Anything	2-5	anything	1-9	anything	0	Any Age, Unmarried, Has Children

Figure 7-19 Logic Statement for Variable Construction

Region of Residence (REGION)

REG V4 (1:10) Geog. I.D.	REGION	
2, 9	1	(Northeast)
1, 6, 7	2	(North Central)
3, 4, 5	3	(South)
0, 8	4	(West)

Age of Head Bracket (AGEB)

AGE V17 (1:34-35) (Age of Head)	AGEB (Age Bracket)
00-24	1
25-34	2
35-44	3
45-54	4
55-64	5
65-99	6

Figure 7-19 (cont'd.)

of the logic. Every logic statement should be checked, whenever possible, by another person. When it is added to the permanent record of the study, it will provide excellent documentation about the actual construction of variables used in the study.

For each variable to be constructed, the composition of each code value is completely spelled out. The construction of AGEB is the most straightforward. The value of 1 for AGEB is to represent all respondents whose age was less than 24. Thus, it includes all values of age from 0 to 24 inclusive.

The life-cycle variable is the most complex. It requires information from five different variables. Thus, each code value represents a rather complex combination of age, marital status, employment status, family size, and children's ages. Each relationship is explicitly spelled out and should be consistent with the categories described in the code addition. The particular combination of specific code values of the variables involved should sensibly yield the characteristic described as "under age 45, unmarried, no children (and, by default, any employment status or number of associated adults)." A check of the code values in Chapter 5 should convince the reader that this is so.

Once the logic statement has been checked thoroughly, it is translated into an executable procedure that will actually construct the variables required and add them to the existing data set. There are two basic strategies that can be followed at this point, one using an existing program with the necessary variable-generation capabilities, the other involving the writing of special-purpose computer programs to accomplish the task. To those with at least slight familiarity with any modern programming language such as FORTRAN, it should be clear that the steps of the logic statement could be easily written in program form. The approach used should depend on the adequacy of available library routines that have variable-generation capacity, the complexity of the tasks to be accomplished, and available programming skills. Since any illustration using a library program would be of little value because of its specific nature, an example of the construction of the three variables using a FORTRAN program will be shown. The language of many library programs (such as SPSS) is similar in form and structure.

Expanding on the logic of the process illustrated in Figure 7-19, the following steps must be followed in the construction of each variable:

1. The variable to be generated must be represented in the program by a unique name, preferably a mnemonic that readily identifies it and relates it to the logic statement. The variable must be initialized (given a value for each record) each time a record is read to ensure that the variable is defined; otherwise, the value from the last record could be assigned by default. It is generally useful to assign an initial value which, if left unchanged, will indicate a classification error (i.e., not be a meaningful code value, but a number that the program will recognize as an error and report to the researcher). The value may also be a legitimate code which is altered to another acceptable value if some of the other logical conditions are met.
2. The statements used to generate the variable must be logically exhaustive of *all* subsets of the data to be submitted to it. A record ordinarily would not satisfy two different logical conditions that generate different code values. But to guard against this possibility, the statements must be internally consistent or self-corrective (i.e., the code value assigned to the new variable may change several times until the proper one is found).
3. At the end of each construction process, the program must check to see that the code value of the variable being built is not equal to the initialized value when that value serves as an error indicator. When such an error is detected, the program should print out a message indicating that a problem is detected, and should then print out all the input data used in the process, including the identification number of the respondent. The latter makes it possible to look up the offending record in the files to see what went wrong.
4. The program should provide documentation of the variable-generation process by printing out (for a reasonable number of records) the values of all the input variables and the value of the variable that is being constructed. For example, printing out the computations for every

100th record in a sample of size 3000 would yield enough information to verify that the procedure was properly generating the variables.

Let *X* represent a variable that is to be generated which has four acceptable codes, 1, 2, 3, and 4. *Y* and *Z* are input variables to be combined to form *X*. *Y* and *Z* have two states each, *Y*1 and *Y*2, and *Z*1 and *Z*2. The logic of the mapping rules for this variable in FORTRAN statements might appear as in Figure 7-20. This sequence sets the value of *X* to 9, a code that could be used for "missing data" but has no meaning here except to indicate that the values of *Y* and *Z* for the record being processed did not satisfy any of the four logically exclusive conditions of the mapping function: $X = F(Y, Z)$. This could occur because either *Y* or *Z* or both took on values other than *Y*1, *Y*2, *Z*1, *Z*2, perhaps as a result of a failure to clean up wild codes earlier in the processing of the data.

After *X* is initialized to a value of 9, the values of *Y* and *Z* are checked to assign the proper value of *X*: 1, 2, 3, or 4. Once through these statements, the program checks to make sure that the value of *X* has indeed been changed, and if it has not, notification of the error is made. The values of *Z* and *Y* and the interview number of the record being processed should be printed out to assist

```
   X=9
   IF(Y.EQ.Y1.AND.Z.EQ.Z1)X=1
   IF(Y.EQ.Y1.AND.Z.EQ.Z2)X=2
   IF(Y.EQ.Y2.AND.Z.EQ.Z1)X=3
   IF(Y.EQ.Y2.AND.Z.EQ.Z2)X=4
   IF(X.EQ.9)WRITE(6,10)INT,Y,Z
10 FORMAT(1HO,'ERROR IN X, INT=',I4,5X,'Y=',I1,5X,'Z=',I1)
```

Values of Y	Values of Z: Z1	Z2
Y1	X=1	X=2
Y2	X=3	X=4

Figure 7-20 Variable Generation Procedure

the researcher in reconciling the problem. Frequently, the default category will be a legitimate code—a miscellaneous category, for example. Thus, it will often not be necessary to change the default value written out on the new record, since there will be no other disposition of the problem but to leave it in such a cate-

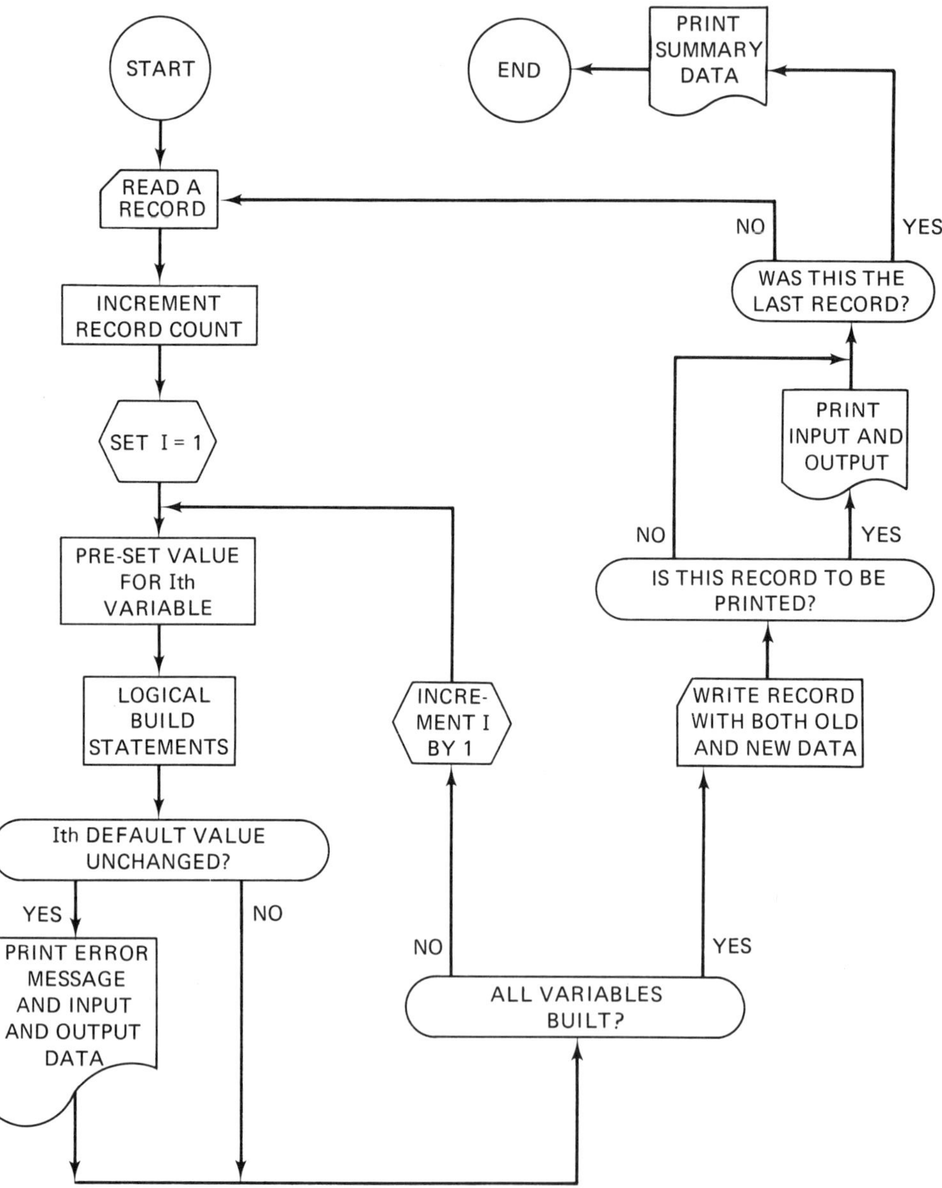

Figure 7-21 Flow Chart for Variable Building Process

gory. If this is not the case, the record will have to be physically changed, as in the wild code and consistency checks.

The general structure of a variable-generation program is illustrated in Figure 7-21. After a record is read in, the record counter is incremented. Then, the value of each variable to be generated is initialized before the conditional statements begin. This ensures that it will have a legitimate code value that is not the code left over from the last record processed. After the execution of the logical generation statements, the program checks to see if the initialized default value has been changed. If it has not, appropriate information is printed out to enable the researcher to find the cause of the problem. Then all the remaining records in the file are similarly processed.

When variable construction is complete and all the records have been processed, the summary data are printed out. The program also has printed every *n*th record, where *n* is determined so as to print out enough records to verify the functioning of the building process. All input data and output data for these records are printed to document fully the functioning of the program. About 30 to 50 records would typically be adequate for a survey with 400 to 500 cases.

The printed records are examined by the staff for correctness. If any errors are found that resulted from a logical or programming error, the program can be corrected. If there appears to be a problem with the logic of the code itself, this can be corrected by changing the generation statements. If the errors appear to reflect a problem with the data, the researcher has the necessary information to determine the disposition of each problem and to indicate the physical corrections to be made to each erroneous record. This process can be repeated until all the variables are generated without errors.

Figure 7-22 illustrates a FORTRAN program written to accomplish the

```
      Tab
1         6  7

C            PROGRAM TO BUILD AGE BRACKETS, LIFE CYCLE, AND REGION
C            772 PGM 01: W. DUNKELBERG/J.SONQUIST, DECEMBER 24, 19--
C            INPUT REQUIRED: MATCH-MERGED FILE OF 772:01 & 772:06 ON 4-5; 6-9
             IMPLICIT INTEGER (A-Z)
             DIMENSION IM(14)
             N = 100
             CC = 0
C            IM IS A CARD IMAGE OF DECK 01
        1    READ (5,10,END=999) DK1, INT1, REG, AGE, ADULTS, AGEYNG, MSTAT,
          1  (IM(I), I=1, 14), DK2, INT2, EMSTAT
       10    FORMAT (3X, I2, I4, I1, T34, I2, T40, I1, T43, I1, T46, I1, T1, 14A4,
```

Figure 7-22 FORTRAN Variable Generation Program

```
        Tab
             1     3X, I2, I4, T49, I1)
C                  ACCUMULATE CARD COUNT AND CHECK THE MERGE
                   CC = CC+1
                   IF (DK1.EQ.1.AND.DK2.EQ.6.AND.INT1.EQ.INT2) GO TO 20
                   WRITE (6, 15) INT1, INT2, DK1, DK2
          15       FORMAT (1H1, 'MERGE ERROR, INT1=', I4, 5X, 'INT2=', I4,5X,
             1     'DK1=', I2, 5X, 'DK2=', I2)
                   GO TO 999
C                  BUILD AGE BRACKETS, AGEB. SET AGEB=1, CHANGE IF AGE NOT
C                  BOUNDED BY 18 AND 24
          20       AGEB=1
                   IF(AGE.GE.25.AND.AGE.LE.34) AGEB=2
                   IF(AGE.GE.35.AND.AGE.LE.44) AGEB=3
1            6     7

                   IF(AGE.GE.45.AND.AGE.LE.54) AGEB=4
                   IF(AGE.GE.55.AND.AGE.LE.64) AGEB=5
                   IF(AGE.GE.65) AGEB=6
C                  BUILD LIFE CYCLE. USES AGE BRACKET JUST CONSTRUCTED
C                  SET DEFAULT VALUE OF LC=10
                   LC=10
                   IF(AGEB.GE.4) GO TO 30
                   IF(MSTAT.GE.2) LC=1
                   IF(MSTAT.EQ.1.AND.ADULTS.GE.2.AND.AGEYNG.EQ.0) LC=2
                   IF(MSTAT.EQ.1.AND.ADULTS.GE.2.AND.(AGEYNG.GE.1.AND.
             1     AGEYNG.LE.5)) LC=3
                   IF(MSTAT.EQ.1.AND.ADULTS.GE.2.AND.(AGEYNG.GE.6.AND.
             1     AGEYNG.LE.8)) LC=4
                   GO TO 40
          30       IF(MSTAT.EQ.1.AND.ADULTS.GE.2.AND.AGYNG.GE.1)LC=5
                   IF(MSTAT.EQ.1.AND.ADULTS.GE.2.AND.AGYNG.EQ.0.AND.
             1     (EMSTAT.EQ.6.OR.EMSTAT.EQ.7) LC=6
                   IF(MSTAT.EQ.1.AND.ADULTS.GE.2.AND.AGYNG.EQ.0.AND.
             1     (EMSTAT.NE.6.OR.EMSTAT.NE.7) LC=7
                   IF(MSTAT.GE.2.AND.AGYNG.EQ.0.AND.(EMSTAT.EQ.6.OR.EMSTAT.EQ.7)
             1     LC=8
                   IF(MSTAT.GE.2.AND.AGYNG.EQ.0.AND.(EMSTAT.NE.6.OR.EMSTAT.NE.7)
             1     LC=9
```

Figure 7-22 (cont'd.)

```
      Tab.
       40      IF(LC.EQ.10.AND.MSTAT.GE.2.AND.AGYNG.GE.1) LC=0
1         6    7

C              CHECK FOR RECORDS THAT DID NOT FIT THE PATTERN.
               IF(LC.EQ.10)WRITE(6,50)INT1,AGEB,MSTAT,ADULTS, AGYNG,
          1    EMSTAT,LC
       50      FORMAT(1HO,'LIFE CYCLE ERROR, INT=', I4,5X,'AGE=', I1,5X,
          1    'MSTAT=', I1,5X,'ADULTS=', I1,5X,'AGYNG=',I1,5X,'EMSTAT=',I1,
          2    5X,'LC=',I1,
C              BUILD REGION FROM DECK 01, COL.10.SET REGION=1, NORTHEAST
               REGION=1
               IF(REG.EQ.1.OR.REG.EQ.6.OR.REG.EQ.7) REGION=2
               IF(REG.GE.3.AND.REG.LE.5) REGION=3
               IF(REG.EQ.0.OR.REG.EQ.8) REGION=4
C              PUNCH OUT A DUPLICATE OF DECK 01 WITH NEW VARIABLES
               WRITE (2,100) (IMAGE(I),I=1,14), AGEB,LC,REGION IF(LC.EQ.10)LC=0
      100      FORMAT(14A4, 3I1)
C              PRINT EVERY 100TH RECORD
               CHECK=CC-N
               IF(CHECK.NE.0) GO TO 250
               WRITE (6,200)DK1,INT,REG,AGE,ADULTS,AGEYNG,MSTAT,EMSTAT,AGEB,LC,REGION
      200      FORMAT(1HO,'CHECK,DK=',I2,5X,'INT=',I4,5X,'REG=',I1,5X,'AGE=',
          1    I2,5X,'ADULTS=',I1,5X,'AGEYNG=', I1,5X,'MSTAT=',I1,5X,'EMSTAT=',
          1    I1,5X,'AGEB=', I1,5X,'LC=',I1,5X,'REGION=', I1)
               N=N+100
      250      CONTINUE
C              END OF PROCESSING, GO READ THE NEXT RECORD
1         6    7

               GO TO 1
      999      WRITE(6, 1000) CC
     1000      FORMAT(1H1,'END OF PROCESSING,RECORDS=', I4)
               STOP
               END
```

Figure 7-22 (cont'd.)

variable generation documented in Figure 7-19. Input to the program is a match-merged file of deck 01 and deck 06. The program reads the variables that it needs from the two decks and rereads deck 01 in its entirety (IM vector) so that it can be reproduced along with the new variables. The program will produce a new deck 01, with all the old data and the new variables added. Every record is then checked to see that deck 01 precedes deck 06 and that the interview numbers of the two decks are the same for each interview. If both conditions do not hold, the execution of the program is terminated immediately, and an appropriate error message is printed out.

The program shown is oriented toward the use of cards or their images on tape or disk. The output is a new deck of cards which will replace the original deck 01. The content of the new deck 01 is shown in Figure 7-23, a single-card form of deck 01, showing the three new variables that have been added. The input and output are easily altered to be compatible with other modes of data management. For example, if the data were stored on tape or disk as a continuous string of 120 variables, the program would input all 120 of these variables and then write them out on a new tape with the three new variables added at the end (numbers 121, 122, 123). Note that the 80-column-card form indicates which program generated the data which those variables represent. This reference is also attached to the description of each variable in the code addition (at the far right) shown in Figure 7-18.

The first variable generated by the program is a bracket code for "age of family head." In the program, this variable is represented by AGEB. It is initialized with the value 1, the code for age 18–24 years. The strategy is then to check and see if the actual age is anything different than 18–24, and if it is, to give AGEB another value corresponding to the proper age bracket. Clearly, any one respondent will satisfy only one of the conditional statements. If none are satisfied, the respondent's age must be in the 18–24 age bracket and AGEB retains the initial value of 1. No check is made for a default error here, since the building process is straight forward and all cases will be assigned a value by the procedure. Clearly, the program "assumes" no wild codes.

The next variable to be generated is "family life cycle." It is a more complex variable, being a combination of several other variables. The possibility also exists that some respondents might not fit any of the categories as defined, so an initial value for LC is chosen that is not one of the acceptable codes. AGEB must be used in the program and therefore must be generated prior to the construction of the life-cycle variable. Again, the FORTRAN statements define mutually exclusive groups. A respondent can fit into only one of the categories described by the conditional statements. In this case, the program does check for cases that did not fit into any of the 10 categories. If LC is still 10 after the record has passed through all the conditional checks, the interview number of the respondent and all the relevant input data are printed out to assist the researcher in resolving the problem.

The final variable to be constructed is "region of residence." This process simply reduces the information contained in column 10 of deck 01 into a four-category variable. The same structure is used for the FORTRAN statements as was used to construct age brackets.

SINGLE CARD FORM

Project Number; 772	Project Name: Survey of Consumers	
Project Director: Phone:	Card Layout By: Phone: Data:	
Deck Number: 01	Source Document:	Trf. from Cards:

Remarks: Example of card layout for Deck 01: Demographics

Columns 1-40

FROM Card	FROM Col		POSSIBLE CODES X	Name	Field Size
		1	1	Study Number (772)	3
		2			
		3			
		4	2	Deck Number (01)	2
		5			
		6	3	Interview Number	4
		7			
		8			
		9			
		10	4	Geographic I. D.	1
		11	5	Primary Sampling Unit	1
		12	6	Urbanization Code	1
		13	7	Dwelling Unit P.S.U. Identific.	2
		14			
		15	8	County Code	1
		16	9	Secondary Selection	1
		17	10	Belt Code	1
		18	11	Size of City	1
		19	12	Distance from City	1
		20	13	Interviewer Social Security Number	9
		21			
		22			
		23			
		24			
		25			
		26			
		27			
		28			
		29	14	Interview Date	1
		30	15	Length of Interview	3
		31			
		32			
		33	16	Sex of F.U. head	1
		34	17	Age of F.U. head	2
		35			
		36	18	Age of wife	2
		37			
		38	19	Is respondent head?	1
		39	20	Sex of respondent	1
		40	21	Number of Adults	1

Columns 41-80

FROM Card	FROM Col		POSSIBLE CODES X	Name	Field Size
		41	22	Adults over 65	1
		42	23	Children under 16	1
		43	24	Age, youngest child	1
		44	25	Age, oldest child	1
		45	26	Age/sex, head	1
		46	27	Marital status, head	1
		47	28	Years married	2
		48			
		49	29	Education, head	1
		50	30	Education, wife	1
		51	31	Race	1
		52	32	Number of calls	1
		53	33	Who present at int.	1
		54	34	Type of structure	1
		55	35	Neighborhood type	2
		56			
PGM	01	57	36	Age, head (interval)	1
PGM	01	58	37	Family life cycle	1
PGM	01	59	38	Region of resid.	1
		60			
		61			
		62			
		63			
		64			
		65			
		66			
		67			
		68			
		69			
		70			
		71			
		72			
		73			
		74			
		75			
		76			
		77			
		78			
		79			
		80			

Figure 7-23

With all the variables built, the program then writes out a duplicate of deck 01, with the three new variables added (AGEB, LC, REGION). Then it checks to see if the record count (not the interview number) is a multiple of 100. If so, it prints out all the input and output data for the record as documentation of the variable-generation step. The next record is then read and processed. When all records have been processed, the program prints out the record count and indicates that the operation is complete. The deck 01 that was used as input should be carefully labeled and disposed of as soon as it is clear that the program faithfully reproduced the information contained in it.[16]

This set of examples has illustrated the sequence of operations that typifies the variable-generation process. The actual set of FORTRAN instructions that implements the mapping rules is an ordered sequence of steps performed one at a time on each observation, not a rule mysteriously applied all at once to the whole file.

Propositions about the values of variables are simply expressed as FORTRAN "IF" statements that define the subsets of the observations in the input to which the associated function is to apply. In most cases the latter are simply executable substitution statements such as REGION $= 3$. They can be more complex (e.g., $Y = .7X + 2$). These "IF" statements and assignment statements are executed in sequence for each observation, and they are executed in the order written unless more complex contingencies are written into the procedures.

One last word—to those who expect to be more than very peripherally involved in analyzing survey data. If you did not understand this FORTRAN example, you should place an introductory computer course high on your priority list. The penalties for not doing so are high, and the payoff from a relatively small investment in time is equally high.

EXTRACTION OF DATA FOR WORK FILES

A work file contains a subset of the original data. It is constructed by selecting certain variables, cases, time periods, or units. Any number of these files may be created for various purposes during the processing of a survey, kept for some period of time, and then discarded. The types of subfiles constructed depends on the size of the data base, the analysis objectives, and the requirements and capabilities of the particular hardware/software combination in use.

There are many reasons for creating work files: the need to reorganize the data according to the study's theoretical scheme rather than for efficient data

[16] It is generally a good idea to keep dated and well-labeled input decks in storage until there is no doubt that the reproductions with the added variables are indeed complete. In fact, copies of all decks should be kept. Reproducing data decks is cheap, but it is expensive to repunch a deck from the original code sheets and recheck and correct it.

collection, the possibility that several analysts will be working with the data base, and the simple need to cut the totality of the survey analysis into a series of manageable parts. The high computer costs associated with repeated reading of very large data bases and with clerical problems associated with the maintenance of large code books and dictionaries which keep changing as new variables are constructed also make the creation of subfiles sensible. Sometimes data files have to be reformatted to meet program or statistical requirements. Complex file structures have to be rectangularized, and when new variables are generated by aggregation over subunits, or contextual variables are assigned to units in groups, the result is generally a new file. This section reviews the survey processing problems that lead to the use of subfiles, the considerations that underlie the way in which such a work file is structured, and outlines the procedures that are involved in creating one.

Why Work Files?

The sequence of items in the data-collection instrument should be determined by interviewing considerations (accuracy and cost being the main ones), as well as by theoretical study objectives. It may be desirable to separate questions about employment from those dealing with income. A sequence of attitude questions might be split up and buried among factual material rather than being placed together to avoid positive response sets. Yet, for analysis purposes, it may be highly desirable to bring each set back together. Sometimes worksheets are used for this purpose during editing, but the most reliable and least expensive procedure is to use computing equipment.

Since, in a typical survey, one is dealing with a great many raw variables, systematizing them according to the theoretical schema is usually a worthwhile operation, facilitating the planning of analyses and helping to prevent the inadvertent failure to include a variable in an important multivariate analysis. The time to do this file reorganizing is after the first main variable-building phase of the study. If several analysts need to work on the same data base, separate files make for a much more convenient arrangement, avoiding coordination problems, problems in keeping documentation up to date, bottlenecks and queuing in the processing, and the hard feelings that invariably attend even partially adequate solutions to these kinds of problems. Arranging to break up the data into subfiles, each to be used for one or more specific analysis purposes and containing the relevant variables and cases, is an integral part of the analysis planning.

There are technical reasons for using work files. Despite the fact that most computers can read in all the variables for a given observation at once, this is expensive if it is done repeatedly, and it is not necessary. The expense comes partly from billing procedures that make charges not only for each individual access to the storage medium on which the data are stored, but for the amount of storage used by the program. Even if one is charged only for the time the program is on the computer, the charges will reflect the extra time taken to execute the instructions that read, format, and convert to binary internal representation all the data for the survey. For many survey processing operations this may represent as much as 90 per cent of the instructions executed! Clearly, ways of organizing data to cut down the I/O (input–output) time are desirable. One answer is to make one run extracting from the main storage files those variables and observations that will be needed for an intensive analysis, and then to work with the small file.

It is the case sometimes that even a large computer is short of space because so many people are using it and the immediate access memory available for a single user is not sufficient to hold the data for a study in which a large number of variables are used. Even the user in a time-sharing environment may be in trouble if several blocks of storage are used for input and a big program is to be used.[17] In addition, the requirements of library programs written for some special purpose at one installation and then moved to another without adequate generalization and revision can sometimes only be met by creating a special file, possibly with variables appearing in a specific order.

The size of the study can also have its effects. Just the sheer reduction in clerical effort in going through the whole code book to find the needed variables every time it is desired to run a frequency distribution can become at least a small part of the motivation for dividing up a large main storage file.

These problems are particularly acute when study objectives include a considerable amount of experimentation with different forms of the variables. This may require trying one set of recoding rules, running a few statistics on the results, looking at a few distributions, repairing mistakes that were made, checking to see whether the results appear to represent the underlying concepts properly, and then repeating the process. With many such computer runs, costs can become very large indeed if the whole study has to be read and rewritten each time a variable is changed.[18] The clerical problems associated with keeping all the codes up to date while these objectives are being achieved also contribute heavily to the motivation to split the files.

In this case it sometimes turns out to be convenient to set up an index construction file which includes (1) those variables that constitute the raw data input, and (2) specific other variables that will be needed during the index-construction phase of the study. The new indices are later re-entered into the main file all at once.

[17] Many installations apparently restrict the use of very big partitions during prime time, and very large programs like SPSS cannot even be run. The use of "virtual" memory permits such runs to be made, but at high cost.

[18] These problems are largely solved (or perhaps replaced by others) if the data-management capabilities being used use a transposed file structure in which a record consists of all the information for one variable over all cases as opposed to the usual method of storing all the variables for one case. Only a few systems use this storage method, however (e.g., IMPRESS and PICKLE). Alternatively, a system using random access rather than sequential storage would solve the problem.

When the study contains design complexities such as data obtained over several time periods, or several units of analysis, or when contextual variables are to be processed, the use of work files becomes almost a necessity. The reason for this is simply that many survey-processing systems and statistical programs in use at this time will not accept as input anything except a rectangular data matrix in which the rows are units of analysis and the columns are variables. In some cases, missing data cannot even be processed. In others, the input variables must appear in a specific order. Analyses with data such as these generally need a good programmer.

When a very large data base is being analyzed, it often makes good sense to take a stratified random sample of the observations in the big file rather than to attempt to use them all for statistical analyses. It should also be clear from this discussion that the smaller the study and fewer the number of variables, the simpler the analysis plan; and the fewer the complexities in the data structure, the less the need to do anything except use the main file. Analysts with under 500 observations and 50 variables in rectangular form should probably not use work files unless they are using a very small computer.

Selection of Variables and Cases for Subfiles

The purpose for which a subfile is to be created obviously should determine which variables and which observations are to be included in it. In most explanatory surveys, a particular analysis plan requires the inclusion of a few dependent variables the behavior of which is to be explained, and a number of variables that are candidates for inclusion in an explanatory model.[19] Or the plan might be aimed at discovering what the correlates of a particular behavior or condition are.[20] If the study is primarily descriptive, the analyst would need to include variables which define those subgroups in the sample that he wishes to compare and contrast. He would, of course, need to include those variables which comprise the dimensions along which the comparisons are to be made. If the analysis has among its objectives the refinement of concepts, a great many items relating to these concepts would be among the variables transferred to the subfile, to be used in obtaining evidence of criterion or construct validity.[21] In a typical explanatory analysis, a common use of subfiles would be to carry out separate analyses for subgroups in which the explanatory factors appeared to operate differently (e.g., males versus females).

Often, a particular phase of the analysis for which a work file is being constructed has several allied purposes. These all need to be thought out carefully ahead of time and the variables for each listed. A fundamental principle to

19 See Sonquist (1970) for a number of examples.
20 See Davis (1971) for examples.
21 See Phillips (1971) for an extended discussion.

remember in constructing work files is that every analysis leads down some paths which are not anticipated by the initial theoretical orientation. To be able to follow these up requires being liberal in transferring variables into subfiles without taking far more than is needed. This is an art that can be learned only by experience. Figure 7-24 provides a checklist of the types of uses to which variables included in work files might be put.

In laying out a subfile the analyst must decide which groups of interviews, which time periods, which variables, and which subunits, if any, are to be copied into the file. The subset of variables and time periods is indicated simply by

All Files:

Unit identifiers
Time identifiers
Contextual identifiers
Sub-unit identifiers

Sampling identifiers
Weights
Random half sample identifiers
Accuracy indicators

Exploratory Analysis and Variable Generation:

Scale items
Raw variables for index construction
Subgroup identifiers
Correlates for criterion validity

Correlates for constant validity
Alternative forms of the same variable

Descriptive Analysis:

Description variables
Variables compatible with other studies or past times

Subgroup delimiter variables
Alternative forms of the variable

Explanatory Model Building and Hypothesis Testing:

Dependent variables
Independent variables
Antecedent variables
Intervening variables
Variables relating to the respondent's position in a structure.

Contextual variables
Moderators
Suppressors
Specifiers
Competing explanatory factors and controls for spuriousness

Residuals from previous models
Belief's, values, expectations
Current experiences, situational factors and constraints
Recent events affecting, respondent
Background factors

Response Rate Analysis File: All variables common to sample response and non-response Units.

Figure 7-24 Checklist: Types of Variables Needed in Work Files

enumerating them in a list (e.g., Time-2 AGE, RACE, ALIENATION). The units and subunits would ordinarily be indicated by writing a subset description [e.g., urban males (URBAN = 2 AND SEX = 1)].

In each file it is generally a good idea to include unit identifiers, such as interview number, family number, and so on, in case problems encountered later make necessary printing out the records. Including these makes it possible to look up the corresponding interview if the need arises. Or the file can be matched against another file by use of these identifiers. Variables that identify which interviewing "wave" or time period is associated with the data would also be included where relevant together with any identifiers that mark contextual groups (e.g., plant or work group), subunits (e.g., automobile number within family identification), and sampling blocks. If weighted data are used, weights would be included. Sometimes random-half samples are used in an analysis for cross-validation purposes, and the variables indicating which random-half strata the observation is in would ordinarily be included. Finally, if measures are obtained that pertain to the quality of the data, such as indications of respondent bias, these would be included.

When the primary purpose of the analysis is exploratory, certain other kinds of variables would be added to those listed above. Clearly, the raw items to be included in scale and index constructions would be included. However, since some analysis would typically be done once the scales are constructed, those variables with which the scales should correlate (construct validity) would be included. If alternative measures of the construct the scale purports to measure are available, they would also be included (criterion validity). Sometimes these correlations should be examined within important sample subgroups, so the measures defining these subgroups would also be included. If recoded versions of individual measures are already available, several forms of these variables might be included.

Descriptive analyses that take place after the initial index construction and scale computations are complete need somewhat less complex files. In addition to those variables needed in all subfiles, what is needed are those dimensions along which important subgroups are to be compared, and those variables which define these subgroups. If an objective of the study is to study trends over time, the analyst must be sure to include recoded versions of both subgroup and descriptor variables whose codes are compatible with past information. The analyst may also need alternative forms of his variables if he is to do additional descriptive work that has no compatibility restrictions.

The most complicated work file is that to be used for model building or hypothesis testing. In addition to those variables that should be included in all subfiles, the investigator would include dependent variables, independent variables, other antecedent and intervening variables, competing explanatory factors and variables to be used as controls for spuriousness, and contextual variables that define the external conditions under which each model operates. If multivariate analysis is to be used, he would need to include variables thought to moderate or suppress the relationship between the independent and dependent variables. If the analysis is a multistage one in which background factors have been held constant, the residuals or the predicted values from previous analyses would be included.

A special type of work file is used for conducting a response-rate analysis. It requires one record for each unit of analysis from whom a usable questionnaire or interview was obtained, plus one record for those from whom an interview should have been obtained. The variables included are all of those for which data have been obtained from both respondents and nonrespondents, usually observational data such as house type, urban/rural, region, and interviewer number.

Procedures for Creating Work Files

It is useful to break down the process of creating a work file into a discrete series of steps. These include:

1. *Planning.* Writing up the file definitions; specifying the units to comprise the file and the rules for sequencing them; making up the list of variables to be included; drafting the format of the variables in the file and, where appropriate, working out what structural changes (i.e., in units of analysis) that will be needed; mapping out the relationship between the file and its physical storage on cards, tape, disk, or other storage media.
2. *Assessing the need for preliminary steps.* Where summarization is over time, subunits or portions of the file will be needed; working out the sequence of steps required, implementing them, and checking the results.
3. *Performing checks and setting up the runs.* Reviewing file organization drafts with all concerned people to make sure that the proposed configuration of variables, units, and file structure are compatible with the expected uses of the file. Doing the technical work necessary to set up the file extraction. Reviewing the technical work with at least one other technically knowledgable person who is familar with the study.
4. *Working out procedures for proving the accuracy of the procedure.* Planning at least for a comparison of N's with previous information to show that all the observations were extracted. Comparison of frequency distributions of variables in the file with others from old files is far superior, since this also ensures that the right versions of the variables were moved. (The more analysis to be done on the file, the more important the proof of its accuracy.)
5. *Drafting the documentation for the file.* Writing up the procedures for inclusion in the project files, drafting codes for the new file, and

writing up documentation on the file and its location for inclusion in project data file control records.

6. *Initiating and checking* the computer runs necessary to create the file.
7. *Taking the steps necessary* to ensure that backup copies of the file are made where appropriate, in the form of listings or tape or disk copies.

The need for repeated checkpoints in these steps cannot be overemphasized. Mistakes made here are far more costly than those involved in computing statistics, since these are early in a long sequence of operations, and errors made here can invalidate successive operations. Nor can the importance of adequate documentation be overemphasized. Having a clear, readable record of when each file was created where it is located, how it can be accessed, what versions of each variable are in it, and how these were constructed makes it possible for the researcher to proceed into the analysis of his file conveniently, and with some confidence.

COMPLICATING FACTORS

Mention has been made more than once of the various factors that complicate the variable-generation and work-file construction process. This section reviews some of the more difficult-to-cope-with problems and indicates the type of ad hoc remedy that will have to be undertaken by most present-day survey analysts confronted with them. There are two alternatives to these remedies: (1) designing the study so that they are not needed in the first place, and (2) improving the computer programs available to the survey analyst who refuses to be bound by technological constraints to rectangular files.

These complicating factors are considered here only as they relate to variable-generation and work-file construction, although they apply in principle to the entire survey processing procedure. Perhaps the best course of action is to hire a programmer to deal with these problems. The difficulties to which we refer are: data collected at several points in time; contextual variables and the process of imputation; sociometric and other structural data; multiple units of analysis and the process of aggregation; multiple data bases and record matching; and mixtures of semantic differential and conventional survey data.

A number of practical problems confront the analyst who collects survey data from the same respondents at two or more points in time. He cannot reach some of his previous respondents, so respondents are added who were not interviewed previously. The questionnaire or the codes for the questions asked at two points in time may change, and some questions may be dropped and others added. This means that to make the data acceptable to some variable-generation library programs, dummy fields of missing-data codes must be generated for respondents who dropped out of later waves of the study and for those who were not present in earlier waves. This will permit a representation of overtime data as a rectangular file. If an adequate library program is not available, a special-purpose program must be written to rectangularize the file. Figure 7-25 shows what such a "rectangularized" file looks like. Of course, the problem is immensely simplified if respondents who were not interviewed both times are simply dropped from the file and if questions and codes are kept identical over both waves of data collection. This is hardly ever possible, however, if cross-sectional analyses are to be performed as well as overtime analyses.

A rectangularized multiwave file would be stored as one logical record for each respondent. Each record would have four groups of variables, as shown in Figure 7-25. With the file in this form and with comparable codes for common variables, ordinary variable-generation procedures can be used, since summarization can take place across variables contained in the same logical record. The procedure necessary to rectangularize the file involves: (1) sorting each time-period file into ascending sequence by respondent number, and (2) matching the two input files on the computer. This produces an expanded data set with dummied missing-data codes. Respondents must be given unique identifying

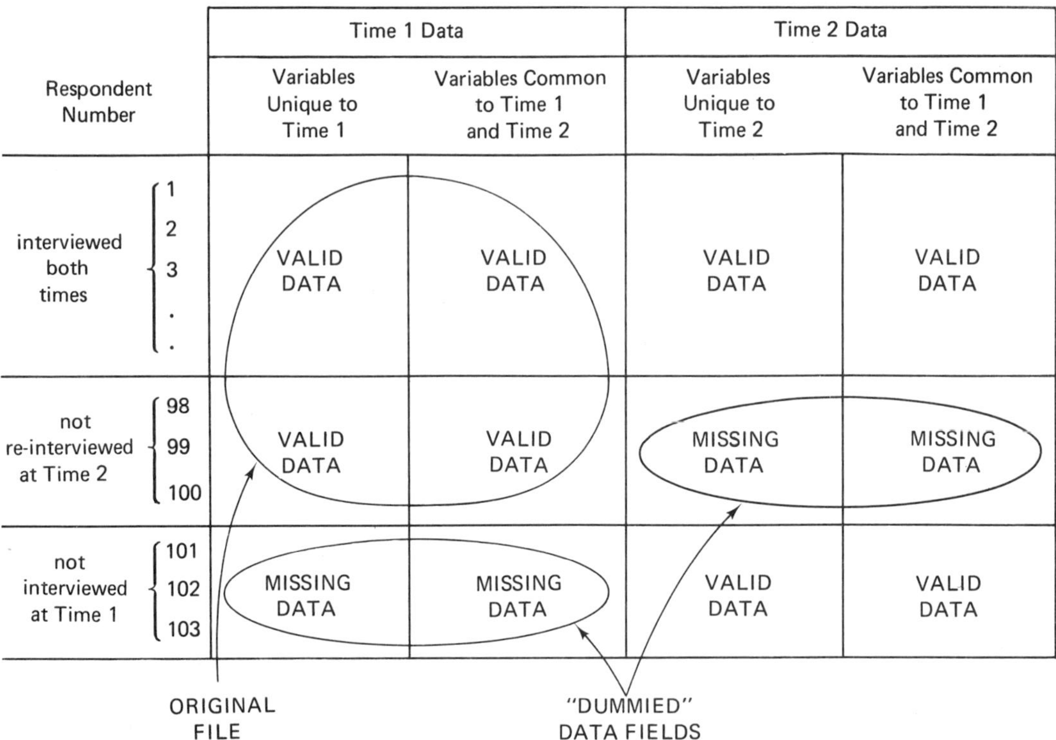

Figure 7-25 Rectangularized Overtime Data

numbers over both time periods for this to work, a task easily overlooked at the time interviews are coming in from the field during the second wave of interviewing.

A second type of complexity that may produce problems during the process of generating variables is the need to compute contextual variables and to reintroduce these into the original file. This type of variable, in which each respondent is characterized by some attribute of his environment, is no problem when the number of environments is small, say 15 or less; but when it is large, then either very cumbersome variable-generation instructions must be written or a special-purpose program written to attach the value of the environmental attribute computed for it to the record of each respondent for whom that environment is relevant. For example, each employee can be characterized by the average morale level and productivity of his work group, and this related to other measures, at an individual level, such as alienation or absenteeism.

Where the number of work groups is small and the work-group identifier is present in the employee records, average (or median or model) morale and productivity can be computed for each work group. Then sets of employees in high, medium, and low groups on each variable can be identified using work-group codes and set-enumeration techniques used to recode the work-group code into a variable that represents membership in a high, medium, or low group with respect to that variable.

Where the number of work groups is large, it may be necessary to record the work-group statistics in a file, sort both the work group and employee file into ascending sequence on the work-group identifier, and then read both files sequentially, transferring (sometimes termed "imputing") the work-group (master) information into the matching employee (detail) records. Sometimes the utility-report generation programs available at most computing facilities can be set up to do this.

Multivalued variables present a different kind of variable-generation problem. When the nature of a question is such that any number of answers can be given in response to it, the analyst generally has to limit the number of possible responses. These have to be represented as separate, individual variables. During the index construction phase, these often must be recoded into single-valued variables, since most statistical programs will not otherwise accept them.

Multiple levels of analysis present more serious problems: for instance, that of aggregating the data from the smaller units before conventional variable generation can take place on the larger ones. Suppose data are collected about each automobile owned by a family. Some statistics are to be computed using the automobile as the unit and others using the family as a unit. If some of the family variables are derived from the characteristics of the owned automobiles, then a procedure is followed such as that described above for coping with a large number of work groups. The automobile and family files are sorted separately into ascending sequence according to the identifier "family." The data from the first family and all its automobiles are read. The family-level variable is computed from the automobile file (e.g., year model of the newest car owned which was bought new), and the result is transferred into a file also containing the corresponding family information. Subsequent families are read and processed similarly. The matching operation must take proper care of families with no cars, however.

Structural data, such as sociometric choice information, are sometimes collected along with survey data. They can be recorded like the multiple-response variables described above; that is, each person is given a number and the numbers of those "chosen" by the respondent in question are simply recorded in a sequence of adjacent fields. The number of responses has to be limited at some point, in order for record lengths to remain fixed. However, methods of using structural information in conjunction with other survey data are still in a sufficiently experimental state that we shall not attempt to treat them further (Runkel and McGrath, 1972, p. 364). The analyst is advised simply to hire a competent programmer and write special-purpose programs adapted to the processing needs.

When survey data must be combined with other data bases, serious file-matching problems are likely to occur. The principal reason is that each record in such an external file must have an identifier field in the survey file. However, often codes do not map uniquely between files. When a match exists for every survey file record, the problem can be taken care of by the type of imputation procedure mentioned above in connection with contextual variables.

The survey data with which this book is primarily concerned can be characterized as single-stimulus proximity or dominance data (Runkel and McGrath, 1972, pp. 260–262); that is, the value of a variable is a relation between a respondent and a single stimulus. Alternatively, some of the data may reflect preferences between stimuli. It is when the data generated by the survey are of still another type, and the researcher tries to use them with computer programs and analysis models appropriate for single-stimulus or preference data that he will run into the most serious processing problems. The reason is that these types of data lead to different kinds of data matrices, despite the fact that they may have been collected by "survey" methods. Some are proximity matrices that tell the extent to which each possible pair of stimuli (or respondents) is alike. Semantic-differential techniques generate such data. Others compare discrepancies between pairs of stimuli. It remains a challenge for those who would develop tools for researchers to use to provide the computer programs to interface the various types of data. Much remains to be done.

STATISTICAL ANALYSIS OF SURVEY DATA

The preceding chapters have covered most of the topics that must be dealt with in the preliminary processing of survey data. Statistical analysis, the last step in this long line of action, comes next. In an adequately designed study, the file structures, the characters used, and the codes have all been designed with a view to the eventual use of a particular configuration of programs for analysis.

The last steps in the process are the selection of the subsets of the data that are to be used in particular analyses, selection of the final versions of the variables to be used, decisions about what statistics are to be calculated, setting up the computer runs to produce these statistics, making the runs, checking the output to make sure that it is correct, documenting the runs, interpreting the results, and then going back to compute more statistics.

This chapter will review the basic concepts underlying the functioning of statistical programs, provide an overview of alternative analysis objectives typical of survey research, and discuss the concrete problems that must be dealt with when using a complete, well-documented file to generate a set of usable statistics upon which the analysis is to be based. The final section suggests strategies for dealing with the inevitable—what to do when, despite all efforts, a computer run fails.

BASIC IDEAS UNDERLYING STATISTICAL PROGRAMS

In addition to understanding both the logic of the decisions to be made in the course of analysis and the statistical procedures to be used, it is helpful to know something about the logic of the programs being used to compute the statistics. This section outlines what the analyst ought to know about the statistical programs to be used and provides guidelines for developing the processing strategies discussed earlier in this book. Accordingly, the level of discussion will be more on the order of explaining what an automatic transmission on an automobile does and how to make the best use of it rather than explaining how it works in engineering terms.

Statistics books are full of formulas, but seldom furnish adequate algorithms or procedures for machine-aided computation of those formulas. However, the analyst must know both formulas and algorithms. For example, what a computer actually does in the process of computing a mean is only partially reflected in the familiar expression for it:

$$\bar{X} = \frac{\sum X}{N}. \qquad (8\text{-}1)$$

The formula for the mean, or average, is simply the sum of all the values divided by the number of items added together. A machine-supported procedure for computing it requires the following steps, not well defined from an examination of the formula:

0. Set the count of the number of X's read to 0.
1. Set to 0 the register that will be used to accumulate the sum of the Xs.
2. Read the "next" X. (This is the first X the first time through.)
3. Add the X to the accumulation register. Add 1 to the count register.
4. Determine if there are any more X's to be read. If there are, go to step 2. It there are not, go on to step 5.
5. Divide the sum by the count.
6. Print the sum, the count, and the mean.
7. Stop.

The X's are assumed to appear in a continuous stream, one after the other, and to have a delimiter between them so that one can be distinguished from the next as they are being read. The ages of the respondents in a study, might look like the data elements on the cards in Figure 8-1.

In actual practice, data would typically be recorded as shown in Figures 8-2 or 8-3. The M's and F's of Figure 8-2, indicating sex of the respondent, might have been recorded as 1's and 2's, and the R's and D's, denoting political-party preference, might have been recorded as digits. In addition, the blank spaces between numbers would generally be omitted. Thus, the data would usually appear as indicated in Figure 8-3. The data, the formulas, the computation algorithm, and the researcher's objectives must all be compatible for a program to be usable.

With data like these, control information must be provided to the program, indicating which variable to use in computing the mean and where the variable

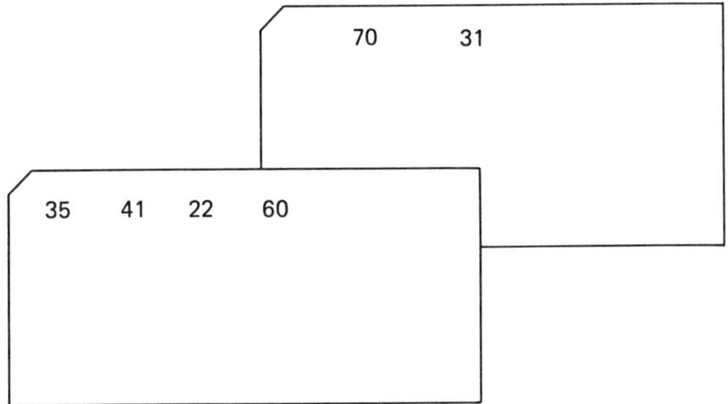

Figure 8-1 A Stream of Numbers on Cards

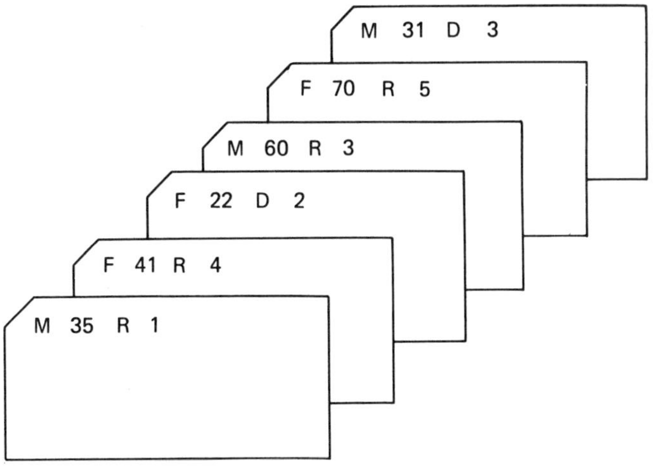

Figure 8-2 Vectors of Variables, One per Interview

is to be found in the file. This type of information is often supplied in the form of a dictionary, or directory, of locations of all the variables kept in the file, together with an input parameter, or pointer that indicates the variable to be used on a given run of the program. The directory might well contain the information contained in Figure 8-3 as well as information as to the number of decimal places to be used, what its missing-data codes are, and so on.[1] With the dictionary kept at the front of the data file, we might have a structure such as that shown in Figure 8-4.

If, as illustrated in Figure 8-4, the file is preceded by a pointer identifying

[1] Dictionaries for various statistical systems contain varying configurations of information and generally are not compatible.

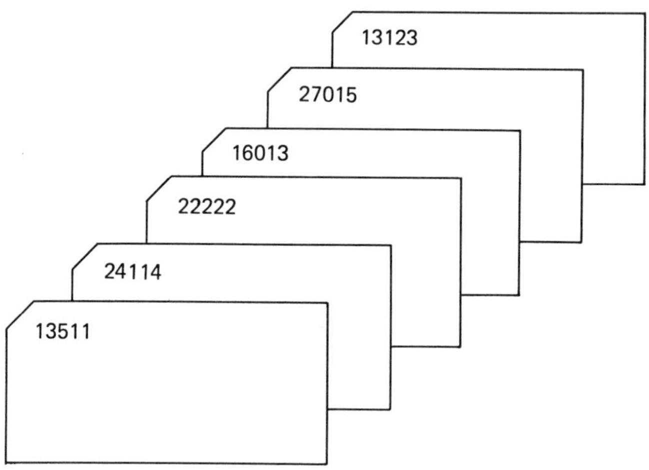

Figure 8-3 Formatted Vectors of Variables

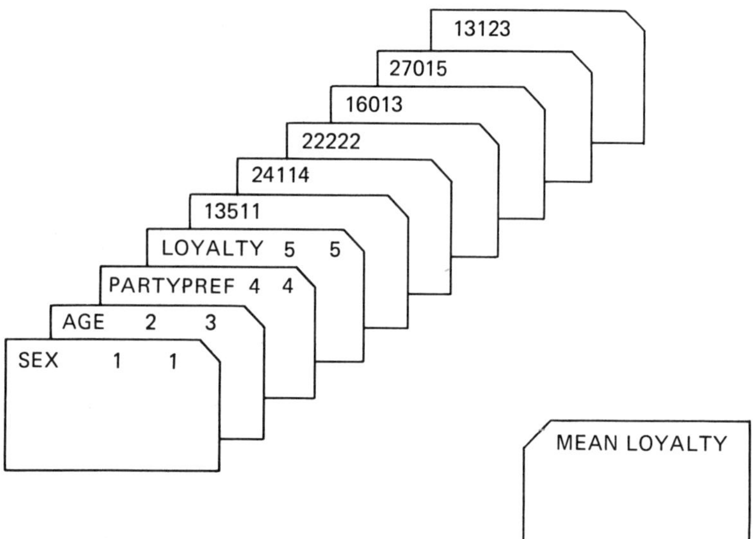

Figure 8-4 Complete File with Dictionary and Pointer Card

the name of the variable to be used in computing the mean, and if the algorithm is modified to read in the pointer and dictionary and to use them to guide the calculations, the result is a simplified approximation of what a typical statistical program does. It reads control information to tell it what to do, and formatting information describing where the variables are located in the storage medium. Then it reads in all the information in the file, extracts those variables which are needed, and performs the required operations. After all the data have been read and the computations have been completed, the indicated summary calculations (which must be postponed until all the data have been read) are completed. Finally, the results are printed out. What the analyst sees are the data and dictionary submitted, the pointers supplied as control information, and the resulting output. The algorithm thus modified might look as follows:

1. Read and save pointer card information.
2. Read and save dictionary information.
3. Look up pointer card information in dictionary and retrieve column locations from which the data are to be extracted.
4. Set the accumulation and count registers to 0.
5. Read all the numbers for the next interview.
6. Using the dictionary card-column information, extract the data from those columns from the interview just read.
7. Add the resulting number to the accumulation register; add 1 to the count register.
8. Determine whether or not there are any more interviews to be read. If there are, go to step 5; if not, go to step 9.
9. Divide the sum that has been accumulated by the count.
10. Print the name of the variable obtained from the pointer, together with the sum, the count, and the mean.
11. Stop.

It can be seen that it would be relatively simple to add further modifications that would provide for additional analytical capability. The algorithm could be set up to compute averages for data from many different studies. The average is simply computed over whatever interviews are contained in the file submitted to the computer. Simply by changing the pointer and rerunning the program, any single variable can be averaged in one "pass" of the file through the program. Missing data could be taken care of by establishing a unique code for them and to including a step to bypass the processing of that observation.[2] Any number of observations can be used, since the program simply reads them one at a time and adds values obtained to the partial sum being built up in the accumulation register. Only one interview at a time is "in" the computer, and the storage space that it occupies is subsequently used for another one.

To use an algorithm such as this, the analyst must (1) desire to compute means rather than some other statistic, (2) have an implemented version of the

[2] If missing information for age was denoted "99" as in the example in Chapter 7, the program could be designed to delete it from the calculations.

program on an available computer, (3) set up the data files to meet the program's input requirements, and (4) remove missing data from the file or modify the algorithm as indicated above. In this example no mention was made of decimal points, negative numbers, population versus sample formulas, or other considerations. In practice one would need to be aware of program restrictions pertaining to these considerations.

Here are some of the more important considerations to be kept in mind when using statistical programs:

1. They accept certain kinds of data, not others; and they produce certain statistics, not others. Using the computer requires data acceptable to the program as well as to the computer and a program that does what you want done.
2. Programs generally require that format information be supplied to indicate where in the storage medium the desired variables are located. They require control information to indicate what processing options are to be exercised also.
3. Programs often require that the data, format information, and control information be coded in a specific form and appear in a specific sequence. Errors arising from failure to meet these requirements are not always easily detectable.
4. The most common problems can be avoided by learning how to use programs before the time actually comes to use them on the study data and by a thorough checking of the format and control information supplied.
5. Good documentation is a prerequisite for effective use of any computer program.
6. Statistical program operation is heavily dependent on (a) the operating system control programs of the computer on which it runs, and (b) utility data-management programs provided by the manufacturer. Knowledge of both is imperative for effective use of statistical programs.
7. Many errors can be detected ahead of time by running tests on a small subset of the data.

There are a great many computer programs already written and available for use by survey analysts, provided that (1) the analyst's data set is organized properly, (2) the analyst needs those exact computations and data manipulations they perform, and (3) the analyst desires the particular results they print out. Having located a program that runs on an available computer, the next task is to determine whether these conditions are, in fact, met. If the documentation is adequate, the easiest way to do this is to start by examining the program write-up or user's manual. A detailed discussion of this documentation follows.

Usually, the principal object in a user's manual is to explain the language that is used to communicate control information to the program. The sum total of all "legal" permutations and combinations of control-language parameters constitutes the *scope* of what the program can do. The logical capabilities of the computer are used as indicated above to interrogate this control information and set the program to follow any one of a number of possible paths of computation.

For example, some programs can accept data from cards, magnetic tape, or disk storage. At the beginning of the program, before any data are read, information must be supplied that answers this question: Where are the data that are to be used? This answer is simply stored away for further use. When the section of instructions that actually reads data is about to be executed, this answer is interrogated and the program goes ahead to use that medium to which it had been referred. It is important to note that if the information stored ahead of time as the answer to a question about storage media had been "printer" or "%Q+a7" the program would fail, since neither of these pieces of information is a meaningful answer to the question "Where are the data?" Of the three types of information about a computer program mentioned here, the input data requirements are often the least well documented in many users' manuals. The others, statistical computation options and output options, are more often governed by control-language parameters and so receive explicit treatment by the writer of the documentation.

By far the vast majority of the computer programs available for use in computing statistics accept row vectors from a complete rectangular data matrix as input. This type of matrix has all the cells present; that is, every row has as many elements as every other row, and every column has as many cells as every other column. It is assumed that there is one row for every unit of analysis over which the calculations are to take place, that there is one column for every variable, and that there is exactly one value in each cell. The cell entry is the value of the variable in whose column it appears, which was obtained from that unit of analysis (case) in whose row it appears. A data-unit vector is one of these rows. As such, it contains one value of each of the variables for one case. It is generally assumed by programmers that this vector corresponds to one logical record in the data-storage medium. These may be blocked into longer physical records, usually by operating-system routines rather by than the statistical program. (See Chapter 9.)

Statistical programs generally are written to accept a file in which all the vectors (one for each case in the analysis) have been written as a sequential file. Figure 8-5 illustrates such a file. Data that contain variations from this type of file structure can still be used with programs that require it if they can be reorganized and reformatted so as to present this appearance (i.e., "rectangularized").

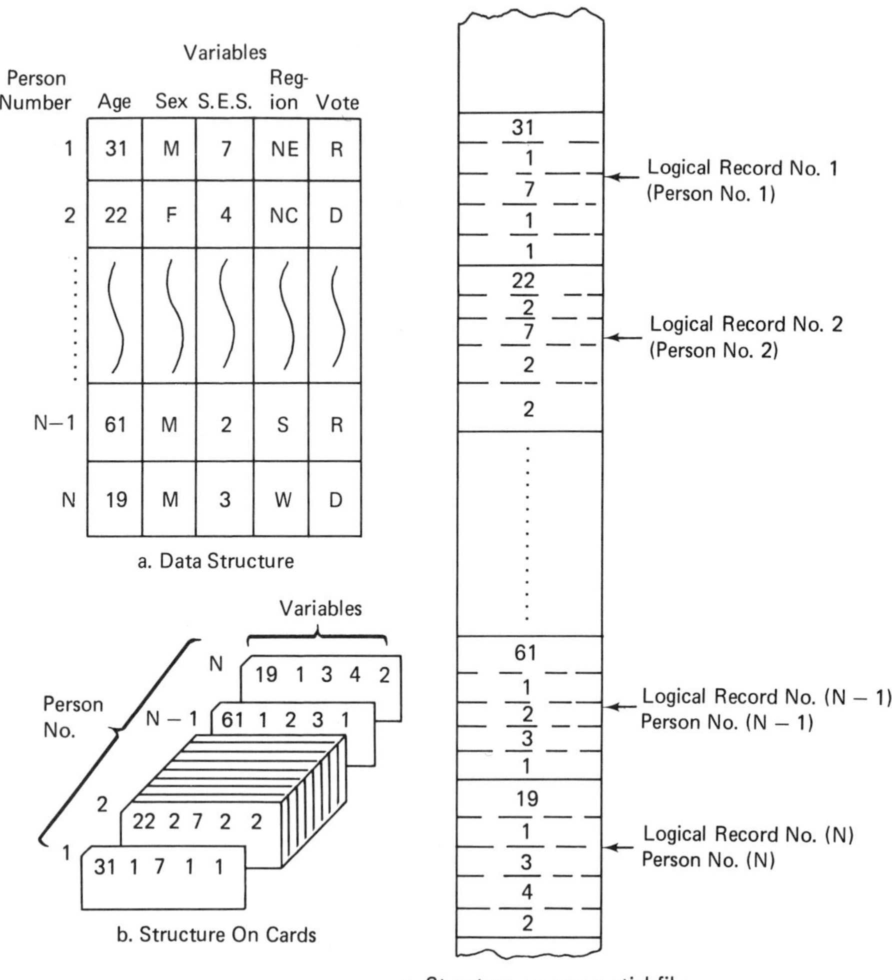

Figure 8-5 Data Matrix Structure, on Cards, as Sequential File

The most frequent departures from the complete matrix structure are missing data and multiple answers to questions. To maintain the rectangular structure, code values are generally supplied for variables which are inapplicable to some respondents or for which information is otherwise missing, thus maintaining the fixed-format, fixed-length-row, fixed-length-column format of the data matrix. A more serious problem is the presence of multiple answers to the same question which may be coded as multivalued variables. Chapter 2 discussed procedures for dealing with this type of data structure and suggested procedures for rectangularizing the data set. Once this is done, the problem is then typically reduced to that of dealing with missing data, since missing-data codes are commonly used to equalize the length of these variable-length vectors across all the observations.

Each statistical program can accept only those problems in which the data are compatible with the character set acceptable to the computer on which the program runs. (See Chapter 2.) However, there are generally additional character set restrictions on data input to a statistical program. Many programs further limit the range of values that data can take on and still remain acceptable as input. Some typical limitations include all positive and negative real numbers, all positive and negative integers, positive integers in the range 0–9, all positive and negative real numbers in the range −9999.9999 to +9999.9999 (decimal points are not punched on the cards), and all positive integers and the capital letters A–Z. Most statistical programs will accept all positive and negative real numbers. In determining whether the scope of a program meets the needs of a study, it is necessary to find out what the restrictions are on data values far enough ahead of time so that it is possible to code the data to meet them. However, if the data do not match a newly acquired program's requirements, changing character sets is not a difficult task for a capable programmer. On the other hand, modifying a program to accept character strings as input is often difficult. It is generally better to change the data to meet the program's requirements, not vice versa.

Once data have been found to meet the program requirements for character representation and matrix structure, missing-data codes, and single-valued cell entries, the next issue to examine is the extent to which the computations meet the analyst's needs. Will the program compute and print (or save in machine-readable form) the statistics that are needed? If not, possibly the program's printout of intermediate results may provide enough information to permit finishing the job on a desk calculator. Or does the program compute statistics that are close to, but not exactly, what is needed? The question of interest is the match between the researcher's definition of the problem and the scope of the input, computation, and output of the program.

Program Control

Almost all computer programs provide the user with options. Printing of statistics can be suppressed, input may come from cards or tapes, one formula rather than another may be used. Options are controlled by parameters whose values are supplied by the user at the time the program is executed. The alternative values of the parameters that can be supplied define the range of options available. These alternatives request that some task be performed or skipped, or indicate a choice between alternative tasks. Sometimes options are independent of one another—one can choose any of those associated with one control parameter and still choose any value of a second control parameter with the program executing properly. In learning to use a program, it is important to find out which options are dependent, which are independent, and what happens if parameter dependencies are violated.

Sometimes information governing all options must be submitted, but in many cases control information is *defaulted* (i.e., the programmer provided a preset answer that the user has the option of changing). For instance, data may be assumed to come from a disk file unless something different is specified explicitly. When default values for parameters are written into a program, the user generally needs to provide values for only those parameters that are to be changed. It may even be possible to omit any reference to a defaulted parameter in the input control stream, even to the omission of cards on which it would otherwise be punched. Control information that has not been defaulted is *required*, and values must be supplied for each such parameter.

Since mistakes in the control information submitted to computers are one of the most frequent sources of error, it is useful for the survey analyst to understand the basic principles governing the most frequently used types of control-language syntax. There are two commonly used methods of conveying control information to a statistical program, positional and syntactic. When *positional notation* is used, the program "knows" what the information is to be used for by its position in the input control stream. The programmer writes an instruction that effectively says something like, "Look at the contents of columns 4 and 5 on the next input card to find the answer to the question, 'How many variables are being input?' and use the information you get for that answer." Whatever appears in columns 4 and 5 on the next card is then used as the answer to that question. Positional parameters punched in the wrong columns account for many failures.

One of a great many possible syntactic substitutes for this example might require that somewhere in the control information stream must appear the character string 'NOVAR = ' and that whatever number appears right after that is to be used as the answer to this question. 'NOVAR = 56' then would mean "56 input variables." More precisely, the parameter whose name is NOVAR is to be assigned the value 56. Syntactic parameters are subject to fewer errors than positional notation, but names must still be spelled correctly. Gone are the requirements that parameters must be entered in a fixed sequence and in their proper place. The important thing to be noted here is that the analyst needs to know whether the parameter languages being employed are positional or syntactic, and, if the latter, what the syntax rules are that govern communication with the program.

Illegal parameter values may be treated in several ways, depending on the sophistication of the programmer:

1. No checks may be made to see if parameters are out of legitimate ranges. The program simply goes ahead to use parameters and data in sometimes mystifying ways.

2. The program checks the value of each parameter received and writes an error message if it is out of range or inconsistent with other parameters upon which it is dependent, but does not stop execution. This is a nonfatal error identified for the user by a warning message.
3. The program may detect an illegal value of a parameter and stop execution with no error message.
4. The program may detect an error, stop execution, and print a fatal-error message.

Sometimes all parameters are checked by a program before aborting (sometimes termed "abending"). Other programs may stop execution without ever checking the remaining input parameters. *All computer output should always be checked for nonfatal warning messages and other evidences of trouble* (*e.g., improbable marginal distributions, zero variances, very skewed distributions, wrong number of observations, etc.*) *before any interpretation is made of the output.*

Program Options Statistical programs may be coupled together to form a statistical "package" or "system," or they may be discrete and even incompatible. Programmers may write them so as to make possible the use of output from one as input to another. When a system is used, the first task faced by the analyst is to get the data into the standard format established for the package of programs intended for use. In some cases, individual programs in the system can be used to make a few preliminary runs without going through a complete conversion to create the required files. If only a few runs are to be made, the savings in time and expense gained by not setting up the standard files may offset the increases in machine costs on the few runs to be made.

Not all statistical systems for processing survey data make use of standardized special files and not all have options for using more than one type of file as input. Discovering what the system requirements are should not be left to the statistical computation phase of the study. Where the multiple-input capability is present, it can generally be recognized by an option that is built into the control-language syntax which recognizes parameters for informing the program whether to expect "standard" versus "nonstandard" files as input. Generally both have the same basic file structure, a rectangular data matrix, but standard files ordinarily have a permanent code book, a machine-readable description of where all the variables are in the file, and so on, which may be stored with the data and not repeatedly read into the computer. Often standard files are binary numbers that may be read into the computer without conversion from ASCII character strings, a time-consuming and expensive process. Some statistical systems (e.g., IMPRESS, PICKLE) have their rectangular data matrix stored column-wise instead of row-wise for greater efficiency in statistical processing. Here standard file-conversion costs may be even greater than if row-wise storage is used, and long-run usage of the converted data set for statistical computation must be even greater if total cost and convenience benefits are to be gained from conversion to standard file format. However, the cost savings and increase in convenience from the use of such transposed standard files may be dramatic if the data are to be used repeatedly. If nonstandard files are an option in the program use, electing to use them will almost certainly result in substantial increases in the amount of information that must be submitted to the computer each time the data are used. The decisions about input the analyst must make include the following:

1. Is it necessary to include a processing step in the statistical analysis to convert the data into a standard file format?
2. If this is an option, what advantages in time, accuracy, error reduction, and economy are to be gained from the costs of establishing an extra file? Over what period of time will these advantages be enjoyed?
3. Can the data be coded so as to minimize conversion costs?
4. Do there exist easy-to-use conversion programs? If not, can needed programming skills be acquired? Is an adequate character-manipulation programming language available for writing such programs?

Obtaining the answers to these questions requires a thorough knowledge of the data, the *data input options* of all the statistical programs to be used, and the programming support facilities available, including staff and programming language resources.

Some statistical programs have options for accepting the files they are to process from cards, tapes, disks, or in some cases directly from a computer terminal. The capabilities of the locally available statistical programs for accepting data in various media are the primary factors determining which storage media should be used. Since this decision has to be made early in the process of planning the study, it follows that the analyst should investigate the available media input options as early as possible, not when the major statistical analysis is about to be started.

In general, analysis programs that will operate from disks will also operate from tapes, and vice versa. This flexibility often is not present when one of the media is cards, unless the programs are simple and do not reread portions of the data during the processing. The analyst must know:

1. Whether the planned storage medium is acceptable as an input source to all the programs to be used.
2. If there are options as to which storage medium to use, what considerations would lead to selection of one over another. Total data volume is one such consideration.

3. What utility programs are available to convert data from one storage medium to another, what their capabilities are and how they are used.

A few rules can be suggested to simplify matters:

1. Always try to keep data in the storage medium that represents the normal mode of input for the programs that are used most frequently.
2. Subject to budgetary and computer-center policy restrictions, try to keep data in a storage mode that minimizes the amount of physical handling necessary to get it into the statistical programs to be used.
   (a) On-line disk storage is most convenient and usually the most costly if data sets are large.
   (b) Specially loaded disk packs are good if the schedule is such that they can be loaded once or twice a day for intensive use. Repeated handling takes time and is sometimes expensive.
   (c) Tapes are generally better than cards, provided one is careful about making backup copies and recopying masters occasionally.
3. Learn to use computing center data-handling utility programs and operating system file-handling facilities thoroughly.

When punched cards were the universal mode of storage for survey data, the sorter was an indispensable adjunct to the commercial accounting equipment which had been adapted to calculate and tabulate statistics. Its use permitted the analyst to physically segregate the subsets of observations for which statistics were to be computed. The sorter was used to arrange records in sequence for these operations as well as to select out those to be used.

When tape or disk storage is employed now, the computer is used to physically segregate those observations that constitute the subsets of the data over which computation is to take place. The simplest procedure for selecting subsets is to make one pass over all the observations and to omit processing on those not needed for the computations. The program examines each of the observations according to the specifications of a set of inclusion and exclusion parameters that are supplied as a part of the control information. Such a *subsetting option* is generally defaulted to include all the observations contained in the file submitted to the computer unless the subset selection capabilities are invoked by submission of a description of the subset of observations that are to be used (included) or a description of its complement (those to be excluded).

The need to compute statistics for a subsample appears through out many different types of statistical analyses. For example, one might wish to compute descriptive statistics just for females, or for urban families, or for all regions except the Northeast. Alternatively, one might wish to develop an explanatory model for those between the ages of 18 and 65 who were either employed or looking for work. Syntactical parameter expressions are often used for defining subset inclusion or exclusion parameters. Assume that the codes for males and females are 1 and 2 and the name of the associated variable is "V27." The expression INCLUDE (V27=1) is an example of the type of subset description that might be included in a computer run over males in the sample.

It is difficult to set up a program to accept fixed-format positional parameters that permit much flexibility in subset selection. Hence, the use of syntactic notation and complex programming to interpret the expressions is becoming more prevalent. The need for considerable flexibility in the control parameters is illustrated by the example above. One might write INCLUDE AGE = (18 TO 65) AND EMPLOYMENT = (1 OR 2).

Early statistical programs tended to require that only those variables that were actually to have statistics computed for them during that particular run were to be input into the computer. To use them, special work files had to be created which had no extraneous variables in them. The variables sometimes had to be in a specified order in the file. More recently, programs have been designed to permit entry of the entire data record for each observation. *Variable selection options* have been included to extract those variables which are to be used in the analysis.

Extracting variables from the long character string comprising an input data vector for one observation requires information describing where each variable is in the string, what the character set is that defines the legal values of the variable, and (if the variable is numeric) where the decimal points are. In the standard file structure used by most statistical systems, this information is stored once, and permanently, at the time the data are originally read into the storage medium. A *variable name* such as "AGE" or "REGION" or a number such as V26 is attached.[3] It is kept in an internal *dictionary* of variable description information. References to individual variables by the user are accomplished after that simply by giving the variable name or its number. This *pointer* serves to permit retrieval of the rest of the information about the variable. Since programs of this type use names that are limited in length, the user must make sure the names for all the variables are all distinct and that they are recorded in the code book. (See Chapter 5.) Misspelled names on the control cards can result in an error message if there is no other variable spelled that way, or in statistics generated for the wrong variable. Generally, such a name must have a letter as its first character, but may have numbers as succeeding characters.

Some analytical packages (e.g., OSIRIS, SPSS) assign sequential numbers to variable names, such as V1, V2, or VAR056. This facilitates referring to a block of variables: one can write expressions such as V2, V7, V11-V67 (OSIRIS) or VAR2, VAR7, VAR11 THRU VAR67 (SPSS). The disadvantage lies in not having a mnemonic reference to the content of the variables and the consequent

[3] For example, Sonquist and O'Brien (1960) used the syntax INPUT LIST IS NAME1, NAME2, . . . , NAMEN to attach names to variables that had been read in. Names could be up to six characters long.

need for continual referral back to the code book in setting up runs and in interpreting output. In some programs, detailed variable descriptions can be supplied optionally. Use of program labeling options substantially aids in the interpretation of output and reduces the possibility of inadvertent reporting of results for the wrong variable.

Some statistical programs also have the option for the inclusion of *random* or *systematic subsets* of observations as input into statistical computation. Systematic subsetting may take several forms. In some programs the first N records in the file may be selected, or the *i*th through the *j*th records, or every *k*th record starting with the *j*th. Selection of a set of records on the basis of their position in the file assumes that those records in the file have been presorted, generally by means of a utility sort program of the type generally available at a computing installation. Sometimes provisions are made (SPSS) to use an individual record on a probability basis (i.e., a random sample can be drawn from the total file). This is especially useful when a holdout sample is required for replication.

Early statistical systems and individual statistical programs often had only rudimentary capabilities for recoding variables, collapsing categories, or providing mathematical transformations either on a temporary or on a permanent basis. Nor did they have the more advanced capabilities of combining several variables into indices. Systems developed more recently ordinarily have both capabilities. The analyst's decision to use temporary *variable-generation capabilities* depends on the analysis objectives and on the extent to which the data have been coded in the form needed. It may be necessary to:

1. Combine or assign missing information.
2. Establish a dichotomy or trichotomy from data that were collected in much more detail.
3. Try various alternatives in establishing a "bracket" code for data originally coded as an interval measure.
4. Perform a mathematical transformation on an interval variable to reduce skew or deal with other distributional problems.
5. Combine items together to form a scale or index that more adequately represents the concept to be studied.

In each case, it may be necessary to experiment with various versions of the recoded variable or index to decide which one finally is to be used in the analysis. This experimentation generally requires at least running frequency distributions on the new variable and may involve cross-tabulations and more complex correlational statistics. The general problem is to transform the variable so that its code structure achieves as close to an optimal form as possible to represent the underlying concept. Having the capability to obtain several simultaneous versions of the same variable is often useful.

It is most important to note that where temporary variable recoding and index construction facilities are not available as control-language options on statistical programs, the analyst must make provisions for separate recoding operations and must provide for code additions and temporary work files containing the experimental versions of the variables to be recoded before the statistical analysis can be started. This requires careful control over the records of which versions of the recoded original variables have been assembled in work files. Airtight code-book control is imperative.

A commonly used option establishes what role each input variable is to play in the analysis. For example, age may be used as an independent variable in a cross-tabulation, region as a predictor in a regression or multiple classification analysis, and an index of authoritarianism as the dependent variable in an analysis of variance. In a positional-parameter control language, each *role definition parameter* "points" to the variable which is to be used for the specific purpose controlled by that parameter. By inserting the name or number of a specific variable as the value of that parameter, that variable is assigned a role in the computation. In a syntactic parameter language this would typically be accomplished by an assignment (e.g., DEP_VAR=AGE). Since several analyses frequently can be obtained in one run, the list of variables that constitutes the control information and defines which variables are to be used in each analysis is often independent of the list of initial input variables. Such an arrangement is used in SPSS. For example, input may have included variables A–Z, but REGRESSION = A WITH B, C, D would define A as a dependent variable and B, C, and D as independent variables. Other statements that request regressions might use other variables. In each case the syntax establishes that these particular variables are to be used to perform the functions indicated. Identifying the variable by its name in the REGRESSION = statement accomplishes the assignment of the role that it is to play.

If samples are used in which subsections of the population are selected with differing probabilities, then weights may be used to reestablish the proper proportions.[4] Statistical programs designed for use with surveys in which probability sampling methods are used ordinarily provide optional capabilities for the use of a *weight variable*. Not all statistical programs that are used to process survey data have these capabilities, however, and if the programs lack them, it will be necessary to "explode" the sample in order to process the data using the weighting scheme.[5]

When the proportion of observations in a particularly important subgroup in the population is small, say, 10 to 15 per cent, then a very large sample would have to be interviewed to obtain enough data for the small group for which statistics are to be computed. For example, if it is desired to estimate the pro-

[4] See Kish (1965).

[5] "Explosion," involves actually making multiple copies of those observations weighted by values exceeding 1. The multiple copies are then added to the original files and the statistics run "unweighted."

portion of black families having life insurance, as compared with white, a sample of 100 families is scarcely large enough, since, if the sample is representative of the U.S. population, it will yield about 10 interviews with the heads of black families. This is not a large-enough base to use for estimating the proportion with life insurance. Since interviews are very expensive to obtain, a likely approach is to increase the probability that a black family is selected in the sample. In effect, the selection rule is:

> Pick a family. Determine if the head is white or black.
> If the head is white, include the family with probability $P = .1$.
> If the head is black, include the family with probability $P = .5$.

If the population contained 900 white families for every 100 black families, we should now expect to get about ($.1 \times 900 = 90$) white and ($.5 \times 100 = 50$) black families in a randomly chosen sample that began with 1000 families.

However, unweighted estimates of parameters for the total population would now be biased because we have too many black families in the sample. It is no longer representative. The proper proportions can be restored by weighting each group by the inverse of its probability of being picked. This requires generation of a new variable for each observation, called a *weight*. It has the value ($.1/.5 = .2$) if the observation is from an interview with a black family and ($.1/.1 = 1$) if the interview is from a white family.[6] The weight is used in the statistical program essentially to count how many times that observation is to be used in calculating statistics.[7] It must be able to accept input parameters that indicate which variable is to be used as the weight, and it must have the numerical precision to be able to deal accurately with the very large numbers that can easily be accumulated when weighted sums of squares of five- or six-digit variables are used. Large rounding errors can easily occur if care is not taken to prevent them. Lastly, the program must produce information based on both weighted and unweighted data in the output for documentation of the weighting procedure. Printed cautions should appear when weights are used, since the concept of degrees of freedom, an important one in hypothesis testing, requires reinterpretation in the presence of weights, as observations are no longer independent.

The control language of the program should reflect the presence of these capabilities and they should be documented in the write-up. If no mention is made of them, it should be assumed that the program cannot make use of weights. Clearly, it is in order to ascertain whether programs that are candidates for prospective use have these capabilities before a commitment is made to a sample design that is not self-representing. Adequate capabilities for handling weighted data generally include the use of *double-precision* computer arithmetic

[6] See Kish (1965, pp. 429–430 and Chap. 1).

[7] For example, Kish (1965, p. 430) gives the formula for calculating the mean in this type of problem (in which sample weights are normalized to sum to 1) as the product of the weight times the value of the variable, summed over all observations.

computer instructions in the program rather than single-precision methods, to avoid serious and undetectable computation errors that result from rounding and truncation.[8]

The conditions likely to cause these truncation errors are field widths of four or more characters, weights of two or three digits, or sample sizes that exceed 1000. If two or more of these conditions are present, the analyst is cautioned to proceed as follows:

1. Choose the widest variable (width = number of characters in the field in which it is recorded).
2. Estimate what the weighted sum of squares is for this field for the whole sample.
3. Subtract from this number the product of the smallest value that appears in this field and the smallest weight.
4. If the result of this subtraction is smaller than the precision available for single-precision floating-decimal numbers in the computer to be used, steps should be taken to prevent truncation errors by such steps as transforming the original data by subtracting their mean, by a z-score transformation, or by sorting the data into ascending sequence on the magnitude of the field before submitting them to the computer.

These considerations all reinforce the importance of becoming familiar with the limitations of the statistical programs to be used before the study is ready for analysis. If a computer program write-up does not specifically say that floating-decimal arithmetic operations are carried out in double precision, or discuss truncation error, then it is usually safe to assume that single-precision methods were used.

Statistical-program control languages are sometimes designed so as to permit the analyst to screen out extreme values of variables that are involved in the computations. *Subset selection options* are an especially desirable capability in

[8] The presence of weighted data can lead to serious errors in product-moment statistics (e.g., correlation coefficients). The reason is that multiplying the square of a four- or five-digit variable by a weight that has two digits and then summing over the N characterizing the typical survey, say 1000 observations, can lead to an accumulated sum of squares of considerable magnitude, perhaps as large as 10^{13}. When the last observations are added to this partially accumulated sum, there is the strong probability that small values may not be added at all. This is called *truncation error* and can lead to distortions, particularly if variances are small. If the discrepancy between a partially accumulated quantity and a new value to be added to it is more than the number of significant digits carried by the computer hardware, the new value is added in as a zero. As a consequence, the sum of squares is too small by some unknown amount and the standard variance formula then applied may produce downwardly biased results, possibly even having negative values. The proper solution is for the program to use double-precision arithmetic. An alternative is to sort the data into ascending sequence on the absolute magnitude of the field in question, causing small values to appear first. This does not work for cross-products. A better solution is to use a z-score transformation. Simply rescaling the data or the weights may solve the problem.

programs in which least-squares techniques, such as analysis of variance, are used. If the distribution of the variable in question is skewed, a few very extreme cases can distort the findings considerably. More often than might be suspected, extreme values turn out to be coding errors that should have been eliminated by earlier consistency checks. The important thing for the analyst is to recognize the possibility of extreme cases, to obtain distributional measures of the potentially troublesome variables, and to utilize data-screening capabilities judiciously.

Alternatively, it may be desired to filter out observations that are coded "miscellaneous" or "inapplicable," or "they have some, but we couldn't tell how much." If codes for these various forms of partial data are established, then the same type of screening capability can be used to eliminate these troublesome observations from the computations. The analyst must learn the exclusion capabilities of the programs and then code the data so as to take advantage of them.

In addition to the subset selection capabilities that may apply to all the statistics being computed during one "run," some programs provide screening capabilities to further restrict the cases to be used in particular computation.[9] For instance, it may be desirable to run a number of cross-tabulations on interviews taken from urban areas, excluding those from rural areas. In each of several tables to be produced, it may be desirable to exclude those observations coded "inapplicable" on the independent variable and also on the dependent variable. These groups would differ somewhat from table to table, yet they could all be produced efficiently on the same "pass" of the data through the computer if adequate global and local filtering capabilities are provided.[10]

Excluding observations that are coded as "inapplicable" is often necessary when multivariate techniques are used. The reason is that the set of observations which are inapplicable on one variable may coincide with the set which are inapplicable on another variable, or these two sets may have a sizable common subset. For instance, in developing a least-squares prediction equation with income as a dependent variable, it is reasonable to use both occupation and weeks of unemployment during the past year as sets of dummy independent variables.[11] However, if one of the occupation categories is "self-employed," another is "farmers," and a third is "retired," which is often the case, and if by definition these people cannot be "unemployed" since they work "for" themselves (or do not "work" at all), considerable disturbance occurs in the correlation between the two variables. The correlation will be spuriously high, and the correlations of both variables with other variables will partially reflect this overlap. This

[9] These are sometimes termed local and global subsetting, exclusion, or filtering capabilities. The global capability applies to the run, the local to the individual statistics.

[10] A knowledge of set theory and some skill in the use of Venn diagrams will be of considerable use to the serious survey analyst who must convey to a statistical system with a sophisticated control language what is to be done to include and exclude data. See Chapter 7 for an exposition of these concepts in the context of variable generation.

[11] For a detailed description of the use and interpretation of dummy-independent variables, see Dunkelberg (1973).

leads to ill-conditioned correlation matrices and results in output from multivariate statistical techniques which may have distortions of unknown magnitude. Moreover, most statistical programs have no built-in methods of revealing the extent to which distortions such as this may be occurring, so it is up to the analyst to make sure that the data put into them have these conceptually overlapping subsets removed. Necessary subgroups can be removed by proper use of filtering options.[12]

A similar kind of problem occurs when the amount of missing information due to refusals is more than just a few per cent. The problem is that refusing to answer one question is often correlated with refusing to answer others, or with certain other variables. There appear to be four methods of coping with this: (1) excluding the missing-data cases, (2) including these cases and leaving the missing data "as is," (3) assigning the missing data to one or more of the non-missing-data categories, or (4) randomizing the missing data. The analyst must deal with missing data within the constraints of the computer programs to be used.

Many computer programs have no provisions for dealing with *missing information*; it simply never occurred to the programmer that anyone would submit a file in which not all of the information was present. Therefore, if the user has missing information coded as 0 or as a padded field of 9's (see Chapter 3), the program will treat these fields as though they were legitimate values of the variables. Obviously, this cannot be permitted to happen; all the offending observations must either be removed from the file before it is submitted as input, or recoded.

Removing all observations with at least one missing value is a time-consuming task when the data are stored on cards. The file must be run through a sorter or collator and any observation that turns up with such a value is removed and placed in a "hold" file. After all fields have been examined, the remaining observations can be used as input to the no-missing-data statistical program. When the information is stored on tape or disk, removal can be accomplished by a complex subsetting operation that makes a copy of the file containing only those observations which are not missing information on any of the relevant variables. It is likely that a special-purpose program may have to be written to accomplish this, and the analyst should plan accordingly if this is the route to be taken. It will be expensive, since it will have to be done once for each analysis that uses a different set of variables. Consequently, this method should be avoided if there is much missing data. Excluding observations with missing data on any variable can mean that the number of cases left for analysis may be very small. Excluding the observation when the variable has missing information on the dependent variable or on one or two critical independent

[12] Often the missing-data categories are included in the regression analysis, since eliminating all missing data on all predictors may remove too many observations. Including the group coded "missing" in the analysis empirically determines which known group they are most like in influence on the dependent variable.

variables seems more reasonable and often can be accomplished easily if global and local subsetting capabilities are available.

Many computer programs have the ability to assign missing data to one of the non-missing-data categories. This is simply an application of the univariate code-collapsing and recoding capabilities that are often built into statistical routines. However, if the program does not have this capability, it will be necessary to make this a separate step. Ordinarily, the modal value (or mean, in the case of a continuous variable) would be used unless there appear to be good reasons for using one of the other substantive categories. This does not avoid the conceptual overlap problem; rather, it hides it from the analyst, as well as from the eventual readers of the report. It is used primarily when the amount of missing information is small and randomizing techniques are not available, or when the primary purpose of the analysis is descriptive. It is probably the most frequently used method for coping with missing data.

Assigning missing information by randomizing it among the non-missing-data categories is a better alternative than the one just described. Missing values are assigned according to the probability that the observation in question actually belongs in that class. Although there are many possible models for probabilistic assignment, using the proportion of known cases in each class seems the most reasonable basis for estimating this probability. This method has the advantage of representing unknown information as a random variable with the same distribution as the known cases (or possibly with a normal distribution). However, most statistical programs do not have this type of recoding capability as an option, and it may be necessary to carry out these assignments as an extra step in the processing. This should be done as soon as the data are "cleaned up" and initial non-missing-data distributions are available on all the variables. Any analysis can then be undertaken without getting involved in missing-data problems.

It cannot be overemphasized that time spent in a thorough cleaning up of the data, including assigning the missing information on a random basis, will be recovered many times over at later stages in the data processing. This point can be stressed by the observation that programs may vary in their treatment of missing data. Some allow the user to control what is to be done with them through assignment or exclusion; others automatically exclude from the statistical computations observations coded in certain ways; still others may make no provisions for dealing with the problem. If automatic exclusion is used by some programs, the user's codes must conform to the code conventions for missing information required by those programs. But these conventions may be incompatible with those of other programs to be used, and recoding will be required if both are to be employed. Unless the analyst checks each program's users' manual very carefully before using it, missing-data conventions are likely to be overlooked. This may be a serious problem, since user errors in defining missing data are not ordinarily detectable by the program! The results may be automatic deletion of the wrong cases, or incorrect inclusion of data that should have been removed—all without any error messages or other warnings. The only check on this problem appears to be a carefully run set of marginal frequency distributions against which the number of observations actually used in the statistical computations can be checked.

Computation and *output options* are almost always among those that are built into statistical programs. Such programs are usually designed to perform several different types of computations, and the user is given the option of what is to be done. These options may include the printing of intermediate results, user-supplied tolerances and critical points, use of one formula or another, single- or double-precision arithmetic, choice of statistics to be printed, and the form in which the output is to be received.

Electing to obtain intermediate results as option is likely to be an expensive proposition with a limited payoff. These options often have simply been left in the program, having been put there for the programmer's use when it was checked for accuracy. Unless there is a specific reason for wanting printed statistics such as covariance matrices, or sums and sums of squares, the analyst will generally do better to suppress printing of this type of information. Specific reasons for obtaining intermediate results might include documentation of suspected program bugs, results that do not agree with those from other programs (possibly due to differences in computational formulas), searching for possible conceptual overlap of variables, and other suspected troubles. When a programming error is suspected, it is often desirable to run the program with all output options "on" to gain a maximum of information to be used in diagnosing the trouble.

Many programs provide for user-supplied *tolerance* or *convergence* criteria, generally defaulted, but available for the user to change, depending on the problem. These include constants to be used as a test for completion of an iterative process, such as the maximum difference to be permitted between two successive estimates, a count of the maximum number of times that a computation is to be performed, minimum or maximum values of a quantity computed by the program, or incremental constants. Some typical examples include communality estimates (factor analysis), F-levels (step regression), and the maximum number of factors to be extracted (factor analysis). Other types of constants include those that are interrogated to direct which computation process will be used. For instance, the text "TYPE = RAO" might initiate a procedure aimed at maximizing the correlation between a set of hypothesized factors and a set of data variables. Generally, a variety of computational procedures are available, and the control language is used to obtain a match of the capabilities of the program with the analyst's particular problem.

Some *data-output options* provide for the computation of residuals or predicted values. Other programs require that variable-generation routines be used for this purpose in a separate run. Since these require adding new variables to the data file, the procedures to be followed and the problems to be solved are essentially those discussed in Chapter 7. Caution must be exercised in computing residuals, however, since (1) the model may not be applicable to every case, as a result of missing data or estimation for a subgroup only; (2) both positive and negative residuals must be allowed for in the codes and the data formats; (3) an adequate number of decimal places must be allowed for (at least one more than in the original dependent variable); (4) adequate documentation of the run that generated the residuals must be kept; (5) prompt updating of code books must take place; and (6) proof that all of the file was processed satisfactorily is needed.

One of the most common options relating to output is the provision for *run labeling* information to be printed along with the statistics. This should be provided by hand if not available as an option, and, if available, should be used religiously. Every page of computer output should contain a header that contains a sequential job number for the project, the date, the name of the input file, the name of the program, and the name of the person responsible for the run. If page-heading facilities are not available, this information should be entered by hand, at least onto the first page of each major section of computer output.

Output options are sometimes available to retain *intermediate results* in machine-readable form, on disk, tape, or cards. This type of option is most frequently available for covariance, correlation, or cluster analysis matrices. Occasionally, it is advantageous to compute a large correlation matrix and then to use this as input to a regression program that is capable of computing a number of equations based on subsets of the variables in the correlation matrix. Where this capability is available, it can save much in the way of time and effort, since usually more than half of the computer time involved in a statistical operation is taken up simply by reading the data into the computer. The costs for computing one large correlation matrix are likely to be considerably less than the costs of a number of smaller correlation matrices. As with other options that present-day computing equipment makes available, using a big matrix requires planning ahead. Using large correlation matrices or other intermediate data as input for a final statistical analysis may not pay off if the variables are not defined in exactly the way one wants them, or if the sample subset over which they are computed is not what the analyst needs. The problem of missing data must be handled carefully and completely in these types of aggregation.

Program Use Strategies

Statistical programs sometimes come in several variations. Each may be able to perform similar operations, but one may be far more efficient than the others for a restricted set of standard operations. For instance, SPSS has an optional cross-tabulation module which operates much faster than the more flexible regular routine. It can handle a larger number of computations, but requires additional control-card preparation, and can handle data coded only as zero or positive integers. OSIRIS has several routines for computing tables of means and standard deviations or for performing analysis of variance; the optimal choice depends on the number of control groups defined by the code categories of the independent variable. It may be possible to divide a large run into several parts to take advantage of the savings in computer time to be gained by using this type of facility.

The nature of batch-processing computing technology has an impact on program use. Delays between "shots" at the computer may run from a miraculous 5 minutes to a frustrating overnight wait, or worse. For this reason, it is sometimes good strategy to run extra tables and individual statistics to tide the analyst over until it is possible to get back at the computer. The fact is that computer time is really cheaper than human time (despite the fact that poor accounting procedures produce figures that emphasize dollar machine costs), and it may well pay to run a few extra things once the data are in the computer, since, if needed, it will take an extra day to obtain them. Because one would have to make an extra "pass" of the data if the extra statistics were run separately, and because present program capacities are often not approached, the strategy of making the extra computations is reasonable. Overdone, however, it leads to a rather large number of statistical tables and difficulty in indexing and storing the results. The best guard against this problem is a clear set of research objectives, a well-controlled schedule, and at least two ounces of theory to every pound of input control cards.

If the data have been collected at two or more points in time, or if the study has more than one unit of analysis, or uses list variables, or includes measures of group attributes or structural relations between units instead of merely attributes of those units, then the analyst is faced with some special problems in the statistical analysis. Little study has been given to the formal structural properties of data collected by survey analysts. Yet, panel studies and relational and contextual analysis promise to yield much more adequate information about social phenomena than simple case-classification studies. Practical experience indicates that a large proportion of the headaches associated with processing nonstandard data can be minimized (but not avoided completely) by making the data look as if they are completely cross-sectional and were gathered from a single unit of analysis. An extensive review of this situation has been presented in an earlier discussion of data structures. Here these points are simply to be emphasized again and their relevance to statistical programs noted.

Almost all of the statistical programs aimed at surveys and extant at the time of writing assume that data will be stored as a series of logical records, each containing a vector of scalar values (variables) representing the measurements of the various attributes of a single unit (usually an interview).[13] This is illustrated in Figure 8-6. Recording of over-time data so that it looks like a vector from a standard cross-section study can be done in one of several ways. Which

[13] The IMPRESS statistical system developed at Dartmouth College is a notable exception and assumes storage of a transposed data matrix. However, the structure of a rectangular data matrix is assumed.

Inter-view Number	X_1	X_2	...	X_{v-1}	X_v

Figure 8-6 Cross-sectional Data Vector

one is chosen should depend on the input requirements of the statistical programs to be used in processing it. One way is to record all the variables for a single observation at time T_1 followed in the same record by all the same variables for the same observation at time T_2, with appropriate missing-data codes if either block is missing. This is illustrated in Figure 8-7(a). An alternative is to record blocks of variables rather than blocks based on interviewing times. Thus, data on one variable at two time periods are placed adjacently. See Figure 8-7(b).

Sometimes the study design calls for a survey in which respondents are selected so as to produce a quasi-experimental design in which matched pairs of observations are obtained. This type of data can be made to look like rectangular data vectors by recording information for the pairs as the unit of analysis. In this case, data might be organized so as to look like Figure 8-8 in structure. All the measurements for all attributes of both members of the pair are stored in one vector. The important point is that statistical programs generally have data structure restrictions or assumptions that may require making a complex data

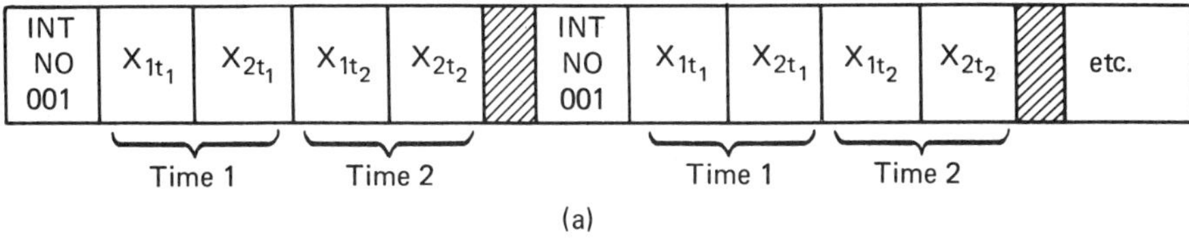

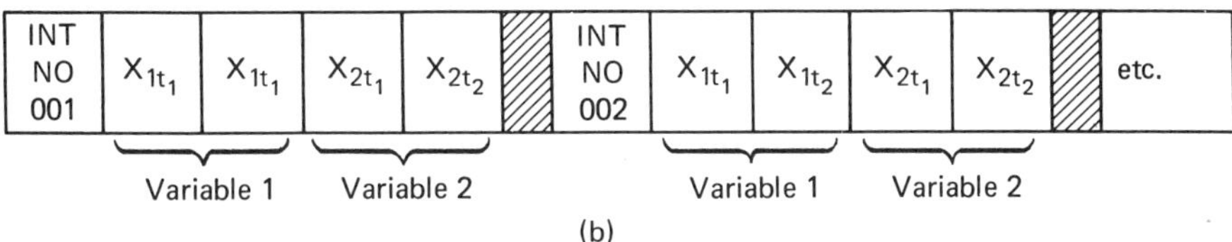

Figure 8-7 Over-Time Data as a Vector

Pair Number 1	X_1 Person "A"	X_1 Person "B"	X_2 "A"	X_2 "B"	etc . . .		Pair Number N	X_1 "C"	X_1 "D"	etc.

Figure 8-8 Data Vector for Matched Pairs

structure appear like a cross-section data vector. Data from several times or from a pair of observations are simply recorded and stored as elements in a single data vector in the storage medium. The purpose of the present discussion has simply been to call attention to this and to the fact that if programs which are to process data like these are to be used without severe delays, the data storage structure they require must be anticipated in advance and suitable arrangements must be made to record the data in an acceptable structural framework right from the start.

There are some notable exceptions to the usual situation in which slight departures from row-wise rectangular data matrices cause input incompatibility. Some statistical programs, frequently those designed by biological scientists or psychologists interested in experimental design, may accept rectangular data matrices stored column-wise; that is, one record contains all of the values for one variable measured at one point in time. Thus, the information generated from examining many observations is kept in one record instead of information from many variables on only one observation. Sometimes information about the attributes of the experimental group in which these observations were taken is also recorded in this vector (i.e., design matrix information).[14] A number of advanced interactive statistical systems for processing surveys use such a transposed data matrix for storage purposes.[15] They contain transposition programs, and their limitation lies not so much in the need to have data submitted to them in column-wise data records rather than row-wise records as it does with the requirement that the data matrix be rectangular. In this respect, they share the limitations of the large bulk of generally available survey processing programs.

Program options are not always designed to be exercised independent of one another. Setting one option to activate a particular program capability or to suppress it may preclude setting another parameter in one or more ways. The parameters are *dependent*. Or the program may be *data-dependent*. The latter refers to a program written so that the presence of data values outside the range anticipated by the programmer causes the program to behave differently from the manner intended. For example, in a cross-tabulation program, a programmer may set up a 10×10 array to count the joint occurrences of values of two attributes. The data for which the program was written all ranged between 0 and 9, and the program was written to use the value of each of the variables to decide where to count the observation—but no check was made to ensure that the range of the input data values was, in fact, between zero and nine. Later, the program is used with data whose values range between 1 and 10. The first time a 10 is encountered the count will be placed outside the matrix of accumulated frequencies. Potentially, this could even alter one of the instructions in the pro-

[14] For example, see General Electric Corp. Statistical Programs available under Mark II Timesharing.

[15] See Meyers (1973) and Shanks (1972).

gram! Even if the latter never occurs, all the counts will have been placed in the wrong cells and the labeling of the output will be entirely erroneous. There may be no way for the analyst to discover this except to compare the results with those from another program. The best defense against such problems is to use a much-used, well-documented statistical package, if one is available.

A. REFERENCE MANUAL

I. Abstract. A brief description of the program purpose.

II. Table of Contents.

III. Definition of terms used in the documentation.

IV. Description of system functioning. Contains: Description of how the program relates to others in this application area and to user's manual processing systems; review of the assumptions made by the program about what the user has done with his data (and codebook) prior to using the program; list of expected uses to which the output will be put; flow of processing described both in narrative and, where applicable, by flowchart.

V. Description of input. Contains: A listing of the data input requirements, structure, files used; sequence requirements, capacities and restrictions, character sets, standard and non-standard file acceptance, treatment of missing data, weights, multiple response variables, alphabetic variables, codebook or other declarative information processing capabilities, decimal points, checks made on input error conditions, a list of things in the data not checked for that the user should guard against.

VI. Description of output. Contains: A description of the specific functions of the program; formulas (and bibliographic references as needed); accuracy and precision; verbal descriptions of algorithms (e.g. matrix inversion); references to the literature, where appropriate. (A later section deals with a specific description of what is printed, written on tape or disks or punched.)

VII. Summary of restrictions. All capacities and limitations of the program with reference to both input data and values of parameters should be listed here in abbreviated, though readable, form.

VIII. Set-up instructions. This should include references to such control card coding forms as are available and samples and should also include:

a. Complete description of the JCL required.
b. A list of the input control file sequence in the order in which it should be submitted (types of cards and their sequence).
c. Storage options as to input files (other than that described in JCL).
d. Several examples of the set-up, including JCL. One example should be provided for each type of input file (or output file) capable of being handled by the program.
e. A description in detail of each type of control card, including formats, parameters values, the results that can be obtained by alternative settings, the effects of each control statement variation. Input sequence of control parameters.
f. Instructions to be given to computer operators by the user if any.
g. Checks made on accuracy of control statements, checks not made that user might want to take steps to guard against, and procedure for user testing of setup correctness.

Figure 8-9 Program Documentation Outline

IX. Description of Output. Describes the order of items on the printed output, and their meanings, with references to literature as necessary; format of punched card output, format of tape output, unit of output (one record per xxx). Options and limitations should be described in detail. A description of what a normal termination looks like should be included. Information, such as records processed, used for proof of successful run, that is supplied by the program should be noted.

X. Error handling and error messages. A complete summary of all the erroneous conditions checked for should appear here, together with an indication of how each is handled by the program. This should be followed by an error message listing with an associated list of things causing each error message and the remedial action to be taken.

B. PROGRAMMER'S GUIDE

I. Table of contents.

II. Introduction and design philosophy (modularity, speed, capacity, accuracy, purpose, etc.).

III. Glossary of terms.

IV. Hardware assumed.

V. Software and operating system environment.

VI. Interfaces to manual elements in processing system.

VII. Program system requirements flow charts and interfaces with other programs in use.

VIII. Programming considerations, interfaces with other modules, communication regions, common storage, etc.

IX. Entry conditions, exit conditions, functions of module with respect to other module.

X. Identification of parts of this module (entries, exits, functions).

XI. Processing options and control language specifications, parameters and way in which they are supplied, functions of each parameter, limits of parameters.

XII. Input and output formats and structure of records.

XIII. Errors and error messages.

XIV. Storage requirements and allocations, label table, array structures and functions of each array, relocatability, common (communication) regions.

XV. Main program.

XVI. Subroutines used.

XVII. Formulas, accuracy analysis, precision requirements, verbal descriptions of algorithms used, (references as necessary).

Note: I-VII are prepared once for each system of programs
VIII-XVII repeated for each individual program

XVIII. Flow charts. Revised in final version to agree with machine code. Index flow charts to statement labels in program.

XIX. Symbolic listings should be included as a part of programmers reference with subroutines used in symbolic form. All listings should be annotated in detail with comments on cards. Indicate dates of all revisions.

XX. Append programmers reference documentation for all subroutines used in program.

Figure 8-9 (cont'd.)

A final trap that the survey analyst needs to know about is poor *documentation* of statistical programs. Although great care and effort is sometimes expended on system documentation, this is, unfortunately, the exception rather than the rule, especially for single programs. Figure 8-9 provides a list of the kinds of topics that should be covered in the documentation for a statistical program. If these topics are not covered, experimentation with the program will generally be necessary to ascertain how it works, or correspondence with the writer of the program may be required.

THE LOGIC OF STATISTICAL DATA PROCESSING

This section provides an overview of the types of objectives that typically characterize a survey project. A given study may encompass several of them, while retaining a primary focus. The complexity or multiplicity of the objectives will be reflected in the complexity and sometimes contradictory requirements of the data processing. First, an overview of typical survey objectives is presented. Using this framework, the discussion then turns to a consideration of the analysis procedures relating to the assessment of reliability and validity. These procedures tend to be common to all surveys, regardless of their major focus.

A section follows which deals with descriptive analysis objectives and their implications for the data processing. The following section reviews some of the approaches to statistical analysis of data in which the objectives are conceptual refinement, the construction of typologies, and the development of improved measures.

Finally, an approach to the explanatory analysis that is the primary focus of most surveys is outlined. The discussion does not distinguish between inductive exploratory research and surveys in which the primary purpose is hypothesis testing. Rather, the view taken is that the hypothetical–deductive rhetoric (inherited largely from a mistaken view of the methodology of the physical sciences of past decades) is more fruitfully replaced by a perspective that focuses on multivariate explanatory models which are improved by successive studies. This orientation has its roots in the biological sciences and in econometrics and receives an excellent exposition by Tukey (1962) and Tukey and Wilk (1966). In this view, inductive and deductive phases of research are cyclical, even within the same study, and the emphasis is not on adducing evidence for or against an isolated hypothesis, but on extracting information from data with a view to making as many theoretically interesting improvements in a model as will stand up to the canons of parsimony, cross validation, and replication. The emphasis is on the fit of the model, its scope, its internal structure, and on the theoretical and practical import of the concepts embodied in it.

Fellin, Tripodi, and Meyer (1969) have classified empirical research into three major categories, according to the main objectives of the research.[16] *Experimental studies* have as their main objective the production of empirical generalizations; that is, hypotheses integrated into well-articulated models and supported by well-documented evidence. Such studies generally seek to establish system input–output or cause–effect relationships by ruling out the effects of extraneous factors through random assignment of subjects to experimental and control groups. But they often use or are based on the data-collection methods of the survey. They face many similar data-handling and processing problems. The research logic, and thus that of the statistics and the procedures used to generate them, is heavily deductive.

Another type of study, termed *quantitative–descriptive*, often has a much wider range of simultaneous objectives than hypothesis testing, which comprises almost the entirety of the goals of laboratory and field experiments. These studies may not only seek to test hypotheses, but also to describe populations or combine these tasks into a design which enables judgments to be made about the effectiveness of a program of action. They may attempt to approximate rigorous statistical designs in an attempt to develop, inductively, a variety of ex post facto middle-range causal models of behavior. The logic is both deductive and inductive. Most applications of survey techniques fall into this area.

A third type, the *exploratory study*, is oriented primarily toward the initial formulation and development of hypotheses and preliminary models. Such studies may seek to clarify and articulate the relationships between concepts and develop methodological approaches and specific measuring techniques. A variety of research techniques may be used, including the type of interviewing usually associated with quantitative–descriptive studies. However, in these studies, the use of systematic measuring procedures to generate statistics picturing accurate quantitative relationships between variables is a secondary concern at best. Such a study may combine survey-type interviews with special data-collection techniques, such as sociometric measures or experimental manipulation. A specific objective may be the development of scales and indices. The research logic is essentially inductive. The important point for this discussion is that data collected using survey methodologies may have exploration as the motivation for its collection and that the statistical analysis carried out will reflect this.

All these objectives must necessarily be reflected in the data processing as well as in the statistical techniques chosen. If a given study is primarily oriented in the direction of model building, or toward hypothesis testing, the bulk of the statistical data processing will derive its characteristics from these objectives. But even in these studies, subsidiary objectives may include description, the development of measures, and conceptual clarification—and analyses reflecting them will require computer usage patterns appropriate to these primarily methodological goals.

Surveys, then, almost always have many objectives. Because of this, one

[16] See Fellin, Tripodi, and Meyer (1969).

cannot just start analyzing the data for the whole study. A series of analysis plans must be developed relative to each specific objective. Each needs to be limited to an achievable set of specific goals, yet be open-ended in case unexpected findings appear. Exploratory objectives will be reflected in analysis plans seeking conceptual clarification, improved measurement, discovery of extreme conditions, typical and unusual configurations of variables, improvements in data-collection procedures, and the like. Program evaluation objectives will reflect the need to isolate the impact of membership in the treatment group(s) as distinct from confounding factors and the need to determine whether unanticipated consequences of the program occurred. Descriptive objectives call for the computation of selected measures of central tendency and dispersion for population subgroups deemed to be of interest. Analysis plans for hypothesis testing or model-building surveys are generally more complex and open-ended, since the analyst has a more difficult task in planning for unanticipated results. In a model-building or hypothesis-testing analysis, the survey analyst must consider the following problems (among others):

1. Will the explanatory model apply to everyone in the sample, or will it be necessary to determine if it applies to all, thereby requiring the inclusion of subsetting variables in the analysis plan?
2. Among the predictor variables, are there conceptual overlaps either between themselves or with the dependent variable, including pseudo-overlaps resulting from common inapplicable codes, missing data, or excluded groups?
3. What are the appropriate units of analysis?
4. Is the analyst's familiarity with the statistics to be used adequate? Are the program mathematical and logical requirements met? Are the assumptions of the technique met?
5. Will it be necessary to compute residuals for later analysis?
6. Have variables been included in the file to provide controls to rule out alternative explanations, correlates that would shed light on possible spuriousness? Are all potential explanatory factors in their proper form, including test factors and suppressor variables?
7. Have adequate plans been made to investigate the types of cross-product terms needed to cope with additivity assumptions?

The statistical data processing will reflect the principal rhetoric of the study logic: that is, inductive—seeking to develop explanatory models by inferring them from the analysis of the data—or deductive—seeking to test and refine models that have been set forth in considerable precision by previous research efforts. If the former is a primary objective, then the statistical analysis will be likely to focus on the measurement process itself rather than on dealing meticulously with theoretical problems. A consideration of several specific objectives of the analysis of survey data and the data processing implied by the choice of these objectives will bring these issues into focus.

Assessment of Reliability and Validity

When a major objective of the study is the development of measuring techniques, the questions of reliability and validity become central to at least one phase of the statistical analysis of the data. Indeed, even when larger objectives are sought after, the assessment of the adequacy of the measures used in the study generally is an intermediate objective that must be accomplished with success if the results of the study are not to be called into serious question by critics.[17]

Reliability The main question at issue when the reliability of a scale or index is being considered is the extent to which the data-generation process is repeatable. The same investigator using different measures of the same underlying construct or dimension, or different analysts using the same measure, should generate results that agree if the knowledge based on them is to be termed scientific. Of course, replicability is not an all-or-nothing characteristic of the measurement process. The extent to which findings can be replicated is a matter of degree, not of kind.

There are two types of factors that contribute to the unreliability of measurements: systematic biases which may or may not be correlated with different facets of the phenomenon under investigation, and measurement errors which appear to be random. We shall not be concerned here with bias or with the details of why a consideration of reliability is relevant to the statistical analysis of survey data. Rather, we shall assume that random-appearing factors that contribute to nonreplicability are of importance in any study and shall point out their implications for data processing. A discussion of bias will be taken up later.

Of course, even being able to repeat measurement exactly does not guarantee the validity of the measurements. This is a nonstatistical question of the extent to which a scale measures the type of behavior which experts agree it is supposed to measure. A respondent's reports of absence from work because of illness may be highly reliable, but they would not necessarily constitute a valid measure of alienation from the economic system. A measure cannot be valid without being reliable; if the respondent's description of absences varies capriciously and randomly, it cannot be used to measure anything with any degree of validity, let alone alienation. Clearly, reliability is a necessary condition for validity, but it is not sufficient.[18]

[17] For a useful discussion of sources of error, see Deming (1970). Heise (1974) discusses the implications of error for later analyses.

[18] For an extended discussion, see Thorndike (1951), Nunnally (1967), and Heise and Bohrnstedt (1970).

Scales and indices are composed of a number of items. If one is willing to make some simple assumptions about these items, evidence of the reliability of a Likert-type scale can be obtained from an examination of the intercorrelation matrix of its components. Although items are never actually sampled randomly from a universe of possible items, it is useful to conceptualize them as constituting a sample or series of samples from the domain of items tapping the attribute being measured. After all, one cannot use all of the items in the domain to place an individual on a scale representing an attribute, so some are selected and used to estimate where the individual would have been placed had all the items been used.

The distribution of sample scale or item scores around such a hypothetical true score reflects differences in the extent to which the items used actually tap the dimension, differences in respondents' interpretations of words in the items, and the whole host of factors present in the interview situation which affect the probability that one answer rather than another will be given in response to a given question. Because there are many such factors pushing in opposite directions, the actual item scores can reasonably be thought of as differing from a hypothetical "true" answer (their mean) on a random basis, and so can be expected to be normally distributed. It is reasonable to assume that different samples of items should produce different results, but that averages of statistics based on these samples of items should provide unbiased estimates of what investigators would obtain if they used up all the items in the domain. In the latter case, all scale results would be identical for any one respondent. Thus, reliability can usefully be thought of as the correlation of a given scale with this "true" score.

These assumptions lead to a series of simple statistical manipulations that can be used to estimate the reliability of a scale based on a series of items. The fundamental assumption is that it is reasonable to use all the items actually administered to estimate the scale position of the respondent that would have been obtained if all possible item configurations in the domain had been employed. To the extent that individual items or a scale based on a subset of the items correlate highly with a scale based on the entire set of items, the individual items, or the scale based on them, can be deemed reliable.

If all the possible items had been used, the average intercorrelation between them would constitute an estimate of the extent to which they have some kind of common referent. The variation of the interitem correlations around this average would indicate the extent to which the items varied in tapping this common attribute. The correlation of any given set of items with a scale based on all possible items can be estimated under these assumptions. It employs the average intercorrelation of all the scale items as an estimate of reliability. Thus, a measure of the reliability of a scale with k items is given by

$$r_k = \frac{kR_{ij}}{1 + (k - 1)R_{ij}}, \tag{8-2}$$

where k is the number of items in the scale and R_{ij} is the average intercorrelation of the items comprising the scale. Also, it turns out that r_k is the expected value of the correlation of any scale with k items with any other k-item scale composed of items from the same domain. Thus, r_k is termed the *reliability coefficient* for a k-item scale determined from the intercorrelation matrix of items comprising the scale.

A simple and often-reported measure of reliability is the split-half measure given by

$$r_s = \frac{2r_{12}}{1 + r_{12}}, \tag{8-3}$$

where r_{12} is the correlation between the scale scores computed from two subscales to which items have been assigned ramdomly and r_s is the reliability of the whole scale using all the items. Both of these formulas are equivalent to the reliability coefficient, sometimes termed *coefficient alpha,* and to the version of coefficient alpha sometimes referred to as the *Kuder–Richardson formula 20* (KR-20). Computations for the latter are simpler than our formulas (8-2) and (8-3), but the ready availability of computing equipment makes the construction of the basic correlation matrix an easy task. Even if the available program does not do the final computation of formula (8-2), this is easily accomplished using desk calculating equipment.[19]

The basic assumption underlying the use of this measure of reliability is that the average correlation of each item with the others is the same for all items. To the extent that this assumption is violated, r_k or r_s give only rough approximations of the actual reliability. However, the indications are that when the number of persons to whom the scale items are administered is about 300 (well under the sample sizes of most surveys), reliability estimates are quite precise, even when the scale in question has as few as 10 items.[20] This discussion of reliability leads to a useful observation.

There is a limit on the correlation between any two scales. If one scale has a reliability of 1.0, then a second scale can only correlate with it as high as the square root of its own reliability coefficient. The expected value of the correlation between two perfectly reliable scales is given by

$$R_{12} = \frac{r_{12}}{r_{11}r_{22}}, \tag{8-4}$$

where R_{12} is the expected correlation if both variables were perfectly reliable, r_{11} is the reliability of scale 1, r_{22} is the reliability of scale 2, and r_{12} is the correlation between scales 1 and 2. Thus, if estimates of reliability are made, research conclusions can be made that take into account the probable level of measurement error. The basic data are simply obtained from a correlation matrix of the items from both scales and the scales themselves.

19 Krippendorf (1970) proposes alternative procedures.

20 The reader is referred to Nunnally (1967, Chap. 6) for a more detailed discussion.

What standards of reliability are acceptable? There appears to be no generally accepted criterion. It has been argued that for most purposes in basic research, reliabilities of the order of .5 or .6 are adequate and that efforts to increase reliability beyond .8 might be better spent elsewhere.[21] The position taken here is to the contrary—that serious efforts should be made to develop measures that have reliability levels of at least .7 or .8. Among the factors to be considered in deciding the level of effort to be expended in increasing reliability is the number of items in the scale. Increasing the number adds to the difficulty of administration, which may take its toll in a poorer response rate or in poorer answers to questions located near the end of the interview when respondent motivation is lagging. Another consideration is the nature of the decision to be made on the basis of the measurements. If the data are to be used to allocate welfare funds, to admit students to medical school, or are to be brought to bear on other kinds of important decisions, then even small amounts of unreliability cannot be tolerated.

From a practical point of view in data processing, the methods of achieving reliability are straightforward. But they depend on having thought about the problem at the time the research instrument was initially designed. It will be remembered that this type of measurement in survey research is ordinarily aimed at assessing the position of a respondent on a particular attribute. Items to be used in constructing a scale to be used in placing individuals on this attribute are useful only if they tap the attribute. Thus, they should be homogeneous in content and should have high and similar correlations with each other and with the total scale score. Obviously, it is necessary for interviewing instructions and coding techniques to be carefully standardized, and care should have been taken during interviewing to minimize interviewer and situational effects. Choosing items with more than two possible answers will generally make for higher inter-item correlations; hence, the five- or seven-point response pattern is preferred over the dichotomous agree–disagree configuration.

A recommended procedure for subjecting items to statistical analysis with a view to establishing a scale with the required reliability level is as follows:

1. Select the pool of items from the questionnaire or interview schedule that is to be used in constructing the scale.
2. Compute scale scores for all respondents using all items.
3. Use a multiple regression program of the step-regression variety to construct a prediction equation of the scale score from the items. Force single items to enter the equation until all have entered. The first item in the equation will be the one correlating most highly with the total scale score. It will be followed by others in order of decreasing explanatory power.

[21] See Nunnally (1967, Chap. 6) for a thorough review of both reliability and validity.

4. Compute the reliability r_k of the scale with the desired number of items. If this is considerably above or below the desired reliability level, add or delete items in the order in which they were entered into the step regression, recomputing r_k each time. Repeat until either an acceptable balance of reliability and number of items has been achieved or until the addition of items results in a vanishingly small increase in reliability.

Because this method capitalizes to some extent on chance, it is desirable to add items until the reliability is slightly higher than is initially specified. Alternatively, one may simply start with two or three items, adding items until further additions fail to achieve much increase in the reliability.

This procedure should work adequately unless intercorrelations among items are all low, or unless the items are markedly different in content. In the latter case, a factor analysis may be called for to investigate the dimensionality of the item pool. The reliability of the resulting scale must be kept in mind when it is used later in a multivariate model. Poor measurement of a factor always results in an underestimation of its explanatory power and may result in an incorrect estimate of the profile of its effects.[22]

Another approach to assessing validity and reliability problems is the multitrait–multimethod matrix technique (Campbell and Fiske, 1959; Althauser and Heberlein, 1970; Summers, Seiler, and Wiley, 1970; Alwin, 1974). The basic data are intercorrelations among variables presumed to measure the same underlying traits, but which have been obtained using different types of methodologies. A rectangular data matrix is assumed.

More extended discussions of reliability can be found in Cronbach (1951), Guilford (1954), Guilford (1965), Gulliksen (1950), and especially in Nunnally (1967). Recently, path-analytic approaches to the assessment of measurement error have been developed (e.g., Blalock, 1969, 1970; Siegel and Hodge, 1968; Blalock, Wells, and Carter, 1970). The major point is that reliability is all too often ignored by survey researchers (Blalock, 1965). But this need not be; using available computing equipment and standard programs it is relatively easy to assess.

Although an explicit rationale for the use of ordinal measures of association in the reliability formulas still appears to be missing, it seems preferable to "promote" the data and use product-moment statistics rather than to ignore the problem.[23] If the development of measures is an important aspect of the research, or if the data are to be used for prediction or other purposes with important social consequences, then the omission of reliability calculations or failure to at least publish the interitem correlation matrix is inexcusable.

[22] For a further discussion, see Cleary, Linn, and Walster (1970).

[23] Alternatively, Multiple Classification Analysis (Andrews et al., 1973) or dummy-variable regression (Lansing and Morgan, 1971, pp. 273–276, 315–329) may be used if the items are not dichotomous.

Validity Two main areas of concern are sometimes lumped together under the general rubric of "validity." One is sometimes termed *external validity* and is concerned with questions of to which population the results may be generalizable. This is really a sampling problem; or, in a smaller form, it may be one of specification—For what groups in the sample does a model "work" well? In either case, the question is one related to inferences about the population from which the sample was drawn.

The second block of questions addressed when the analyst confronts validity problems are deceptively simple. "Does my scale (index, variable) measure the concept I want it to measure?" "Does it predict what it is supposed to predict?" "Does it correlate with other measures of the 'same' construct?" "Does it correlate with other constructs the way it should if it measures what it is supposed to measure?" This section discusses some of the questions that take statistical forms when these issues of *internal validity* are confronted. Their implications for data processing will be pointed out.

It is important once again to note that fuzzy, unclear concepts cannot have associated with them measuring instruments that have much validity. To the extent that the concept is itself multidimensional, this is necessarily reflected in the measurement. Social science ultimately must be based on concepts that are clear and precise, and on measuring devices which, as far as practicable, measure the respondent's position on that dimension and not also on something else. It is precisely the desire to clarify and refine concepts that leads to statistical analyses revolving around the validity of the measures used in a survey.

Perhaps the most fundamental fact of validity questions is that they do not really have statistical answers. The term *face validity* simply refers to agreement among professionals that a measure taps what it is supposed to tap. This is really a problem of the extent to which the items sampled to form a scale are representative of an agreed-upon content universe of behavior. The resolution of this question requires the achievement of consensus among one's colleagues about the items. The latter have to be judged in terms of their presumed relevance to the task of placing survey respondents along an underlying dimension. This consensus building usually operates through negotiation of the boundaries of the domain of the observable variables thought to be related to the underlying construct. The principal method of resolving such questions is controversy at professional meetings and in the literature, which centers around the items alleged to lie just outside the agreed-upon domain. These often acrimonious arguments frequently proceed without recognition of the fact that validation of a scale does not take place once and for all, but in the context of using it for a particular purpose which is itself only a small part of the validation. The analysis of item intercorrelations helps to resolve such conceptual disagreement.

When it is evident from the literature that certain concepts need explication and improvements in clarity and precision, redefinition at a higher level of abstraction, and revision so as to achieve greater theoretical relevance, then a specific objective in the analysis of survey data may be to generate information that will bear on these problems. Indeed, research exploring the validity of measures purporting to tap a dimension of important theoretical status may be a required phase in the study of a particular problem area before adequate descriptive, model-building and testing, or program-evaluation research can even take place. Explication of a concept leads to a more unitary and clearly defined construct, as well as to information about the relationships between the items that tap it and proxy variables representing other constructs. Again, the principal analysis mode is correlational.

In a few cases, *predictive validity* may be the primary concern. This question is often put in terms of the practical problems of assessing the correlation between a scale and some criterion, such as "success" in college or performance in an occupation. This emphasis is misplaced. The practical task is really to compare the average performance of respondents selected through use of the scale in question with that of those selected through other methods. Even if the correlation between the selection score and performance is low, the improvement in average performance may justify use of the measuring instrument in practice.

The validity problem in statistical analysis centers around the fact that even clear and precise constructs, or concepts, that are sufficiently abstract to be broad in scope and thereby of theoretical interest, generally cannot be measured directly. Constructs are the stuff of hypotheses, models, and theories; but they have to be represented by observable, concrete, proxy variables, often combined into scales. Each construct may be thought of as having a domain of variables related to it.[24] The investigator must make the assumption that the variables or items used in the scale belong in the construct's domain (i.e., that they are valid indicators of the construct). The purpose of statistical analysis is to obtain evidence that bears on this assumption.

The problem of *content validity* or *face validity* is best tackled at the beginning of the study rather than at the statistical-analysis phase. The real task is to have thought through the concept well enough to have developed a series of items that are representative of the domain of the concept in question and to do a careful job of incorporating them into a clear, understandable set of questions which mean the same thing to each respondent. They must also be minimally subject to the difficulties that sometimes beset the interviewing process. Only then is it possible for statistical evidence bearing on validity problems to be maximally useful.

The evidence is of two sorts. The items should correlate "properly" with each other and with other measures of the "same" construct; and the scale built from them should correlate properly with proxies for other constructs. For example, items purporting to measure "intelligence" should correlate positively with

[24] Subsets of this domain may be of particular relevance to a specific investigator with a unique set of values and research problem, so the validity question is not one that is ever solved permanently, even for that investigator.

each other. The scale built from them should correlate positively with other scales purporting to measure intelligence, and it should correlate positively with variables that intelligence correlates positively with. It should also correlate negatively with variables that commonly correlate negatively with measures of intelligence. The analyst demands internal consistency and unidimensionality of the scale, agreement with other measures that purport to measure the same construct, and a scale that "behaves" the way it is supposed to in its intercorrelations with other variables.

In this process, the analyst uses theory to hypothesize what other constructs (and thereby proxies for them) should be related to the scale in question. These must be relationships that have already been well substantiated because they must be used as assumptions. The same logic is used to hypothesize which variables should not be correlated with the items and the scale. The relevant correlations are computed (provided that someone has thought to collect data on them) and their size and sign are examined and checked to see if their profiles or slopes are as conjectured. The test is not whether the correlations are significantly different from zero, but whether they are significantly different from values expected on the basis of those already found elsewhere. Ideally, they should be checked to see if they hold up in important subgroups in the data, and should be checked to see if they hold up when social desirability or other factors that might lead to spurious relationships are partialed out. In general, it is most useful to correlate the proposed new scale with others for which reliability and validity investigations have already been carried out.[25]

When items and the scale built from them are correlated with other measures that purport to tap the same or a similar construct, the procedure is sometimes termed *criterion validation*. Nunnally (1967) questions the usefulness of such procedures on several grounds. Why develop a new measure at all if the old one was valid? How was the old one validated? If the old measure was not valid, why test out a new one by correlating it with the old one?

Although these questions have some merit, it seems useful to treat criterion validation as a special case of *construct validation*. This is the primary validation strategy that can be called into play during the statistical analysis of the data. Put most simply, evidence is adduced to assess the extent to which the scale behaves the way it is supposed to in its patterns of intercorrelations with a variety of other variables. Some of these may be measures of the same construct; others may tap different concepts. The validity evidence is as good as the total pattern of intercorrelations, the quality of the evidence for the reliability and validity of the measures studied as correlates, and the evidence supporting the theory upon which the assumed correlational patterns are based.

The latter is of no small importance. As already noted, test variables must

[25] For example, see Robinson, Rusk, and Head (1968), Robinson, Athanasiou, and Head (1969), and Robinson and Shaver (1969) for a compilation of measures pertaining to a wide variety of concepts.

be chosen so that hypotheses about their intercorrelations with the items and the scale in question already have enough evidence so that they may safely be taken as assumptions. The logic is:

1. Construct X is correlated with construct Y at level Z with sign W (assumption from theory A).
2. Variable U has already been found to be a valid scale based on members of the domain of variables tapping Y (assumption from theory A or other theory).
3. Variable V is a valid scale based on members of the domain of variables tapping construct X (hypothesis about the scale being investigated).
4. Then variable V should correlate with variable U at level Z_1 with sign W_1 (conclusion that would be drawn given the assumptions, if the hypothesis is correct).
5. If V and U correlate as expected, we have evidence to support the validity claim (not proof!).
6. If V and U do not correlate as expected, either V is outside the domain of X and thus cannot be a valid indicator of a respondent's position on X, or we must modify concept X so that it is reasonable to include V in its domain.
7. If we choose the latter, then we must make other assumptions about the intercorrelations between X and Z. If we choose the former, then we omit V from consideration as an indicator of X, or modify it and repeat the correlational process.

It is not likely that the total pattern of correlations will be observed exactly as predicted, so the analyst is faced inevitably with the question of whether to treat the results as being sufficiently discrepant from the assumed patterns as to warrant modifying the item content of the scale, or whether to change the verbal definition of the concept. (See Davis, 1971, Rosenberg, 1968, and Nunnally, 1967, for further discussions of these decision criteria.) In all these cases, the practical data-processing problems are similar.

The computing problems arising from the confrontation of validity problems are primarily those related to generating correlation matrices. The analyst will generally be dealing with two-variable correlations, sometimes computed over subsets of the data in order to replicate other investigators' samples. Figure 8-10 illustrates the type of data matrix needed for a typical validity analysis. The variables required include all the items (1, 2, . . . , K) from the scale, the scale score itself (K + 1), those variables that are to be used for construct-validation purposes (K + 2, . . . , L), and other criterion scales which measure the "same" construct, (L + 1, . . . , M). In addition, other variables will generally be needed,

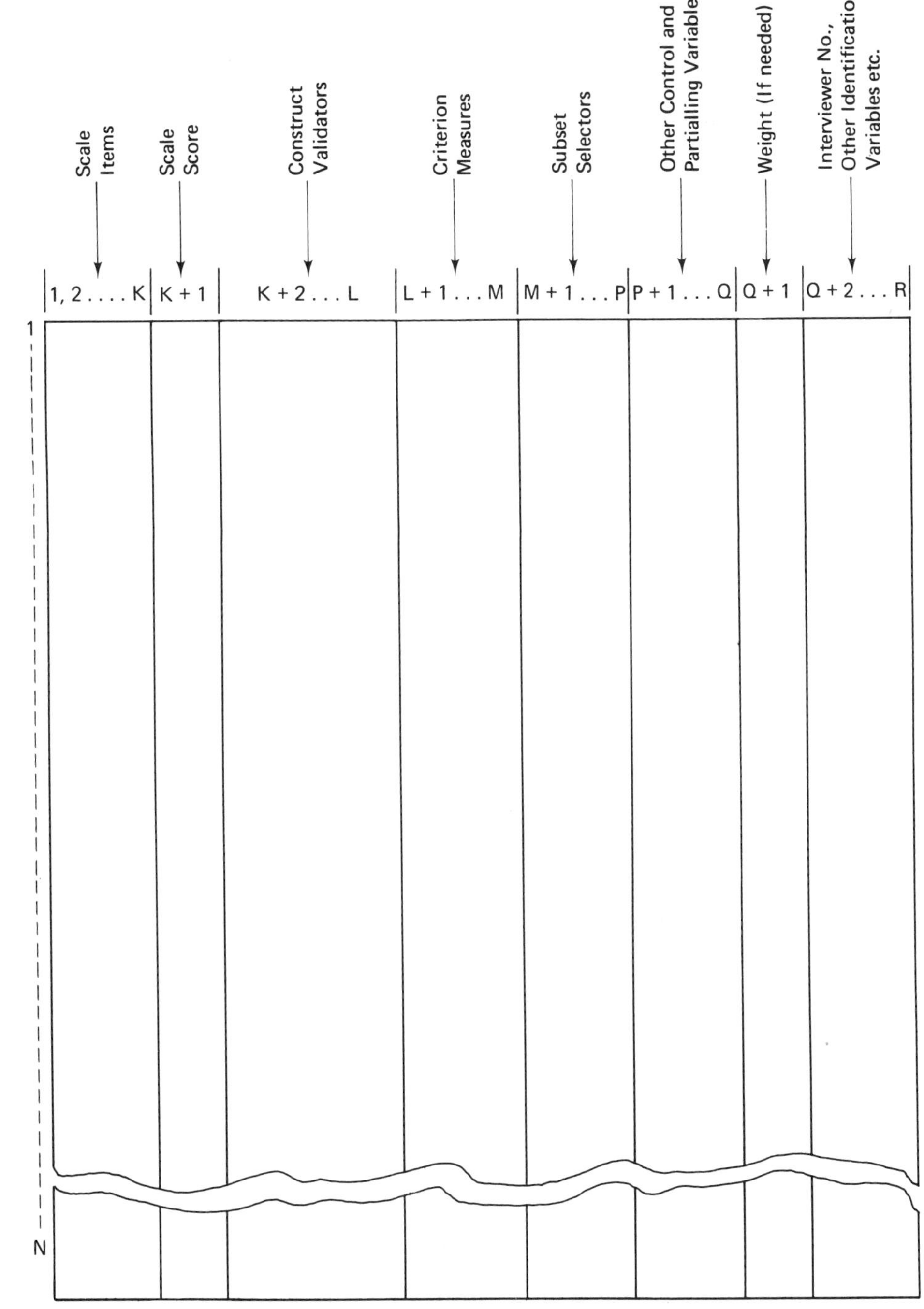

Figure 8-10 Data Matrix for Validity Analysis

including subset selectors ($M + 1, \ldots, P$); other variables for controlling and partialing out other effects ($P + 1, \ldots, Q$); a weight ($Q + 1$), if needed for sampling requirements; identification variables, such as the sample book number and interview number; and measures of the coding accuracy of each data item, if available ($Q + 2, \ldots, R$).

These variables function as input into a *strip-correlation* procedure; that is, a subset of rows of a correlation matrix is computed. (See Figure 8-11.) The intercorrelations between the items, the correlation of the items with the scale score, and correlations of all of these with criterion- and construct-validation measures make up the *strip*. The remainder of the larger matrix is not usually computed, unless supplementary analysis goals or computer program limitations are present.[26]

When product-moment statistics are used and there is no missing information, this computation is not likely to be a costly proposition. However, if rank-correlation statistics, such as Kendall's tau, are to be used, or if missing data require the omission of selected pairs of observations, then costs may be

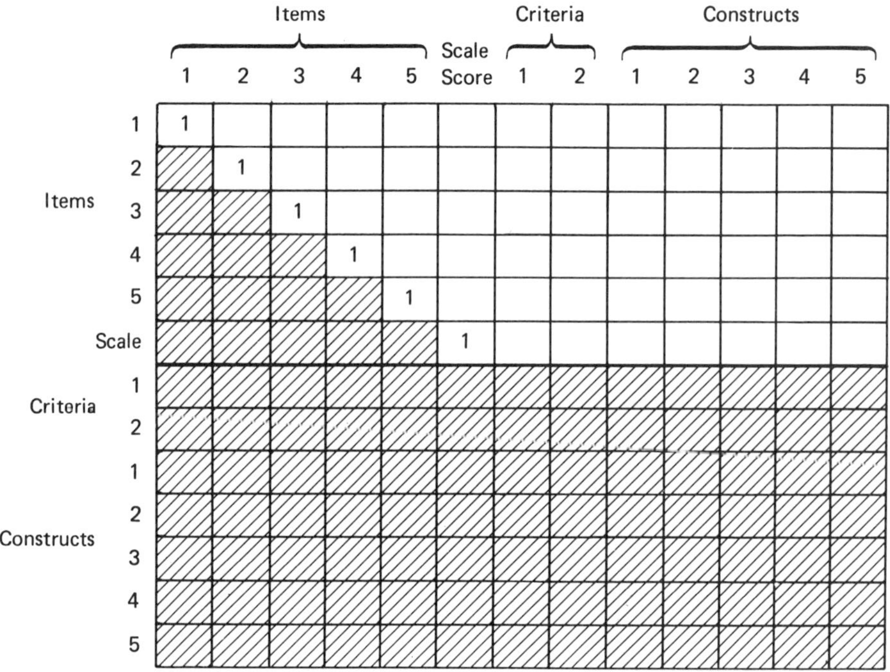

Figure 8-11 "Strip" Correlation Matrix for Validity Analysis

[26] Computation of the desired correlation strip may require the generation of unwanted sections of the total matrix simply because the available programs compute only the latter.

high. Often the value of a measure of relationship for ordinal variables can only be obtained at the cost of also obtaining a printout of the cross-tabulation of the two variables. The large number of such tables needed uses computer memory space, results in a large number of printed lines, and is generally expensive. Missing-data correlation matrix runs require approximately seven times the computation and storage as do runs with data in which all missing information has been assigned. In any case, test runs and very careful checking of input control cards are in order.

Exploratory Analyses

In Chapter 7 a rationale was presented for measurement and index construction operations that can be termed *monothetic* (Bailey, 1972) and which is based on theory rather than on the characteristics of the data in question. The investigator chooses the variables to use, forms types by partitioning the range of each variable into sets, forms unions of these sets, identifies each with a code, and then assigns observations to the resulting unions.

This type of index is multidimensional (i.e., the proxy variables or indicators are not assumed to represent the same underlying construct). Family life cycle was our example. The procedures for assigning observations to life-cycle categories represent the establishment of a code for a multidimensional typology, the configurations of which have been established by theory, experience, or previous research. The computer program example illustrating family-life-cycle computations implemented a rule for assigning observations to type categories. The set of types was mutually exclusive and exhaustive. This particular typology was not established by an ivory-tower process of speculation about "ideal types," but actually evolved from experimentation over the years in combining age, marital status, number of children, and so on, in various ways, and discovering that the resulting configurations made sense both theoretically and practically.

An essential property of such a monothetic typology is that there exists a necessary and sufficient set of characteristics that a family must possess before it can be classified as that particular type. The configuration of attributes comprising a given type is unique. Each attribute is necessary, and the set is sufficient to classify the family as a particular type. It is not important what the level of measurement of the relevant variables is—the important thing is that boundary lines are drawn at fixed points. If variables are continuous, then minor differences on either side of these points are ignored.

In contrast to family life cycle, a scale computed as the sum or the average of a series of items, based on a factor analysis and weighted accordingly, displays other properties. The data-processing operations were based on the assumptions that the proxy variables or scale items had been determined to have at least face validity in representing a single underlying dimension. Thurstone, Guttman, or Likert assumptions are required. If the heads of families are characterized by a scale of alienation based on factor scores, two families may have the same factor score even though one of them possesses a high score on a particular item and the other does not. A high score on one item may compensate for a low score on another. Families are grouped together in the resulting scale because of their overall similarity, not because of the presence or absence of a particular configuration of attributes. No single attribute is either necessary or sufficient for a particular factor score.

Typologies such as this, in which grouping is based on a measure of overall similarity rather than on a particular configuration, are termed *polythetic* (Bailey, 1972). The distinction between monothetic and polythetic typologies is trivial in the univariate case. The usual problem in survey research is to develop meaningful typologies based on a relatively large number of variables.

Dealing systematically with typology construction involving more than two variables was virtually impossible until the advent of computing equipment. The only alternative was arbitrary combining of cells (Bailey, 1972, pp. 92–95) in a cross-tabulation of the relevant variables.[27] The advent of computing made possible the development of cluster-analysis and factor-analysis techniques. These enable the analyst to reduce the complexity of multivariate typologies by reducing the number of dimensions that must be dealt with.[28]

Bailey (1972) terms all these techniques *functional reduction methods*. They either create clusters of objects (*Q*-analysis) or of variables (*R*-analysis). In either case, clusters are formed which exhibit high degrees of overall similarity. The members of the cluster are more alike than their resemblance to members of other clusters. Because factor analysis splits up the variance of each variable, the latter can be assigned to several clusters rather than one, whereas typical clustering methods assign an object or a variable to exactly one cluster.

The research output of a cluster or factor analysis is thus a conceptual scheme for categorizing objects or variables. Both techniques function by defining sets, the members of which have been found to be similar according to an overall measure; at least, more similar to each other than to those in other clusters. An important distinction between factor analysis and clustering is that the latter can be used with data that are ordinal, or even nominal, and thus cannot meet the tighter interval assumptions.

Once the clusters have been established, the analyst seeking to develop typologies and refine concepts asks: "What do these elements have in common that gives rise to the clustering?" When the clustered elements are variables, the answer is given in terms of the extent to which they measure the same underlying dimension. When the clustered items are objects, the answer is given in terms of a hypothesized underlying process that accounts for the clustering. For example, in some biological applications, the underlying theory has been that

[27] Bailey (1972) also makes a further distinction between arbitrary numerical and pragmatic reductions in types.

[28] Ad hoc methods of combining cells do not reduce the number of dimensions; rather, they reduce the number of types defined by the configuration of dimensions.

objects from closely related species should cluster together and that more distantly related species should appear in separate clusters. The clustering structure is sometimes thought of as hierarchical, corresponding to concepts of genus, species, or whatever. The clustering methods used should reflect both the underlying theory and the levels of measurement used. When the measure of relationship is between objects and defines social relationships such as attraction, liking, or the amount of communication rather than similarity or dissimilarity, clustering objects yields an analysis of group structure and places individuals in positions vis-á-vis that structure (Gleason, 1969).

One of the objectives of science is to have unitary constructs, clearly and precisely defined, which permit measurement of a respondent's position on just one attribute. If one is seeking to interpret a correlation and each of the two measures taps a multitude of dimensions, how can a meaningful view of the substantive significance of that relationship be chosen? Factor analysis provides one procedure for assessing the extent to which a measure is unitary. If a variable loads only on one or two factors (i.e., is factorially "pure"), its meaning is clear. If it is factorially complex (i.e., loads on a number of factors), there will be difficulty in developing a meaningful interpretation of its relationship to other measures.

Factor analysis also provides a set of criteria for weighting items that are to be combined into an index, as well as a means for ascertaining the extent to which the underlying dimension tapped by the index is well defined. Some factors may be general, having high loadings associated with all or many variables. Others may be specific, loading high only on some variables. Generally, the survey analyst's objective is to achieve a compelling structure in which the factors are relatively pure. Indices constructed using them will then have well-defined meanings. More will be said about this topic below when simple structure is discussed. For the present, it is sufficient to point out that the analyst, having obtained information about the conceptual structure of items, is in a position to reformulate question wordings so as to improve their reliability and validity with respect to the underlying concepts that it is desired to tap. Simultaneously, information is obtained on how best to combine items into scales that tap the underlying dimensions revealed by the factor analysis.[29]

As used in much survey work, the typical role of factor analysis is as a tool to assist in determining the extent to which it is reasonable to interpret the intercorrelations among many items as resulting from their tapping of a few common underlying factors. This assumes a measurement problem, not one of causality or explanation. It typefies the question that is asked of the data when an objective of the study is the development of scales and the appropriate weights for the items comprising them. Thus, a factor analysis of survey measures would ordinarily be aimed at conceptual clarification and the development of improved

[29] An extended discussion of concepts underlying factor analysis is not presented. The reader is referred to Kerlinger (1973), Schuessler (1971), Nie, Bent, and Hull (1973), Rozebloom (1966), Rummel (1967), Cattell (1965), and Harman (1967).

measuring instruments, not at model building, hypothesis testing, or project evaluation.[30] Usually, the development of carefully constructed and factorially pure measures should precede the latter tasks.

The usual assumption of factor analysis is that a set of latent dimensions accounts for the observed pattern of correlations between variables, not because somehow the items are conceptually distinct from and causally related to them, but because they all measure these dimensions. Each is, to some extent, a proxy for one or more of the underlying dimensions of interest. The analyst's strategy is to use factor-analytic techniques to summarize the data so as to reveal the dimensionality of the system of proxy measures, finding out how many dimensions are required to tap the domain of the items adequately. Then, by examining what the items have in common that load on each factor, the analyst obtains information of use in refining the content of the concept corresponding to that underlying dimension. This process increases the specificity and precision of the procedures for measuring the positions of respondents on each attribute. The analysis reveals how several variables of a domain can be combined to produce maximum discrimination among individuals along each underlying dimension. On a broader plane, the procedure is commonly used in attempts to generate constructs that reflect the similarities and differences between blocks of items. Names applied to factors are constructs that will ultimately be applied (perhaps even ex post facto in the same study) in the development of explanatory models.

Ideally, correlations used as input to factor analysis should be based on continuous variables with distributions approaching normality. In practice they will not always meet these requirements and may even be based on variables that are ordinal or nominal in measurment level. Yet practical experience indicates that the technique is robust when used as a heuristic device for improving measuring instruments. While geometric interpretations usually associated with the technique are not possible if interval measurement levels are not achieved, it is possible to factor a matrix of correlations between attributes and make useful inferences about the underlying dimensions that the nominal or ordinal measures presumably express (MacRae, 1970).

Input to many programs can be raw data. Others require standardized (z-score) measures or a correlation matrix. Some programs permit input of a factor matrix and communalities for experiments with rotation. Where some of the data are missing, preliminary steps should generally be taken to assign these values unless provisions exist in the programs to be used for computation of correlations on a pairwise basis or for deletion of the cases with some data absent. Generally, factor-analysis programs require rectangular data files with single-valued variables.

[30] It can also be applied to test hypotheses. Factor theory may be formulated to predict the presence or absence of a particular factor structure. However, this usage is relatively uncommon in most survey research. For a further discussion, see Kerlinger (1973, p. 685).

The communality of a variable is the proportion of its variance attributable to the common factors, and thus is heavily dependent on which other variables have been included in the correlation matrix. It is obtained by summing the squared factor loadings across rows of the factor matrix.[31] For the principal-axis method in general use, communalities are required at the start of the factoring process; but, since they are computed from the common factors that have yet to be extracted, they must be estimated initially. The objective in estimating communalities is usually to choose values that will yield the smallest number of factors.

Since a communality is a proportion of the total variance of a given variable, it cannot be larger than unity, nor can it be smaller than the squared multiple correlation between the variable in question and the other variables in the correlation matrix. Although there is not complete agreement between authorities as to the best estimating procedure, several have been suggested (Schuessler, 1971, pp. 89–91). Sometimes unity is used for each diagonal element (communality) in the input correlation matrix, sometimes the squared multiple correlations are used, and sometimes the highest correlation in a given row is used. At other times, previous data on reliability and validity are used to determine what values should be used.

When communalities are estimated initially and then computed exactly by iteration, the assumptions underlying the associated mathematical model more closely correspond to the type of assumption usually made about variables measured in a survey than do those implied by the use of unities in the diagonal. In the latter case, the assumption is that all the variance in the correlation matrix can be accounted for by an underlying factor structure. On the other hand, when communality estimates less than unity are used, the implied assumption is that only some facets of the variables are involved in the patterning of factors, and that if common factor sources of variation are removed, the correlations between variables will approach zero. More explicitly, this approach assumes that part of the variation in any individual variable is simply not involved to any significant extent with any of the other variables currently in the correlation matrix. Replacing diagonal elements with communalities implies analysis only of the variation in the correlation matrix which is shared with other variables. The remaining portion of variation in each variable is ignored, being ascribed to sources other than the underlying common factor structure. Thus, there are three commonly used estimating procedures available: (1) it may be desired for theoretical reasons to factor using unities in the diagonals, (2) independent data on reliabilities may lead to theoretically determined communalities, or (3) estimation followed by iteration and refactoring may be the most appropriate. The first

[31] Summing the squared factor loadings down columns instead of across rows (so the summation takes place over variables instead of over factors) and dividing by n, the number of variables, gives the proportion of the aggregate variance in the entire matrix which can be ascribed to each factor.

method is used when a principal-components analysis is desired.[32] The third is the most usual case.

If communalities are to be estimated, it is desirable for the prospective program to have the capability of factoring the matrix using the initial communality estimates, computing new communalities from the factor matrix so obtained, and recomputing the factor matrix using these new communalities, iterating until the communalities stabilize. A good method of estimating the communalities initially is to use the squared multiple correlation coefficient of each variable with the others as the initial estimate. If iterations are not possible, this is regarded by some authorities as the best method of estimating.[33] However, when iteration capabilities are available, the initial selection does not appears to be critical. The highest correlation in each row may be used, or even zeros. Cost factors are present, however, since convergence of the communalities during iteration will be more rapid if initial estimates are not too far off. Moreover, the squared multiple correlation sometimes provided by principal-axis programs is generally more convenient to use; otherwise, an intervening inspection of the correlation matrix must be made. A common rule is to iterate on the communalities until no estimate changes by as much as .005 on successive iterations. The procedure for iterating to estimate communalities is not independent of the number of factors, so these two decisions should be made together.

As many factors may be extracted as there are variables in the correlation matrix—but to do this denies achievement of the fundamental objectives of parsimony and clarity of description. Moreover, even a random correlation matrix can always be described by fewer factors than there are variables. Hence, there is no point in extracting more than M factors, as indicated in formula (8-5):

$$M = \frac{(2n + 1) - \sqrt{8n + 1}}{2}. \tag{8-5}$$

Table 8-1 provides a guide to the maximum number of factors that can be extracted from a correlation matrix of N variables.[34] In practice, only as many factors as are statistically significant should be extracted, using a preselected criterion. One guide, proposed by Schuessler (1971), derives from the assumption that the standard deviation of the residuals after factoring should be equal to $1/\sqrt{\mathrm{N}}$, where N is the number of cases in the sample. If the kth-order residual variance is larger than this, additional factors may still be extracted. A second rule, due to Kaiser (1958) and widely used, is to keep all those factors that contribute at least $1/n$ to the explanation of the aggregate total variance.[35]

[32] In this case, an exceptionally thorough review of the principal-components literature should precede the analysis.

[33] See Guttman (1955) and Harman (1957, p. 86). Schuessler (1971) has an excellent discussion of the communality estimation issue.

[34] When factors are extracted initially for the purpose of iterating to stablized communality estimates, generally one factor is extracted for each variable in the correlation matrix. Other criteria are then used to cut down the number of factors in subsequent iterations.

[35] When all measures are in standard form, the total variance is exactly equal to n, the number of measures in the correlation matrix.

TABLE 8-1 Maximum Number of Factors That Can Be Extracted from N Variables (N up to 80)[a]

N	M	N	M
1	0	41	33
2	1	42	34
3	1	43	35
4	2	44	36
5	3	45	36
6	3	46	37
7	4	47	38
8	5	48	39
9	6	49	40
10	6	50	41
11	7	51	42
12	8	52	43
13	9	53	44
14	10	54	45
15	10	55	45
16	11	56	46
17	12	57	47
18	13	58	48
19	14	59	49
20	15	60	50
21	15	61	51
22	16	62	52
23	17	63	53
24	18	64	54
25	19	65	55
26	20	66	55
27	21	67	56
28	21	68	57
29	22	69	58
30	23	70	59
31	24	71	60
32	25	72	61
33	26	73	62
34	27	74	63
35	28	75	64
36	28	76	65
37	29	77	66
38	30	78	66
39	31	79	67
40	32	80	68

[a] M is the maximum number of factors extractable.

According to Cooley and Lohnes (1971, p. 104), this rule works well when the number of cases is small or intermediate but may be too conservative for larger sample sizes. These writers suggest that the best results will be obtained when the number of factors extracted is determined by trial and error. The criteria for judging whether enough factors have been extracted also include the extent to which residual correlations from a given number of factors are small and normally distributed with mean zero. Thus, a program that permits inspection of the residual correlation matrix at late stages in the factoring is desirable. The proportion of the variance in the correlation matrix explained by the jth factor is the sum of squares of the factor loadings in the jth column divided by the number of factors:

$$P_j = \frac{\sum_{k=1}^{p} s_{kj}^2}{p} = \frac{\lambda j}{p}, \tag{8-6}$$

where s_{kj} is the factor loading for the kth test on the jth factor, and p is the number of items.[36] The variation explained by the whole factor structure is this quantity summed over the entire factor matrix:

$$E = \sum_{j=1}^{n} \frac{\sum_{k=1}^{p} s_{kj}^2}{p}. \tag{8-7}$$

The communality computed from the factor structure is the sum of the squared factor loadings in the kth row:

$$h_k^2 = \sum_{j=1}^{n} s_{kj}^2. \tag{8-8}$$

When the factoring is complete, based on the final iteration and recomputed communalities, the task is one of rotation to simple structure.

Since the technical problem faced by the analyst who seeks conceptual clarification is to discover a configuration of reference axes that has a clear and compelling interpretation, extraction of a factor structure is only the first step in the analysis. Many possible factor structures can account for the configuration of intercorrelations equally well, but not all achieve a maximum reduction in the complexity of the interpretation of the underlying structure of dimensions. Thurstone's (1947) simple structure concept provides a set of criteria that meets these parsimony requirements. The factor structure is rotated so that each variable is affected only by some of the factors and each factor contributes to some of the variables (Thurstone, 1947, p. 156). These standards are scarcely ever met in practice, but are the criteria lying behind almost all rotational algorithms. Kaiser's (1958) varimax and other rotational algorithms are not substitutes for simple structure; rather, they optimize a specific criterion and produce simple structure as a by-product. These simple structure principles are as follows (Thurstone, 1947, p. 335; Harman, 1967, pp. 97–99):

[36] These formulas apply when the items have been standardized with mean zero and variance 1. This may not be the case when nominal or ordinal data are used and other than product-moment correlations are used in the matrix to be factored.

1. Each row (variable) of the factor matrix should have at least one entry close to zero.
2. For each column (factor) of the factor matrix, there should be at least as many variables with near-zero loadings as there are factors.
3. When factors (columns) are considered in pairs, there should be several variables with loadings on one factor which do not load on the other. All pairs should have this characteristic.
4. When there are four or more factors, most of the variables should have very small (close to zero) loadings on any given pair of factors.
5. For every pair of factors in the factor matrix, there should be only a few variables which have sizable nonzero loadings in both columns.

These criteria essentially define the requirements that each variable be loaded on as few factors as possible, and that each factor be well defined by a subset of the variables which do not also serve to define other factors. A mathematical summarization of the data which meet these requirements will be maximally helpful in conceptual clarification and parsimonious in its representation of the data. The analyst who uses rotation to simple structure as a heuristic device for gaining insight into what the study variables may mean and how they can be redefined to better achieve clarity and unidimensionality has a reasonable and defensible position.

There are a number of rotational methods. Orthogonal rotations maintain the 90-degree angles between the originally inserted reference factors. Thus, the latter remain uncorrelated. Some authorities insist that maintenance of orthogonality is unrealistic, since attributes in real life are usually correlated (Thurstone, 1947, pp. 139–140; Cattell, 1965, pp. 116–123). This school of thought also asserts that simple structure criteria are better achieved when oblique rotations are employed. Others insist that orthogonality is more parsimonious, that orthogonal variables are more useful, and that oblique rotations are extremely difficult to interpret. Experimentation with several methods seems a reasonable strategy.

The use of factor-analysis procedures can be broken down into several stages: preparation of the correlation matrix, extraction of the initial factors, rotation, and computation of factor scores. Associated with each stage are a set of decisions to be made, and given each decision, a set of problems to be solved. Each of the four stages is reviewed in the next sections.

This first decision is closely related to the more general goals of the research. The analyst must first decide whether the correlations to be used are between variables (*R*-analysis) or between people (*Q*-analysis). The former is the more usual case and ordinarily has as its objective the development of improved measures of a hypothesized underlying dimension. It seeks to develop pure concepts by means of the study of the common elements of variables which are grouped together because they have large loadings on a single factor. On the other hand, the factor-analytic study of intercorrelations between people ordinarily has as its objective the study of the structure of attitudes within individuals, a much less frequent objective in a survey.[37]

A second decision related to the computation of the initial correlations is the selection of the measure of association to be used. If the variables are ordinal or nominal, it may be desirable to consider one or another of the cluster analysis techniques rather than to factor-analyze a matrix of ordinal or nominal measures of association, such as Kendall's tau, or phi.[38] In any case, nondirectional measures should be used rather than those which assume one dependent and one independent variable. If the items to be factor-analyzed are Likert scales, one choice is to make the trace-line assumptions discussed in Chapter 7 and compute a product-moment correlation matrix.

Related questions arc the selection of relevant variables and analysis units. In selecting cases it must be kept in mind that surveys are generally conducted over highly heterogeneous populations and that this may result in some spurious common factor variance. Thus, there are some arguments for separating the survey file into several segments (providing there are enough cases) and factor-analyzing each segment. If the sample is divided into homogeneous subgroups, spurious correlations due to sex, social class, education, or age may be avoided. Tests for differences between factor structures (OSIRIS, 1973) can be employed to assess dissimilarities in the resulting factor structures, and, if they appear insufficient to warrant separate treatment, the entire sample may then be combined. If enough cases are available, random-half samples appropriately mapped onto the sample design provide a one-degree-of-freedom estimate of the stability of the factor structure.

An important consideration in the computation of the correlation matrix is the treatment of missing data. Three options, reviewed earlier, are possible. A case may be deleted if any of the variables to be intercorrelated have missing information; individual coefficients in the correlation matrix may be calculated using only those cases for which both values were present; or missing information may be assigned ahead of time. Assignment of missing information for each variable separately, using random procedures based only on thc distribution of known cases, is inexpensive and the recommended procedure.

It is often convenient to compute the correlation matrix as a separate step in the factor analysis. This permits inspection of pairwise correlation coefficients, a review of the N's for each, and the acquisition of a feel for the data before factoring criteria and a rotational scheme must be decided upon. The correlation

[37] Conventional *Q*-technique as set forth by Stephenson (1953) and modifications of factor-analytic technique termed the semantic differential (Osgood, Suci, and Tannenbaum, 1957) will not be discussed. The reader is referred to the excellent discussions in Kerlinger (1973).

[38] For example, see Kruskal (1964), Roskam and Lingoes (1970), and the OSIRIS III Manual (University of Michigan, 1973).

matrix should generally be saved in machine-readable form for later rereading into the factor-extraction routines if this input option is available.

Some factor-analysis programs may require that input variables already be in z-score form (mean zero and unit variance); hence, preliminary processing may be required. It may be desired to delete some of the variables before factoring. This may result from the use of items which, it is discovered, are so highly intercorrelated that one of them must be dropped from the analysis before factoring can proceed. Consequently, a program that has the ability to select rows and columns of a larger correlation matrix for factoring is desirable.

The second phase of the analysis is the actual extraction of a set of factors. The major decisions to be made are the selection of a factoring procedure and the method to be used in estimating communalities. The principal-components algorithm with communalities set to one and with no iterations to compute communalities is generally used only when the purpose of the analysis is to transform a given set of variables into a composite, orthogonal set. This is a relatively unusual objective in survey analysis. A more usual one would be to estimate communalities using the multiple correlation of each variable with all the others, and then, using a principal-components algorithm, to iterate until they stabilize.

Other factoring methods, termed *canonical factoring* (Rao, 1955), *alpha factoring* (Kaiser, 1963), and *minres* (Harman, 1967), are less well known than the approach described here.[39] In some cases (e.g., Nie, Bent, and Hull, 1970), the computer programs have options for computing factors, using a variety of optional methods. Analysts with minimal mathematical sophistication are urged to use principal-axis solutions as a computational procedure with squared multiple correlations as initial communality estimates, and iterations to recompute communalities.

Additional decisions to be made at this point include setting the number of factors to be extracted, deciding upon the maximum number of iterations to be performed in computing communalities, and establishing the convergence criteria for the iteration procedure. Unless there are severe problems with rows in the correlation matrix that approach linear dependence, or other numeric problems, 25 communality computation iterations should suffice for most analyses of matrices up to about 80×80 in size when a communality convergence criterion of about .001 is used.[40]

Ordinarily the control parameters for the maximum number of iterations would not take effect unless the communalities failed to stabilize. The "maximum number of factors to be extracted" parameter would not usually control the behavior of the program unless a built-in stopping criterion failed to halt the

[39] For a discussion of a variety of newer methods, see Harris (1964).

[40] The convergence criterion is used to stop the iterative procedure. When all communalities change less than .001 from one iteration to the next, the iteration stops.

factor-extraction process.[41] However, programs differ in the sequence in which stopping criteria are employed, and the analyst is advised not only to read program documentation carefully, but to experiment ahead of time using small sets of contrived data.

Several methods of halting the factoring process are used. One method, employed by Nie, Bent, and Hull (1970), allows the user to specify a minimum-eigenvalue criterion or a maximum-number-of-factors criterion. In the former, only those factors with eigenvalues greater than or equal to unity are retained, requiring that a component account for at least as much variance as the average variable. Schuessler (1971) also recommends this stopping rule. Some programs (e.g., OSIRIS, p. 609) also provide for a minimum percentage of variance to be explained before the factoring stops. The procedure recommended by Schuessler (1971) appears to have much to recommend it, keeping in mind that it is probably conservative when large samples (e.g., 500 cases and over) are used.

There are a number of troubles that beset the factoring process. One is due to matrices that are sometimes ill-conditioned. This usually arises because of several variables which have very high intercorrelations with one another and thus have very similar patterns of intercorrelations with other variables. It can be caused by correlated missing data when pairwise computation of correlation matrices is used. The result is that some rows of the correlation matrix can be expressed as approximate linear combinations of other rows (within some level of error). When this happens, the mathematical properties of the matrix that permit carrying out of the factoring process no longer hold. This is not an all-or-nothing condition; rather, ill-conditioning is a matter of degree. Its symptoms may appear as communalities greater than 1, or the determinant of the correlation matrix being close to zero, having a negative sign, or becoming infinite. The only alternative appears to be to inspect the correlation matrix carefully and then to drop one or more of the offending variables from the analysis or combine them into a single measure.

A second problem is related to the fact that numbers in a digital computer are only approximations. The use of double-precision arithmetic operations to avoid rounding errors was discussed earlier. The six-place accuracy characterizing many present-day computers usually presents no single-precision rounding problems unless the correlation matrix is very large (over 80×80) or is based on a weighted sample of 2000 or more. Then correlations, matrix inverses, and factor loadings may be accurate only to one decimal place, rounding errors having occurred during computation of sums of squares. Large matrices are also subject to rounding error during the factoring process. Unfortunately, the computer printout will not disclose the problem. When weights are three digits or more, or more than 80 variables are to be factor-analyzed, consultation with a competent numerical analyst may be advisable.

The third decision to be made is the choice of a rotational technique.

[41] For an additional discussion, see Nie, Bent, and Hull (1973).

Factor solutions are not unique. Rather, there are always an infinite number of equivalent solutions. One can be transformed into another without violating the mathematical properties of the technique or its underlying assumptions. While this may be mathematically unsatisfying, it is not necessarily unfortunate scientifically. Some solutions are more parsimonious than others, or lead to insights, or stimulate serendipitous speculation. The analyst attempts to choose a rotational algorithm that leads to a final configuration that meets the type of parsimony requirements typified by Thurstone's (1947) simple structure criteria, while conforming to the theoretical and practical constraints of the problem at hand.

The primary decision to be made is whether to use orthogonal or oblique rotations, and, in either case, what rotational algorithm is to be used. The goal of each is an approximation of simple structure. The oblique methods are more flexible and more likely to achieve a more compelling structure. However, they are more likely than orthogonal methods to capitalize on chance. Nevertheless, they have an intuitive appeal in that they do not require the sometimes substantively unrealistic assumption that the underlying dimensions be uncorrelated. The oblique solutions also provide information about the extent of the intercorrelation between the dimensions. Thurstone's (1947) simple structure criteria assure that many points will lie near the axes, some will be near the origin, and only a few will be distant from both axes (Harman, 1967, p.99).

The quartimax procedure seeks to reduce the complexity of the structure of variables by rotating so as to cause them to load highly on one factor and low on the others. Because the method attempts to simplify rows (variables), the first factor tends to have high loadings on many variables (i.e., it is often a general factor). Subsequent factors tend to have higher levels of purity. Orthogonality is maintained.

The varimax algorithm, perhaps the most frequently used, attempts to simplify columns (factors) rather than rows. In maximizing the variance of the entries of each column, it tends to produce conceptually pure factors rather than conceptually pure variables. It, too, maintains the orthogonal structure.

The covarimin procedure minimizes the sum of the covariance between columns. As such, it is an oblique analogue to the varimax and is not affected by the amount of correlation between factors.

The oblimin algorithm minimizes the cross-products of the factor loadings on the reference axes. The oblimax procedure maximizes the kurtosis of the distribution of correlations between variables and factors. An important consideration is whether or not to insist on orthogonality of the rotated matrix.[42]

All these methods of rotation should be viewed as heuristic aids for attaining simple structure. As such, committing oneself ahead of time to one or

[42] For good introductory discussions of this topic, see Schuessler (1971) and Kerlinger (1973). Ahmavaara (1954, 1963) and Shoneman and Carroll (1970) discuss methods of comparing factor structures in several groups.

another seems less likely than experimentation with several procedures to move the analysis toward discovery of a simple structure that seems compelling. One additional consideration is to be emphasized. The ability to communicate the results of a factor analysis to scientific and lay people is invariably an objective. Obscure rotational schemes are hard to communicate, and the mathematical sophistication, or lack thereof, in the prospective audience for the research should always be taken into account.

Once a satisfactory rotation has been achieved, it is often the objective to compute scores for each respondent on the factors isolated during the analysis, and then to store these back in the survey data file with the rest of the variables pertaining to the respondent.[43] Some factor-analysis programs provide capabilities for doing this; others simply print the regression weights for the scores. In the latter case, the computations must be done using available index construction programs, or by writing a special-purpose program. Still other programs require the analyst to compute the weights from the rotated factor matrix. The factor score computation process is beset with problems, ranging from discovering late in the analysis that the survey staff needs a programmer, to dealing with missing data on the input variables.

Factor score coefficients can be calculated through a regression estimating procedure defined by

$$S_{jk} = \sum_{k=1}^{n} f_{ji} z_{ik}, \tag{8-9}$$

where S_{jk} is the score on the jth factor for person k, f_{ji} is the factor coefficient for the jth factor for the ith variable, and z_{ik} is the standard score for the ith variable for the kth person. The coefficients are computed by

$$F = S'R^{-1}, \tag{8-10}$$

where F is the factor score coefficient matrix, S the rotated factor structure matrix, and R the matrix of intercorrelations between variables. Thus, the transpose of the factor structure matrix is postmultiplied by the inverse of the correlation matrix.[44]

It is of some importance for the computation process to note that the standard score is computed by subtracting the mean from each observation and dividing the results by the standard deviation. If a program for computing standard scores is not available, the computations can sometimes be performed with the variable-generation facilities available in one of the statistical packages, or programming may be necessary.

[43] For additional references, see Harman (1967, p. 352). The coefficients are usually rounded, since the level of precision of measurement in survey data scarcely warrants the pretense of much accuracy.

[44] See Kaiser (1962) for an additional discussion of computation of factor scores. Armor (1974) outlines a complete strategy for the assessment and improvement of scale reliability and improved conceptual clarity based on factor-analytic procedures.

If missing data exist, several extra steps may have to be performed:

1. If the correlation matrix was computed over a subset of the observations in the file, all those not in the subset must be assigned an inapplicable code for the factor score.
2. If the correlation procedure deleted observations from the computations, and if any of the associated variables had one or more missing values, factor scores are undefined for these cases and should be assigned missing-data codes.
3. If the correlation procedure used pairwise deletion, factor scores may be estimated for observations with some values missing by using the available ones. It is suggested that if a specified proportion of these values is missing, say, one third, that the factor score for that observation be assigned a missing-data code.

In most cases the file must also be recopied, the new variables added, and then codes and file documentation updated.

These considerations suggest that if it is not possible to assign missing-data values early in the study, a visual inspection of the correlation matrix should be made before factoring takes place, with a view to finding out what the distribution of observations is with one, two, three, . . . , missing values among the variables scheduled for inclusion in the factor analysis. If the problems are sufficiently severe, it may be best to drop the offending cases (if the missing information is highly concentrated in them) or to assign missing values, using randomizing procedures at this point in the analysis.

This section has reviewed the use of factor analysis in answering measurement questions. Reviewed were the form the input data must take, the problem of estimating communalities, how many factors to extract, and the concepts of simple structure and rotation.[45] Four phases of the analysis were discussed; preparation of the correlation matrix, extraction of the factors, rotation to simple structure, and computation of factor scores. Table 8-2 summarizes these topics in a checklist for the analyst about to undertake the use of a factor-analysis program.[46]

Cluster Analysis The analysis objectives of clustering procedures other than factor analysis are similar despite the differences in tradition. The objective is generally to clarify and make more precise the conceptual apparatus for dealing with a particular phenomenon by reducing the number of dimensions that must be coped with, and by relaxing the monothetic requirements for inclusion of

[45] For a further exposition, see Nie, Bent, and Hull (1970, p. 216).

[46] The reader is referred to Harman (1967, p. 334–341) and to Rummel (1970) for additional details.

TABLE 8-2 Checklist for Review of Factor-Analysis Program

1. Input requirements: raw data vs. correlation matrix; requirements for data to be normalized to mean 0 and variance 1 (z-scores); maximum size of correlation matrix; ability to accept missing data; deletion of observations with missing data vs. computation of pairwise correlation coefficients; provision for handling a subset of variables in the file; provisions for computations over a subset of observations; computation of z-scores; factor matrix input.
2. Factoring options: R- and Q-analysis; principal components; canonical factoring; alpha factoring; image factoring; minres; maximum likelihood; ability to factor a subset of the matrix; methods of controlling maximum and minimum number of factors.
3. Communality estimating procedures: squared multiple correlations; largest correlation in row; reliabilities supplied as input; iteration procedures and stopping criteria.
4. Error flags for troublesome correlation matrices: matrix inverse; determinant available as output.
5. Rotation options: orthogonal vs. oblique; varimax, quartimax, equimax, oblimax, covarimin, biquartimin; normalization options; controls over extent of obliqueness; defaults and recommended iteration and criterion values.
6. Output print options: means and standard deviations of variables; correlation matrix; correlation matrix inverse and determinant; communalities; eigenvalues and proportion of total and common variance; initial and final values of communalities; initial factor matrix; transformation matrices and rotated factor matrices; factor score coefficients; plots of rotated factors.
7. Output file options: means and standard deviations; z-scores; simple correlations and subset of correlations; factor matrix and communalities; factor score computations; insertion of factor scores into raw data input file.

an observation into a class. As in factor analysis, either variables or objects can be clustered, and the choice depends on the particular theoretical framework invoked by the investigator. The most common use is undoubtedly R-analysis, in which variables are clustered and the objective is conceptual clarification. A very large number of procedures and theoretical rationales have been developed and will merely be listed here. The reader is referred to the sources for theoretical rationales, mathematical procedures, and computer programs.

Bailey (1972) provides a particularly lucid overview of the basic ideas. Other overviews are provided by Gower (1967), Fliess and Zubin (1969), and Wallace (1968). Bijnen (1973) reviewed a great many clustering algorithms and evaluated them. Guttman's facet-theoretical approach receives an exposition in several publications (Guttman, 1954–1955, 1957, 1968) and is further elaborated by Lingoes (1968). Early approaches to the problem of reducing complexity in typologies are illustrated by Lazarsfeld and Barton (1951) and by Barton (1955). Sokol and Sneath (1963) apply clustering concepts to biological problems of numerical taxonomy. Beckner (1959) discusses the important differences between polythetic and monothetic typologies.

Computer programs for smallest-space analysis (SSA) have been developed by Lingoes (1965a, 1965b, 1966a, 1966b, 1968). Lingoes (1966a, 1970) provides improved computer programs and capabilities for both *R*- and *Q*-analyses. Roskam and Lingoes (1970) provide further improvements in large-scale computer programs. Another approach is provided in a program due to Guthrey, Spaeth, and Thomas (1968). Bloombaum (1968a, 1968b) provides several illustrations of smallest-space analysis. Other references include Kruskal (1964) and Shepard (1962), whose algorithms have been widely used (cf. OSIRIS III). A variation of Johnson's (1967) hierarchical algorithm has also been widely distributed (cf. OSIRIS III). A useful comparison of factor, cluster, and smallest-space analyses is provided by Gullahorn (1967).

The required data for clustering and scaling algorithms is generally either a raw rectangular data matrix of observations and variables, or a matrix consisting either of correlations between variables (*R*-analysis) or measures of similarity or dissimilarity (*Q*-analysis). If the input is a raw data matrix, variables which have missing values often must be assigned ahead of time, since many algorithms have not been programmed to deal with missing data.

Depending on the algorithm, input measures may be dichotomous or ordinal, with the maximum number of ranks and the maximum number of input variables depending on the constraints of various computers. In general, variables may not be multivalued. Weights generally are not permitted except when the program has been incorporated into one of the larger survey analysis systems. When a stand-alone program is used, the analyst is advised to make advance runs on it well in advance of the time the actual analysis is to take place to assure a mesh between program requirements and input data, and to check out documentation.

Descriptive Analyses

In many studies a specific objective is precise description of populations of individuals, families, organizations, automobiles, union members, or whatever the unit of analysis is. In order to make precise statements about the values of population or subgroup parameters, complex sampling methods are often used. Because of the high costs of data collection, interviews may last an hour or more and generate a large number of variables by which populations can be described. In some studies, an objective will be to obtain trends over time, or to compare one population with another. In others, description is the precursor to explanation and model building. Descriptive study content may not necessarily be limited to "hard" data, although in economic surveys with primarily descriptive objectives, this is sometimes the case. More often, studies may seek to explore and describe using a variety of hard data, such as demographic characteristics, and "softer" information, such as attitudes and opinions.

Despite complex content and procedures similar to those in studies where the objectives are model building and explanation, the correlational logic comprising the paradigm of the latter is not the statistical rhetoric used in achieving descriptive objectives. Studies aimed at description do not seek to discover correlations among variables which are then to be used as the basis for ex post facto models which are basically causal in nature (even though they may not use the terminology of causation). Rather, descriptive studies simply focus on answering questions of fact using measures of central tendency and dispersion and confidence intervals. Incorporated into study objectives are the answers to such questions as, "Are there differences in various characteristics relevant to the study among important population subgroups?" Although an *F*- or *t*-test might be used to answer the question, the objectives are different than those associated with the use of the same statistics in explanatory studies. They do not include the generation of answers to the question of why the differences might occur.

There is often confusion about study objectives where both description and explanation are sought. One of the reasons is probably the widely held, but mistaken, view that one cannot "be scientific" unless one is testing hypotheses that are explanatory in substance. This focus precludes establishing other objectives explicitly, even though they must still be achieved. Another is the confusion between the statistical concept of a hypothesis and the substantive proposition which underlies it. This confounding obscures the different substantive rhetoric underlying the use of a statistic in descriptive versus explanatory contexts. In the model-building or hypothesis-testing survey, the analyst is concerned with assessing the evidence bearing on the proposition that, for an individual case, having a large value on one variable somehow affects the value of another. One corresponding statistical implementation of this question is to examine a measure of central tendency of the dependent variable "controlling for" or "conditional on" values of the independent variable. The logic is that of statistical control substituting for the experimental control of factors believed to be responsible for behavior. The statistics used are correlations.

On the other hand, when the objective is descriptive, the concern is not with why two means are different (even though this may ultimately be of considerable interest). Rather, it is simply to obtain as carefully drawn a picture as is possible of what the differences are, in fact, between population groups of interest. The paradigm is not correlational, even though the statistics used may involve the same *F*- or *t*-tests comparing measures of central tendency in two or more groups.

In both cases, sampling variation has to be ruled out as a possible explanaion for perceived differences. However, when the objective is explanatory, then the analyst also needs directional correlation measures, perhaps couched in PRE (proportional reduction in error) terminology, a definition of the subset for which the relation holds, a description of the behavior of the variables, as well as some type of objective decision procedure (i.e., a significance test). In this case, the test is used for deciding whether to treat the variables as causally related or not. When the objective is only description, the correlational measure is not needed.

Failing to distinguish between descriptive and explanatory objectives results in confusion in the data processing because the tasks associated with description are simpler than those required for explanation and hypothesis testing.

The objective of a descriptive analysis is to characterize one or more theoretically relevant subsets of the sample cases using measures of central tendency and dispersion of the variables serving as indicators of the constructs of interest to the study, and to include appropriate confidence intervals.

To accomplish this typically implies the following:

1. Performing the necessary preliminary code-collapsing, variable-generation, and scaling operations; mapping the descriptor and subset definition variables into both theory and past research as well as into the current problems of interest to the analyst and the study sponsors.
2. Computing marginal distributions and measures of central tendency and dispersion for the total sample, and establishing such distribution-based class intervals (e.g., percentiles) as may be needed for the descriptor variables, and then recoding variables to reflect these class intervals.
3. Computing marginal distributions and measures of central tendency and dispersion for the variables which are to be used to divide the sample into subgroups for comparison. This will typically include face-sheet variables such as age, education, region, urbanization, sex, socioeconomic status, and race, as well as other subset definition variables of interest to the study.
4. Dividing the sample into the relevant subgroups and computing measures of central tendency and dispersion for the sample subgroups for each of the variables used in the descriptive process.
5. Computing confidence intervals and sampling error statistics; reviewing bias and data-collection problems associated with all the variables used.
6. Extracting several interviews from each important population subgroup for intensive reading with a view to illustrating and amplifying the descriptive statistics.

The first task, variable generation and scaling, was discussed in Chapter 7. For the remainder, it will be useful to work backward from the desired output.

TABLE 8-3 Education, Age, and Race by Total Family Income in 1968[a]
(Percentage Distribution of Families)

Family Income	*Education of Family Head*								
	0–5 Grades	*6–8 Grades*	*9–11 Grades*	*12 Grades*	*12 Plus Noncollege Training*	*Some College*	*College Degree*	*Advanced Degree*	*Total*
Less than $3000	21	37	17	6	3	12	3	1	100
$3000–3999	15	31	17	10	10	9	7	1	100
$4000–4999	9	18	22	18	13	10	8	2	100
$5000–5999	6	22	24	16	9	15	6	2	100
$6000–7499	5	24	19	18	14	9	9	2	100
$7500–9999	3	17	18	22	13	15	8	4	100
$10,000–14,999	1	11	16	21	14	19	12	6	100
$15,000 or more	1	8	12	14	11	19	22	13	100
All families	7	20	17	16	11	14	10	5	100

Family Income	*Age of Family Head*								*Race of Family Head*		
	Under Age 25	*25–34*	*35–44*	*45–54*	*55–64*	*65–74*	*Age 75 or Older*	*Total*	*White*	*Nonwhite*	*Total*
Less than $3000	12	4	6	7	15	29	27	100	79	21	100
$3000–3999	15	12	11	14	20	17	11	100	71	29	100
$4000–4999	14	15	9	13	15	22	12	100	85	15	100
$5000–5999	19	19	8	13	21	16	4	100	86	14	100
$6000–7499	9	32	14	13	17	10	5	100	88	12	100
$7500–9999	12	27	18	19	13	7	4	100	90	10	100
$10,000–14,999	4	30	25	21	15	4	1	100	94	6	100
$15,000 or more	1	12	29	30	19	8	1	100	96	4	100
All families	9	20	17	17	16	13	8	100	88	12	100

[a] Source: Katona et al. (1970, p. 12). Used by permission.

Several examples will illustrate the types of tables needed for this type of description. Table 8-3 illustrates frequency distributions showing the interrelationships between several face-sheet variables. The percentages could have been computed in either direction. Table 8-4 provides an example of a basic descriptive variable, family income, broken down by face-sheet variables: education, occupation, ubanization, race, age, and family life cycle. The distribution, mean, and median are displayed. Footnotes are supplied which provide definitions of terms and handling of N.A. cases. The units of analysis are specified in the table (unlike the definition of the population which is supplied in associated text). Percentages are rounded to the nearest whole percentage, since sampling errors make them only approximate anyway. Means and medians are rounded to the nearest $10 for a similar reason. The number of cases is specified for each subgroup to make possible reconstruction of the exact frequency distributions and to make possible judgments by readers of the probable sampling errors of the means and medians. Standard errors of means and proportions are not reported on in the table; rather, they should be dealt with more extensively in a separate appendix.[47]

Table 8-5 illustrates trends in the distribution of family income over the years 1961–1965. To show trends in the distribution of dollars among rich and poor over the period, the share columns are included. Means and medians are

TABLE 8-4 Total Family Income—Within Various Groups[a]
(Percentage Distribution of Families)

	Mean Income in 1968	*Total*	*Less Than $3,000*	*$3,000 –4,999*	*$5,000 –7,499*	*$7,500 –9,999*	*$10,000 –14,999*	*$15,000 or More*	*Number of Cases*	*Median*
PART A										
Education of family head[b]										
0–5 grades	$ 4,000	100	52	22	13	7	4	2	143	$ 2,920
6–8 grades	6,300	100	33	16	19	14	13	5	410	5,170
9–11 grades, some high school, plus noncollege	8,820	100	17	15	20	17	22	9	402	7,260
12 grades, completed high school	9,480	100	6	12	18	24	29	11	415	8,940
Completed high school plus other noncollege	9,890	100	5	14	18	20	31	12	264	9,060
College, no degree	10,830	100	14	9	12	17	31	17	329	9,610
College, bachelor's degree	13,030	100	6	10	14	13	29	28	239	11,240
College, advanced, or professional degree	16,460	100	3	6	6	15	31	39	109	13,120
PART B										
Occupation of family head										
Professional, technical	$13,670	100	2	7	12	16	36	27	301	$11,800
Managers, officials	16,260	100	—	4	11	16	30	39	203	13,150
Self-employed businessmen, artisans	11,830	100	3	12	23	10	31	21	114	10,320
Clerical, sales	10,520	100	5	12	14	23	31	15	215	9,530
Craftsmen, foremen	10,750	100	2	5	18	22	38	15	358	10,430
Operatives	8,720	100	5	11	25	27	27	5	334	8,360
Laborers, service workers	6,390	100	21	19	24	18	15	3	238	5,960
Farmers	8,750	100	15	21	17	20	17	10	78	7,140
Miscellaneous groups	5,000	100	34	28	16	11	10	1	130	4,150
Retired	5,400	100	49	19	13	8	7	4	346	3,000

[a] Source: Katona et al. (1970, pp. 13–15). Used by permission.
[b] Data for 14 cases for which education of head is not ascertained are omitted.

[47] For an example, see Katona et al. (1970, pp. 279–288).

TABLE 8-4 (cont'd.)

	Mean Income in 1968	*Total*	*Less Than $3,000*	*$3,000 –4,999*	*$5,000 –7,499*	*$7,500 –9,999*	*$10,000 –14,999*	*$15,000 or More*	*Number of Cases*	*Median*
PART C										
Belt										
Central cities of 12 largest SMSA's[c]	$ 8,690	100	11	19	18	18	21	13	252	$ 7,680
Central cities of other SMSA's	7,970	100	23	17	17	16	18	9	331	6,150
Suburban areas of 12 largest SMSA's	12,460	100	5	7	10	13	40	25	328	11,820
Suburban areas of other SMSA's	10,540	100	12	11	13	20	28	16	344	9,180
Adjacent areas	8,530	100	20	13	19	19	19	10	435	7,300
Outlying areas	7,770	100	29	14	20	13	16	8	461	6,050
PART D										
Race[d]										
White	9,710	100	16	12	16	17	25	14	2027	8,360
Black	5,490	100	36	22	16	11	11	4	238	3,970
PART E										
Age of family head										
Under age 25	$ 5,800	100	23	21	24	22	9	1	188	$ 5,450
25–34	9,420	100	4	9	22	23	35	7	519	9,160
35–44	11,820	100	7	8	12	17	35	21	469	10,900
45–54	11,760	100	7	10	12	19	29	23	491	10,300
55–64	9,430	100	17	14	20	13	21	15	382	7,400
65–74	7,550	100	40	20	16	9	7	8	165	4,110
Age 75 or older	3,790	100	59	19	9	9	2	2	103	2,460
PART F										
Life-cycle stage of family head[e]										
Under age 45										
Unmarried, no children	$ 5,650	100	33	19	23	14	8	3	120	$ 4,790
Married, no children	10,070	100	3	13	19	18	36	11	149	9,610
Married, youngest child under age 6	9,910	100	3	8	19	27	33	10	511	9,330
Married, youngest child age 6 or older	12,420	100	1	4	14	19	41	21	295	11,440

[c] A Standard Metropolitan Statistical Area is a county or group of contiguous counties (except in New England) which contained at least one city of 50,000 inhabitants or more in 1960. In addition to the county or counties containing such a city or cities, contiguous counties are included if, according to certain criteria, they are essentially metropolitan in character and sufficiently integrated with the central city. In New England, standard metropolitan areas have been defined on a town rather than on a county basis.

[d] Data excludes Oriental, Puerto Rican, Mexican, Cuban, and "other" categories, owing to the small number of cases.

[e] The term "no children" means no children under age 18 living at home. Unemployed people and housewives age 55 or older are considered retired; unemployed people and housewives under age 55 are considered to be in the labor force.

TABLE 8-4 (cont'd.)

	Mean Income in 1968	*Total*	*Less Than $3,000*	*$3,000 -4,999*	*$5,000 -7,499*	*$7,500 -9,999*	*$10,000 -14,999*	*$15,000 or More*	*Number of Cases*	*Median*
Age 45 or over										
Married, has children	12,700	100	5	6	15	19	31	24	327	10,770
Married, no children, head in labor force	12,020	100	5	10	19	16	24	26	326	9,920
Married, no children, head retired	6,050	100	31	25	15	12	11	6	139	4,580
Unmarried, no children, head in labor force	7,420	100	19	29	18	14	14	6	145	5,270
Unmarried, no children, head retired	4,680	100	71	15	5	4	3	2	155	1,920
Any age										
Unmarried, has children	5,640	100	29	29	18	11	11	2	150	4,340
All families	9,220	100	18	13	16	17	23	13	2317	7,860

TABLE 8-5 Distribution of Families and Distribution of Total Money Income, by Income Groups, 1961–1965[a] (Percentage Distribution of Family Units)

	Family Units[b]					*Share of Total Income*				
Income Groups	*1961*	*1962*	*1963*	*1964*	*1965*	*1961*	*1962*	*1963*	*1964*	*1965*
Under $1000	6	4	4	4	3	1	c	c	c	c
$1000–1999	10	9	10	9	8	2	2	2	2	1
$2000–2999	9	9	9	8	9	4	3	3	3	3
$3000–3999	9	8	8	8	8	5	4	4	4	3
$4000–4999	10	10	9	8	7	7	6	6	4	4
$5000–5999	12	12	10	9	8	10	10	8	7	6
$6000–7499	14	14	16	14	13	14	14	16	12	11
$7500–9999	14	16	15	17	17	19	20	20	19	19
$10,000–14,999	11	12	14	15	17	19	22	24	23	26
$15,000 or more	5	6	5	8	10	19	19	17	26	27
Total	100	100	100	100	100	100	100	100	100	100
Mean family income[d]	$6480	6800	6710	7680	7940					
Median family income	$5310	5820	5900	6320	6670					

[a] Source: Katona et al. (1967, p. 15). Used by permission.

[b] Family units include (a) single person unrelated to other occupants in the dwelling unit; (b) a person living alone; and (c) two or more people living in the same dwelling unit related by blood, marriage, or adoption.

[c] Less than 0.5 per cent.

[d] Mean income is obtained by dividing aggregate money income by the number of family units.

also supplied. Rounding practices and definitions of terms are dealt with as noted above.

Table 8-6 illustrates a more complex type of description. The proportion of families in each life-cycle group is given for the time periods in question. The proportion of new cars purchased by families in each group is given. Then the per capita consumption of new cars for each life-cycle group is given (actually the consumption per 100 families is used).

TABLE 8-6 New Car Purchases by Family Life Cycle[a] (Figures Are in Per Cent)

	Distribution of All Families				*Shares of New-Car Purchases*				*Ratio of New Cars Purchased to Number of Families*			
Life Cycle	*1961*	*1962*	*1963*	*1964*	*1961*	*1962*	*1963*	*1964*	*1961*	*1962*	*1963*	*1964*
Under age 45												
Single, no children	6	5	5	5	3	3	1	5	4	5	3	12
Married, no children	5	6	5	5	10	11	7	6	16	20	13	14
Married, child under 6	26	22	22	21	28	17	21	20	9	8	11	12
Married, oldest child 6 or over	10	11	10	10	11	12	14	12	9	12	14	15
Age 45 or over												
Married, children	12	15	14	13	11	21	21	16	7	14	16	15
Married, no children:												
Head in labor force	12	14	16	17	17	20	19	25	13	15	13	18
Head retired	7	9	8	8	11	6	6	5	13	7	7	7
Single, no children:												
Head in labor force	7	5	7	7	3	4	7	5	4	9	11	9
Head retired	8	8	9	9	3	4	2	3	3	5	3	4
Any age												
Unmarried with children	7	5	4	5	3	2	2	3	4	4	4	7
All families	100	100	100	100	100	100	100	100	8	10	11	12

[a] Source: Katona et al. (1966, p. 76). Used by permission.

Table 8-7 illustrates the description of a very small, but growing, segment of the population in detail. Some N.A.'s were excluded from this table. Age groups were broken down into very small groups to permit a detailed examination of differences. The table is actually a compilation of figures in which comparable age, retirement, and income distributions were used, and in which the definitions of families and the sampled populations were the same (Katona et al., 1967).

Tables 8-8 and 8-9 again show trend data, organized so as to permit a comparison of home ownership on a cohort basis as well as by a combination of

TABLE 8-7 Age and Income of Retired People[a]
(Percentage Distribution of Families)

	Family Income							
Age of Head	*Less than $2000*	*$2000–2999*	*$3000–3999*	*$4000–7499*	*$7500 or More*	*Total*	*Median Income*	*Number of Families*[b]
Younger than age 60	20	11	13	23	29	100	$3770	115
60–64	28	11	17	20	21	100	3650	71
65–69	20	19	18	25	17	100	3610	147
70–74	32	26	10	21	10	100	2690	155
75 or older	44	17	14	13	10	100	2350	187
All retired	33	18	14	20	16	[b]	3140	675

[a] Source: Katona et al. (1967, p. 148). Used by permission.

[b] Percentages do not add to 100 because 2 per cent not ascertained on income are excluded from the table.

TABLE 8-8 Home Ownership by Age Cohort Groups[a]
1950–1965
(Per Cent of Nonfarm Families)

						Increase in Ownership by Cohort Group Over 10-Year Period[b]	
Age of Head	*1950*	*1955*	*1960*	*1965*	*Increase in Ownership 1950–1965*	*1950–1960*	*1955–1965*
18–24	15[c]	15	14	19	4		
						29	32
25–34	37	43	44	47	10		
						27	26
35–44	52	59	64	69	17		
						17	16
45–54	65	61	69	75	10		
						−3	10
55–64	68	66	62	71	3		
						−3	5
65 and over	65	63	65	71	6		
All nonfarm families	54	55	58	63	9	—	—

[a] Source: Katona et al. (1966, p. 118). Used by permission.

[b] The table shows, for example, that there is a 29 percentage point difference between the 15 per cent of those 18–24 years old in 1950 owning their homes and the 44 per cent of those 25–34 years old 10 years later, in 1960.

[c] Arrows indicate those in same age cohort group over 10-year period.

TABLE 8-9 Home Ownership by Population Group and Income Quintile[a] (Per Cent of Nonfarm Families)

Population Group and Family Income Quintile	*Per Cent Owning Their Home*		
	1955	*1960*	*1965*
Married, under age 45, no children			
Lowest or second quintile	23	18	24
Third quintile	27	37	38
Fourth quintile	34	40	44
Highest quintile	49	32	64
Married, under age 45, children, lives in large city[b]			
Lowest or second quintile	14	14	17
Third quintile	30	35	42
Fourth quintile	55	65	54
Highest quintile	64	63	91
Married, under age 45, children, does not live in large city			
Lowest quintile	43	38	8
Second quintile	47	38	45
Third quintile	54	57	64
Fourth quintile	67	80	82
Highest quintile	82	86	91
Married, age 45 or older, lives in large city			
Lowest quintile	46	61	64
Second quintile	41	60	51
Third quintile	65	52	68
Fourth quintile	62	47	80
Highest quintile	76	76	84
Married, age 45 or older, does not live in large city			
Lowest quintile	66	61	68
Second quintile	72	75	70
Third quintile	79	82	87
Fourth quintile	81	83	88
Highest quintile	81	91	91
Not married, under age 45			
Lowest quintile	3	6	0
Second quintile	11	10	10
Third quintile	18	9	14
Fourth or highest quintile	[c]	14	15

[a] Source: Katona et al. (1966, p. 119). Used by permission.
[b] A large city is one with a population of over 50,000.
[c] Too few cases.

TABLE 8-9 (cont'd.)

Population Group and Family Income Quintile	*Per Cent Owning Their Home*		
	1955	*1960*	*1965*
Not married, age 45 or older, lives in large city			
Lowest quintile	29	31	36
Second quintile	22	40	32
Third quintile	46	39	55
Fourth or highest quintile	56	47	62
Not married, age 45 or older, does not live in large city			
Lowest quintile	51	47	60
Second quintile	40	59	66
Third quintile	56	55	81
Fourth or highest quintile	81	66	78

family-life-cycle and income-level groups. Note that the tables apply to nonfarm families only.

The last illustration, Table 8-10, illustrates estimation of the total number of persons in the population (continental United States) in each income and family size group. It is simply obtained by multiplying the frequency distribution of families in each cell by the number of persons in the family and then multiplying the result by the reciprocal of the study sampling fraction.[48] From the table, one can make such estimates as, "There are approximately 3 million elderly single-person 'families' in the United States with incomes of less than $3000 per year."

The considerations that are related to sampling are always a part of survey research, simply because of the way in which data must be gathered. Typical populations are spread out over a large area and are heterogeneous. According to Lazerwitz (1968), samples should be representative, be obtained by a probability process in order to permit them to be related back to the population from which they came, be as small as precision requirements will allow, and be designed so as to maximize efficient data-collection procedures. When cluster samples are used to achieve these goals, the clustering process itself introduces complexities into the statistical computations. Numerators and denominators of means are no longer completely independent, and the differences between two means or other statistics may not be statistically independent. The problem is not that the sample statistics such as means and variances are biased; they are not, but their standard errors are biased downward.

[48] The latter is obtained by estimating the number of families from U.S. census data and multiplying by the observed sample proportion.

TABLE 8-10 Estimated Population According to Family Size, Family Income, and Whether Anyone 65 or Older in the Family[a]
(Millions of People)

		No One 65 or Older in the Family							
		Number in the Family							
Family Income	*All Family Sizes*	*One*	*Two*[b]	*Three*	*Four*	*Five*	*Six*	*Seven*	*Eight or More*[c]
Less than $1000	2.1	0.7	0.4	0.4	0.2	0.1	[d]	0.2	0.1
$1000–1999	6.7	1.0	1.3	0.8	1.2	1.0	0.5	0.5	0.4
$2000–2999	7.7	0.7	1.6	0.9	1.0	1.2	0.4	0.9	1.0
$3000–3999	9.9	0.7	1.8	1.8	1.7	1.3	1.1	0.3	1.2
$4000–4999	12.3	0.5	1.5	2.1	1.8	2.4	1.5	1.0	1.5
$5000–5999	15.5	0.5	2.5	2.6	3.6	2.6	1.9	0.8	1.0
$6000–7499	25.9	0.5	3.3	4.3	7.0	4.2	2.5	1.7	2.4
$7500–9999	34.1	0.6	3.8	5.0	9.9	6.3	3.6	1.4	3.5
$10,000–14,999	30.1	0.3	3.3	5.5	7.4	6.0	4.1	1.4	2.1
$15,000 and over	13.9	0.2	2.1	1.6	4.5	3.2	1.4	[d]	0.9
Total	158.2	5.7	21.6	25.0	38.3	28.3	17.0	8.2	14.1

		One or More Persons 65 or Older in the Family							
		Number in the Family							
	All Family Sizes	*One*	*Two*	*Three*	*Four*	*Five*	*Six*	*Seven*	*Eight or Morer*[c]
Less than $1000	1.7	1.0	0.5	0.1	[d]	0.1	[d]	[d]	[d]
$1000–1999	4.5	1.4	2.1	0.5	0.1	0.2	0.1	0.1	[d]
$2000–2999	3.8	0.6	2.3	0.1	0.3	[d]	0.1	0.1	0.3
$3000–3999	2.8	0.2	2.1	0.3	0.1	0.1	[d]	[d]	[d]
$4000–4999	1.7	0.2	1.2	0.3	[d]	[d]	[d]	[d]	[d]
$5000–5999	2.0	0.1	1.0	0.3	0.1	0.2	0.2	[d]	0.1
$6000–7499	2.1	0.1	0.7	0.6	0.3	0.2	0.2	[d]	[d]
$7500–9999	2.5	0.1	0.7	0.7	0.4	0.3	[d]	0.3	[d]
$10,000–14,999	3.2	[d]	0.7	0.8	0.7	0.7	0.1	0.2	[d]
$15,000 and over	2.2	0.1	0.7	0.3	0.2	0.7	0.2	[d]	[d]
Total	26.8	3.8	12.0	4.0	2.2	2.5	.9	.7	.4

[a] Source: Katona et al. (1966, p. 25). Used by permission.

[b] Table reads: Top of third column: There are .4 million people in families of two people with family income of less than $1000 and no one 65 or older in the family.

[c] Assume nine individuals per family.

[d] Fewer than .05 million.

The best way of dealing with this problem is exact sampling error computations for the statistics upon which the major study findings are to be based. If careful population description is an important study objective, this is imperative and involves extended computations that are beyond the scope of this book.[49] But in many instances either this will not be financially possible, or the necessary computational capabilities will not be available. Yet standard errors must still be computed if the analyst is to fulfill the obligation to provide the reader with information to be used in assessing the precision of the description.

Many computer programs provide standard errors and *t*-values based on simple random sampling (SRS) formulas. These should not be used with other than simple random samples without some adjustment in the interpretations based on the standard errors they produce. According to Frankel (1971), the use of SRS formulas with clustered samples appears to result in the understatement of true standard errors by about one-third for means, proportions, and differences between them; one-fifth for simple and partial correlations; about 10 per cent for regression coefficients; and 50 per cent or more for multiple correlation coefficients.

Knowing these biases permits the analyst to make appropriate adjustments and to revise interpretations accordingly. Such adjustments are based on the presuppositions that there is some unknown, but nonzero, pattern of intercorrelations between the variables studied and the clustering pattern, an assumption that seems likely to hold true for every study. Until further work on the relationship between simple random-sampling formulas and statistics computed from clustered samples is completed, the analyst should follow the guidelines furnished by Frankel's work when exact computations cannot be made.

Data-Processing Considerations The analyst typically must make a simpler set of decisions when the objective is description than when explanation is an objective, although many are the same. The most important of these decisions are noted below and some of the considerations related to each are discussed. In many cases, the decision will have been made at the time the study is designed, but in a complex study with multiple units of analysis, or with data collected over time, this cannot be the case.

Units of analysis and dimensions of description must be selected. Scales or proxy variables for those dimensions must be chosen. Relevant sample subsets must be defined in order to establish the groups over which the statistics are to be computed. If differential sampling fractions have been employed, a decision must be made on the use of weights in the computations. These all depend on the nature of the theory giving form to the study, on the practical problems to be confronted by the study findings, on the value system the study staff brings to bear on these problems, and on the organizational setting and the political and economic context of the study. If replication or comparability with other studies is desired, both descriptor and subset definition variables may have to be recoded to ensure consistency of definition.

[49] The reader is referred to Lazerwitz (1968), Kish (1965), Schuessler (1971), Frankel (1971), and especially to Kish, Frankel, and Van Eck (1972).

Once these fundamental decisions are made, a set of summarizing techniques must be decided upon. What measures of central tendency shall be used? Shall percentile or absolute class-interval definitions be employed? What measures of dispersion skewness and kurtosis shall be computed? If the analysis deals with inequalities in the shares of an economic or other good or commodity, shall Lorenz curves be employed?[50] What estimates of standard errors or confidence intervals are to be provided? With what precision are the results to be reported? What display devices (e.g., tables, graphs, charts, etc.) are to be employed? Are population estimates (i.e., absolute quantities) to be reported or are sample proportions and means adequate? Again, comparability with other findings should be a consideration in the decision. At the time the variables are selected for use, coding and editing reports should be scanned for evidence of bias and inaccuracies and a note made to accompany the findings.

To help convey a sense of the personal, one- or two-unit subsets of the data corresponding to different portions of the tables should be retrieved from the data base, the interview numbers identified, and the interviews pulled out and read. The analyst's summary of these interviews should be incorporated into the report dealing with this portion of the analysis. This simple expedient at once helps prevent misinterpretation of the data and goes a long way toward helping respondents not to become mere statistics.

Description eventually merges into explanation as differences (or unexpected similarities) between substantively interesting population groups emerge and the analyst cannot help conjecturing "Why?"[51] Description also merges into conceptual clarification when several variables are used jointly to describe a population. The following section takes up explanation as a study objective.

Explanatory Analyses

Most surveys which seek to go beyond mere description tend to have only a few specific hypotheses to be tested which are formally deduced from theory. Their major focus is likely to be on the formulation and improvement of explanatory models. These describe the functioning of a specific aspect of a particular kind of behavior; and, as such, constitute a middle-range theory dealing with specific groups of people (Blau, 1960). They are often ex post facto, since it is left to a later study to assess the adequacy of the model put forth, although substantiating evidence in the form of internal consistency or random-half validation may be produced. Replication is a necessary part of this approach, and further studies respecify and improve the model.

[50] See Hainsworth (1964) and Morgan (1962) for examples.

[51] In fact, the question "why" must always be asked even if the purpose of that phase of the study is strictly descriptive. The answers "because of data-collection errors" and "because of sampling errors" must both be ruled out if the analyst is to have confidence in the results.

Such models are explanatory in the sense that subsequent individual events are seen as objective instances of the class of behavior described by the model (Popper, 1959). The value of each dependent variable for a given object is seen as such an instance. The configuration of initial conditions is interpreted as the causal factors responsible for its observed behavior. The model describes both a class of objects and the functional relationships between the attributes of the objects comprising the class. It explains variation between objects along specified dimensions. The power of the model comes from its ability to make accurate predictions about the behavioral outcomes that result from various combinations of the feasible initial conditions.

Most such models assume a number of explanatory factors, which operate simultaneously to affect the outcome (i.e., they are multivariate). Some factors may contribute only a small-sized push on the effects (e.g., bread has fewer calories than a chocolate sundae) and still be considered worthy of being included in the model. Similarly, assessment of each variable's relative importance and its profile of influence requires holding constant all the other factors which, according to the pattern of causal assumptions in force, operate directly and simultaneously.[52] The description of the class of objects to which the model applies is an integral part of the theory in which the model is embedded and is ordinarily expressed as a multivariate monothetic set definition. Figure 8-12 outlines the topics of explanatory analysis.

Specification The use of such models is based on the assumption that there is a greater or lesser correspondence between the variables measured and the underlying factors, which, if they could be measured directly, would provide maximal explanatory power for the various outcomes of the phenomenon studied. Since only some of these factors are measured by methods approximating direct measurement, others only indirectly, and still others not at all, part of the analysis problem is to figure out how to combine the measured variables in such a way as to best represent each underlying factor's effect on the phenomena to be explained. "Best" always represents several considerations: parsimony, closeness of fit to the data, theoretical relevance, and the current purposes of the analyst in doing the research.

These explanatory factors, as represented by the indicators obtained in the survey, do not necessarily affect measures of the dependent variables in ways which are both linear and additive.[53] In particular, the presence of contextual effects or the differential effects of variables operating at different times may require the use of interaction terms in the model which are quite complex (Sonquist and Morgan, 1964; Sonquist et al., 1974).

Each explanatory proposition in the model is to be given mathematical form and precision by representation as a function depicting the simultaneous

52 For a further discussion, see Hirschi and Selvin (1967, 1970).

53 See Alker (1966). Tufte (1969) also confronts many related problems.

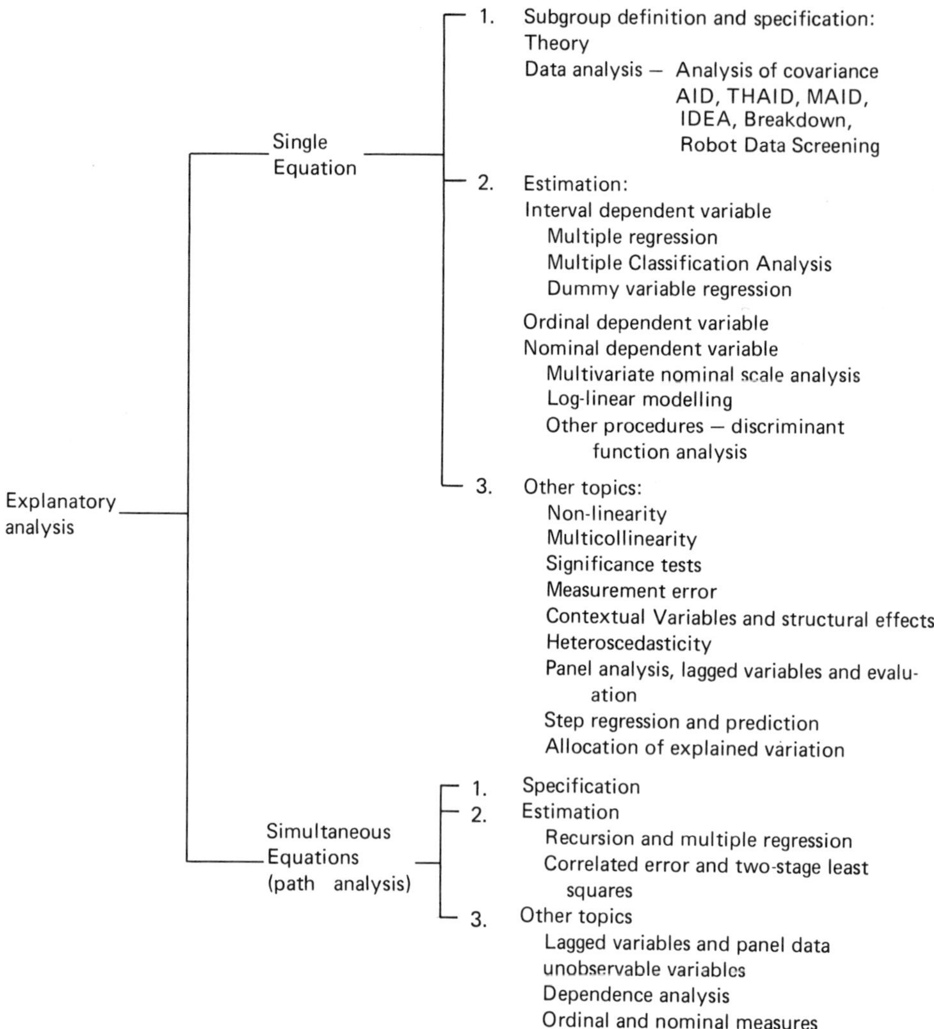

Figure 8-12 Topics in Explanatory Analysis

net effects of a set of explanatory factors on a dependent variable. This function is usually expressed in least-squares form and explains the variation in the dependent variable:

$$Y = f(X_1, X_2, \ldots, X_n) + e. \tag{8-11}$$

The stochastic term is included for several reasons—and part of the task of the survey analyst is to find ways to minimize it. Included in its value are errors in the measurement process and variation in the dependent variable associated with explanatory factors uncorrelated with those already in the model.[54] If the analyst has combined the measured variables so that they do not represent the underlying factors well, or if they are combined so as not to represent the joint effects of the factors optimally, the error term may be unnecessarily large. Since many factors are assumed to be at work and pulling in opposite directions, it is assumed that small positive and negative values of the error term should appear more frequently than large ones.

Thus, part of the task of the survey analyst is to decide how many equations to use in modelling the phenomenon and what terms to use in each. In each equation it may be necessary to combine some subsets of the available variables into theoretically interesting terms that will minimize the error. Nonlinearities and interactions are the most usual problems. Determining the configuration of the equations and terms is termed *specification* by econometricians and is of central concern in explanatory survey analysis.

Specification actually consists of two tasks, not one. Not all models will apply to the entire study sample. It may be that several quite different models are required to represent the influence of the independent variables on the phenomena to be explained. For example, the effect of education on income has been found to be different for black and white heads of families in the United States. The effect of age on hospitalizations is different for men and women. Such variables as race, sex, and social class may "interact" with so many other variables in a model that parsimony is better sacrificed to predictive accuracy by the formulation of several models rather than just one complex one, perhaps even with different predictors. This second specification task, then, is to define the group to which each explanatory model is to apply. Ascertaining the need for several models rather than one is a task that must be undertaken along with the rest of the decisions to include variables as predictors and to generate interaction terms from them. Information relevant to all these decisions is obtained partly from theory and partly from examining the data.

Other specification problems include dealing with mixtures of nominal and ordinal data, highly correlated variables, conceptual overlap, correlated measurement errors, logical priorities and chains of causation, and nonlinearities.

It is often useful to start the specification process simply by examining two-way tables or frequency plots. A bivariate statistical finding should contain three reported parts. Usually these would consist of a profile of the observed relationship between the variables, a summary of the extent to which the variables are related, and a statement of the level of confidence the researcher has in the interpretation made of the findings. The profile may be a bivariate frequency distribution, or the slope and intercept of a regression line; the measure of the extent of the relationship would ordinarily be some type of directional

[54] This reinforces the need for developing these a priori models prior to the construction of the questionnaire to be used to collect relevant data.

correlation coefficient; and the measure of the trust held in the interpretation of the results would be provided by a significance test or confidence interval supported by reports of reliability and validity analyses and by interviewing and coding reports.

But a series of bivariate tables is not the only avenue to be taken. Computing equipment makes possible the use of new kinds of strategies for analyzing survey data. These are not substitutes for old ways of doing things but should form a complementary part of the tool kit available to help formulate models which aid in the understanding of human behavior.[55] Computing equipment has helped to make it possible to tackle directly problems earlier left to the analyst's serendipity. These are the ones directly associated with model specification, with induction, with the problem of pulling up social science theory by its bootstraps to the point where it is precise enough to enable testable hypotheses to be deduced. It provides a vehicle for examining data systematically when theory is weak and poorly formulated, to discover what patterns appear to be there.

Research always alternates between deductive and inductive phases (Tukey, 1963; Tukey and Wilk, 1966). These cycles are both long and short term. A given study may be primarily focused either on discovery or on model testing, but invariably moves into the alternative rhetoric for short periods of time (Anscombe and Tukey, 1963; Riley, 1954). Most survey analysts who seek more than description will either be primarily focused on formulating middle-range explanations of a multivariate nature, or on testing them out and modifying them (Morgan and Sonquist, 1963). Inductive statistics carry with them the rhetoric of curve fitting; deductive rhetoric is that of the significance test.

There are a number of reasons why a model-building, model-revising approach is a necessary complement to the deductive rhetoric associated with the hypothesis-testing logic inherited from experimentalists. Existing theory simply is often not stated in a form sufficiently precise that individual hypotheses can be deduced formally and tested statistically against a null hypothesis. Second, there are often severe validity problems in survey data. The investigator often has only hints from the literature as to what the relevant variables are and seeks to discover the best formulation of them. The process of specification involves using the data to generate hints as to what is relevant, and to suggest the pattern of association among the explanatory factors. This is a process of discovery, not deduction. Third, it is inherent in the nature of survey methods to collect data on many variables. Many interrelated problems are often investigated, and variables collected originally for one purpose may turn out to be of use in dealing with another. Sometimes the data are gleaned from an archive, and the analyst must pick and choose from the available variables. Finally, gathering, processing, and analyzing survey data is time-consuming and expensive. Consequently, it behooves the analyst to maximize the scientific return on

[55] For a further discussion, see Fen (1968).

every interview, to examine the data thoroughly. The result is a richness that often requires formulating the initial explanatory analysis problem as one of reducing the number of potential explanatory variables down to a manageable size, to sift out the combinations of variables that are most likely to pay off in insight, and to discard the ones most probably useless.

This was strictly a problem to be solved by laborious examination of many cross-tabulations until computing equipment became available. The very presence of the computer has encouraged the development of ways to apply it directly to these problems. Obviously, the primary guidelines to analysis should come from theory, but there are good reasons for supporting theoretical hints about which explanatory factors to explore with information from the data. After all, no one ever collects data which theory suggests will be useless.

The absence of a rhetoric for the use of statistics inductively in model-building efforts has led to fears (not altogether unrealistic) that naive analysts will be seduced into mechanistic "data dredging" (Selvin and Stuart, 1966). However, neither can the testing of isolated hypotheses suffice in a nonexperimental environment in which computers permit the development and manipulation of complex multivariate models. The use of multivariate explanatory structures to model complex phenomena demands a statistical rhetoric in which one first can construct a model, add terms, delete some, explore possible revisions of the model, and then fit these revisions to new sets of data. Even just to test whether one explanatory factor should be retained requires controlling for the simultaneous effects of the remaining factors in an appropriately specified framework. None of this could even be contemplated without computing equipment, the necessary software, and a statistical orientation that balances improved predictability from adding a new term to a model against losses in degrees of freedom, replicability, and degraded parsimony.

Computer-supported causal modeling can be described in terms of the four interrelated kinds of tasks that form an iterative cycle: this is illustrated in Figure 8-13. These include conceptualization, specification, estimation, and modification of the model. When something new is learned, the cycle starts over again. At some point the analyst runs out of variables, time, money, or interest; writes up the results at hand; and begins a new data-collection effort. The emphasis in any particular analysis on model building versus model testing and modification depends on the previous state of conceptualization, the available levels of measurement, and the precision with which past models have been stated.

The analyst often proceeds to get initial leverage on the overall task by examining zero-order profiles of the effects of the independent variables on the dependent ones, and by comparing their explanatory power in various important subsets of the data. Then variables are at least implicitly ranked on a scale ranging from potentially useful to utterly useless. It may be necessary to return to the data at various times to get additional information relevant to a decision as to how to treat a variable. A tentative model is then specified (Sonquist,

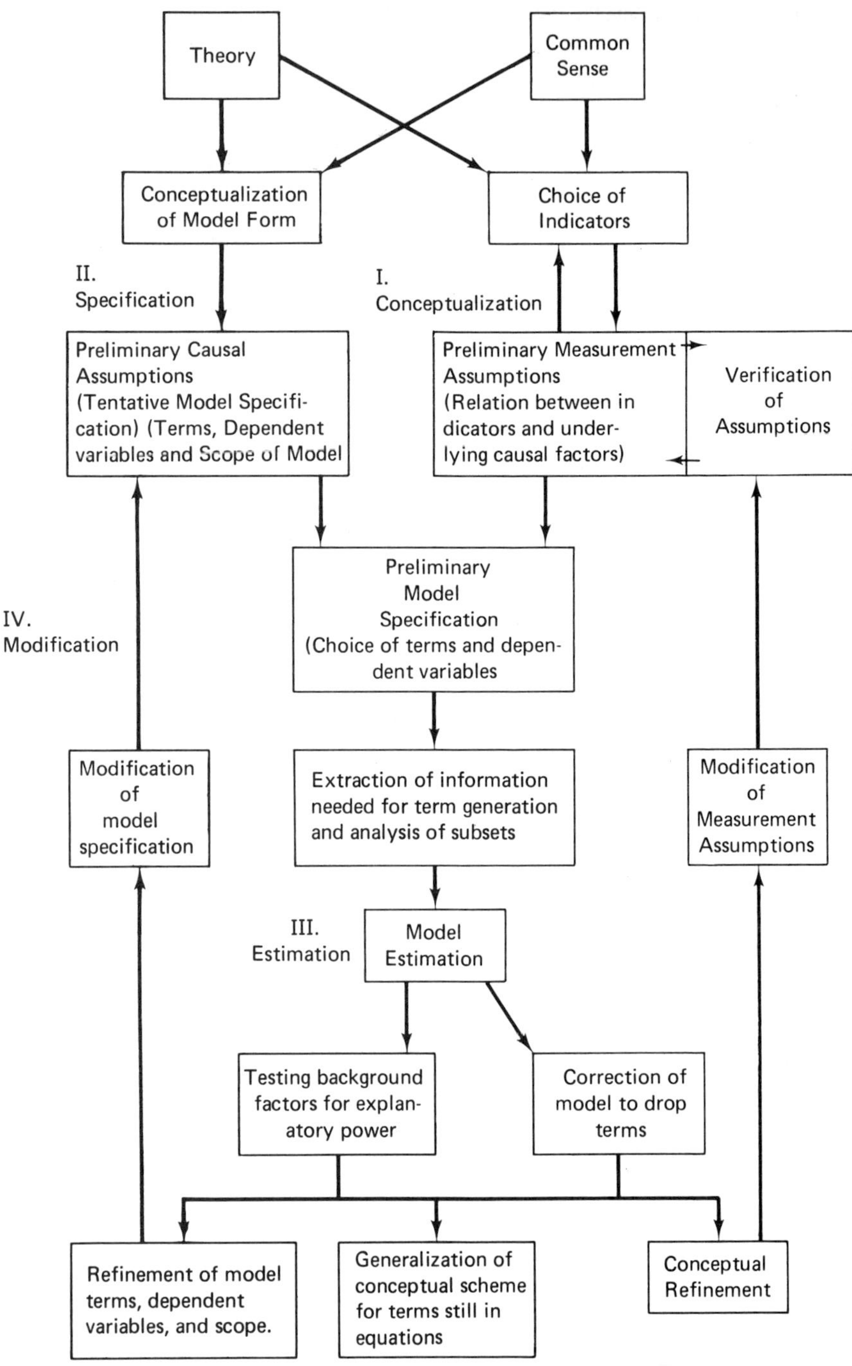

Figure 8-13 Inductive Model Building as a Process

1969, 1970). Others are combined into indices or interaction terms. Still others are excluded. In many cases, the analyst can write down an arbitrary decision rule for including or excluding variables usually involving a significance level or amount of explained variation. It is useful to note that when rules can be written down, they can usually be programmed on a computer.

Sterling et al. (1969) suggest some requirements for a formal decision algorithm to select variables for inclusion into a multivariate model. According to these writers, such a procedure must have:

1. A rule for rating variables and combinations of variables on a scale ranging from relevant to nonrelevant.
2. A scanning procedure with a practical number of steps for applying the rules.
3. Decision rules for the selection of the variables.

They suggest that stepwise sequential selection procedures make good sense because of the intuitively reasonable assumption that the most likely candidates for inclusion at a given step are those which passed the selection test at the previous step. Such procedures are heuristic; that is, they are designed to aid in a solution to a problem, not to guarantee one.

A number of sequential heuristic algorithms exist which serve the function of eviscerating the data so as to generate information useful in specification and in gaining insight into the behavior of the variables under various circumstances. These include algorithms due to Sonquist and Morgan (1964), Sterling et al. (1969), Gillo (1971), Sonquist et al. (1974), Morgan and Messenger (1973), and Press, Rogers, and Shure (1969). Finifter (1971, 1972) and Staelin (1970) have provided additional statistical guidelines for the use of some of these procedures.

Every survey-analysis statistical package (e.g., SPSS, OSIRIS, DATA-TEXT) has conventional statistical procedures such as the analysis of variance, *t*-test computations, cross-tabulations, and ordinal measures of association which are typically used to extract information from the data for these initial evisceration tasks. SPSS has an algorithm (subprogram "BREAKDOWN") which, although it does not use heuristics to assist in obtaining potentially useful summarizations of the data, performs a similar function (Nie, Bent, and Hull, 1970).

What all these sequential display algorithms have in common is that they partition the sample into a number of divisions and compute measures of relationship between the candidates for independent variables in the model and the dependent variable. They produce information helpful in assessing whether several models may be needed for different subgroups, and whether interaction terms may be needed in each model. It must be emphasized again that any heuristic which derives its information from the data at hand is likely to capitalize on idiosyncratic characteristics. Hence, use of these techniques needs to be carefully guided by available theory and constraints need to be placed on the algorithm to ensure adequate stability of results.

Estimation

After a model has been specified and the scope of its application defined, the problem is to estimate its parameters. According to Johnston (1972), this step performs a number of functions: (1) it is desirable to see the extent to which the data conform to the a priori specification, (2) the relative impacts of the various independent variables should be assessed, (3) understanding the behavior of the entire model requires knowledge of the parameters, and (4) it may be desired to make forecasts.

An important aspect of the estimation process is to obtain information about how close the model conforms to the data. If this is grossly inadequate, the specification process must begin anew, possibly with some variables added, others deleted, or new terms constructed. This may have to await a new data collection if it is evident that additional variables may be needed. Indeed, in many analyses a major objective is to gain insight into which factors these might be and what form the terms representing them should take.

The type of estimating procedure invoked in dealing with single-equation models depends on the level of measurement of the dependent and independent variables. When the dependent variable is interval or dichotomous, multiple regression (Johnston, 1972) is the frequent choice if the independent variables meet the measurement assumptions. When the independent variables are ordinal or nominal, multiple classification analysis (MCA) (Andrews et al., 1973), or dummy-variable regression (DVMR) (Johnston, 1972), can be used. (See Table 8-11.) At the other extreme, when the dependent variable is a polytomy, discriminant function analysis (DFA) is an appropriate choice when the independent variables are all interval or dichotomous (Cooley and Lohnes, 1971). Dummy variables can be introduced into the predictors if some or all are ordinal or nominal (DVDFA).

When all predictors and the dependent variable are nominal, a number of recently developed techniques are appropriate. One such procedure (MCTA) is due to Goodman (1965, 1969, 1970, 1971, 1972a, 1972b) and explicated in a summary by Davis (1974). Another (MNA) is described by Andrews and Messenger (1973) and by Messenger and Mandell (1972). Further methods are reported by Coleman (1970); Bock and Yates (1973); Kolakowsky and Bock (1973); Haberman (1973); Fienberg (1970); Miller (1964); Walker and Duncan (1967); Theil (1970); Grizzle, Starmer, and Koch (1969); and Entwisle and Knepp (1970). Discriminant-analysis techniques are set forth by Miller (1962) and by Overall and Klett (1972). Background information on measures of association is set forth by Goodman and Kruskal (1954) and by Lazarsfeld (1961). An informative comparison of techniques is given by Andrews and Messenger (1973).

TABLE 8-11 Selected Multivariate-Analysis Techniques Grouped by Levels of Measurement

	Dependent Variable		
Independent Variables	*Interval or Dichotomous*	*Ordinal*	*Nominal*
All interval or dichotomous	Multiple Regression	[a]	Discriminant Function Analysis (DFA)
Some interval or dichotomous, some ordinal	Multiple Classification Analysis (MCA)	[a]	Dummy Variable (DFA)
	Dummy-Variable Regression (DVMR)		(DVDFA)
All ordinal	MCA, DVMR	[a]	DVDFA
Some ordinal	MCA, DVMR	MNA[b]	MNA, MCTA,
Some nominal		MCTA[c]	DVDFA
All three levels present	MCA, DVMR	MNA, DVDFA	MNA, MCTA, DVDFA
All nominal	MCA, DVMR	MNA, DVDFA	MNA, MCTA, DVDFA

[a] See the text for a discussion.
[b] Multivariate Nominal Scale Analysis (Andrews and Messenger, 1973).
[c] Multivariate Contingency Table Analysis (Goodman, 1972; Davis, 1974).

The literature on multiple regression and on the use of dummy variables is extensive, and only general guidelines for the analyst confronted with the choice of techniques will be set forth here. Good general discussions of multiple regression are given by Cohen (1968), Darlington (1968), Gordan (1968), Goldberger (1968), Draper and Smith (1966), Kerlinger and Pedhazur (1973), and Van de Geer (1971). More advanced treatments are given by Johnston (1972), Tatsouka (1971), Valavanis (1959), Snedecor and Cochran (1967), Morrison (1967), Rao (1965), Dempster (1969), Bock (1974), and Coleman (1964). Introductory expositions are given by Kerlinger (1973); Mueller, Schuessler, and Costner (1970); Nie, Bent, and Hull (1970); and Armor and Couch (1972).

A large number of recent articles deal with special topics in regression which are of potential interest to the analyst considering its use. Goldberger and Jochem (1961) discuss step-regression techniques and the analysis of residuals. Goldberger (1961) reviews issues in the allocation of variation in step regression. McGee and Carleton (1970) provide an additional discussion of step-regression problems. Blalock (1965) provides an excellent discussion of the concept of statistical interaction in explanatory models, and in Blalock (1963) the problem of high intercorrelations among predictors (multicollinearity) is reviewed.

Farrar and Glauber (1967) provide an extended treatment of the same topic. Fuguitt and Lieberson (1974) discuss problems of spurious correlation relating to the use of ratio measures and difference scores in regression. Costner and Wager (1965) discuss problems related to dichotomized variables. The use of a dichotomous dependent variable is also reviewed by Neter and Maynes (1970). Bohrnstedt and Carter (1971) review the robustness of regression technique when its assumptions are violated. Overall and Spiegel (1969) discuss the use of regression in dealing with experimental or quasi-experimental designs. Dummy variables are used to represent the design. A good example of the use of regression in survey analysis is given by Blau and Duncan (1967).

In *dummy variable regression*, nominal or ordinal predictors can be used along with interval variables. For such variables each class except one is represented as a separate variable in the equation. Each of these dummy variables is coded 1 if the observation is a member of that class; otherwise, it is coded zero. If the observation is a member of the omitted class, all variables for the set are coded zero. Generally, the excluded class is a large and fairly typical group. The unstandardized regression coefficients can be interpreted as discrepancies between the means of the classes represented by the dummy variables and the mean of the excluded class. The technique also permits curvilinear predictors to be represented with no restrictions on the form of the relationship. Interaction between two sets of dummy variables can be represented by "and's" and "or's."

General expositions of dummy-variable regression techniques can be found in most of the general treatments of multiple regression; in particular, Johnston (1972) and Cohen (1968). Other general expositions include Ward (1962), Bottenberg and Ward (1963), Fennessey (1968), Burke and Schuessler (1974), and Dunkelberg (1973). Sweeney and Ulveling (1972) relate the regression statistics to conventional regression parameters. Boyle (1966) shows the correspondence to Coleman's (1964) effect parameters. Melichar (1965) provides a lucid exposition of the relationships between dummy-variable regression and the corresponding analysis-of-variance formulation (multiple classification analysis). Other general expositions are developed by Jennings (1967) and by Bradley (1968). Kish and Frankel (1970) deal with sampling error problems in multiple classification and dummy-variable regression. Brownlee (1960, Chap. 18) develops useful F-tests for interaction in dummy-variable or multiple-classification-analysis models. Kramer (1957) also provides some useful tests for the significance of the dummy-variable coefficients. Goldberger (1964, pp. 173–177, 218–231, 248–255) treats problems of relative importance and dummy dependent variables. Some examples of the uses of dummy variables in research are Morgan, Sirageldin, and Baerwaldt (1965); Jackson and Burke (1965); Cohen (1968b); Benus (1970); and Dunkelberg (1973).

In much survey data a multiple classification analysis formulation used with an interval or dichotomous dependent variable is more easily interpretable than conventional dummy-variable specification. Formula (8-12) indicates the equation used:

$$Y = M + a_1 + b_2 + \cdots + e. \tag{8-12}$$

As in the analysis of variance, the MCA model assumes that each criterion score is composed of a series of additive components, or main effects, corresponding to the particular category in which that observation stands on each predictor (Andrews et al., 1973). The main-effect coefficients are formulated as deviations from the grand mean. A least-squares procedure in which the constant term is constrained to the grand mean, the technique is appropriate for any mixture of nominal, ordinal, and interval predictors. The last are input as class intervals. Since survey data generally have intercorrelated predictors, part of each observed zero-order effect is really contributed by that variable's correlation with other predictors, so that conventional multidimensional analysis of variance is inapplicable. The MCA model fits a set of coefficients to obtain values for the a_i, b_j, etc., which fit the least-squares regression model, and which represent the effects of the variables in the desired form: that is, after adjustment for the effects of their intercorrelations. The proportion of variation explained by these main effects together provides a measure of the adequacy of the fit of the model in its entirety.

This formulation is the mathematical equivalent of dummy-variable regression methods, but is more easily interpretable because of the analysis-of-variance formulation and because the constant term has been constrained to the grand mean. It provides both profiles of effects and measures of relative importance, as well as handling missing information (just another class), nonlinear effects of interval predictors, and explanatory factors which could only be measured by ordinal or nominal scales. Ordinal predictors are essentially demoted to nominal levels. Its biggest limitation is the same as that of multiple regression, the need to determine in advance how various predictor variables are to be combined, where necessary, into interaction terms which will constitute the best possible specification (Morgan and Sonquist, 1963; Sonquist and Morgan, 1964; Sonquist, 1970; Sonquist et al., 1974). F-tests for interaction can be computed comparing the explained sum of squares with interaction terms substituted for main effects with that explained by main effects only. Some examples of its use include Morgan, Sirageldin, and Baerwaldt (1965) and Bachman (1970). Dunkelberg (1973) demonstrates the equivalence of MCA and dummy-variable regression.

Strategies in Explanatory Analysis One of the unsolved problems in multivariate modeling, whether using single- or simulateneous-equation path-analysis models, is the problem of how to deal with mixtures of variables. Another is how to deal with ordinal measures (Somers, 1962, 1970; Wilson, 1971). In the absence of a well-worked-out general theory of correlation, competing claims exist about the advisability of "promoting" ordinal measures of relationship to a higher (interval) level and then using multivariate statistics in which the strong measurement assumptions cannot be tested.

One school of thought exemplified by Nunnally (1967), Mayer (1972), and by Labovitz (1970) suggests that, in the absence of well-grounded ordinal multivariate techniques, research will be best served by promoting ordinal measures to interval. Under careful constraints, multiple regression and other powerful techniques can be used, provided that results are interpreted conservatively. Wilson (1971) takes the opposite stance. Hawkes (1971) has partially developed an integrated interval–ordinal–nominal multivariate rationale, but many questions remain unanswered.

Various means of coping with ordinal measures in explanatory models have been proposed. Lyons (1971) develops a method of dummy-variable regression coding for ordinal variables. Boyle (1970) discusses ordinality problems in path analysis. Smith (1974) proposes a complete set of ordinal analogues to interval path coefficients based on Hawkes' (1971) and Somers' (1970) rationales.

At the present juncture, it is clear that, when the dependent variable is at the interval level, many techniques can be used. Dummy-variable coding can handle both nominal and ordinal predictors (Lyons, 1971). When the dependent variable is nominal, dummy-variable discriminant function analysis can handle any combination of levels of predictor measurement. If, in addition, all predictors are demoted to nominal status, then MCTA or any other procedure for dealing with all nominal variables can be used. However, the amount of information lost through demotion and the consequences of this loss are unknown.

When the dependent variable is ordinal, it can be demoted to nominal status and the nominal procedures such as MNA or DFA can be used. Alternatively, it can be promoted to interval status. It is not clear whether promotion or demotion is preferable, however.

If the Hawkes– Somers–Smith proposals become more solidly grounded, the foundation will have been laid for dealing with any combination of predictors and dependent variable without promotion or demotion. But until the work receives further mathematical elaboration, analysts using this frame of reference doubtless will need to buttress conclusions drawn from models with promoted or demoted variables with additional evidence, such as consistency with other findings, deductions from the fitted model that prove out, validation of the model on a random-half sample, and replication of the study on new data.

Clearly, it is highly desirable to devote considerable effort to achieving interval measurement on variables that are to be used as dependent variables (Wilson, 1971), and interval measurement is to be striven for on predictors. Since the controversy over the use of ordinal measures in path analysis has just begun, it seems wise in many substantive areas to focus on using single-equation models in an attempt to locate as many of the major sources of variation as possible. When the objective is one of maximizing explained variation, as it would be in this case, rather than making detailed substantive path interpretations of regression coefficients, promotion of ordinal variables to interval status will not have such serious consequences. These considerations all emphasize the need for viewing the ordinality and promotion controversies in a larger perspective. Until strategies are employed to uncover variables which, will explain a much larger proportion of variation than is typical of most current models, the analyst will not be able to determine whether the size of the error term is due primarily to measurement error, incorrect specification, or just omission from the study of important variables.

The person who has a small tolerance for error should avoid research. Explanatory data analysis is a series of difficult decisions, based on information by definition inadequate, in which later ones compound errors from those made earlier. The principal use of significance tests in explanatory analyses is in guarding against making decisions that are likely to have regrettable consequences and in reducing the likelihood of making certain kinds of errors.

Generally, survey samples are so large that almost any correlation which looks interesting substantively will be significantly different from zero, statistically. The real task is not to report statistically significant effects, but to locate major sources of variation The main issue in explanatory analysis is importance, not significance. Yet decisions must be made as to how to view relationships between variables, and reproducible rules need to be attached to them. Significance tests provide consistent, reproducible rules. They prevent ignoring the effect of one variable at a certain magnitude while focusing on another. They provide a means by which disagreements over whether or not a term is worth including in the model can be resolved when inspection does not produce immediate consensus. They provide a standard against which judgments of substantive significance can be made. Significance should be a necessary prerequisite for inclusion of a term in an explanatory model, but it is not sufficient. It is merely evidence that one mathematical model, a random process, does not fit the data and thus provides confidence in a decision to treat the term as relevant to the model under consideration.

Other factors may influence the size of a correlation or regression coefficient much more than chance variation, however, and although significance tests should be used when adding terms (particularly interaction terms) to a model, using them should not obscure the need to examine carefully other potential explanations of why the observed parameters are the size they are. Other candidates for inclusion in these explanations include measurement error, suppressor variables, nonlinearities, coding errors, and possibly even inadvertent use of unintended variables in the analysis.

Treatments of significance tests are presented by Acock, Libby, and Williams (1971); Henkel and Morrison (1971); Pierce (1971); Labovitz (1970, 1971); Morrison and Henkel (1970); Walster and Cleary (1970); Gold (1969); Winch and Campbell (1969); Morrison (1969); Rulon and Brooks (1968); and Kruskal (1968). Finifter (1972) explores the use of random-sample replication (jackknifing) as an alternative to significance tests in drawing conclusions about parameter values. Confidence intervals based on jackknife techniques will doubtless prove more useful in the long run than significance tests for both descriptive and explanatory analyses.

Explanatory analyses are plagued by the presence of missing values. When more than about 30 per cent of a variable is missing, there is enough question about its reliability and validity to suggest that the analyst should simply discard it from use. Yet, when the data are to be used, explanatory analysis techniques must be adapted to deal with them. A prerequisite is that missing data codes be separable and identifiable. Assignment was discussed earlier in this chapter and in Chapter 7. Several alternative treatments were reviewed, including assignment via an actuarial table based on previous multivariate analysis, pairwise exclusion from correlation computations, exclusion of an entire case, and assignment from a random-number distribution, either normally distributed or with the same shape as the cases with valid data. Some authors recommend assigning the mean of the valid observations. Another alternative is assignment of the mean and coding of a dummy variable indicating whether or not the factor was assigned. Including the dummy variable in the analysis retains all the information. Probably the best compromise, when engaged in an explanatory analysis, is to assign a random number from a normal distribution with the same mean, standard deviation, and range as the known observations. This represents unknown information as "white noise," and should have a minimal disrupting effect on estimates of that variable's effects on dependent variables, since it is uncorrelated with other variables. This can be accomplished using a recoding procedure with a random-number generator early in the study. When data are missing from a dependent variable, the observation should simply be excluded from the analysis. In the latter case, it may be useful to perform a discriminant function analysis on a dummy variable which is coded 1 for missing data on the original dependent variable and zero for the non-missing-data cases. Then information can be extracted to define the population groups to which the model applies.

The handling of missing data for explanatory analyses differs from that appropriate for analyses in which the objectives are conceptual clarification or description. In the latter cases, it may be better to compute the multiple regression of each item on all the remaining items, using the data for which all the variables are known, and then to estimate the missing values from these equations. Problems in handling missing data are given a careful review by Elashoff (1970), Miller (1970), Siegle (1967), and Afifi and Elashoff (1966, 1967).

When surveys are used to study interacting groups of people, such as work groups in organizations, union locals, discussion groups, or graduate student associations in university departments, individual observations can be classified according to the characteristics of the environment in which they function. Even when surveys are based on national samples, modern technology makes possible the merging of census and survey data so that observations can be classified according to the characteristics of the neighborhood in which they live. For instance, median income in the census tract is a typical such variable. Every observation from a particular group is simply assigned the value of a parameter describing the group. Since some variables can characterize both an individual and the group in which that individual functions, correlations can be computed on a group or on an individual basis. The former are often termed "ecological correlations," and this discussion will not be concerned with them.[56] Blau (1960); Davis (1961); Davis, Spaeth, and Huson (1961); Lazarsfeld and Menzel (1961); and Tannenbaum and Bachman (1964) put forth strategies for assessing the impact of group structures on individual behavior. The essential thrust is that of correlating behaviors Y and X at the individual level while controlling for X at the group level. Sills (1961) provides a substantive example. The logic is further developed by Werts and Linn (1968); Lipset, Trow, and Coleman (1970); and by Coleman (1970). Harder and Pappi (1970); provide a multiple regression framework for incorporating *contextual variables* of this type into an explanatory model. Kish (1965) reviews sampling problems related to the selection of such groups.

The implications for the data processing are that variables must be created at the individual level in a form suitable for *aggregation* to the group level. Then computation of measures of central tendency and dispersion must take place at the group level. These variables are then imputed downward to every observation in the group.

The first step is a straightforward index construction or variable-generation problem. The second involves computation of possibly a great many statistics, depending on how many groups there are. The third may also be conceptualized as a variable-generation problem. The imputed values are assigned as a function of the group identifier variable associated with each observation. The data-processing problems stem from the fact that if there are a large number of groups, this variable-generation procedure is likely to be extremely complex. It can be simplified by first sorting the observations into sequence by group, computing all the required group statistics and saving them in a file in which there is one record per group. Then both the original file and the group file are reread, and since they are in the same order (by group number), the assignment is straightforward. This procedure generally requires the use of special-purpose programs, as aggregation, group-level computation, and storage of parameters followed by imputation, are not always available as part of the statistical packages in general use.

Untangling the joint effects of correlated independent variables is the main reason for using least-squares techniques such as MCA or regression. At stake are immediate questions about whether a given predictor should be included in an explanatory model or abandoned, and ultimate questions about which predictors subject to policy decisions are the most likely to produce changes in the distribution of *Y*-values if they are changed. If one variable explains a relatively large amount of variation in another, one may wish to study it further, to look

[56] For an examination of the problems associated with making inferences about individuals from partially aggregated data, see Goodman (1959), Robinson (1950), Lord (1967), Slatin (1969), Theil (1954), and Cartwright (1969).

in greater detail to discover what it is about having a particular value that makes for an extreme value of the dependent variable. On the other hand, if it explains little of the variation after the effects of other variables are held constant, one may choose to look elsewhere for factors that will help to develop an adequate model.

Because the assessment of relative importance is so central to explanatory analyses, the problem has received a great deal of attention. In this exposition the recommendations of various writers will not be summarized; rather, illustrative points of view will be listed. An important point is the fundamental insight of path analysis that variables can have both direct and indirect effects on a dependent variable, the latter deriving from their influence on other independent variables, which themselves affect the dependent variable directly.

In addition to those writers noted in previous sections who dealt directly with multiple regression as a technique, others have focused on the relative merits of alternative methods of assessment of explained variation. Chase (1960) gives a method for apportioning variation among predictor variables. Blalock (1961) considered the topic in an extensive review. Hoffman (1962) suggested that the improvement in explained variation when each predictor is added to the equation is the best measure. Wisler (1968) also provided a review of alternative methods. Werts (1968, 1970) raised the problem of the influence of specification on the way in which explained variation and apparent importance is distributed among predictors. Blalock (1968) discussed the relative merits of standardized and unstandardized measures. Bell (1968) provided a general review. Ward (1969), Linn and Werts (1969), and Werts and Linn (1969) all discuss alternatives. Cain and Watts (1970) discuss the practical limitations of making policy inferences from standardized regression coefficients.

Duncan (1970) makes a persuasive argument that the establishment of a satisfactory system for partialing out explained variation is of far less importance than gaining an adequate understanding of the implications of alternative specifications of the variables. He argues that no interpretation of explained variation is possible at all except on the basis of specific assumptions about the causal structure of the system of variables. According to Duncan, judgments that result in the elimination of a variable from the equation(s) are, in fact, based on either implicit or explicit causal assumptions which should be carefully included by the analyst in an explication of the rationale for the decision. The contribution of path analysis, in his view, is to make explicit the need for the formulation of an integrated and explicit set of causal assumptions that must precede the meaningful allocation of variation. An important point to be added is that in the presence of large amounts of unexplained variation, large standardized regression coefficients probably indicate that the variable in question is correlated with a number of major explanatory factors that have not yet been included in the model. When this is the case, tentative assignations of explanatory power should serve primarily as clues to what factors these might be, not as the basis for closely reasoned theoretical argument.

In many instances, the analyst seeks to explain a single phenomenon as a function of a set of predictors. Restricting the analysis in this way may be a reasonable strategy because not enough is known about potential causal factors even to identify many of them, because measurement precision and reliability have not progressed to the point where multiple-equation models are a reasonable objective, or because it appears impossible to establish agreed-upon criteria for specifying causal priorities sufficient to meet multiple-equation assumptions. Single-equation model builders then look to obtaining clues as to what the causal ordering of the obtained variables may be, seeking eventual establishment of a multiple-equation model.

According to Heise (1969), a specific objective in an explanatory survey may be to define an entire set of path equations which permit predictions of how changes in one of the variables impact other variables in the system. The causal paths in the system are to be identified, and parameters estimated, so that the amount of influence each variable has on the others is depicted with considerable precision. Spurious correlations must be accounted for, and chains of causation and conditioning variables (interactions) need to be specified. Of interest is the attachment of a value to the contribution of each path between variables, to be used in explaining variation in those farther down the chain. The emphasis is on the system of variables as an integrated whole, not just with a single dependent variable.

The model must be theoretically reasonable as well as reproducible. It must reproduce the observed data well and make good predictions. Of particular importance is the precision allowed by the model in breaking down correlations into parts which may have several underlying processes behind them. Assessing the impact of several underlying processes on all the factors involved makes possible the assessment of the impact on all variables of a change in any one or several. It is also possible to make explicit how a change in the structure of the system affects the behavior of the units studied.

Path analysis is adaptable to both over time and cross-sectional data. In studies over time or even in experiments, variables observed at earlier times can be correlated with later behavior. In the cross-section study, a snapshot in time is taken, and the assumption is made that certain persons have experienced some types of conditions and others not. Correlational techniques are used to untangle the complex web of current behavior and configurations of past experience. The further assumption is made that experiences in the past which influenced presently observed values can be replicated in the present—in other words, if changes are made in the experience patterns of other people, they will become like those studied in the past.

As with single-equation models, there are two analytic tasks, specification and estimation. In addition to the simpler specification tasks listed above, questions of causal priority must be addressed in detail. Variables must be ordered on this criterion—a task easy in principle, but difficult in practice, since verbally stated theory is not always equal to the task. The scope of the model must also be defined.

The second task is to estimate the unknown path coefficients from available empirical data. To do this it is necessary to make several assumptions. One is that disturbances (unexplained variation coming from outside the system of variables) are uncorrelated. Every disturbance term is assumed to represent variables not in the model and not correlated with those in it. Put another way, this assumption is that all background exogenous variables having an impact on those dependent variables in the system have been included in the model.

Specifically, the assumptions required are:

1. Functions are linear and additive. Variables involved in interactions have been replaced by appropriate terms.
2. There are no feedback loops in the system, although lagged correlations can be used.
3. Causal chains and priorities are clearly specified and capable of being agreed upon.
4. Disturbance terms (unexplained variation) associated with each dependent variable are uncorrelated (i.e., all major sources of variation are incorporated into the analysis).
5. The usual multiple regression assumptions are met (observations independent of one another, reasonable approximations to interval scales, homoscedasticity, absence of severe multicollinearity, etc.).
6. Variables must have high reliability.

The assumption that the sources of variation for each dependent variable have uncorrelated disturbance terms implies a level of conceptual distinctness frequently absent when several attitude measures are to be used as predictors.

These assumptions can be weakened considerably without making the technique unusable, provided it is made clear that the interpretations have correspondingly less confidence behind them. Curvilinear correlations can be straightened out using transformations. Interaction terms may be used instead of raw variables. Feedback loops can, in fact, be dealt with but at the cost of considerable mathematical complexity. Even when it is not possible to get agreement on causal priorities, the technique may be useful to formalize the differences in conceptualization and to gain insight into the implications of accepting alternative models. Given a clearly specified system, it is possible to identify those causal linkages which appear to have zero path coefficients, and thus to simplify the associated theoretical model.

The assumptions required for path analysis are not really very different from those that usually underlie older cross-tabulation techniques used in explanatory analyses; they are simply more explicit. When they can be met, the precision provided by the method enables the formulation of well-articulated and clear explanatory models.

Although causal inference models based on path analysis fit some data well, the assumptions required mean that much research is not eligible to use them. The offending assumption is often the specification of causal ordering or the need for building feedback loops into the model. The implications are not that other techniques should be used instead for explanatory model building, but that the high-level objectives achieved when the assumptions are met are beyond reach. Perhaps an important thrust of path analysis has been to legitimize the idea that the central problem in explanatory analyses is not to test hypotheses carefully deduced from well-defined theory, but to unscramble the effects of a multiplicity of variables related in obscure ways to the phenomenon to be explained. This invariably involves an iterative series of eviscerations of data, followed by model construction efforts. The view is toward convergence on a model that has face validity, is tied adequately to other theory, fits the data well, and is replicable.

In the simple, recursive case, the task of constructing a complete model from a set of variables is to specify and then estimate a set of equations. The relationships among the equations and the variables entering into them are asymmetrical. The ordering of the variables must correspond to an agreed-upon causal sequence. The system of linear equations has the form

$$\begin{aligned} Y_1 &= e_1 \\ Y_2 &= a_{21}Y_1 + e_2 \\ &\vdots \\ Y_n &= a_{n1}Y_1 + \cdots + a_{n-1}Y_{n-1} + e_n. \end{aligned} \tag{8-13}$$

The e_i are random variables which are assumed to be independent of each other. The Y's are causally ordered in the sense that any Y_i is affected by the variables preceding it and, in turn, affects those following it. In this framework, zero-order correlations are spurious if the relevant path coefficient is zero.

The path coefficients are standardized regression coefficients (betas), and the technique can be viewed as an extension of multiple regression.[57] The important extension is to provide a framework for considering all of the dependent variables simultaneously. Each is considered once as a dependent variable and as an independent variable, as many times as the theoretical formulation deems to be appropriate.

Path diagrams constitute a convenient shorthand for representing the system of relationships which conform to these assumptions. The causal relations

[57] The issues of interpreting standardized versus unstandardized regression coefficients in path analysis have not been resolved; for example, see Schoneberg (1972).

are represented by unidirectional arrows. Noncausal relationships between exogenous variables in the system are distinguished by curved, two-headed arrows. Residual variation is represented by a unidirectional arrow leading to the dependent variable. The quantities entered next to each arrow are the numerical values of the path and correlation coefficients of the specified causal and correlational relations.

The path coefficients measure the direct influence on the dependent variable in terms of the fraction of its variance due to the independent variable in question, when other factors are held constant. More specifically, the squared path coefficient measures the proportion of the variance in the dependent variable for which the independent variable is directly responsible. The path model is represented by the set of structural equations which are estimated using least-squares equations. A problem of some importance is whether or not the parameters of the structural model can be estimated uniquely from observed data. If there is a simple one-to-one correspondence between the parameters of the structural equations and the least-squares estimators, this is no problem. Not all models have this property, however, and over- or underidentification is often a problem. The unexplained variation in each dependent variable is assumed to be entirely uncorrelated with variables in the system and corresponds to the commonly defined coefficient of alienation.

When the system is exactly identified, the standardized path coefficients and path regression coefficients can be estimated by the standardized and raw partial regression coefficients from ordinary multiple regression. The correlation of an exogenous variable and the dependent variable is the sum of its direct effect (the path coefficient from that variable to the dependent variable) and the indirect effects it has through its correlations with other exogenous variables and their path coefficients. A compound path coefficient is the product of the basic path coefficients between the variables in question.

The assumptions of path analysis enable the construction of well-defined criteria for defining direct and indirect effects in terms of explained variation. The total effect of an exogenous variable on an endogenous variable is simply the correlation between the two. The direct effect is measured by the path coefficient between the two variables, and the indirect effect is measured by the product of the correlation between the exogenous variable with another exogenous variable times the path coefficient of the latter with the dependent variable. Path analysis thus provides a method of assessing the direct and indirect effects of explanatory factors in a multivariate causal chain. The total aggregate effect of an exogenous variable takes place through all its direct and indirect paths. In this frame of reference, the concept of explained variation has meaning only in the context of a given causal structure.

In recursive systems such as that illustrated above, multiple regression equations may be used to estimate each of the path coefficients directly. In those cases where the form of the structural equations deviates from this simple model, other methods, such as two-stage least squares, must be used.[58] Johnston (1972) provides an excellent introduction to 2SLS.

Path-analysis logic and multiple regession have formed a strong basis for the study of change through panel surveys. An early statement by Zeisel of the panel study as an explanatory tool is contained in Denzin (1970). Additional treatments of multiple regression in the study of change are contained in Harris (1967), including a review by Lord (1967) of elementary models of change. Cross-lagged correlational techniques were proposed by Pelz and Andrews (1964). Further discussions assessing causal direction in panel data are given by Yee (1968) and by Rozelle and Campbell (1969).

Path-analysis techniques were brought to bear on change problems in an article by Boudon (1967); and articles by Duncan (1969), Heise (1970), and Goldberger (1970) continued the development of panel applications. Pelz and Lew (1970) provide an illuminating example of Heise's (1970) techniques. Duncan (1972) considered the impact of unmeasured variables and emphasized the need for adequate model specification if panel analysis is to lead to causal inferences that are not misleading. Hibbs (1974) considered problems of estimation and causal inferences in time-series models. Other treatments of the analysis of panel data in explanatory analyses include Coleman (1968), Werts and Linn (1970), and Cronbach and Furby (1970). Bohrnstedt (1970) provides a lucid overview of problems in the area. Davidson (1971) compares several panel-analysis strategies in a realistic setting.

A parallel problem to that of causal analysis in panel data is that of evaluating the impact of an action program designed to achieve some specific change (Weiss, 1972a, 1972b). In studies such as this, the crucial problems are

[58] Introductory treatments of path analysis are given by Nygreen (1971), Land (1969), Heise (1969), and Duncan (1969). A classic exposition is that given by Duncan (1966). Background and early treatment of path-analysis topics are given by Wright (1934), Englehart (1936), Tukey (1954), Wright (1954), and Wold (1964). Much more extended treatments are provided in books by Blalock (1964), Lerner (1965), Linn and Werts (1969), Goldberger (1969), and Blalock (1971). Blalock (1966) considers problems associated with identification. Boudon (1965) proposes certain modifications to earlier proposals which were critiqued by Goldberger (1970). Hilgendorf and Irving (1967) suggested the combined uses of path and linkage analysis in modeling. Land (1970) discusses problems associated with assessing the impact of unmeasured variables, as did Hauser and Goldberger (1971). Forbes and Tufte (1968) considered questions of interaction and multicollinearity and provided a critical review of unsophisticated use of the technique. They underlined the need to specify models carefully before estimation. Polk (1962) provided a discussion of asymmetric models. Schoenberg (1972) raised questions about the use of standardized versus unstandardized path coefficients. An example of the application of the technique is provided by Werts (1968). Other general discussions include those by Li (1968) and Blalock (1967). Examples of the use of path-analytic techniques in various disciplines include education (Werts, 1968; Hauser, 1971; Yee, 1968), political science (Goldberger, 1966; Alker, 1966), and sociology (Duncan, Haller, and Portes, 1968; Hauser, 1969; Spaeth, 1968; Sewell and Shah, 1967).

to assess whether or not specific changes took place, whether they appear to be due to participation in the program being evaluated, and whether unanticipated consequences occurred. When data are collected at several points in time on experimental and control groups, or, in a weaker design, just on the experimental group, path-analysis techniques developed for working with explanatory models based on panel data have direct applicability. The dimensions along which change was to have taken place are specified as dependent (endogenous) variables measured at the end of the experiment. Other variables appear as endogenous variables characterizing the program and the participant's role in it at earlier times. The characteristics of the participant at the start of the experiment comprise the set of exogenous variables.

The most frequently available computer program is generally one for multiple regression. Hence, if the assumptions required for simple recursive-path models are met, the estimation computations are straightforward. However, this may mean that data collected by survey techniques must be assigned, since many regression programs have no missing-data capability. This may require a special-purpose assignment program written expressly for that purpose and may require advance computation of means and standard deviations.

The analyst who wishes to use structural equations with correlated error terms, lagged variables, and so on, must generally rely on two-stage least-squares techniques. These programs are relatively common also, but will not generally be known to those using survey methods. Generally developed for use with econometric models using simultaneous equations, they can usually be obtained through economics departments and econometrics laboratories, rather than through more usual sources of survey data-processing programs. Rectangularization of panel data files is generally a prerequisite. If interactive facilities are available, routines which make use of correlation matrices as input may be particularly helpful, since it is often useful to experiment with respecification and reestimation of models. Alternatively, it may be necessary to return to raw data matrices if these efforts require cross-product terms.

If a two-stage least-squares program is not available, ordinary multiple-regression programs can be used to regress each endogenous variable on the exogenous variables prior to it in the structure and to replace its raw values with predicted values from the regression equation. Even if the regression programs compute residuals and predicted values, however, the latter are often printed instead of being stored in machine-readable files, so this process is liable to require an extra keypunch and match step. Alternatively, it may be possible to modify the output routines of these programs to store predicted values in a file, and then to merge them back into the file containing the original raw variables. The results are used as independent variables for estimating endogenous variables on down the line. Smith (1972) and Nygreen (1971) discuss interactive computer routines.

Control Parameters in Regression Programs

Since the most frequent vehicle for model estimation is likely to be a multiple-regression program, a review is presented of the decisions that will have to be made in using one. Not all programs have each "handle" mentioned here, but good ones should. Most provide for user control over input, computational options, printing options, and residual or matrix output to be stored in machine-readable form.

Input

1. Is a correlation or raw data matrix to be used?
2. If raw data are to be used, what format should the file be written in? Is rectangularization necessary?
3. What are the options for deleting missing information? Is a pairwise deletion of cross-products available? Is there a parameter that can be set to terminate the run if there is too much missing data? Must it be preassigned?
4. Are contextual variables to be used? If so, will preliminary aggregation, computation, and imputation steps be required to store the contextual variables as a file?
5. What sample subsets are to be used in the computation? How are they defined in terms of a monothetic rule specifying the union or intersection of sample subsets? Can the regression program select the proper subset from the file, or must this be done by a prior step?

Specification of the Equation

1. Which variables are to be used as independent variables, dependent variables, weights? What program options are there for multiple dependent variables or repeated regressions over sample subsets?
2. What indices, ratios, cross-products, or other terms must be generated? Is the capability included in the regression package itself? Can dummy variables be generated?

Control over Computational Sequences

1. What controls are there over the sequence in which variables enter the equation? Can they be entered singly and in blocks under user control? If the system is a step regression that selects the next variable on the basis of an *F*-test, does it step up, increasing the number of variables,

or does it step down, deleting useless variables? Can the user enter a block of variables and then enter successive ones either under parameter control or by means of selection through F-tests?

2. What is the maximum number of variables? Cases? What is the criterion for stopping the entry of variables? (Typical criteria include adding variables until the increase in explained variation is less than a constant or until a value of Student's t is less than a constant; adding k variables; and adding k variables and then using other criteria.) A regression program should terminate if a pivot element in its matrix inversion is detected as too small, or if the determinant of the matrix approaches zero (e.g., $d < .00001$ in single precision and $d <$ .00000001 in double precision). A desirable option is to permit use of the maximum pivot element for entry of a variable if intermediate steps are not to be used.
3. Can F-levels be used to enter and remove variables? Is an option provided to restrict the constant term to zero (available for use only if raw data input is used)? Are options for the use of sample or population formulas provided?
4. Is there an option for pairwise deletion of missing data? If there is, correlations are then based on different N's. According to Armor and Couch (1972), more than 30 per cent missing data on a given variable is likely to cause serious trouble. Error terms in path analysis are likely to be correlated if means are used to estimate missing values. Observations with missing data on the dependent variable must be excluded as well as those that are inapplicable on any variables (more problems for multiple-equation models).

Output

1. Are there options for printed output for univariate (not pairwise) means, standard deviations, N's, maximum and minimum values? Is run labeling provided?
2. Are pairwise correlations and sample-size statistics available as an option if pairwise deletion is used? In this case, is printing of the variance–covariance matrix also available? Is the matrix of $(k - 1)$-order partial correlations available as an option?
3. Do the available options include variable labeling, unstandardized regression coefficients with their standard errors, and standardized coefficients and their standard errors? Can one obtain a t-test value for each coefficient and its degrees of freedom, the $(k - 1)$-order partial correlation coefficient between that variable and the dependent variable, and the multiple correlation coefficient (squared) between the

predictor and all $k - 1$ other predictors? Do the options include a printout of the increase in explained variation due to entering the last variable, explained variation for the final equation and this quantity adjusted for degrees of freedom, the determinant of the matrix, the constant term, the reason for stopping, an F-level for the significance of the entire regression, and its degrees of freedom and significance level? The standard deviation and mean of the residuals should also be available.

4. Do printed output options include plots of the residuals against any variable in the regression, an option to normalize the residuals to a normal (0, 1) distribution, and the Durbin–Watson statistic?
5. Does optional machine-readable output include predicted values, residuals, and the ability to transfer a case identifier and any or all variables from the input file to an output file together with the residuals and predicted values? Is there control over accuracy and rounding of residuals? Is there provision for assignment of missing-data codes, for undefined predicted values and residuals due to missing data, and for deletions arising from inapplicable cases?
6. Is output of the correlation matrix and vectors of means and standard deviations in a standard machine-readable format available as an option?

SETTING UP AN ANALYSIS SEQUENCE

The variables measured in a survey do not necessarily correspond exactly to the attributes of critical theoretical import to the study. Indeed, one of the major objectives of the analysis is often to discover those measurable attributes which appear to be most closely tied to the phenomenon of interest. Thus, the setting up of an anlaysis plan requires translating a research problem, stated in terms of underlying concepts, into a far more precise statistical question usually involving both variable generation and descriptive or explanatory statistics.

For example, Katona, Mandell, and Schmiedeskamp (1971, p. 19) sought to ascertain whether there were differences in the use of credit by blacks and whites. The alternative statistical translations are: "Are black families more likely than whites to have installment debt obligations?" "For families with installment debt obligations, is the amount of such obligation larger for blacks or smaller?" Research questions are translated into propositions about the values of variables or the shape of the distribution of installment debt outstanding. The conceptualization of the research question permits an answer couched in statistical terms. It is translated eventually into the language of specific variables to which the statistics are to be applied. (See Table 8-12.) Units of

TABLE 8-12 Amount of Installment Debt Outstanding by Race[a] (Percentage Distribution of Families)

Debt Status	Race: White	Race: Black[b]
Have none	53	38
Have debt	47	62
$1–199	7	17
$200–499	7	14
$500–999	9	11
$1000–1999	11	10
$2000 or more	13	10
Total	100	100
Number of cases	(2250)	(279)
Mean debt for those having debt	$1320	$950
Median debt for those having debt	$1040	$500

[a] Adapted from George Katona, Lewis Mandell, and Jay Schmiedeskamp, *1970 Survey of Consumer Finances*, Institute for Social Research, University of Michigan, Ann Arbor: 1971, p. 29, by permission.

[b] Forty-seven other families of other races were excluded from the analysis.

analysis are defined which reflect the conceptualization (the family is the principal economic unit, with single individuals being counted as one type of "family"). The variables involved are race and installment debt outstanding at the time of the interview. Although obtaining the answer to a single question is not a very complex analysis plan, it illustrates the type of question that is put together with others to make up such a plan. The units of analysis are defined, the appropriate form of the variables chosen, the appropriate statistical technique chosen, and certain observations excluded as inappropriate. In this example, the authors elected to present the distribution of the amount of debt owed rather than to compare means or medians. They concluded:

> "Black families are far more likely to have some installment debt obligations than white families, although the amount of their obligation is generally smaller. . . . 62 percent of black families have some installment debt outstanding, as compared to only 47 percent of white families. However, 24 percent of white families have at least $1000 of installment debt as against 20 percent of black families. . . (Katona et al., p. 19)."

The plan for the analysis had to specify which variables were to be used as input into a statistical procedure, and which recoding or variable-generation procedures were to be used (debt was collapsed into intervals). It required that all debt information be consolidated into total outstanding debt, and assumed that this had all been done in advance. Groups other than whites and blacks were excluded from the analysis. In addition, it was necessary to specify the way in which percentages were to be computed. Since the analysis was intended as descriptive, no measure of relationship between race and pattern of outstanding debt was specified: no control variables were needed for the analysis. After the data were organized for tabular presentation, the findings were translated back into the original language in which the problem had been phrased.

When such a task is first started, the analyst must consider a variety of specific statistical and technical details. A number of these are listed in Figure 8-14. They range from problems related to the data, its distribution, measurement level, and the sampling, to computational problems associated with the way in which survey data interact with statistical programs, to technical problems associated with the use of computer output. Some of the more common problems are inventoried in Figure 8-15.

Statistical Problems Related to the Data

Extreme cases do occur—wealthy individuals are interiewed, some people live to a very old age. A few extreme cases exert a disproportionate amount of influence on least-squares procedures and the data need to be examined for their presence before substantive conclusions are drawn about means, variances, correlation coefficients, or slopes of regression lines involving these cases. In explanatory analyses it may sometimes be better to omit them from the computations and restrict the definition of the population to which the conclusions apply. In addition, some statistical programs require that input variables be limited in their range (e.g., negative numbers may not be permitted, maximum values may be limited to 9999, etc.) Thus, transformations such as conversion to z- or t-scores may be required before a given program can be used.[59]

Not infrequently the researcher will discover that the survey has produced too few observations to compute statistics for a particular subgroup of the population. In many cases, little or nothing can be done to correct this problem except to incorporate this group into another one. A related problem is one of badly skewed distributions. One convenient method for minimizing the latter is to convert variables into class intervals based on percentile points in the distribution. Then, if the distribution is badly skewed, an extra amount of detail may be included at one end. For example, Katona et al. (1967, p. 64) report home-ownership patterns among families in each income quintile; that is, for the bottom 20 per cent of the families arranged in order by family income, the next 20 per cent, and so on. This technique has the advantage of equalizing the number of cases in each category. Had it been necessary to preserve the skewness of

[59] In the z-score transformation, the variable has mean zero and standard deviation 1; in the t-score version, the resultant variable has a mean of 50 and a standard deviation of 10; thus, negative scores are avoided.

CHECKLIST OF LOGICAL AND STATISTICAL PROBLEMS WITH SURVEY DATA ANALYSIS

I. Data problems
   A. Distributional problems
      1. Extreme cases, range problems.
      2. Small N's.
      3. Skewed distributions.
   B. Measurement problems
      1. Missing data.
      2. Inapplicable variables.
      3. Correlated missing data and "inaps".
      4. Correlated reliability and validity problems.
      5. Scales that didn't meet the assumptions of their scaling model very. well. Absence of multiple measures of important variables.
      6. Classifications or ordinal scales, as opposed to interval or ratio.
      7. Non-linearity of measures.
   C. Sampling problems
      1. Multi-stage probability samples may lead to weighting or explosion of cases.
      2. Response rate problems may lead to weighting or explosion of cases.
      3. Difficult interpretation of tests of significance.
      4. Underestimation of variation.

II' Problems associated with survey statistical programs
      1. Serious failures of data to meet assumptions required by models.
      2. Truncation and rounding error
      3. Heteroscedasticity.
      4. Non-linearity of relationships.
      5. Non-additivity of relationships.
      6. Failures of programs to provide all relevant statistics.
      7. Correctness and appropriateness of formulas.
      8. Poor or no temporary variable generation capability.
      9. Restrictions on number of variables.
      10. Amount of time and storage required to run the problem.
      11. Complex set-up parameter structure inadequately documented
      12. Input incompatibility with other programs.
      13. Dependence on locally programmed subroutines.

III. Output problems
      1. Failure of programs to provide exactly the statistics desired.
      2. Poor labelling and annotation of report, difficult to decipher.
      3. Failure to provide references to texts or articles reporting on the characteristics of the algorithms used.
      4. Output incompatibility with other programs, especially ability to output factor scores or regression residuals in a form suitable for re-entry into the original file.
      5. Failure to provide options for output of intermediate results.
      6. Poor error messages.

Figure 8-14 Checklist of Logical and Statistical Problems with Survey Data Analysis

CHECKLIST FOR COMPLETION OF SETTING UP AN ANALYSIS

I. Prerequisites completed:

A. All preliminary processing has been completed

1. Work files constructed.
2. All variables needed for the whole analysis included.
3. Proper cases included, subset definitions worked out.
4. All data have been cleaned, missing data taken care of and assignments made, no illegal characters.
5. Codes for all variables are up-to-date and all codebooks properly updated.
6. Information on possible errors in measurement in the variables to be used has been included in the workfile.
7. Necessary subset descriptor variables, attribute descriptors, weights, explanatory variables, multiple dependent variables, covariates, Intervening variables, contextual variables, suppressors, contingent or conditioning variables have been included.
8. Raw variables for constructing indices not yet constructed have been included.
9. Variables are in proper form (e.g. class intervals, scales, dummy variables, etc.).

B. Data are in appropriate rectangular or other structure needed for the analysis. Provisions for handling multi-valued or other list variables have been made and checked out.

II. Clearly worked-out set of objectives for the analysis has been drafted, discussed and finalized. Logical priorities and causal assumptions have been agreed upon.

III. Clear plan for computational sequence leading to the desired statistics is ready, including some dummy tables. The level of familiarity with the statistical techniques to be used and their robustness is adequate. Sampling errors and significance test problems have been resolved.

IV. Needed computer programs have had dry-runs made on them for test purposes, and staff familiarity with the control languages is adequate. Rounding errors or other numerical problems have been explored.

V. All file merging needed has been completed. Plans for merging of factor scores, contextual variables, residuals or predicted values have been completed.

VI. If the analysis plan is to replicate a previous analysis by another study, have all the variables been included which have codes which are as nearly identical an possible to the other study; can the data be broken into subsets that will replicate those?

VII. Attempts have been made to anticipate problems of conceptual overlap and multicollinearity, missing data, "inapplicable" codes, skewness, extreme cases, small N's, reliability of measures, correlated measurement errors, ranges for plots and graphs, weights.

VIII. Codes for factor scores, residuals, predicted values or aggregate files have been worked out, including substantive codes, inapplicable, missing data, variable names, decimal places, negative signs, character sets, record formats. File storage updates have been prepared for both printed and machine-readable files.

Figure 8-15 Checklist for Completion of Setting up an Analysis

the income distribution, the top quintile could have been divided into the two top deciles. An alternative is to collapse adjacent class intervals until adequate numbers of cases are achieved. A general rule, which we repeat here, is not to base any calculation of a mean or percentage on less than 30 cases, preferably 50. Class intervals generally should not be collapsed to create dichotomies simply to permit the use of easy-to-calculate statistics. It is desirable to maintain as much detail in the data as possible up to the 30- to 50-case rule. Collapsing a continuous variable into five to seven categories will retain almost all of the information contained in its distribution. Skewed distributions can also be made easier to use in multivariate analyses by using logarithm or square-root transformations. Descriptive analyses must also deal with a measurement problem put succinctly by Davis (1971, pp. 19–20); beware of one-variable survey findings unless they are based on ratio scales. Some surveys attempt to estimate the absolute amount of some characteristic of the population. But ordinal and interval scales have arbitrary zero points, and even nominal scales often have very arbitrary classification rules. Hence, the fundamental survey findings presented should generally involve at least a comparison between two subgroups in the sample with respect to the characteristic in question.

Missing information often presents formidable problems during the statistical analysis, and various ways of dealing with it have been discussed at various places in this book. In planning an analysis, the researcher will have to consider evidence as to whether the missing information is correlated or randomly distributed. If it is random, then assignment may be the most satisfactory procedure. But if it is correlated, the fact that respondents could not or would not answer questions may be highly important and the missing data code may require treatment as a substantive category. This generally requires earlier coding of "don't know" responses differently from inapplicable and substantive answers. Each no-answer type is simply treated as another category. When ordinal, interval, or ratio scales are employed, missing data must be assigned or omitted from the computations. The purposes of the analysis should influence the choice of missing-data handling procedures. Assignment by means of prediction equations or actuarial tables appears desirable when conceptual clarification or population description are the objectives. Assignment by means of random assignment from a distribution with the same mean and standard deviation as the known cases appears the best choice in an explanatory or hypothesis-testing analysis. In the long run, there is no substitute for careful measurement.

Codes reflecting the inapplicability of an attribute to a particular respondent may be even more troublesome than missing information. Such observations should not appear in a statistical analysis that purports to be explanatory. Rather, the model should be restricted in its application to the population for which they are defined and they should be excluded from the analysis. In a descriptive analysis, they can simply be placed in a separate category, excluded from the base of percentaged tables, and omitted from calculations of means and the like.[60]

The use of scales or single measures of an attribute that do not meet the underlying assumptions of the scaling model used may also produce problems during the analysis phase of the study. For example, if Guttman scales are used with items that actually have trace lines that correspond to the Likert or Thurstone models, correlations with other variables will be lowered. What happens to slopes or other specific patterns of the profiles of the relationships between two variables is not clear. Generally, the analyst should seek evidence that the variables are not burdened with problems like this before entering into the statistical analysis of the data. Far too many surveys receive complex and detailed interpretations of multivariate analyses using variables whose measurement is open to serious question.

Statistical Problems Related to Sampling

Multistage probability samples, especially those which are not self-weighting, present special problems. Observations are no longer independent, and conventional statistical assumptions associated with simple random sampling cannot be invoked. One reasonable approach to dealing with this is to normalize the weights to sum to the sample size, and then assume that estimates or variation are biased downward. Confidence intervals can be estimated that take the sampling design into account, however. (See Kish, 1965; Frankel, 1947.) If computer programs are not available that accept weighted data, it will be necessary to "explode" the data deck, using integral weights that will restore the proper proportions to the sample strata represented. This usually requires normalizing the weights so that all are integral, and then using a specially written computer program to duplicate as many copies of each unit of analysis as is specified by the integral weight. The analysis programs are then run with this augmented file as input. It is easy to see that the assumptions of independence of observations which underlie most significance tests are not met. Variances are biased downward. When using weights, the analyst is admonished to follow Kish (1965) or Frankel (1971) if feasible, and to use tests based on simple random sampling formulas if not: but, in the latter case, to interpret results very conservatively, and to report procedures faithfully and completely. Despite the fact that sampling designs often make the use of significance tests difficult, there remain good reasons for using them, albeit conservatively. When interpretation

[60] Meyers (1973) provides a good introductory discussion of the strategies of omission of the offending case, substitution of the mean of the valid observations, assignment of a random variate, prediction from other variables, and utilization of only those sets of observations for which all required values are present.

of the observed magnitudes of the correlation between variables is questioned by reasonable professional colleagues on the basis of inspection, some rules must be agreed upon. Otherwise, there is no basis for agreement on the substantive import of results. Moreover, scientific endeavors demand some consistency from the investigator. One relationship of a given size should not be ignored while another of similar magnitude is given substantive significance. The function of a statistical significance test in most survey situations is to provide an agreed-upon rule for decisions such as whether to treat two groups as the same or different, and whether to include a variable in a model or to discard it; significance tests keep researchers honest with themselves.

A significance test provides evidence that one mathematical model, a random process, does not fit the data. It answers the question, "Could the data reasonably have been produced by this model?" Having ruled this out, the analyst can then assume that the phenomena under study (as measured by the instruments) functioned in some way as to have generated the data. It is necessary to rule out the random model because research is almost always conducted on samples instead of on populations, and samples do produce slightly different results upon replication. The important point for the analysis plan is that the research questions really only start with statistical significance; they do not end there.

A related decision to be made at this point is the choice of a significance level. In much analysis of survey data, this functions principally as a rule for deciding whether or not to retain a variable in a model. As such, significance levels are agreed upon by a historical consensus-building process about what works well in practice. A 0.05 level of significance may be too conservative for much exploratory work. It may be better to take greater risks of falsely including variables in the models used than is permitted by this choice. In the last analysis, the researcher's attention must eventually be focused on the sizes of observed correlation coefficients and on ruling out other reasons for why the observed results came to be. This process must dispose of the arguments that measurement errors, uncontrolled variables, conceptual overlaps, coding and interviewing errors, differential response rates, and the like are responsible for the size of the observed correlation coefficient and the profile of relationships between variables. These sources of confusion in the findings ultimately may require as much attention as the possibility that random-sampling fluctuations may have something to do with the observed results.

Other Statistical and Mathematical Problems

Additional decisions that confront the analyst relate to the questions, "Can I use this particular statistic with my data? Do they meet its assumptions?" Such questions usually relate to ordinal measures. The reader is referred to

Nunnally's (1967) excellent discussion of "promoting" ordinal variables for use with statistical techniques requiring "interval" measures. Promotion may have two consequences, criticism from one's colleagues and misinterpretations of the slopes of the relationships, the latter resulting from nonlinear relationships to the underlying attributes they are supposed to measure. However, correlation coefficients are probably not seriously affected by promotion. The advantage is that, by promoting, the analyst is often enabled to use powerful multivariate techniques, thus obtaining leverage on the problem of too many explanatory variables. The risk of error is traded for multivariate power, which can be used if it is applied with caution and slopes are not interpreted in detail.

A further problem is overlap between the conceptual referents of various measures. An example illustrates the problem. It would surprise no one to discover a high correlation between the number of acres comprising a farm and the income received from crops grown on it. Acreage should be a reasonably good predictor of such income and can reasonably be termed an independent variable (predictor, cause, input variable, etc.) in explaining farm income. As concepts, acres and dollars are not easily conceived of as measures of a single underlying dimension; intuitively, they seem conceptually distinct. Nor is acreage easily thought of as something "caused" by the dollars received for crops. Acreage is in some sense antecedent to crop receipts, not vice versa. This conceptual clarity is less obvious in the variables used in many political, sociological, or pychological investigations. Attitudes are used to predict other attitudes with little regard for the possibility in many cases that it might be more reasonable to view the pair of attitudes as items tapping the same underlying attribute. The results may be correlations which are high, not from causal relationships, but from the properties of the measuring instrument, and which are all but impossible to use in multivariate analysis. Sometimes it may be necessary to disregard one variable.

Another set of problems about which decisions must be made relates to the assumptions that underlie the use of significance tests. These include homoscedasticity, normality, linearity of relationships and additivity. In the context in which much survey research takes place—that of discovery—and in view of the robustness of most commonly used tests of significance as well as the probable size of measurement errors in survey data, spending much time checking homoscedasticity and normality assumptions appears to be misplaced effort. The same cannot be said for additivity and linearity. There are good reasons for obtaining scatter-plots of all correlations of much substantive import, especially if they do not appear to be as large as might have been expected from theory. Additivity assumptions also have been claimed to be less applicable to social science data than have been cavalierly assumed (Sonquist, 1970). Thus, decisions to use powerful multivariate techniques which require these assumptions should be backed up by an analysis plan which checks their appropriateness for the body of data at hand. The balance is the cost of modest extra efforts against the cost of models which fit less well than they might, and failure to discover possibly important relationships between variables.

Universality is an assumption which deserves to be questioned. There is no reason why the whole sample must always be used in analyzing the data, yet this is often done, despite abundant evidence that large groups of people behave very differently. Sex, race, age, and social class are almost always measured in surveys and are constantly being used as predictors. But these attributes demarcate vastly different life experiences and role patterns in society. The idea that factors used to explain behavior should apply in exactly the same way to old and young, males and females, blacks and whites, and slum dwellers and millionaires deserves to be tested rather than taken for granted. Hence, most plans for analysis of survey data should include demographic variables as "specifiers." Variables should also be included which are relevant to the possibility that several separate analyses should be conducted to see if different patterns of explanatory factors are operative in different population groups.

Skewness is a statistical term that refers to the bunching up of observations on one end or the other of the frequency distribution of the variable in question. Its effect in survey analysis is often to reduce the correlation of that variable with others in the survey analyst's model. The practical implications of skewed variables are the need to run marginal distributions for important theoretical subgroups of the data as an early step in an analysis, and the need to recode measures so as to minimize skewness. One strategy for handling skewness is to collect detailed information on the values of continuous variables, and then to recode them as quintiles or deciles.

The problem of multicollinearity has been mentioned above, in its substantive form, as conceptual overlap. In its statistical form it occurs as a substantial correlation between the two variables in question (i.e., of the order of .5 or more when the variables are dichotomized and Yule's Q is used; see Davis, 1971, p. 49). It typically occurs when the analyst has included two factors in the analysis which initially were thought to be two separate attributes, but which might more profitably be thought of as two measures of the same thing. Since severe multicollinearity will cause unstable results, large standard errors, and the like, in multivariate statistical analyses it behooves the analyst to check out the data before embarking on a costly and time-consuming detailed analysis using these techniques.

The data-processing strategy suggested is to obtain preliminary correlational statistics on the variables in the work file which are to be used in the analysis. This can be done by using a frequency distribution cross-tabulation program if the number of variables is small, or by looking at measures of relationship such as Kendall's tau–beta. If a larger number of such variables must be examined, the table programs can sometimes be set to suppress printing of the table so that only the measure of the strength of the relationship is obtained. If interval measures are used, a product-moment correlation matrix provides the needed information. Since the problem is merely one of locating troublesome variables, there would appear to be no arguments against using product-moment statistics, even when the variables are merely ranks. Pearson product-moment statistics are much easier to compute than measures of relationship based on bivariate cross-tabulations, so costs are likely to be significantly lowered if they can be used.

Survey analysts will almost always have to contend with failure of the programs to provide exactly the statistics desired. Sometimes this can be dealt with by reprogramming, but at the expense of some time taken away from substantive research. A frequent adaptation to this problem is merely to confine the analysis to the available routines. A more insidious problem is poor labeling and annotation of statistical program output. The answer is to do this by hand immediately when the output is received. Six months later one is likely to have forgotten whether a multiple correlation coefficient has or has not been adjusted for degrees of freedom. When computer program documentation refers to texts or articles describing the algorithms used, these should be obtained and reviewed by the analyst. When they are not available, correspondence should be initiated with the writer of the program to secure them. Failure to do this is almost to ensure misinterpretation of some of the output.

A major output problem touched upon elsewhere in this book is the need to store factor scores, residuals, correlation matrices, or aggregated variables for further processing. These problems have only recently been tackled by statistical system designers, and current methods for coping with them are often less than completely satisfactory. If such processing is anticipated, it is necessary to review early, and carefully the capabilities of the programs to be used, and if they appear likely to be inadequate to add a competent programmer to the staff.

Two final problems the analyst should expect to encounter are failure to provide options for the output of intermediate results and poor error messages. The former are needed whenever trouble is suspected. For example, one will not need to know the N associated with every pairwise correlation, but if the study has a substantial amount of missing information, this may be a crucial piece of information in deciding how to handle a correlation matrix to be factor-analyzed. If problems such as this are anticipated, programmers can sometimes make trivial patches in programs to dump out the information.

Error messages are a more serious problem. A well-designed statistical analysis program will examine all its control information and check it for logical correctness before starting any of the processing. Error messages will appear in natural language instead of in "programmerese" and will provide clues to the source of the trouble. These will be further documented in the user's reference manual for the program, if not necessarily explained in detail in the primer. However, these standards are not universally followed. If clear documentation of error messages is not available, the analyst would be well advised to have a programmer go over a program that must be used extensively, locate the error exits, and prepare a list of the circumstances under which the program terminates execution unsuccessfully, matched to the symptoms that mark each illness.

Other types of error messages come from the operating-system control programs. These are often written in a jargon understood only by systems programmers. The analyst generally must depend on computer-center consultants for interpretation. What these sources often will be unable to do is to develop an explanation of what caused the error message in terms of the interaction of the data submitted to the program and the control information supplied with it. To solve problems involving errors for which these are the only clues, a conference between computer-center consultants, the analyst with the problem, and other users of the program is the most likely source of a solution.

Keeping in mind all these problems, the analyst can proceed to set up an analysis sequence typically using several statistical programs. Figure 8-16 provides a checklist of specific topics to remember.

CHECK LIST FOR PREPARATION OF
DATA FOR STATISTICAL PROGRAM INPUT

1. All previous processing pre-requisites completed and no errors.
2. All variables needed for the analysis are in the file in the proper recoded version. Program recoding capabilities can do what is needed. Newly recoded variables to be saved. Checks on recodes established to prove proper computation.
3. Variables included for subsetting of file, (both global and local) for each statistic; for assignment basis; weights; dependent and independent variables, etc.; processing controls to prove adequacy of subset; interview numbers and identifiers; variables measuring errors in data.
4. Match of missing data codes and inapplicable codes to program.
5. Over-time, nested units of analysis, paired data structures mapped onto row vector.
6. Multiple response codes taken care of by program.
7. Contextual or relational variables already generated.
8. Physical condition of data storage medium ok. No missing cards, back up tape etc. ok.
9. Bracket, decile and field codes all available for use.
10. Multiple measures of important variables available for use.

Figure 8-16 Checklist for Preparation of Data for Statistical Program Input

Coping with Very Large Data Files

Typical survey designs generate files ranging in size from about 8000 characters to as much as 1.5×10^{11} characters for a census-sized study. There is usually little reason to use all the data for all objectives in a study. A very large data set should generally be sampled for analysis, and only infrequently would this work file need 10,000 cases. Even if the characteristics of interest occur infrequently, efficient sampling techniques can usually generate a sufficient number of cases without increasing the total to more than this amount. Few problems will require more than 3000, a very large proporation can be handled with 1500, and many can be adequately treated with as few as 500 cases. The sample should obtain the smallest number of cases that can be used to answer the questions with adequate precision. A useful rule of thumb is to have not less than 30 observations in the smallest group for which a mean or percentage is to be based. Fifty is more desirable. Working backward from this minimum requirement and employing dummy tables of the type to be employed in the analysis lead to a determination of the required sample size. Use of the entire data base is costly and cumbersome, often requiring that runs be made only at night, and it is usually unnecessary.

Training and Documentation

There are two modes of setting up runs on statistical programs. In one case, the analyst sets up the run using the program control language; in the other, an explanation of the problem is given to an assistant, preferably supplemented by a written specification of what is to be performed. In either case, runs should be planned in a series, each forming part of an integrated series of steps leading to a well-defined objective. If this is not done, and runs are planned on an ad hoc basis, the processing functions that are necessary to later stages will almost invariably be overlooked.

Even if runs are to be performed by an assistant, it is highly desirable for the analyst to have a thorough knowledge of the characteristics, capabilities, and control-language options available on the programs to be used. Figure 8-17 provides guidelines for training both analyst and assistant in program use. In addition, it is necessary for the assistant to be thoroughly conversant with the objectives of the analysis and the role that each run is to play in it. Without these common understandings, delays and mistakes will be unnecessarily common and are certain to become serious problems. With adequate understanding on both parts, the assistant is in a position to bring detailed technical knowledge of the programs' behavior to bear on the analysis plan, and the analyst learns of things that can be done with the data that might otherwise be overlooked merely because of ignorance.

There is a last rule that applies in either case. All information pertaining to a run on a statistical program should be filed and kept indexed and readily accessible until the project's last report has received its reviews from professional colleagues and clients. This is especially true when the analyst is doing the computer work and there is an almost irresistible tendency to get on with the analysis and not to keep written records of what was done and in what sequence.

There are four types of information needed to set up a run on a statistical program and which need to be documented in hard copy: input specifications,

CHECK LIST FOR LEARNING TO USE AN UNFAMILIAR STATISTICAL PROGRAM

1. Read the documentation thoroughly, and be sure that it agrees with the version of the program that is on your computer.
2. Read the statistical references given in the write-up.
3. Examine the control language for the program carefully for uses of default values.
4. Determine what can be accomplished by departing from default values of parameters.
5. Check parameter language for dependencies.
6. Determine if a configuration of parameter values can be established that will do what you anticipate needing. Plan ahead for as many analyses as seems reasonable.
7. Allow the time to experiment with making test runs on the program, either using contrived data or previously analysed data.
8. Where possible, compare output from tests with known answers.
9. Identify un-clear or missing topics in the write-up and confer with other users of the program both in your own discipline and in other disciplines. Find out from the computer center who the other users are. Find out from them what bugs and documentation inaccuracies exist, and what typical costs and run timing are.
10. Start this process early enough so you have time to become thoroughly familiar with the program before you actually have to use it.
11. Examine its requirements for file structures, input media, subset selection capabilities, temporary variable generation capabilities, output and intermediate output options, computational options, conventions and options for dealing with missing data, potential for errors from rounding or use of weights.
12. Review the write-up to find out exactly what the scope of the program is.
13. Examine the restrictions placed on the user: maximum number of input variables, maximum number of variables used for each purpose, restrictions on the ranges of variables,treatment of missing data, output of intermediate results, ability to store intermediate and final results in machine-readable form, graphic display capabilities, subgroup selection capabilities, temporary variable generation capabilities.
14. Check hardware, compiler and operating system requirements the program requires.

Figure 8-17 Checklist for Learning to Use an Unfamiliar Statistical Program

temporary recoding instructions, output specifications, and scheduling requirements marking the place of the run in the sequence of analysis computations. Table 8-13 summarizes the types of information that should be committed by the analyst to paper and filed in the sequential log book of computer processing tasks. It is strongly recommended that all processing specifications of this type

15. Check use of external subroutines or other programs as adjuncts.
16. Verify input storage media requirements (cards, tape, disk, terminal, etc.).
17. Check amount of computer storage required of various types to run the program using the data that you expect to use (core storage, auxiliary disk or tape storage for intermediate results, etc.).
18. Develop procedures for estimating the time and costs of runs on the program.
19. Learn methods for supplying the program with descriptions of the data to be used (e.g. machine-readable codebooks, or Fortran format statements, etc.).
20. Develop specially written subroutines that must be supplied by the user.
21. Check input requirements to determine whether list variables, list structures or other complex data structures can be input.
22. Investigate whether test runs can be made on the program to check out the correctness of the control language syntax without actually submitting data.
23. Determine whether the program can make multiple "passes" on the same dataset to produce a large amount of output in smaller blocks, or to accomplish computation of a problem too large to be taken care of in one run.
24. Check if program requires transposition of the data files from storage row-wise to column-wise.
25. Check if proposed input requires preliminary processing to put it into a form required by the program, e.g. some regression programs require a correlation matrix as input, rather than raw data.
26. Check what problems, if any there would be in handling weighted data.

Figure 8-17 (cont'd.)

TABLE 8-13 Checklist of Information To Be Supplied and Permanently Recorded When Setting Up a Run on a Statistical Program

I. Input information.
   1. Files to be used and function each file is to play. File names, number of records, storage location, and all other information listed on the file storage records.
   2. File sequencing requirements or grouping of observations.
   3. Variables to be used from the file, names, and category labels.
   4. Subsets of observations to be used or excluded.
   5. Check to ensure that all preliminary processing on each file has been completed as required for this run.
      a. Updating or addition of observations or variables.
      b. Creation of new variables or complex recoding tasks, indices.
      c. Aggregation or imputation from other units of analysis.
      d. Merging of data from new time periods, etc.
      e. Preliminary processing of list variables.
      f. Computation of weights, if needed.
   6. Compatibility of character sets and missing-data codes.
   7. Check to see that data meet program restrictions on variable ranges and sample sizes, and use of list variables.

TABLE 8-13 (cont'd.)

8. Check to see if reordering of sequences of variables or reformatting of file is necessary. Data formats as needed.
9. Exact instruction for recoding temporary variables if needed.

II. An exact description of the computations desired, and program used.

1. Listing of the role each variable is to play in the computations (e.g., control variable, weight, dependent variable).
2. Exact specification of which computational options are to be exercised on the program to be used.
3. Control parameter values for *all* parameters available on the program. Specify default if that is what is desired, rather than omitting mention of the parameter value. Provide exact values for parameters, prescribing maximum number of iterations, stopping criteria, *F*-levels, dimensions of tables, percentage options, formulas to be used (including optional choices), structures of tables.
4. Instructions for repeating computations over various subgroups in the data.
5. Handling of missing data.
6. Use of weights.
7. Use of double-precision arithmetic, if needed.
8. Order in which computations are to be performed, if relevant.
9. Structure of control variables in ANOVA or cross-tabulation programs (e.g., crossed and nested designs; design matrix).
10. Where appropriate, statistical text references to procedures or page references in program manuals where statistical information is obtainable.

III. Output information to be supplied. In many cases, computation options specified will also produce the requisite output.

1. Printed output options to be elected, files to be written.
2. Page numbering, labeling, and decimal-point-control information.
3. Files to be used and the function each is to play; names, units of analysis, number of records, storage locations, and all information listed on the file storage records.
4. Subsets of observations or other results to be written in the file.
5. File groupings and sequencing; file formats and structure.
6. Values that are to be supplied for missing information.
7. Merging operations that are to be performed on the output files.
8. Labeling and tape or disk use for output files, holding and scratching requirements.
9. Plotting information, scales, page widths, maximum and minimum values, plotting keys.
10. Specify media on which output files are to be saved, and formats.
11. If factor scores or predicted values and residuals from multivariate analyses are to be computed, specify the form they are to be saved in and where they should be stored for further use.

IV. Temporary recoding instructions.

1. Population over which the variable is defined.
   a. Units, groups.
2. Input fields; location, treatment of minus signs, handling of inapplicable values, missing-data treatment, maximum and minimum values, decimal places.

TABLE 8-13 (cont'd.)

3. Output fields: location, field width, decimals, range, inapplicable and missing-data codes.
4. Computational formulas; constants, tables, group definitions, sequences of computation, examples.

V. Scheduling requirements and the place of the run in the analysis plan.
1. Operations that are to be performed on output files; names of programs that are to use them and an instruction to verify the compatibility of each output file with the requirements of the program that will use it.
2. Requirements for combining output files by merging data from them back into input files (e.g., saving residuals).
3. Scheduling time and alternatives for the proposed run.
4. Estimated timing information on the run, estimated output file sizes, and page estimates. Recommendation to use optional computer-center "rapid turn-around" services if available.

be filed, together with those earlier ones that deal with keypunching, editing and consistency checking, and variable generation; numbered sequentially; and carefully kept up to date. All output from statistical runs, like that from all other computer runs, should be indexed and kept in binders, not scattered unbound. The output is numbered like the specification sheets. If multiple copies are needed, they can be distributed to the staff, since they are easily obtained from most computer centers. The important thing is that a master be kept.

WHEN RUNS FAIL

One of the most dismaying things that can happen to a survey analyst is to pick up output from an "abended" (abnormally ended) statistical program. Such an aborted run will have cryptic or even humorous error notations and (hopefully) some explanation produced by the program as to what kind of error condition was detected. The following suggestions are recommended strategy for discovering what the problem was, what caused it, and what can be done to rectify it. The reader is urged to keep in mind what kinds of strategies might be pursued to prevent such problems from occurring.

1. Even when all desired output appears to be present and correct, always carefully inspect all pages to make sure no error comments are printed.
2. Distinguish whether each error message comes from the program or the computer's operating-system monitor programs. Computer-center consultants will generally be able to identify and interpret system messages. If they cannot figure out what a message means, the source is probably your program.

3. If the error message does come from the system, the consultants will generally be able to help figure out what to do to correct the problem. If it is a message from the applications program, consultants often will not be able to help you. Never waste time experimenting with trial and error solutions; contact an experienced user of the program that you are working with to get help. Keep all input and output to show consultants.
4. Do not assume that there must be some error within the program itself. Follow a detective-like strategy in tracking down the cause of the symptoms.

Regardless of whether the message came from the program in use or from the operating system, it is likely that there is something about the combination of control information and data that was submitted to the computer, rather than an error in the program itself, that is responsible for the erroneous results. A checklist of possible sources of error is presented below. In tracking down the cause(s) of a problem, start at the top of the list, the most likely sources of errors. If a hypothesis that completely accounts for all the program behavior does not prove out, add the next item on the list as a possible "suspect." Do not stop adding items until your hypothesis accounts for *all* of the observed troubles.

1. Incorrect formulation of program control-language information.
2. Incorrect formulation of job-control-language information.
3. Bad data (off-punched card columns, nonnumeric data in numeric fields, etc.).
4. Incompatibility of program and data.
5. Impossible task.
6. Communication-system malfunction.
7. Logical error in the program being used.
8. Logical error in the compiler or operating system.
9. Computer operator error.
10. Computer hardware error.

An incredibly high proportion of errors can be traced to incorrect program control information. Here is a list of common mistakes made by analysts in setting up programs:

1. Control information or input data in wrong sequence.
2. Misspelled variable or parameter keyword names.
3. Syntax errors in control language, incorrect punctuation, and the like.

4. Incorrect format for control information, wrong card columns.
5. Omitted information that should have been supplied.
6. Inconsistent control information.
7. Program options not independent and incompatible tasks requested.

A common type of error is incorrect or inconsistent logic in earlier variable-generation phases of the study. This may result in variables that cannot be described correctly by the control information used in the statistical program. Alternatively, incorrect logic used in variable generation may result in failure to obtain the subset of observations desired for the analysis. A typical symptom is the discovery that there are too few cases in the analysis. This may be due to failure to make missing-data codes conform to those "expected" by the program, so that some cases are inadvertently omitted. (A worse case is when they are inadvertently used in the computations usually with values of zero or a field full of nines.) An additional problem which is similar results from the incorrect use of "and" and "or" in index construction or subset selection specifications. The English language is inconsistent in everyday usage, but in a subset description the operator "and" means the intersection of two sets, and "or" means their union. Incorrect usage is often revealed by a run with the wrong number of observations used as a basis for the computations.

Misspelled names of keywords are readily identifiable from error comments produced by most programs. If a variable name is misspelled and no other variable has that spelling, the error will be readily identifiable. However, if a second variable exists whose name is identical, it may simply be used and no indication of error may occur. This can happen easily on a study with many variables and several recoded versions of many of them. It is discovered when the marginal distributions of the variables used are found to be different from that expected.

Syntax errors are a frequent cause of aborted runs. Computer programs generally have rigid, fixed rules about how parameter information is to be inserted. Commas often must be placed exactly where the write-up of the program specifies. Blank spaces often must appear where specified, and keywords must be spelled properly.

Where the control information for the program is punched in fixed format, it is necessary to check extremely carefully to ensure that parameters are punched in exactly those columns specified in the program documentation. In most cases, numeric information must be right-adjusted in the field provided for it (moved as far as possible to the right in the field); alphabetic or character-string information must sometimes be moved to the leftmost positions of the field if the number of characters is insufficient to fill up the alloted space.

A typical problem is an out-of-range parameter. If the program was designed to handle correlation matrices up to a certain size, you may not inform it that the job to be done this time is a matrix larger than that size. A more difficult problem is the situation in which the program allocates storage dynamically during execution according to needs that are dependent on the properties of the data. One may receive an aborted run that has run out of space or time. The only answer may be to break up the problem into smaller runs.

Omitted information is often a hard-to-diagnose problem. Some statistical programs provide "default" values for control information; omitted values are supplied by the program. In some cases, these may be appropriate for the data; in others, not. Some programs supply default values for some parameters but not for others. Others provide no defaults. Whether or not a value for a particular parameter must be supplied may depend on whether an option controlled by another parameter is exercised. A good program will permit the omission of a value for an unused parameter.

The action most likely to lead to a successful diagnosis and remedy of a problem due to omitted control information is:

1. Rereading the program write-up.
2. Explaining in detail to an experienced user of the program what tasks you wanted to do, what your data looked like, and exactly what you did.
3. Showing the expert the input and output.

The actions most likely to forestall this problem from occurring are:

1. To assign a project staff member the explicit responsibility of keeping program documentation up to date and of keeping in contact with other users about problems they have had.
2. To check runs before they are submitted by having a project staff member other than the original writer check the problem definition and its proposed solution.

The second most frequent type of error is inaccurate or incorrect submission of information to the computer to define which program is to be used, which data files are to be used, or what the attributes of the file are. The operating systems used on many large-scale computers provide great flexibility but in some cases require that a complex jargon be used to invoke the operation of a program or series of programs, to assign system resources such as disk or tape drives to particular functions during computation, and to link requests for information from files from the program to particular tapes or disks mounted on specific drives. Termed *job control language* (JCL) on the IBM 360/370 series of computers, jargons such as these were designed for professional programmers rather than for users submitting their own runs on statistical or data-management programs. They are subject to a wide variety of possible errors in use. Learning to use them requires a considerable investment of time and energy—and is required of at least two people on the project.

The strategy most likely to result in a quick diagnosis of a suspected problem of this type is similar to that suggested above:

1. Check the job control information on previous successful runs of the program made by one's own staff and by other users. Check the program write-up instructions pertaining to this subject.
2. Bring all the input and output from the run and check it with computer-center user-services personnel. Bring along the copy of the program write-up used to set up the run.

The action most likely to prevent this type of problem from arising in the first place is to assign one project staff member the responsibility of becoming an expert on the local job control jargon. Then set up the job submission procedures so that others ask that person to check their runs before they are submitted. Have them attend computer-center staff meetings regularly, if possible, or otherwise make sure that there is close contact with those computer-center staff members responsible for job-control-language problems brought in by users. Be sure they keep all project copies of job control manuals up to date.

If the data and program have never been used together, it is desirable to run a check by printing out the first 10 and last 10 records to make sure the file is all there and in proper form. Errors in the data or incompatibility of program and data may be responsible for the trouble. Program control information indicating where variables are to be read from should be checked closely. If the data set is not too large, a listing of the entire data set is a good procedure. Format errors are common, particularly if FORTRAN format descriptors are the method used to inform the program where the data are to be read from. Check the program write-up to make sure the type of data file structure used is acceptable to the program. Check the character set required by the program against that used in the file. Make sure that the records in the file are in the sequence required by the program, if any. If a match-merged file of cards was used as input, one or more cards may be missing or out of sequence. Verify the program handling of missing information and the way in which the subsetting of observations for input takes place. Check to see that previous recoding of variables was correct. In particular, scan the data-set code books for inapplicable codes, use of alphanumeric characters, and the presence of blank fields. Examine the codes to see if extreme values of data are outside program limits. Missing observations, missing variables for certain observations, or duplicate observations may be at the root of some trouble.

If the data are erroneous or incompatible, it may be necessary to write a special-purpose program to bring them into the required form. Sometimes a utility program available from the computing facility can be set up to do this. Unless file structures are incompatible, a special-purpose program to make the data fit the program is not a long task for a capable programmer. The problem essentially is figuring out what is wrong.

Less frequent are mathematical problems which cause problems. Sometimes missing information and small groups combine to produce a very small group (i.e., one case). The variance in such a group is undefined. Unless anticipated by the programmer, and bypassed, application of the sample variance formula yields a zero divisor and an unexplained error message from the operating system. Rounding errors can lead to similar problems when sample sizes are small or when weights are three or four digits. Sometimes a combination of incorrect logic in sample subset selection or in inconsistent recoding of variables may lead to exclusion of a large fraction of the observations, also producing very small groups, and leading to the same observed divide-by-zero. A more serious problem are the overlapping concepts which lead to ill-conditioned correlation matrices which, when used in a multiple regression or factor analysis, are plagued by severe numerical problems. The remedy is as above—always have a senior staff member on the project check analysts' plans and computer setups for their basic logic.

In an interactive environment, telephone lines may be damaged or other communications gear fail to function properly. Interactive operating systems are subject to overload and some "crash" with an undesirable frequency. If lines are bad, the principal alternatives are: (1) sign off and call on another line if possible, or (2) sign off and wait until the problem is cleared up. A more serious problem is the possibility of loss of files when the crashed operating system must be regenerated. This means that when the project uses an interactive computer a strategy of file backups on tape or removable disks must be established and followed religiously to prevent loss of files. Since computer-center backup of user files is not always satisfactory in its scheduling, care must be taken.

Programmers are usually conscientious, but often rushed, or poorly supervised, and frequently unacquainted with good programming and testing techniques. "Bugs" may yet remain in the code. The more complex the program, the more likely it is that some combinations of data and options will not work properly. The older the program, the less likely that the observed trouble is due to this problem.

When the more likely sources of error have been eliminated and a program bug appears, check with experienced users. Then, if there appears to be a problem that they cannot circumvent, find another program immediately or shift analysis strategy as needed. Do not wait for the bug to get fixed. An exception to this rule, of course, is a program written by a project staff member.

A logical error or "bug" in the compiler or operating system is an unlikely, although possible, source of error in batch computer systems. It is a frequent cause of error in time-sharing systems. However, in the latter its manifestations are likely to be loss of files or inability to access the computer at all rather than aborted runs or indecipherable output. If this problem is suspected, treat it like a suspected hardware error (see below). Modern operating systems leave little leeway for operator errors affecting users' output. This is an unlikely cause of problems. Batch computing systems are now quite stable. Few hardware errors occur. The same is not true for time-sharing systems. As noted above, however, the time-sharing symptoms are not likely to lead to a detective-like attempt to diagnose what the underlying causes of the troubles are. On time-sharing systems, files will be lost, continuing a terminal session will be impossible, or another readily apparent problem will be manifest. If, in a batch environment, other sources of error have been tentatively cleared of suspicion, and if hardware errors are believed by user-service personnel to have been frequent on the day the job was run, then rerun it exactly as it was originally submitted. However, if other errors are suspected, even remotely, check them out; do not waste time on this potential source. On the other hand, it is desirable to keep in close-enough touch with computer-center consultants to know what the system crashing patterns have been currently. If there has been a fair amount of recent downtime, this should be the first instead of the last on the list of possible causes of failure. Sometimes the job will run if different output units or disk or tape drives are used.

The logic behind this sequencing of probable sources of error is the frequency with which errors have been found to occur in practice. About 80 per cent of the reasons for aborted runs are either program control information errors, job control information errors, or trouble with the data. Most of these can be traced to failure to check the program documentation thoroughly before using the program, to misunderstanding it, or to inadequate documentation. A large fraction of the remainder are due to simple clerical errors in setting up the input. Where punched cards are used as data storage, physical deterioration of the cards and errors arising from replacing worn cards will also be found to be frequent sources of errors, as well as missing cards.

A very large fraction of these problems can be avoided by the simple expedient of having a project staff member check every run thoroughly after it is completely set up and ready to be submitted to the computer, and by keeping careful cumulative records of what has been done to the data. Running test runs on small data sets or on contrived data will also uncover many potential errors. The more complex the run, the higher the payoff from using a test. These factors are precipitating causes of trouble and often arise from two more basic factors—using programs that simply were not designed to take the type of data employed, and failure to train research assistants adequately.

Another type of problem can occur for which there are no error messages. The use of procedures for solving sets of simultaneous linear equations programmed by persons inexperienced in numerical problems in computation can lead to serious errors undetectable from the computer printout. The mathematical problems are discussed by Wampler (1970). For this reason, it is desirable to review the numerical procedures employed in a multiple-regression or factor-analysis program with a competent numerical analyst or statistician before it is used in the analysis. Even when this is done, however, problems that are basically conceptual in nature can lead to ill-conditioned correlation matrices in which some rows approximate linear functions of others, and which are extremely unstable. This may be due to a combination of subsetting, sample size, and missing information which leads to an extremely small number of cases in some cells. These, in turn, can lead to mathematically possible but patently absurd results, such as factor loadings greater than 1.0. Other types of mathematically possible but seriously misleading results from multivariate statistical procedures are treated by Sonquist (1970), Wilson (1971), and Andrews et al. (1973).

These remarks are an explicit emphasis on a caution. Numbers printed by a computer have no more meaning than if they were scrawled by a child's pencil. The important thing is not that they are printed by a computer, but that they are correct. The computer makes possible bigger mistakes than ever before.

This chapter provided guidelines for the intelligent use of the analytical power available through the use of statistical techniques unavailable without a computer. The problems identified are typical of all types and sizes of research projects, and the suggestions made will apply correspondingly. Avoiding problems is better than solving them, and this requires planning ahead. It means taking the time to become familiar with the available systems, organizing the data so that they can be entered into the programs, planning for supplementary manual procedures, and careful checking of control information submitted to the computer.

9 ADMINISTRATION

Every survey, no matter what its size, needs organized procedures for recording analysis plans, data-collection procedures, editing and coding procedures, computer runs, and data storage and management. Either the researcher or an assistant or both must become familiar with the hardware and software configurations available and the institutional environment in which these are maintained.

With these needs in mind, we turn to the three foci of this chapter. First, managing the study operation requires technical knowledge about interactive and batch computer systems and their characteristics. It requires that the analyst understand the differences among card, tape, and disk storage media. In short, the researcher must become familiar with his computer environment. A second theme is software and the capabilities that available computer programs must have if typical survey processing tasks are to be accomplished. The third focus is on a broader array of management tasks: dealing with the computer center, coping with turnaround problems, organizing survey data files, training project staff members, and establishing and maintaining the record-keeping system that is the main organizing tool for the data processing. Together, these topics put into perspective the more specific technical apparatus and concepts discussed to this point.

TECHNICAL CONSIDERATIONS IN PROJECT MANAGEMENT

Although it is not the objective of this book to provide it, the survey analyst should have a thorough technical background in computing. Accordingly, he should at least become familiar with an introductory text on computer science.[1] The discussion here will be limited to the implications of using batch versus interactive computing resources for study data-handling strategy, and for the way in which data are organized on storage media. Survey analysts can expect to have one or more of three types of computing available to them: batch, rapid or remote batch, and interactive. There are advantages and disadvantages to each. The tasks are to know and understand their strengths and weaknesses, and to take the best advantage of what is available.

Batch Computing In a batch-oriented computing system the unit of work done by the computer is the *job*. Jobs may have one or several *steps*. Each step involves the execution of a program and the acceptance of input and the production of output. Steps can be set up to *execute* one after the other without physical intervention. This is sometimes called *chaining*. A step in a multistep job generally either accepts input and control information and leaves files in the computer for subsequent steps, or it accepts files from tapes, disks, or other storage media and prints output. Sometimes both will be produced. Frequently, if an early step aborts or *abends* (*ab*normal *end*ing) the files required by subsequent steps are not prepared and those steps fail, too. In the case of either failure or success, all the output from all steps is collected and delivered in one piece to the *user* who submitted the job. He generally has no access to his control information or his data after the job has been *submitted* (either by turning a deck of cards in to an operator at the computer center, or loading the coded computer instructions directly into a reading device).

In this type of computing environment, *turnaround* (i.e., elapsed time between submitting a job and receiving both control input and output back) may range from several minutes to 24 hours. This turnaround time depends on how busy the computer is relative to its capacity, the length of time needed to run the job (longer jobs are often postponed until evening or night hours when the load on the system is lighter), the priority scheduling system used by the computer center (some classes of jobs get more rapid service), and the personal relationships between the user and the computer-center operations staff. Because of the turnaround time in batch environment, it is generally advisable for the survey analyst to make use of any high-speed printing capacity available to print the relatively large blocks of computation that may be generated.

The output from all jobs in a given priority level is generally placed in a queue and printed in the order in which they were executed. Printed materials are generally placed in bins where users can come to pick them up, or, in commercial systems, may be delivered to the user by messenger.

Because it is easy to make errors when setting up computations, the slow turnaround time generally available to the batch user can result in delays in the analysis. Procedures for having several people check the control and format

[1] For example, see Gear (1973) and the companion volume by Bohl and Walter (1973), or the Forsythe et al. (1970) volumes.

input, as well as the job control information for invoking the programs to be used, have very high payoff.[2]

A useful method of circumventing the problems of long turnaround and large amounts of unusable output is the use of check runs. The job is submitted complete except that the large data file containing the survey is replaced by a small one containing only a few observations (some output may also be left out). Frequently, programs can be written so that the syntax of the control and formatting information can be checked for errors but actual execution of the statistical parts of the program is suppressed. Since syntax checking takes only a short time, the job can be put in a high-priority queue if available and so turnaround is very short. When the errors thus revealed have been corrected, the large data set is referenced and the production job submitted.

Programs designed to run in batch mode generally have been written to do a large number of tasks and to produce a relatively large amount of output. This can lead to a "do-everything-at-once" approach to computer-based analyses. Medium-sized runs are a better strategy, permitting more effective debugging and often saving computer time spent on job steps otherwise executed on the faulty inputs generated by errors in preceding steps.

Most frequently, batch processing of survey data is initiated by punching format and control information on cards. Programs can usually be kept on random-access storage devices such as disks. Most statistical programs accept data from disk or tape storage, as well as from cards, so it is usually necessary only to write data onto tape or disk storage once. Generally, computer centers have utility programs for copying card files to tape or disk. Information about these will not generally be available from the write-ups of the statistical program that the analyst wishes to use. It must be obtained separately from computer-center consultants. These utility data-handling programs are generally provided by the computer manufacturer.[3]

Rapid Batch Mode Delays in actually getting batch jobs to go into execution due to errors in the operating-system control language and the desire for convenient access to input and output units are leading to increasing use of "rapid" or "remote job entry" batch systems. In such a system, limits are usually placed on the amount of computer storage that can be used by jobs sent through it, on the length of time each job can execute, and on the programs or data that can be used. A card reader, punch, and printer are set up in a convenient location away from the central computer center, together with keypunch and consultation facilities. The configuration is geared to provide turnaround times of a few seconds to 5 minutes, returning the user's job input file to him immediately, and

[2] One experiment showed that, on one type of widely used equipment, errors in specifying instructions to the operating system were by far the largest single cause of blown jobs.

[3] Sometimes such utility programs may be obtained commercially, and may be of greater usefulness for the problem at hand than those supplied by the manufacturer. For example, see the Utility-Coder/360 Manual.

directing his output back to that particular printer. Sometimes the amount of output is also limited, since the printing equipment usually placed in such an installation is intermediate in its capacity between a slower teletype and the high-speed line printers normally used for regular batch printing.

An arrangement like this permits the use of existing batch programs, but cuts down the time needed to get a job to run properly, reduces time spent in going to the computing facility itself, and thus reduces the penalties for making errors. Long or large jobs must still generally be run in regular batch mode, however. Remote batch service facilitates use of smaller increments in the computer processing plan, and makes debugging and supplemental analyses much simpler.

An extension of the remote batch mode is an arrangement whereby a batch job can be initiated from a remote teletype or other typewriter-like terminal, and the results sent out through the central batch printer. In some arrangements, enough information is made available to the terminal so the user can at least tell whether the job ran properly. In some cases results can be stored on disk files. Printed output must be picked up at the computer center. The combined abilities to edit control-card text and to submit and retrieve jobs in such a system result in dramatic decreases in the total time required for processing data.

Interactive Processing A more recent innovation is the introduction of equipment and operating systems that permit the statistical program running in a computer to interact directly and continuously with the analyst via a teletype, or other computer terminal, and telephone lines. Use of the computer is allocated in rapid succession to the programs being used by a large number of terminals. It looks to each user as though he has the whole computer for his exclusive use. In actual fact, the user's messages are being accepted and held until the program is brought into operation from disk or other random-access storage where it is being kept. Then it goes into execution from the point where it left off when it was "swapped" onto the computer's disk or drum storage in favor of another user's program. Such interactive programs can print out results directly at the user's terminal, or write any output generated into a disk file. Alternatively, output can be sent to the regular printing queue for later printing via the batch "background" output stream. Batch jobs can also be started from such terminals.

An important feature of this environment from the survey analyst's point of view is that turnaround is essentially instantaneous. Errors can be corrected immediately. Most importantly, if programs making use of the interactive capability are available, the analysis of the data can proceed in small steps which need be planned only a short time before the program is used.

This is not to suggest that the restrictions mentioned earlier—that data must fit the program and that it must in fact do what you want—do not apply; rather, the process between deciding to use a usable program and getting back usable output has been considerably shortened. Because of the input and output limitations of such a console, the output and input volumes must be small.

Analysis Strategies and Interactive Versus Batch Computing The nature of the analyst's communication process with the computer necessarily has a profound effect on the analysis strategy. Much of what has been said in this book is predicated on the use of batch technology rather than on truly interactive communication. The nature of batch technology limits the researcher's rapid accomplishment of small amounts of work. Someone must prepare input control sequences without any feedback from the computer as to errors, and wait a substantial period of time before receiving output. Printed output is produced through very high-speed line printers, and large amounts can be produced efficiently. The computer center is often located in an area removed from the researcher's normal place of work, even if remote-batch card read and print stations are used. The user submits his job and usually goes away and does something else until he can return to pick it up; or it may even be delivered sometime later by messenger. All these factors suggest a strategy for the researcher that involves considerable planning ahead and a commitment to fairly large amounts of computing between examination of results and decisions as to what to do next. Choosing too small a bite for computation or data processing carries with it the cost of many more computer jobs turned in, more dependence on frequently unpredictable computer-center turnaround time, and too much total elapsed time for the study.

On the other hand, in an interactive environment, where the analyst can retain minute-by-minute control over the computational process, other strategies are often preferable. Using software geared to time sharing, the analyst can obtain smaller amounts of computation, can explore hunches as they occur to him, and can return to batch mode later to obtain the results of a large-scale computation that he would not wish to wait for at his terminal. The slower output speeds of most time-sharing terminals call for programs that are far more economical in their presentation of information about the data than are most programs designed for batch use. The growing availability of full graphical capabilities makes for vastly improved capabilities that the analyst can use in obtaining a visual analog of the relationships between variables in his data. When good interactive capabilities are available, although analysis plans should still be directed toward specific goals, they should provide for the flexibility and time to explore the side issues that come to light during the course of interactive sessions.

The use of interactive capabilities poses new problems, however. The analyst with only a soft-copy graphics character display terminal will not be able to keep a card file copy of successful setups to programs. He will have to devise a means of building up this record of how-to-do-it experience in some other fashion, perhaps in a file kept on the computer itself.

The main point of this discussion is to call the attention of analysts using interactive equipment to the possibility that the large chunks of computation and sometimes incredible volumes of output characteristic of batch-oriented survey processing systems should not necessarily be a part of their strategy. If they have the opportunity to intervene, control, and direct the course of computation, new strategies of computer use which take advantage of this capability provided by interactive technology may prove useful.

Storage of Survey Data Files

There are three commonly used modes of storage for survey data: cards, tapes, and random-access devices such as disks. Each has its advantages and disadvantages. Each computer center has its own particular capabilities and limitations vis-à-vis these media, and the study director needs to make sure that the storage medium to be used is one for which they have good processing capabilities.

Most surveys usually start their machine-readable life as one or more *decks* of cards. For computer processing with medium- and large-scale equipment, and with small computers having very slow, minimal card-reading equipment, tape or disk storage will be preferred. Cards have other disadvantages, including being easily lost; "folded, spindled, and mutilated"; and higher computer processing costs than tapes or disks since they take so much time to pass through the input and output equipment. So, unless the data set is quite small, it will generally pay off to move it from cards to tape or to random-access storage, depending on the computer center's strengths and weaknesses.

Tape Storage of Survey Data Computer tape is nothing more than audio tape-recorder tape made bigger and produced to more rigid specifications. Like audio tape, it is plastic and has one side covered with a metallic oxide coating. Like audio tape, it can be read and written on over and over again. When something is written, the previous contents are erased. When it is read (played back), the contents are not affected, so it can be read as many times as desired. Tape is written and read by passing it through a set of read and write *heads* similar to those on a tape recorder. Tapes already containing data can be protected from accidental erasure by means of a plastic ring on the reel containing the tape. When the ring has been removed, the tape *units* or *drives* cannot write on the tape. Tapes are normally stored with these rings removed ("ring out"). When it is desired to write on a tape, written instructions to the computer operator must be supplied requesting insertion of a *write ring*. This ring will be left "in" until the program is finished with the tape. When the tape is dismounted by the operator at the end of the job, he will remove the ring if so instructed.

Information is written on tapes in bursts called *physical records*. When the computer writes on a tape, it first starts the drive and accelerates it to the proper speed. This takes about $\frac{1}{4}$ inch of tape. When the tape is moving past the heads at the proper speed, the drive starts transmitting information, usually as a continuous stream of characters. The characters are written at one of several densities which can be chosen by the program. These range from 556 to 1600 characters per inch or higher. After the computer stops transmitting data, it stops the tape drive. About $\frac{1}{2}$ inch of tape passes the heads while the drive is slowing down. Computer tape contains blocks of information separated by these *inter record gaps* with no information in them.

Most computing equipment represents information as a pattern of *bits*. Each bit can have the value 1 or zero. Eight bits make a *byte*. Various patterns of bits in the byte represent characters. There are several schemes used by manufacturers for encoding characters. These include Extended Binary Coded Decimal Interchange Code, EBCDIC (IBM) and American Standard Code for Information Interchange, ASCII (most other manufacturers). An earlier scheme was Binary Coded Decimal, BCD (IBM), which used six-bit bytes. Tapes written in one mode cannot always be read by equipment normally using another mode.

A byte is recorded magnetically on a track on tape (see Figure 9-1). These tracks run parallel to the length of the tape. One character is recorded by magnetizing a certain combination of tracks across the tape at that point. The combination of tracks represents the pattern of 1's and 0's that constitute the character. Tape drives normally write on nine tracks on the tape. [Earlier (BCD) drives used a seven-bit code.] The extra track is used to write a *parity* bit. This is used to check for loss of information or damage to the tape. If the character has an odd number of 1's, the parity bit is usually set to zero. It is set to 1 if there is an even number of 1's. When *odd parity* is used, the result is always an odd number of bits. Nine-track drives typically operate at odd parity. Seven-track drives can operate either in odd or even parity (Figure 9-1).

The computer always reads back what it has just written and checks the parity of the character. It also checks parity of information when it is reading tapes. If a parity check fails, it tries several more times to perform its read or write operation. If it still cannot succeed, it stops processing on that drive and prints an error message. Usually, the job is then terminated. When this happens, one can have the tape cleaned and try to run the job again later. If the parity checks still fail, one either has to use another tape or make provisions in the program being used to skip that record on the tape. Tape reliability is good; perhaps several years of weekly use without unrecoverable errors is not an unrealistic expectation. However, data are usually too precious to take chances with, and copying a tape is cheap. A backup tape is one of the best investments that a survey analyst can make.

Most survey processing programs that use card input will also accept tape input. When putting survey data on tape, several decisions must be made. These include the use of one tape or several (if there are several files of data) and decisions about tape length, blocking factors, and recording density. Computer-center utility programs are usually available for such file conversions.

Density on a tape is defined as the number of characters written on 1 inch

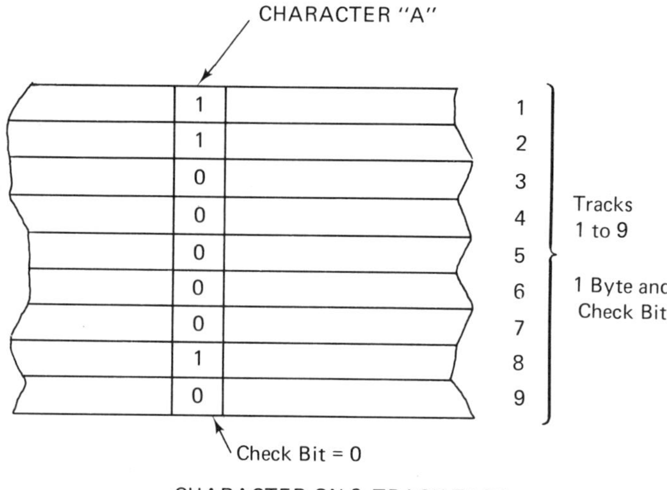

CHARACTER ON 9-TRACK TAPE

0 C
1 A
1 B
0 8
0 4
0 2
1 1

Check Bit
and
Tracks A, B, 8, 4, 2, 1

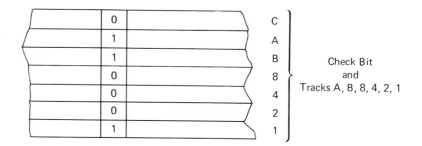

CHARACTER ON 7-TRACK TAPE

Figure 9-1 Characters on 7- and 9-Track Tapes

of tape. It is measured in bits per inch (bpi). Many nine-track tape drives are *defaulted* (set up in advance) to write at 800 bpi unless otherwise instructed via system controls. Alternative densities are 200, 556, 1600, or sometimes 3200. With seven-track drives, densities of 200, 556, and 800 are available (here the user must always specify which density). In general, it is advisable to use the highest density available unless tapes must be shipped to installations where capabilities are more limited.

When data cards are put on tape, they can be written so that the information from one card is placed in a single record. This means that the tape would consist of records, each consisting of 80 characters (at 800 bpi, this is $\frac{1}{10}$ inch) and an interrecord gap of $\frac{3}{4}$ inch. Thus, most of the tape would be interrecord gaps. This is needlessly wasteful of tape storage space and potentially expensive, since computer centers frequently charge for the number of physical records they have to read and write.

The concept of *blocking* is the simple expedient of combining several (perhaps many) short character strings into one long one before writing them on tape. For example, if one had a survey with five cards of information per respondent, it would be reasonable to combine the five cards into one block of $5 \times 80 = 400$ characters per respondent and write them on tape that way. Alternatively, the five separate "decks" could each be blocked, say, at 10 cards per record, and then these files sorted and merged. In either case, the final file would consist of the desired 400-character record. In turn, these records could be blocked, say, 20 to a record, for further savings in tape and time.

Records in a file in which all have the same number of characters are termed *fixed-length.* Operating system programs take care of blocking and unblocking, and the survey data-processing programs need only be written to deal with the number of characters that are transmitted in a single "logical" record. At this point a more formal definition of some terms applicable to data-storage technology seems in order:

Physical Record: the block of information written on the storage medium as a consecutive string of characters. It is always written by the operating-system programs.

Density: the number of bytes written per inch of tape.

Logical Record: a string of characters or block of information sent to or from the program to the operating-system programs. It is transferred from a single read or write instruction in the program. A program never writes on the storage medium; it sends the character string to the operating system programs, which then block one or more logical records together into a single physical record.

Blocking Factor: the number of logical records that are put together to make a single physical record. If it has the value 1, then one logical record equals one physical record and the file is said to be *unblocked.*

Blocksize: the number of characters in one physical record.

Interrecord Gap: the blank section in the storage medium that separates physical records.

Buffer: space in the computer set aside for the operating system to use for reading and writing records. It contains space for the characters required to read or write one physical record.

Information about the logical record length (number of characters) in each logical record (e.g., blocking factors) generally must be supplied to the operating system when a program is executed. Sometimes most of this information can be kept in the machine-readable label at the front of a tape file.

Tapes are available in several lengths, for example, 1200 or 2400 feet. How much tape is needed to store the data from a survey depends on several factors: the blocksize, the density, the number of records to be written, and the blocking factor. Formula (9-1) gives the number of feet of tape needed in terms of these factors:

$$L = \left(\frac{B}{D} + .75\right)\left(\frac{N}{12F}\right) + 35, \tag{9-1}$$

where L = length of tape needed, feet,
N = number of logical records to be written,
F = blocking factor,
B = blocksize,
D = density at which the tape is to be written, bpi.

The formula has three terms: the length of a block, the number of physical records to be written, and a conversion to feet instead of inches. The constant 35 provides an allowance for extra tape at the beginning and end of the reel. For example, if cards are written onto a tape unblocked with a density of 800 bpi, each card (80 characters) takes (80/800) = .1 inch for the data plus .75 inch for the interrecord gap. If the blocking factor is 1, then 100 cards would take ($.85 \times 100$) = 85 inches or, divided by 12, this would be a little over 7 feet. If the cards were blocked at 10, then 10 cards would take 1.75 inches, including the gap, and 100 cards would only take up about 17.5 inches of tape. Blocking at even higher factors results in better tape utilization and is limited only by the core storage available to the user's problem program. Blocks of forty-four 80-character cards (blocksize = 3520) often result in efficient processing.[4] In addition to the tape required for data storage, about 20 feet at the beginning and 15 feet at the end are needed for leader and trailer space.

Tapes can be purchased or leased (or, occasionally, borrowed). Computer installations will generally make arrangements to sell tapes to users if desired. This probably results in as inexpensive an outlay as can be made by negotiating directly with suppliers. With either lease or use of one's own tapes, computer centers require that tapes be registered and that users conform to certain labeling and use regulations. Generally, a serial number is assigned to each individual reel of tape. All references to that tape are via this number. Registered tapes can generally be restricted as to who can use them or can be declared to be public, by option of the owner. Similarly, they can be protected in terms of how they can be used (i.e. for reading, writing, or unlimited use).

[4] This is largely because of the physical characteristics of the Model 2314 disk-drive units commonly used on IBM equipment. Other values would be needed to match the physical characteristics of other manufacturer's units.

Generally, registration and usage information is stored in files internal to the computer. When a request is received to mount a tape, the operating-system programs check to see whether this user is entitled to use the tape and whether his job specification cards call for reading, writing, and so on, in conformity with the usage restrictions. If the instructions do not agree with the regulations established by the owner, the tape cannot be used for that job. The owner can request that the tape librarian change his tape-usage rules. This type of system has a large number of variations, depending on the installation. It protects users against the possibility of someone else accidentally writing on their tape and destroying the data stored there. For further protection, tapes should be labeled.

Provisions are generally made for writing machine-readable *labels* on the front end of each tape. If this information is omitted, or its use is bypassed, programs can run with the wrong tape mounted accidentally. When labels are used, the operating system can check the label specified on the job setup instructions with the label it reads from the tape. If they do not agree, the program will not run.

Tapes can be labeled or left unlabeled. On an unlabeled tape, the data are simply written starting with the beginning of the reel. The end of the data is denoted by a special character called a *tapemark*, which marks the end of a data file. A tape can hold as many files as there is physical space for. Conversely, a very large data set might extend over several tapes. The end of the *last* set of data on a tape is marked by two tape marks instead of one. The second tape mark, which appears immediately following the first, informs the computer that no more data follow on that reel and that the end of that file is present. This second tape mark is erased automatically when additional data sets are added to the end of the tape. When several sets of data are written on unlabeled tapes, each new data file begins right after the tape mark which denotes the end of the preceding set. When it takes two or more tapes to contain a single data set, only the last tape has two tape marks; the earlier ones have only one. Unlabeled tapes look somewhat as shown in Figure 9-2.

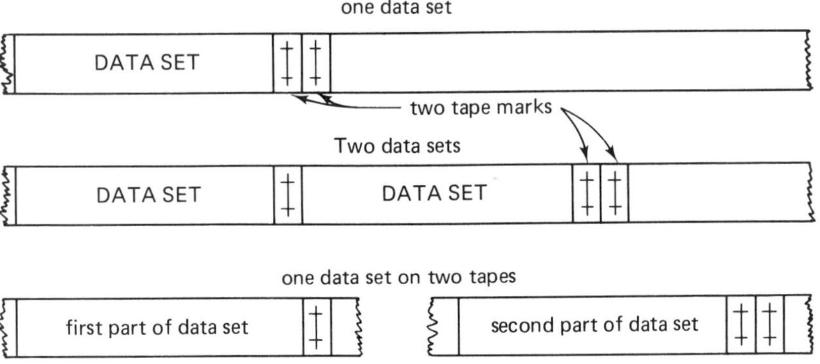

Figure 9-2 Files on Unlabeled Tapes

Labels appear as extra records written before and after a data file on tape. They are used for safety and convenience. When the tape is being read, the operating system can check to see that the correct one has been mounted, and that the correct file is being read, by comparing label specifications in the job setup to labels written on the tape. If an expiration date is used as a label component, the operating system can protect files from being overwritten by mistake. Such data characteristics as the length of the physical records in the tape and record formats can be stored in the label. Since users forget which files are on which tapes, utility programs are usually available that will print only the labels, providing clues as to what is on a tape. In general, labeling should always be used unless the tape is to be transferred to or from an installation using another manufacturer's equipment, in which case the labels will not generally be compatible.

Tapes with standard labels are illustrated in Figure 9-3. In some cases header and trailer labels may have several records in them. Data-set labels include the following kinds of information: the *name* of the data set; the *serial* number of the tape; a *sequence* number, indicating whether the data file is the first, second, . . . , file on this tape; an *expiration date*; *security* information such as a password required to read the file; a count of the *number* of blocks in the file; and the record *format*, *blocksize*, *logical record length*, *tape density*, and type of *parity*. Trailer records contain similar information, plus an actual *count* of the number of records and an indication of whether the file *continues* on another tape volume.

There are several reasons why it is better to keep only one or two files on one tape unless additions are not to be made to the files and the tapes are not

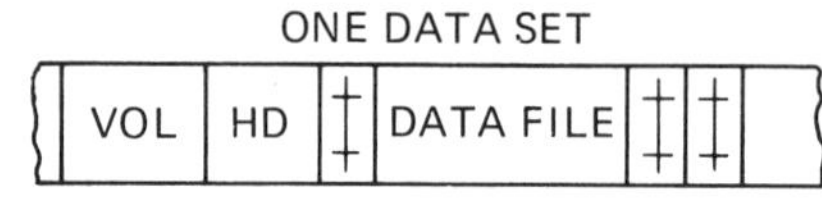

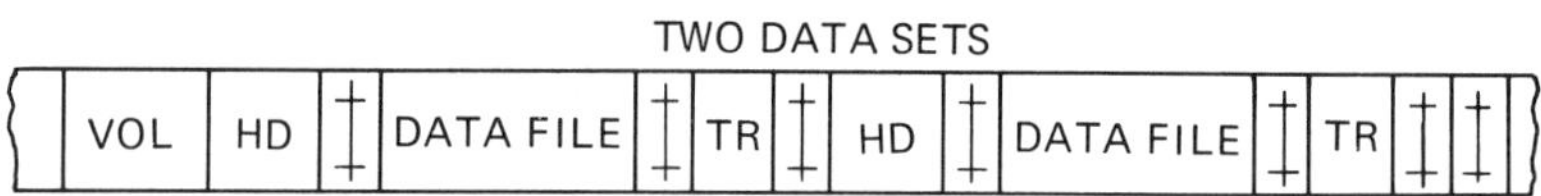

Figure 9-3 Labeled Files on Tape

to be used too often. Tape is cheap. Searching for files on the end of a long tape takes a lot of computer time, as much as 5 minutes. Every record of every file in front of the desired one must be read. In addition, if it is necessary to overwrite one of the earlier files on a tape, the later files that have been previously written cannot be used. A much better alternative is to use several smaller reels with one or two files on each reel. Three-hundred-foot tapes are often ideal for survey data-storage use.

Tapes are probably the best storage medium for survey information that is no longer in constant use. They are durable and inexpensive. When use is infrequent, the cautions not to put many files on a single reel do not apply, since accessing of files will be infrequent and up-dating or rewriting of files will not occur.

One caution must be observed, however. Every storage tape needs a backup tape, since physical deteriotation does occur. This is a simple task involving only computer-center-supported utility-file copying programs. In addition, every storage tape should be hung on a tape drive and read, and the file rewritten, at least once in 24 months. The reason for this is that when layers of tape stay next to one another on the reel for a long period of time the magnetized particles of oxide on which information is recorded tend to induce a copy of themselves on the adjacent layer of oxide. This *print-through* causes tape reading errors and eventual loss of some records. Reading the tape and rewriting it changes the physical contact pattern just enough to prevent the problem.

Obviously, accurate records have to be kept as to what is on the tape storage reels. This is discussed in the sections dealing with code books and data storage control.

Disk storage of Survey Data Disk drives provide another alternative to cards and magnetic tape as a storage medium that is machine-readable and which can be used to hold survey data for machine processing. Disks are *direct-access* devices. If a file is set up for random access, an individual record in the middle can be read without having to first read all those records that precede it. Alternatively, processing can be set up to read through the records sequentially, as is required with the use of cards and tape. Which mode is used depends on the program. One set up to read files sequentially can access data on cards, tape, or disk; one set up to access data directly requires disk storage.

Information is recorded magnetically on *tracks* on the surfaces of a stack of whirling platters. As with tape, these surfaces are covered with oxide that can be magnetized. Unlike tape, where the read–write heads are stationary, most disk heads are placed on arms which can move between concentric tracks. One typical disk pack contains 4000 tracks of space. A disk pack can hold about as much as a 2400-foot reel of magnetic tape. Disks range in their storage capability from about 250,000 characters to over 40 million characters.

Characters are recorded on disks as they are on tape; that is, they are recorded sequentially on a single track. The tracks form concentric circles on the surfaces of the disk. On a typical disk pack, the IBM Model 2314, there are 10 such surfaces. Each surface has its own read–write heads. These heads can move inward or outward across the tracks, which revolve continuously under them. Since the 10 heads all move simultaneously, 10 tracks of information can be accessed simultaneously.

There are 400 tracks on each surface, each requiring a different position of the read–write heads. The bank of 10 tracks corresponding to one of these positions is called a *cylinder.* So a cylinder consists of one track from each of the 10 disks. A single 2314 disk has 400 cylinders or 4000 tracks. Each track can hold up to 7294 characters. However, like tape, there must be interblock gaps. These may be as much as 100 characters. Therefore, if a single block of data is to be written to a single track, it should not exceed approximately 7240 characters. The largest blocksize for two blocks to fit on one track is 3520 characters. One block of data ordinarily may not overflow onto more than one track. If cards are written onto a disk file, a maximum of 35 will fit into one track if they are not blocked. But if they are blocked at 3520, then 88 cards will fit on one track; if blocked up to 7200 characters, 90 will fit. Thus, an IBM 2314 disk capacity is 900 cards per cylinder ($10 \times 90 = 900$) and ($400 \times 900 = 360{,}000$) cards per disk unit.

Some disk units (sometimes termed "packs") are removable and, like tapes, can be purchased or leased. Alternatively, computer centers frequently will provide arrangements for leasing a certain number of cylinders or tracks on their own disk packs. Leasing arrangements for complete packs can sometimes be made with manufacturers or computing suppliers. As with tapes, these have to be registered with the computing center used. This registration is taken care of by the computer center. The disk is labeled and a few tracks are allocated to contain a table of contents which will have entries made in it later, showing the names of the data sets stored there and their locations. Read–write checks are then made on all the tracks.

Removable disks can either be kept *on-line* (i.e., in the disk-drive unit all the time) or they can be kept *off-line* in storage and mounted whenever the files they contain are needed. On-line storage is desirable if the data files are to be used frequently. Off-line is better if the usage is less frequent than a few times each day. As might be expected, the survey analyst has to balance convenience against cost. Whether tapes or disks are used for working storage should depend on the adequacy of computer-center hardware, storage facilities, and procedures for processing each.

Disk files generally have labels. The labels contain the following types of information: *date* on which the file was written, expiration date, disk *serial number*, volume *sequence* (if the data set takes up more than one volume or disk pack), *security* information (such as a password that must be given by a prospective user), the record formats, *blocksize*, *record length*, number of tracks *allocated* for use by the data set, number of tracks actually being used, and so on.

Data can be organized in various ways on disks, and programs written for processing survey data make use of various methods. If the records in a file are always to be written consecutively, one after the other, and if they are to be retrieved in the same way, the file is *sequential.* Tape files are always sequential, simply because of the nature of the storage medium and the tape drives. Any program that uses sequential files can generally be set up easily to accept data from cards, tape, or disk. It is not possible to change existing data on a sequential file without also changing all records that follow the data to be changed. It is possible to add records to the end of a sequential file, however.

A second mode of data organization on disk is *random.* If this mode is used, a key, or address, is assigned to each record. When the file is written, the operating system keeps a list of the keys showing where the records have been put. To retrieve the records the system uses the key to calculate the track number where the record has been stored. The important thing is that it is not necessary to read all the records in order to retrieve or modify one of them. Unlike the procedure for writing tapes, rewriting a disk record does not erase the beginning of the next one. The mode of data file organization on disk is chosen by the programmer who writes the program for processing the survey. Generally, files with different organizing principles can exist together on the same disk.

Disks are typically designated as "public" or "private" by the computer center. Private disks are specially mounted for running a particular job. Public disks may be used to store data sets through a track-leasing arrangement. On a time-sharing interactive system files are generally saved on public disks by a command from the terminal. They are catalogued under the user's identification number and can be retrieved any time. Users of such systems are advised to have backup tapes made regularly and often, perhaps every few weeks. A variety of password and file protection codes are generally available to restrict use of a given file by others who have access to public disks. The important thing to take note of is that capabilities are generally available to the survey analyst to protect data and programs from being overwritten, to restrict access to them, to provide for backup copies in the event of trouble, and to facilitate program and data use and record keeping. Accordingly, the survey analyst should:

1. Investigate the data-protection and accessing capabilities available at the computer center, both by reading the available manuals thoroughly and by talking with consultants at the facility.
2. Work with these staff members to set up a file protection system that meets study requirements.
3. Spend the time to supervise the operation of the file control system, to watch how it is being used, and to make improvements or corrections to procedures where necessary.
4. Ensure that periodic backup files are created.

5. Take the time at the end of the project to make sure that written documentation of all files is complete, that those files to be kept are all written on tapes for storage, and that appropriate backups and periodic rereading procedures have been instituted.

SOFTWARE CONSIDERATIONS IN PROJECT MANAGEMENT

Computing knowledge is not just technical. Moreover, the technical knowledge of computer programming obtainable from the first course in computer science that many readers of this book will have taken will not fully equip them for dealing with the administrative problems that plague users of new technologies that remain new because of constant change. This section reviews the general types of computer software systems available for use in processing survey data, lists the computer-based capabilities ordinarily needed in processing a survey from beginning to end, suggests strategies for use in searching out programs, and outlines a series of factors to review when considering the use of a program. The problems associated with writing needed programs not otherwise available are reviewed, together with a set of criteria for deciding when not to use the computer at all. Specific recommendations are sometimes absent, because decisions must depend on local circumstances.

Types of Programs for Processing Survey Data

Most computer facilities will have at least one of the large statistically oriented survey-processing and data-management systems, which include an integrated set of routines for doing much of the processing required to prepare survey data for analysis. They are generally well documented, carefully debugged, centrally maintained, and can generally be depended on not to have incorrect statistical formulas and other serious logical errors in them. Some examples are SPSS, OSIRIS, DATATEXT, SAS, and IMPRESS. Anderson (1972) lists many others.

A second type of software generally available was developed for the analysis of large amounts of data in engineering research or experimental analysis in the biological or psychological sciences. Some examples include the BIMED and General Electric MARK II libraries. The quality of the programming is usually excellent, but prospective users should make a careful investigation of the match between file-handling and missing-data conventions implemented in these programs and their own data.

A third type of survey data-processing environment is a miscellaneous collection of programs, usually both local and imported. The analyst will be faced with problems of poor documentation, incompatible input requirements, user service consultation from his computer center that is less adequate than that ordinarily provided for the larger statistical packages, and a smaller user group from whom answers to troublesome questions can be obtained.

Each of these environments presents the researcher with a different set of managerial problems. These difficulties must, as much as possible, be anticipated to ensure the success of the project. Some advance planning and investigation will help avoid costly delays and errors. A first step requires an examination of the processing needs of the project. These include the tasks of sorting and sequencing data; merging, altering, and updating files; checking and correcting records; variable generation; subsetting files; and file storage. An extensive, but not exhaustive, list of these needs is shown in Table 9-1. For smaller surveys, much of the listed capability may not be needed.

TABLE 9-1 Basic Survey Processing-System Capabilities

I. File entry processing, error detection, and error correction
  A. Data.
    1. Labeling of magnetic tapes.
    2. Utility routines for manipulation of card-image files; addition and deletion of cards; corrections to fields on cards.
    3. Printing of cards and card-image files from tape or disk.
    4. File duplication and copying between media: card, tape, and disk.
    5. Reformatting of tapes between IBM and other manufacturers' equipment —ability to read any kind of tape.
    6. Ability to copy all the files on a tape or disk.
    7. Capability for reading multiply-punched card images and creating files using only the standard computer character set.[a]
    8. Checking for matching and/or missing records and cards from files.
    9. Ability to retrieve and display one or a few records from a file, or selected fields within the record.
    10. Conversion of card-image data to standard statistical system files; two versions, one defaulted for extreme simplicity in producing a standard system file.
  B. Processing of information about the data.
    1. Good text-editing and text-management program.
    2. Programs to list and check machine-readable code-book information; ability to merge and combine code books from different studies and different waves of a panel study.

[a] Only required if old data or other data using non-character-set punching patterns are to be used. Use of card-punching patterns outside the character set of the computer to be used should be avoided.

TABLE 9-1 (cont'd.)

II. Error detection and correction; file updating and data-management programs
   1. Addition of records to standard statistical system files; addition of variables, addition of data collected at different times or by different instruments; ability to dummy-in data for rectangularizing.
   2. File correction procedures; deletion and replacement of sets of records; correction of fields or sets of fields.
   3. File-merging capabilities.
   4. Error-detection procedures:
      a. Sample book check for completeness of file against sampling frames.
      b. Wild-code check for illegal characters or values.
      c. Consistency checking of data fields within and between records.
   5. Data-set listing: subsetting of variables and observations for display.
   6. Creation of subfiles; subsets of variables and observations.
   7. Sorting and sequencing programs for files.
   8. Explosion of records by weighting factors.
   9. Rectangularization of complex files, dummying of missing blocks of data.
   10. Conversion of tape or disk into punched cards or card-image files.

III. Data transformation and index construction capabilities
   A. Index construction.
      1. Mathematical.
      2. Logical.
      3. Distribution analysis (percentiling).
      4. Guttman, Likert, and Thurstone procedures.
      5. Factor score and predicted value (multiple regression).
   B. Aggregation and imputation: transfer of data from one unit of analysis to another.

IV. Data-analysis programs
   A. Descriptive statistics: means, marginal distributions, percentiling,
   B. Analytic statistics; two- and *N*-way cross-tabulations.
   C. Visual and printed graphical displays: scatter plots and histograms.
   D. *T*-tests and analysis of variance.
      a. One-way analysis of variance.
      b. Two- and three-way ANOVA designs.
      c. Multivariate analysis of variance (MANOVA) designs.
   E. Interaction and specification analysis and generalized least-squares analysis, including regression and dummy-variable regression, automatic interaction detection, multiple classification analysis, including predicted values and residual computations.
   F. Correlation computations excluding missing information that can provide input into multivariate programs.
   G. Partial correlation and path-analysis programs.
   H. Subgroup regressions, analysis of covariance, discriminant function analysis, strip correlations.
   I. Two- and three-stage least squares and analysis of residuals.
   J. Other multivariate-analysis techniques.
      1. Factor analysis: comparison of factor structures.

TABLE 9-1 (cont'd.)

2. Canonical correlations.
3. Clustering and hierarchical clustering techniques.
4. Multidimensional scaling and smallest-space analysis.
5. Log-linear modeling.

K. Nonparametric techniques.
1. Matrix generators (Goodman–Kruskal's tau; Kendall's tau, gamma; etc.).

L. Panel-analysis techniques.
1. Cross-lagged correlation techniques.

M. Structural-analysis programs.
1. Sociometric analysis (e.g., graph-theory programs).
2. Programs for converting structural into contextual variables.

V. Special-purpose programming languages for nonsystem applications
A. Algorithmic compilers; FORTRAN, BASIC, COBOL, PL/1, ALGOL, etc.
B. Special-purpose data-manipulation languages: Utility-Coder-360.
C. List-processing languages: SNOBOL, LISP.
D. Simulation languages.

VI. Project management programs
A. Project scheduling, control, and accounting (PERT, CPM).
B. Data-file control system.
C. Miscellaneous utility routines (e.g., for testing tapes and disks, printing tape labels, file labels, and disk contents listings).
D. Generator for producing test data with arbitrary correlations and model or specification structure.
E. Document retrieval and topic search system.
F. Keyword-in-context (KWIC) indexing routines and routines for constructing bibliographies.

Strategies in Searching Out Computer Programs

Since checking out a heretofore unused program takes time, the search must be started *far* in advance of the time when it will be needed. When it becomes necessary to "import" programs it is desirable to obtain them from users of equipment as similar to your own as possible.[5] Programs entirely written in ANSI FORTRAN will generally be easiest to move. Those written in the Assembly Language code for a particlar computer will, in general, be almost impossible to move, even if these sections comprise only a relatively small portion of the total program.

Treat any newly acquired program as though it had just been written for you by a semicompetent programmer who had not yet had time to check it out. Plan on using it only after having obtained an actual run on it (with test data)

[5] See *Communications of the ACM*, **15**, 12 (1972), p. 1093.

to determine (1) whether your data will fit into it, (2) whether it really uses the computational methods you require, and (3) if it produces the output you need. Modifying programs to accept data in a new format is generally expensive, time consuming, and risky. A better strategy is to write a program to convert study data into the form required by the new program. Writing modifications to a program to print the output you need is less risky than modifying input, but it is still frequently expensive. Table 9-2 provides a list of questions to ask of any program documentation under consideration for use.

TABLE 9-2 Check List for Computer-Program-Use Evaluation

1. Acceptance of character set and file structure of survey.
2. Restrictions on input variable ranges and sample sizes.
3. Subsetting capabilities or combination with file extraction program.
4. Conventions for inapplicable and missing-data codes.
5. Computation of desired statistics, computational formulas, acceptance of weights.
6. Suitability of output options, overview of control language options, and review of potential sources of error.
7. Input storage media options, recoding and variable-generation options, and cross-product matrix input options.
8. Compatibility of input and data output with other programs.
9. Potential rounding problems, precision, pivot-element, and other numerical analysis problems.
10. Check with experienced users for troubles, bugs, etc,. and provisions for mutual self-help. Locate active users.
11. Review adequacy of documentation and obtain supplementary information and copies of setup examples from other users. Provision for acquiring and maintaining documentation.
12. Locating and checkout of companion programs as needed to do sample subsetting, file transposition, reformatting, or variable generation.
13. Access required system job control information and documentation of rules and limits.
14. Facilities for documenting output, and proof that all computations have been done properly; planning for labeling.
15. Provisions made by computer center or others for consultation and handling of program bugs, type of support available for error diagnosis; plans for continuation of support and updated versions of program.
16. Extent to which program is integrated into system for handling other survey processing needs.
17. Probable extent of use to be made of program and evaluation of alternatives.
18. Need for programmer to use program versus setup runs by survey analyst. Staff to use program has had adequate training ahead of time.
19. Cost and timing information.
20. Will it run on available equipment?

When Not to Use the Computer

Since the advent of well-documented survey data-processing packages, there has been some tendency to assume that all phases of survey processing must be done on the computer. There are several principles that govern when to use a computer, and several circumstances in which it will generally pay to use it only minimally or not at all.

For small surveys (less than 100 observations and 10 variables) it is generally a waste of time to use the computer for anything except the computation of statistics. For studies with 50 or fewer observations, obtaining access to a high-quality electronic desk calculator will prove far more useful than processing the study on a computer. The use of an engineering-oriented statistical package in a time-shared environment may also be an effective way to handle the processing and analysis of a small survey, providing missing-data incompatibility problems can be solved. For sorting and merging small files, and even for wild-code and consistency checking, a counter–sorter may still provide the cheapest and quickest way to handle the data.

Program Documentation and Maintenance

Rapid technological change and the installation of updated versions of programs that supposedly are free of the bugs that plagued earlier users force the study director to institute procedures which will ensure that the documentation his staff is using is up-to-date and complete, and that it actually corresponds with the version of the program currently available to him.

This problem is compounded by the facts that documentation often is simply not very good and that far too many computer centers have an incredibly haphazard system for maintaining up-to-date documentation for themselves of the programs they make available, let alone making sure that users have adequate and timely information. Thus, it is necessary to assign one person on the survey staff not only to maintain weekly contact with that person in the computer center responsible for documentation, but also to maintain contact with the *original* supplier and distributor of the software. The objective is to discover what bugs have been discovered in the programs and what "fixes" are available for them, to obtain copies of changes in documentation that apply to the version of the programs being used, to maintain the copies of the program manuals used by the survey staff in an up-to-date and complete form, and to work with the computer center to ensure the availability of an up-to-date version of the program.

In addition, he would have the responsibility for making sure that all other staff members, including the study director, are kept aware of changes in program documentation and are apprised of the availability of new and "improved" versions of the software when they are found to be available.

This person maintains a master set of manuals, places update pages in the manuals assigned to various staff members, and removes obsolete and out-of-date information about programs no longer in existence. He also keeps a dead file of old program documentation until such time as the last report from the project has been published and there is no longer any need to reconstruct what was done with that program to the data.

OTHER ADMINISTRATIVE CONSIDERATIONS

The five remaining topics in this chapter were not left to last because they are the least important. Rather, they bring us full circle, to where this volume started, to the larger process of survey research and the central place of computer-based data processing in it. First considered are problems in dealing with local-computer-center staff and then problems of turnaround time and the scheduling of computer runs. A larger topic is treated, which is often overlooked in technical treatments of survey research, the organization of survey data files. Then come questions that should be dealt with in training survey staff members in the use of available computing facilities. Finally, a topic is covered which places all of this in a larger context, a review of the record-keeping devices that enable the analyst to keep control of the data processing and an articulation of their relationships to other project files.

Negotiating with Computer-Center Personnel

In most computer installations, social-science users are johnny-come-latelys. Computing was for many years the exclusive province of engineers, mathematicians, and physicists, with an occasional venturesome chemist, biologist, or business school graduate student haunting the user's rooms at night. Most computer centers set up their user-service groups to provide the type of consultation support and help needed by the majority of their users. These still are largely either computer-science students or sophisticated users who have written their own programs and whose primary needs are for information about advanced uses of FORTRAN, or the intricacies of the operating system, or who are themselves doing research on computing. Thus, user-service groups are often simply not set up to provide the type of help and guidance needed by a social-science user who has discovered that by implementing and using one of the available statistical-survey-processing packages, he or she could facilitate the computation and processing of substantive research data.

Early social science users often complained bitterly about the unwillingness of the computer-center user-service organizations to provide them with the support and consultation they needed. The complaints continue. One problem is not knowing what questions to ask the consultants.

Given this situation, the following strategies are suggested:

1. Try to place the major responsibility for the data processing for the study in the hands of a person who has taken at least one introductory course in computing.
2. If the study will require extensive use of computer facilities, the study director should at the very beginning of the project confer with the computer-center director, explain what the study is doing, indicate the staff's level of knowledge of computing, and get the center director's suggestions how best to make optimal use of the computer's user support group. The study director should find out what the computer center's peak load periods are and, where possible, find ways to do his work so as to avoid them.
3. The study director and the persons with primary responsibility for the data processing should meet together with the computer-center user-services staff to go over the services available from the group (and pricing policies for services) and to inform the group about the project. This discussion can form the basis for setting up such training sessions for project staff as appear desirable. Do not expect the user-services group to be able to conduct training sessions on the specific survey-data-processing programs you will be using. They probably will not know them any more thoroughly than you do. Ask for training sessions on the topics suggested in Table 9-3.
4. When the user-services group is particularly helpful on some phase of a project, *the study director should see to it that both the user-services chief and the computer-center director know about it.* Computer-center people receive a far greater number of complaints than kudos, simply because people tend to remember only the troubles they had. Throwing bouquets as well as brickbats is the best basis for good working relationships. Remember that most failures in the execution of computer programs are the fault of the user, not the computing-center staff or the programs. Smile and be polite when asking for assistance.

Turnaround Time and Computer Scheduling

Find out what the computing center's peak-load pattern is and avoid it if possible. There are two types of peak-load patterns, those occurring daily and those occurring over periods of several months. In a university or college setting

TABLE 9-3 Checklist of Topics To Be Covered in Training Sessions with Computer-Center User-Service Staff Members

1. Description of facility
   a. Hardware
   b. Software
   c. Services offered
2. Operating-system job control language: usage and most frequent errors
3. Input–output gear available and potential use for project
4. Job submission procedures
5. Typical machine-room operation procedures, including quality-control checks
6. Use of utility programs
   a. Copying to new media
   b. Updating
   c. Inventorying files, etc.
   d. Scratching files
   e. Display of one or more records
   f. Compression, blocking, deblocking, etc.
7. Other program libraries of potential use to the study
8. Error recovery and abend procedures; how to find out what error messages mean
9. Recommended backup procedures
10. File security procedures
11. Program write-up standards
12. Input devices available (punches, cassettes, mark-sense, etc.)
13. Who to see about what problem
14. How to use, sort, and merge utilities
15. Where the manuals are and how to use them
16. Available subroutine libraries and how to use them
17. Who are the other users of the programs to be employed
18. Procedures for leasing space on disks, cataloguing, and scratching procedures and backup
19. Refund policies and procedures
20. Procedures for handling tapes, disks to be hung, long jobs for overnight, use of special input–output gear such as the plotter
21. Training in use of terminals
22. Maintenance policies on software to be used
23. Accounting system and sources of timing information; how charges are computed, and the rationale for them
24. Job-stream-scheduling practices
25. Other users with jobs similar to those to be run
26. How to obtain account numbers and description of practices for controlling use of accounts
27. Arrangement for regular review of adequacy of computing service
28. Arrangements for billing for computing time and services
29. Clarification of study personnel assignments to computer-center people
30. Way in which users are assigned partitions to use in multiprogrammed computer
31. Long-range computer-center plans for maintenance of software to be used
32. Make arrangements for you and your data-processing assistant to be placed on the computer center's mailing list for bulletins
33. Find out where to obtain copies of all relevant manuals and how to keep them up to date

it is likely that late afternoons and any time toward the very end of the semester or quarter will be peak-load times. Where possible, the survey analyst should try to plan the computing schedule to avoid these times.

Many facilities have prices that vary inversely with the demands on the computer. Nights are frequently the cheapest time to run, especially for long jobs which produce large quantities of printed output. If immediate turnaround is needed, high-priority time may be available, although at higher cost. A short job queue, useful for debugging programs, may also be available. Check the job-queue setup at your computing center. Some strategies are:

1. Plan your daily schedule so that you and your assistants have things to do if a run is delayed by 24 hours.
2. Keep close tabs on what the current computer-center turnaround times are.
3. Check, double-check, and triple-check the control-card setups for jobs submitted to the computer center in periods where turnaround times are more than 1 hour.
4. If the computer center offers a fast turnaround service for which you have to pay a premium price consider the possibility of using it, since your staff costs will almost certainly be more than the price differential.
5. Submit large runs broken down into several smaller jobs, where possible, so that if one fails, others may still run.
6. If you will have some very large runs coming up, it may be necessary to inform the computer-center staff ahead of time.
7. Learn to make accurate estimates of the time it will take to run a job and the amounts of output that can be expected. Job failures are expensive, and overestimating the time required may unnecessarily delay your job.

In a time-sharing environment where the analysis is conducted interactively through a remote keyboard terminal, the same strategies are used with respect to avoiding peak-load periods, if possible. One other point is relevant. Time-sharing system terminals operate in two modes. Some are wired directly to the computer, others communicate through regular switched telephone lines. When the telephone-line network is heavily loaded, degradation of the signals carried over the lines may cause transmission errors. This can sometimes be remedied by signing off the system and redialing to obtain another line. More often it calls for taking a break and coming back at a less busy time.

Organization of Survey Data Files

The primary purposes of a data-storage system for the survey staff are to keep track of the physical storage devices that are used to store the data (e.g., tapes, disks, cards) and to keep track of the location, contents, and physical attributes of each file.

When the survey is a small one, lasting only a short period of time, the data storage system should be kept uncomplicated. The data control log system described here illustrates the type adequate for most modest survey projects.

However, when there are several analysts working on the project, each with one or more research assistants helping him by preparing computer runs, and the like, the problems of coordination are greater. Under these circumstances the project director will generally find it necessary to formalize the system somewhat more, and perhaps add additional directories to the log records suggested here. Useful first additions might well be listings of all project files alphabetically and by responsible person.

Data Control Log The simplest method of keeping written control over the various files that are invariably created during the processing of a survey is to list them in a directory. This data control log (DCL) is used together with the codes for each file and the more compact listing of the names of the variables contained in each file. The codes and variable lists provide an inventory of the contents of the file, and the DCL relates the file to others and to the various storage media used. Where several projects share the same physical storage media, be it card file cabinets, a rack of tapes, or one or more disk packs, some type of data control log is essential.

Data are often entered into the storage media one file at a time, and the documentation of the survey file is entered into the data control system when the new file is created. Additions must be made to the file description when new variables or observations are added. However, information about the contents, structure, and location of a file must be retrieved from the data control logs each time a run is made on the computer. These patterns suggest contradictory principles of organizing the file description data. On the one hand, it would appear desirable to keep together information about files located on the same physical storage unit. On the other, an alphabetical listing of files under the name of the person responsible for a group of files would probably be most useful for the study staff, since retrieval of the information about each file is based on the need to use the file, not the storage medium on which it is located. Either mode of organization would work for a small project and both are probably needed for a large one.

On a small project, information about the physical location of each file should be kept with the codes for that file. The codes are the materials the staff will normally be working with in processing the data. Information about the details of the structure and general contents of all the files stored on a particular tape reel or disk should be kept in one place, the data control log.

Thus, the data control log can usefully be organized as indicated in Figure 9-4. Its use presupposes that each card file and drawer is given a unique number or other label, each tape reel is given an identifying number, and each disk is given a number. Each storage unit then is given its own file directory.

Card, Tape, and Disk Files File description information for card files can usefully be kept in sequence by project identification number and deck number. Card files may be located anywhere in the card file cabinets, but it is preferable

I. Disk Files:
   A. On-Line files (files listed alphabetically).
   B. Files kept on demountable packs (listed alphabetically within each pack).

II. Tape Files:
   A. Scratch Tape Pool (listed serially by tape number).
   B. Temporary Work Tapes (listed serially by tape number within name of person to whom tape is assigned: files are kept track of by that person).
   C. Data Storage Tapes (files listed in serial order within the tape on which they are located: tapes listed in ascending sequence by tape identification number).
   D. Back-up Tapes (files listed in serial order within the tape on which they are located: tapes listed in ascending sequence by tape identification number).

III. Card Files:
   A. Data decks stored by project and deck number.
   B. Work file storage space assigned by person.
   C. File of control cards for successful computer program runs; kept in chronological order.
   D. File of source decks for computer programs written for use on the project; kept in order in which used to process the data.

IV. File records for all scratched files; ordered alphabetically by file name within responsible person.

V. Tape and Disk Inventory Files:
   A. Disk Pack Inventory Forms.
   B. Tape Reel Inventory Forms.

Figure 9-4 Organization of a Data Control Log

for all of the data to be kept in a consecutive sequence of file drawers in one cabinet. Each deck should be assigned a specific set of drawers. Additional card file drawers are assigned to project staff members as working space and are simply labeled with each individual's name. Figure 9-5 illustrates a card file record sheet.

An important card file that should always be kept is a chronological file of all control cards submitted on successful computer runs. This chronological file of computer input control cards is probably the most useful block of information that the survey staff can develop to facilitate building up an adequate culture of shared expertise in handling the data, and it will eventually cut the number of aborted computer runs if conscientiously added to and consulted before each run is made.[6] An additional file contains final source-language versions of all computer programs specifically written or modified especially for use on the project. Figure 9-6 illustrates the record sheets for these other card files.

[6] Often the bulk of the control cards simply can be duplicated using a keypunch, thus providing a considerable saving in time and clerical errors in setting up subsequent runs.

CARD FILE RECORD

CABINET NO._______
DRAWER NO._______

Project Number:____________________ in Columns:____________________

Project Name:____

Card Deck Number:____________________ in Columns:____________________

Interview Number in Columns:____

Other Identification:____________________ in Columns:____________________

Deck Contents:____

Expiration Date:____________________ Backup Location:____________________

Total Number of Cards:____________________ Unit of Analysis:____________________

Number of Cards per Analysis Unit: (   ) Fixed (   ) Variable

Continuation from/to______________(Cabinet No.)______________(Drawer No)

Processing Step Creating File:____

Program Creating File:____

Responsible Person:______________________________ Phone:______________

Permission to
Scratch Given by:______________________________ Date:______________
(Signature)

Remarks:

Figure 9-5

Card files will contain four sections: data files for the project, in sequence by deck number; individual work files assigned to each staff member (with the contents kept track of by that staff member); control-card packets stored in chronological order; and source decks for computer programs written for use in processing the data.

The section of the DCL devoted to tapes can usefully be broken down into four categories: scratch tapes, temporary work tapes, data-storage tapes, and backup tapes. Scratch tapes comprise a pool from which staff members withdraw individual reels for use. No records are kept in the DCL of what is on these reels.

When a tape is withdrawn from the pool, it is moved to a new status as a temporary work tape and is assigned to one staff member for his or her exclusive use. Still, no central record is kept of its contents, although it is presumed that the staff member will keep track of whatever sequential files are written on it. All that is recorded in the DCL is that the tape has been assigned to that person.

Unlike work tapes, those used for data storage have central records kept of the files written on them. The information for each file is kept sequentially

CONTROL CARD FILE

Date	Run Number	Program	Purpose of Run	Person Making Run	Remarks

STAFF WORKSPACE CARD FILES

Name	Cabinet Number	Drawer Number	Date Assigned	Remarks

COMPUTER PROGRAM STORAGE FILES

Program	Programmer	Use in Study	Date	Remarks

Figure 9-6 Control Card, Workspace, and Program File Inventory Forms

for each tape, in the order in which the files appear on the tape. These groups of file records are themselves kept sequentially according to the identifying numbers of the tapes on which they are located. Thus, all the descriptive information for tape number one, including files one, two, three, and so on, comes first. This is followed by the descriptive information for all the files on tape number two; and so on. Backup tapes comprise the fourth subcategory. Information about the files on them is stored in the same order as that for the data-storage group. Figure 9-7 gives an example of a tape file record sheet.

TAPE FILE RECORD FORM

Tape No.____________
File No.____________

File Name:______________________________ Date Written:______________________

Contents of File:____

Expiration Date:___________________________ Password:______________________

Length of Records: ( ) Fixed ( ) Variable ( ) Other:______________________

Blocking Factor:___________________________ Block Size:_____________________

Logical Record Length:_____________________ No. of Logical Records:_____________

Continuation from/to Tape No.:______________ No. of Variables:_________________

Unit of Analysis:___________________________ Back-up Location:________________

Processing Step
Creating File:_____________________________ Program
Creating File:_____________________________

Responsible Person:______________________________________ Phone:____________

Project No:_______________________________ Project Name:____________________

Permission to
Scratch Given By:____ Date:____________
(signature)

Remarks:____

Figure 9-7

Unlike tapes, disk packs would not generally be assigned to individual staff members, since each disk pack can hold a very large number of files, many more than one staff member would normally use. Moreover, it is not necessary to read over each file on a disk in order to locate a given file for processing. Files may be updated at any time without destroying others that have been written later; so there is no need to keep an exact sequence of file records for the pack in the order in which they were originally written. For these reasons, the data describing the files on a disk drive, showing the number of records, block-size, and so on, are best organized alphabetically, by the name of the file. Data for each demountable disk would be placed together. Data on files kept on-line at the computer-center would be kept separate from those on demountable packs and would simply be kept in alphabetical order by file name. Figures 9-7 and 9-8 illustrate the type of file records that need to be kept for tapes and disks.

Data Librarian In a major survey project, control over data files can be best kept by giving one staff member the specific responsibility for maintaining them. The objectives of the data librarian are to (1) maintain the data base and its

DISK FILE RECORD FORM

DISK FILE FORM Disk No.:__________

File Name:____________________ Date Written:____________________

Contents of File:____

Expiration Date:____________________ Password:____________________

Length of Records: ( ) Fixed ( ) Variable ( ) Other:____________________

Blocking Factor:____________________ Block Size:____________________

Logical Record Length:____________________ No. of Logical Records:__________

Continuation to/from Disk No.:__________ Access Method: ( ) Sequential ( ) Other

No. of Variables:____________________ Unit of Analysis:____________________

Processing Step Creating File:____

Program Creating File:____

Back-up Location:____

Project No.:____________________ Project Name:____________________

Responsible Person:______________________________ Phone:__________

Permission to Scratch Given By:______________________________ Date:__________
(signature)

Remarks

Figure 9-8

integrity, (2) facilitate the use of the data by the project staff, and (3) organize the data base so as to make for the most efficient use of both staff time and computer resources. The data librarian's duties can be summed up as follows:

1. Prepare and maintain the data control log.
2. Maintain the physical storage of tapes and card files and control the return of tapes and card decks to storage after usage.
3. Assist other staff members in using the data-storage system.
4. Review periodically with other staff members the various storage media used by the project to determine whether expiration dates have passed, and if so, what is to be done with the expired files.
5. Monitor the frequency of file usage and the organization of the disk packs used by the project to ensure that they do not inadvertently

get filled up with files which are no longer used even though their expiration dates have not yet arrived, and which should be scratched or moved to more permanent storage on tape.

6. Periodically reorganize the disk data files to scratch unneeded data sets and move others to the most appropriate types of storage for their usage pattern.
7. Provide for periodic backup of data sets kept on disks.
8. Review periodically the status and usage of work tapes.
9. Periodically initiate runs to reread backup tapes to ensure that print-through does not occur.
10. Maintain password logs for all project files.
11. Plan for and take responsibility for acquiring new tapes, disk packs, leased disk space, and data-storage supplies as needed and budgeted. See to it that they are registered appropriately in the computer center, listed in the appropriate sections of the DCL, and assigned storage space.
12. Maintain liaison with computer-center operations and user-service personnel to establish and maintain cooperative procedures for efficient handling of cards, tapes, and disks, and for maintenance of the integrity of the data.
13. Develop and maintain skills in the use of the utility programs offered by the computer center for data manipulation and in the use of the job-control-language facilities relating the data base to the programs used by the project.
14. Monitor problems and assist in the development of solutions for problems related to the management of the project's data.
15. Read the literature on data-base management and data organization and on technology related to data storage, and advise the project director on improved procedures.

Many of these tasks are shared with others. The important point to be made here is that one person should be given the primary responsibility for maintaining the data and the authority and resources to do a thorough job. The alternative is confusion and probable loss of important data files.

Operation of the System The functioning of the system can be illustrated by describing several of the typical transactions that take place. These include receipt of new reels of tape, a staff member getting a scratch tape from the pool to use as a temporary work tape, creation of files on a data-storage tape, creating backup copies of tapes and disks, returning tapes to scratch pool status, and scratching disk files.

DISK PACK INVENTORY

Disk No.:__________ Date Purchased:__________

Owner:__________ Manufacturer:______ Type:______

Responsible Person:__________ Phone:__________

Date of Last Certification:__________ Vendor:__________

Remarks:

TAPE REEL INVENTORY

Tape No.:__________ Date Purchased:__________

Manufacturer:__________ Type:__________

Responsible Person:__________ Phone:__________

Owner:__________ Date of Last Certification:__________

Length:__________ Channels ( ) 7 ( ) 9 Density:__________ bpi

Label Status: ( ) Labelled ( ) Unlabelled Vendor:__________

Remarks:

Figure 9-9

When a new reel of tape or a new disk pack is acquired, the data librarian registers it at the computer center and writes up the appropriate information in the tape and disk inventory files. (See Figure 9-9.) Information items included in the inventory file are the newly acquired registration number, the date purchased, the manufacturer's name and product identification code, the name of the owner of the tape reel, its length, number of channels, labeling status, vendor from whom purchased, and, where appropriate, the recording density to be used.[7] The librarian sets up storage space for it in the tape racks or shelves, and the inventory record is then placed in the appropriate section of the DCL. In addition, a tape file record, blank except for the tape number, is placed in the scratch tape pool. A similar procedure would be followed for a newly acquired disk pack, except that the blank disk file record would be placed in a new section of the demountable pack section of the DCL. The new disk pack would ordinarily receive storage space at the computer center. The new storage unit is then ready for use.

When short-term files are to be created by a staff member for his own use,

[7] Ordinarily, it will be best to decide what density to use and then to keep this constant for the whole study, despite the fact that some exceptions may have to be made if tapes are ever to be shipped to other installations. Of course, in these cases other densities may have to be used and appropriately recorded.

it may be best simply for that staff member to keep track of them. In this case several options are open, depending on the facilities offered by the computer center and the project's arrangments with them. The staff member may create a disk file on-line without registering it in the project's DCL, obtain a temporary work tape for the file, or write the file on one of the demountable disks—again with no entry in the DCL. Having the flexibility to do this without going through the extra paper work of making entries in the DCL is often desirable, especially if the file is temporary. However, if this practice is followed, it is absolutely necessary to have a completely understood, regular, and public schedule for scratching files that have no entry in the DCL. This is the responsibility of the data librarian. Of course, if the staff member uses a temporary work tape, this problem does not arise. It is sufficient to sign out a tape from the scratch pool, moving the blank tape file record to thc section listing the staff member's own work tapes, listing himself or herself as the person now responsible for the tape. If the staff member creates private files in this way, it is desirable also to borrow a few blank tape or disk-file record forms and to maintain a temporary DCL log for his or her own files.

The decision where to place the new file will depend, in part, on the facilities offered by the computer center and the characteristics of the programs to be used, as well as on cost factors. If the file is to be used extensively for a short period of time, on-line storage may be best. If it is a very large file, a temporary work tape may be best. If it is part of a series of operations using computer programs which are already stored on a demountable disk pack, locating the file on this pack would generally be desirable. Both cost and convenience factors influence the decision.

If the staff member has a reasonable expectation that the file will be needed after the next regularly scheduled scratching of files from the disks, he or she should register it in the DCL and put an expiration date on it. If it has been placed on a temporary work tape, its status should soon be changed to that of data-storage tape. It is good practice to restrict temporary work tapes to files destined to last a few days at most.

Data-storage tapes should be reviewed by the librarian every few months to determine which ones should be copied for backup. Anything worth saving at all is generally worth backing up. A number of shorter tapes can be copied onto a single long tape. This can generally be done during off-hours when computer rates are likely to be lower. Backup copies are not made for temporary work tapes.

Backup procedures for disk files are of critical importance because of time-sharing operation-system crashing problems which can cause loss of information, even on "private" demountable disks (although the likelihood of loss is much less than if data is kept on-line). All disk files should therefore be copied onto tape at intervals appropriate for the frequency of operating system problems typically encountered, and the amount of changes made in the files during a given period. Particularly important files should be backed up as soon as they are written, however. Computer centers do their own disk-file backup, often on a weekly basis, and the librarian should become familiar with these procedures and take advantage of them where possible.

When a file is created as part of the regular data-storage system, the tape or disk file record should immediately have *all* the entries completed (except the permission to scratch), and should be placed promptly in the appropriate place in the DCL. It should be carefully reviewed for completeness and accuracy by the data librarian.

When a periodic review of the files' status with project members reveals that one or more files may be scratched, the librarian obtains written approval of these decisions, writes the files on a "drainhole" tape, and returns the storage medium to scratch status.[8] For a tape, returning to scratch status simply means transferring the file records for all the files on the tape to the alphabetically organized "scratched-file" section of the DCL, setting up a new blank tape file record with only the number entered on it, and placing this in the scratch-tape section of the DCL. For a file on a demountable disk pack, the disk file records would be held in a queue for the next regular disk scratch and reorganization computer run. Urgent needs for disk space would speed the scheduling of this run.

As with tapes, the file records scratched from disk storage are simply transferred to the scratched-file section of the DCL. Their retention here permits later reconstruction of the file processing sequence if errors have to be tracked or lost files reconstructed. A record of the control cards and programs used to build the data file facilitate this, should it become necessary.

As soon as a complete copy of all the basic consistency-checked data for a study has been written on tape or disk, a single extra copy of its backup should be made and stored in another location; at the residence of the study director, in a bank vault, or in some other safe location away from the main data-storage location.

There are several additional complications when several persons are working simultaneously with the study files. To add observations, make corrections, or add variables to an existing file, a staff member should first notify the person responsible for the file. When additions have been made they should be proved by counting the records in the file at the end of the procedure, or by printing out the first few and last few records. A new description of the modified file should immediately replace the DCL entry for that file. The record for the old file is marked "update"; a reference to the new description is inserted, together with the date; the old information is crossed out *in readable fashion* (not erased); and the old record is transferred to the scratched-file section of the DCL. Then a new backup for the updated file is made and the old backup should not be reused until the new copy of the file has proved itself in use.

[8] The drainhole tape is kept for 3 months and then returned to scratch status. Use of such a tape involves some computer costs, but it can be used selectively. It has saved more than one potential disaster.

Physical Condition of Tapes and Disks Although the reliability of these storage media has been vastly improved, wear and tear do take place. Arrangements should be made by the librarian with the computer center to undertake periodic review and certification of the tapes and disks used by the project. Certification involves the use of a test program that reads and writes on the tape, checking its physical characteristics with special electronic instruments. Bad tapes can be cleaned and shorted. Careful attention once a year to this problem can prevent the inadvertent use of a bad unit and loss of data. A good computer-center accounting routine can easily generate tape- and disk-usage statistics, which can be kept as part of the tape and disk inventory, for use in these periodic reviews.

Training Study Staff Members in Data Processing

Study directors planning for the data processing of a survey sometimes start this phase of their planning process after all the interviews have been received from the field. This is too late. For one thing, study staff members (often including the study director) will not have sufficient time to familiarize themselves with the computer programs, control languages, computer-center procedures, output formats, and data-processing procedures to be used.

This suggests that a major task during the earlier phases of the study should be training the staff members who are to handle the data processing. At least three effective training methods can be employed: staff participation in planning the data-processing sequences, lectures and demonstrations from computer-center personnel on operating procedures, and practice using the computer programs with contrived data.

Table 9-3 provided an inventory of a list of topics to be covered in a series of meetings between study personnel who will be involved in data-processing for the survey and computer-center user-service personnel. Arrangements should be made early in the project for a regular series of meetings between computer-center user-service people and survey staff. All these topics should be gone over at least once even if survey staff members have had previous experience in processing this type of data using that particular computer. Procedures change and it is of the utmost importance that people working with the data on a day-to-day basis be completely familiar with current practices.

The need for familiarizing survey staff members with the programs to be used *before* the actual processing takes place cannot be overemphasized. Even a study director, experienced in using the statistical system to be employed, forgets the details of control-language syntax in the time period since he last used the program. Experience has shown repeatedly that merely reading the manual is no substitute for actually trying to set up a run on a program. The more complex the control language for the program, the more the need for dry runs.

A recommended method for training staff is to take the practice interviews set up for the training of coders, and editors and prepare the corresponding machine-readable records. A few of the regular interviews can be added to make a small file that can be used to make test runs inexpensively on the programs to be used. Where possible, dry runs should be made on every single program to be used in the study about 2 weeks preceding its actual use. This can be accompanied by phone calls to or conferences with other users of the program to find out about the existence of any recently discovered bugs (errors) or other problems. This ensures that a usable copy of the program is actually available at the computer center, and it gives the study staff a chance to ask questions about the input parameters. Rather than taking extra time, this will be found to cut the *total* time for processing the data significantly as well as reducing total computing costs.

Dry runs will also reveal the extent to which the staff do not have adequate familiarity with the data structures, the codes, the problems to be solved using that particular program, the computer-center operating procedures, the procedures for ensuring that errors are kept to a minimum and caught when they occur, and the record-keeping procedures for keeping track of computer runs.

Checklists of topics for review by computer users are included here as a reminder of the topics that must be considered. The first (Table 9-4) is a guide for reviewing the characteristics of a program about to be used for the first time by the project, the second (Table 9-5), for outlining a procedure to be used in setting up a computer run, the third (Table 9-6) for the materials ordinarily needed when setting up a computer run, and a final list (Table 9-7) of topics to review when actually preparing a computer run. There are overlaps between the checklists, but use of each as a starting point will prevent inadvertently overlooking a factor that later proves troublesome.

TABLE 9-4 Checklist for Computer Program About To Be Used

1. Check sample size and number of variables, other program restrictions and limits. Make sure problem will fit into program.
2. Review documentation and make test or practice run.
3. Review temporary recoding, subsetting, and input storage media options.
4. Review missing-data requirements and check against data characteristics.
5. Review control parameters, output options, and sequence of control input, independence of options.
6. Review job-control-information requirements.
7. Check with other users for recent information on bugs and bad documentation or program version updates, and current cost patterns. Find out if similar runs made.
8. Check for updated documentation and local check-out status of program.
9. Locate and review past runs and setups. Review past output.
10. Locate copies of current versions of coding forms and setup aids.
11. Develop cost and time estimates.
12. Work out labeling for runs.

TABLE 9-4 (cont'd.)

13. Check precision and rounding problems.
14. Check with computer-center staff and other users for assessment of recent problems users have had.
15. Review job control language that relates program to data and to operating system.
16. Review formulas.
17. Check for problems with list variables.
18. If this is the first time the program is to be used on these data, elect to obtain as many of the output options that are feasible. If past experience indicates they are not needed, omit them.
19. On statistical programs always obtain a profile of the relationships between variables, a summary measure of the extent of the relationship, and a significance test.
20. Do not assume that you understand how a particular program parameter works until you have actually used the program with variations of the parameter.
21. Check to see that all the data you need are in your file and do not have to be aggregated, imputed, or transferred from another file.
22. Some programs require that data be sorted before input as a separate step—check input-data-sequence requirements and status of file. If others are also using the file, include sorting steps as needed. Do not depend on past sorts.
23. Are the forms of the variables to be used in the run consistent with program requirements? Some programs require class intervals, others continuous variables. Some may require that a variable have not more than 10 class intervals. In many cases several recoded versions of variables may be available. The right ones must be selected. If class intervals are used, are they to be based on percentiles of the distribution or on specifically chosen breakpoints?
24. Review handling of over-the-field amounts and inapplicable codes.

TABLE 9-5 Procedure for Setting Up a Computer Run

A. Assemble needed materials, description of desired processing, and:
    1. Program write-ups.
    2. Codes for files to be used as input.
    3. Computer-center account number, passwords, etc.
    4. Job submission information about computer-center procedures.
    5. System-control information for invoking execution of the program.
    6. Coding forms and other aids to setting up the run of the program.
    7. Examples of past control-card packets and past output of program.
    8. Timing and cost information for calculating expected time and page estimates.
    9. File control information on physical location of input files, blocking factors, record lengths, number of variables, formats, file structures, etc.
    10. Scratch tapes, etc., as needed.
B. Check with others who have used the program recently to see if there have been any unresolved problems with it.
C. Code the control information for the program run.
    1. Output.
    2. Computations.
    3. Input.

TABLE 9-5 (cont'd.)

4. System job control language for invoking the program.
5. Operator's instructions for tape hanging, etc.

D. Desk-check the run setup for errors.
1. System job control language.
2. Program control information.
3. Data sequence.

E. Have a colleague or supervisor desk-check the setup for errors, using the original description of processing required.

F. If schedules permit, and if the run will be a large one, make a test run using a very small subset of the input data; purpose: computer syntax check of control language and check of job control language.

G. Make run.

H. Go over output extremely carefully:
1. For error messages due to either job control language or program.
2. To see that the job, in fact, ran to completion.
3. Examine any checks for errors that had been built into the run (e.g., proper number of cases; frequency distributions agree with those from previous run, etc.; proper handling of missing data).

I. File control cards and description of desired processing in control-card file and processing file, respectively, and update indexes to these files.

J. Distribute copies of runs as needed, placing master copy in project computer output file.

TABLE 9-6 Checklist for Materials Needed in Setting Up Computer Runs

1. Data file information: File name, number of records, blocking factor, record length, file storage media location, backup-file information, units of analysis, file sequencing information, subset of observations.
2. Variable information: code book, marginal distributions, questions, questionnaire, variable numbers or names, location in storage file, format information, character sets, missing data codes, decimals, ranges.
3. Past processing information on file: printed output from all programs that have written into that file. Descriptions of processing that generated all variables in the file; output from programs that generated those variables. Subsetting information if file is subset.
4. Coding forms and setup aids used with program and instructions for their use.
5. Computer program user's manual for program being used.
6. Account numbers and authorizations for computer use and data storage.
7. Job-control-information manuals.
8. Computer-center procedures and requirements for submission of jobs, especially as they apply to submission of cards, disks, tapes, etc., with jobs, where these apply.
9. Examples of past use of program and copies of complete sets of control information exactly as used. Old output from past runs, examples of parameter values, etc., especially where task is similar to present task.
10. Administrative information: processing log books.

TABLE 9-7 Checklist of Topics To Review When Setting Up a Computer Run

1. Has a careful check been made of the input parameters, sequence, and format?
2. Have these been checked with at least one other person?
3. Have adequate entries been made in the study documentation files showing the purpose of the run and a description of what's being done?
4. Have all the required tapes been acquired and checks made to see that disk space is available as needed?
5. Have adequate tests for the run been set up?
   a. Main logic
   b. Exception conditions
   c. High and low values
   d. Missing data
   e. End-of-file processing
   f. What to do if run aborts
6. Is the run relatively routine, or is it an unusual situation requiring extra checks?
7. Have all the required input subfiles been created?
   a. Variables
   b. Cases
8. Has all the required variable generation been accomplished?
   a. Summarization
   b. Aggregation
   c. Imputation
9. Is the logic of the subsetting and variable-generation description correct?
10. Are the correct formulas being used?
11. Are the names of the input files and their locations correct? Are they matched up to the required program input streams?
12. Have the input files been properly sequenced? Are there files that must be concatenated or merged?
13. Have the requirements for printed and machine-readable file output been met?
14. Have all previous processing steps on this file been completed and the results verified?
15. Have all variables needed in the file been transferred in or properly recoded? Is an extra variable-generation step needed? Are the ranges of the variables compatible?
16. Have the records of the accuracy of the previous recoding operations on this file been checked to prove the correctness of the recoding?
17. Are all the variables needed for subsetting and assigning missing data, weights, dependent variables, independent variables, and identifiers present? Are they in the right form?
18. Has information been assembled for easy reference that pertains to the adequacy of measurement of the most important variables in the analysis (e.g., coding and editing decisions, interviewer comments about respondent vagueness in answering these questions)?
19. Have error checks been built into the run to catch potential errors?
   a. Correct subgroups included and excluded
   b. Correct versions of variables
   c. Logic of recoding operations
20. Are observations to be excluded from the run? On what basis? Missing information on dependent variable? Other missing information? Exclude subset of data to whom model does not apply?

TABLE 9-7 (cont'd.)

21. Have all the provisions for any output files been made properly? Codes and variable category labels? Missing-data codes, inapplicable cases, file names, and tape or disk storage arrangements? Decimal points in output variables, plus and minus values? Blocking factors for files, record lengths? Subfile structures?
22. Have all the necessary provisions for proper handling of multivalued variables been made?
23. Do category labels need to be supplied for any of the variables? Are they adequate for the purposes of the analysis?
24. Is the run labeling information adequate to describe the data input, the purposes of the analysis, the sequence of the run in the processing, date, person running the program, etc.?
25. Are the formats for all the control information correct? Is all the control information in the correct sequence?
26. Are the control parameters prescribing computation options consistent with past practice, or have new requirements been responsible for changes to unusual values?
27. Is there an output option that has inadvertently been overlooked or left out because nothing was said about it in the processing specifications?
28. Are there dependent parameters whose values are inconsistent?
29. If several versions of the input variables were present in the input files, has the correct one been used in all cases?
30. Does the specification sheet itself make sense in terms of what the data-analysis objectives are known to be?

Organizing All the Files for the Study

Taking up this topic brings us back to the beginning—to a consideration of the overall place of data processing in the study. Files directly concerned in one way or another with the processing of survey data can be organized conveniently into four parts: sampling the field operations, coding and editing, data processing, and general study files. Figure 9-10 contains a checklist of the various types of files the study director will generally need to maintain.[9] The following section presents an overview of the contents of each of these files as well as a short discussion of some of the alternative physical implementations for storage.

General Study Files In addition to the obvious correspondence and administrative files, certain others are suggested. A bibliographic file of 3- by 5-inch cards containing references to the literature pertinent to the study and cross-referenced by subject matter as well as by author will generally prove to be worth while. If either the library call numbers or the sequential numbers (for publications which the project has copies of) are written on the cards, retrieval of the material is straightforward. The sequential numbers are attached to books,

[9] The numbering system suggested has worked well. Undoubtedly omissions and rearrangements would be required for any individual study.

CHECK LIST OF SURVEY FILES

I GENERAL STUDY FILES

1.0 Index to and description of study files.
1.1 Correspondence.
1.2 Bibliography:
  1.2.1 Index.
  1.2.2 Documents.
1.3 Spare Copy.
1.4 Carbon Log.
1.5 Personnel (study staff, interviewing and sampling staff, coding and editing staff, consultants).
  1.5.1 Name and address file.
1.6 Study Objectives:
  1.6.1 Proposal.
  1.6.2 Working Papers.
  1.6.3 Interviewer and Coder Explanations.
  1.6.4 Press Releases.
1.7 Draft Reports and Reprints.
1.8 Accounting and Cost distribution:
  1.8.1 Budget.
  1.8.2 Expenditures by Category.
  1.8.3 Computer Cost Accounting.
1.9 Memoranda Book.
  1.9.1 Project scheduling, target dates and task precedence charts.

II SAMPLING AND FIELD OPERATIONS FILES

2.1 Sample Design Working Paper.
2.2 Field Operations Working Paper.
2.3 Sample Book and Address Listings.
2.4 Interviewer Production Control Sheets.
2.5 Interviewer Correspondence Files.
2.9 Memoranda Book:
  2.9.1 Sample Book Check Report.
  2.9.2 Sampling Cost Report.
  2.9.3 Sample Coverage and Population Representation Report.
  2.9.4 Field Quality Control Report.
  2.9.5 Response Rate Report.
  2.9.6 Interviewing Cost Report.
  2.9.7 Interviewing Supervisor Reports.

Figure 9-10

reprints, or copies of journal articles, which are then kept sequentially in a separate location.[10]

If a spare copy file is established which can be used to keep extras physically

[10] Where a computer-based bibliographic capability is provided, its use will provide convenience and flexibility. The FAMULUS system (University of London, 1972) is a typical example.

III EDITING AND CODING FILES

3.1 Master Editing Instructions:
- 3.1.1 Edit Instruction Master and Changes.
- 3.1.2 Edit Change Log Book.
- 3.1.3 Editing Decision Book.

3.2 Master Codes:
- 3.2.1 Variable Index's.
- 3.2.2 Master Codes and Changes.
- 3.2.3 Code Change Log Book.

3.3 Interview-work-sheet packet files:
- 3.3.1 Interviews and work sheets.
- 3.3.2 Cover Sheets.

3.4 Pack Sign-out Book.

3.5 Bound Code Sheets.

3.6 Edit and Code Quality Control File:
- 3.6.1 Training materials, practice Interviews and their code sheets, Check-edit and
- 3.6.2 Check-edit and Check-code and variable quality control inventory records.

3.9 Memoranda Book:
- 3.9.1 Edit Progress Reports.
- 3.9.2 Coding Progress Reports,
- 3.9.3 Editing and Coding Costs Reports.
- 3.9.4 Interviewer Reports on questionnaire problems.
- 3.9.5 Coder and Editor Reliability and Variable-Quality memo, evaluation of problems with codes.
- 3.9.6 Coding Procedures memo.

IV DATA PROCESSING FILES

4.1 Data-Processing Job Specification Book.

4.2 Computer Output Files.

4.3 Computer Program Manual File.

4.4 Computer Cost Summary and Error File.

4.5 Computer Program Job Set-up file.

4.6 Data File Control Log (DCL)
- 4.6.1 Storage Media Register
- 4.6.2 Data File Indices:
  - 4.6.2.1 Project
  - 4.6.2.2 File name.

4.7 Dead Storage Index.

4.8 Statistical Table Book.

4.9 Memoranda Book:
- 4.9.1 Codes for PSU's, Occupation, etc.
- 4.9.2 Keypunch, Data-structure and File organization.
- 4.9.3 Sample Book Check.
- 4.9.4 Weight Computations
- 4.9.5 Data Processing Cost and Error summary memo.

Figure 9-10 (cont'd.)

removed from master copies and other do-not-lose articles, unfortunate losses can be avoided. Here should be kept extras of letters sent to respondents announcing the study, press releases, extra questionnaires, show cards, cover sheets, worksheets, pages for log books, interview and coder explanations of what the study is all about, and the like. They can usefully be organized into sections that parallel the total file organization (i.e., general, field and sampling, editing and coding, and computation and data processing).

The carbon log is intended to provide some redundancy in the record keeping and to provide a trace of the activity of the survey over time. It is simply a binder with one extra copy of absolutely everything that comes from the secretary's typewriter, dated, punched for binding, and kept in the order in which it was produced.[11]

A copy of the original research proposal, working papers on research objectives, explanations of these given to coders and to interviewers, and press releases should be kept on file. A working paper should be prepared which defines survey objectives, schedules, concepts, units of analysis, data-collection units and theoretical constructs to be used. Dependent and explanatory variables should be used. Dependent and explanatory variables should be sketched and important sample subgroups should be outlined. The paper should set forth the types of statements about the population in question that the analyst wishes to be able to make on the basis of the data. Interview and coder explanations and press releases are, of course, abridged versions. These general files are an appropriate place to keep master copies of reports and reprints of printed materials based on the findings of the study. Extra copies would, of course, be kept separately in the spare copy file.

Keeping administrative control of the highly complex project that a survey can be is probably the most underexplained topic (relative to its importance) in survey research methodology texts. It seems within the scope of this book to comment that this cannot be accomplished without (1) a budget having meaningful cost-distribution categories, (2) an accurate and timely expense-accounting system that corresponds to the budget categories *and which the surveyer does not have to design and implement*, and (3) an inclination on the part of the analyst to feel sufficiently responsible to sponsors and staff that some time is spent in this mundane and intellectually unrewarding activity. Of particular importance is our admonition to survey analysts to keep close control over their expenditures as regards computing both salary and machine time. This requires a computing-center accounting system that permits job submission and cost data to be reported back to the survey project director every few weeks, and with the reporting basis being a unit useful to the project director.

The last item in the project general file is the planning and scheduling memorandum. This is needed for even the least amount of efficiency in the use

[11] Project management will be much simplified if everything of any importance is typed, labeled with a project identification number or code, dated, and if all documents are identified with the writer's or designer's name or initials.

of staff time during the interviewing, editing and coding phases, and acts as a checklist and organizer for the entire processing sequence of the study.

Sampling and Field Operations Files The primary items in the sampling and field files are the working papers on these topics and the sample book itself. These are supplemented by control sheets, correspondence files, and reports dealing with what was actually done. The sample design working paper should contain sections relating the sample design to the study objectives. Two kinds of topics should be covered: the actual sample design and the rationale for using it, as well as the procedures to be followed in implementing it. Definitions of the population, the sampling frame, units of sampling, and data-collection and analysis objectives should be set forth. It should also outline the types of interviews to be obtained and the strata to be used. It should record sampling fractions to be applied to these strata, desired sample size, and the rationale used in the selection of this configuration. It should specify procedures for selecting the exact individuals to be interviewed and should specify the methods to be used in calculating sampling errors.[12]

The field-operations working paper should cover the methods of data collection to be used and the rationale for this selection. It should specify and explain the measurement methods to be used; define the length of the interview desired; specify supervisory roles and interviewer training procedures and evaluation methods; outline the types of instructions that are to be written for interviews; and specify calling and call-back procedures. Eventually, this document is to be combined with field reports from supervisors. Hence, standards by which interviewer performance is to be measured should be set forth.

The sample book itself constitutes a major subfile. It contains a detailed description of each address in the sample, its location and stratum, and its assignment to an interviewer for coverage. Eventually, it will have attached to it the sample book numbers of the cover sheets associated with it by the interviewer and the interview numbers of those interviews obtained from the data collection associated with that address. Ordinarily, correspondence files would be maintained for each interviewer since interviews often have to be returned from editing with questions. When this and all sample book checks have been completed it may be desirable to remove this file and the file of cover sheets (which is the only link between interview and address) to the safety of vault storage.

A number of reports should be written on the basis of information generated by the sampling and field operations. These are generally needed eventually as methodological documentation of the study. They ordinarily could be placed in the sampling and field operations memorandum book, and would include reports on the sample book check, sampling and interviewing cost reports,

[12] For a more detailed exposition of this process, see Lazerwitz (1968), Kish (1965), and Lansing and Morgan (1971).

interviewing supervisor's report, a more general interviewing quality report, a response-rate analysis, and a sample coverage and population representation report.

The sample book check documents (1) that all addresses comprising the sample were visited and that cover sheets were obtained for every interviewing unit associated with those addresses; and (2) that there is, in fact, exactly one interview, noninterview form, or nonsample form for each sampled address, or, where there are multiple interviewing units located at that address, appropriate accounting for each such interview. This requires checking to ensure that all multiple interviews located in the same sampling address were accounted for.

A parallel objective is to verify that sampling-frame identification codes, locality information codes such as county identification, and so on, have been correctly transferred from the sample book listings to the cover sheets, interviews, and noninterview or nonsample forms; to the code sheets; and ultimately to machine-readable form. In addition, the report should contain a tally of the types of errors found and an identification of the most frequent sources of error. It should establish exact control figures for the number of interviews, number of noninterviews, and number of nonsample addresses. Further evidence as to whether the interviews were, in fact, obtained from the correct interviewing unit, the right respondent, whether there should have been additional interviews obtained (or whether too many were obtained), and whether or not respondents were correctly identified, and so on, will be obtained during later editing phases.

The principal difference between the sampling coverage and population representation report and the original sample design working paper is that the report documents what was *actually done.* Thus, it includes definitions of the population, the sampling frame, units of sampling, and the sample design and rational for using it; the type of strata actually used; actual sampling fractions; formulas for estimating population figures from sample statistics; and adaptations that had to be made in sampling and interviewing strategies as the study progressed.

The field quality-control report summarizes experiences in pretesting, describes interviewer selection and training procedures, summarizes experiences in using the interview schedules, and points out problems with certain questions and the strategies that were adopted for solving them, with an assessment of the outcome.

The objective of the response-rate report is to assess the extent to which findings from the sample can be generalized to the sample that it purports to represent. It presents statistics that show the proportion of completed interviews resulting from the coverage of the sampling frame, broken down by sampling units and by other relevant variables; comparisons between observational data obtained from interviews and noninterview households; and comparison between sample characteristics and data from other published sources.[13]

[13] For an example, see Lansing and Morgan (1971), pp. 255–268.

The interviewing cost report provides guidance in estimating data-collection costs for future projects and reveals cost differences between interviewers that could lead to discovery of fraudulent interviews supplied by dishonest interviewers, as well as facilitating control over interviewer expense accounts. Ordinarily it would be written by that project staff member having primary responsibility for the data-collection process, together with field supervisory staff.

Interviewing supervisor reports provide documentation on interviewer performance and describe experiences with sections of the questionnaire that presented problems during the interviewing process. They provide evidence summarizing the data-collection problems that inevitably occur in urban areas and can provide valuable guidelines to interpretation during the analysis phases of the study when variables correlate in unexpected ways.

Editing and Coding Files These documents are generated at the time codes and editing instructions are finalized, during the editing and coding processes, and after their completion when these raw materials are summarized for later inclusion in the methodological appendices of reports to be written on the study findings.

In addition to the master copy of the editing instructions with all dated changes, the log book showing each change, the reason for it, and the date on which it was implemented should be included. The editors' decision book forms the third section of this group of files. It provides the major documentation of the way in which study concepts are actually operationalized.

The master code files are similar to the editing files. Included are the master copy of the codes themselves, the log book in which all code changes, the date on which they were implemented and the reasons for implementation, and the files of 3- by 5-inch cards on which were written unclassifiable responses which resulted in the generation of the new codes. A valuable addition is an index that not only relates each variable to its position in the file, and maps it into the questionnaire, but relates it to appropriate concepts in the theoretical edifice that informs the study. If this can be made machine-readable and adequate cross-indexing obtained, it can be an exceedingly helpful aid. It is a necessity if the study is longitudinal.

The third, fourth, and fifth sections of the editing and coding files contain the actual packets of 10 interviews together with their associated worksheets, the pack sign-out book, and the bound code sheets. Cover sheets linking interviews to addresses should be kept in a separate file and kept under lock and key to ensure confidentiality of the respondents. The interview pack sign-out book records the coding and editing history of each pack of 10 interviews and provides a continuous and up-to-date progress report on the state of the coding and editing. Code sheets returned from keypunching should be bound in interview number order and kept as a part of the study files.

The editing and coding quality-control file contains all the training materials used in these phases of the study, practice interviews, check-editing records, and records of all efforts to ensure quality during these two phases. These constitute the raw materials from which the coding and editing quality-control memorandum or working paper is later written.

As with the two preceding major file sections, the editing and coding section contains a memorandum book. It contains short working papers summarizing the editing and coding operations that were performed on the data, reporting the level of quality achieved, and documenting unsolved problems. These working papers take little time to write if undertaken right at the close of that phase of the processing and can be used to good advantage later during the analysis to clarify why certain variables behaved statistically the way they did, as well as for planning later studies and training future staff members.

This memoranda book contains the progress reports supplied weekly by the editing and coding supervisors detailing procedures used, number of interviews processed, problems encountered, and solutions implemented. The editing and coding cost reports, written at the end of these phases, summarize total costs and present per-interview and per-coder figures. Their objective is to provide guidelines for future budgeting and to facilitate financial control over the editing and coding operations. These reports might often be combined with coder and editor reliability figures and summaries of problems encountered with specific variables. They are indispensable during the later analysis of the data. The coding-procedures memo, drafted at the start of the editing and coding phases and finalized after all changes have been completed, provides a summary description of what was actually done and is useful for the methodological appendix of a study monograph.

Data-Processing Files The importance of thorough documentation of computer-based processing of a survey cannot be overemphasized, and specific procedures were suggested earlier to aid in keeping track of what has been done in the course of converting coded interviews into a finished report. Rather than being bureaucratic "busy work," these files serve to reduce the effort required to keep track of numerous steps, some of which may be performed in parallel, and others which require the successful completion of previous ones.

The heart of the data-processing file system is the job-specification book. It contains the written specifications for every processing step undertaken on the data, revised as needed after the processing step is completed to conform with what was actually done. It is advisable to have these written by one staff member and checked by another *after* it has been typed. It should be marked with the date of writing, date of processing start, and completion date. The names of the writer and checker should be on the job specification. Even if the project director is doing all the data processing in a one-person survey, this file should be established and kept up to date. The specifications include a three- to five-line summary of the purposes of the processing block, references to other processing blocks, references to other processing steps that must be completed before this one is started, a target date, and a complete description of exactly what is to be done with the data. If several steps are described in one specification block, they should be numbered and sequence requirements spelled out. The data to be used as input should be clearly and completely specified (e.g., file, units of analysis, variables, subset of the file for which the operations are defined). The processing requirements should be given in detail (e.g., what variables are to be generated, mapping rules for variable generation, computational requirements, handling of inapplicable cases, missing information, decimal points, zero values and negative numbers, use of weights) Output requirements, both in terms of files and reports, should be listed (files, variables, location in the file, codes and variable names, etc.). Processing specifications calling for statistical computations should contain all the details necessary to set computer-program parameters to meet the analysis requirements. The details of exactly what needs to be specified are reviewed in the other chapters of this book.

It is generally useful to identify a written processing specification with a serial number so that references to it are concise, accurate, and convenient. One method is simply to assign ascending numbers to these specifications as they are written. A better procedure is to assign serial numbers within broad categories. Processing specifications can be divided into tasks that correspond roughly to the chapters in this book. Thus, it makes sense to establish categories of processing specifications which are identified with letters and *within which* processing specifications are assigned serially. One possible breakdown is:

(P) Preliminary data processing on other studies.

(S) Sample book check and keypunching specifications, listings of data, file creation, etc.

(R) Response-rate analysis.

(C) Consistency checks and checks for wild codes.

(V) Variable generation and file manipulation.

(S) Statistical-analysis computer runs.

Specifications are then filed under the category in which they occur (e.g., SO1, SO2, SO3). Carbon copies can be used by staff members in setting up computer runs, in checking computer output to ensure that it met the specifications, and in writing up reports. Processing serial numbers should always be included in the run-labeling text provided by almost all computer operating systems or analysis programs, providing positive identification that can be indexed through the processing specification file. Generally, computer output should be bound either in chronological order or in serial-number order by category type, and kept in binders. If multiple copies are obtainable, one can go to the master file and the other to the analyst needing to work with it. However, it is the analyst's pencil-marked copy that should eventually wind up in the master file, and the temporary "master" can be destroyed or recycled.

The computer-program manual file often receives the least attention from the project director, yet almost everthing done to the data is heavily dependent on this being complete and up to date. Copies of manuals of all programs used by the project should be kept in the main project working area and formal arrangements made with the computer center and the original distributors of the programs to keep them up to date. This file should include programming language manuals and programmers' guides for the languages in which the programs are written (e.g., FORTRAN, PL/1, BASIC), as well as user's manuals and primers. In addition, it should contain those operating-system manuals most likely to be of use. These will generally be utility-program and error-message manuals. The contents of this library should be the responsibility of one staff member, who should maintain close liaison with the computer center, implementing formally agreed-upon arrangements for keeping the manuals and the programs up to date.[14] It is poor policy to rely on borrowed manuals or on those kept in computer-center users' workrooms. Whenever sections of the manuals are found to be unclear, incomplete, or inaccurate, the staff member discovering this should mark the area in the manual in pencil and add clarifying notes in a supplementary loose-leaf section kept at the end of the manual. These should be discussed regularly at project staff meetings.

Using a computer to process survey data is both costly and error-prone. If it is possible to establish an atmosphere among the staff that recognizes this and in which staff members help each other to control costs, prevent errors, and to recover from those that inevitably occur with as little delay as possible, the project will fare much better than if costs are ignored by all but the study director and errors are hidden in fear and embarrassment. For this reason, aborted jobs should not be thrown out but annotated as to what caused the problem and bound chronologically. Cost information is almost always printed on computer output, and a project staff member can be given the responsibility periodically to review the file and make recommendations for future prevention of the most serious errors. At the end of the project, cost summaries for various phases of the project can be obtained that will reflect a somewhat different and far more accurate picture than that obtained from the file of usable computer output. Control of computer costs occurring early in the project may make the difference in being able to perform certain important analyses at the end rather than foregoing them.

Another file often omitted by a project is the computer-program job-setup file. This is simply a file arranged in chronological order, containing the control-card packets used to make all the usable computer runs. The easiest way to set up a computer run is to copy and then modify a control-card package that worked previously, with the help of a manual and preferably with the help

[14] If the project must also maintain its computer programs, a programmer should be employed who is familiar with program library maintenance methods.

BIBLIOGRAPHY

ACM, "ACM Reference Guide to Special Interest Groups," *Communications of the Association for Computing Machinery* **15**, no. 12 (Dec. 1972), p. 1093.

ACOCK, A. C., LIBBY, R. W., and WILLIAMS, J. S., "Statistical Inference," *Pacific Sociological Review* **14**, No. 2 (Apr. 1971), pp. 163–170.

AFIFI, A. A., and ELASHOFF, R. M., "Missing Observations in Multivariate Statistics I. Review of the Literature," *Journal of the American Statistical Association* **61** (Sept. 1966), pp. 595–604.

———, and ELASHOFF, R. M., "Missing Observations in Multivariate Statistics II. Point Estimation Simple Linear Regression," *Journal of the American Statistical Association* **62** (Mar., 1967), pp. 10–29.

AHMAVAARA, Y., "The Mathematical Theory of Factorial Invariance Under Selection," *Psychometrika* **19** (1954).

———, *On the Mathematical Theory of Transformation Analyses.* Helsinki: 1963.

Alberta, University of, *APL-STATPACK Computer Program Manual,* 1972.

ALEXANDER, H. W., "A General Test for Trends," *Psychological Bulletin* **43** (1946), pp. 533–555.

ALKER, H. R., JR., "Causal Inference and Political Analysis," J. Bernel (ed.), *Mathematical Applications in Political Science*, Vol. II, Dallas, Tex.: The Arnold Foundation, Southern Methodist University, 1966.

———, "The Long Road to International Relations Theory: Problems of Statistical Nonadditivity," *World Politics* (July 1966), pp. 623–655.

ALLERBECK, K. R., "Data Analysis Systems: A User's Point of View," *Social Science Information* **10**, no. 3 (1971), pp. 23–35.

ALMOND, G. A., and VERBA, S., *The Civic Culture: Participation and Civic Involvement in Five Countries.* Princeton, N.J.: Princeton University Press, 1963.

Althauser, R. P., and Heberlein, T. A., "Validity and the Multitrait–Multimethod Matrix," E. F. Borgatta and G. W. Bohrnstedt (eds.), *Sociological Methodology*. San Francisco: Jossey-Bass, 1970.

Alwin, D. F., "Approaches to the Interpretation of Relationships in the Multitrait–Multimethod Matrix," H. L. Costner (ed.), *Sociological Methodology*. San Francisco: Jossey-Bass, 1974.

American Psychological Association, *Standards for Educational and Psychological Tests and Manuals*. Washington, D.C.: American Psychological Association, 1966.

Anastasi, A., *Individual Differences*. New York: Macmillan, 1958.

Anderson, N., "Scales and Statistics: Parametric and Nonparametric," *Psychological Bulletin* **LVIII** (1961), pp. 305–316.

Anderson, O. W., and Feldman, J. J., *Family Medical Costs and Voluntary Health Insurance: A Nationwide Survey*. New York: McGraw-Hill, 1956.

Anderson, Ronald E., "A Bibliography of Social Science Computing", *Computing Reviews*, July, 1974, pp. 247–261.

———, *Introduction to Lansor* (*Language for Social Research*). Minneapolis, Minn.: Sociology Data Center, Department of Sociology, University of Minnesota, 1969.

Anderson, T. W., "The Use of Factor Analysis in Statistical Analysis of Multiple Time Series," *Technical Report No. 12, AF41 (657)–214* 1967.

Andrews, F. M., and Messenger, R. C., *Multivariate Nominal Scale Analysis*. Ann Arbor, Mich.: Institute for Social Research, University of Michigan, 1973.

———, Morgan, J., Sonquist, J., and Klem, L., *Multiple Classification Analysis*, rev. ed. Ann Abor, Mich.: Institute for Social Research, University of Michigan, 1973.

Anscombe, F. J., and Tukey, J. W., "The Examination and Analysis of Residuals," *Technometrics* (May 1963), pp. 141–160.

Armor, D. J., "Developments in Data Analysis Systems for the Social Sciences," *Social Sciences Information* **9**, no. 3 (June 1970), pp. 145–146.

———, "Theta Reliability and Factor Scaling," H. L. Costner (ed.), *Sociological Methodology*. San Francisco: Jossey-Bass, 1974.

———, and Couch, A. S., *Data-Text Primer: An Introduction to Computerized Social Data Analysis*. New York: Free Press, 1972.

Astin, A., "Criterion-Related Research," *Education and Psychological Measurement* **XXIV** (1964), pp. 807–822.

Babbie, E. R., *Survey Research Methods*. Belmont Cal.: Wadsworth, 1973.

Bachman, J. G., *Youth in Transition: The Impact of Family Background and Intelligence on Tenth-Grade Boys*, Vol. II. Ann Arbor, Mich.: Institute for Social Research, University of Michigan, 1970.

Bailey, K. D., "Polythetic Reduction of Monothetic Property Space," H. L. Costner (ed.), *Sociological Methodology*. San Francisco: Jossey-Bass, 1972.

Ball, G. H., "Data Analysis in the Social Sciences," Proceedings, Fall Joint Computer Conference. New York: Spartan, 1965, pp. 533–560.

BARGER, R., *The University of Wisconsin Data Management System.* Madison, Wis.: University of Wisconsin, 1967.

BARLOW, R., BRAZER, H., and MORGAN, J., *The Economic Behavior of the Affluent.* Washington, D.C.: Brookings Institution, 1966.

BARTLETT, M., "The Use of Transformations," *Biometrics* **III** (1947), pp. 39–52.

BARTON, A. H., "The Concept of Property-Space in Social Research," P. F. Lazarsfeld and M. Rosenberg (eds.), *The Language of Social Research.* New York: Free Press, 1955, pp. 40–53.

BEAN, J. W., KIDD, S., SADOWKSY, G., and SHARP, B., *The Beast—A User-Oriented Procedural Language for Social Science Research.* Washington, D.C.: The Brookings Institution, 1968.

BECHTOLDT, H., "Construct Validity: A Critique," *American Psychologist* **XIV** (1959), pp. 619–629.

BECK, C., MCKECHNIE, J. T., and STEWART, D. K., "Open-Ended Data Files: A Format for Ragged Data Sets," *Social Science Information* **VI-5** (Oct. 1967), pp. 129–131.

BECKNER, M., *The Biological Way of Thought.* New York: Columbia University Press, 1959.

BELL, R. Q., "A Reinterpretation of the Direction of Effects in Studies of Socialization," *Psychological Review* **75** (1968), pp. 81–95.

BENUS, J., "Transportation of the Poor" (Working Paper from the OEO Study of Family Income Dynamics). Ann Arbor, Mich.: Survey Research Center, University of Michigan, July 1970.

BIJNEN, E. J., *Cluster Analysis: Survey and Evaluation of Techniques.* Rotterdam, The Netherlands: Tilburg University Press, 1973.

BISCO, R. L. (ed.), *Data Bases, Computers, and the Social Sciences.* New York: Wiley, 1970.

BLALOCK, H. M., JR., "Causal Inference, Closed Populations, and Measures of Association," *American Political Science Review* **61** (Mar. 1967), pp. 130–136.

———, *Causal Inferences in Non-experimental Research.* Chapel Hill, N.C.: University of North Carolina Press, 1964.

———, *Causal Models in the Social Sciences.* Chicago: Aldine, 1971.

———, "Correlated Independent Variables: The Problem of Multicollinearity," *Social Forces* **42** (1963), pp. 233–237.

———, "Estimating Measurement Error Using Multiple Indicators and Several Points in Time," *American Sociological Review* **35** (Feb. 1970), pp. 101–111.

———, "Evaluating the Relative Importance of Variables," *American Sociological Review* **XXVI**, No. 6 (Dec. 1961).

———, "The Identification Problem and Theory Building: The Case of Status Inconsistancy," *American Sociological Review* **31** (1966), pp. 52–61.

———, *Measurement in The Social Sciences.* Chicago: Aldine (in press).

———, "Multiple Indicators and the Causal Approach to Measurement Error," *American Journal of Sociology* **75** (Sept. 1969), pp. 245–263.

———, "Some Implications of Random Measurement Error for Causal Inferences," *American Journal of Sociology* **71** (July 1965), pp. 37–47.

———, "Standardized and Unstandardized Measures," H. M. Blalock, Jr., and A. B. Blalock (eds.), *Methodology in Social Research.* New York: McGraw-Hill, 1968.

———, "Theory Building and The Statistical Concept of Interaction," *American Sociological Review* **30**, No. 3 (June 1965), pp. 374–380.

———, and Blalock, A. B., *Methodology in Social Research.* New York: McGraw-Hill, 1968.

———, Wells, C. S., and Carter, I. F., "Statistical Estimation with Random Measurement Error," E. F. Borgatta and G. W. Bohrnstedt (eds.), *Sociological Methodology.* San Francisco: Jossey-Bass, 1970.

Blau, P. M., "Structural Effects," *American Sociological Review* **25** (1960), pp. 178–193.

———, and Duncan, C. D., *The American Occupational Structure.* New York: Wiley, 1967.

Bloom, B., et al., *Taxonomy of Educational Objectives. Handbook I: Cognitive Domain.* New York: Longmans Green, 1956.

Bloom, S. W., *The Doctor and His Patient.* New York: Russell Sage Foundation, 1963.

Bloombaum, M., "The Conditions Underlying Race Riots as Portrayed by Multidimensional Scalogram Analysis: A Reanalysis of Lieberson and Silverman's Data," *American Sociological Review* **33** (Feb. 1968), pp. 76–91.

———, "Tribes and Traits: A Smallest Space Analysis of Cross-Cultural Data," *American Anthropologist* **70** (Apr. 1968), pp. 328–330 (B).

Bock, R. D., *Multivariate Statistical Method in Behavioral Research.* New York: McGraw-Hill, 1974.

———, and Yates, G., *Multiqual: Log-Linear Analysis of Nominal or Ordinal Qualitative Data by the Method of Maximum Likelihood.* Chicago: National Educational Resources, Inc., 1973.

Bogue, D. J., *Skid Row in American Cities.* Chicago: Community and Family Study Center, 1963.

Bohl, M., and Walter, A., Introduction to PL/1 Programming and PL/C. Chicago: Science Research Associates, 1973.

Bohrnstedt, G. W., "Observations on the Measurement of Change," E. F. Borgatta and G. W. Bohrnstedt (eds.), *Sociological Methodology.* San Francisco: Jossey-Bass, 1970.

———, and Carter, T. M., "Robustness in Regression Analysis," H. L. Costner (ed.), *Sociological Methodology.* San Francisco: Jossey-Bass, 1971.

Bonacich, P., "Techniques for Analysing Overlapping Memberships," H. L. Costner (ed.), *Sociological Methodology.* San Francisco: Jossey-Bass, 1972.

Boneau, C., "A Note on Measurement Scales and Statistical Tests," *American Psychologist* **XVI** (1961), pp. 260–261.

Borgatta, E. F., *Sociological Methodology 1969. San Francisco:* Jossey-Bass, 1969.

———, and Hayes, D., "Some Limitations on the Arbitrary Classification of Non-Scale Response Patterns in a Guttman Scale," *Public Opinion Quarterly* **16** (1952), pp. 410–416.

Borko, H. (ed.), *Computer Applications in the Behavioral Sciences.* Englewood Cliffs, N.J.: Prentice-Hall, 1962.

Bottenberg, R. A., and Ward, J. H., Jr., *Applied Multiple Linear Regression.* Air Force Systems Command AD413-128, Lackland AFB, Tex., Mar. 1963.

Boudon, R., "A Method of Linear Causal Analysis: Dependence Analysis," *American Sociological Review* **30** (1965), pp. 365–374.

———, "Methods of Analysis for Panel Surveys," *Social Science Information* **VI-5** (Oct. 1967).

Boyle, R. P., "Causal Theory and Statistical Measures of Effect: A Convergence," *American Sociological Review* **31**, no. 6 (Dec. 1966).

———, "Path Analysis and Ordinal Data," *American Journal of Sociology* **75** (Jan. 1970), pp. 461–480.

Bradley, H. E., "Multiple Classification Analysis for Arbitrary Experimental Design," *Technometrics* **10** (1968), pp. 13–28.

Braithwaite, R., *Scientific Explanation.* New York: Cambridge University Press, 1951.

Brownlee, K. A., *Statistical Theory and Methodology in Science and Engineering.* New York: Wiley, 1960, Chap. 18.

Buhler, R., *P-Stat: An Evolving User-Oriented Language for Statistical Analysis of Social Science Data.* Princeton, N.J.: Princeton University Computer Center, 1968.

Burke, P. J., and Schuessler, K., "Alternative Approaches to Analysis of Variance Tables," H. L. Costner (ed.), *Sociological Methodology.* San Francisco: Jossey-Bass, 1974.

Bussel, R. L., Costa, I. A., Spencer, R. E., and Aleamoni, L. M., *MERMAC Manual: Test and Questionnaire Analysis Programs for the IBM and System/360.* Urbana, Ill.: University of Illinois Press, 1971.

Cain, G. G., *Labor Force Participation of Married Women.* Chicago: University of Chicago Press, 1966.

———, and Watts, H. W., "Problems in Making Policy Inferences from the Coleman Report," *American Sociological Review* **35** (1970), pp. 228–242.

Cambridge Computer Associates, *Crosstabs II.* Cambridge, Mass.: Cambridge Computer Associates, 1970.

———, *Utility Coder/360 Manual.* Cambridge, Mass.: Cambridge Computer Associates, 1970.

CAMILLERI, S. F., "Some Problems of Induction in Sociology," *Journal American Statistical Association* 1959.

———, "Theory, Probability and Induction in Social Research," N. K. Denzin (ed.), *Sociological Methods*. Chicago: Aldine, 1970.

CAMPBELL, A., and KATONA, G., "The Sample Survey: A Technique for Social-Science Research," L. Festinger and D. Katz (eds.), *Research Methods in the Behavioral Sciences*. New York: Holt, Rinehart and Winston, 1953.

———, and SCHUMAN, H., *Racial Attitudes in Fifteen American Cities*. Ann Arbor, Mich.: Institute for Social Research, University of Michigan, 1968.

———, CONVERSE, P. E., MILLER, W. E., and STOKES, D. E., *The American Voter*. New York: Wiley, 1960 (abridgement, 1964).

———, GURIN, G., and MILLER, W., *The Voter Decides*. Evanston, Ill.: Row, Peterson, 1954.

CAMPBELL, D., "Factors Relevant to the Validity of Experiments in Social Settings," *Psychological Bulletin* **LIV** (1957), pp. 297–312.

———, and FISKE, D. W., "Covergent and Discriminant Validation by the Multitrait–Multimethod Matrix," *Psychological Bulletin* **56** (1959), pp. 81–105.

———, and STANLEY, J., *Experimental and Quasi-experimental Designs*. Skokie, Ill.: Rand McNally, 1963.

CANNELL, C., and KAHN, E., "The Collection of Data by Interviewing," L. Festinger and D. Katz (eds.), *Research Methods in the Behavioral Sciences*. New York: Holt, Rinehart and Winston, 1953.

———, and KAHN, R., "Interviewing," G. Lindzey and E. Aronson (eds.), *Handbook of Social Psychology*, 2nd ed., Vol. III. Reading, Mass.: Addison-Wesley, 1968.

CAPLOVITZ, D., *The Poor Pay More: Consumer Practices of Low Income Families*. Glencoe, Ill.: Free Press, 1963.

CARTWRIGHT, D. S., "Ecological Variables," E. F. Borgatta and G. W. Bohrnstedt (eds.), *Sociological Methodology*. San Francisco: Jossey-Bass, 1969.

CATTELL, R. F., *Factor Analysis*. New York: Harper & Row, 1952.

———, "Factor Analysis: An Introduction to Essentials: (I) The Purpose and Underlying Models; (II) The Role of Factor Analysis in Research," *Biometrics* **21** (1965), pp. 190–215, 405–435.

———, and ADELSON, M., "The Dimensions of Social Change: P Technique," *Social Forces* **30**, (1951), pp. 190–201.

CENTERS, R., *The Psychology of Social Class: A Study of Class Consciousness*. Princeton, N.J.: Princeton University Press, 1949.

CHASE, C. I., "Computation of Variance Accounted for in Multiple Correlation," *Journal of Experimental Education* **28**, no. 3 (1960), pp. 265–266.

———, and LUDLOW (eds.), *Readings in Educational and Psychological Measurement*. Boston: Houghton Mifflin, 1966.

CLARK, W. E., "A Relocatable, Associative Data Structure for Spatial Information," *SIGSPAC Bulletin* **3**, no. 1 (May 1969), pp. 16–27.

CLEARY, T. A., LINN, R. I., and WALSTER, G. W., "Effect of Reliability and Validity on Power of Statistical Tests," E. F. Borgatta and G. W. Bohrnstedt (eds.), *Sociological Methodology*. San Francisco: Jossey-Bass, 1970.

CLIFF, M., and HAMBURGER, C., "The Study of Sampling Errors in Factor Analysis by Means of Artificial Experiments," *Psychological Bulletin* **LXVIII** (1967), pp. 430–445.

CLYDE, D., CRAMER, E., and SHERIN, R., *Multivariate Statistical Programs*. Coral Gables, Fla.: Biometric Laboratory, University of Miami, 1966.

COAN, R., "Facts, Factors, and Artifacts: The Quest for Psychological Meaning," *Psychological Review* **LXXI** (1964), pp. 123–140.

COHEN, J., "Multiple Regression as a General Data-Analytic System," *Psychological Bulletin* **70** (1968), pp. 426–443.

———, "Prognostic Factors in Functional Psychosis: A Study in Multivariate Methodology," *Transactions of the New York Academy of Sciences* **30** (1968), pp. 833–840.

COHEN, M., *A Preface to Logic*. New York: Meridian, 1956.

———, and NAGEL, E., *An Introduction to Logic and Scientific Method*. New York: Harcourt Brace, 1934.

COLEMAN, J. S., *The Adolescent Society: The Social Life of the Teenager and its Impact on Education*. New York: Free Press, 1961.

———, *Equality of Educational Opportunity*. Washington, D.C.: Government Printing Office, 1966.

———, *Introduction to Mathematical Sociology*. Glencoe, Ill.: Free Press, 1964.

———, "The Mathematical Study of Change," H. M. Blalock and A. B. Blalock (eds.), *Methodology in Social Research*. New York: McGraw-Hill, 1968.

———, "Multivariate Analysis for Attribute Data," E. F. Borgatta and G. W. Bohrnstedt (eds.), *Sociological Methodology*. San Francisco: Jossey-Bass, 1970.

———, "Relational Analysis: The Study of Social Organizations with Survey Methods," N. K. Denzin (ed.), *Sociological Methods*. Chicago: Aldine, 1970.

———, KATZ, E., and MENZEL, H., *Medical Innovation: A Diffusion Study*. New York: Bobbs-Merrill, 1966.

Computer Usage Company, *QUIP Manual*. Palo Alto, Cal.: Computer Usage Company, 1972.

CONANT, J., *Science and Common Sense*. New Haven, Conn.: Yale University Press, 1951.

CONRAD, A., et al., *Automobile Accident Costs and Payments: Studies in the Economics of Injury Reparation*. Ann Arbor, Mich.: University of Michigan Press, 1964.

COOLEY, W., and LOHNES, P., *Multivariate Data Analysis*. New York: Wiley, 1971.

———, and Lohnes, P., *Multivariate Procedures for the Behavioral Sciences.* New York: Wiley, 1962.

Coombs, C. H., "Theory and Methods of Social Measurement," L. Festinger and D. Katz (eds.), *Research Methods in the Behavioral Sciences.* New York: Holt, Rinehart and Winston, 1953.

———, "A Theory of Data," *Psychological Review* **LXVII** (1960), pp. 143–159.

———, *A Theory of Data.* New York: Wiley, 1964.

Costner, H. L., and Wager, L. W., "The Multivariate Analysis of Dichotomized Variables," *American Journal of Sociology* **70** (1965), pp. 445–466.

Cronbach, L. J., "Coefficient Alpha and the Internal Structure of Tests," *Psychometrika* **XVI** (1951), pp. 297–334.

———, "Test validation," R. Thorndike (ed.), *Educational Management*, 2nd ed. Washington D.C.: *American Council on Education*, 1971, pp. 443–507.

———, and Furby, L., "How We Should Measure 'Change'—or Should We?" *Psychological Bulletin* **74**, no. 1 (1970), pp. 68–80.

———, and Meehl, P., "Construct Validity of Psychological Tests," *Psychological Bulletin* **LII** (1955), pp. 281–302.

———, et al., *The Dependability of Behavioral Measurements: Theory of Generalizability for Scores and Profiles.* New York: Wiley, 1972.

Cureton, E., "Measurement Theory," R. Ebel, V. Noll, and R. Bauer (eds.), *Encyclopedia of Educational Research*, 4th ed. New York: Macmillan, 1969, pp. 785–804.

Darlington, R., "Multiple Regression in Psychological Research and Practice," *Psychological Bulletin* **LXIX** (1968), pp. 161–182.

Dartmouth College, *Basic Manual*, 5th ed. Hanover, N. H.: Dartmouth College Computer Center, 1970.

Davidson, T. N., "Evolution of a Strategy for Longitudinal Analysis of Survey Panel Data." Ann Arbor, Mich.: Unpublished Ph.D. Dissertation, University of Michigan, 1971.

Davidson, W. I., *Information Processing: Applications in the Social and Behavioral Sciences.* New York: Appleton-Century-Crofts, 1970.

Davis, J. A., "Compositional Effects, Role Systems, and the Survival of Small Discussion Groups," *Public Opinion Quarterly* **25** (1961), pp. 574–584.

———, *Elementary Survey Analysis.* Englewood Cliffs, N.J.: Prentice-Hall, 1971.

———, *Great Aspirations: The Graduate School Plans of Amercian College Seniors.* Chicago: Aldine, 1964.

———, "Hierarchical Models for Significance Tests in Multivariate Contingency Tables: An Exegesis of Goodman's Recent Papers" H. C. Costner (ed.), *Sociological Methodology.* San Francisco: Jossey-Bass, 1974.

———, Spaeth, J. I., and Huson, C., "A Technique for Analyzing the Effect of Group Composition," *American Sociological Review* **26** (1961), pp. 215–225.

DEMING, W. E., "On Errors in Surveys," N. K. Denzin (ed.), *Sociological Methods.* Chicago: Aldine, 1970.

DEMIRMEN, F., "Multivariate Procedures and FORTRAN IV Program for Evaluation and Improvement of Classifications," *Computer Contribution* **31**. Lawrence, Kan.: University of Kansas State Geological Survey, 1969.

DEMPSTER, A. P., *Elements of Continuous Multivariate Analysis.* Reading, Mass.: Addison-Wesley, 1969.

DENZIN, N. K., *Sociological Methods.* Chicago: Aldine, 1970.

DIXON, W. J. *BMDP—Biomedical Computer Programs.* Berkeley, Cal.: University of California Press, 1975.

———, Statistical Packages in Biomedical Computation, R. W. Stacey and B. D. Waxman (eds.), *Computers in Biomedical Research.* New York: Academic Press, 1965, pp. 47–64.

——— (ed.), *BMD: Biomedical Computer Programs.* Berkeley, Cal.: University of California Press, 1970.

DOBY, J. T., "Logic and Levels of Scientific Explanation," E. F. Borgatta and G. W. Bohrnstedt (eds.) *Sociological Methodology.* San Francisco: Jossey-Bass, 1969.

DOUVAN, E., and ADELSON, J., *The Adolescent Experience.* New York: Wiley, 1966.

DRAPER, N., and SMITH, H., *Applied Regression Analysis.* New York: Wiley, 1966.

Duke University Computation Center, *TSAR System User's Manual.* Durham, N.C.: Duke University, 1967.

DUNCAN, O. D., "Contingencies in Constructing Causal Models," E. F. Borgatta and G. W. Bohrnstedt (eds.), *Sociological Methodology.* San Francisco: Jossey-Bass, 1969.

———, "Partials, Partitions, and Paths," E. F. Borgatta and G. W. Bohrnstedt (eds.), *Sociological Methodology.* San Francisco: Jossey-Bass, 1970.

———, "Path Analysis: Sociological Examples," *American Journal of Sociology* **72** (1966), pp. 1–16.

———, "Some Linear Models for Two-Wave Two-Variable Panel Analysis," *Psychological Bulletin* **72** (Sept. 1969), pp. 177–182.

———, "Unmeasured Variables in Linear Models for Path Analysis," H. L. Costner (ed.), *Sociological Methodology.* San Francisco: Jossey-Bass, 1972.

———, HAILER, A. O., and PORTES, A., "Peer Influences on Aspiration: A Reinterpretation," *American Journal of Sociology* **74** (Sept. 1968), pp. 119–137.

DUNKELBERG, W., "Dummy Variables-Their Use and Interpretation," unpublished manuscript, Stanford University, 1973.

EBEL, R., "Estimation of the Reliability of Ratings," *Psychometrika* **XVI** (1951), pp. 407–424.

———, "Obtaining and Reporting Evidence on Content Validity," *Educational and Psychological Measurement* **XVI** (1956), pp. 269–282.

EDWARDS, A., *Experimental Design in Psychological Research*, 3rd ed. New York: Holt, Rinehart and Winston, 1968.

———, *Techniques of Attitude Scale Construction*. New York: Appleton-Century, 1957.

ELASHOFF, R. M., "Regression Analysis with Missing Data." R. Bisco (ed.), *Data Bases, Computers, and the Social Sciences*. New York: Wiley, 1970.

ELDERSVELD, S. A., *The Citizen Administrator in a Developmental Democracy*. Glenview, Ill.: Scott, Foresman, 1968.

ENGELHART, M. D., "The Technique of Path Coefficients," *Psychometrika* **1** (1936), pp. 287–293.

ENTWISLE, D. R., and KNEPP, D., "Uncertainty Analysis Applied to Sociological Data," E. F. Borgatta and G. W. Bohrnstedt (eds.), *Sociological Methodology*. San Francisco: Jossey-Bass, 1970.

FARRAR, D. E., and GLAUBER, R. R., "Muticollinearity in Regression Analysis: The Problem Revisited," *Review of Economic and Statistics* **49** (Feb. 1967), pp. 92–107.

FELLIN, P. TRIPODI, T., and MEYER, H. J., *Exemplars of Social Research*. Itasca, Ill.: Peacock, 1969.

FEN, SING-NAN, "The Theoretical Implications of Multivariate Analysis in the Behavioral Sciences," *Behavioral Science* **13** (1968), pp. 138–142.

FENNESSEY, J., "The General Linear Model: A New Perspective on Some Familiar Topics," *American Journal of Sociology* **74** (1968), pp. 1–27.

FESTINGER, L., and KATZ, D., *Research Methods in the Behavioral Sciences*. New York: Holt, Rinehart and Winston, 1953.

FIENBERG, S. E., "The Analysis of Multidimensional Contingency Tables," *Ecology* **51**, no. 2 (1970), pp. 419–433.

FINIFTER, B. M., "ERIV: A Computer Program for Evaluating Relative Importance of Variables in the Analysis of Interaction Effects," *Behavioral Science* **16**, no. 5 (Sept. 1971), pp. 511–512.

———, "The Generation of Confidence: Evaluating Research Findings by Random Subsample Replication," H. C. Costner (ed.), *Sociological Methodology*. San Francisco: Jossey-Bass, 1972.

FLIESS, J. L., and ZUBIN, J., "On the Methods and Theory of Clustering," *Multivariate Behavioral Research* **4** (1969), pp. 235–250.

FORBES, H. D., and TUFTE, E. R., "A Note of Caution in Causal Modeling," *American Political Science Review* **62**, no. 4 (1968).

FORSYTHE, A. I., KEENAN, T. A., ORGANICK, E. I., and STENBERG, W., *Computer Science: A First Course*. New York: Wiley, 1970.

———, KEENAN, T. A., ORGANICK, E. I., and STENBERG, W., *Computer Science: FORTRAN Language Programming*. New York: Wiley, 1970.

FORSYTHE, G. E., and MOLER, C. B., *Computer Solution of Linear Algebraic Systems*. Englewood Cliffs, N.J.: Prentice-Hall, 1967.

FRANKEL, M. R., *Inference from Survey Samples.* Ann Arbor, Mich.: Institute for Social Research, University of Michigan, 1971.

FREE, L., and CANTRIL, H., *The Political Beliefs of Americans.* New Brunswick, N.J.: Rutgers University Press, 1967.

FRENCH, J., EKSTRAM, R., and PRICE, L., *Manual for Kit of Reference Texts for Cognitive Factors.* Princeton, N.J.: Educational Testing Service, 1963.

FUGUITT, G. V., and LIEBERSON, S., "Correlation of Ratios or Difference Scores Having Common Terms," H. L. Costner (ed.), *Sociological Methodology.* San Francisco: Jossey-Bass, 1974.

GAGE, N. L., *Handbook of Research on Teaching.* Chicago: Rand McNally, 1963.

GALTUNG, J., *Theory and Methods of Social Research.* New York: Columbia University Press, 1967.

GEAR, C. W., *Introduction to Computer Science.* Chicago: Science Research Associates, 1973.

General Electric, *Statistical Analysis System User's Guide* (*Statsystem*). General Electric Corp. Information Services, 1971.

GILLO, M. W., "MAID: A New Interactive Version of AID, with Applications." Lawrence, Kans.: Working Paper, Department of Psychology, University of Kansas, 1971.

GLEASON, T. C., *Multidimensional Scaling of Sociometric Data.* Ann Arbor, Mich.: Institute for Social Research, University of Michigan, 1969.

GLOCK, C. Y., *Survey Research in the Social Sciences.* New York: Russell Sage Foundation, 1967.

———, and STARK, R., *Christian Beliefs and Anti-Semitism.* New York: Harper & Row, 1966.

———, SELZNICK, G., and SPAETH, J. L., *The Apathetic Majority: A Survey Based on Public Responses to the Eichmann Trial.* New York: Harper & Row, 1966.

GOLD, D., "Statistical Tests and Substantive Significance," *The American Sociologist* **4** (1969), pp. 42–46.

GOLDBERGER, A. S., "Discerning a Causal Pattern Among Data on Voting Behavior," *American Political Science Review* **60** (Dec. 1966), pp. 913–922.

———, "Econometrics and Psychometrics: A Survey of Communalities," *Social Systems Research Institute Workshop Paper EME 7013.* Madison, Wis.: University of Wisconsin, Mar. 1970.

———, *Econometric Theory.* New York: Wiley, 1964, pp. 173–177, 218–231, 248–255.

———, "On Boudon's Method of Linear Causal Analysis," *American Sociological Review* **35** (Feb. 1970), pp. 97–101.

———, "Stepwise Least Squares: Residual Analysis and Specification Error," *Journal of the American Statistical Association* **56** (Dec. 1961), pp. 998–1000.

———, "Structural Equation Models in Sociology," *Social Systems Research Institute EME Workshop Paper*. Madison, Wis.: University of Wisconsin, Nov. 1969.

———, *Topics in Regression Analysis*. New York: Macmillan, 1968.

———, and DUNCAN, C. D., *Structural Equation Models in the Social Sciences*. New York: Academic Press, 1973.

———, and JOCHEM, D. B., "A Note on Stepwise Least Squares," *Journal of the American Statistical Association* **56** (1961), pp. 105–110.

GOODE, W., and HATT, P., *Methods in Social Research*. New York: McGraw-Hill, 1952.

GOODMAN, L. A., "A General Model for the Analysis of Surveys," *American Journal of Sociology* **77** (1972), pp. 1035–1086.

———, "A Modified Multiple Regression Approach to the Analysis of Dichotomous Variables," *American Sociological Review* **37** (Feb. 1972), pp. 28–46.

———, "The Multivariate Analysis of Qualitative Data: Interactions Among Multiple Classifications," *Journal of the American Statistical Association* **65** (1970), pp. 226–256.

———, "On Partitioning Chi Square and Detecting Partial Associations in Three-Way Contingency Tables," *Journal of the Royal Statistical Society, Ser. B*, **31** (1969), pp. 486–498.

———, "On The Multivariate Analysis of Three Dichotomous Variables," *American Journal of Sociology* **71** (1965), pp. 290–301.

———, "Partitioning of Chi-Square, Analysis of Marginal Contingency Tables, and Estimation of Expected Frequencies in Multidimensional Contingency Tables," *Journal of the American Statistical Association* **66**, (1971), pp. 339–344.

———, "Some Alternatives to Ecological Correlation," *American Journal of Sociology* **64** (1959), pp. 610–625.

———, and KRUSKAL, W. H., "Measures of Association for Cross Classifications," *Journal of the American Statistical Association* **49** (1954), pp. 732–764.

GORDAN, R. A., "Issues in Multiple Regression," *American Journal of Sociology* **73** (1968), pp. 592–616.

Government Printing Office, *Dictionary of Occupational Titles*, Vol. II. Washington, D.C.: Government Printing Office, 1965.

GOWER, J. C., "A Comparison of Some Methods of Cluster Analysis," *Biometrics* **23** (Dec. 1967), pp. 623–637.

GRIZZLE, J. E., STARMER, C. E., and KOCH, G. G., "Analysis of Categorical Data by Linear Models," *Biometrics* **25** (1969), pp. 489–504.

GROSS, N., MASON, W., and MCEACHERN, A., *Explorations in Role Analysis: Studies of the School Superintendency Role*. New York: Wiley, 1953.

GUILFORD, J. P., "Factorial Angles to Psychology," *Psychological Review* **LXVIII** (1961), pp. 1–20.

———, *Fundamental Statistics in Psychology and Education.* New York: McGraw-Hill, 1965, Chap. 17.

———, *Psychometric Methods*, 2nd ed. New York: McGraw-Hill, 1954.

GULLAHORN, J. E., "Multivariate Approaches in Survey Data Processing: Comparisons of Factor, Cluster, and Guttman Analyses and of Multiple Regression and Canonical Correlation Methods," *Multivariate Behavioral Research Monograph No. 67–1.* Society of Multivariate Experimental Psychology, 1967.

GULLIKSON, H. ,*Theory of Mental Tests.* New York: Wiley, 1950, Chaps. 1–8.

GURIN, G., VEROFF, J., and FELD, S., *Americans View Their Mental Health.* New York: Basic Books, 1960.

GUTHREY, S. B., SPAETH, H. J., and THOMAS, S., "FASCALE, a FORTRAN IV Multidimensional Scaling and Factor Analysis Program," *Behavioral Science* **13** (Sept. 1968), p. 426.

GUTTMAN, L., "The Development of Nonmetric Space Analysis: A Letter to John Ross," *Multivariate Behavioral Research* **2** (1967), pp. 71–82.

———, "A General Nonmetric Technique for Finding the Smallest Coordinate Space for a Configuration of Points," *Psychometrika* **33** (1968), pp. 469–506.

———, "Introduction to Facet Design and Analysis," *Proceedings of the Fifteenth International Congress of Psychology, Brussels.* Amsterdam: North-Holland, 1957.

———, "An Outline of Some New Methodology for Social Research," *Public Opinion Quarterly* **18** (Winter 1954–1955), pp. 395–404.

———, "The Quantification of a Class of Attributes: A Theory and Method of Scale Construction," P. Horst et al., *The Prediction of Personal Adjustment.* New York: Social Science Research Council, 1941, pp. 319–348.

HABERMAN, S. J., *C-TAB: Analysis of Multivariate Contingency Tables by Log-Linear Models, a FORTRAN Program.* Chicago, Ill.: National Educational Resources, 1973.

HAINSWORTH, G. B., "The Lorenz Curve as a General Tool of Economic Analysis," *Economic Record* (Sept. 1964).

HANSEN, M., and HAUSER, P., "Area Sampling—Some Principles of Sample Design," B. Berelson and M. Janowitz (eds.), *Supplement to Reader in Public Opinion and Communication.* New York: Free Press, 1953.

HARDER, T., and PAPPI, F. U., "Multiple Regression Analysis of Survey and Ecological Data," *Social Science Information* **8**, no. 5 (1970), pp. 43–67.

HARMAN, H., *Modern Factor Analysis.* Chicago: University of Chicago Press, 1967.

HARRIS, C. W., "Some Recent Developments in Factor Analysis," *Educational and Psychological Measurement* **XXIV** (1964), pp. 193–206.

——— (ed.), *Problems in Measuring Change.* Madison, Wis.: University of Wisconsin Press, 1963.

HART, J. F., CHENEY, E. W., LAWSON, C. L., MAEHLY, H. J., MESZTENY, C. K., RICE, J. R., THACHER, H. G., and WITZGALL, C., *Computer Approximations.* New York: Wiley, 1968.

HAUSER, R. M., "On 'Social Participation and Social Status'," *American Sociological Review* **34** (Aug. 1969), pp. 549–553.

———, *Socioeconomic Background and Educational Performance* Washington, D.C.: American Sociological Association, 1971.

———, and GOLDBERGER, A. S., "The Treatment of Unobservable Variables in Path Analysis," H. L. Costner (ed.), *Sociological Methodology*. San Francisco: Jossey-Bass, 1971.

HAWKES, R. T., "The Multivariate Analysis of Ordinal Measures," *American Journal of Sociology* (Mar. 1971), pp. 908–926.

HEISE, D. R., "Causal Inference from Panel Data," E. F. Borgatta and G. W. Bohrnstedt, *Sociological Methodology*. San Francisco: Jossey-Bass, 1970.

———, "Problems in Path Analysis and Causal Inference," E. F. Borgatta and G. W. Bohrnstedt (eds.), *Sociological Methodology*. San Francisco: Jossey-Bass, 1969.

———, "Some Issues in Sociological Measurement," H. L. Costner (ed.), *Sociological Methodology*. San Francisco: Jossey-Bass, 1974.

———, and BOHRNSTEDT, G. W., "Validity, Invalidity, and Reliability," E. F. Borgatta and G. W. Bohrnstedt (eds.), *Sociological Methodology*. San Francisco: Jossey-Bass, 1970.

HENKEL, R. E., and MORRISON, D. E., "On the Non-utility of Significance Tests," *Pacific Sociological Review* **14**, no. 2 (Apr. 1971), pp. 171–172.

HENRY, A., "Method of Classifying Non-scale Response Patterns in a Guttman Scale," *Public Opinion Quarterly* **16** (1952), pp. 94–106.

HESS, R., and TORNEY, J., *The Development of Political Attitudes in Children*. Chicago: Aldine, 1967.

HIBBS, D. A., JR., "Problems of Statistical Estimation and Causal Inference in Time-Series Regression Models," H. L. Costner (ed.), *Sociological Methodology*. San Francisco: Jossey-Bass, 1974.

HILGENDORF, L., CLARK, A. W., and IRVING, B. L., "The Combined Use of Linkage and Path Analysis in the Development of Causal Models," *Human Relations* **20**, no. 4, (1967), pp. 375–385.

HIRSCHI, T., and SELVIN, H., *Delinquency Research: An Appraisal of Analytic Methods*. New York: Free Press, 1967.

———, and SELVIN, H. C., "False Criteria of Causality in Delinquency Research," N. K. Denzin (ed.), *Sociological Methods*. Chicago: Aldine, 1970.

HOFFMAN, P. J., "Assessment of the Independent Contributions of Predictors," *Psychological Bulletin* **59**, no. 1 (1962), pp. 72–80.

HOLLEY, J. W., and GUILFORD, J. P., "A Note on the G Index of Agreement," *Educational and Psychological Measurement* **24** (1964), pp. 749–753.

HORST, P., *Factor Analysis Matrices*. New York: Holt, Rinehart and Winston, 1965.

HOYT, C., "Test Reliability Obtained by Analysis of Variance," *Psychometrika* **VI** (1941), pp. 153–160.

HYMAN, H., *Survey Design and Analysis*. Glencoe, Ill.: Free Press, 1955.

JACKSON, D., and MESSICK, S., *Problems in Human Assessment*. New York: McGraw-Hill, 1967.

JACKSON, E. F., and BURKE, P. J., "Status and Symptoms of Stress: Additive and Interaction Effects," *American Sociological Review* **30**, No. 4 (Aug. 1965), pp. 556–564.

JANOWITZ, M., *The Professional Soldier*. Glencoe, Ill.: Free Press, 1960.

JENNINGS, E., "Fixed Effects Analysis of Variance by Regression Analysis," *Multivariate Behavioral Research* **2** (1967), pp. 95–108.

JOHNSON, S. C., "Hierarchical Clustering Schemes," *Psychometrika* **32** (1967), pp. 241–254.

JOHNSTON, J., *Econometric Methods*, 2nd ed. New York: McGraw-Hill, 1972.

JONES, K. J., "The Multivariate Statistical Analyzer," *Behavioral Science* **10** (1965), pp. 326–327.

JONES, L., "The Nature of Measurement," R. Thorndike (ed.), *Educational Measurement*, 2nd ed. Washington, D.C.: American Council on Education, 1971, pp. 335–355.

JORESKOG, K. G., "RMLFA: A Computer Program for Restricted Maximum Likelihood Factor Analysis," *Research Memorandum RM-67-21*. Princeton, N.J.: Educational Testing Service, 1972.

KAHN, R. L., *Organizational Stress: Studies in Role Conflict and Ambiguity*. New York: Wiley, 1964.

———, and CANNELL, C., *The Dynamics of Interviewing*. New York: Wiley, 1957.

KAISER, H. F., "Formulas for Component Scores," *Psychometrika* **27**, no. 1 (1962), pp. 83–87.

———, "Image Analysis," C. W. Harris (ed.), *Problems in Measuring Change*. Madison, Wis.: University of Wisconsin Press, 1963.

———, "The Varimax Criterion for Analytic Rotation in Factor Analysis," *Psychometrika* **XXII** (1958), pp. 187–200.

———, and COFFRY, J., "Alpha Factor Analysis," *Psychometrika* **30** (1965), pp. 1–14.

KALTON, G., "A Technique for Choosing the Number of Alternative Response Categories in Order to Locate an Individual's Position on a Continuum," Three Memos, Dated Nov. 7, 1966, Feb. 10, 1967, Mar. 10, 1967. Ann Arbor, Mich.: Institute for Social Research Sampling Section, Survey Research Center.

KAMMEYER, K. C. W., and ROTH, J. A., "Coding Responses to Open-Ended Questions," H. L. Costner (ed.), *Sociological Methodology*. San Francisco: Jossey-Bass, 1971.

KATONA, GEORGE, et al., *Survey of Consumer Finances*. Ann Arbor, Mich.: Institute for Social Research, Monograph Series 1960 through 1971.

KEMENY, J., and SNELL, J., *Introduction to Finite Mathematics*, 2nd ed. Englewood Cliffs, N.J.: Prentice-Hall, 1966.

KERLINGER, F., *Foundations of Behavioral Research*, 2nd ed. New York: Holt, Rinehart and Winston, 1973.

——, "Research in Education," R. Ebel, V. Noll, and R. Bauer (eds.), *Encyclopedia of Educational Research*, 4th ed. New York: Macmillan, 1969, pp. 1127–1144.

——, "Social Attitudes and Their Criterial Referents: A Structural Theory," *Psychological Review* **LXXIV** (1967), pp. 110–122.

——, "A Social Attitude Scale: Evidence and Reliability," *Psychological Reports* **XXVI** (1970), pp. 379–383.

——, and PEDHAZUR, E., *Multiple Regression in Behavioral Research*. New York: Holt, Rinehart and Winston, 1973.

KERSHNER, R., and WILCOX, I., *The Anatomy of Mathematics*. New York: Ronald Press, 1950.

KIRK, R., *Experimental Design: Procedures for the Behavorial Sciences*. Belmont, Cal.: Brooks/Cole, 1968.

KISH, L., "Sampling Organizations and Groups of Unequal Sizes," *American Sociological Review* **30**, no. 2 (1965), pp. 564–572.

——, *Survey Sampling*. New York: Wiley, 1965.

——, and FRANKEL, M., "Balanced Repeated Replications for Standard Errors," *Journal of the American Statistical Association* **65** (Sept. 1970), pp. 1071–1093.

——, FRANKEL M. R., and VAN ECK, N., *Sampling Error Program Package*. Ann Arbor, Mich.: Institute for Social Research, 1972.

KLUCKHOHN, F. R., and STRODTBECK, F., *Variations in Value Orientations*. Evanston, Ill.: Row, Peterson, 1961.

KNOTT, G. D., ANDERSON, W. J., and MCKAY, J. A., "A Table-Making Language," *Proceedings of the IEEE* **54**, no. 12 (Dec. 1966), pp. 1779–1787.

KOLAKOWSKI, D., and BOCK, R. D., *LOGOG: Maximum Likelihood Item Analysis and Test Scoring: Logistic Model for Muitiple Item Responses*. Chicago: National Educational Resources, 1973.

KORNHAUSER, A., and SHEATSLEY, P., "Questionaire Construction and Interview Procedure," C. Selltiz (ed.), *Research Methods in Social Relations*, rev. ed. New York: Holt, Rinehart and Winston, 1959, APP. C.

KOSOBUD, R., and MORGAN, J. (eds.), "Consumer Behavior of Individual Families over Two and Three Years," *Monograph* 36. Ann Arbor, Mich.: Institute for Social Research, University of Michigan, 1964.

KRAMER, C. Y., "Extension of Multiple Range Tests to Group Correlated Adjusted Means," *Biometrics* **13** (1957), pp. 13–18.

KRIPPENDORFF, K., "Bivariate Agreement Coefficients for Reliability of Data," E. F. Borgatta and G. W. Bohrnstedt (eds.), *Sociological Methodology*. San Francisco: Jossey-Bass, 1970.

KRUSKAL, J. B., "Multidimensional Scaling: A Numerical Method," *Psychometrika* **29** (1964), pp. 1–27.

——, "Multidimensional Scaling by Optimizing Goodness of fit to a Nonmetric Hypothesis," *Psychometrika* (**B**)**29** (1964), pp. 115–129.

———, "Transformation of Data," *International Encyclopedia of the Social Sciences*, Vol. 16. New York: Macmillan, 1968, pp. 182–193.

Kruskal, W. H., "Tests of Significance," *International Encyclopedia of the Social Sciences*, Vol. 14. New York: Crowell Collier, 1968, pp. 238–250.

Labovitz, S., "The Assignment of Numbers to Rank Order Categories," *American Sociological Review* **35** (June 1970), pp. 515–524.

———, "The Nonutility of Significance Tests: The Significance of Tests of Significance Reconsidered," *Pacific Sociological Review* **13**, no. 3 (Summer 1970), pp. 141–148.

———, "The Zone of Rejection," *Pacific Sociological Review* **14**, no. 4 (Oct. 1971), pp. 373–382.

Land, K. C., "Formal Theory," H. L. Costner (ed.), *Sociological Methodology*. San Francisco: Jossey-Bass, 1971.

———, "On the Estimation of Path Coefficients for Unmeasured Variables from Correlations among Observed Variables," *Social Forces* **48**, no. 4 (June 1970), pp. 506–511.

———, "Principles of Path Analysis," E. F. Borgatta and G. W. Bohrnstedt (eds.), *Sociological Methodology*. San Francisco: Jossey-Bass, 1969.

Lansing, J., and Morgan, J., *Economic Survey Methods*. Ann Arbor, Mich.: Institute for Social Research, 1971.

Lazersfeld, P. F., "The Algebra of Dichotomous Systems," *Item Analysis and Prediction*. Stanford, Cal., Stanford University Press, 1961.

———, "The Use of Panels in Social Research," B. Berelson and M. Janowitz, *Supplement to Reader in Public Opinion and Communication*. New York: Free Press, 1953.

———, and Barton, A. H., "Qualitative Measurement in the Social Sciences: Classification, Typologies, and Indices," D. Lerner and H. D. Lasswell (eds.), *The Policy Sciences—Recent Developments in Scope and Method*. Stanford, Cal.: Stanford University Press, 1951.

———, and Menzel, H., "On the Relation Between Individual and Collective Properties," A. Etzioni (ed.), *Complex Organizations*. New York: Holt, Rinehart and Winston, 1961, pp. 422–440.

Lazerwitz, B., "Sampling Theory and Procedures," H. M. Blalock, Jr., and A. B. Blalock (eds.), *Methodology in Social Research*. New York: McGraw-Hill, 1968.

Lennon, R. T., "Assumptions Underlying the Use of Content Validity," *Educational and Psychological Measurement* **XVI** (1956), pp. 294–304.

Lenski, G., *The Religious Factor*. New York: Doubleday, 1961.

Lerner, Daniel (ed.), *Cause and Effect*. New York: Free Press, 1965.

Levin, J., "Three-Mode Factor Analysis," *Psychological Bulletin* (1965), pp. 442–452.

Li, Chang-Chu, "Fisher, Wright, and Path Coefficients," *Biometrics* **24** (1968), pp. 471–483.

Likert, R., "A Technique for the Measurement of Attitudes," *Archives of Psychology*, no. 140 (1932).

LINDZEY, G., and ARONSON, E., *Handbook of Social Psychology*, (2nd ed., Vol. II. Reading, Mass.: Addison-Wesley, 1968.

LINGOES, J. C., "A General Survey of the Guttman-Lingoes Nonmetric Program Series," R. Shepard, A. K. Romney, and S. Nerlove (eds.), *Multidimensional Scaling: Theory and Applications in the Behavioral Sciences*. Stanford, Cal.: Stanford University Press, 1971.

———, *The Guttman-Lingoes Nonmetric Program Series*. Ann Arbor, Mich.: Mathesis Press, 1973.

———, "An IBM 360/67 Program for Guttman-Lingoes Multidimensional Scalogram Analysis—III," *Behavioral Science* **13** (Nov. 1968), pp. 512–513.

———, "An IBM 360/67 Program for Guttman-Lingoes Smallest Space Analysis—PI," *Behavioral Science* **15** (Nov. 1970), pp. 536–540.

———, "An IBM 7090 Program for Guttman-Lingoes Multidimensional Scalogram Analysis—I," *Behavioral Science* **11** (Jan. 1966), pp. 76–78. (A)

———, "An IBM 7090 Program for Guttman-Lingoes Smallest Space Analysis—I," *Behavioral Science* **10** (Apr. 1965), pp. 183–184. (A)

———, "An IBM 7090 Program for Guttman-Lingoes Smallest Space Analysis—II," *Behavioral Science* **10** (Oct. 1965), p. 487. (B)

———, IBM 7090 Program for Multi-dimensional Scalogram Analysis II, *Behavioral Science* **11** (July 1966), p. 322. (B)

———, "The Multivariate Analysis of Qualitative Data," *Multivariate Behavioral Research* **3** (1968), pp. 61–94.

———, "New Computer Developments in Pattern Analysis and Nonmetric Techniques," *Uses of Computers in Psychological Research—The 1964 IBM Symposium of Statistics*. Paris: Gauthier-Villars, 1966, pp. 1–22.

———, "Recent Computational Advances in Nonmetric Methodology for the Behavioral Sciences," *Proceedings of the International Symposium: Mathematical and Computational Methods in Social Sciences*. Rome: International Computation Centre, 1966, pp. 1–38.

———, and GUTTMAN, L., "Nonmetric Factor Analysis: A Rank Reducing Alternative to Linear Factor Analysis," *Multivariate Behavioral Research* **2** (1967), pp. 485–505.

———, and VANDENBERG, S. G., "A Nonmetric Analysis of Twin Data Base on a Multifaceted Design," *Louisville Twin Study Research Report*, **17** (1966), pp. 1–17.

LINN, R. L., and WERTS, C. E., "Assumptions in Making Causal Inferences from Part Correlations, Partial Correlation, and Partial Regression Coefficients," *Psychological Bulletin* **72** (1969), pp. 307–310.

———, and WERTS, C. E., "Path Analysis: Psychological Examples," *Research Bulletin RB*-69-82. Princeton, N.J.: Educational Testing Service, Sept. 1969.

LIPSET, S. M., TROW, M., and COLEMAN, J. S., "Organizational Analysis," N. K. Denzin (ed.), *Sociological Methods*. Chicago: Aldine, 1970.

———, TROW, M., and COLEMAN, J. S., *Union Democracy: The Internal Politics of the International Typographical Union*. Glencoe, Ill.: Free Press, 1956.

LOEVINGER, J., "Objective Tests as Instruments of Psychological Theory," *Psychological Reports* **III** (1957), pp. 635–694, Monograph Supplement 9.

LOHNES, P., and COOLEY, W., *Introduction to Statistical Procedures; With Computer Exercises*. New York: Wiley, 1968.

LORD, F. M., "Elementary Models for Measuring Change," C. W. Harris (ed.), *Problems in Measuring Change*. Madison, Wis.: University of Wisconsin Press, 1967.

———, "Further Comments on 'Football Numbers,'" *American Psychologist* **IX** (1954), pp. 264–265.

———, "A Paradox in the Interpretation of Group Comparisons," *Psychological Bulletin* **68** (1967), pp. 304–305.

LYONS, M., "Techniques for Using Ordinal Measures in Regression and Path Analysis," H. L. Costner (ed.), *Sociological Methodology*. San Francisco: Jossey-Bass, 1971.

MACCOBY, E., and MACCOBY, L., "The Interview: A Tool of Social Science," G. Lindzey (ed.), *Handbook of Social Psychology*, Vol. I. Reading, Mass.: Addison-Wesley, 1954.

MACRAE, D., JR., *Issues and Parties in American Voting*. New York: Harper & Row, 1970, Chap. 5.

MARGENAU, H., *The Nature of Physical Reality*. New York: McGraw-Hill, 1950.

MARKS, E., and MARTIN, C. G., "Further Comments . . . ," *American Educational Research Journal* **10**, 1973, pp. 179–191.

MATHEWS, D. R., and PROTHRO, J. W., *Negroes and the New Southern Politics*. New York: Harcourt, Brace and World, 1966.

MAYER, L. S., "Using Monotone Regression to Estimate a Correlation Coefficient," H. L. Costner (ed.), *Sociological Methodology*. San Francisco: Jossey-Bass, 1972.

MCCRACKEN, D., *A Guide to FORTRAN IV Programing*. New York: Wiley, 1965.

MCGEE, V., and CARLETON, W. T., "Piecewise Regression," *Journal of the American Statistical Association* **65** (Sept. 1970), pp. 1109–1124.

MCINTOSH, S., and GRIFFEL, D., *The Current Admins System for Non-textual Data*. Cambridge, Mass.: Center for International Studies, 1967.

MCTAVISH, D., "A Method for More Reliably Coding Detailed Occupations into Duncan's Socio-Economic Categories," *American Sociological Review* **29** (1964), pp. 402–406.

MELICHAR, E., "Least Squares Analysis of Economic Survey Data," Proceedings of the Business and Economic Statistics Section, American Statistical Association, 1965.

MESSENGER, R. C., and MANDELL, L. M., "A Modal Search Technique for Predictive Nominal Scale Multivariate Analysis," *Journal of the American Statistical Association* **67** (1972), pp. 768–772.

MEYERS, E. D., JR., *Time Sharing Computation in the Social Sciences*. Englewood Cliffs, N.J.: Prentice-Hall, 1973.

MEYERS, E. D., JR., "Interactive Systems and Social Science Research and Instruction," Project Impress, Dartmouth College, Hanover, N.H. (Paper presented at Conference on Social Science Computer Capabilities, New York, Jan. 30, 1969.)

———, "Interactive Systems and Social Science Research and Instruction," *Social Science Information* **9**, no. 3 (1970), pp. 157–171.

MILLER, D. R., and SWANSON, G. E., *The Changing American Parent: A Study in the Detroit Area*. New York: Wiley, 1958.

MILLER, J. R., "DATANAL: An Interpretive Language for On-Line Analysis of Empirical Data," *Sloan School Working Paper 275–67*, 1967.

MILLER, R. G., "Regression Estimation of Event Probabilities," *Technical Report 7411–121, Contract CWB 10704*. Hartford, Conn.: The Travelers Research Center, Inc., 1964.

———, "Some Ways of Handling Missing Data," R. Bisco (ed.), *Data Bases, Computers, and the Social Sciences*. New York: Wiley, 1970.

———, Statistical Prediction by Discriminant Analysis, *Meteorological Monographs* **4**, no. 25 (1962).

MILTON, R. C., and NELDER, J. A. (eds.), *Statistical Computation*. New York: Academic Press, 1969.

MORGAN, J. N., "The Anatomy of Income Distribution," *Review of Economics and Statistics* **XLIV**, no. 3 (Aug. 1962).

———, and MESSENGER, R. C., *THAID: A Sequential Analysis Program for the Analysis of Nominal Scale Dependent Variables*. Ann Arbor, Mich.: Institute for Social Research, University of Michigan, 1973.

———, and SONQUIST, J. A., "Problems in the Analysis of Survey Data: and a Proposal," *Journal of the American Statistical Association* **58** (1963), pp. 415–435.

———, DAVID, M., and BRAZER, H., *Income and Welfare in the United States*. New York: McGraw-Hill, 1962.

———, SIRAGELDIN, I., and BAERWALDT, N., *Productive Americans*. Ann Arbor, Mich.: Institute for Social Research, University of Michigan, 1965.

MORRIS, P., *Prisoners and Their Families*. London: Allen & Unwin, 1965.

MORRISON, D. E., *Multivariate Statistical Methods*. New York: McGraw-Hill, 1967.

———, and HENKEL, R. E. (eds.), *The Significance Test Controversy*. Chicago: Aldine, 1970.

———, and HENKEL, R. E., "Significance Tests Reconsidered," *American Sociologist* **4** (May 1969), pp. 131–140.

MUELLER, E., and LANSING, J., *The Geographic Mobility of Labor in the United States*. Ann Arbor, Mich.: Survey Research Center, University of Michigan, 1967.

MUELLER, J. H., SCHUESSLER, K. F., and COSTNER, H. F., *Statistical Reasoning in Sociology*. Boston: Houghton Mifflin, 1970.

MURPHY, R., and ROBERTS, R., "Occupational Situations, Subjective Class Identification, and Political Affilliations," *American Sociological Review* **26** (1961), pp. 383–392.

MUSSEN, P. (ed.), *Handbook of Research Methods in Child Development*. New York: Wiley, 1960.

NETER, J., and MAYNES, E. S., "On the Appropriateness of the Correlation Coefficient with a Zero-One Dependent Variable," *Journal of the American Statistical Association* **65** (June 1970), pp. 501–509.

NEWCOMB, T. M., KONIG, K., FLACKS, R., and WARWICK, D., *Persistence and Change: Bennington College and Its Students after 25 Years*. New York: Wiley, 1967.

NIE, N., BENT, D., and HALL, C., *SPSS: Statistical Package for the Social Sciences*. New York: McGraw-Hill, 1970.

NORTHRUP, F., *The Logic of the Sciences and the Humanities*. New York: Macmillan, 1947.

NUNNALLY, J., *Psychometric Theory*. New York: McGraw-Hill, 1967.

NYGREEN, G. T., "Interactive Path Analysis," *American Sociologist* **6** (Feb. 1971), pp. 37–43.

O'CONNOR, E. F., "Extending Classical Test Theory . . . ," *Review of Educational Research* **42** (1972), pp. 73–97.

OSGOOD, C., SUCI, G., and TANNENBAUM, P., *The Measurement of Meaning*. Urbana, Ill.: University of Illinois Press, 1957.

OVERALL, J. E., "A Note on the Scientific Status of Factors," *Psychological Bulletin* **LXI** (1964).

———, and KLETT, C. J., *Applied Multivariate Analysis*. New York: McGraw-Hill, 1972.

———, and SPIEGEL, D. K., "Concerning Least Squares Analysis of Experimental Data," *Psychological Bulletin* **72**, no. 5 (1969), pp. 311–322.

PARTEN, M., *Surveys, Polls and Samples*. New York: Harper & Row, 1950.

PELZ, D. C., and ANDREWS, F. M., "Detecting Causal Priorities in Panel Study Data, *American Sociological Review* **29** (Dec. 1964), pp. 836–854.

———, and LEW, R. A., "Heise's Causal Model Applied," E. F. Borgatta and G. W. Bohrnstedt (eds.), *Sociological Methodology*. San Francisco: Jossey-Bass, 1970.

PETERSON, D., "Scope and Generality of Verbally Defined Personality Factors," *Psychological Review* **LXXII** (1965), pp. 48–59.

PHILLIPS, B. S., *Social Research: Strategy and Tactics*, 2nd ed. New York: Macmillan, 1971.

PIERCE, A., "A Rejoinder to Labovitz's 'The Non-utility of Significance Tests,'" *Pacific Sociological Review* **14**, no. 2 (Apr. 1971). pp. 173–176.

POINCARÉ, H., *Science and Hypothesis*. New York: Dover, 1952.

POLK, K., "A Note on Asymmetric Causal Models," *American Sociological Review* **27** (Aug. 1962), pp. 545–548.

POPPER, K. R., *Logic of Scientific Discovery*. New York: Basic Books, 1959.

PRESS, L. I., ROGERS, M. S., and SHURE, G. H., "An Interactive Technique for the Analysis of Multivariate Data," *Behavioral Science* **14** (1969), pp. 364–370.

QUENOUILLE, M. H., *Analysis of Multiple Time Series.* Darien, Conn.: Hafner Press, 1968.

RAO, C. R., "Estimation and Tests of Significance in Factor Analysis," *Psychometrika* **20** (1955), pp. 93–111.

———, *Linear Statistical Inference and its Applications.* New York: Wiley, 1965.

RATTENBURY, J., and VAN ECK, N., *OSIRIS: Architecture and Design.* Ann Arbor, Mich.: Institute for Social Research, University of Michigan, 1973.

RIESS, A., DUNCAN, O., HATT, P., and NORTH, C., *Occupations and Social Status.* New York: Free Press, 1961.

RILEY, M. W., "Sources and Types of Sociological Data," R. E. Faris (ed.), *Handbook of Modern Sociology.* Chicago: Rand McNally, 1964.

———, et al., *Sociological Studies in Scale Analysis.* New Brunswick, N.J.: Rutgers University Press, 1954.

ROBINSON, J. P., and SHAVER, P. R., *Measures of Social Psychological Attitudes.* Ann Arbor, Mich.: Institute for Social Research, University of Michigan, 1969.

———, ATHANASIOU, R., and HEAD, K. B., *Measures of Occupational Attitudes and Occupational Characteristics.* Ann Arbor, Mich.: Institute for Social Research, University of Michigan, 1969.

———, RUSK, J. G., and HEAD, K. B., *Measures of Political Attitudes.* Ann Arbor, Mich.: Institute for Social Research, University of Michigan, 1968.

ROBINSON, W. S., "Ecological Correlation and the Behavior of Individuals," *American Sociological Review* **15** (1950), pp. 351–357.

RORER, L., "The Great Response-Style Myth," *Psychological Bulletin* **LXIII** (1965), pp. 129–156.

ROSENBERG, M., *The Logic of Survey Analysis.* New York: Basic Books, 1968.

ROSKAM, E. E., "Metric Analysis of Ordinal Data in Psychology." Leiden, The Netherlands: Ph.D. Dissertation, University of Leiden.

———, and LINGOES, J. C., "MINISSA-1: A FORTRAN IV (G) Program for the Smallest Space Analysis of Square Symmetric Matrices," *Behavioral Science* **15** (1970), pp. 204–205.

ROSS, D. L., *BASIS: Burroughs Advanced Statistical Inquiry System.* Detroit, Mich.: Burroughs Corporation, 1970.

ROSSI, P. H., *Why Families Move.* New York: Free Press, 1955.

ROTH, J., "Hired Hand Research," N. K. Denzin (ed.), *Sociological Methods.* Chicago: Aldine, 1970.

ROZEBLOOM, W. W., "Foundations of the Theory of Prediction." Homewood, Ill.: Dorsey, 1966.

ROZELLE, R. M., and CAMPBELL, D. T., "More Plausible Rival Hypotheses in the Cross-Lagged Panel Correlation Techniques," *Psychological Bulletin* **71** (Jan. 1969), pp. 74–80.

RUBLE, W., *Stat Technical Report*. Lansing, Mich.: Agricultural Experiment Station, Michigan State University, 1967.

RUGGLES, R., and RUGGLES, N., "Data Files for a Generalized Economic Information System," *Social Science Information* **VI-4** (Aug. 1967).

RULON, P., and BROOKS, W., "On Statistical Tests of Group Differences," D. Whitler (ed.), *Handbook of Measurement and Assessment in Behavioral Sciences*. Reading, Mass.: Addison-Wesley, 1968.

RUMMEL, R. J., *Applied Factor Analysis*. Evanston, Ill.: Northwestern University Press, 1970.

———, "Understanding Factor Analysis," *Conflict Resolution* **II** (1967), pp. 444–480.

RUNKLE, P. J., and MCGRATH, J. E., *Research on Human Behavior*. New York: Holt, Rinehart and Winston, 1972.

SCHOENBERG, R., "Strategies for Meaningful Comparison," H. L. Costner (ed.), *Sociological Methodology*. San Francisco: Jossey-Bass, 1972.

SCHONEMANN, P. H., and CARROLL, R. M., "Fitting One Matrix to Another Under Choice of a Central Dilation and a Rigid Motion," *Psychometrika* **35** (1970), pp. 245–255.

SCHUESSLER, K., *Analysing Social Data*. Boston: Houghton Mifflin, 1971.

SCHWARTZ, M., *Trends in Whites Attitudes Towards Negroes*. Chicago: National Opinion Research Center, 1967.

SEARS, R., MACCOBY, E., and LEVIN, H., *Patterns of Child Rearing*. New York: Harper & Row, 1957.

SEIGLE, D., "Some Aids in the Handling of Missing Data," *Social Sciences Information* **VI-5** (Oct. 1967), pp. 133–150.

SELLTIZ, C., et al., *Research Methods in Social Relations*, rev. ed., New York: Holt, Rinehart and Winston, 1962.

SELVIN, H., and STUART, A., "Data Dredging in Survey Analysis," *The American Statistician* (June 1966), pp. 20–23.

SEWELL, W. H., and SHAH, V. P., "Socioeconomic Status, Intelligence and the Attainment of Higher Education," *Sociology of Education* **40** (Winter 1967), pp. 1–23.

SHANKS, M., Berkeley Transposed File Statistical System (PICKLE). Berkeley, CA.: Survey Research Center, University of California (1973) Unpublished manuscript.

SHEPARD, R. N., "The Analysis of Proximities: Multidimensional Scaling with an Unknown Distance Function," *Psychometrika* **27** (1962), pp. 125–140, 219–245.

SIEGEL, P. M., and HODGE, R. W., "A Causal Approach to the Study of Measurement Error," H. M. Blalock and A. B. Blalock (eds.), *Methodology in Social Research*. New York: McGraw-Hill, 1968.

SILLS, D. L., "Three Climate of Opinion Studies," *Public Opinion Quarterly* **25**, (1961), pp. 571–573.

SKINNER, B. F., "The Operational Analysis of Psychological Terms," H. Feigl and M. Brodbeck (eds.), *Readings in the Philosophy of Science*. New York: Appleton, 1953.

SLATIN, G. T., "Ecological Analysis of Delinquency: Aggregation Effects," *American Sociological Review* **34** (1969), pp. 894–907.

SMITH, R. B., "Neighborhood Context and College Plans: An Ordinal Path Analysis," *Social Forces* **51**, no. 2 (Dec. 1972), pp. 199–218.

———, "Continuities in Ordinal Path Analysis," *Social Forces* (Dec. 1974), pp. 200–299.

SNEDECOR, G., and COCHRAN, G., *Statistical Methods*, 6th ed. Ames, Iowa: Iowa State University Press, 1967.

SOKAL, R. R., and SNEATH, P. H. A., *Principles of Numerical Taxonomy*. San Francisco: W. H. Freeman, 1963.

SOLOMON, R., and LESSAC, M., "A Control Group Design for Experimental Studies of Developmental Processes," *Psychological Bulletin* **LXX** (1968), pp. 145–150.

SOMERS, R. H., "A New Asymmetric Measure for Ordinal Variables," *American Sociological Review* **27** (Dec. 1962), pp. 799–811.

———, "A Partitioning of Ordinal Information in a Three-Way Cross-Classification," *Multivariate Behavioral Research* **5** (Apr. 1970), pp. 217–239.

SONQUIST, J. A., "Finding Variables that Work," *Public Opinion Quarterly* **31**, no. 1 (Spring 1969), pp. 83–95.

———, *Multivariate Model Building*. Ann Arbor, Mich.: Institute for Social Research, University of Michigan, 1970.

———, and MORGAN, J. N., *Detection of Interaction Effects*. Ann Arbor, Mich.: Institute for Social Research, University of Michigan, 1964.

———, and O'BRIEN, T. C., "Uses of the Computer in Social Science Research." Paper presented at American Sociological Association Meeting, 1960.

———, BAKER, E., and MORGAN, J. N., *Searching for Structure*, rev. ed. Ann Arbor, Mich.: Institute for Social Research, University of Michigan, 1974.

SPAETH, J. L., "Occupational Prestige Expectations among Male College Graduates," *American Journal of Sociology* **73** (Mar. 1968), pp. 548–558.

SROLE, L., et al., *Mental Health in the Metropolis: The Midtown Manhattan Study*. New York: McGraw-Hill, 1962.

STAELIN, R., "A Note on Detection of Interaction," *Public Opinion Quarterly* **34**, no. 3 (Fall 1970), pp. 408–411.

STANNON, S., and HENSCHKE, C., "Stat-Pak: A Biostatistical Programming Package," *Communications of the ACM* **10** (Feb. 1967), pp. 123–125.

Statistical Service Unit, University of Illinois, *SSUPAC—Manual of Computer Programs for Statistical Analysis*. Urbana, Ill.: University of Illinois, 1967.

STEPHENSON, W., *The Study of Behavior*. Chicago: University of Chicago Press, 1953.

STERLING, T. D., and POLLACK, S., *Introduction to Statistical Data Processing*. Englewood Cliffs, N.J.: Prentice-Hall, 1968.

———, Binks, R. G., Haberman, S., and Pollack, S. V., "Robot Data Screening: A Ubiquitous Automatic Search Technique," R. C. Milton and J. A. Nelder (eds.), *Statistical Computation*. New York: Academic Press, 1969.

Stevens, S., "Mathematics, Measurement and Psychophysics," S. Stevens (ed.), *Handbook of Experimental Psychology*. New York: Wiley, 1951.

———, "Measurement, Statistics and the Schemapiric View," *Science* **CLXI** (1968), pp. 849–856.

Stouffer, S. A., *Communism, Conformity, and Civil Liberties*. Garden City, N.Y.: Doubleday, 1955.

———, "Some Observations on Study Design," *American Journal of Sociology* **LV** (1950), pp. 355–361.

———, et al., *The American Soldier:* Vol. 1, *Adjustment During Army Life;* Vol. 2, *Combat and Its Aftermath*. Princeton, N.J.: Princeton University Press, 1949, 1950.

Summers, G. F., Seiler, L. H., and Wiley, G., "Validation of Reputational Leadership by the Multitrait-Multimethod Matrix," E. F. Borgatta and G. W. Bohrnstedt (eds.), *Sociological Methodology*. San Francisco: Jossey-Bass, 1970.

Sweeney, R. E., and Ulveling, E. F., "A Transformation for Simplifying the Interpretation of Coefficients of Binary Variables in Regression Analysis," *The American Statistician* **26** (1972), pp. 30–32.

Tannenbaum, A. S., and Bachman, J. G., "Structural Versus Individual Effects," *American Journal of Sociology* **69** (1964), pp. 585–595.

———, and Kahn, R. L., *Participation in Union Locals*. Evanston, Ill.: Row, Peterson, 1958.

Tatsuoka, M., *Mutivariate Analysis: Techniques for Educational and Psychological Research*. New York: Wiley, 1971.

Theil, H., *Linear Aggregation of Economic Relations*. Amsterdam: North-Holland, 1954.

———, "On the Estimation of Relationships Involving Qualitative Variables," *American Journal of Sociology* **76** (1970), pp. 103–154.

Thompson, G., *The Factorial Analysis of Human Ability*. Boston: Houghton Mifflin, 1951.

Thorndike, R. I., *Concepts of Over- and Underachievement*. New York: Teachers College Press (Columbia University), 1963.

———, "Intellectual Status and Intellectual Growth," *Journal of Educational Psychology* **LVII** (1966), pp. 121–127.

———, "Reliability," E. F. Lindquist (ed.), *Educational Measurement*. Washington, D.C.: American Council on Education, 1951, pp. 560–620.

——— (ed.), *Educational Measurement*, 2nd ed. Washington, D.C.: American Council on Education, 1971.

———, and HAGEN, E., *Measurement and Evaluation in Psychology and Education*, 3rd ed. New York: Wiley, 1969.

THURSTONE, L., *Multiple Factor Analysis*. Chicago: University of Chicago Press, 1947.

TORGERSON, W., *Theory and Methods of Scaling*. New York: Wiley, 1958.

TRYON, E., "Reliability and Behavior Domain Validity: Reformulation and Historical Critique," *Psychological Bulletin* **LIV** (1957), pp. 229–249.

TUCKER, L. "Three-Mode Factor Analysis," *Multivariate Behavioral Research* **2** (1970), p. 139.

TUFTE, E. R., "Improving Data Analysis in Political Science," *World Politics* **21** (1969), pp. 641–654.

TUKEY, J. R., and WILK, M. B., "Data Analysis and Statistics: An Expository Overview," *Proceedings, Fall Joint Computer Conference, American Federation of Information Processing Societies*, 1966.

TUKEY, J. W., "Causation, Regression and Path Analysis," Oscar Kempthorne et al. (eds.), *Statistics and Mathematics in Biology*. Ames, Iowa: Iowa State College Press, 1954, pp. 35–66.

———, "The Future of Data Analysis," *Annals of Mathematical Statistics* **XXXII** (Mar. 1962), pp. 60–61.

———, "The Inevitable Collision Between Computation and Data Analysis," *Proceedings of the IBM Symposium on Statistics*. White Plains, N.Y.: Data Processing Division, IBM, Oct. 1963.

UNDERWOOD, B., *Psychological Research*. New York: Appleton, 1957.

United States Bureau of the Census, *1960 Census of Population, Alphabetical Index of Occupations and Industries*. Washington, D.C.: Government Printing Office, 1960.

University of London, *FAMULUS Users Manual*. London: Computer Centre, University College, University of London, 1972.

University of Michigan, "Interviewers' Manual, Survey Research Center," rev. ed. Ann Arbor, Mich.: Institute for Social Research, University of Michigan, 1976.

———, *OSIRIS/III—Organized System of Integrated Routines for Investigations with Statistics*. Ann Arbor, Mich.: Institute for Social Research, University of Michigan, 1973.

University of Minnesota, *UMST—Statistical Computer Programs Manual*. Minneapolis, Minn.: Computer Center, University of Minnesota, 1968.

Valavanis, S., *Econometrics: An Introduction to Maximum Likelihood Methods*. New York: McGraw-Hill, 1959, Chap. I.

VAN DE GEER, J. P., *Instroduction to Multivariate Analysis for the Social Sciences*. San Francisco: W. H. Freeman, 1971.

VELDMAN, D., *FORTRAN Programing for the Behavioral Sciences*. New York: Holt, Rinehart and Winston, 1967.

WALKER, S. H., and DUNCAN, D. B., "Estimation of the Probability of an Event as a Function of Several Independent Variables," *Biometrika* **54** (1967), pp. 167–179.

WALLACE, D. L., "Clustering," D. L. Sills (ed.), *International Encyclopedia of the Social Sciences*, Vol. 2. New York: Macmillan, 1968, pp. 519–524.

WALSTER, G. W., and CLEARY, T. A., "Statistical Significance as a Decision Rule," E. F. Borgatta and G. W. Bohrnstedt (eds.), *Sociological Methodology*. San Francisco: Jossey-Bass, 1970.

WAMPLER, R. H., "A Report on the Accuracy of Some Widely Used Least Squares Computer Programs," *Journal of the American Statistical Association* **65** (June 1970), pp. 549–565.

WARD, J. H., JR., "Multiple Linear Regression Models," H. Buros (ed.), *Computer Applications in Behavioral Sciences*. Englewood Cliffs, N.J.: Prentice-Hall, 1962.

———, "Partitioning of Variance and Contribution or Importance of a Variable: A Visit to a Graduate Seminar," *American Educational Research Journal* **6** (1969), pp. 467–474.

WEBB, W., "The Choice of a Problem," *American Psychologist* **XVI** (1961), pp. 223–227.

WEISS, C. H., *Evaluating Action Programs*. Boston: Allyn and Bacon, 1972.

———, *Evaluating Research: Methods of Assessing Program Effectiveness*. Englewood Cliffs, N.J.: Prentice-Hall, 1972.

WERNER, J., and WERNER, R., *Bibliography of Simulations: Social Systems and Education*. La Jolla, Cal.: Western Behavioral Sciences Institute, 1969.

WERTS, C. E., "The Partitioning of Variance in School Effects Studies," *American Educational Research Journal* **5** (1968), pp. 311–318.

———, "The Partitioning of Variance in School Effects Studies: A Reconsideration," *American Educational Research Journal* **7** (1970), pp. 127–132.

———, "Path Analysis: Testimonial of a Proselyte," *American Journal of Sociology* **73** (Jan. 1968), pp. 509–512.

———, and LINN, R. L., "Considerations when Making Inferences within the Analysis of Covariance Model," *Research Bulletin 69–28*. Princeton, N.J.: Educational Testing Service, 1969.

———, and LINN, R. L., "A General Linear Model For Studying Growth," *Psychological Bulletin* **73**, no. 1 (1970), pp. 17–22.

———, and LINN, R. L., "A Regression Model for Compositional Effects." Princeton, N.J.: Educational Testing Service. Unpublished paper, 1968.

WHELPTON, P. K., CAMPBELL, A. A., and PATTERSON, J. E., *Fertility and Family Planning in the United States*. Princeton, N.J.: Princeton University Press, 1966.

WILSON, J., and BROPHY, H., *A Generalized Table Generator*. Canberra, Australia: Commonwealth Bureau of Census and Statistics, 1968.

WILSON, T. P., "A Critique of Ordinal Variables," *Social Forces* **49**, no. 3 (Mar. 1971), pp. 432–444.

———, "Measures of Association for the Bivariate Ordinal Hypothesis," H. M. Blalock, Jr. (ed.), *Measurement in the Social Sciences*. Chicago: Aldine, 1974, pp. 327–342.

———, "A Proportional Reduction in Error Interpretation for Kendall's TAU-B," *Social Forces* **47** (Mar. 1969), pp. 340–342.

WINCH, R. F., and CAMPBELL, D. T., "Proof? No. Evidence? Yes. The Significance of Tests of Significance," *American Sociologist* **4**, no. 2 (1969).

WISLER, C. E., "On Partitioning the Explained Variation in a Regression Analysis," *U.S. Office of Education Technical Note No. 2.* Washington, D.C.: U.S. Office of Education, Jan., 1968.

WOLD, H., "Forecasting by the Chain Principle," H. Wold (ed.), *Econometric Model Building—Essays on the Causal Chain Approach* (Contributions to Economic Analysis No. 36). Amsterdam: North-Holland, 1964, pp. 5–36.

WRIGHT, S., "The Interpretation of Multivariate Systems," O. Kempthorne et al. (eds.), *Statistics and Mathematics in Biology*. Ames, Iowa: Iowa State College Press, 1954, pp. 11–34.

———, "The Method of Path Coefficients," *Annals of Mathematical Statistics* **5** (1934) pp. 161–215.

YARROW, L., "Interviewing Children," P. Mussen (ed.), *Handbook of Research Methods in Child Development*. New York: Wiley, 1960.

YEE, A. H., "The Source and Direction of Causal Influence in Teacher–Pupil Relationships," *Journal of Educational Psychology* **59** (1968).

———, and GAGE, N. I., "Techniques for Estimating the Source and Direction of Causal Influence in Causal Data," *Psychological Bulletin* **70** (1968), pp. 115–126.

ZEISEL, H., "The Panel," N. K. Denzin (ed.), *Sociological Methods*. Chicago: Aldine, 1970.

INDEX